Letters of Thomas Attwood Digges

THOMAS ATTWOOD DIGGES
(attributed to Sir Joshua Reynolds)

Letters of Thomas Attwood Digges
(1742–1821)

Edited by
Robert H. Elias
and Eugene D. Finch

 University of South Carolina Press

*Publication of this book was aided by the
Hull Memorial Publication Fund of Cornell University*

Copyright © University of South Carolina 1982
FIRST EDITION
Published by the University of South Carolina Press,
Columbia, South Carolina
Manufactured in the United States of America

Library of Congress Cataloging in Publication Data
Digges, Thomas Attwood, 1742–1821.
Letters of Thomas Attwood Digges (1742–1821)
1. Digges, Thomas Attwood, 1742–1821—Correspondence. 2. Novelists, American—Colonial Period, ca. 1600–1775—Correspondence. 3. United States—History—Revolution, 1775–1783—Sources. I. Elias, Robert H. II. Finch, Eugene D. III. Title.
PS787.D35z48 1982   813'.1 [B]   81-16450
ISBN 0-87249-412-8   AACR2

Contents

PREFACE	xi
ACKNOWLEDGMENTS	xvii
ABBREVIATIONS OF LOCATIONS AND SOURCES	xxi
INTRODUCTION	xxiii
THE TEXT	lxxix

1767

To Francis Street, Feb. 23	1

1777

To Ralph Izard, Sept. 8	2
To Matthew Ridley, Nov. 20	4
To John Thornton, [Nov. 30]–Dec. 1	7

1778

To Arthur Lee, Aug. 30	11
To [⟨Jonathan Loring Austin⟩], Aug.	15
To Benjamin Franklin, Sept. 18	18
To David Hartley, Nov. 26	19
To Benjamin Franklin. Dec. 19	21

1779

To Benjamin Franklin, Jan. 31	26
To Benjamin Franklin, Feb. 7	31
To Benjamin Franklin, Apr. 9	36
To Arthur Lee, Apr. 18	37
Oath of Allegiance, May 3	40
To Benjamin Franklin, May 4	41
To Benjamin Franklin, May 12	42
To Benjamin Franklin, May 14	45
To Benjamin Franklin, May 18	46
To Benjamin Franklin, May 21	48
To Benjamin Franklin, May 25	50
To Benjamin Franklin, May 31	52
To Benjamin Franklin, June 11	55
To Benjamin Franklin, June 18	62
To Benjamin Franklin, June 25	65
To Benjamin Franklin, June [⟨26⟩]	66
To Benjamin Franklin, July 6	67
To Benjamin Franklin, July 14	70
To David Hartley, [July ⟨31⟩]	71
To Benjamin Franklin, Aug. 10	72
To Benjamin Franklin, [Aug.] 13	75
To Benjamin Franklin, Sept. 4	78
To Benjamin Franklin, Sept. 6	81
To Benjamin Franklin, Sept. 20	85
To Benjamin Franklin, Oct. 8	90
To Benjamin Franklin, Oct. 8	91
To Benjamin Franklin, Oct. 12	95
To Benjamin Franklin, [Oct. 26]	97

v

vi   CONTENTS

To Benjamin Franklin, Oct. 30	98	To David Hartley, Feb. 7	155
To Benjamin Franklin, Nov. 9	103	To Benjamin Franklin, Feb. 10	158
To Benjamin Franklin, Nov. 10	104	To John Adams, Mar. 3	160
To Benjamin Franklin, Nov. 15	106	To Benjamin Franklin, Mar. 3	164
To Benjamin Franklin, Nov. 15	107	To John Adams, Mar. 7	170
To Benjamin Franklin, Nov. 26	112	To Benjamin Franklin, Mar. 7	171
To Benjamin Franklin, Nov. 30	115	To John Adams, Mar. 10	172
To Benjamin Franklin, Dec. 3	118	To Benjamin Franklin, Mar. 10	173
To Benjamin Franklin, Dec. 4	121	To Benjamin Franklin, Mar. 15	174
To Benjamin Franklin, Dec. 17	126	To Benjamin Franklin, Mar. 17	175
To William Temple Franklin, Dec. 20	127	To Benjamin Franklin, Mar. 20	180
To David Hartley, Dec. 21	129	To John Adams, Mar. 28	181
To Benjamin Franklin, Dec. 24	131	To John Adams, Apr. 6	183
To David Hartley, [Dec. ⟨24⟩]	133	To Benjamin Franklin, Apr. 6	185
To David Hartley, Dec. 28	134	To John Adams, Apr. 14	189
To David Hartley, Sat. [1779–1780]	135	To Benjamin Franklin, Apr. 14	191
To David Hartley, Thurs. [1779–1780]	136	To Benjamin Franklin, Apr. 17	194
		To Benjamin Franklin, Apr. 17	195

1780

		To Benjamin Franklin, Apr. 22	198
To Benjamin Franklin, Jan. 9	137	To John Adams, Apr. 28	198
To Benjamin Franklin, Jan. 10	141	To Benjamin Franklin, Apr. 28	202
To Benjamin Franklin, [Jan. ⟨10⟩]	142	To John Adams, May 2	205
To William Temple Franklin, Jan. 10	146	Certificate, May 10	207
To Benjamin Franklin, Jan. 11	147	To Benjamin Franklin, May 24	209
To David Hartley, Jan. 26	148	To John Adams, M⟨ay⟩ 26	211
To Benjamin Franklin, Jan. 28	150	To Benjamin Franklin, May 29	212
To Benjamin Franklin, Feb. 4	153	To Benjamin Franklin, May 30	214
		To John Adams, June 8	215
		To Benjamin Franklin, June 10	223
		To John Adams, June 29	226

To Benjamin Franklin, June 29	230
To John Adams, July 12	234
To Benjamin Franklin, July 12	238
To William Temple Franklin, July 12	240
To John Adams, July 17	241
To Benjamin Franklin, July 17	243
To John Adams, July 25	245
To John Adams, July 28	246
To Benjamin Franklin, Aug. 18	247
To John Adams, Aug. 24 [⟨22⟩]	252
To John Adams, Aug. 25	253
To Benjamin Franklin, Aug. 25	254
To John Adams, Aug. 29	256
To Benjamin Franklin, Aug. 29	260
To Benjamin Franklin, Sept. 1	261
To Benjamin Franklin, Sept. 8	263
To Benjamin Franklin, Sept. 12	267
To John Adams, Sept. 15	269
To Benjamin Franklin, Sept. 18	272
To John Adams, Sept. 20	277
To Benjamin Franklin, Sept. 20	279
To John Adams, Sept. 26	281
To Benjamin Franklin, Sept. 26	284
To John Adams, Sept. 29	286
To Benjamin Franklin, [Sept. 29]	289
To John Adams, Oct. 3	291
To Benjamin Franklin, Oct. 3	293
To John Adams, Oct. 6	294
To Benjamin Franklin, Oct. 6	295
To John Adams, Oct. 10	296
To Benjamin Franklin, Oct. 10	298
To John Adams, Oct. 17	299
To Benjamin Franklin, Oct. 17	301
To John Adams, Oct. 20	303
To John Adams, Oct. 22	304
To John Adams, Oct. 24	305
To Benjamin Franklin, Oct. 24	305
To John Adams, Oct. 27	307
To Benjamin Franklin, [Oct. 27]	309
To John Adams, Oct. 31	310
To Benjamin Franklin, [Oct. 31]	314
To John Adams, Nov. 3	316
To Benjamin Franklin, Nov. 3	318
To John Adams, Nov. 8	319
To John Adams, Nov. 10	320
To Benjamin Franklin, Nov. 10	322
To Benjamin Franklin, Nov. 13	323
To Benjamin Franklin, Nov. 13	324
To John Adams, Nov. 14	329
To John Adams, Nov. 17	331
To Benjamin Franklin, Nov. 17	333
To Benjamin Franklin, Nov. 21	335
To John Adams, Nov. 22	337
To John Adams, Dec. 12	339
To John Adams, Dec. 22	340
To John Adams, Dec. 26	341
To Benjamin Franklin, Dec. 29	343

1781

To John Adams, Jan. 5	345
To John Adams, [Jan 9]	348
To John Adams, Jan. 23	349
To John Adams, Feb. 11	350
To John Adams, Mar. 8	351

1782

To John Adams, [Mar. 20]	352
To Benjamin Franklin, Mar. 22	354
To John Adams, [Mar. 26]	362
To John Adams, Mar. 26	364
To David Hartley, [Mar. 29]	364
Memorandum for Lord Shelburne, [Mar. 30]	365
To John Adams, Apr. 2	367
To John Adams, Apr. 9	371
To John Adams, Apr. 16	373
To John Adams, Apr. 23	375
To Lord Shelburne, Apr. 26	376
To John Green, June 11	377

1783

To Robert Traill, Mar. 3	379
To William Carmichael, Apr. 3	383
To Matthew Ridley, Aug. 20	392
To Charles Steuart, Aug. 29	396
To Charles Steuart, Nov. 17	398

1784

To Thomas Trant, May 5	399

1786

To ———, [Aug.]	401

1788

To Thomas Jefferson, May 12	408
To Samuel Huntington, Sept. 13	411

1790

To Theobald Wolfe Tone, [Nov. or Dec.]	418

1791

To Thomas Jefferson, Apr. 28	422
To George Washington, July 1	428
To George Washington, Nov. 12	434

1792

To Alexander Hamilton, Apr. 6	436

1793

To Thomas Jefferson, Mar. 10	441
To Thomas Pinckney, Mar. 12	446
To Thomas Pinckney, Mar. 21	449
To Thomas Pinckney, Apr. 6	452

1794

To Joshua Johnson, Mar. 10	456

1797

To Rufus King, Nov. 25	457
To Rufus King, Nov. 27	459

1798

To George Washington, Apr. 10	463

1801

To Thomas Jefferson, Nov. 17	464

1803

To Thomas Jefferson, Oct. 28	466

1804

To John Carroll, June 3	467
To Thomas Jefferson, Dec. 13	472

1806

To Thomas Jefferson, June 30	473
To Thomas Jefferson, Sept. [19 or 20]	476
To Thomas Jefferson, Dec.	479

1807

To Thomas Jefferson, Feb.	481
To Thomas Jefferson, Mar. 11	482
To Thomas Jefferson, July 29	483
To Henry Dearborn, Sept. 15	485
To Thomas Jefferson, Sept. 15	487

1808

To Thomas Jefferson, Feb. 14	489
To Thomas Jefferson, Feb. 23	491
To Henry Dearborn, Mar. 11	492
To Henry Dearborn, Mar. 17	495
To Henry Dearborn, Mar. 21	497
To Philip Barton Key, May 28	499
To Thomas Jefferson, Aug. 4	505
To Thomas Jefferson, Sept. 20	508
To Thomas Jefferson, [Oct. 24]	510

1809

To Thomas Jefferson, Feb. 20	511
To John Smith, Mar. 15	512
To Thomas Jefferson, Sept. 11	514

1810

To Paul Hamilton, Nov. 29	517

1811

To Paul Hamilton, July [23]	518
To John Rodgers, July 26	519

1812

To Paul Hamilton, Jan. 4	521
To James Madison, Feb. 9	522
To John Carroll, May 27	523
To Paul Hamilton, May 28	529
To Paul Hamilton, June 23	530
To Paul Hamilton, Dec. 22	530
To John Borlase Warren, Dec. 28	531

1813

To John Borlase Warren, Jan. 14	538
To Jehu Chandler, Jan. 19	540
To James Patton, Apr. 24	541
To William Jones, Aug. 16	547

1814

To John Armstrong, Mar. 23	549
To John Armstrong, Apr. 9	550
To John Armstrong, Apr. 14	551
To John Armstrong, Apr. 18	551
To John Armstrong, May 3	553
To John Armstrong, July 2	554
To John Armstrong, July 22	555

To James Madison, Aug. 30	558	To George Graham, Nov. 6	606
To James Monroe, Sept. 25	561	To George Graham, Nov. 20	607
To James Monroe, Sept. 27	562		
To James Monroe, Sept. 28	564		
To James Monroe, Sept. 30	564		

1815

To James Monroe, Feb. 27	565		
To George Graham, June 24	567		
To George Graham, Aug. 10	569		
To John Carroll, Aug. 18	571		
To [⟨George Graham⟩], Aug. 24	576		
To George Graham, Nov. 11	578		
To James Madison, Nov. 27	580		
To George Graham, Dec. 22	582		

1818

To John C. Calhoun, Feb. 25	608
To John C. Calhoun, Mar. 7	609
To Christopher Van Deventer, Mar. 15	610
To John C. Calhoun, [May 19]	612
To Thomas Jefferson, May 30	614
To James Madison, July 17	618
To John C. Calhoun, Aug. 16	621
To John C. Calhoun, Sept. 15	623

1816

To William H. Crawford, Oct. 26	584
To James Monroe, Oct. 26	586
To George Graham, Nov. 6	589

1819

To J. W. Harris, Dec. 8	624

1820

To Pierre Charles L'Enfant, [July 30]	627
To John C. Calhoun, Aug. 14	629
To ———, Aug. 26	631
To ———, Aug. 30	632
To [⟨Paymaster General's Office⟩], Sept. 5	633

1817

To George Graham, Mar. 5	590
To George Graham, Apr. 16	591
To Charles Bagot, May 30	595
To George Graham, July 11	596
To George Graham, Aug. 7	598
To George Graham, Aug. 19	599
To George Graham, Aug. 25	600
To George Graham, Oct. 9	602
To George Graham, Oct. 19	604

1821

To James Monroe, Mar. 4	634
To [⟨William Dudley Digges⟩], Mar. 29	636

❦ Preface

We have collected and annotated for publication nearly three hundred letters written by Thomas Attwood Digges of Maryland (1742–1821)—all that we have been able to find—which as a compilation constitute both a useful contribution to American political and literary history and an intrinsically engaging story.

Until the mid-thirties, when we two editors, quite independently and unknown to each other, began our researches, Digges was known primarily as the subject of footnotes to Benjamin Franklin's career in France and as a member of a prominent family on the Potomac with whom George Washington was long intimate. Historians, when they did more than just mention Digges, suggested that he was an American of uncertain loyalties, possibly a spy for the British, possibly a double agent, who, while helping Franklin dispense funds for the relief of Americans imprisoned in England during the Revolution, had engaged in shady dealings to his own advantage and embezzled some of the money intended for the detained Americans. What we have found is different, both less simple and more arresting.

We had started our investigation as graduate students interested in the beginnings of American fiction, and in the New York Public Library had each come across what we thought might be "the first American novel": *Adventures of Alonso: Containing Some Striking Anecdotes of the present Prime Minister of Portugal. By a Native of Maryland*, some Years resident in Lisbon (London: Printed for J. Bew, 1775). Although we were aware that the attribution of authorship to a Marylander could be merely an enticement and itself a fiction, we were struck by the additional fact that someone years earlier had penciled across the title page: "By Mr. Digges of Warburton in Maryland." It was not long before we concluded that the attribution was correct and that the author was the Thomas Attwood Digges of dubious repute. He had, we learned, in the presence of Franklin in Paris, in 1779, formally taken an oath of allegiance to the United States of America, which meant that although most of the action in *Alonso* takes place in Portugal and Brazil, and although it was printed in London, *Alonso* was apparently the first novel to have been written by someone born in this country who also came to affirm his citizenship here. Charlotte Lennox (1720–1804), author of *The Life of Harriot Stuart* (London, 1750), had left New York for England at the age of fifteen and never returned; William Hill Brown (1766–1793) did not publish *The Power of Sympathy* until 1789. However one defined it, the place of *Alonso* in American literary history was distinctive, and we believed that the career of its author might, if we could but pursue our many leads, constitute a lively tale. Those leads we could not at the time pursue as readily as we imagined. Because of our individual professional commitments, one of us could work only sporadically, and the other decided to suspend his search for Digges entirely—until the mid-seventies, when we exchanged letters that led to collaboration in the present enterprise. The effort has been rewarding. We cannot say that we have recovered a forgotten man of letters, but we have recovered an individual whose correspondence illuminates both American and British politics during the revolutionary and early national periods and thereby clarifies some of the new republic's first concerns.

Digges's life before 1767, when he left home for Lisbon, has had to be reconstructed from fragmentary evidence embedded in sparse family records, scanty legal documents, and casual comments by individuals who knew him or his relatives. The years in Lisbon are even less easy to describe, with the most tantalizing of the clues confined to two brief allusions in unpublished passages of Robert Southey's memoirs, where we are told of a short-lived romantic attachment between Digges and Southey's aunt, Elizabeth Tyler. But after Digges's arrival in England, on the eve of the American Revolution, his letters, along with those of other Americans abroad and of some Englishmen as well, survive to offer a wealth of details that place him close to the center of an Anglo-American group in and about London who were sympathetic with the colonists' efforts to win their independence. Ralph Izard, Arthur and William Lee, Matthew Ridley, William Carmichael, David Hartley, Lord Shelburne, as well as Franklin and John Adams, appear among Digges's correspondents and acquaintances, and in their generally cordial and often genuinely friendly relationship to him show how active and useful he was as an informant about impending motions in Parliament, the state of public opinion regarding the war, and plans for military movements. In distributing the prisoners' relief in Franklin's behalf, he was, his letters also disclose, in continual touch with captured Americans and was often instrumental in helping escapees reach France or Ireland or return more directly to the United States. Because of the risks attending such activity, he had to do much that he did with extreme circumspection, resorting to the use of nearly thirty pseudonyms in correspondence directed across the Channel and even then not always managing to prevent the interception of his letters. In England he suffered the seizure of his papers and was interrogated by suspicious authorities. Because, amid these risks, he succeeded in circulating freely among British liberals and American sympathizers, his reports on politics, especially on the struggles for power within Parliament and the political and personal dissensions among American representatives abroad, have an authenticity that gives them value for historians of the period in our own time. Similarly, his letters enable us to understand better than we could before now just how American news reached London, Paris, and Amsterdam and how pro-American propaganda found its way into the British newspapers.

Beyond his roles of agent assisting prisoners and of informant, Digges throughout his stay in England was, his letters reveal, a diplomatic courier and active supporter of independence generally. Through him letters passed between Franklin and Hartley; through him, during Henry Laurens's imprisonment in the Tower late in 1780, Laurens and the American commissioners communicated. He carried a peace feeler from Lord North to Adams in 1782, giving the unfortunate appearance of some double-dealing. He contributed advice to Theobald Wolfe Tone and other leaders of the United Irishmen in 1790. He assisted Rufus King in 1797 in getting to the bottom of the Blount-Chisholme conspiracy to seize Spanish territories. And he did what he could to promote economic and industrial self-sufficiency in the United States, smuggling machinery and artisans from the British Isles to American ports, recruiting indentured servants to assist with crops in the South, and providing Washington, Alexander Hamilton, Thomas Jefferson, and Thomas Pinckney, among others, with news about the new power-driven looms, the minting of coins, and the results of technological progress in Great Britain.

After regaining his home in Maryland in 1798, he continued to write letters expressing his political and economic concerns. State and national politics, agriculture and animal husbandry, the role of Catholics in local elections—these are the principal subjects of correspondence with Jefferson, James Madison, and Archbishop John Carroll. Because Warburton Manor became, early in the century, the site of Fort Washington, Digges had frequent occasion to refer to the progress of construction there, both before the War of 1812 (some episodes of which he reported) when Major Pierre Charles L'Enfant, who lived at Warburton, was chief engineer, and after that war, when he became preoccupied with money the government owed him for the land it had bought and for damages done to his fisheries by the soldiers and the construction crews. During this later war he was again, briefly, a diplomatic courier, providing liaison between members of the administration and Admiral John Borlase Warren.

A few of Digges's letters have been published elsewhere, though seldom accurately transcribed, and others are scheduled to be included within the next two decades in the volumes devoted to the papers of Adams, Franklin, Hamilton, Jefferson, and Madison. But we have felt that Digges also deserves his own volume, so that instead of remaining a small part of the context of other lives, he gains a life of his own. The letters of prominent men do not always indicate what was said in the coffee houses, the corridors, and the parlors. Minor figures often, in fact, occupy more central positions and thereby play distinctively critical roles. It is precisely because of these various roles that Digges's letters are of interest to anyone seriously wanting to know about the American past.

Preface

The locations of the manuscripts are many and widely scattered. Some have long been accessible to all accredited scholars, but others have become accessible only to us at this time because of our intention to bring together as much of Digges's correspondence as we could collect. We are thus, we hope, both making available to specialists materials that can serve as the sources of numerous individual studies and offering to more general readers clusters of interrelated documents that systematically afford a unique view of the public events of the time.

We have introduced the letters with a biographical sketch that will help frame the collection. When, occasionally, this account anticipates annotations of individual documents that follow, such repetitions are deliberate, serving in this very full volume as reminders rather than as redundancies; for our aim in headnotes and footnotes has been to enlarge contexts and identify elusive references rather than to provide heavy editorial emendations. The details of our method are outlined below, but one editorial decision may be puzzling enough to require explanation. In a few instances Digges wrote Adams and Franklin *almost* identical letters, and we have preserved the duplication. Never pervasive, this duplication is important to reproduce because one charge against Digges has been that he did not always tell Adams and Franklin the same story, and anyone wishing to do Digges justice should be able to make comparisons firsthand and not rely, as has been done in the past, on editors' substituted summaries. After all these years the adventurous author, agent, and citizen should receive his due.

R.H.E.
E.D.F.

Acknowledgments

The location or source of each document printed in full or quoted in part in this volume is designated wherever the text of that document appears. For facilitating our access to those texts and for granting us when necessary the right to print them, we are grateful to the many individuals and institutions thus cited. More specifically, most of the correspondence included here appears by the courtesy and permission of

Adams Manuscript Trust
American Philosophical Society
Archdiocese of Baltimore
Berkshire Record Office, Reading, England
William L. Clements Library, University of Michigan
D. A. Hartley-Russell
Historical Society of Pennsylvania
Houghton Library, Harvard University
Huntington Library, San Marino, California
Library of Congress
Maryland Hall of Records
Maryland Historical Society
Massachusetts Historical Society
Massachusetts State Archives
National Archives and Records Service
Trustees of the National Library of Scotland
Trustees of the National Maritime Museum, Greenwich, England
New-York Historical Society

Manuscripts and Archives Division (Astor, Lenox, and Tilden Foundations), New York Public Library
Public Record Office, London
South Carolina Historical Society
Carrow Thibault, Jr., Radnor, Pennsylvania
Board of Trinity College, Dublin
U.S. House of Representatives
University of Notre Dame Press
Charles Patterson Van Pelt Library, University of Pennsylvania
Lord Vernon, Sudbury House, Derbyshire, England
Yale University Library

We wish also to thank the Columbia Historical Society, Washington, D.C., for letting us reproduce the photograph of the portrait of Digges that was first published in their *Records* in 1904. We had intended to provide a full-color reproduction of the original painting, but unfortunately, during the settling of an estate, the painting left the custody of the family in 1957, and no surviving relative or member of the banking and law firms that participated in the settlement knows of its whereabouts.

In making such formal acknowledgments we do not wish to exclude recognition of what numerous individuals associated with the various repositories have contributed to our project. They, along with friends, colleagues, fellow editors, and members of reference staffs in other institutions, have provided indispensable help in locating manuscripts, solving orthographic problems, and identifying obscure persons. We cannot, unfortunately, name them all here; but on the time and goodwill of some we have made such unusual or repeated claims that we want to single them out for special appreciation: Henry Adams, Adams Papers; Whitfield J. Bell, Jr., American Philosophical Society; Ruth M. Blair, Connecticut Historical Society; Julian P. Boyd, Papers of Thomas Jefferson; Dorothy W. Bridgwater, Papers of Benjamin Franklin; Stuart Lee Butler, National Archives; David R. Chesnutt, Papers of Henry Laurens; Frederick S. DeMarr, Prince George's County Historical Society; Donald D. Eddy, Cornell University; Elaine C. Everly, National Archives; Diane P. Frese, Maryland State Hall of

Records; Miss A. Green, Berkshire Record Office; Philip M. Hamer, Papers of Henry Laurens; Minnie Mosher Hill and Katherine A. Kellock, Washington, D.C.; James G. King, New York City; Robert W. Krauskopf, National Archives; Gregory L. Lint, Adams Papers; Frank MacDermot, Dublin; Sir Ewan Macpherson-Grant, Ballindalloch, Banffshire, Scotland; Sally B. Marks, National Archives; LeRoy Morgan, Washington, D.C.; Kathryn M. Murphy, National Archives; Linda J. Pike, Lafayette Papers; Catherine M. Prelinger, Papers of Benjamin Franklin; Mrs. M. B. Prior, South Carolina Historical Society; Robert A. Rutland, Papers of James Madison; Arlene P. Shy, William L. Clements Library; Brother Thomas W. Spalding, Louisville, Kentucky; David Spinney, Blandford, Dorset, England; Rev. John J. Tierney, Archdiocese of Baltimore; Lord Vernon, Sudbury House, Derbyshire, England; Celeste Walker, Adams Papers; and Waverly K. Winfree, Virginia Historical Society. We want also to note that regularly over a period of five years, sometimes on a weekly, and sometimes even daily, basis, we have found ourselves heavily indebted to the extraordinary resourcefulness of the reference department of the John M. Olin Library at Cornell University.

At Cornell in addition we have profited immeasurably from the work of students who at varoius times have enthusiastically committed themselves to us as research assistants. Without their professional collaboration, we would have been severely stalled in our labors. It gives us pleasure to name these co-workers: Elizabeth Grant, Ilisa Hurowitz, Nancy Ann Jaqua, Kathy Lefferts, Ellen Amanda McCollister, and Kenneth John Myers. For enabling Elias to enlist their assistance, as well as to defray other expenses, we thank the Humanities Faculty Research Grants Committee of Cornell's College of Arts and Sciences and especially the College's dean during our most critical period, Professor Harry Levin. Likewise, we are indebted for the extensive research conducted abroad to the two sabbatical years and travel allowances that Phillips Exeter Academy granted Finch.

Abbreviations of Locations and Sources

AB	Archives, Archdiocese of Baltimore
APS	American Philosophical Society
BRO	Berkshire Record Office (Reading, England)
HEH	Huntington Library
HSP	Historical Society of Pennsylvania
HU	Harvard University (Houghton Library)
LC	Library of Congress
MHS	Massachusetts Historical Society
MdHR	Maryland Hall of Records
MdHS	Maryland Historical Society
MdLRO	Maryland Land Record Office
MoHS	Missouri Historical Society
NA	National Archives
NLS	National Library of Scotland (Edinburgh)
NMM	National Maritime Museum (Greenwich, London)
NYHS	New-York Historical Society
NYPL	New York Public Library (Manuscripts and Archives Division—Astor, Lenox, and Tilden Foundations)
PAH	*Papers of Alexander Hamilton*, ed. Harold C. Syrett (New York: Columbia University Press, 1961–)
PRO	Public Record Office
PTJ	*Papers of Thomas Jefferson*, ed. Julian P. Boyd (Princeton: Princeton University Press, 1950–)
SCHS	South Carolina Historical Society
SH	Sudbury House, Derbyshire, England (Collection of Lord Vernon)
B. F. Stevens, *Facsimiles*	B. F. Stevens, *Facsimiles of Manuscripts in European Archives Relating to America, 1773–1783* (London: Maltby & Sons, 1889–1898)
Thibault	Collection of Carrow Thibault, Jr. (Radnor, Pennsylvania)
TCL	Trinity College Library (Dublin)
UM	University of Michigan (William L. Clements Library)

ABBREVIATIONS

UP	University of Pennsylvania (Charles Patterson Van Pelt Library)
USC	University of South Carolina (Caroliniana Library)
VHS	Virginia Historical Society
WTF, *Memoirs*	William Temple Franklin, *Memoirs of Benjamin Franklin* (London: Henry Colburn, 1817)
YU	Yale University Library

❧ Introduction

Thomas Attwood Digges was born about six in the morning of July 4, 1742, at Warburton Manor, Prince George's County, Maryland. He bore a name distinguished in both England and America. Some of his more famous forebears were Thomas (d. 1595), a mathematician, architect, engineer, and muster master general for Queen Elizabeth; and Sir Dudley (1583–1639), ambassador to Prussia, commissioner to Holland, and Master of the Rolls. Great-great-grandfather Edward (1621–1675), the first of the Diggeses in America, had been governor of Virginia (1654–1656) and agent in England for the colony. For two centuries the Diggeses of Kent had been men of education, wealth, and influence. The family seat of Chilham Castle bespoke their social consequence.

The Attwoods, Catholics of Worcestershire, though well connected by marriage, had taken less part in public life. Digges family papers trace the ancestry of Ann Attwood, Thomas's mother, on her mother's side back four generations to William, Lord Petre, baron of Writtle, and to Catharine, daughter of Edward Somerset, earl of Worcester. Ann's grandfather, George Attwood, of the parish of Claines in the county of Worcester, had four sons: William, Thomas, Peter, and George. George, Ann's father, took up large estates in land in Virginia, some of which he mortgaged to his brother William. Whether Ann, his only child, was born in America is not known. She was married to William Digges on June 3, 1739. Her father, soon after, sold his estate, Widow's Purchase, near Bladensburgh, and came to live with her at Warburton. When he died on September 26, 1744, he left her 3,300 acres "considerable way back in Virginia"—specifically, in Loudoun County.

The fortunes of her husband had been well established by his grandfather, Colonel William Digges, and his father, Charles. Not much is known of either of these men. William was born at Chilham, came to Charles County, Maryland, in 1679 or 1680, married Elizabeth Sewall, daughter of Henry Sewall of Patuxent, widow of Dr. Jesse Wharton, and stepdaughter of Charles Calvert, Lord Baltimore. He died in 1695 and was buried at the Woodyard, Prince George's County.

Charles on September 15, 1710, married Susannah Maria, youngest daughter of Colonel Henry Lowe, a nephew of Lady Baltimore. They had five children, of whom only three reached maturity: William, Thomas Digges's father, was born February 19, 1711, and died March 28, 1783; Mary, born January 17, 1715, married Clement Hill of Upper Marlborough; Anne, born November 22, 1721, married Dr. George Stewart of Annapolis. Sometime between May 1717 and April 1720, Governor John Hart and the two Houses of the Assembly served notice on the "Principall Papists" of Prince George's County to appear at a certain time "to make appear what right or Privileges of theirs (as they have given out in Speeches) are Infringed by the present Administration of Government . . . ."[1] The group included Charles, his brother John, his brother-in-law Henry Darnall, his subsequent son-in-law Clement Hill, his son William, and son William's subsequent wife's uncle, the priest Peter Attwood.

In 1717 Charles bought from Luke Gardiner the larger part of Warburton Manor on the Potomac, across from Mount Vernon. Just when Charles removed to Warburton from his estate of Charles Town in Charles County is uncertain, but for three generations of Diggeses of Charles's line, Warburton Manor was to be the family seat. Here William remained after his marriage and here his children were born.

Of William's various sons Thomas should eventually have become an unchallenged beneficiary of Charles's purchase. Charles died

---

[1] *Archives of Maryland* (Baltimore: MdHS, 1913), 33:516, 621.

in 1743 or 1744. His will, witnessed by Ann and Henry Darnall (sister and brother-in-law), George Attwood, and Henry Rozier, was sworn to as the will of the deceased testator by Attwood and Rozier on May 28, 1744.[2] By the will William inherited various properties without limitation, but Warburton Manor and the adjoining tract of Frankland were specifically entailed after William's death to his eldest son Charles, and then if Charles died without a son to William's second son, Thomas Attwood Digges, and if Thomas died without a son, to the third son, George, and so on through William's sons. At about the same time Ann Attwood Digges had inherited not only the tracts in Loudoun County, Virginia, bequeathed by her father, but also, from her uncle, Dr. Thomas Attwood of Powick, near Worcester, various property. Thus, upon the death of Thomas Digges's elder brother Charles in 1769, Thomas was heir both to his mother's estate and to Warburton and Frankland. But Warburton and Frankland would pass at his death if he had no male heir to his younger brother or his younger brother's eldest son. From this disposition of family property much trouble was to come.

The growth of William's family is best presented in what appear to be William's own words:

    My son Charles Attwood Digges was born on the 17th day of May 1740—about 10 Oclock had the small pox 1748 and died the 5th of April 1769

    My daughter Frances Digges was born on the 13th day of May 1741 about 12 Oclock at night had the small pox 1742 May & dyed 16th of November 1748

    My son Thomas was born the 4 July 1742 about 6 Oclock in the morning

    My son George was born the 4 July 1743 about 6 Oclock in the morning

    My Daughter Teresia was born the 7th of October 1744

    My Son Henry was born the 9th of Feby. 1745/6

    My Son Joseph was born the 19th of March 1746/7

    1748 May the 28th My Daughter Susane was born and dyed September 21st 1773

    1750 June the 1st My Daughter Ann was born

    1751 Augt. 23d My Daughter Mary was born and dyed the 23d of Jany. 1761 at 12 Oclock

[2] MdHR: Prince George's County, Original Wills, 1774, box 6, folder 50.

1753 August 4th My Daughter Elizh was born
1755 Feby. 18th My Daughter Jane was born
1757 Augt. 14th My Dear Wife Depd. this life 3 oclock in the morg.[3]

Twelve children in eighteen years of married life, nine or ten of whom apparently reached maturity. Not much is known about the way he provided for and educated this family. As receiver of his lordship's land rents for Prince George's County in 1739, he was admonished by the Lower House of the Assembly for "irregular and oppressive conduct" of his office.[4] His indebtedness to the house of John Glassford and Company of Glasgow for such items as nails, fabrics, rum, and books went over a hundred pounds in the 1770s, but a gentleman planter did not do a cash business, and there seems to have been no question about his credit.[5] Most significant is the fact that in the three years following William's death in 1783 the income of the estate sufficed to pay little more than the interest on his indebtedness of about £4,000 sterling. Hospitality at Warburton must have been costly. What facts there are support the legend of an expansive manorial life at Warburton. The exchange of hospitality between Warburton and Mount Vernon is well documented in the Washington diaries for the period between 1768 and 1775. Washington Irving, in his *Life of Washington*, wrote of the barge with liveried oarsmen who on signal came over to Mount Vernon from the Maryland shore.

It seems likely that the four boys who lived to grow up were educated abroad. Charles, according to Katharine Kellock, "must have had some merchant apprenticeship, . . . since at the time of his sudden death in 1769 he was a partner of a London merchant, Thomas Philpot."[6] The family legend is that Thomas and George went to Oxford, but no proof has been found. It is certain that Joseph studied medicine at the University of Edinburgh for three years, 1764–1767. As his name is not in the list of graduates, and there is no record

---

[3] MdHS: Ms. 246.
[4] *Archives of Maryland*, 40:303.
[5] LC: Glassford Papers.
[6] Katharine A. Kellock, *Colonial Piscataway in Maryland* (Accokeek, Md.: Alice Ferguson Foundation, 1962), p. 17.

of a thesis for the M.D., he must have completed his studies elsewhere, possibly with his uncle Dr. George Stewart in Annapolis.

Of the upbringing of the girls, one can only guess. When their mother died in 1757, the oldest of them, Teresia, was just short of thirteen; the youngest, Jane, two and a half. Of the seven girls, two died young; one, Susane, lived to the age of twenty-five and died single "with Fits from the Cradle." From the Washington diaries, one would suppose that there were only four girls, Teresia (Tracy), Ann (Nancy), Elizabeth (Betty, Betcy), and Jane (Jenny). Teresia married Ralph Forster in 1783 and died October 11, 1784. Ann died single, December 28, 1805. Elizabeth married Daniel Carroll of Rock Creek. Jane married Colonel John Fitzgerald of Alexandria, Virginia, in 1779. John Fitzgerald was an aide-de-camp of Washington during the Revolution. Washington recommended him to Jefferson in 1787, "despite his being a native of Ireland," and mentioned his marriage "with one of the most respectable families, Digges of Maryland."[7]

About Thomas Digges's youth and early manhood in Maryland, one can again only guess. It is obvious that this second son of the owner of Warburton Manor had many social and financial advantages. We know he grew up to be a tall and handsome young man. But what he was really like we have no way of knowing. Only one bit of evidence has come down to us, and that is touched by rumor and scandal. William Hodgson, a London merchant, attacking Digges's character in a letter to Benjamin Franklin, May 8, 1781, alludes to "Storys told of him during his Residence in America that affect his honesty very much." And among Sir Ewan Macpherson-Grant's family papers in Ballindalloch, Banffshire, Scotland, is an undated, unsigned document, apparently an intelligence report of 1782 or thereabouts, that reads in part: "Thomas Digges a Native of Maryland of an exceeding bad character in that Country altho of a good family there, and obliged to leave it long before the Rebellion." And Arch-

---

[7] May 30, 1787, *PTJ*, 11:387–88. For the dates of births, marriages, and deaths see MdHS: Ms. 246; Gaius Marcus Brumbaugh, *Maryland Records* (Baltimore: Williams & Wilkins, 1915), 1:110; and Edith Roberts Ramsburgh, "Sir Dudley Digges, His English Ancestry, and the Digges Line in America," *D.A.R. Magazine*, 57 (Mar. 1923):130.

bishop John Carroll in 1792 could write to the archbishop of Dublin: "He is of respectable family and connections in this country, no one more so; in his early youth he was guilty of misdemeanours here, indicating rooted depravity, but amazing address, but even this could not screen him, and his friends, to rescue him from the hands of justice, and themselves from dishonour, sent him out of the country. He went first to Lisbon, where fresh misconduct compelled him to seek refuge elsewhere."[8]

What is troubling in these three references to Digges's misconduct is their vagueness. Had he, like the hero of the novel he was later to write, *Adventures of Alonso*, had an affair with a married woman and been disowned by his father? And had he, like Alonso, then raised money on his father's credit? Whatever his misconduct was, it would appear that when at the age of twenty-four he set out, in midwinter, for Portugal, a country unknown to him, carrying gold or bills of exchange, he was a disowned son.

Twenty-six months after he left the country, his elder brother Charles died. Thomas, as second son of William, was next in the entail. Third son George stood next. Within a month of Charles's death William and George took steps to dock the entail. Of these steps Thomas wrote some thirty-five years later, in this way:

> William Digges and George Digges gave a Deed of Leading Uses & Common Recovery (calld *fine & Recovery*) for docking the Entail of Warburton Manner & Frankland—to Geo. F. Hawkins 1st May 1769 very unfairly & intirely unknown to Thos. Digges until he was shewing His papers to His Council Mr. Mason in 1805—and who has written His opinion on the back of the said Deed (see Copy) as follows

> William Digges son of Charles by the Will of His Father took only an Estate for Life in the Warburton Manor & Frankland Estates, and therefore was not competent to suffer a common Recovery of those Lands or do any other act to defeat the Entail which was limited to his Sons
> Signed
J.F.M. Octo. 1, 1805[9]

---

[8] *The John Carroll Papers*, ed. Thomas O Brien Hanley (Notre Dame, Ind.: University of Notre Dame Press, 1976), 2:25–26. Editor's interpolation omitted.
[9] MdHS: Ms. 246.

In the Judgments of the Provincial Court, May and October terms, 1769, dealing with this deed, William and George Digges appear as inheritors from Charles. No mention is made of the entailing of the estate upon Thomas Digges, nor does Thomas's name appear. Whatever rights he had in the transfer of title were ignored, and the entail was thus docked.[10]

Two years later, Frank Leeke and George Digges, administrators of the estate of Charles Digges, petitioned the Lower House of the Assembly, "praying An Act may pass to impower them to sell a Lot of Ground in Upper Marlborough which Charles Digges late of that County deceased purchased from a certain John Weldon, for the Payment of the Debts of the said Charles Digges." From the Act, signed by the Lower House, November 11, 1771, and by the Upper House, November 16, 1771, it appears that Charles devised all his estate to William Digges, his father, and appointed him executor, but that William renounced executorship and letters of administration were granted Frank Leeke and George Digges, who administered; that considerable debts remained; that Charles Digges neglected to republish his will; and "that the said Lot of Ground devolved by Descent upon Thomas Digges Junior as Heir at Law to the said Charles Digges & that the said Thomas Digges is beyond Sea in Parts unknown & in all Probability will never return into this Province."[11] By the Act, then, Leeke and George Digges were allowed to sell the property, rightfully Thomas's.

Whether William and George made further use of their power over property entailed upon Thomas is not clear. Since neither mentioned Thomas or the entailed property in his will, it is impossible to say whether they attempted to will property rightfully Thomas's to their heirs. But it is clear that when Thomas returned to Maryland in 1798 he returned as owner of his ancestral home, his by his grandfather's will, and that though Warburton and Frankland had been held by George from his father's death until his own nine years later in 1792, Thomas billed George's estate for rents on Warburton, Frank-

---

[10] MdHR: Provincial Court Judgments, DD15, fol. 598, and DD16, fol. 277.
[11] MdHR: Laws of Maryland, 762347, RG: 121–23.

land, and the Virginia property for the nine years of George's tenure.

After Charles' death, Joseph, William's fifth son, was the next to die. He had been appointed surgeon to the Maryland Marching Militia, September 4, 1777, and must have served, for on January 6, 1778, the Council ordered the payment to him of forty-three pounds and ten shillings "balance of Account due him as Surgeon to the Maryland Militia." On October 23, 1778, the Council voted permission for him to go to Bermuda for the recovery of his health, "Doct. Joseph Diggs of this State having some time past been in bad Health."[12] He drew his will on February 11, 1780, leaving to George all his estate, lands, Negroes, goods, chattels.[13] His sisters and John Fitzgerald are remembered. Although Thomas is not mentioned, he must have been in touch, if not with Joseph, at least with the family, for he could write Benjamin Franklin, May 31, 1779, that his younger brother, a doctor and a consumptive, should have arrived in Bilbao from Maryland about February 1, 1779, and that he fears Joseph is dead.[14]

Thomas's father died March 28, 1783. His will, dated July 17, 1780, names his children as George, Teresia, Ann, Jane, and Elizabeth. To George he bequeaths Charlestown and "all other tenements, Lands, and real Estate which I have possess or have a right to in Maryland or elsewhere." If George should die without issue, then the estate is to be divided among his sisters, Teresia, Ann, Jane, and Elizabeth. Very specific provisions are made: to Elizabeth, lots in Carrollsburgh; to Jane, lots in Alexandria; to Teresia and Ann, should they marry within three years of their father's demise, ten Negroes each. The intent of the testator is emphatic and explicit: ". . . It being my will and desire to give and bequeath and devise all and every Estate and Estates in Lands, Tenements, or Hereditaments which I have Possess, or have a right to in the world to my said son George in tail with remainder to my Daughters as aforesaid in fee."[15] The exclusion of Thomas seems to be as complete as though he had never existed.

When George Digges made his will on November 13, 1792, he

[12] *Archives of Maryland*, 16:362, 454; 21:222.
[13] MdHS: Ms. 246.
[14] All Digges letters cited will be found in the present volume.
[15] MdLRO.

mentioned only his wife Catharine, his daughter Anna Maria, and his son William Dudley.[16] To George, who had been silent for twenty-three years about his and his father's attempt to dock the entail of Warburton, the drawing of this will must have offered some problems.

In the light of the attempt to dock the entail and of these wills of Thomas Digges's father and two brothers, *Adventures of Alonso* takes on added interest. On June 7, 1775, it was announced for publication by *Lloyd's Evening Post* in these terms:

> Next week will be published Neatly printed on a fine Writing Paper, in Two Volumes, Duodecimo, Price 4s. sewed, or 5s. bound
> Adventures of Alonso
> Containing some striking Anecdotes of the present Prime Minister of Portugal.
> Printed for J. Bew, No. 28, Pater-noster-row.

Between June 7 and June 9 the same announcement was made in the *London Chronicle for 1775*, the *Morning Chronicle and London Advertiser*, the *Morning Post and Daily Advertiser*, the *Gazetteer and New Daily Advertiser*, and the *Daily Advertiser*. The next week all of these papers announced the publication of the work on Thursday, June 15. The *London Review* and the *London Magazine* both noticed the publication in their June issues but did not review the work. The *London Chronicle* on July 1 gave the novel considerable space. First it summarized:

> Alvares, A Merchant in one of the principal towns in Portugal, situated upon the sea coast, having determined to bring up his only son Alonso in business, resolves to send him to England (where his connexions in trade mostly lay) for instruction and improvement in the English language. Alonso when about fifteen years of age was accordingly sent to London, and put under the care of Mr. Stephenson, his father's correspondent, with whom he continues five years, at the expiration of which he returns to Portugal.
> Soon after his arrival, he became acquainted with Donna Eugenia de Miranda, a young Lady of great beauty, who visited his mother and sisters; with

[16] MdHS: Ms. 246.

this Lady he became deeply enamoured, and having frequent opportunities of engaging her attention, he soon inspired her with the kindest sentiments towards him. Eugenia, however, was already married, having been forced by the avarice of her parents to wed Don Pedro, a Captain of the Portuguese cavalry, upwards of three-score years of age. Alonso having prevailed on Eugenia to elope with him, disguised in man's apparel, they leave Portugal, and after several adventures, arrive at Cadiz, where they are kindly received by Pacheco, an old friend and schoolfellow of Alonso. Alonso acquaints Pacheco, that he had formed a design of obtaining a settlement in some of the Spanish colonies in America; this Pacheco dissuades him from, and advises him to return secretly to Lisbon, and embark with the Goa ship for the East Indies. Alonso and Eugenia accordingly depart for Lisbon, and on their arrival, Alonso, on an interview with his friend Mr. H——, a Gentleman belonging to the English factory, he is again dissuaded from pursuing his voyage to the East Indies, and advised to sail with the fleet going to the Brazils, where a more extensive line would be opened to him than in the East Indies.

Alonso sailed to the Brazils (Eugenia having been with much difficulty prevailed on to stay in Lisbon and retire to a Convent during his absence) and soon after his arrival was appointed to a considerable employment in the Diamond mines. While he was thus engaged, a negro offered him three very large diamonds worth at least 50,000£ he had found means to conceal (these large diamonds being all the property of the king) which Alonso purchased for between two and three ounces of gold dust, but in his attempt to secrete and carry them off, was detected and flung into prison, from which he escapes by making a friend of the Jailor. Alonso afterwards meets with a variety of adventures, and at last is taken prisoner by a Barbary corsair in his passage on board a ship bound from Panama to Cadiz, and carried a slave to Sallee, where after some time having obtained his liberty, he gets to Cadiz, and makes himself known to his old friend Pacheco, who acquaints him that Eugenia is alive, and her husband Don Pedro dead, and that his father was reconciled, and earnestly wished to embrace him. This good news is however much damped, when he is informed that Eugenia had taken the veil, and was for ever lost to him. Alonso immediately embarks for Lisbon, where he is most affectionately received by Alvares, and being determined to visit Eugenia, he arrives at the Convent just time enough to be a spectator of her funeral obsequies, which were then performing. Alonso returned to his father, and became a comfort to him while living, and at his death inherited his great riches.

This summary is followed by an extract "to enable the Reader to judge, in what manner the Author has executed this work," of pages

59 to 68 of Volume II, which cover a dialogue between Alonso, the governor of Guadalajara, a merchant of Cadiz, and two Spanish officers on such subjects as the openness of the Spanish colonies to conquest, the great loss to Spain through emigration to the colonies, the advantages of trade, and the success of the count d'Aranda in getting the people of Spain to adopt the garb of the rest of the world. All of this material was accorded space on the front page.

The *Monthly Review* in September gave the novel two sentences: "The author of this Novel has contrived to mix just so much political anecdote and reflection with his love tale, as to make it dull and tedious. It is one of those performances, which though it may not shock the reader with glaring faults, will be read without emotion, and forgotten as soon as it is laid aside."

Although the work was anonymous, a later issue bore on the title page the words, "By a Native of *Maryland*, some Years resident in *Lisbon*." A copy of this issue in the New York Public Library, with the bookplate of Sir Walter Blount of Sodington in the County of Worcester, carries on the title page the penciled note, written in a contemporary hand, possibly Digges's own, "By Mr. Digges of Warburton in Maryland." This copy also identifies Captain J—— as Captain Jarvis, and "Mr. H——, (an English gentleman belonging to the factory, a friend of his father's, with whom he was intimately acquainted) . . . ," as Mr. Hake. These two identifications, apparently trustworthy, invite a further reading of the novel as autobiography. Despite the ever-changing scene, the exploitation of coincidence, the adventures that Pacheco said "ought not to be hid from the world," the romantic sensibility linked with many instances of the imperfections of man, there are strong suggestions of the pattern of the eighteenth-century novel "founded on fact." It seems likely that Thomas, like Alonso, was sent to England for training under the direction of a merchant, Mr. Stephenson in both cases. Like Alonso he returned to his native country, where he soon lost his father's favor as a result of scandal and was forced to seek his fortunes abroad. His mother, like Alonso's, died early. Both had numerous sisters. Although Thomas probably never got to South America or experienced Moorish slavery, and although we do not know that he ran off with a married woman, the friend of his eldest sister, the parallels between the book and his life are plentiful.

The thought of the book, reflecting Digges's views of Portugal, Spain, and Britain, appears in discussions of such topics as assassination and superstition in Portugal, the character of the English, the question whether time has brought an increase in human happiness, the state of the armies of Portugal and Spain, and the question whether Spain with her colonies is not at a disadvantage in opposition to England with her manufactures. The method is simply to recount the conversation of Alonso and his fellow passengers on three ocean voyages, a device used most successfully and extensively in Alonso's voyage from Lisbon to Rio de Janeiro. The passengers include a Franciscan friar, an army major, a merchant, and a lawyer. Through the friar, we get various ribald laughs at the immorality of his order—indeed, he offers it for laughter; through the major, the importance of patronage if one is to rise in the army; through the merchant, the folly of monopoly in the trade with Brazil; through the lawyer, the decay of law and justice because of the avarice of Pombal; and through Alonso, many judgments upon the character and rule of the Portuguese prime minister and dictator, Pombal.

It cannot be said that the twelve pages devoted to him make good on the promise carried on the title page of "Some STRIKING ANECDOTES of the present PRIME MINISTER OF PORTUGAL." Strictly speaking, there are no anecdotes of Pombal, though a fairly accurate account of his life and character is given. "Few states," says Alonso, "have felt more severely the despotism of a minister than our own under the present government," and although Pombal may be considered a great man in many parts of Europe, "that is more than he is by his own countrymen. . . . Our commerce languishes, and is almost ruined by the monopolizing companies of the Brazil trade; the laws are trampled upon, and even private property is not secure against his venality; the army is like a body without a soul; in short he has exhibited such instances of rigour and cruelty, that he is the dread of the whole nation.—Every domestic confidence is destroyed by the emissaries he is known to employ.—Perhaps, when his avarice is satiated, and he is arrived at the summit of power, he may, like Augustus, do good to mankind; but believe me, at present there is no order, no rank in society, but what detests him." Anecdotes to illustrate these judgments are missing. It is true that the Franciscan friar bound for Rio tells of gaining influence by winning the love of Pombal's brother's mistress, whose acquaintance he made through the archbishop of Evora and the Franciscan confessor of the young woman. And the major tells of the banishment to Angola of a brother officer of his for speaking too freely of the minister. But these are offered as fictions, not anecdotes of Pombal.

The only striking anecdote the book contains is the story of the attack of John de Sousa on the king at the Villa Viçosa, December 3, 1769. The major says he was on guard in the palace that day and proceeds to tell a story the historical accuracy of which appears from a comparison of the anecdote as given by Digges and the reports of the incident sent from Lisbon on December 6 and 12, 1769, to Lord Viscount Weymouth in Whitehall by the ambassador to Portugal, William Henry Lyttelton.

Adventures of Alonso (I, 116–119)

This madman, then, (for though he was not a lunatic, he deserves no other name) after serving the greatest part of his life as a soldier in the artillery, was discharged as unfit for service. The king remained in arrears to him six years pay; and, besides, he claimed the value of a mule, which had been pressed from him during the war, for his majesty's service.—He set forth his claims in a petition to the king, which he presented himself.—After waiting some days in fruitless attendance, he presented another, which the king likewise received, and gave to one of his suit.—However, as this met with the same fate as the first, he determined to present a third; but the king recollecting the man's face again, pushed it on one side, and said to him, "Fellow, why do you plague me thus with your petitions?"—The old soldier was obliged to retire, but sullen and thoughtful, thus he reasoned with himself—"I have served the king the best part of my life—I am old, and he owes me money—yet treats me with contempt—I will have satisfaction."

Accordingly he provided himself with a long stout stick, with which he was resolved to give his majesty a drubbing the next morning as he went a-hunting;—he therefore planted himself, very composedly, at the park gate; and just as his majesty passed through, he fell most heartily upon him; and if he had not been immediately seized, he would probably have brought the king to the ground—The attendants in their fury would instantly have dispatched him, if they had not been prevented by the king, who called out to them to spare his life. He was ordered into strict custody; and, soon after, all his friends and relations, and those with whom he had any intimacy or acquaintance, were sent to prison, in order to find out who it was that had instigated him to so rash an action;—but all their enquiries proved fruitless, and it did not appear that he had any accomplices, but had acted merely from a principle of taking satisfaction for the injustice the king had done him.— What became of the poor fellow afterwards, God knows;—but the army owe him, at least, this piece of service, that sometime afterward their arrears were paid.

Lyttelton, December 6

His Most Faithful Majesty has for the second time very narrowly escaped losing his Life by the hands of an Assassin; The Particulars of the Fact as I have collected them from private Persons are as follows; On Monday last the 4th instant at eight in the Morning His Majesty accompanied by the Queen & His usual attendants was going out on Horseback to Hunt in the neighbourhood of Villa Viçosa, and being somewhat advanced before Her Majesty & the rest of His Suite as far as to the Arch of a Gateway through which there is an Entrance into a Park, was there assaulted by a tall strong Man in the Habit of a Peasant who was arm'd with a long Staff one end whereof was knotty & heavier than that which formd the handle, and who aimd therewith three blows at the King: the first which was intended to have fall'n on His Majesty's Head was received upon His Shoulder, the Second on His left Hand with which He held His bridle, & the third on the Crupper of His Horse. The Count de Prado one of the Lords of His Majestys Bedchamber rode up to defend Him and in so doing is said to have been wounded in the wrist, but at the same time one of the Kings Huntsmen named Bartholomew closed in with the Villain, His Majesty calling out with a loud Voice that they shoud not kill him, & other Persons coming up he was secured. I have not been able to learn who he is, much less what motives appear to have actuated him to perpetrate so execrable a Deed, but am told he was observed to be lurking for three days together at or near the same Place waiting for a favourable opportunity to put his Design in execution, but as his Purpose was not in the least suspected no further Notice was taken of him.[17]

Lyttelton, December 12

The Ruffian defended himself desperately & besides striking the Count de Prado . . . it is said wounded the Huntsman who seized him who is a vigorous active Man accustom'd I am told, at Bull Feasts to leap on the Necks of

[17] PRO: SP 89/69.

those Animals. Coud the Wretch have disengaged himself he was perhaps not without a hope, however vain, of escaping, as there is, if the description I have had of it is a just one, a Park wall on one side of the spot where he assaulted the King, and on the other irregular broken ground with olive yards & thickets where it wou'd have been very difficult to have follod him. I hear he is a native of the Province of Beira & servd for some time in a Regiment of Artillery but has of late subsisted by following the occupation of a muleteer, & that his Beasts having been taken for the King's use during the Journey of the Court to Villa Viçosa, one of them by hard driving perish'd, whereupon he presented a petition to His Majesty praying to be indemnified and also to receive some arrears of Pay due to him as a Canoneer & it is said that the Reason he gave when he was askd immediately after being taken at Villa Viçosa what coud have induced him to commit so horrid a Deed, was that his said Petition had been disregarded. By some Persons he is represented as a Man not in his right Wits, but as he arrived here only the night before last and I have not yet had any account of this Black Affair from the Count d'Oeyras or any other Minister of His Most faithfull Majesty I choose to avoid giving your Lordship any conjectures upon so delicate a subject which may prove ill founded & have the honor to be with great respect.[18]

Adventures of Alonso may have been reissued by Bew in 1785, if the appearance of a critical notice in the July *Critical Review* is an indication—a copy of it with this date has yet to be found—but, curious evidence of more distinction, it was translated into German and published in Leipzig in 1787[19] More curious, though, is Digges's silence about his book. It appears to have been his only literary effort; he made no reference to it in any letter of his thus far found; and the only person whose correspondence contains any allusion to his authorship is Robert Southey, who in 1821 mentioned it in the course of the reminiscences that he was addressing to his friend John May.[20] Whether Digges's silence is biographically significant is a question for conjecture. He may have turned his back on the novel very much as his father had turned his back on him. He may have been simply embarrassed by the tepid reception. Or, more likely, he may have considered it less as an effort to establish himself as a novelist than as a kind

---

[18] Ibid.
[19] Robert H. Elias, "The First American Novel," *American Literature*, 12 (Jan. 1941):434.
[20] Robert H. Elias and Michael N. Stanton, "Thomas Atwood Digges and *Adventures of Alonso*: Evidence from Robert Southey," *American Literature*, 44 (Mar. 1972):120.

of open letter to British readers calling attention to their government's perilous colonial policies. Although *Adventures of Alonso* interests literary historians today because of its position at the beginning of a tradition of political fiction that has flowered in our own century in many forms, it appears to have been not so much the work of an aspiring man of letters as one of the many activities of a restless man of action. Certainly, in its treatment of historical and political matters *Adventures of Alonso* reflects concerns and presents arguments that Digges's correspondence shows preoccupied him as an advocate of independence throughout the revolutionary period as he entered dangerous scenes that required more than a novelist's talents.

When Digges arrived in Britain is uncertain, the evidence confusing or contradictory. From Carroll's letter one would infer that he was soon forced to leave Lisbon for fresh misconduct. Yet in a letter to William Carmichael of April 3, 1783, he refers to having been in Lisbon in 1770, 1771, 1772, and 1773. He writes in a letter of November or December of 1790 to Theobald Wolfe Tone that he was in Madrid during the winter of 1774. But in a letter to John Borlase Warren of December 28, 1812, he alludes to "our primary meeting—afterwards in Lisbon—with passage to Falmouth—subsequent scenes in London . . .—Your L: Marlow scenes of Election to Parliament—. . . ." Warren won his seat in Parliament in Marlow in 1774. Moreover, providing additional support for dating Digges's arrival in London in that year is a story that Southey included in his reminiscences about his mother's half-sister, Elizabeth Tyler, a strong-minded, imprudent, and "remarkably beautiful woman," who in 1774, at the age of thirty-four, having inherited a small estate, visited Lisbon and there "gave more encouragement than was prudent to an American Adventurer, who followed her to England. His name was Digges."[21] Though the relationship came to nothing—perhaps, Southey speculated, because one of the two discovered the other's "fortune to be very inferior"— Digges was to refer to Lisbon as a place where he had spent "some of the happiest years of [his] life";[22] and though he often wished to do so, he was not to visit there again.

[21] Ibid.
[22] Digges to Thomas Jefferson, Feb. 23, 1808.

Introduction

xxxix

Within six months of the publication of *Adventures of Alonso*, his activities were thought worthy of the attention of Lord North, and he was to learn more and more in the next eight years of the hazards of being a loyal and energetic American in Britain.

On December 24, 1775, an anonymous informer in Bristol wrote to the treasury office:

> This Second Intrusion on Your Lordship is in Consequence of a promise made in a former Letter; and to acquaint Your Lordship that the Vessel which I then mentioned to have been bought by Mr. Diggs of Maryland for the supposed purpose of conveying Intelligence to America has been for some time in the Bay of Swanzea near the Mouth of the Severn—She is a small Brigantine with bright Sides—deep waisted & has Port Holes for Ten Guns & had while at Kingroad Eight of them mounted tho' the Pilot who gives me this Information says She has none now upon Deck. This Vessel was purchased in Bristol but has not yet been cleared out. When the Captain is asked his destination He says He is bound to St. Johns in the Gulph of St. Lawrence with Implements for settling some Lands which Mr. Digges & Sir John Warren have purchased there but from the Depth of the Vessel it is not improbable She has some Military Stores on board—When Mr. Digges was last in Bristol I heard him enquiring the Market Price of Salt Petre & I have reason to suppose he shipped some & also some lead on board this Vessel—I heard not many days ago He was in Bath to which place I shall go tomorrow and if I get any further intelligence from him, Your Ld.ship shall have it in a P:st. [Postscript]—My reason before as well as now for secreting my Name is the fear of a Discovery which might hurt me & effectually ruin my only Son who has property in America & in actual Service in the provincial Camp. My reason for now troubling Your Lordship is solely to give an Opportunity to some of the Cruizers in the Channel to stop this Vessel which may too probably convey some material assistance to the Provincial Army. I know She has been waiting some time only to carry out the Resolves of the present Parliament and Administration with regard to American measures.
> Bath 25th
> P.S.—On Enquiry here for Mr. Digges I find He went last Friday into Wales and not improbably to dispatch away his Ship.[23]

This information John Robinson of the treasury laid before Lord North late on the night of December 27, too late to transmit it to Lord Suffolk, secretary of state.[24] By Lord North's orders, Robinson wrote

---

[23] PRO: SP T1/518.
[24] PRO: SP 37/22.

the collector of the port of Bristol and sent his letter express the following morning directing him, after summarizing the foregoing letter, "to forthwith look out for such Vessell and to examine & search her if found, and in Case She shall appear to have on board any Military Stores, Saltpetre or Lead without due Licence that You do seize & detain her & report the same immediately to me for their Lordships Information. . . ."[25] The collector, Daniel Harson, sent one P. Wright, assistant to the surveyor at Pill, to Swansea. Wright reported on January 4 that on the first, with the collector of Swansea, he had surveyed all Swansea Bay "from hash point to the mumble Head & all vessels in Swanzey road." On the second he had examined all creeks and docks in the river at Swansea, but he could not find nor could he get intelligence of any vessel of the description of Robinson's letter.[26] This information was conveyed by Robinson to William Eden "for the Information of the Earl of Suffolk" on January 7.[27] It seems likely that the story of sending implements to Prince Edward Island was a shield because in 1812 Diggs could ask Sir John Borlase Warren what he had done with his lot of twenty thousand acres on St. John's Island in the Bay of Fundy and whether he had fixed settlers on it "as we contemplated in 1777."

Thomas's brother George was in London in the early part of 1776. Though Thomas corresponded with him, it does not appear that he came to London to see him. The reason may be guessed at from a letter of John Robinson from treasury chambers, January 15, 1777, to Sir Stanier Porten:

SIR,
    The Lords Commissioners of His Majesty's Treasury having received Information that Mr. Diggs an American Gentleman of considerable Property in Maryland has been busily employed at Bristol for some days past to collect & send forward all the American Captains, Seamen & others acquainted with the coasts of North America to the Ports of Bourdeaux Dunkirk & Nantz where there are people to receive & employ them—that He has already got five Captains to go & has a promise of Eight or Ten more Seamen—That Mr. Diggs has during the last Summer & Fall, shipped from Bristol in Spanish

---

[25] Ibid.
[26] PRO: SP 37/23.
[27] Ibid.

Bottoms to Bilboa several Boxes & Casks cleared out as wrought Iron which the Informer is certain were Musquet Locks, & that He has now in a Store on the Quay & near about to be shipped, several Casks under the Appearance of Nails, which the Informer is equally certain cover near Thirty Thousand Musquet Locks—that He has got some Baggage on board of a Spanish Vessel now in the river bound to Bilboa & is to set out in a week or two thro' France to some part of Spain where He is employed to transact some Business for the Congress & where he has been very lately called either by a letter from Dean at Paris or from Dr. Franklyn who is an Acquaintance of his—That this Mr. Digges has lived there three or four Years lately in Spain & Portugal & is exceedingly well acquainted with the Trade Manners & Language of Spain—He has been seen frequently last Week on board a Spanish Vessel at the Quay in Bristol & very often talking Spanish with the Captains on the Exchange—that one of the Captains who has been employed by him told the Informer that He was certain Mr. Diggs would very soon appear in Spain as an Agent for the Congress & that the reason for his employing American Seamen to go to France was by an order from Mr. Dean, who under Licence from that Court had prevailed on many French Merchants to fit out upwards of Twenty armed Vessels to trade to Virginia for Tobacco, Rice & Indigo & that these Captains and Seamen were to act as Pilots on board them—; I am directed by their Lordships to transmit this Intelligence to You for the Information of Lord Weymouth. I am, Sir, Your most obedient humble Servant John Robinson.[28]

It is unlikely that either Silas Deane or Franklin had asked Digges to serve as an American agent in Spain, but the informer's intelligence that Digges had cleared out musket locks in Spanish bottoms from Bristol to Bilbao was sound.[29]

As a result of Robinson's letter, Lord Weymouth of the state department wrote, February 14, 1777, to Lord Grantham, the ambassador at Madrid:

Information has been received that a Mr. Lee who is employed as an Agent for the Colonies in rebellion has set out for Spain. If he should come to Madrid, Your Excellency will pay such attention to his motions and applications as may be consistent with your situation. It has also been represented that a Mr. Diggs who is likewise an agent from the American Congress has sent on board several Spanish Vessels to Bilbao sundry Casks under the appearance of Nails, which cover a large number of Musquet Locks, from

---

[28] Ibid.
[29] See the letter of Apr. 10, 1777, from the American informer Isaac Van Zandt to William Eden, quoted in note 2, Digges to Arthur Lee, Aug. 30, 1778.

thence it is proposed to send them to America. Your Excellency will endeavour to find out whether this information is founded, and take such measures as may be proper to frustrate the Design."[30]

Lord Grantham was able to present a circumstantial account of Lee's doings, but nothing about Digges appears in his dispatches.

Specifically, little is known of Digges's activities in the first half of 1777. He was in London in February. Sometime in midsummer, at George Washington's request, he sent him some books. He was corresponding with Arthur Lee and Matthew Ridley, according to a letter he sent from Worcester to Ralph Izard on September 8, the first letter known since, ten years before, he had written to Francis Street just before embarking for Cadiz. The letters of the interim, covering his life from the age of twenty-four to the age of thirty-five, in Portugal, Spain, and England, appear to be forever lost. But from 1777 until 1821 there is no extensive gap in the flow of letters. There are still biographical puzzles, but there are few black holes.

A letter to Ridley of November 20, 1777, makes it clear that Digges had been engaged for some time in getting out munitions from Birmingham to America. Though eager to get to London and doing everything to get away from Birmingham, he fears he "may be calld back on a future day on similar business, & therefore [wishes] to stand well with those who have done things of some consideration by my recommendation & to whom I may again have occasion to apply." The "getting out useful articles," he later wrote Franklin (April 9, 1779), had employed him for nearly two years.

One other matter that had occupied him was a claim he made in Worcester as heir at law through his mother to Attwood properties. A document apparently in Digges's hand headed "Attwood Family" shows a family tree that would support the note carried by the document, "Doctor Thomas Attwood of Beverly late of Powick, near the City of Worcester and died at Powick on the (th) [sic] and Thomas A. Digges was heir at Law to him and did sell real estates viz. Houses and lots in the City of Worcester in the years 1779 and 1780 which could not Be sold without his then reversionary *Title*."[31] And an indenture

---
[30] PRO: SP 94/203.
[31] MdHS: Ms. 246.

of November 17, 1777, "between Thomas Digges of Warburton . . . Heir at Law of Mary Attwood late of the City of Worcester Spinster deceased . . . only surviving Daughter and Heir at Law of William Attwood late of Beverly . . . by Elizabeth his Wife both deceased and Sister and Heir at Law of Ursula Attwood late of the City of Worcester aforesaid Spinster deceased of the one part and William Lilly of the City of Worcester . . . of the other part" shows that Lilly paid Digges £200 to give up all claim to the property that had been willed to Lilly on February 10, 1770.[32]

The indenture completed and proper leave taken in Birmingham, he was in London by December 18, probably by way of Portsmouth, for he sent to John Thornton a careful, detailed list of American prisoners in Forton Prison as of December 1. Though he may have wavered later, he apparently had made his choice between service on the Continent, which the Lees were offering him and for which he was eminently qualified by his knowledge of Spain and Portugal, his command of the languages, his commercial experience and connections, and service in England. It had been mentioned to him, he had written Matthew Ridley on November 20, that "a person is wanted to make some distributions of assistance to some confined unfortunates in this Country." He continued: "As it was never in my power to give a personal assistance where perhaps it was most wanted, I have long eer this pledgd myself to do every thing in my power, & think this business could be done without any material personal risque."

The personal risks did not include bullets, but they were very real, as Digges was to discover. Isaac Van Zandt, a New Yorker who regarded Digges as "a particular friend," was already a paid informer of the British and had exposed to his employers Digges's letter of November 2 to William Carmichael, secretary of the American commissioners in Paris.[33] Lee's secretary, John Thornton, to whom Digges sent the December 1 list of prisoners in Forton, was very soon to accept British pay. Loyalties were uncertain. The mails were watched, letters read, and often withheld. The shipping was watched. The

[32] PRO: c. 54/6475, 19010, 15–18.
[33] B. F. Stevens, *Facsimiles*. no. 298.

agents of government were many. Some, like Edward Bancroft, Paul Wentworth, and John Vardill, were clever and able. Digges was not to come through his agency unscathed. Far from it. His record would open him to serious charges, but no evidence has been found that he did not mean what he had written to Ridley or that he ever wavered in loyalty to his country.

On December 24, 1777, at a meeting held at King's Arms Tavern, Cornhill, for relief of American prisoners, a committee of twenty was formed, which, headed by John Sawbridge and Frederick Bull, aldermen, included Thomas Digges and men who figure in his life: Benjamin Vaughan, Edward Bridgen, William Hodgson, Matthew Ridley, Edmund Jenings. Among the most generous donors were Thomas Day, Sir George Savile, the bishop of St. Asaph (Jonathan Shipley), and the earl of Shelburne, with all of whom Digges had subsequent dealings. John Thornton subscribed £100.[34]

Digges must have seen his brother George during this stay in London, because George subscribed five guineas in late January. But Thomas was soon out of London again. Ridley reported on March 14 that Digges was well and "busy in the old way."[35] The Lees were still writing to him. In April he saw Governor George Johnstone in Portsmouth just before the departure of the peace embassy—Lord Carlisle, Johnstone, and William Eden—for America and secured from Johnstone an order for the release of Dr. James Brehon from Forton. The commissioners must have asked Digges to go with them, for Ridley wrote Digges April 23, 1778: "I do not wonder at their wanting you to go with them or any Person they thought might have influence. To my certain knowledge Johnstone has applied to Americans in a very middle line even for the Names of those of Fortune and influence in America. To take one with them therefore who knows them would be a still greater advantage."[36]

Curiously enough, the *Courrier de l'Europe* on August 11, 1778, published an extract of a letter of an officer of General Henry Clin-

---

[34] *London Evening-Post*, Jan. 3, 1778.
[35] Ridley to Joshua Johnson, Mar. 14, 1778 (MHS: Ridley Papers, Norton Gift, Letter Book, 1776–1778).
[36] MHS: Ridley Papers, Norton Gift.

INTRODUCTION

xlv

ton's army to one of his friends, dated June 20, 1778, which reads in part:

Quelques jours avant de quitter *Philadelphie*, j'y ai vu le Gouverneur *Johnstone*, & j'ai eu quelque conversation avec lui: par l'entremise du Commandant en chef & de M. *Galloway*, il a fait parvenir des lettres de recommandation personelle a quelques particuliers puissants; il en avoit, entre autres, une d'une maison *Quaker* etablie dans la cité de Londres, pour M. *Morris*, l'un des principaux membres du Congrès, et trois autres pour le général *Washington*, M. *Johnson* Gouverneur du *Maryland*, & M. *Carmichael* ci-devant Sécretaire des Commissaires du Congrès résidants à *Paris*; ces dernieres lettres lui avoient été données par un particulier du *Maryland*, établi actuellement à B * * * & qui avoit été à bord du Trident visiter les Commissaires avant qu'ils partissent de Spithead: toutes ces lettres furent présentées au Général *Clinton*, qui fit partir M. *Brown* avec un parlimentaire, pour les faire passer à leur destination: à en juger parce qu'on m'en a dit, l'objet de ces lettres est purement d'introduire le Gouverneur *Johnstone*: les personnes qui les ont écrites ajoutent seulement qu'elles desirent ardemment que leur recommandation donne lieu à une entrevue & à quelque pour-parler, dont un accomodement honorable pour les deux nations puisse être la suite; *Washington* répondit le lendemain, & nous ne regardons pas sa réponse comme un présage favorable à la paix.

[A few days before leaving *Philadelphia*, I saw Governor *Johnstone* and had some conversation with him: through the good offices of the Commander in chief and Mr. *Galloway* he had some personal letters of recommendation sent to several influential persons; there was, among others, one letter from a *Quaker* business established in London for Mr. *Morris*, one of the principal members of Congress, and three others for General *Washington*, Mr. *Johnson*, Governor of *Maryland*, & Mr. *Carmichael*, former Secretary of the Commissioners of Congress living in *Paris*; these last letters had been given him by an individual from *Maryland*, presently established in B * * * & who had been on board the Trident in order to visit the Commissioners before they left Spithead: all these letters were presented to General *Clinton*, who had Mr. *Brown* leave with a parliamentarian in order to deliver them: judging by what I was told, the purpose of these letters is simply to introduce Governor *Johnstone*: their writers add simply that they ardently wish that their recommendations may bring about a meeting and some negotiation, which might result in an honorable accommodation for the two countries; *Washington* answered the following day, & we do not consider his reply auspicious for peace.]

There follows a letter from Washington to Johnstone of June 18, which includes the words, "& je suis très obligé à mon ami de l'intention qu'il à eue de nous rapprocher l'un de l'autre [& I am much obliged to my friend for his wish to bring us together]."

Although Digges is not named, it is hard to doubt that he was the Marylander, established at B*** [Bath?], who had seen Johnstone before the departure of the commissioners, who had given letters introducing Johnstone to Washington, Carmichael, and Thomas Johnson, and finally, to whom Washington could have referred as his friend. Were the letters the price of securing the release of Brehon?

On August 30 Digges wrote Arthur Lee supporting him in his quarrels with Bancroft, Deane, and Franklin. But on September 18, from Birmingham, he wrote Franklin offering his services and giving as references Izard, the Lees, Joseph Wharton, Carmichael, Ridley, and Joshua Johnson. Ridley was in Paris in September. By October he was doing business in Nantes. He wrote Christopher Johnston in Baltimore on October 26 telling of his removal from London, asking for consignments from any of the states, and continuing: "The very disagreeable situation I was in, in England, where I was closely watchd for some time past prevented me writing you anything particular on business," a remark that throws some light on what Digges was offering to do for Franklin.[37] On October 31 Ridley forwarded a letter from Thomas to his brother George, who in August had appeared before the governor and Council to take his oath of fidelity to the state of Maryland, having been "in Great Britain and other Parts beyound the Seas for about three years last Past and hath lately that is to say within three months now last past returned into this State."[38] Thomas wrote Franklin from Bristol on December 19 that he was much with David Hartley, with whom Franklin had been corresponding about the prisoners and the cartel. And on February 7, 1779, he explained to Benjamin Franklin that he "[made] it [his] business to be as much among the Lords & minority members as [he could]." A week before, in another letter to Franklin, he had referred to Lord Shelburne as his acquaintance. It is hard to understand how he could have done so well in such a short time without the "amazing address" that Archbishop Carroll later wrote of.

[37] MHS: Ridley Papers, Nichols Gift, 6, Letter Book.
[38] *Archives of Maryland*, 21:182.

On May 3, 1779, before Franklin in Paris, he swore allegiance to the United States, renouncing all allegiance or obedience to George III. Soon back in Britain he was involved in what appears to have been his first assignment, putting out peace feelers through Hartley. They reached Lord North but slowly died. On July 6 he wrote Franklin that his business would take him to Lisbon in a few months and that he had rejected three offers to attend Arthur Lee as secretary, having "no prospect of comfort . . . by living with a Man or Men who are apt to quarrel." In August he complained that the Lees were implying that he was cool to the cause. On August 31 he was brought into serious danger by the arrest of Thomas Hutchins, an American captain in the British army, charged with "treasonable correspondencies with Dr. Franklin, Mr. S. Wharton & other Americans." Hutchins was closely questioned about his correspondents, one of whom was Thomas Digges. This led Digges to write Franklin that he kept his papers distant from himself. His letters do not indicate that he was shaken as he makes it clear that Hutchins was by the severity of his treatment. Yet such a paragraph as came out in the *Morning Post and Daily Advertiser* of October 16, 1779, might well have excited a little alarm:

> The superior lenity of this country over all others, as to the treatment of spies and prisoners, is in no instance more conspicuous than in the suffering a *certain American* to go about the kingdom unmolested, who is agent for Congress, and in the confidence and correspondence of the traitor Franklin. It is well known, and has been proved under a late examination, that he has very extensive credit with disaffected foreign merchants in the City, by which he has been able to remit considerable sums lately in English specie to Holland, and through that channel sent very great supplies of soldiers clothing, ammunition, &c. &c. which the *new* and *mighty* allies of America could not supply her with. Under the appearance of leading an intriguing, dissipated life at Bath, pleading poverty from the times, wishing reunion between the two countries, when he would rejoice to see this ruined, and artfully insinuating himself with some of the first circles, he goes on doing much secret and hidden mischiefs to the country he is permitted to go at large in, and finds a great many gulls among the leaders of the opposition, who swallow, with avidity, every piece of bad news he gets transmitted from France and America.

Digges confessed alarm at the difficulties caused by the American prisoners who escaped and came to him for help. Ridley had found the expense intolerable, and so did Digges. At least five times in the fall of 1779 he wrote Franklin mentioning his financial embarrassment from this cause, most eloquently on November 10: "We are at length informd that the Cartel Ship will be soon on float again the new passport for Morlaix having arrivd. I hope to God they will clear both prisons in a trip from each, & not make more for some time. I cannot describe to You the trouble I have with these people; and the expence is so heavy on me at times that even with my curtaild and oeconimic mode of living I am put to extreem difficulties. It is not trifles that will do for men who come naked by dozens & half dozens, & it is harder still to turn ones back upon them."

Five days later he mentioned the danger involved in helping the escaped prisoners: "The delays of Office are so great here that I fear another squad may be inducd to break Prison before they can be convincd that the Cartel will go on again—These breaking outs, are not only disagreeable, but at times highly distressing & dangerous to me and they seem to fly to me as one who was obligd whether it was convenient or not, to supply them."

The hazards of Digges's position were growing.

In December he made another offer to be a go-between for the cause of peace. He wrote David Hartley on December 28 about John Adams's appointment as a peacemaker and stated: "I . . . would sacrafice every thing I possess to be even instrumental in bringing . . . [peace] about; My time or the Expence of going is no sort of object, but as the partys are not arrivd & I have not yet got the true ground on which He [Adams] comes an immediate journey would be premature." The delay he suggests lasted until March of 1782.

Whether Digges heard in these months from his brother Joseph is unknown. Joseph, a prisoner on parole in Port Orotava, Teneriffe, was dying of consumption. He sent George Washington a pipe of wine and wrote him on November 1 a personal and pathetic letter in which he said that he had not heard from Warburton, that the family must think him dead, that he wished to get to southern France, and that he would die soon if he had to stay on Teneriffe. He died on Teneriffe a few months later.[39] He was thirty-four.

[39] Joseph Digges to George Washington, Nov. 1, 1779 (LC: Washington Papers, Series 4); MdHS: Ms. 246.

INTRODUCTION

In March of 1780 the correspondence began with John Adams that was to continue for the next two years through many trying times for Digges, times when he wished to leave Britain. He had thought of going to America by way of St. Eustatius as early as January of 1780, according to a letter Anne Ridley wrote her husband on January 14.[40] On July 12 he wrote Adams offering to serve in Portugal in a subordinate way, saying that he knew every corner of that country and every merchant of eminence there. This was apparently a bid for a salaried post. No evidence has been found that he was receiving anything for his services to the prisoners, nor, if we can believe what he wrote Robert Traill on March 3, 1783, did he ever have any allowance or stipend for his agency. But Congress on July 11 had appointed their agent in Lisbon. No doubt Digges could have gotten out of Britain, as Ridley and Johnson had, but he was caught up in increasing difficulties and complications. One difficulty was his continuing financial embarrassment. For instance, on April 6 he had to ask Franklin to send on to Adams the newspapers and pamphlets Franklin was receiving from Digges, "which may save me an expence of sending duplicates—my present finances obliges me to be thus oeconomical." It seems possible that when Adams found himself receiving Digges's pamphlets only through "another Gentleman"—Franklin—his pique led to these words in a letter to Digges, April 15:

Let me beg of you to send me duplicates, of Pamphlets, as they come out, when you send setts to another Gentleman—any Banker in London who will draw upon Me or Mr. Grand the Banker for the Expense of them, shall be punctually paid, or I will get Mr. Grand to desire some Banker of his Correspondence to pay you, or the Book seller if any one, will undertake to send them to me. Political Pamphlets I mean respecting the present War, and the actual State of Things.—It is of much Importance to me, and perhaps to others, that I should have all these Things as soon as possible and that they should be my Property that I may have the Use of them to myself as long as I please, and send them where, and as soon as I please.[11]

Over and over in the next months Digges complained to Franklin of the hardships imposed on him by the demands of the prisoners and other Americans. Except for the bill drawn by Dr. James Brehon,

[40] MHS: Ridley Papers, Nichols Gift, 2.
[41] MHS: Adams Papers, Reel 96.

he had "never had a bill paid, nor any remittance from any one of his Countrymen pushing home." On November 14 he wrote Adams that the few guineas Manley and Conyngham got from him he could "very ill afford."

On December 5 Franklin wrote asking him for a complete statement of his accounts.[42]

Hard pressed for cash, questioned about his payments to the prisoners, and deeply engaged in getting out English goods to America, he was soon dangerously involved in the affairs of Henry Laurens and John Trumbull. This time he did not escape unscathed.

He managed very well with Laurens, the American commissioner to the Netherlands who, captured at sea on his way to his post, had on October 6, 1780, as Digges reported to Adams the same day, been committed "a close prisoner to the Tower" with "orders that no person whatever speaks to Him." Adams answered October 14, asking Digges: "Pray inform me constantly of every Thing relative to him."[43] On October 24 Digges wrote Adams and Franklin that he had found means of communicating with Laurens and offered them this access. On October 27 he was able to send each of them a copy of a note he had had from Laurens that included the injunction, "Continue to keep those friends F[ranklin] and A[dams] informd, & communicate intelligence from them as speedily as possible—" along with the words, "A million of thanks to W. S. C.——[Thomas Digges]." One would suppose from this note that without Digges Laurens would have been cut off from Adams and Franklin. In the letter of that date to Franklin Digges said of Laurens: "His disorder being contagious I am afraid to visit him—He is getting better & I hear from Him and he from me now & then." On October 31 he reminded Franklin that "the friend whom I have lately wrote to You about, *has his communications,* & very lately expressd an expectation of hearing from You." On November 3 he informed Franklin that though Laurens's friends are "absolutely denyd any further admittance—yet *communications* are kept up." On the tenth he wrote Franklin: "I hear now & then from the friend I have lately mentiond in Letters to you, & he express's

[42] LC: Franklin Papers, Series 1, 4:319.
[43] MHS: Adams Papers, Reel 102.

wishes to hear from others & to know what can be done in His case. His son is now with me."

Laurens had been in the Tower less than six weeks when Colonel John Trumbull, the artist son of Governor Jonathan Trumbull of Connecticut, was jailed on a charge of treason—in retaliation for Major John André's death, said Digges to Franklin, November 21, commenting: "Good God what a degree of Wickedness folly & weakness are we Englishmen reducd to." The next day, when Digges, Henry Laurens, Jr., Leendert de Neufville, of the Amsterdam house of Jean de Neufville, and Gilbert Stuart, the American portrait painter and protégé of Benjamin West, went to see Trumbull, they were taken to a magistrate to declare what they knew of Trumbull.[44] Whether they had come to see him as a group is uncertain but possible. Digges and de Neufville were friends, Henry Laurens, Jr., was staying with Digges, and Trumbull and Stuart were friends. On November 23 the *London Evening-Post* told of Trumbull's being brought up from New Prison for reexamination at the Public Office in Bow Street. One of the letters read in evidence against him was from William White of Lyme in Dorset to Trumbull in care of Mr. Waters, No. 23, Villars-street, Strand. Under interrogation Trumbull identified Waters as Digges. The *Political Magazine* for November identified William White as William Brailsford, an American who had lived "some time since" with his father in Bristol before moving to Lyme. "Trumbull's saying he knew him but as a chance acquaintance must be false."

When de Neufville, who had quickly retreated to Amsterdam, wrote Franklin on December 21 that he had left Digges in a disagreeable situation, Franklin asked for details. The response on February 8 was this:

The disagreeable Situation of Mr. Diggs I alluded to was then caused by Mr. Trumbulls mentioning his name in his trial & his thus becoming a more immediate object of Ministrys attention while on the other hand some Americans that owed their escape to his care had behaved rather imprudently by telling their story to the Capt. of the vessel they came over in; but I am sorry to say that this is a good deal worse than [?] at present. Mr. Warren Mr. Brailsford both taken up the latter with a recommendation letter in his

[44] Digges to John Adams, Nov. 22, 1780.

pocket Signed T. D. Your Excellency knows I suppose that this Mr. Brailsford was said to be author of the letter found with Mr. Trumbull signed White; Thus I find that the suspicion falling on Mr. Dgs. he is oblidged to keep much out of the way for fear that the same insolence might extend to himself. Young Mr. Warren was suspected on account of his correspondence with Colo. Tyler but which I believe had been found innocent. I hope that Mr. Digges will come away in time as the example of Mr. Trumbull shows that innocence cannot avail against the inveterate rage of a corrupted Ministry.[15]

It is possible that the "corrupted Ministry" acted after Digges had prudently removed to Bath on February 21. Hodgson wrote Franklin on May 8 that he had been informed that Digges had "very lately" been arrested in Bath.[46] He gives no reason for the reported arrest, and no further evidence has come to light. But that Digges's papers were seized at about this time is beyond doubt. They were not to be recovered until after a visit to John Adams in Amsterdam in March of 1782. Meanwhile Digges's character was being assailed by Franklin and Hodgson, who were convinced that Digges had pocketed money sent him for the relief of the prisoners in Mill and Forton. By August of 1781 Digges's character had been, in Hodgson's words, blasted, and his regular correspondence with Franklin and Adams had ceased. It had been maintained with Franklin from September 18, 1778, to April 25, 1781, and with Adams from March 3, 1780, to March 8, 1781. It had been maintained under difficult and dangerous circumstances by a man well aware of the value of intelligence and propaganda, an American with connections with shippers, Spanish, Portuguese, French, and Dutch, with English manufacturers, with the London press, and, most important, with members of the British opposition. He had been able to write of Benedict Arnold's treachery before the *Courant* reported it. He had been able to provide Adams with accounts of Laurens for the European press. He had been able to get out needed munitions to America. There were not many like him in England with the desire, the opportunity, the daring, and the ability to serve. His faults may have been many, but his services were great.

Hodgson wrote Franklin on May 8, 1781, that he did not think

---

[45] APS: Franklin Papers, 21:54.
[46] Ibid., 22:12.

INTRODUCTION

Digges would appear again in London.[47] But he was there by February 12, 1782, and was soon sent by Lord North to see Adams in Amsterdam and make inquiries that might lead to peace, his way eased by letters to Franklin and Adams from David Hartley. Adams's impression of Digges's embassy is best seen in Ridley's record in his journal, May 20, 1782, of what Adams had told him of it:

On asking the question Mr. Adams informed me Mr. Laurens had been in Holland, that he came to know what had passed between Mr. Adams & Mr. Thos. Digges who had been here & to be sure how far his & Mr. Adams's opinion coincided in case of offers of Peace—Their opinions are the same. He staid only a few Hours. The affair of Digges is as follows. He came to Holland.—Put up at the Parliament of England & sent to Mr. Adams to know when he could Have the honor of waiting on him—Sending him at the same 2 Letters from Mr. Samuel [actually David, not Samuel] Hartley wherein Mr. Hartley said Mr. Digges was sent to Holland for the purpose of Interview with Mr. Adams & he had authority to say he was sent by Persons of the first distinction.—Mr. Adams returned for answer to D. that he could have no meeting with him unless in the presence of a third Person & even not then unless he was left at Liberty to publish to the world if he thought necessary what might have between them and send it to Comte de Vergennes at Versailles for he would have no secrets, that the third Person he should propose would be his Secretary Mr. Thaxter—If he D. chose to see him on those conditions he might call the next morning—D. accepted them & came—He informed Mr. Adams he was sent by Lord North that England was desirous of a Peace but did not know if the same disposition prevailed with the other parties or if it would be listened to—Mr. A. told him whenever the English Ministry chose to apply in a proper way they would be attended to but while they continued to do otherways no attention would be paid to what they said. D. said they had understood that Mr. A. was inclined to Peace but D[r.] F. was against. Mr. A. said it was impossible for any one to know his sentiments for he had never declared them to any one that the making Peace did not depend upon him. Congress had named five Persons (one of which Mr. Jefferson of Virga. was not yet arrived, the other four Dr. F. Mr. Jay. Mr. Laurens & himself[)] that any Offers made for Peace must be made at Paris—D. mentioned the difficulty of collecting such a number together. Mr. A. told him that would be no difficulty if England made such propositions as might be listened to—if she did not—certainly there would be no meeting & that America would make no Peace but on such terms as should satisfy France as well as America & that it must be made in conjunction with Comte de Vergennes—A Copy of the

[47] Ibid.

Commission for making Peace laying at Mr. Adams's hands he told Digges there was a Copy of the Commission & read it to him—D. said he should report what had Pass'd & I think Mr. Adams told me talked of writing to Mr. Adams. Mr. A. told him he might write but he need expect no Answers from him & that he should think himself obliged to communicate to Dr. Franklin & Comte de Vergennes whatever he received—Thus the Interview ended—D. returned to England. Lord North was then out & he made his report to Ld. Shelburne who had come into office & it is said added that Mr. A. had promised to correspond with him which Mr. A. flatly & roundly denies."[48]

Back in London, Digges with his new consequence as a go-between seems to have offended Hodgson, who wrote sourly to Franklin on July 13: "The Fellow appears with all possible Effrontery—especially since he was sent or pretended to be sent by the old Ministry to Mr. Adams and the Hague."[49] Digges wrote Adams on April 9, 1782: "I have had every indulgence shewn me towards the recovery of my papers; but altho I have a Chart Blanch to search in the office things are not yet so en train in the new offices as to have things in proper order for looking over.—Notwithstanding the savage practice of every Minister when he goes out of office making a sweep & taking all papers he likes with Him, I have yet the hopes of soon getting the material part of mine. . . ." Though he may not have recovered all his papers, he got others of great importance to Lord George Brydges Rodney, General John Vaughan, and the English merchants who had been supplying the United States, via St. Eustatius, with the essentials for carrying on the war. Thirty-one years later he could write: "At the Close of that war I obtain bags & sacks full of Letters *opend* during the naval warfare, as a *donation* from the succeeding minister to Ld. North (Rockingham) for my trouble & vigilence as messenger under them for the first overtures for Peace (*Independance the prelimary article*) to Amsterdam & Paris. The day of my return, in 8 days to & from Lord Rockinghams, I did not sleep or hardly eat until I got a coachfull of those documents & Letters from the then foreign office of G. Jackson in Cleveland row."[50]

Whatever papers he recovered, they were not apparently enough

[48] Ridley Papers, Norton Gift, box 5.
[49] HSP: Franklin Papers, 3:30.
[50] Digges to James Patton, Apr. 24, 1813.

INTRODUCTION

lv

to permit him to face Franklin in Paris and clear himself of the charge of embezzlement. And of course with the change of ministry, his services as an emissary were no longer required. Throughout the rest of 1782 and most of 1783, he remained in London pursuing his shipping interests.

Why Digges in late 1783 or early 1784 should have gone to Ireland is a question. His father had died March 28, 1783. Digges knew of his death by August 20, when he referred to it in a letter to Ridley. With the death of his father, what was holding him up from claiming Warburton, which was legally his, and settling down to the life of a country gentleman? Certainly not mercantile success. He wrote Robert Traill on March 3, 1783, that he had "for the last Six years been Distressd Exceedingly for money, and in times as much in want as any American prisoner I had the care of." Times were hard for traders to America. Remittances were hard to get. Bankruptcies were many. William Hodgson, who had contributed so much to Digges's troubles, "in a fit of despair," took his life with a pistol October 20, 1784.[51] Ridley wrote in this period of the number of failures in France.[52] In October of 1783 John Bondfield wrote Arthur Lee of "Mr. Diggs draft on Waterman of London which has been return'd protested for nonpayment."[53] Did he fly from his creditors?

It is possible that he was drawn to Ireland by the growing market in America for indentured servants, a market about which he and Ridley were corresponding by February 25, 1783 (see headnote, Digges to Ridley, Aug. 20, 1783). In April of that year he wrote William Carmichael: "There is a great appearance of *vast* Emigration to America, & I encourage it all I can; hundreds of People *with money in their pockets* are moving.—They look to that Country as an Elezium, & seem certain it is *there* only where nature opens her broad lap to receive the perpetual accession of new comers, & to supply them with food." After speaking of his meaning "to set out in 8 or 10 days to see the northern manufactories & thence to Ireland & Scotland," he con-

[51] *Political Magazine*, 7 (Oct. 1784): 244.
[52] Ridley to Ridley & Pringle, Sept. 12, 1783 (MHS: Ridley Papers, Norton Gift, Letter Book, 1783–1785).
[53] HU: Lee Manuscripts, 7:116.

tinues, "I take this tour principally to serve my Brother in Law Mr. Jno. Fitzgerrald settled in an extensive Commercial way in Alexandria." Fitzgerald was interested in the building of the Potomac Canal and was looking for laborers. Digges wrote Ridley from Brighton on August 20 that he had been getting away a ship for Virginia. "She will sail on Sunday for Potomack & carrys out about 8 or 900£s worth of Goods & some 16 or 17 Indentures viz. 2 Black Smiths, 3 Ship wrights, a Sadler, a Shoemaker & Tanner of some property, and 10 or 12 excellent Husbandmen. It is uncertain if She goes to Richmond where the owners Brother wishes to settle or to Alexandria but I am in hopes to get Her to the later." Digges was well prepared on May 5, 1784, to answer the enquiry of the Cork shipper Thomas Trant of "the probable benefits on a Cargoe of Indented Servants from hence to Virginia." Nothing, he said, could be sent from Ireland "to greater prospect of success." He spoke of dispatching the *Washington* with 200 or 250 such servants to John Fitzgerald in Alexandria and was convincing enough with his detailed counsel to get Trant to send a cargo on his ship the *Angelica* to the same address. The two ships arrived almost simultaneously in late July.

But whatever was Digges's success in forwarding indentured servants and tradesmen, it did not save him from his creditors. By January 1, 1785, he was in debtor's prison in the Four Courts Marshalsea in Dublin. Exactly when he entered and who put him there are unknown, but he was certainly there from January 1, 1785, until at least January 23, 1786, as shown in his announcement, December 6, in the *Dublin Gazette* of his intent to take benefit of the Act for the Relief of Insolvent Debtors. Jonathan Williams wrote Franklin from Dublin June 17, 1785: "You will not be much surprised when I tell you, that Mr. Diggs, who had so much of our Prisoners money is in . . . Four Courts Marshalsea; He has been playing the Rogue in this Country, but like all other cunning Rogues shewn himself to be a Fool also, and is now paying severely for his Folly & Wickedness."[54] What Williams could have been referring to has not come to light. Digges wrote from Dublin to Samuel Huntington September 13, 1788, ". . . my having a

[54] APS: Franklin Papers, 38:158.

INTRODUCTION   lvii

heavy Chancery Suit to look after in this Country has brought me often to it, & causd a frequent residence in it since 1784." But all that is certain is that Digges was in prison for debt. One wonders whether he appealed for help from his brother-in-law Fitzgerald, or from his brother George, who in July 1785 was ordering from France such items as claret, burgundy, brandy, champagne, silk hose, and kid gloves. Unless Digges had funds that his creditors could not get at, he must have suffered. The life of the penniless debtors in Four Courts Marshalsea, according to contemporary accounts, was truly horrifying. One account, in the *Dublin Journal* of April 14, 1784, asks: "Would it not be more reconcileable with humanity to deprive them of life in a summary way, than to starve them by a tedious and lingering process?"

No letter written by Digges during the time of his imprisonment has been found. He may have written to his family at Warburton, but there is no evidence of it. In fact no family letter of his has surfaced. The public man is shown in many guises; the private man seldom appears. While he was in prison, it is possible that he wrote a puff for the Potomac Canal published in the *Volunteer's Journal* of Dublin, August 12, a puff which referred to Washington, John Fitzgerald, Thomas Sim Lee, and Thomas Johnson. More curious is an item in the same paper of February 10, 1786, an extract of a letter from New York dated December 10, 1785, which spoke of a publication "handed about with avidity," called, "A Representation of the State of Politics, Commerce, and Manufactures, in Ireland, in 1785, dedicated to the Congress of the United States of America, by a Citizen of Maryland. To which is added, some Hints to the Rulers of America, towards forming a Commercial Treaty with Great Britain and Ireland." The author "appears to have been an Agent for Congress in England." The article adds that the book "seems to have been privately published in Dublin at the expense of the author, and is not sold here." No copy has been located thus far. It should be remembered that *Adventures of Alonso* had carried on the title page "By a Native of Maryland," and that Digges was not ignorant of the uses of a good press.

The press he was soon to get over the loss of the St. Eustatius papers proved to be bad. When Admiral Rodney and General Vaughan took the Dutch island of St. Eustatius February 3, 1781, they confiscated the property of most of the English merchants doing business there as the property of traitors supplying the enemy. Their papers were sent to the office of George Germain, secretary of state for the colonies. Upon these papers Rodney and Vaughan came to depend for defense against the suits of the merchants who had lost their property and whose claims amounted to a sum greater than the proceeds of the capture. But the papers had disappeared, and as the search for them went on, their disappearance became more puzzling and complicated. Some of the complications were these: There were two transmissions of papers from St. Eustatius. William Knox, undersecretary of state for America, 1770–1782, testified in the House of Lords on the second reading of the St. Eustatius bill in 1786 that, fearing prosecution for the commitment of Samuel Curson and Isaac Gouverneur, the American agents at St. Eustatius who had been sent prisoners to London for high treason, he had, on the fall of North's ministry, secretly held back from the new minister, Shelburne, "one part of those Papers which contained the principal Evidence of [Curson's and Gouverneur's] criminality."[55] The second shipment of papers, a large one, was studied beginning in May 1781, and précis were made under the direction of Knox's colleague in Germain's office, Sir Benjamin Thompson (known later as Count Rumford), by Daniel Leonard and Arthur Savage. One of their notes reads: "Saml. Hartley of London appears to be Privy to a Concern of largely Shipping Goods from Great Britain to the revolted Colonies in America, (see the original letter directed to T—— D—— under his cover.)."[56]

Digges had, as he wrote in the letter of 1813 already quoted, been allowed to search for his papers in March or early April of 1782, and on the day he got back from seeing Adams, had taken "a coachfull of . . . documents & Letters from the then foreign office" of George Jackson, second secretary to the admiralty. Whether these included St. Eustatius papers is uncertain. In May 1782, Curson recovered his and Gouverneur's papers and "threw in a good many others that were

[55] PRO: TS 11/2080/658.
[56] UM: Shelburne Papers, 84:83.

among them to fill the Trunks."[57] In late January of 1783 Arthur Savage received an order "from the best authority" to deliver a part of the papers he and Leonard had worked on to the Bermuda merchant, Richard Downing Jennings. In his long search for them, Savage "found many of the Books and Papers we had examined in 1781 removed, or taken away."[58] So that of the St. Eustatius papers, Digges, Knox, Curson, Gouverneur, and Jennings all had some.

But it was Digges who interested the newspapers most. Besides being named in the inaccurate article enclosed in Digges's letter of August 1786 to an unidentified recipient, he was glanced at by the *Morning Chronicle and London Advertiser*, July 3, the London *Public Advertiser*, July 4, the *Dublin Journal*, July 6, and the Dublin *Volunteer's Journal*, July 7. Their almost identical accounts read: "It turns out that when Lord S[helburne] came into office, he suffered the St. Eustatius papers to be withdrawn from the Secretary's office; and upon inquiry it is suspected they were delivered to the known agent of the Americans." The attack upon Digges continued for two years as the suits against Rodney and Vaughan ground on. The Dublin *Volunteer Evening Post* noticed him on April 7, April 14, and May 26, 1787. The London *Public Advertiser* on September 15, 1788, commented:

By the loss of the St. Eustatia papers, which appear now to have been unaccountably got out of the Secretary of State's Office in the year 1783 by the then American agent, or some other political vermin, the late trials before the Lords of Appeal were reduced to one mass of confusion and gave their Lordships much trouble and vexation, such papers only being partially produced or suppressed as the agents in each party chose: It is supposed, however, at the next sittings of the Lords of Appeal, some lights may be thrown on the matter, and the St. Eustatia captors, in a great measure, relieved from the heavy suits and damages given against them in the Courts, as some of those papers after a five year loss, have, of late, come to light.

This article was reprinted in the *Dublin Chronicle* of September 18, 1788. One may well wonder what the source of the papers lost for five years was. It could hardly have been Digges, there being no evidence

---

[57] Ibid., 122.
[58] PRO: TS 11/2080/658 ("Copy of a letter from Mr. A. Savage proposed by him to be inserted in one of the Public Prints," July 10, 1786).

of his sudden prosperity. Two years out of debtor's prison and cognizant of what the government had inflicted upon Laurens, Trumbull, Curson, and Gouverneur, Digges must have felt the need of caution and circumspection.

His concern could not have been lessened by his activities, well reflected in his letters to Washington, Jefferson, and Hamilton during the next four years, in getting out skilled workers to develop manufactures in America. The penalty for seducing artisans to emigrate, "highly dangerous to those concernd," was £500 and a year's imprisonment. In his letter to Jefferson of May 12, 1788, Digges wrote of having been "a little hurt since my arrival in Ireland through my endeavours to get some useful mechanicks to my home near Alexandria," but he gave no details of how he had been directly affected. He could hardly have been pleased to read in the *Dublin Journal* of April 3, 1790:

> Among other secret resolutions of the Federal Congress, there has lately been discovered one of a serious nature to the mechanic and the manufacturing interests of Great Britain and Ireland. They not only suffer bounties to emigrant artists, but the different states give premiums upon the introduction into the United States of all kinds of manufacturing machinery; and it is a well known fact, that there are now, and have been for some time past, two or three agents (men of cleverness and consequence in that country) employed by congress for the special purpose of travelling about and inveigling away artists and their tools from England, Scotland, and Ireland, to stimulate emigrations from these countries, which have increased lately in the North of Ireland to an alarming degree.

He might, however, have been pleased by the notice (indeed he might have written it) in the *Belfast News-Letter* of June 25–29, 1790, which, after recording the death of Franklin, goes on:

> It is said his store of MS. papers, memorandums, and correspondatory letters will afford a vast scope for literary publications upon philosophy, mathematics, legislature, and circuitous politics, prior to and during the late war. His correspondence seems to have been with men of the first abilities and genius, and not confined to any part of the globe. He found means to get communications of the first rate authority even from Asia as well as Africa, and the principal places of Spanish and Portuguese America. It is said that his valuable collection is not a little added to by a series of letters written to him while at Paris between the years 1775 and 1783, in a stile similar to that of the Jewish

Spy, by a Mr. D——s, (who was employed in England during that time as Agent for America, and is since gone to India) and are fraught with much political as well as commercial information, describing in a particular manner the manufactures, and giving characters and anecdotes of the leading men of Great Britain.

By late 1789 or early 1790 Digges had moved to Belfast. Here he had become acquainted with Thomas Russell, the Irish patriot, and was in on the heady days of the founding of the United Irishmen. It is clear from Russell's diary that Digges made a great impression upon him. The Madden Papers in Trinity College Library contain "Memoranda drawn up by the late Capn. Russell nephew of Thomas Russell chiefly in relation to certain remarks on Russell's character that appeared in an article published in Frazer's Magazine, and attributed to John Wilson Croker": "—was Lt. in Belfast—in 64 Regt. went bail for Thos. Diggis—An American (a man who appeared a patriot—plausible—) who was arrested for £200—Mr. Thos. Brown—a Merchant—advised T. R. not to persist in offering himself as Bail, as he little knew the character of the Man he had to deal with—who would infallibly leave him to pay every farthing—T. R. persisting—was obliged to sell his commission—to raise the money—" In the margin against this passage are the words, "*Diggs* Stole a pair Silver Spurs from Sam Neilson." Whatever the truth of Russell's persisting in offering himself as bail, or of Digges's stealing Neilson's spurs, it is true that Russell sold his commission as reported in the *Dublin Gazette*, September 22–24, 1791: "64th Regiment of Foot. Mr. James O'Grady to be Ensign, vice Russell, resigned."

Another story is told in "A Sketch of the Life of Thomas Russell" in the *Ulster Magazine* of January 1830:

Among the acquaintances which Russell formed in Belfast, was a Medical gentleman, an American by birth. This man, who was extremely plausible, though somewhat superficial in his manners, had contrived to win the confidence, not only of Russell, but also of the principal merchants of Belfast. The citizen of a young and rising republic, he seemed privileged to descant with more freedom than those about him, on that liberty and equality which the Presbyterians of the North prized in their hearts, though they had still too much regard for constituted authority, to talk so largely on the subject. He was, moreover, a complete theophilanthropist; and his views for promoting the happiness of the human race, were so extensive and enlightened, that

Russell loved him for his political sentiments, despite of the heterodoxy of his religious opinions. In speaking thus of this person, it is not meant to throw out any direct imputations on the opinions of the conscientious sceptic. There are hypocrites of every creed; and when villains are occasionally found among professing Christians, it is nothing extraordinary that a disciple of Tom Payne should sometimes prove to be a scoundrel.

The conduct of this Transatlantic theophilanthropist, however, would, in the opinion of many, completely justify all the sarcasms which the wit of Canning and the eloquence of Burke have vented against the sect. He had contrived to get in debt to one individual to the amount of £200, and the creditor beginning to suspect that all was not right, had him arrested. In this extremity, he applied to Russell. Unsuspecting and generous, the latter could not bear the idea that the man whose free-born soul could scarcely brook to be chained down for a season to this little world, should be incarcerated in a dungeon; and that he, whose enlarged benevolence embraced the whole human race, should suffer hardship for a paltry sum. He became security for the American Physician, and the latter was immediately set at liberty. Shortly after this, a party was formed in Belfast for an excursion to Scotland; and the American Doctor was one among the number. Scotland was not then the classic ground which the "Great Magician" since has made it, and the excursion of the Tourists was chiefly confined to Edinburgh and Glasgow. In the latter town it happened, that the Belfast Ladies and Gentlemen entered a Silk Mercer's shop, where one of the party wished to make some purchases. While these matters were in progress, Russell's theophilanthropic friend, who had been the life and soul of the expedition, threw, with a gallantry and grace peculiarly his own, a rich piece of lace, round the neck of one of the ladies who were present; and the next instant, observing the shop-men to be busily engaged, he adroitly conveyed the entire web into his pocket. Though this was done with a dexterity that would have done honour to a Chinese Juggler, the movement did not escape the keen eye of the Scotch trader. The Belfast folk withdrew; but scarcely had they arrived at the Hotel, when the Police Officers paid them a most unceremonious visit, arrested their American friend, and appeared very much disposed to take the whole party into custody. The surprise and vexation of these good citizens of our Northern Athens, may be better imagined than described; but their astonishment and indignation was still further increased, when the officers of justice proceeded to examine the trunks and wardrobe of the prisoner. So practical had been the philosopher's ideas concerning community of property, that there not only was not one among the Tourists, but scarcely a single acquaintance of his in Belfast, from whom he had not contrived to purloin some valuable article, and appropriate it as his own! To do the fellow justice, however, it is necessary to add, that with the most philosophic *nonchalance*, he drew up, and signed a paper, exculpating the Belfast gentry from any participation in his plans for procuring some little mementos of the several places which he visited. He handed the paper to a gentleman who was present, bowed politely to his *quondam* friends, and withdrew with the police officers, from whom, however, he shortly afterwards contrived to effect his escape. Poor Russell now saw himself the dupe of his generosity; but true to his principles, which the breath of dishonour never tarnished, he immediately sold his commission and paid the debt.

A copy of this article in the National Library, Dublin, has marginal notes made by Captain John Hamilton, son-in-law of Captain John Russell, nephew of Thomas Russell, identifying the "Medical gentleman" as "Digges—6 feet 2 inches high—good looking." One is inclined to disregard the article, if not for its showy literary graces or its coming thirty-eight years after the events recorded, then for its identification of Digges as a doctor and its dating Russell's selling his commission after rather than before Digges's arrest in Glasgow. Although search in Glasgow has turned up no record of an arrest or a trial, there is clearly some truth in the account. At least Tone and Russell believed in the reported arrest, for Tone recorded in his journal July 12, 1792: "Digges, the Hero of my last journal a Shop lifter; taken up at Glasgow for stealing muslin neckcloths: got a letter from P:P: [Russell] to that effect and am heartily sorry that neither of us can doubt the truth of the story—Poor Digges!"[59] Tone's reference to Digges as the hero of his last journal is not an overstatement. On his visit to Belfast, where he had first met Digges, he had seen Digges on fifteen of the seventeen days he was there. His admiration of Digges is reflected in a passage in the *Life of Theobald Wolfe Tone* dealing with Tone's "Plan of a Settlement in the Sandwich Islands": "Mr. Russell, of the 64th foot, to whom I had communicated all my proceedings hitherto, had gone to Belfast to join his regiment, and there became acquainted with Mr. Digges, an American gentleman, who had, during the war which terminated in the emancipation of his country, served Congress in various official situations. He was a man who, to a most ardent zeal for liberty and a universal regard for the welfare of man, joined the most cool, reflecting head, the most unshaken resolution, a

[59] TCL: Tone Papers, Journal, E 1792.

genius fertile in expedients, and a most consummate knowledge of commerce and politics."[60]

Frank MacDermot in his biography of Tone speaks of Digges's being "a fatal friend" to both Tone and Russell: "He ruined Russell by inducing him to back a bill on which he defaulted, and Tone by betraying a confidential letter of his to the Irish Administration."[61] That Tone and Russell did not regard Digges as a "fatal friend" is suggested by Tone's recording in his journal on July 13, 1792, the day after hearing of the Glasgow episode: "Belfast not half so pleasant this time as the last: Politics just as good, or better: everything else worse. Grievous want of P:P: [Russell]—Miss that unfortunate Digges—weather bad; afraid for tomorrow every way: Generally in low spirits—" Two weeks later he recorded: "—pleasant breakfast: tell Grattan about Digges. Grattan eager to know him: promise to send him Digges's letter on trade &c." Of Henry Grattan, eloquent and influential member of the Irish Parliament, Tone was a great admirer. It would seem from this entry in the journal that Tone had spoken well of Digges to him. Tone's harshest words came in a journal entry of June 20, 1798, and those are tempered by praise: "Digges was a rascal, but he was a man of great sense and observation." Judging by a letter Russell had had from his brother John from London (September 18, [1793]), he must have tried to aid Digges in spite of the charge of shoplifting and the suspicion that Digges had sent to the Irish administration a letter Tone had written Russell, for John wrote: "As to Diggs—I told you—before—that he was *not* arrested by me—I only laid a detainer on him—Your release would do him no good—it *would not liberate him*—he swindled every one here that he could—so say no more of him."[62] Digges may well have kept the friendship of Tone and Russell, but he never saw fit to return to Ireland.

Where Digges went from Glasgow is a question. He may have sought out his cousin David Stewart in Perthshire, but no evidence has been found that he did so. There is no trace of him until March 10,

---

[60] *Life of Theobald Wolfe Tone*, ed. William Theobald Wolfe Tone (Washington: Gales & Seaton, 1826), 1:529.
[61] Frank MacDermot, *Theobald Wolfe Tone* (London: Macmillan, 1939), p. 53.
[62] TCL: Russell Papers.

1793, when he wrote Jefferson from Birmingham about recent advances in both weaving and the minting of coins, a gap of nearly a year in the known correspondence. In that interval George Digges, the last of Thomas's brothers, had died (November 17, 1792). Sometime in March 1793 Digges put in a claim of £1010.15.0 against George's estate for "Rents &c. due upon the estates of Warburton and Franklyn manor, also for rents and arrears of rent due upon the Green Hill and the Goose creek estates in Loudoun county Virginia from the day of the decease of the late Mr. Wm. Digges up to December 1792, and also for cash and other advances made to said G. Digges during his residence in England."[63] He swore to this bill on April 5, 1796, before alderman and magistrate of London, R. Clark, his friend Joshua Johnson attesting and adding the United States consular seal: "Thomas Digges of Digges Landing of the state of Maryland but now of the city of London Gentleman this day appeared before me and maketh oath that the above account is justly and truly due and owing to him from the Estate of George Digges late of Maryland deceased."[64]

In his letter of March 10, 1793, Digges told Jefferson that he had been trying to get leasehold or annual tenants for his lands, meaning Warburton, and that he meant "to Embark for America in May or June." Two days later he wrote Thomas Pinckney that he had been in England some months trying to get his Virginia lands sold or let. He referred to George's death and the difficulties he faced in having more land than he could properly till or occupy. He said he meant to go toward Bristol and London and might go to New York in June or July.

Why he did not leave for home in May, June, or July is probably explained in two ways. First, he must have thought there was a chance that he could lay some claim upon Chilham Castle, the ancestral seat of the Diggeses, and its lands. At any rate he investigated very carefully his chances. He must have reached London by February 1794, for on February 17 an anonymous letter to Lord Grenville, the for-

[63] MdLRO: Chan 40, fol. 210.
[64] Ibid.

eign secretary, informed him: "... there are two Persons *now* in London of the names of *Cuthing* [James Cutting], and *Digges* who are well worthy your *particular attention*,—as Emissaries from France &c.&c."[65] The latter "emissary from France" had a legal opinion of his claim upon Chilham from one J. Meddowcroft, Bedford Row, [London], March 9, 1794, sent to him in Canterbury, from which one concludes that he was committed seriously to the venture. Meddowcroft raised doubts but was not discouraging.[66] The letters show that Digges was on his way to Kent from somewhere to the west by March 10. On March 14, in the *Kentish Chronicle*, he advertised his lands in Virginia for sale or lease. He was in the neighborhood of Chilham certainly in April and May, during which time he interviewed many people, as recorded in a forty-four-page booklet in Digges's hand called "Memorandums concerning the Family and Pedigree of *Digges*—of *Chilham Castle* in *Kent* and the now Heirs and decendants of it in *The State of Maryland*." The testimony he gathered is fairly well suggested by the following:

> They also told me that a large part of that Estate was bought & is now in the Park or inclosures of Sir Henry Oxendens Estate, and that the present Family is now made very uneasy by my appearance and stay in the County of Kent. The reasons, says they, is that the real Heir in tale to this Estate and also to the Chilham mannor property went out to The American Colonies (at a time when there was two or three lives between Him & the property) and altho He was wrote to and twice sent for to be inducd over in order to dock the Entail and by so doing that it might be rightfully passd away or Sold, He never could be prevaild upon to come back to England, and therefore the Entail, which was a very strict one, was never broken. For want of which, and the Family loosing The English *male* heir, who getting ruind by Gambling in the famous South Sea bubble of Mr. Law about the year 1720 or 1721, The Estates sold but for a trifle comparatively to what The Chilham Castle Estate & Manor was worth; and the whole Country then, a long since knew that the descendant of The Digges's of Chilham who went out to The American Colonies was the True & Lawful Heir to Chilham, as well as a great part of The Digges Court or Barham Estate, and to about 450£s a year now under inclosures and in Sir Heny. Oxendens Park.[67]

[65] PRO: HO 42/28.
[66] MdHS: Ms. 246, "Memorandums concerning the Family and Pedigree of *Digges*."
[67] Ibid.

But whatever his hopes, Digges must have given up by midsummer on his role as the American claimant.

Meanwhile he was in danger of losing his Maryland estate. As long as George Digges had been living, title to all of the Maryland and Virginia property had apparently been secure, although in 1790 Benjamin Brookes of Prince George's County had given information "to the executive of this state" that Warburton Manor and Frankland were liable to confiscation, "being the property of a certain Thomas Digges, of Great-Britain."[68] In April 1794, while Digges was in Chilham and Canterbury, his brother-in-law John Fitzgerald wrote George Washington as follows:

Alexandria April 14th 1794

DEAR SIR

When I last had the honor of dining with you in this town, I mention'd the information given by some people in Maryland to the executive of that state respecting the Estate of Thomas Digges, & wishing to bring it under the confiscation Law. This Business is now drawing to a Crisis, & it may possibly be brought to trial next Month in the General Court. I am possess'd of a great variety of Proofs in support of Mr. Digges's Agency & Activity during the American War, which I believe were exerted at the utmost peril, as he was strongly suspect'd & narrowly watched in England at that time. Upon mentioning the observations you were pleased to make respecting Mr. Digges's conduct my Lawyers think it highly essential that your testimony on this matter should be obtained, as that will immediately silence the Gentry who wish to enrich themselves in this summary way. Your love of justice I well know, would induce you to set matters right on any common occasion, where circumstances happen'd within your knowledge but in this I feel a flattering confidence, that you will with pleasure step forward, & testify what you know of Mr. Digges during & since the War, as you will thereby not only do justice to his patriotic Character, but perhaps save an Estate to the Descendants, of an old friend & neighbour, & to a family which from a strong habit of intimacy with yours, I have every reason to believe you honor with your friendship.[69]

Washington replied on April 27:

DEAR SIR:

Your letter of the 14th instant came to hand in due course of post, and would have received an earlier acknowledgement had I not been pressed with other business.

[68] Laws of Maryland, 1795, chap. 76.
[69] LC: Washington Papers, Series 4.

I have no hesitation in declaring that the conduct of Mr. Thomas Digges towards the United States during the War (in which they were engaged with Great Britain) and since as far as the same has come to my knowledge, has not been only friendly, but I might add zealous.

When I conversed with you on this subject in Alexandria, I thought I recollected a special and pointed instance of beneficial service he had rendered this Country in sending me between the leather and pasteboard cover of a book, some important intelligence; but upon reflecting more maturely on the matter since, I am unable to decide *positively* whether it was from him, or another gentleman this expedient was adopted to elude the consequences of a search. Be this however as it may, it is in my recollection that various *verbal* communications came to me, *as from him*, by our Captives, who had escaped from confinement in England; and I think I have received written ones also: but the latter (if at all) must have been rare on account of the extreme hazard of discovery, and the consequences which would follow, both to the writer and bearer of such corrispondences.

Since the War, abundant evidence might be adduced of his activity and zeal (with considerable risque) in sending artizans and machines of public utility to this Country I mean by encouraging and facilitating their transportation as also of useful information to the Secretary of State, to put him on his guard against nefarious attempts to make Paper, &ca. for the purpose of counterfeiting our money. Until you mentioned the doubts which were entertained of Mr. Digges' attachment to this country, I had no idea of its being questioned. With esteem, &c.

P.S. Since writing the foregoing letter, I have seen and conversed with Mr. John Trumbull respecting Mr. T. Digges. The former, before he was committed to the Tower of London, was well acquainted with the latter in England, and much in his company. To him Mr. Digges always appeared well attached to the rights and interests of the United States. *Knows* that he was active in aiding our citizens to escape from their confinement in England; and *believes* he was employed to do so by Doctr. Franklin. Mr. Trumbull has never seen Mr. Digges since he left the Tower, but has heard that a difference arose between him and the Doctr. not from any distrust entertained by the latter of disaffection in the former; but on the settlement of their accounts.

The preceding statement is made from the best recollection I have of the subject. The expression might (if I had had more leisure) be more correct, but not more consonant with truth. Such as it is you are welcome to make what use you please of it.[70]

Although the property remained in some jeopardy at least through 1795, Warburton and Frankland were not confiscated.

---

[70] *Writings of George Washington*, ed. John Fitzpatrick (Washington: United States Government Printing Office, 1940), 33:340–41.

Introduction

The other reason for Digges's continued stay in England was probably trouble with his creditors. In May 1808, writing to Philip Barton Key, he said he had been in danger of being brought in as a partner in the bankrupt firm of Lane, Son, and Frazer because he had endorsed some of their paper. To free himself from this risk he had assigned property in Virginia and Prince Edward Island and had named Thomas Holmes, to whom he was indebted, as a trustee of this assignment. But Holmes, advised by Samuel Hartley, who sought to advance a claim of his own, had had him arrested for debt and "fell upon my Virginia property." Digges continued: "At this period I had obtained the appointment, & was prepared to attend Mr. T. Pinkney from London thro Paris as Secretary to Mr. Pinkneys then successful Embassy to Madrid—*where*, but for this rascal Hartley I might yet probably have been Agent or Minister." How long Digges's arrest continued is unknown. It may be significant that facts about his life are lacking between May 1794, when he was in Kent, and April 5, 1796, when he swore in London to his claim of £1010.15.0 against the estate of George Digges. Even if free from his creditors he lingered in London. On October 16, 1797, Robert Brent, George's widow's brother, wrote him from Washington that Digges's friends were well and had expected to see him before this.[71] In November Digges was attempting to gather intelligence concerning the Blount conspiracy for the United States ambassador to Great Britain, Rufus King, and still living in the city, at 26 Red Lion Street. As late as April 10, 1798, he sent from London some seeds and seed potatoes to George Washington. But by November of that year he must have reached Warburton. A letter of David Erskine from Richmond, Virginia, November 3, 1798, to his father in England tells of being bound for Mount Vernon and of "travelling with a Gentleman who is going to his house which is opposite to General Washington's." This "very well informed man . . . has been Agent for America in England."[72]

For Digges it must have been a disturbing homecoming. He had left for Lisbon in 1767 when he was twenty-four years old. Now he was fifty-six. He had left behind brothers Charles, George, and Jo-

[71] MdHS: Ms. 246.
[72] Patricia Holbert Menk, "D. M. Erskine: Letters from America, 1798–1799," *William and Mary Quarterly*, 3rd ser., 6 (Apr. 1949): 255.

seph, and sisters Tracy, Susane, Ann, Elizabeth, and Jane, all now dead except for the last three. Ann, the oldest, had been fourteen when he left. Jane, the youngest, now forty-three, had been twelve. The disowned son who had been referred to in 1771 as being "beyond Sea in Parts unknown" whence "in all probability he would never return into this Province" was now at last home after adventures as extravagant as Alonso's.

He was to live on for twenty-three more years. He was to enjoy the friendship of Presidents Washington, Jefferson, Madison, and Monroe and to prove himself an anti-Federalist. He was to see the construction of Fort Warburton and be "at his post" at Warburton when the fort was blown up and abandoned to the British in 1814. He was to have "the pleasure to hear & see dozens of Mortars, Rockets &ca. pass in direction very nearly over [his] house."[73] He was to see the rebuilding of the fort on a larger scale, the destruction of valuable fishing berths, and the erosion of all domestic comfort because of the "ruin & depredations done & doing the Farm by an ungovernable vile Soldiery too close in my vicinity and the nightly plunder of the labouring herd on the Fort works."[74] Through all he was to know exasperating strife with the government, financial embarrassment, and deteriorating health, so that when he died at seventy-nine he must have been ready.

Little is known of the problems Digges faced when he returned in 1798, but they must have been numerous. In the course of the six years since George's death many questions must have arisen demanding the attention not of an agent but of a resident owner. This may account for the fact that letters of 1799 are lacking. Yet in that year Digges had time to dine at Mount Vernon on February 8, May 10, June 11, and August 15.[75] On June 11 the party had included, according to Washington, "Bishop Carroll, Mr. Digges and his sister Carroll"—Bishop John Carroll, who had warned the archbishop of Dublin against Digges in 1792, Thomas Digges, and his sister Elizabeth,

---

[73] Digges to James Madison, Aug. 30, 1814.
[74] Ibid., July 17, 1818.
[75] *Diaries of George Washington, 1748–1799*, ed. John C. Fitzpatrick (Boston: Houghton Mifflin, 1925), 4:297, 304, 306, 311.

wife of Daniel Carroll, the bishop's nephew. It does not appear that Digges ever suspected that the bishop had once attacked his character. On July 5, 1802, Digges for "One Dollar and . . . One Common Prayer Book" conferred upon the bishop and his "successors in the Holy Office of the Church . . . for the full benefit and use of the Roman Catholic Congregation of Piscattaway" all his rights in "the Catholic Chappel formerly built by his Father William Digges and lately put into good repair at Considerable expence by the said T. A. Digges and others of the said Congregation situated on Frankland Mannor . . . together with two Acres of Woodland adjoining to and Surrounding the said Catholic Chappel." The deed stipulated that the two acres with the chapel would revert to Digges or his heirs if ever the church or congregation should "cease useing the Ceremonies of the Catholic Church or the service of Mass."[76] Digges was further useful to the bishop and his family by investigating the status of property in Ireland to which Carroll seemed "to have a legal claim" and to which Digges said William Carroll, the bishop's nephew, "has some Claim as Heir at Law."[77] Digges's friendship with the bishop lasted until the bishop's death in 1815.

Digges's sister Ann died at Warburton December 28, 1804. Her death occasioned a bequest to his remaining sisters, dated June 3, 1806, which reads in part:

Know all men by these presents that I Thomas Attwood Digges of Warburton in Maryland in consequence of request made to me as well as in conformity to the last will & Testament made by my deceased Sister Ann Digges late of Warburton aforesaid bearing date the 13th of Octo. 1800: Wherein she bequeaths me for & during my Natural life All her Negroes Horses Stock of every kind, Plate, bedding and all kinds of House hold furniture: to be used with my own personal property thereby assisting me very much in the tillage of my Land by & with the work of the said Negroes Stock &ca.&ca., And in consideration of her requests and the Natural love & affection I have for and bear to my beloved Sisters Mrs. Elizabeth Carroll and Mrs. Jane Fitzgerald and also for divers good Causes & Consideration me the said Thos. Attwood Digges thereunto moving Have given granted & confirmed and by these presents do give grant & Confirm unto my said Sisters Elizabeth Carroll and Jane Fitzgerald all

---

[76] MdHR: Land Records, Prince George's County, JRM 9, fol. 258–59.
[77] Digges to John Carroll, June 3, 1804.

my goods chattles plate books pictures bedding and Household furniture of every kind, also my Carriages & Horses Carts ploughs Waggons &ca. Brood Mares draft Oxen and all out Cattle Milch Cowes Hogs Sheep &ca.&ca. in whose hands whatsoever they may be within the State of Maryland (such articles only as herein or upon the back of this paper expressly notified and described) To have and enjoy . . . To be divided as they may chuse among the respective children or Familys of the said Elizabeth Carroll and Jane Fitzgerald . . . I the said Thomas Attwood Digges have put the said Elizabeth Carroll and Jane Fitzgerald in full possession by delivering to each of them one Silver Spoon at the time of sealing and delivering of these presents in the name of the whole goods & chattels &ca. hereby granted. In witness whereof I have hereunto set my hand & Seal this third day of June in year of our Lord one thousand eight hundred & Six—

Thos. A. Digges

On the back of which Bill of Sale was thus Endorsed to wit The Articles deeded away and mentioned within are as follows N.B. By my Sisters will she left me a life estate in 30 or 32 Negroes to go to my Sisters Carroll & Fitzgerald after my death—also several articles of Household Furniture &ca. &ca. and not having any Negroes of my own I now deed as follows Vizt. One old Chariot & two Carriage Horses (Lofty & Fairfax) One Gig chaise and Horse Loudoun—One Waggon & Geers entire—Two Ox Carts—3 Dung Carts—eight ploughs—Harrows, Draggs Wheel barrows and all kinds of Axes tools Hoes and farming implements—The Tobacco yet hanging stript & under prize [?] as now remains in two Tobacco Houses—Two Mules—Six draft Horses—three brood Mares and their issue—two Yearling Colts—& two two year old Do. Six Working Oxen Seven Milking Cows—and about thirty head of out Cattle—yearlings Calves &c.—Sixty Sheep—Sixty or Seventy hogs young & old—Two Landscape Pictures in Oil (by Moreland)— Threee family portraits in Do.—fifteen framed & Glazd prints—All the China, Glass's &ca.&ca. Some old plate supposed about 50 or 60 Ounces—All & every kind of Household furniture Bedding Carpets Chairs Tables and all kinds of Kitchen utensils—Two Boats and two Seins with Ropes &ca. about 110 Vols. of used Books.

Thos. A. Digges[78]

Most tantalizing in this indenture are of course the three family portraits in oil, immediately following the mention of "Two Landscape Pictures in Oil (by Moreland)." Family tradition has it that both Thomas and George had their portraits painted by Joshua Reynolds

---

[78] MdHR: Land Records, Prince George's County, JRM 11, fol. 370. This document is a copy not in Digges's hand.

—according to one document among the Digges papers, Thomas's was done between 1775 and 1781. But in the light of the obvious pride Digges took in the print of Reynolds's *Faith* that he sent to Bishop Carroll on August 18, 1815, it is inconceivable that had his own portrait, in all probability one of the three, been by Reynolds he would not have said so.

Digges reported on July 29, 1807, that at Jefferson's request he had had surveyed the part of Warburton designated by Washington as the most favorable station on the Potomac "for annoying Vessels passing up or down." Washington had written Benjamin Stoddert, the secretary of the navy, on September 26, 1798, that "should proper works be erected on Digges point, (which you well know) at the junction of the Potomac and Piscataqua creek, it would not be in the power of all the navies in Europe to pass that place, and be afterward in a situation to do mischief above."[79] When asked by the secretary of war, Henry Dearborn, for his price, Digges responded with expressions of anxiety over the evil of trespass, the inroads to the fort, the "injury to domestic Comforts to the future possessors of Warburton," and the disadvantage of the fort to a valuable fishery and suggested that the price should be left to twelve gentlemen chosen between them. He communicated his anxieties to Jefferson, to whom he also wrote that he hoped that some military gentlemen who had inspected the site might have found a more eligible spot for the fort because it "would be a dreadful inroad upon my retirement in age." He could not have been more prophetic. Driven to name a price, he said $15,000 on March 11, 1808, to which Dearborn responded that if he would throw in his buildings and five hundred acres, the price would be less objectionable, so the price was left to a panel, which set a price of $6,000 for a little over three acres. The indenture of Jefferson of April 15 states that Digges's fishing rights would be respected, but with the unfortunate clause that "in all respects as little injury shall be done thereto to the fishing stations or the banks or soil outside the limits of the fort boundaries . . . as the nature of things will admit."[80] From this clause came endless trouble.

---

[79] *Writings of George Washington*, 36:465–66.
[80] NA: Record Group 77, OCE, Land Papers, Fort Washington, Maryland.

News of this sale apparently spread quickly, for on May 12, 1808, Francis Scott Key was ordered by his uncle, Philip Barton Key, an established attorney, to arrest Digges for the old debt to Holmes and Hartley, "believing he has received $6,000 from Government lately."[81] There is no record of Digges's having been arrested, but the order must have occasioned Digges's letter to Philip Key of May 28, 1808, in which he reviews the history of his Virginia lands and vigorously attacks the character of Samuel Hartley. The outcome of this suit for debt is uncertain; no record has been found thus far that Holmes and Hartley got their money.

On December 24, 1811, through Robert Brent, Digges sold to his nephew William Dudley Digges 650 acres of Warburton, with the buildings, reserving to Digges for his life the use and benefit of the property and in trust for his sister Jane Fitzgerald should she survive him.[82] This sale to the member of the family next in the entail would seem questionable but for Robert Brent's agency. Brent, a lawyer, should have been well able to protect the interest of his sister's son. And it is possible that Brent had moved to protect Dudley's interest. Not all the facts are known, but it seems clear that Dudley had not been consulted and had not benefited from the sale of the site of Fort Warburton. From December 24, 1811, Digges could not sell any of the 650 acres of the home place without the concurrence of his nephew. The price of $6,000 for the land and buildings would appear to be nominal. Another complication is that Digges's claim against the estate of his brother George, Dudley's father, for £1,010 with interest from 1793, was still unpaid and seemingly never was paid, although Digges said in a letter of August 18, 1815, to Bishop Carroll that it was money he had frequently wanted. He went on to complain to Carroll that of a $2,000 payment from the government for additional land for the fort, he had had only $250, the rest being held by his nephew. The complexity of this matter, like that of the Holmes and Hartley suit, is baffling.

With the War of 1812 Digges once more came into some prominence. Though the evidence is slight, it seems certain that he went in

---

[81] Philip B. Key to Phineas Bond, May 12, 1808 (HSP: Cadwalader Collection, Phineas Bond Section, Key Correspondence—*Digges* v. *Holmes & Hartley*).

[82] MdHR: Land Records, Prince George's County, JRM 15, fol. 58–61.

INTRODUCTION lxxv

August of 1813 as an emissary from James Monroe, then secretary of state, to see Admiral John Borlase Warren off Annapolis about the American prisoners in Warren's hands.[83] Digges had written three letters offering his services to his old acquaintance, which Warren, reporting on June 5, 1813, to Lord Melville, first lord of the admiralty, said he had not answered, "as I had not any opinion of him." Warren also said that he remembered Digges "in England in the former War with America acting as Commissary General for prisoners."[84] From the statements made in Digges's letter of December 12, 1812, to Warren and the teasing tone of Digges's review of their association in 1774 and 1775, it appears that Warren was less than candid. It is certain that Warren knew Digges better than his letter suggests. In his letter to Melville, Warren enclosed a letter Digges had sent James Patton, British vice-consul of Alexandria. Although Digges had recommended Patton to Warren's notice on January 14, 1813, Patton seems to have betrayed Digges by sending his confidential letter to Warren with the suggestion that it might "produce a smile."[85] With these undercurrents the meeting of the old acquaintances must have been interesting. Unfortunately there is no record of it.

The war was soon to touch Digges far more closely. On August 27, 1814, Fort Warburton (now better known as Fort Washington) was blown up and abandoned by its garrison. Alexander Cochrane, commander on the American station, reported on September 2 to John Wilson Croker, secretary of the admiralty:

SIR,
I have the honor to acquaint you for the information of my Lords Commissioners of the Admiralty, of the proceedings of His Majesty's combined Sea and Land forces since my arrival with the Fleet within the Capes of Virginia, and I beg leave to offer my congratulations to their Lordships upon the successful termination of an Expedition in which the whole of the Enemy's Flotilla under Commodore Barney has been captured or destroyed, his Army, tho greatly superior in number and strongly posted with Cannon, defeated at Bladensburg—the City of Washington taken—the Capitol with all the public buildings, Military Arsenals, Dock Yard and the rest of their Naval

---

[83] MdHS: Ms. 246.
[84] NMM: LBK2, Admiral Warren's Correspondence with Lord Melville, American War, 1812–1814.
[85] Patton to Warren, Apr. 28, 1813 (SH: Warren Papers, Letters from Various Persons to Admiral John Borlase Warren, 1792–1814).

Establishment together with a vast quantity of Naval and Military Stores, a Frigate of the largest class, ready to launch, and a Sloop of War afloat, either blown up or reduced to Ashes. . . . Previously to my entering the Patuxent I detached Captain Gordon of His Majesty's Ship Seahorse, with that Ship and the Ships and Bombs named in the Margin, [Euryalus, Devastation, Ætna, Meteor, Manly, Erebus] up the Potowmac to bombard Fort Washington (which is situated on the left bank of that River about ten or twelve miles below the City) with a view of destroying that Fort and opening a free communication above, as well as to cover the retreat of the Army should its return by the Bladensburg Road be found too hazardous from the accession of Strength the Enemy might obtain from Baltimore. . . . I have not yet received any Returns from the Ships employed in the Potowmac, the winds having been unfavorable to their coming down; but by the information I gain from the Country people—they have completely succeeded in the capture and destruction of Fort Washington, which has been blown up.[86]

Throughout the action at the fort Digges remained at Warburton. On August 28, according to his letter to Madison of August 30, he had Gordon's promise that his house and property would be secured, but he expressed fears he might lose his Negroes. He had lost "every thing between the Fort & River shore," presumably the buildings for the fishermen who leased the fishing rights, but as he says, a thunderbolt the week before had done him more damage. Everything within the fort, though, was ruined, Digges said, save two Columbiads, and these later proved to be useless but for remelting.

Reconstruction of the fort started within days, with the designer of Washington, Pierre Charles L'Enfant, in charge. Here began an association that lasted until Digges's death. L'Enfant stayed on at Warburton until invited in February of 1824 by William Dudley Digges to come to live at Green Hill. There he died in 1825. His long residence at Warburton was at times an embarrassment. In Digges's words, he had been given in July of 1815 "the go-by" as the engineer of the new fort. He was poor but proud. He apparently scorned demanding what should have been accorded to him. Digges, whose esteem and loyalty never wavered, tried to collect for him money owed by the city of New York and by the government. Fretted by loungers who were prone to make Warburton "a cake house for the idle," Digges wished to remove to Washington, where he could get needed medical attention. But for

[86] PRO: ADM 1/506, letter no. 267.

long he found that impossible. He might lock up his house for a week or two, he wrote to George Graham, chief clerk of the War Department, December 22, 1815, "But how Sir can I do it with The old Major a seeming fixture therein?" He had hoped he might escape from home if L'Enfant found employment with the War Department. After giving a fine tribute to L'Enfant he asked for help in disposing of "this good old Major (whom I would by no means injure)."

Growing afflictions finally forced him to make the move. The last letter addressed from Warburton is dated October 9, 1817. Thereafter the letters come from the Washington Hotel, Tennison's Hotel, Strothers Hotel, and Mansion Hotel, all in Washington. Yet from Strothers Hotel he wrote on December 19, 1819, to J. W. Harris that he had come from his "tatterd & comfortless home on yesterday with a hope that in a warm room (which I keep in it for *going & comeing* purposes) to attain some amelioration in spasm complaints in my ankle joints & Rhuematics in my Shoulders & neck joint, afflictingly bad at times although *internally* in good health."

At Strothers Hotel he died, Thursday, December 6, 1821. The *National Intelligencer* on the eleventh carried the obituary:

In this city, on Thursday last, after a long illness, Thomas A. Digges, Esq. of Warburton, aged about 80 years, an undeviating republican and patriot. The numerous acquaintances of the deceased, in this country and in England, where he spent many years of his life, and all who had enjoyed his interesting society, or partaken of the pleasures of his hospitable mansion, will learn his death with sincere regret.

The location of his grave is unknown.[87]

---

[87] Digges's activities abroad have, since the early 1950s, interested a few other scholars. To enlarge our portrayal see the following: William Bell Clark, "In Defense of Thomas Digges," *Pennsylvania Magazine of History and Biography*, 77 (Oct. 1953):381–438, and "A Franklin Postscript to Captain Cook's Voyages," *Proceedings of the American Philosophical Society*, 98 (Dec. 23, 1954):400–405; Lynn Hudson Parsons, "The Mysterious Mr. Digges," *William and Mary Quarterly*, 3rd ser., 22 (July 1965):486–92; Catherine M. Prelinger, "Benjamin Franklin and the American Prisoners of War in England during the American Revolution," ibid., 32 (Apr. 1975):261–94; Carroll W. Pursell, Jr., "Thomas Digges and William Pearce: An Example of the Transit of Technology," ibid., 21 (Oct. 1964):551–60. In 1943 the United States Catholic Historical Society in New York published a facsimile edition of *Adventures of Alonso* as Volume 18 in its Monograph Series.

The Text

Our editorial practices have been designed to make the presentation of Thomas Digges's letters compatible with the presentation of the letters of those of his notable contemporaries with whom he was most frequently in correspondence—Benjamin Franklin, John Adams, and Thomas Jefferson—and so we have concurred in their editors' decision to adopt the "expanded method," which eschews the two extremes of literal transcription and total modernization. The arguments in favor of this method are now so widely accepted by scholars working in the period that it would be supererogatory to repeat them here, where it should be enough to remind readers of the peculiar difficulties of producing a printed version of hastily written eighteenth-century manuscripts with their notoriously erratic spelling, capitalization, punctuation, paragraphing, and forms of abbreviation, and to admit that we have made some compromises. These compromises have sought to preserve Digges's style and expression on the one hand and to eliminate gratuitous obstacles to twentieth-century accessibility on the other.

I. Generally we have followed Digges's spelling, capitalization, punctuation, and paragraphing, making exceptions only to enhance readability:
   A. When punctuation at the end of a paragraph or between sentences is missing, we have silently provided a period and made certain that the following sentence begins with a capital letter. Likewise, when a period (or a period followed by a dash) is already there but the next sentence begins without a

capitalized word, we have silently provided the capital letter. When, though, the second sentence begins with a coordinating conjunction that appears to function as a link in a compound sentence, or when a dependent fragment is set off by a period and dash, we have simply treated the period as an intended comma. Periods used in series (usually after numerals) without ambiguity we have allowed to remain.

B. We have retained comma splices that produce no ambiguity, but when ambiguity exists, we have silently substituted a period for the comma and capitalized the word following it. Likewise to overcome ambiguity we have on a few occasions silently provided commas within sentences.

C. When marks of punctuation and capitalization are ambiguous, we have tried to follow Digges's usage elsewhere; if that has provided inadequate guidance, we have favored present usage. Parallel dashes (resembling the "equals" sign) we have rendered as ordinary dashes.

D. We have silently corrected unmistakable slips of the pen, such as missing final letters or repeated words, and restored letters lost in holes and tears. If we cannot be sure that an error is a slip, we have bracketed our emendations. Similarly, if a word has been misused, we have inserted an appropriate kind of bracketed correction following it. Square brackets indicate our certainty about what is missing or wrong; pointed brackets within square brackets indicate conjecture.

E. When we are confronted with undecipherable words, tears in the paper, or words obscured by smudges or blots, we have used pointed brackets to record our conjectured substitution.

F. We have retained contemporary forms that nowadays might seem to be abbreviations or contractions but that in Digges's time were common spellings; for example: *coud, woud, wou'd, brot, 'em, tho, tho', thro*. But since he often alternates these with the expanded forms, we have chosen to expand the words as though they were contractions (see below) when instead of an apostrophe he uses a tilde. His spelling of *eer* (the obsolete form of *ere*) we have modified by simply discarding the

The Text

erroneous tilde that he suspends over the entire word. The long-tailed *s* we have modernized.

G. In setting off paragraphs and postscripts we have imposed present-day conventions. We have regularly indented, although Digges does not regularly observe such marks of division. When Digges has left us in doubt about his intentions, we have fallen back on intuition.

H. In the use of quotation marks we have disregarded Digges's outmoded practice of placing such marks before each line in the left-hand margin; we have simply followed today's practice of using them only at the beginnings and ends of the passages quoted.

I. In all but a few instances we have based our text on the original manuscripts, but when they have been unavailable, we have relied on transcripts and printed texts, choosing in each case the earliest version. Letters to and about Digges have been treated the same way as letters by him. Enclosures in his letters are in his hand unless otherwise stated.

II. We have treated contractions and abbreviations with a freer hand than we have spelling and punctuation, but again, we have had in mind the price of every compromise:

A. We have eliminated the tilde and have lowered superior letters to the line of the text to be set in the same size type as the rest of the word.

B. We have expanded ordinary words, using Digges's spelling as consistently as possible: *Dr.*, *Lettr.*, *yr.*, *pr.*, *agst.*, *accot.*, *recd.*, *Eveng.*, *nit.*, become, for example, *Dear*, *Letter*, *your*, *per*, *against*, *account*, *receivd*, *Evening*, *night*. But we have preserved abbreviations in the complimentary close on the ground that they are inseparable from the ritualistic effect. On rare occasions, when Digges is quoting what appears to have been originally abbreviated (such as an address on a package where an abbreviation like *Mert.* [*Merchant*] or *Negot.* [*Négociant*] appears integral), we have retained the words as written.

C. We have retained the ampersand, unusually ubiquitous in Digges's letters, but expanded the thorn (which had not yet come to symbolize quaintness) to make *the* out of *ye*; and we have replaced @ (and *a* used synonymously) with *at*.

D. We have retained abbreviations that continue to be used in our day, or that unambiguously resemble those currently used. These include the days of the week (*Wed.*, *Wedn.*, *Fry.*), months (*Sep.*, *Sepr.*, *Sept.*), titles and positions (*Mr.*, *Sr.*, *Cap.*, *Capn.*, *Capt.*, *Col.*, *Colol.*, *Coll.*, *Commr.*, *H.M.*, *Secy.*), points of the compass or cartographers' designations (*Wt.*, *So.*, *Lat.*), addresses (*St.*, *Str.*, *Stt.*), references to hours of the day (*p.m.*, *oClk.*), weights, measures, and monetary signs and values (*lb.*, *Leags.*, *hhd.*, *HHd.*, *dwt.*, *pr. Ct.*, *Stg.*, *Str.* [sterling]), the jargon of correspondence (*ulto.*, *ulo.*, *inst.*, *int.*), and the conventional *do.* [*ditto*], *i.e.*, *e.g.*, and *viz.* or *vizt.*

E. Proper names have posed difficulties because some are too ambiguous to expand with firm consistency (*Jno.*, *Fr.*). Accordingly, although surnames never resist expansion, the frequently abbreviated given names appear as written. When the full name is known, it usually is spelled out in the annotations and the index. The use of initials, though, has invited a different practice. Generally, an individual's initials punctuated by periods remain as written, with clarification provided by the immediate context or footnotes. But when names of persons or places contain dashes in place of letters (perhaps at times to confuse British intelligence) that the addressee can be expected to supply for himself, we have with the first mention in each item of the correspondence used bracketed insertions to fill in whatever is missing.

F. Geographical references are treated in three ways: (1) when the abbreviations are readily recognizable, we have preserved them; (2) when they require clarification and appear only once or twice, we have explained them in brackets following; (3) when they appear repeatedly in a form that either confuses or distracts, we have silently expanded them: *Ama.*, *Amns.*, *Amm.*, *Gibr.*, *Jama.*, *Phia.* (but not *Philaa.*), for example, become *America*, *Americans*, *Amsterdam*, *Gibraltar*, *Jamaica*, *Philadelphia*.

G. Misspellings of the names of persons and places are repro-

THE TEXT lxxxiii

duced without correction unless obscurity requires bracketed clarification. We have made exceptions when Digges has casually omitted the apostrophe between capital letters in *D'Artois*, *D'Estaing* (and its variants), *L'Enfant*, *O'Brien*, and the like. We there have silently repaired the omission.

 H. In all instances we have regularized the use of periods after those abbreviations for which Digges has supplied no terminal mark, and when the initials of names are used, we have regularized the use of the apostrophe with the possessive (*D. H.'s*), although when the name is spelled out we have respected Digges's consistent indifference to apostrophes, since no ambiguity follows (*Hartleys, Norths, Washingtons*).

III. Format:
 A. The name of the addressee is at the top of each letter, regardless of where it may appear on the actual. If it appears on the face of the letter, it will thus appear twice.
 B. The date and place of the letter are in the upper right-hand corner, often in a continuous line, regardless of where Digges has written them. Ordinarily, unless the information has a function within the text, it will not reappear later.
 C. Whatever Digges has written on the cover of the letter is included at the end of the text. Slashes included in addresses signify the beginnings of new lines. The substance of the endorsement, though, is recorded only when it contributes to an understanding of the correspondence. We have likewise not attempted to reproduce graphically or describe Digges's revisions, deletions, or substitutions unless some significance attaches to them.
 D. The complimentary close, when it is clearly not a part of the preceding paragraph, is separately paragraphed.
 E. Letters written on the same day are arranged alphabetically by addressee.

IV. Annotations:
 A. The first item (unnumbered) following the text identifies the location of the document we have used: see the list of abbreviations.
 B. In the numbered footnotes we try, in conjunction with their

first mention, to clarify allusions to individuals and events not ordinarily considered common knowledge. Some persons have, not surprisingly, remained elusive, and we have had to leave them either wholly unidentified or only partially identified, indicating our inability only where the context has seemed to demand it. Well-known historic personages and events do not, we trust, require equal elucidation.

C. Since sources for many of our annotations are numerous, we have eliminated almost all such secondary footnoting in the interests of proportion when those sources are published ones. When those sources are manuscripts, we have included them.

D. We have occasionally used cross-references for the reader's convenience, but generally have depended on the index to guide those who simply require the page of first mention.

Letters of Thomas Attwood Digges

To Francis Street

New York February 23d 1767—

DEAR SIR,[1]

Your kind favour of the 17th Inst. (which coverd a Letter to Mr. Beekman,[2]) came to my hands this morning, & I believe the tardy delay it met with, was owing to a person in the Post Office who told me a day or two ago it was not then arrivd from Philadelphia.—As it will be out of my power to leave this before Wednesday, I shall have no chance after that time to arrive at Philadelphia soon enough to get a passage in the snow you mention will sail the middle of this week:[3] I have therefore bespoken a passage in a Ship that will sail from this to Cadiz about this day week,[4] and as it is not distant from Lisbon more than 30 or 40 leags. it will not be very inconvenient to me; as I am told there are often oppertunitys both by Land & water from thence to Lisbon. I could have wishd to have seen you at Philadelphia, as I want some account given me of the nature of the Country to which I am bound & which I may probably stand in need of, however I suppose there are many Englishmen in Cadiz, who can direct me which way to take for the most ready conveyance to Lisbon in which place there are some Gentlemen to whom I am personally known & when I get among them I shall think myself snug enough—I am much oblidgd to You for the Line to Mr. Beekman tho his absence from home at present has deprivd me of the pleasure of seeing him as yet—I am at a loss at present to know whether it would be better for me to carry Gold from this to Lisbon or sell it here for Bills of Exchange & as you know the rate it passes for there, I should be oblidged to you to acquaint me which would be most to my advantage. It will be at least this day week before I sail & in which time I suppose a Letter will reach me from you. I am sorry to be so troublesome but hope it will be in my power to do as much for you & whenever you may have occasion I hope you will freely Command

Sir Yr. oblidgd & obt. servt.
Thom. Digges

[Addressed:] To Mr. Francis Street/Mercht./Philadelphia

NYPL: Miscellaneous Papers.

[1] Street was a Philadelphia merchant with interests that ranged from the Newfoundland fish trade to the market for wines and liquors in Maryland.
[2] Probably James Beekman (1732–1807), an importer of fabrics, necklaces, spices, teapots, hemp, and cordage, among other merchandise that he sold at his store in Queen Street, and a merchant who during 1768–1773 did business with Long & Richard of Lisbon.
[3] The *King George* (Capt. J. Potts), cleared the week before for departure to Barcelona, was, according to the Philadelphia papers, the only snow to sail from Philadelphia for the Iberian peninsula from Feb. through Apr.
[4] The *Earl of Hertford* (Capt. John Pym) was at this date the only ship listed in the newspapers with Cadiz or any Portuguese port as its destination, either among the outward entries or among those cleared for departure. The voyage could be expected to take approximately nine weeks.

To Ralph Izard

Ralph Izard (1742–1804), a patriot from South Carolina living in London since 1771, had just moved to Paris with his family. The Continental Congress in May had chosen him to be commissioner to Tuscany, but that government never received him, and he remained in France until 1780, quarreling with Benjamin Franklin (1706–1790) over his uncertain diplomatic role and his unpaid salary.

Worcester, Sept. 8, 1777.

DEAR SIR:—

I did not mean to write to you until I had received a line to inform me in what part of France you had fixed your temporary residence—and given me a direction how to address you—which was promised me in your last letter—but a friend of mine, Mr. Matthew Ridley,[1] formerly of Maryland, and now a merchant in London—being about to take a trip to Paris, (where he will be an utter stranger) I cannot but ask you how you do—nor deny him the pleasure of your acquaintance—by withholding this introductory note.

It is uncertain that Mr. Ridley will meet you in Paris—but should he do it—I am to beg the favour of your assistance, and advice to him.

He will naturally want to speak to our American friends, in Paris—which may be denied him—from a want of knowledge of his worth—and the cast of his Politics—both of which, stand in the highest estimation with me—and I should be very thankful, you could gratify him—should he apply for assistance on this head.

When Mr. Ridley returns—I should be glad of a few lines by him—acquainting me how to write to you, &c. Should you have occasion to command me—I hope you will freely do it. Your usual direction to Bath, would I think be a very safe one.

I write to A. L.[2] by this opportunity, in answer to a letter lately received from him. My best wishes attend you and yours—and I hope you will ever look upon me as

    Your very affectionate friend,
    And obedient servant,
    T. Digges.

Correspondence of Mr. Ralph Izard of South Carolina from the Year 1774 to 1804; with a Short Memoir, ed. Anne Izard Deas (New York: Charles S. Francis Co., 1884), 1:338–39. Mrs. Deas also attributes to Digges a letter of October 10, 1777, signed "D. Wister" and addressed to "Crawford," stating that those were names feigned by Digges and Izard, respectively. But if that letter is by Digges, then probably a letter dated August 8, 1777 (1:320–21), and certainly one dated September 1, 1777 (1:332–34), should likewise be attributed to him; yet the internal evidence strongly argues against our accepting the attribution of any one of those three letters. Without confirmation by resort to the original manuscripts (impossible because the documents are reported to have been destroyed by fire some years ago), we find no justification for including them in this edition.

[1] Born in England in 1749, Ridley (d. 1789) had gone to America in 1770 to manage the Maryland branch of the London mercantile firm of Stewart & Campbell. In 1775 he

had returned to England, where he had married and become active in aiding American prisoners of war, along with Digges and such British sympathizers as Benjamin Vaughan (1751–1835) and William Hodgson (d. 1784), London merchants, raising a fund of more than four thousand pounds for their relief. His visit to France, which lasted until 1779, brought him in touch with the American commissioners, enabled him to join others, both American and French, in arranging for the shipment of merchandise to the new country, and eventually led to his being appointed in 1781 as Maryland's agent to obtain a European loan for that state, an appointment that returned him to Paris in 1782.

[2] Arthur Lee of Virginia (1740–1792) had come to London in 1768 and in 1770 become an assistant to Franklin as agent for Massachusetts. Late in 1776, after a year as secret agent for the Continental Congress's Committee of Secret Correspondence, he had been appointed with Franklin and Silas Deane (1737–1789) to constitute a commission that would negotiate a treaty with France. Not needed in that country, he had gone to Spain and Germany to negotiate for supplies and support. Now back in Paris he began to find himself at odds with Franklin and Deane and to send home complaints that led to his recall two years later.

To Matthew Ridley

B[irmingha]m 20 Nov. 77 /

Dear Sir[1]

I should certainly not have been so long inatentive to your last obliging Letter, had any thing occurd in the interval worth communicating; and indeed I have nothing now to say that will authorise my present intrusion on your time. My Brother[2] writes me that you have an order drawn by Baylor to Mr.———— for five Guis. & desires to know if it be good. It is so, & I will take it up on our meeting in London, which I hope will be before Xmas. I am now here on what I expect will be my last visit, & hope to finish on Saty., when I shall return to Wr. [Worcester] and should be glad to meet there a line from you. I have had two Letters from our Friends[3] since you left them, but nothing in the news way which You are not informd of—indeed they very seldom touch upon that topic to me. I find my intimate is going to Tuscany, & I doubt not from his good understanding and attachment to the cause He will be very useful.[4]

I am anxious to see You & J[ohnson]⁵ & am using every means to get speedely away from this quarter, but it would be highly imprudent in me to do it without finishing, & taking a decent kind of leave. I have fears that I may be calld back on a future day on similar business, & therefore wish to stand well with those who have done things of some consideration by my recommendation, & to whom I may again have occasion to apply.

I have had some hints that I am much wanted abroad, but it will be impossible for me to go before Mar. or Apl. nor perhaps then without I can get releasd from some engagements here. It has also been mentiond to me that a person is wanted to make some distributions of assistance to some confined unfortunates in this Country. As it was never in my power to give a personal assistance where perhaps it was most wanted, I have long eer this pledgd myself to do every thing in my power, & think this business could be done without any material personal risque—but more of this hereafter. I find the Levant Letter [of] Marque of Bristol has sent in a retaken Wine Ship insurd at 15,000 in Londo.⁶—Her Cargoe was 250 pipes of Port, the rest money, which the Capn. of the privateer secured by taking out of the prize.—Two Americans Jno. Scott of Piscataqua prize master, & a Sailor Jno. Pearson of Cape Ann, who belongd to the Civil usage privateer ownd by Jackson & Tracey of Newberry, are now in Newgate at Bristol.⁷ Before these men were put on board the Wine ship, the Civil usage had taken 15 prizes. The Levant is a very strong well fitted Ship of 22 Guns & is cruising on the Coasts of France. She belongs to five or six people in Bristol among whom is *Ware* the Virga. Tobacco Merchant & one Brackenridge who was His Factor in Vira. & whom You might have seen in London with me in Feby. last. I hope his property in the Colony, & Wares Consignment Business from thence, will stigmatise them hereafter.

Pray acquaint me what you think about the late vast reports of the loss of Washingtons army Philadelphia &ca. and if there has been any news from Maryland—Mollison I am told has a Letter from His Brother at Elk Rivr. 2d Sepr.⁸ I hope to God our Countrymen will continue to bear with fortitude the many calamities with which they are surrounded—I cannot divest myself of fears that they are in want of Amunition & many other necessarys.

The trade in this place begins now to diminish, & almost every manufacturer that I speak to tells me it is much hurt altho some particular branc[h]es are yet full of orders. Many of the heads of the addressers have acknowlegd to me they are become heartily sick of the American War—

I am Yrs. &ca.
W. R.

In a Letter from Geo. while he was in London I am informd You receivd safe my last packet. The blank Letter to C[armichael][9] I hope was forwarded according to direction. Pray when did You hear last from him? and is he still bent upon the purpose of leaving Europe.

MHS: Ridley Papers, Nichols Gift, 5.

[1] Ridley, who had carried Digges's Sept. 8 letter of introduction to Izard in France, was now back in London.

[2] George Digges (1743–1792), who had sailed to London two years earlier and was apparently living there.

[3] Possibly Ralph Izard and his wife, but more likely Arthur and William Lee (1739–1795), both of whom were also in Paris.

[4] A reference to Izard's appointment by the Continental Congress as commissioner to Tuscany (see headnote for Digges to Izard, Sept. 8, 1777).

[5] Joshua Johnson (1742–1802), a Maryland merchant involved in commercial ventures before the war and now in Nantes performing a variety of commissions for both the Congress and his own state. He would serve as the first U.S. consul in London, 1790–1797.

[6] The *London Daily Advertiser* had reported on Nov. 11 that the *Levant* and another vessel had taken several ships in the area of Cadiz.

[7] The Newburyport mercantile firm of Jackson, Tracy, & Tracy, founded in 1774 by Jonathan Jackson (1743–1810) and his brothers-in-law John (1753–1815) and Nathaniel Tracy (1751–1796), had prospered and become prominent before the outbreak of the war, but it had then begun outfitting a number of privateers like the *Civil Usage* and suffering heavy losses. With the restoration of peace the firm disbanded. "Scott" (actually Trott) had been on the *Civil Usage* but was prize master's mate on the *Dover* when captured. Both men petitioned for relief in the fall of 1778; Trott was pardoned in Oct. 1778 on condition of his serving in the Royal Navy.

[8] Probably a reference to William Molleson and his brother Robert, Marylanders who were established as London merchants trading with North America. Various documents suggest that William was the one then in England. Both Arthur and William Lee

were suspicious of the Mollesons, believing that intelligence from home was immediately passed along to the government in London. Elk River rises in Chester County, Pa., and runs through Elkton, Md., to Chesapeake Bay.

⁹William Carmichael (ca. 1745–1795) was in Paris as secretary of the American commissioners, collaborating with them in their efforts to obtain aid for the rebellion. When jealousies developed among the commissioners, resulting in the recall of Silas Deane, with whom Carmichael was closely associated, Carmichael in 1778 returned home to represent Maryland in the Congress until 1780, then to become secretary of the American legation in Spain under John Jay (1745–1829) until 1782. On Nov. 2, 1777, Digges had written Carmichael a letter from Birmingham under cover of a letter to "Oliphant" [Ridley], who had forwarded it on Nov. 8. Although endorsed as having been received Nov. 18th, Ridley's letter was intercepted in the General Post Office, where a copy was made of it (see B. F. Stevens, *Facsimiles*, no. 298); Digges's letter has not been found.

To John Thornton

Major Thornton was in England as Franklin's envoy to confer with David Hartley (1731–1813), a friend of Franklin's in Parliament opposed to the American policies of the North government, in order to arrange for alleviating the plight of American prisoners as a step toward Anglo-American reconciliation. To this end Thornton was to report on conditions in the prisons, draw up a list of the prisoners, and distribute relief. At that time Digges was himself already engaged in helping those held in Forton Prison near Portsmouth and in Old Mill Prison at Plymouth. Arthur Lee's journal entry of November 27, 1777, makes Digges's involvement clear: "Wrote to Mr. Digges, in England, to try to furnish necessaries to Capt. Nicholson, [Henry] Johnson, and other prisoners to the amount of £50 sterling" (Richard Henry Lee, Life of Arthur Lee, LL.D. [Boston: Wells & Lilly, 1829], 1 : 356). Digges was, accordingly, familiar enough with the situation to be able to supply Thornton with needed information. Although Thornton, as Lee's private secretary, was about to become an informant for the British, he was faithful in carrying out his mission for the prisoners and successful in providing them with a few of their necessities. Like Lee, who on December 19 recommended to the Committee of Secret Correspondence that they consider Digges for some role in Europe, Thornton doubtless had confidence in Digges.

1 December 1777

American Prisoners in Fortton Prison near Portsmo.[1]

Decr. 1. 1777

Wm. Tryon, Leiut. of a Brigantine from Chs. Town So. Carolina[2] also A French Gentleman who was passenger and seven private men.

—

Captain Harris[3] of the Brigantine Musqueto belonging to Virginia also Capn. Dick of marines,[4] Chas. de La Hay Master,[5] Alexr. Moore Midshipman[6] & Jno. Smith Boatswain.[7]

—

From the Brigantine Montgomery belonging to Philadelphia Jas. Bryant 1st Leiut., Thos. White 2d Leiut, Geo. Seaguer Surgeons mate, Jas. Lee prize master and about 30 privates.[8]

—

Belonging to the Reprisal Capt. Weeks & taken in prizes—six privates.[9]

—

Belonging to Capt. Cunningham—Do. Mr. Jno. Bayley[10] and eight privates.

—

From the Schooner Jenny—bound from france to Virginia Leiut. Arthur[11] & 6 privates.

—

Sloop Hornet belonging to the Congress, Capt. Jno. Nicholson, his Leiut. second Lieutenant, Capn. of Marines, Master, and Surgeon no privates.[12]

—

From the Oliver Cromwell Privateer belonging to Philaa. Eleven privates.

—

From the Lexington Privateer belonging to the Congress Docr. Downing[13]—Privates.

—

There is also Docr. Smith and Docr. Jas. Brehon[14] from Maryland and many others as well officers as privates whose names cannot be recollectd.

—

N.B. There are also in the same prison & treated in a similar manner a French Gentleman an Engineer taken with some others in Fort Washington, another French officer taken with General Lee and two other French officers.[15]

Since the above list was receivd from Portsmouth there has been an addition of about thirty to the prisoners (cheifly officers) takin on the Banks of Newfoundland & brought home in the Men of War from thence.

The Government allowance to these Prisoners is indiscriminately 1 lb. of Bread and ¾ lb. of Beef (raw & including bone) and a quart of small Beer per day for each man. They have each a small hammock, Straw, and one coverled, & are in one general room. The hammocks are swung to Posts & three & four tier deep as the room is much too small to hang them in their usual mode.

Not the least fire or Candle is allowd them & no paper or pen & ink. Any Donations whatever that are sent to them must pass thro the hands of the Agent; and if money, it is witheld by the Agent & given in at *a shilling* per Day. The Prisoners speak exceedingly well of the Captain & Soldiers on Guard, but complain exceedingly of the harsh treatment of the Agent, who often exercises the punishment of the *black* hole upon them—The black hole is a dungeon in the Prison, & the agent has often put individuals into it for many days at a time for harsh language to himself and other trifling incidents.

SIR

The foregoing is every memorandum that I can procure relative to the prisoners at Portsmouth. I have not been able to get any information of those at Plymouth but have good reason to suppose their treatment is very similar and that their numbers are larger—

I am Yr. mo. Obt. Ser.
Tho. Digges

Sunday Evening [November 30, 1777]

For Mr. Thornton

HU: Arthur Lee Papers, 3:89.

[1] Confirmation of much of the information given by Digges can be found in a journal kept by one of Forton's first American prisoners, Timothy Connor, and edited by William Richard Cutter, "A Yankee Privateersman in Prison in England, 1777–1779," *The New-England Historical and Genealogical Register*, 30–33 (1876–1879), printed in brief installments. Additional confirmation and biographical data can be compiled from the extensive literature about the navy, the officers, and the privateersmen of the Revolution, as well as from records in state collections. What cannot be verified is the spelling of some names, characterized as it then was by phonetically dictated variations.

[2] Tryon's ship was the *Notre Dame*. He had been committed to Forton on July 15, escaped, and been captured and placed in solitary confinement on July 30. On Mar. 7, 1778, he again escaped and was again retaken, successfully gaining his freedom on July 23, 1778.

[3] John Harris (d. ca. 1783), of Welsh descent born in Italy, was a man of means from Hampton, Va., owner as well as captain of the *Mosquito*, which had been credited with taking many prizes before being captured by H.M.S. *Ariadne* in the West Indies on June 25, 1777. Harris, with seven others from the *Mosquito*, had been committed to Forton on Aug. 8, tried to escape and failed, and, pardoned on May 31, 1779, was released through an exchange of prisoners, probably in late June or early July 1779.

[4] Alexander Dick (d. 1786), of Fredericksburg, Va., had been captain of marines aboard the *Mosquito* and lodged in Forton along with Harris. He escaped twice: on Dec. 2, when he was quickly retaken, and on Sept. 6, 1778, when he and others broke out and sought refuge with the Rev. Thomas Wren (1725?–1787), the benevolent Presbyterian minister in Portsmouth who had initiated the subscription for the relief of imprisoned Americans and distributed supplies to those in Forton. Soon after, he sought refuge with Digges (see Digges to Franklin, Sept. 18, 1778).

[5] Gaius Marcus Brumbaugh's *Revolutionary War Records: Volume I, Virginia* (Baltimore: Genealogical Publishing Co., 1967), p. 37, lists the sailing master as Charles Dekay (Connor gives the name as Decay). He had been committed to Forton with the others from the *Mosquito* and managed to escape on Dec. 2.

[6] Moore escaped on Dec. 2, was soon retaken, and was pardoned for exchange on May 31, 1779. On Oct. 3, 1779, he was a midshipman on the frigate *Alliance*, consort of the *Bonhomme Richard* in her action with the *Serapis*.

[7] Smith enlisted in the Royal Navy in order to get out of Forton. His pardon enabling him to enlist was issued Dec. 3, 1778.

[8] The crew of the *Montgomery*, taken by the *Levant*, Mar. 8, 1777, had been committed to Forton on Aug. 8. Bryant escaped July 7, 1779. White was pardoned for exchange May 31, 1779, and became an officer aboard the *Alliance*. Seaguer (sometimes listed as Seger, Segar, and Seugure) escaped. The captain, Benjamin Hill, listed by Connor, is not mentioned by Digges because he had doubtless escaped before Digges undertook to compile his list.

[9] The captain of the *Reprisal*, first of the Continental cruisers to operate in European waters, was Lambert Wickes (ca. 1742–1777), who during June 1777 had succeeded in capturing several British ships and their crews. Early in July, however, two had been retaken, and with them, to be committed to Forton on Aug. 9, the prize master, the prize master's mate, and eight crewmen of one of the ships. Some managed to escape; some entered the British service. Wickes himself escaped capture.

[10] Benjamin Bailey (alias Capt. James Smith), prize master on the *Northampton*, had,

according to his allegation, been put aboard that ship after being kidnapped at Dunkirk onto the *Revenge*, commanded by Gustavus Conyngham (1744–1819), who in May had begun the exploits that made him celebrated for the number of British ships he had captured. Nonetheless committed to Forton on Aug. 11, 1777, he was subsequently pardoned to enter the British service in Sept. 1778.

[11] John Arthur, listed by Connor as the prize master of the *Mosquito*, which had apparently taken the *Jenny* as a prize. He was later pardoned to serve the British, May 22, 1779.

[12] John Nicholson, younger brother of the navy's senior captain, James Nicholson (ca. 1736–1804), had assumed command of the *Hornet* late in 1776, been taken on Apr. 27, 1777, and broken out of Forton, Dec. 2, only to be retaken next day. His officers were, respectively, Lt. William Morann (or Moran); 2d Lt. Edward Legear (or Legar or Leger), who escaped on July 23, 1778; Lt. William Radford (of the marines), who had tried to escape with Nicholson and been retaken with him; Master Robert Robertson, who later escaped; and Dr. James Brehon, of Cambridge, Maryland, who had shared Nicholson's and Radford's failure but succeeded in escaping in 1779, this time to seek out Digges for assistance (see Digges's letters to Franklin, beginning May 21, 1779).

[13] Dr. Eliphalet Downer (1744–1806), of Roxbury, Mass., who had fought at Lexington, Apr. 19, 1776, and then served aboard the privateer *Yankee* as a surgeon, had been taken prisoner prior to July 31, 1776, had been confined by order of Aug. 16, and then had either escaped or been released before becoming a passenger on the brig *Lexington*, which had been en route to Boston from France when captured by the British cutter *Alert* on Sept. 19, 1777, when he had once again been made prisoner. Committed to Forton on Oct. 13, he succeeded in escaping Sept. 6, 1778.

[14] Dr. Clement Smith had been a doctor on the *Hornet* and committed to Forton, along with Brehon (see n. 12), from which he had escaped to become surgeon on the *Lexington* before being taken again.

[15] A reference to the capture of Gen. Charles Lee (1731–1782) at Baskingridge, N.J., Dec. 13, 1776. Lee had been held in New Jersey under the jurisdiction of Sir William Howe (1729–1814). The French engineer was Lt. Col. Viebert; the other French officer was Lt. Col. Baubetrang, acting as Lee's aide-de-camp when taken.

To Arthur Lee

Arthur Lee was in the midst of his controversy with Franklin and Deane over the management of American affairs in Europe. The product of complex political, social, ideological, and personal differences, the controversy had reached a crisis when Lee, full of suspicion, had complained to the Congress of his fellow commissioners' conduct and early in 1778 succeeded in having Deane recalled. Lee had resented being excluded from councils to which Franklin had admitted Deane; he had been angered by discovering that Dr. Edward Ban-

croft (1744–1821), employed by Deane as secretary (and later found to be a double agent), had been abusing him to Franklin; and, partly, perhaps, because it had interfered with some Virginian schemes, he had condemned land speculation in the Northwest Territory designed to create a new proprietary colony there, Vandalia, in the interests of a group that included Deane, Franklin, Samuel Wharton (1732–1800) and Joseph Wharton, Jr. (1733–1816), of Philadelphia; Jacques Donatien le Ray de Chaumont (1725–1803); Thomas Walpole (1727–1803), Sir Robert's nephew; and various intimates of George III (1738–1820) and Lord (Frederick) North (1732–1792). When Deane had then sought a hearing to clear himself, Lee must have asked Digges to write him a letter that he could use in support of his accusations.

Bristol, August 30, 1778

It is beyond a doubt that there were very considerable sums done in the stocks by the friends of a certain quondam commissioner,[1] about November and December last, in consequence of the arrival in London of Doctor Bancroft, with the news of the favourable turn given to American affairs by the surrender of Burgoyne's army. The Doctor was in close cog all the time he was in London, and was never visible but to the brothers (meaning the Whartons in London) and one or two other confidants, whom I always shunned on account of their intimacy with Vansittart before & after his apostacy in exposing the letters he bore from American people in London to their friends in Paris, among which were some of mine.[2] During the time I was busy in London getting forward the subscription for relief of American prisoners, and when Mr. Thornton was over about them,[3] I gave that Gentleman a full verbal account of this infamous transaction of Vansittart, in order that it might be made known to your community; and I wrote particularly to you and Mr. Izard, by Mr. Thornton, about it. As I am positive of the facts alledged against him, Vansittart seems to have got his deserts, for I hear he is shunned by your community as well as all his countrymen in France. You may assure yourself that Lord North, Mr. Knox, Mr. Hartley,[4] and some others about the Secretary's Office, knew of Doctor Bancroft's being in London, the former had information of what he was about, and had him dogged more than once to the house of Samuel Wharton, at late hours in the night. I had convincing proofs of this before the Doctor took flight to France, and being then in intimacy with Samuel Wharton (from knowing he had the confidential correspondence of Doctor Franklin, and getting him at times to forward my letters.) I went to him and expostulated with him on the impropriety of Doctor Bancroft's being in London on a stock-jobbing errand, in which it was very visible Mr. Deane was concerned, & that Doctor Franklin was not absolutely ignorant of it. It is natural to me, Sir, to feel much where my country is concerned. I have often wished my feelings less, but at that period of time I was more than usually agitated, and unhappy.

Many hundred American prisoners were in a starving condition from cold and famine; numbers were daily taken at sea, and forced to war against their countrymen, on board English ships. Every person who came from France told me it was but a partial assistance that country was giving to mine, and every month was full of the disunity that subsisted in your small community. That the two first commissioners formed a party against you; that one of them at least, if not both, had united against you, in a manner very unjustifiable, both in respect to yourself and the business you were concerned in; and that a vile combination subsisted to reduce you, not only to a cypher, but to sink you into contempt: That you were not in the confidence of the other two, and a variety of other tittle tattle stories, chiefly levelled at the consequence of yourself and brother, for he too has had his share of abuse, particularly as to the story of the ill consequences of his selfishness in regard to his losing two or three West Indiamen, which were carried into Nantz last summer, and were given up to their owners in London; a lie that both from my Nantz letters, as well as other conviction here, I had in my power to flatly contradict it. There has been a story lately against Samuel Wharton which will make me more cautious than ever I was with him. It is something similar to that of Vansittart, and came originally from the same informant, Mr. Williams.[5] Mr. Wharton has however (as Mr. Craig[6] informed me) cleared up this matter to Dr. Franklin, and satisfied Mr. Williams.[7] He must therefore stand acquitted, whatever we may think. J. Wharton, his brother (who is an honest careless ruined man) has been the principal negociator of stock and gaming policies on a French war; he has repeatedly wished me to join him in such business (which I [n]ever did, and ever shall refuse to do). He once or twice told me his information of the state of politicks came from Mr. Deane, and that there was security in such a gambling scheme; but I much fear from his present circumstances, he has been fatally deceived. In short Sir, there has been much done by the two brothers, Dr. Bancroft and two or three others, and it is evident to me Mr. Deane either had a hand in it, or gave his countenance thereto, & that Dr. Franklin knew of the transaction.

"Extract of a letter from ———— Digges, Esq; to the Hon. Arthur Lee, Esq; dated Bristol, August 30, 1778," in *Extracts from a Letter written to the President of Congress by the Hon. Arthur Lee, Esquire, in Answer to a Libel Published in the Pennsylvania Gazette of the Fifth of December, 1778. By Silas Deane, Esquire.* [Epigraph] (Williamsburg: Printed by J. Dixon & T. Nicolson, 1779), pp. 30–31 [Evans microprint 16319]. This is the earliest version of the text available; it is followed by the phrase "True copy from the original. Ludwell Lee." The original manuscript has not been found. An anonymous handwritten transcript of this "true copy" made by Lee's nephew Ludwell (1760–1836), containing some insignificant variants, is among the Lee papers in the Virginia Historical Society, but, made many years after Ludwell Lee's death, it surely has no greater claim to accuracy than the printed version. Moreover, since it transcribes no more than the published extract and supplies the identical label, the character of the so-called original on which the true copy was based must itself remain in question. What had happened was that Deane, facing delays in his hearing, had become so impatient that he had published in the *Pennsylvania Packet* on December 1, 1778, his "Address of Silas Deane to the Free and Virtuous Citizens of America," an attack on both the Lees that was reprinted in other papers. This action prompted Arthur Lee to publish a reply that quoted part of Digges's letter in support of the charges against Deane.

[1] Silas Deane.
[2] Apparently a reference to the activities of the son of Jacobus Van Zandt, a prominent American merchant. Isaac Van Zandt, whose name is variously spelled by contemporaries, had been recruited as a spy by the Rev. John Vardill on behalf of William Eden, later Lord Auckland (1744–1814). Using the name George Lupton, Van Zandt had from Apr. 1777 to late Jan. 1778 picked up gossip at Silas Deane's dinner table concerning cargoes, sailing dates, and the activities of privateers, passed along the information, not always accurately, to the British government, and exposed American correspondence to British authorities. On Apr. 8 and 10, 1777, in a report to Eden, he

had attributed to Digges the shipping of locks for guns or muskets to America, but requested "no notice . . . be taken as it is already past, and Diggs a particular friend" (Stevens, *Facsimiles*, no. 681, pp. 6–7).

³See Digges to John Thornton, Dec. 1, 1777.

⁴North was the prime minister, Feb. 10, 1770–Mar. 27, 1782; William Knox (1732–1810) was undersecretary of state for the colonies under Lord George Germain (1716–1785); and David Hartley, still a member of Parliament opposed to the war and an advocate of conciliation, was along with the London merchant, William Hodgson, continuing to collaborate with Franklin to improve the lot of American prisoners and to promote their exchange.

⁵Probably John Williams, a cousin of Franklin's and uncle of Franklin's grandnephew, Jonathan Williams, Jr. (1750–1815), the American agent at Nantes. John Williams had tried to use his connections to sell his services to the British, had not been paid money promised to him, and in his anger had threatened to expose Van Zandt to Franklin and possibly also sought to embarrass Wharton, since he had served as a go-between between Vardill and Wharton.

⁶A Philadelphian, James Craig, who was serving as a courier between Digges and others in London and the American commissioners in France; later, he was consul at St. Martin, France.

⁷Jonathan Williams, Jr.

To [⟨Jonathan Loring Austin⟩]

Jonathan Loring Austin (1748–1826), secretary to the Massachusetts Board of War, had been dispatched to France to inform Franklin and the other commissioners officially of the American victory at Saratoga. He had reached Passy on December 4, 1777, and a few weeks prior to February 12, 1778, been sent by Franklin on a secret mission to London to try to convince Lord Shelburne and other members of Parliament opposed to the government's policies that continuation of the war was futile. He had stayed in England until March 23, 1778, when he had returned to France. While in England he had used the name George Brown, to whom this letter appears to have been sent.

Augt. 1778

Mr. Digges would be obligd to Mr. Brown for a line from P[ari]s, as soon as He arrives there to inform him of the success of his journey &ca. &ca.¹ & to give him accounts of the latest news from america. He will be informd from any of our Friends at P——s the mode of conveying Letters to England—mine are directed thus—Mr. Thos. Digges—to the care of Mr. M: Ridley[2] No. 4 Circus Tower Hill London.

Mr. Digges forwarded for Mrs. Macaulay[3] in May last a large paper parcel of Books directed for Dr. F[rankli]n at Paris.—They were for the following persons—

one Vol. quarto—Mrs. Macaulays late History In Letters[4]—for Dr. F——n

four Do.—Mrs. Macaulays History of England—for Count Sarsfield[5]

four Vols. Do. . Do.—— Do.—— for Madm. de Chaumont[6] The parcel being too large for Mr. Austin to carry in his Portmanteau, it was forwarded by a Friend who meant to push his way out to Pensylvania thro France: He went in a Guernsey trader from London to Guernsey and in attempting to get from thence in a hired boat to the Coast of France He was *suspected* & had his baggage seizd together with this parcel of books. They were all lodg'd and are yet in possession of a Custom house officer in Guernsey who writes to my Friend in London they shall be restored. Mr. Digges has made Mrs. Macaulay acquainted with the accident to the books, but She is afraid of being suspected by Her friends in P——s of not being so good as her word, having promisd to send them these books; Mr. D. therefore requests Mr. Brown to make the above circumstances known to Dr. F. and to Mr. Arthur Lee, in order that Madame de Chaumont & Count Sarsfield may know Mrs. Macaulay fulfilld her promise. Mr. D. in the mean time is using every method (thro some Guernsey Merchants in London) to get the things sent back to London & hopes to be more lucky in forwarding them a second time. In his two last letters of June 1st & 28th he particularly mentions these circumstances to his Friend Mr. Ar. Lee, but has not receivd a line from him or his Brother now for many months, altho his late letters to both of them relate to some particular business of their own.[7]

Mr. D—— begs his particular rembrance to them, & if they have any thing to do their commands shall be minutely attended to.

HSP: Franklin Papers, 5 : 47.

¹Austin apparently had made a second trip to England after reporting to Franklin in Mar.

²Matthew Ridley.

³Catharine Macaulay (1731–1791) wrote extensively on political and historical subjects from a point of view likely to appeal to Franklin and American sympathizers in France. Her most ambitious work, *The History of England from the Accession of James I to the Elevation of the House of Hanover*, which had already appeared in at least three editions, with some slight variations in the title, had a libertarian purpose explicitly stated in her introduction: "To do justice . . . to the memory of our illustrious ancestors to the utmost of my small abilities, still having an eye to public Liberty, the standard by which I have endeavoured to measure the virtue of those characters which are treated of in this history. . . ."

⁴This single volume was the first and only published volume of *The History of England, from the Revolution to the Present Time, in a Series of Letters to the Reverend Doctor Wilson* (Bath: R. Cruttwell, 1778).

⁵Probably the third edition of her large work (London: Edward and Charles Dilly, 1769, 1772). Why she sent only four-volume sets of what was in fact a five-volume work is uncertain. Perhaps she considered only the first four volumes a set; they had been published in 1769 and the fifth volume had not been published until three years later. The first four were designated on the title page as "Ed. III" and concluded with the execution of Charles I. The fifth lacked the designation of an edition and concluded with the Restoration of Charles II. The intended recipient of this set was Guy-Claude, comte de Sarsfield (1718–1789), whose seat was at Rennes but who spent much of his time in Paris, where he could entertain and correspond with all Americans of prominence who came to Europe.

⁶*Née* Thérèse Joguer, wife of Jacques Donatien le Ray de Chaumont, a friend of Franklin's who had turned over most of his vast Hôtel Valentinois to the American commissioners, although the de Chaumonts continued to reside in the main apartments. The sieur de Chaumont's mercantile interests and connections with Versailles enabled him to support various military ventures of the French government, to serve as agent in completing arrangements for John Paul Jones (1747–1792) to cruise in the *Bonhomme Richard* in 1779, and, largely because of his hostility to England, to promote Franco-American relations generally.

⁷Arthur Lee was still in Paris. His brother William was in Frankfurt, having been appointed commissioner to the courts of Berlin and Vienna, but, because of war conditions in Europe, was never received. Both the Lees were becoming embroiled in a controversy with Franklin and Deane over the conduct of American diplomacy abroad. No correspondence between Digges and Arthur Lee earlier than Digges's letter of Aug. 30, 1778, has been found, although they had been corresponding since at least March 14. Nor have Digges's letters to William Lee been found, but their correspondence also dates back. By Jan. 9 Lee had known Digges well enough to recommend him in a letter to Richard Henry Lee (1732–1794) as a commissioner in Portugal (*Letters of William Lee*, ed. Worthington Chauncey Ford [1891; rpt. New York: Burt Franklin, 1968], 1:339–40), and the William Lee letterbooks in the Virginia Historical Society contain copies of eight of his letters to Digges, including two that Digges here seems not to have received: June 17, 1778, from Vienna, and Aug. 21, 1778, from Frankfurt (MssL51f 417, pp.

18–19 and 49). These letters, acknowledging two from Digges, respectively thank Digges for help in completing a financial transaction and comment on the progress of the war.

To Benjamin Franklin

Bir[mingha]m Sept: 18./78

SIR

My having an oppertunity to forward this under cover to my freind Mr. I[zar]d, induces me to obtrude a few lines on You. Mr. Alexr. Dick and some companions of his was lately with me,[1] and their situation and circumstances demanded of me every alleviation of their wants that I had in my power to afford them; in the doing of which I was obligd to take Mr. Dicks bill on You dated Bristol Sept. 8, ten days sight, for twenty six pounds Stg., which bill I shall keep until a favourable oppertunity offers of remitting it to some freind in France. As Mr. Dick promisd me to give You the earliest notice of this bill from the first port he might arrive at in France, and to inform You for what it was drawn, who, & what His circumstances were, and also to lodge the needful for its discharge, I make no doubt You are informd of it before this day, & that it will be honord when presented to You.

I hope You will excuse me Sir for this unnecessary intrusion, but I am prompted from an ardent wish to be servicable to You or Your Community, to go further, and make an offer of my services to You. I am unavoidably prevented from giving my personal assistance to a cause I have extreemly at heart, but I am so situated in this Country as to have it often in my power to be servicable to those more actively & openly employd; If You can point out any mode wherein I can be useful, or will place confidence enough in me to transact or do any thing for You here, I promise you Sir it shall be done with zeal punctuality secrecy & honor. It will not be prudent in me to be further explicit. Mr. I——d, Messrs: L[ee]s, Mr. Jos. W[harto]n, Mr. C[a]rm[ichae]l whom I have reason to expect is returnd to You, or any other confidential Freind who has lately gone from England, Mr. R[idle]y, or Mr. J. J[ohnso]n can satisfy You who & what I am; The two first mentiond Gentlemen, & Mr. R——y, can give you my name and direction, and I have lately wrote to the three, to mention a circumstance to You about our people in this quarter, that is deserving Your attention, for I begin to fear their situation will soon be again deplorable—

I have the honor to be Sir Yr. very Ob. Sert.
T. D——

HSP: Franklin Papers, 5:48.

[1] See Digges to Thornton, Dec. 1, 1777, n. 4.

To David Hartley

Digges had become acquainted with Hartley in conjunction with the efforts that had begun late in the previous year to provide relief for American prisoners of war. Remaining in touch with Hartley, Digges managed to learn much about the attitudes of various members of Parliament and to serve both Hartley and Franklin in forwarding messages from one to the other.

Miss Temple
Galloways Buildings Bath
26 No./78

DEAR SIR

I did myself the pleasure to write You on Monday last, & as there was little probability of its meeting You at Southampton I directed the letter to Golden Square.

Since the verdict of the inquest which sat on the body of Count DuBarry,[1] there has been various reports and conjectures on that matter. The town in general seems not to approve either of the verdict or the proceedings of the Coroner as to his intercourse with Ct. Rice prior to empanelling the Jury. Nothing material transpires since I wrote You, save that Mr. Rogers (the second of Ct. Rice) now appears in public, & as yet, no notice taken of him by the civil magistracy—He told me that He knew nothing of the affair prior to Rice's coming to him after He was in bed & about one oClk. in the morning of the day they fought—He saw no material rancor between them, & as He thought it only a common dispute they had to settle by the Sword, He attended Rice; & describes the duel as a very fair one. They were placed at 25 yds. distance, & agreed to advance on each other & fire when they pleasd; & it was at about 15 yds, distance the two wounds was given.

You will see an account of this in the morning post of yesterday signd, W. Brereton M. C. which by every account is totally erroneous[2]—I inclose You a part of the Bath paper with the account of Sr. J. Millers signd J. M.—He was foreman of the jury.—The other signd J. W—— is Mr. Woods account—the magistrate who took up the two drivers & examind them prior to the inquest, & who also attended the Jury.

This affair has raised so much the indignation of several Gentlemen here against Count Rice, that I think it beyond a doubt He will be indigted and tryd at the Sessions.

He is now out of danger—yet in custody of the Coroner & a guard, & no recognisance taken for his appearance &c.

You will observe in the inclosd News paper some articles of News from N. York and from St. Christophers.

The vessel which brought the Officer with dispatches for Government, was bought at St. Kitts for the purpose; as the Messenger would not declare a word of his errand & only insinuated things were very bad indeed in that quarter, His back was scarcely turnd, when the whole city of Bristol was alarmd with the report that St. Kitts and St. Vincents were both taken by the french,[3] & it occasiond a gloom upon the exchange on tuesday that would be difficult to describe. Times are strangely alterd in that quarter—You now hear nothing but curses on the blundering ministry &ca., &ca. I have shewn some of the leading Government people there Your three first letters—they were very much commended & I think the distribution of half a dozen (when they are compleat) in that City will have a good effect. I have sent the others by an oppertunity that almost insures there Safe arrival in America, & noted at the end of the third, that a fourth letter was in the press & should be forwarded out with all care.⁴

I want much to hear the turn of political matters in Parliament—I am pretty confidant no more troops will be sent to the Continent of America whatever may be held out here. I trust you will give me information as to the prisoners business, as well as of any measure that Administration may apparently fix upon for the prosecution of their hitherto blind & destructive measures.

BRO: Hartley-Russell Papers, D/EHy F-86.

¹Jean-Baptiste-Adolphe du Barry (1749–1778) had been killed in a duel on Nov. 18, 1778, by a companion with whom he had quarrelled, Count Rice, from Ireland. The verdict rendered by the coroner's inquest was manslaughter.
²Probably a reference to the *London Chronicle*, Nov. 24–26, 1778, p. 508, where William Brereton's letter, dated Nov. 23, appears, intended to correct reports that the *Chronicle* had published in its two preceding numbers: Nov. 19–21, p. 490, and Nov. 21–24, pp. 498–99.
³St. Kitts (or St. Christopher's) and St. Vincent's are both islands in the British West Indies.
⁴The four letters (dated Sept. 13, Sept. 24, Oct. 11, and Oct. 29, 1778) were bound together and published as *Letters on the American War. Addressed to the Right Worshipful Mayor and Corporation, to the Worshipful the Wardens and Corporation of the Trinity-House, and to the Worthy Burgesses of the Town of Kingston upon Hull* (London: Almon . . . [et al.], 1778).

To Benjamin Franklin

B[risto]l 19th Decr. 1778

DEAR SIR

Encouragd by an offer of getting this Letter deliverd safely by a private hand, I sit down to acknowlege the receipt of Your obliging favor of the 23d Octor. relative to Mr. C: D[ic]ks bill remitted by me; and to thank You Sir for your kind offers of attention therein made.¹

I should think my time very well taken up in writing to you whenever I had any thing material or useful to communicate; and I certainly should at times have done it, had I a proper name & direction to write under; for situated and busey as I am at present, and distant too from the Capital, I do not often hear of private conveyances before it is too late for me to embrace them, and the uncertainty of safety in the common post renders it very discouraging. I have not the honor to be known to you Sir, but those about you are well acquainted who & what I am, and can testify, that altho my personal assistance to the cause You are so deeply engagd in, has been hitherto unavoidably denyd Me, yet my mite has been chearfully given, & I trust with some little success & advantages to My Country.

The Bearer (a Gentleman connected with a freind lately settled at Nantes)[2] will deliver You this, & has my direction & also knows *how* letters may be forwarded under cover to others—A Monr. Monr. Pierre J: Bertrand, Post Office Londo., or Pierre. J. Du Vall post office Bristol, will do for the common post; and I will attend to the signature of Louis Frances, or any other name written in the same hand as the letter of the 23d Octor.—

The parliamentary news of the day I need not attempt to give You, as I know the public papers go regularly abroad. The general opinion is that no more troops will be sent to America, save new recruits sufficient to fill up the vacancies: I am credibly informd that if more men are wanted, Ministry are confidant they can get them in America, and have on more occasions than one, given pretty plain hints that Men enough for their purpose, & who have become tired of the measures of the Congress, may be had for bounties of twenty or thirty Guineas a head, which is a more cheap and eligable mode than sending out Regiments from Europe.—Some people are gone over with secret instructions to get among the Americans by art, & publish to them the bounties offerd by Government for such as will go over or inlist. The mode of war has certainly been orderd from home to be alterd into a more vigorous, I may say infamous one; Fire devastation and plunder is now to be expected, and I but *too* often hear it urged, That it is now the interest & intentions of all England to render the American accession of as little avail as possible to France, You must destroy America or She will destroy You &ca. &ca. &ca. The ministry go on in deceiving the Country Gentlemen & in fact themselves, & parliament is as plyant as usual; What may be their plan of future opperations it is impossible to say; I beleive they have none but what the event of the day suggests, & the occurrence of the following recals; I cannot think at present more is meant by them than to retain actual possessions, to annoy at Sea, destroy unguarded towns & property, and to take the chance of the chapter of accidents. The reenforcements voted, or expected from abroad, are not equal to more active Services. My favourite wish, American Independency, seems to make no proselites but in the minority, and even there, where union is so necessary for the immidiate salvation of this Country, I am sorry to say the opinion is not general in favour of it. Tho they disagree in the end I think they will nevertheless join in the means: As to numbers they stand better than heretofore, and except in the instance of my acquaintance Govr. J[ohnston]e,[3] I see no signs of desertion in the little Corps of Patriots.—Tho the word is so low in credit, I trust the principle exists, & I hope will one day or other revive.

It is surprising that the people swallow with as much avidity as ever the tales & promises of Administration & their runners,—every thing they give out is in some measure beleivd, & consequently finds the effect: The quarrels at Boston with De Estaignes people—the total destruction of His fleet by Adm. Byron—the sunken consequence of Congress—the defection & desertion of almost all Washingtons army —The Revolt of the So. Carolinians & New Englandmen[4]—the almost certainty that the party under Campbell (which saild the 19 Octor. from N. York) would take quiet possession of Chas. Town,[5] with a number of other similar storeys, was to have alterd intirely the face of the drooping cause of England in America: As time & information contradict these reports, there are always others ready cut & dry, & as constantly beleivd—so are they deceivd and so they will be to the end of the Chapter.

The Culloden a 74 & one of Byrons Squadron arrivd a few days ago at Milford-haven—After Byron left N. York on the 19h Octo. His fleet put into R. Island & soon after leaving that place on a cruise (supposd to be to look after De Estaigne) a violent storm seperated the fleet; The Somerset a 64 was lost in it near Cape Cod, & the Culloden (formerly hurt in her Masts) was obligd to fly before it to England. On her way, tho not altogether out of the tract for the Wt. Indies, she took an armd brig belonging to De Estaignes Squadron, the crew of which gave information they were bound for Europe, & this is generally now beleivd. A packet is since arrivd at Falmo. which left N. York the 19th Novr., which confirms the dispersion of Byron—that most of his fleet had got back to R. Island—that De Estaigne had saild on the 4th from Boston but not known *for where*—that Ld. Carlyle, Eden, Cornwallis, Gen. Grey,[6] & other officers of the guards were soon to come home— & that the expedition under Campbell to So. Carolina had also been seperated & dispersd. As Coll. Stewart who bore the dispatches has been now some days in London & not a word of these disagreeable intelligences in the Gazette,[7] it is to be feard they are too true.

I am much with our mutual freind D[avid] H[artle]y, and we are in dayly hopes of something being done for our captive people—their situation is getting worse & worse, & I am but too often put to my utmost tryals to render them assistance and releif.

The fleet for the Wt. Indies said to be 7 of the line and some hundred Merchantmen, are waiting for a wind; This business of the two Admirals has causd a shift of Captains, and will it is feard very much retard the sailing of our fleets.[8] I am on all occasions

Dr. Sir Most respectfully Yrs.

J. W.

HSP: Franklin Papers, 5:51.

[1] A reference to Captain Alexander Dick's bill following his escape from Forton (see Digges to Thornton, Dec. 1, 1777, n. 4, and Digges to Franklin, Sept. 18, 1778). Digges has simply lapsed in his use of the initial of Dick's given name.

[2] The bearer, John Hunt, was a cousin of Matthew Ridley's wife. Ridley had removed to Nantes by Oct. 1778.

[3] George Johnstone (1730–1787) had served as governor of West Florida, 1763–1767, entered the House of Commons in 1768, and although at first a supporter of the administration, joined the opposition members because of objection to the American policies of Lord North, whose measures he viewed as destructive of the constitution. But when in Mar. 1778 the marquis of Rockingham and other critics of North had argued for the recognition of American independence as a means of breaking the newly concluded Treaty of Amity and Commerce between France and America, Johnstone had told the House that "he always had been and still was against the independence of

America," regretted that "gentlemen with whom he had acted" favored it, and rather than "give up the supremacy of this country over America . . . would sooner cross the floor and join those whose measures he had always disapproved" (*Parliamentary History of England* [London: Hansard, 1814], 19:918–20, 951). In June he had gone to America with Frederick Howard, the fifth earl of Carlisle (1748–1825), and William Eden to try to negotiate a peace.

⁴Comte Charles-Henri d'Estaing (1729–1794), the French naval commander, had arrived at the mouth of the Delaware in July 1778 to aid the Americans with a French fleet superior to the British fleet commanded by Admiral Richard Howe (1726–1799), but in the next few weeks a series of events had advantaged the British: American pilots had refused to risk taking the French across the bar at Sandy Hook, N.J.; a furious gale off Rhode Island had prevented a naval engagement; a delay in implementing plans d'Estaing had coordinated with Gen. John Sullivan (1740–1795) for closing in on the British garrison at Newport had given Howe a chance to receive reinforcements from Adm. John Byron (1723–1786), who had been sent from England to find the French; and under orders to revictual his ships in Boston and thence go to the West Indies if he encountered a superior force such as he believed at hand, d'Estaing had taken no risks, sought supplies in the face of a hostile reception in Boston, where townspeople and French sailors fought angrily, and finally sailed away, his fleet intact. Later, on Sept. 6, more serious riots had occurred in Charleston, with many wounded and some killed.

⁵Col. Archibald Campbell (1739–1791) had embarked from New York for the South, but it was Savannah, not Charleston, that turned out to be his first objective. He took possession of the Georgia port on Dec. 29, 1778; Charleston did not surrender to the British until May 1780.

⁶The earl of Carlisle, head of the commission to negotiate a peace in America; William Eden, the undersecretary of state who was in charge of England's spy network and, with Johnstone, a member of the Carlisle commission; Charles Cornwallis (1738–1805), second in command under Sir Henry Clinton (ca. 1738–1795); Charles Grey (1729–1807), promoted to major general after succeeding in a battle at Germantown, Oct. 1777.

⁷But the *London Chronicle* in its issue of Dec. 17–19, 1778 (4:585), had reported: "Yesterday . . . the Hon. Col. Stuart, son of the earl of Bute, arrived at the Plantation-office with dispatches from Gen. Clinton of New York, the contents of which were laid before his Majesty at St. James." These contents were "positively said to confirm the account that several of the southern Colonies have accepted the terms of reconciliation offered them by His Majesty's Commission, and had declared against their independence on [of] the Mother-country, and that several other Colonies would soon follow their example." The French fleet, moreover, was said to have been defeated, suffering considerable losses. Sir Charles Stuart (1753–1801), a lieutenant colonel since 1777, was the fourth son of John Stuart, third earl of Bute (1713–1792).

⁸During the critical conclusion of the indecisive naval battle off the island of Ushant near the Brittany coast, July 27, 1778, Vice-Adm. Hugh Palliser (1723–1796) had failed to provide Adm. Augustus Keppel (1725–1786) with the assistance that might have given the British the victory. Each admiral blamed the other for what had happened; the controversy reached Parliament and was at this time about to culminate in Keppel's court-martial in Jan. Following Keppel's honorable acquittal in Feb., Palliser's

house was sacked and his effigy burned. Ultimately, he, too, was cleared of all charges. What Digges means by "our fleets" is not entirely clear. It became customary for him to write as though he were a loyal Englishman when he feared his letter might be intercepted; although the present letter was entrusted to a reliable courier and is elsewhere that of an American supporter, his reference appears nonetheless to be to England's fleets.

To Benjamin Franklin

31st Jany. 1779

DEAR SIR

Altho my letter if opend in France may have a tendency to render You suspected of improper correspondence, I cannot as an Englishman refrain from congratulating You on the favourable turn of our affairs since my last letter of the 23d Inst: Stocks have got up two pr. Ct. within this few days, principally owing to accounts brought from America by the last arrivals from N. York; the most flattering of which is the apparent disunion in Congress & partys among the people against that vagrant Assembly. The Letters of Mr. Deane & Genl. Lee as publishd in the last weeks papers[1] opens new matters to our Rulers here, & their advocates now see the propriety of Ministry being uniformly averse to give up America; for in the next Campaign these cabals in America, among the leading people too, must accelerate the subjugation of the Revolted Colonies. What egregious fools must the Americans have been after suffering such hardships & severe struggles to thus divide among themselves, & give Us the only opening left for materially annoying them: we have various accounts & some circumstancial ones of their differences, as well as that the people employd by them in Europe, are pulling against one another, & holding secret correspondencies with people in this Country much against the general interests of their own.—Some heavy reflections are levelld at two Brothers[2] whom perhaps You may know or have seen in Paris, & which appear too bad for my beleif altho I am rather open to suspicion; but when a Set of Men (unitedly employd in so great a cause) pull one against the other, hold improper correspondencies, cabal about lucrative appointments where *self* is only in view, & are shy and uncommunicative with each other there must be some thing wrong at bottom & much mischief may be expected from it.

Our Ministers thank God are getting a little more popular, but it may be attributed to good luck.—The Islands are in a better situation in point of Safety than some late accounts seemd to indicate—The rise of the Stocks—some favorable overtures from Holland—The supine state of Spain—but above all the cabals in Congress & different face to affairs in America has given room for praise to our Rulers; Fleets too have saild with safety & carried supplies to our extended dominions, and others are preparing. Ld. Shuldham has returnd to Spithead with 15 Ships, having seen Commo. Rowley with 4 of the line & 40 or 50 Merchantmen 200 leags. Wt.wrd.[3]—A fleet saild from Jamaica about the 29 Novr. (forty sail under convoy of 3 armd Ships) & all was well there at that time—No word of D'Estaigne—The Embargo & martial Law taken off,[4] two of this Convoy are arrivd the others hourly expected, the fleet was seperated in a gale of wind early in the voyage in which one of the armd Ships founderd; and another is arrivd single—private letters to Men of property on the Island do not paint things in the most favorable light; Eleven transports with troops (part of Grants army from N. York) were met near the Island going in, & *report* says, the other division had arrivd to windward, & that Come. Hotham had joind Barrington.[5] A fleet saild from N. York for England about the last of Decr. They were also seperated off Newfoundland the 7th Inst. in a gale of wind. Two Men of War (their convoy) is arrivd & one Transport, the rest about 30 hourly expected; I am sorry to say there was great want in the garrison, & our American friends who had sided with Government were in a very deplorable situation—Clinton was said to be coming home, & Murray is to have that Command[6]—There had been an unsuccessful Expedition up the No. River meant cheifly to surprise & retake Burgoines captive army as they passd So.ward.[7] They had got accounts in N. York that Campbell had landed his 2000 Men near Savanah in Georgia & built much upon the success of it[8]—Byron with 9 ships of the line saild about the

15th Decr. after D'Estaign—it was suppos'd the Cornwal man of war was lost in the same gale with the Somerset, *two* are dismasted, & *two* got to England. A few days ago a *report* was current that Dominica was retaken[9] & I have yet my hopes about it—there has been no arrivals from the Leward or Windwd. Islands, consequently no accounts of their state, of Barrington, or *where* D'Estaign is for which we are all exceedingly anxious—The Jamaica Packet taken by an American privateer on the 7th Inst. has been retaken & carried into Liverpoole—We are in some pain about Senegal. It is said to be taken by the French, & there is no appearance of retaking it or sending out any succour.[10] A fleet of 7 Transports said from Corke for the W. Indies the 17th Int. *Report* says one or two of them have been taken & sent into France—A fleet is collecting there for America & the Wt. Indies which will sail in about 3 weeks, ninety to one hundred Sail in all, & as yet only one fifty a frigate & Sloop of war appointed for their Convoy—The Liverpoole Blues are under order for Jamaica & will probably go in this fleet[11]—doubtless some recruits may be sent to America but I think their numbers will be few if any, so sure are we sir that the Americans are divided in opinions & that the present force will conquer them.—Adml. Huges is still at Spithead (suppos'd he will sail in 10 days). He has 4 of the line and Nine Indiamen and carries out Lord McLoads Regiment of Highlanders about 900 Men and neerly 1100 Recruits for India.[12] Not a word as yet about any cruising fleet to be Sent out to the Bay,[13] but it is a likely measure to be adopted. I am sorry to tell You a *great many* Ships have been lately taken by a french Privateer out of Granville call'd the Amerique—the french cruisers have been equally lucky in the Mediteranean where I believe there is not at present one Man of War of ours, Many letters from merchants in Spain paint that trade (i. e. the Mediterranean) in a deplorable situation.

Keppels tryal still goes on tediously & may last some weeks more. He seems to Stand on good ground altho he did not beat the french handsomlly on the 27 July[14]—it is generally suppos'd on the close of that business, some moves will take place in the Admiralty if not in the Administration, and I have little doubt but my acquaintance Lord

Shelburne will get in as a Secretary tho not prime—He will come in hostile to America, particularly the independence of it, & I make no doubt will try to deceive old Franklin & Lee in obtaining his purposes by holding out false lights as to granting Independence *for a time*[15]—I think I could *help* him in this business, were I the *go between*, for I know a little of Mr. Lee & have seen Dr. F———n.[16] A Member of Parliament Mr. H[artle]y who has done some business for Dr. F. with Lord N., is likely to be soon prosecuted for a book he has lately publishd in favor of the Americans. It is calld Letters to His constituents,[17] pray have You seen it & what is Your opinion about it—I understand the writer means to move something in Parliament favourable to his friends the Americans—but wants to know the *grounds* to go upon— do You think he can justify the Rebels in detaining Burgoines Army? what *reasons* do the Americans give at Paris for their detention of that Army? Has Mr. Deane publishd any thing in America that exposes the offers made by this Administration to purchase french neutrality in this american contest?—probably by Your mixing with some of the Americans at Paris you may get out these facts & you have my direction by Mr. Hunt & in a letter about a bill I some time ago sent You.[18] I would have You attend a little to my hint about *Lord Shelburnes intentions*—I am sure some good may be gatherd from such attention.—I do not mean by my writing to you to draw you into a correspondence, but I should be glad to hear my letters got safe, & you may depend any thing in my power to do, shall be done with secrecy & honor. Altho there is a pretty general opinion got forth, that the Independence of America should not be given up, & that we should prosecute with vigor another Campaign to subjugate her, yet there are people even among us who wish a settlement of the dispute by negotiation, & I am of opinion there have been some persons lately at Paris tampering with the American Agents on this business—I am sure there are some, & of their own Countrymen too, who are now there for the purpose of informing our Rulers what is going on &ca., & I hope they will obtain the rewards such services merit; for sure no man can be overpaid for being an instrument in bringing about so desirable a purpose as peace. *With the assent of France can not there be a suspension of* the Treaty between her & America, so as to leave a door open for some negotiation from hence? I should like to know this, for some good might arise from a *friend of ours* knowing a certain ground to go upon.

I am Yrs. very truly
P. B[ertran]d

[Addressed, in a hand that may not be Digges's:] A Monsieur/ Monsieur F———n/ at Passey

UP: Franklin Papers, 3:2.

[1] Silas Deane's "Address . . . to the Free and Virtuous Citizens of America" had been published first in the *Pennsylvania Packet*, Dec. 1, 1778, and then widely reprinted (see Digges to Arthur Lee, Aug. 30, 1778). Its attack on the Lees exacerbated latent factionalism in the Congress. On Dec. 3 "General [Charles] Lee's Vindication to the Public" had appeared in the same paper, attempting to refute the charges of misconduct at the battle of Monmouth, where Lee had allegedly disobeyed orders, misbehaved before the enemy, and showed disrespect of the commander in chief. Lee's forces had indeed retreated; Washington and he had exchanged sharp words; he had then demanded of Washington an apology, which had been refused, and sought a court-martial, which convicted him in August, resulting in a year's suspension from the army. In his attempt to clear himself he became so abusive of Washington that Colonel John Laurens (1754–1782), an aide of Washington's and a son of Henry Laurens (1724–1792), president of the Continental Congress, subsequently challenged him to a duel that was fought on Dec. 23. Lee was wounded, but not fatally.
[2] Arthur and William Lee.
[3] Adm. Molyneux Shuldham (ca. 1717–1798) had sailed from Spithead on Christmas day to convoy more than three hundred merchantmen partway to North America and the East and West Indies and returned on Jan. 26. Sir Joshua Rowley (1730?–1790) was en route to the West Indies, where as rear admiral he served as one of Adm. Byron's division leaders during the year-long series of engagements with the French.
[4] On Mar. 18, 1778, the king of France had issued an edict to seize all British ships then in French ports; nine days later the British had laid an embargo on all French shipping in British ports.
[5] Commodore William Hotham (1736–1813), who had organized the successful landing of British troops on Long Island two years earlier, had arrived in Carlisle Bay, Barbados, on Dec. 10 with a convoy bringing Maj. Gen. James Grant (1720–1806) and the army Sir Henry Clinton had chosen Grant to lead. Grant, Hotham, and Rear Adm. Samuel Barrington (1729–1800) had then taken and secured St. Lucia.
[6] Lt. Gen. James Murray (ca. 1719–1794), governor of Quebec, 1760–1766, and of Minorca, 1774–1781.
[7] The terms under which Lt. Gen. John Burgoyne (1722–1792) had surrendered at Saratoga Oct. 15, 1777, included the provision that his army be shipped back to En-

gland and its members not bear arms against the colonies again. Burgoyne himself, criticized at home for the disaster, had given his parole and gone to England to defend himself in May 1778, leaving his men behind under detention.

[8] See Digges to Franklin, Dec. 19, 1778, n. 5.

[9] Dominica had been taken by the French Sept. 7, 1778, and remained in French hands until the peace.

[10] A British possession, Senegal did not fall to the French until late Apr. 1779. But British concern arose from the knowledge that the garrison had not been provisioned beyond Christmas and that the ship loaded with replenishing supplies remained in port awaiting a convoy.

[11] The Seventy-ninth Regiment of Foot, consisting of some 1,100 men raised by the city of Liverpool in Jan. 1778, embarked for Jamaica in Mar. 1779.

[12] Rear Adm. Edward Hughes (ca. 1720–1794), in command of the fleet for the East Indies, sailed on Mar. 7, 1779, with a regiment of Highlanders that John Mackenzie (1727–1789), generally, if not properly, known as Lord Macleod, had been permitted to raise following his return from a military career as a volunteer in the Swedish army during the Seven Years' War. Mackenzie had gone to Sweden after being pardoned for his service in the Jacobite army and forfeiting his estates. He was now embarking for Madras and a campaign against Hyder Ali. He became a member of Parliament in 1780 and regained his estates in 1784.

[13] Chesapeake Bay.

[14] A reference to the battle of Ushant and its consequences (see Digges to Franklin, Dec. 19, 1778, n. 8).

[15] William Petty, second earl of Shelburne (1737–1805), secretary of state, southern department, 1766–1777, had resigned from the cabinet when there had been talk of dismissing him. Opposed to the colonial policies of the North ministry, he nonetheless opposed independence for the Americans. He did not reenter the ministry until North's fall from power in 1782.

[16] Confirmation of Digges's having seen Franklin prior to this letter has not been found.

[17] See Digges to Hartley, Nov. 26, 1778, n. 4.

[18] See Digges to Franklin, Dec. 19, 1778. John Hunt had been the bearer.

To Benjamin Franklin

B[risto]l 7 Feby. 1779

SIR

Since my letter by Mr. Hunt I have taken the liberty to write You under cover to Monsr. G[ran]d[1] the 31st ult. The two Gentlemen who will wait on You with this are lately from P[⟨hiladelphi⟩]a, and thinking their accounts (tho not of very late dates) might tend to Your information, I have solicited their call on You on their way to L'Orient & Nantes, whither they are bound on some schemes of their own—They can also give You some accounts from Casco Bay as late as Jany. 1st, which they got from the Crew of a prize lately brought in from thence.²

The fleet from Corke which will consist of about 100 Sail for the Wt. Indies, & a small part for N. York, are under sailing orders, & will probably sail between the 15 and 20th, perhaps a few days later.—Their Convoy is one 60 Gun Ship, one frigate, and a 20 Gun Ship. A fleet is also assembling at Spit-head for a like destination & nearly the same number of Ships—day fixt for Sailing the 12th Int. but it is more than probable they will be a fortnight longer.³ Some Men of War of Force will see this fleet some leagues to the westward, but their Convoy will be but two frigates & one sloop. Six weeks after the Corke fleet sails there will be a Convoy appointed for another fleet, which will be the large *Spring* Fleet. The East India Fleet of four of the line & 10 Company Ships are still at Spithead but will probably sail in a week—there is about 2,500 men going in them to India, cheifly McLoads highlanders, other Scotch Recruits, and kid-napt Company troops.⁴ Some late accounts from Canada via Halifax has producd an order for sending out one Regiment to Quebec to hold in security that Capitol from the native Canadians, who have been lately discoverd to avow Sentiments unfriendly to Government. Some few men are going to Halifax, & by all accounts I can gather they talk of 3,000 For New York—These with nearly a like number intended to be sent in the Portsm. Fleet to the West Indies of which the Liverpoole Blues, about 1100 Men, are part,⁵ is the whole of the Army that is to subjugate America. It is said in the Admiralty that Transports are engaged to carry over fifteen thousand Men to America, but I see no likelyhood of it, nor where they will be able to get the Ships or Men. In order to keep up the farce & appearances, every embarkation is markd down *for America*; Yet the ministry & their friends hold a language, that the American War is not [to] be prosecuted with vigour, nor is the Independence to be given up or peace *as yet* sought for: They seem to be persuing a sort of middle policy or half sighted measures that are incomprehensible to Me. I beleive they build a little upon the reports of disunion in America & in Congress; these reports together with Deanes, & Genl. Lees letters, have had some effect upon the Stocks,[6] & I think has given a little credit to Lord Norths intended loan. It is a general topic *now* that Mr. Lee, thro Lord Shelburne, is soon to offer terms from America short of Independence. You may easily guess what degree of Credit I give to such reports; but it hurts Me that one of Your body should lay Himself thus open to be talkd of at home and to be much hurt in the Eye of his Employers. I write to him frequently without any one motive or purpose but the giving information, & which I am sure has been frequently useful if properly communicated: I write by this conveyance to tell him what I hear & know to be the conversation about him near his home, & let him act as his better judgement sees fit. I have not the least reason to suppose any letters pass between him & Lord Shelburne, further than that formerly there was a strict intimacy between them, & I cannot suppose that if such communication is now open, but that Mr. L. does it to serve the cause he is engagd in. I have dwelt thus long upon a topic perhaps improper to You, but my fears are, that any little differences in Europe may encrease to party cabals & disunion at home, which I am certain will hurt America & its cause more than its most implacable Enemies can do mischief to it from hence. I make it my business to be as much among the Lords & minority members as I can, for it has been in my power at times to give them a little information; I am sorry they do not all pull together so well as I wish; but tho they do not agree in the means, I hope they will succeed in the end. I beleive many of them are at a loss for what ground to go upon—*one* I am sure, (whom I lately mentiond to You & with whom You have lately communicated)[7] would be glad of a hint, and I think it might come servicably; He means to do something by way of motion, & may be helpt by the pro or con to a simple question Whether or not *with the assent of France* a Suspension for a time of the treaty with America, could not be brought about, so as to give an opening for this Ministry to negotiate with Your Community.

A Change in the ministry is more than usually talked of. It is thought Lord Sandwich & Suffolk are likely to go out, the place of [the] former to be given to Lord Howe, & that of the latter to Lord

Shelburne;[8] If this Gentleman gets in He will proceed hostily against America. I have talkd much to him of late & I cannot fathom His politics save that his predominant bent is to the loaves & fishes; It is not unlikely his first effort may be to trick or deceive America, or Her Agents, by holding out some false lights. He has ever been uniform in his opinion to Me that the acknowlegement of Independence cannot nor must not be given, and that He sees a way short of Independence & honourable to both Countries that *may* be brought about—I wish my Country was as free from disunity or civil dissention, as that his Lordship is mistaken. Governor Johnstone, who has been deceivd himself by Galloway, Delancy, &ca.,[9] is going on deceiving others, and has done much mischeif; he seems to be treading the same path which Bernard & Hutchinson formerly did,[10] & has lately declard to some of my acquaintance in Parliament that he has used, & will still use, every effort to perswade Ministry to send out more Men and prosecute the war with vigour.

Since I began this letter I have advices from Falmo. that a packet is arrivd there in 21 days from N. York, which will bring her sailing to about the 15th Jany. There is no material accounts by her save that 7 or 8 Victuallers had arrivd safe from Cork with a seasonable & much wanted supply—You may easily guess what degree of Credit is due to *reports of N. York*, these were that Campbell met with very great success in Georgia & that the Storey of a revolt there was confirmd—that some persons had erected the Kings Standard in So. Carolina; and that Young Laurens had dangerously wounded Genl. Lee in a duel at Phila.[11]—many Stories of dissentions in Congress &ca. &ca.

I am sorry to hear from the bearer of this letter the very exhorbitant prices given for dry Goods throughout America, the depreciation of the paper money &ca.; these evils originate from the same cause *a want of trade*, & this might in a great measure be remidied, if the restrictions of not accepting imports from Gt. Britain were taken off. I wish this could be done in America, & that our friends would think of it.—This restriction has now no longer an effect on the Manufacturers here, & I am convincd many Cargoes to considerable amount would be speedily sent out were they not seizable on their arrival; There are adventure[r]s enough here who would attempt to supply America by collusive clearances, & there are also many who would pack up their *all* & try to set themselves down in a happier Country. I am glad to find from Mr. C——ys[12] that many useful articles which I have forwarded from hence to America thro Spain have got out safely. I am now waiting here the arrival of a Spanh. vessel from Bilboa, & as I shall likely be here for a few weeks longer, a letter will safely find me directed A Mr. Monr. Pierre J. DuVal Bristol. I am

very truly Yr. Obt. He. Servant
T. D.

[Addressed:] Dr. B. F——

UP: Franklin Papers, 3:5.

[1] Ferdinand Grand (1729–1794), principal member of the banking firm in Paris and Amsterdam that handled the accounts of the American commissioners. He had a country seat near the home of the American delegation in Passy.

[2] A report from Portsmouth, Feb. 4, 1779, quoted in the *London Chronicle* for Feb. 4–6, 1779 (45:126), stated: "The 'Effingham,' from Casco Bay to Cadiz . . . is taken and carried into Kingroad by the 'George' privateer of Bristol."

[3] The Cork fleet (about 110 sail) set out on Mar. 1, 1779; the one from Spithead, estimated to be more than 200 sail of West Indiamen, sailed on Mar. 26.

[4] This reinforcement of the India squadron, commanded by Rear Adm. Hughes, was delayed for want of a wind until Mar. 7 (see Digges to Franklin, Jan. 31, 1779, n. 12).

[5] See ibid., n. 11.

[6] See ibid., n. 1.

[7] David Hartley.

[8] John Montagu, fourth earl of Sandwich (1718–1792), who had served as first lord of the admiralty during 1748–1751 and 1763 and as secretary of state, northern department, during 1763–1765, had been reappointed first lord of the admiralty in 1771 and remained in that post until the departure of Lord North in 1782. Henry Howard, twelfth earl of Suffolk (1739–1779), had become secretary of state in 1771 and remained in his post until his death in Mar. 1779. Lord Howe, having resigned his command of the naval forces in American waters to join his brother, Sir William, in securing a parliamentary inquiry into the conduct of the American war, for whose failures they were being blamed, was offered a high post by Lord North in an attempt to silence his criticism. Lord Shelburne, opposed to the ministry's war policy, was also opposed to Sandwich's continuation as first lord of the admiralty.

[9] Johnstone continued to oppose American independence (see Digges to Franklin, Dec. 19, 1778, n. 3). Joseph Galloway (ca. 1731–1803), once a Speaker of the Pennsyl-

vania House of Assembly but never a proponent of independence, was now in England, constituting himself a spokesman for the middle colonies and an advocate of a strategy, accepted by the ministry, of concentrating on one area of the colonies at a time to enable the loyalists to subdue what he represented as a rebel minority in each area. James De Lancey (1732–1800), a politically active New Yorker who preceding 1775 had followed a course between opposition to the ministry's policies and something short of commitment to revolutionary activity, had after the outbreak of hostilities sold his property and returned with his family to England.

[10] Francis Bernard (1712–1779) and Thomas Hutchinson (1711–1780), both former royal governors of Massachusetts, had believed that domestic peace in that colony (to which Hutchinson in particular was deeply attached) would attend stricter control over local government, and, in consequence, had advocated less rather than more independence.

[11] See Digges to Franklin, Jan. 31, 1779, n. 1.

[12] C——gs, perhaps. Unidentified.

To Benjamin Franklin

Londo. Apr. 9. 1779

DEAR SIR

Our friend Mr. B[ridge]n[1] having given me an oppertunity to convey a letter by a safer conveyance than that of the common post, I make free to inclose it to You in order to be forwarded to Mr. W[harto]n[2] should he be out of P[ari]s.

I have but a few minutes before Mr. B—— closes his packet to appologise for the freedom I take & to offer my services here. I am not many hours in London, & shall remain here 'till calld to a western port on the arrival of two Spanish vessels expected there which I guess will be in six or seven weeks. My purpose with these vessels is the same as what has employd me for now nearly two years—the getting out useful articles—The very great wants of which would be much alleviated was an import directly from this Country allowd by mine, for there are hundreds who would adventure largely, & this too without a prospect of *immideate* payment. Not a word of American news, & by what I can gather, it is likely the embarkation of troops & Recruits destind for N. York (in all about 4,500) have been lately countermanded.

The next Wt. Inda. Fleet will sail about the 10 May. 80 to 100 Ships. I cordially wish You every prosperity & am Yours.
                    T. D——

A Monsieur Monsieur Jacques Vincent Drouillard
Bureau des Postes Londres

[Addressed:] A Monsieur/Monsieur B. Franklin

HSP: Franklin Papers, 5:57.

[1] Probably Edward Bridgen (d. 1787), an American-born London merchant, son-in-law of the writer Samuel Richardson (1689–1761), and a sympathetic correspondent of Franklin's and Arthur Lee's.
[2] Both Samuel Wharton and Joseph Wharton, Jr., were in France, but this is probably a reference to Samuel, who in his promotion of the Vandalia claim was the more active correspondent.

To Arthur Lee

London April 18. 1779

DEAR SIR

I have a very great dislike to write upon matters wherein private affairs are to be discussd or mentiond, but in compliance to your solicitation, to the justice that is due to Mr. John Lloyd (whose character I understand is likely to suffer in America by reports that appear to me to be malicious & ill-founded)[1] & from my being entirely free from any restraint as to injunctions of secrecy &ca., I take the opportunity by Mr. P[enn][2] to inform you that I have been repeatedly told by Mr. Joseph Wharton (about the periods of Novr. & Decr. 1777. & Jany. Feby. & March 1778) that he (Mr. J. W.) in conjunction with others & particularly with Mr. R. Champion of Bristol,[3] had engaged deeply in Stock jobbing & Insurances, on Events & consequences of the American war—such as the surrender of Genl. Burgoyne's army at Saratoga, The period of signing the treaty between France & America at

Paris, & on a declaration of war between France & England. Mr. Wharton often solicited me to become an adventurer with him, & urged as a good reason for my doing so that he had the best intelligence from France, & a safe & regular communication with Dr. Bancroft who was at that period in Paris & in confidence with Mr. Silas Deane. Mr. Wharton, the more strongly to induce me to enter into the plan of making money in the funds & by insurances, read to me at times letters which he said were from Dr. Bancroft at Paris, & altho I cannot swear to the hand (having never seen Dr. Bancrofts writing) I have strong reasons to beleive they were from him. One of these letters was dated from Paris about the begining of December 1777 & written in an ambiguous stile, which Mr. Wharton explaind to me as accounts having come to Paris, with the account of Burgoyne's surrender (a circumstance then not certainly known in England) & to take measures as to the Stocks accordingly. Mr. Wharton afterwards & as I beleive in the same month of Decr. 1777 told me Dr. Bancroft was in London in cog for the same purpose of Stock-jobbing, but had not arrived in time to make money by the Secret. He also shewd me a letter I beleive in Jany. 1778 which he said came from the same quarter, & which intimated in a like ambiguous manner, that a certain great event[4] (by which Mr. Wharton told me he meant the signing of the treaty between France & America) was very nearly at hand. I had often in these conferences with Mr. Wharton complaind heavily that such gambling schemes woud hurt the interests of our Country, as they were seemingly carried on by men, who if not publicly employd by Congress, had the confidence of those who were the public servants of America, & I beleive Sir I more than once wrote to you my fears on this head. I talked much to Mr. Thornton[5] about it, when he first came over with proposals for exchange of prisoners, & was the first person who told him Lord North knew of Dr. Bancroft's being in London in cog upon a Stock jobbing errand & in which his Lordship supposed he was connected with Mr. Silas Deane—these were nearly Lord North's words to Mr. Hartley who told them to me on the day he had them from Lord North. Mr. Wharton after this became rather shy of me, but he from time to time very imprudently continued to communicate the contents of Dr. Bancrofts letters to others, in order as I suppose to get them to join him in insurances for or against particular events of the war. Mr. Archer a Banker of London has very lately told me Mr. Wharton communicated such intelligences to him as advices from Dr. Bancroft, & that in consequence of such letters, Mr. Archer's partner Mr. Byde did engage in Sums of money jointly with Mr. Wharton. Mr. Champion of Bristol has also assurd me, that he often lent his name in Bills of Exchange & did join in Insurances with Mr. Wharton to a considerable amount in which he understood Dr. Bancroft was to have a part of Mr. Whartons share. Mr. Champion after hearing Mr. Wharton had in France denyd that Dr. Bancroft gave him such intelligences, & said that they came from Mr. Lloyd then at Nantes to Mr. Champion at Bristol & thro him to Mr. W., came to me in London last month, & shewd me a great number of Letters from Mr. Joseph Wharton, on the plan of their transactions in the Stocks & in Insurances.

By some of these letters there is the fullest proof under Mr. Joseph Whartons hand writing (which I can prove having had many letters from him) that Dr. Bancroft did give him the intelligences; & Mr. Champion told me, he was willing to make oath, that Mr. Wharton repeatedly told him, it was from Dr. Bancrofts advices that he was led into the schemes of insurances & dealing in Stocks; Mr. Champion also declared to me, that he never received any political advices from Mr. Lloyd, more than what was common in the course of his correspondence from Nantes. I think Sir I need not dwell longer on this subject; If more proofs are wanting I daresay Mr. Champion can give them in the fullest manner; as can three or four other Gentlemen of my acquaintance.

       I am Sir
       Your very Obedt. Servant
       (Signd.) Tho. Digges

 True Copy from the original/in the hand writing of Mr. Digges
       Ludwell Lee
Hble. Arthur Lee Esqr.

NA: Papers of the Continental Congress, 1774–1789 (Microfilm M247, Roll 110, Item 83), 2:545–51. Two other copies exist. One is a fair copy of the above in the Papers; the other is a copy, made later, among the Lee Papers of the Virginia Historical Society (Mssl L51all), which differs in spelling, capitalization, paragraphing, and other similar orthographic details. It is possible that the above text and the VHS text were both made from the original—the VHS does not reproduce the Ludwell Lee attestation—but the Ludwell Lee copy here appears to be the earliest: the handwriting closely resembles Ludwell Lee's and thus may be his rather than a contemporary copy of his for the Congress.

[1] Lloyd (1735–1807), a British-born South Carolina planter who had become an ardent supporter of the Revolution and served on the Committee of Secret Correspondence, had settled in Nantes in 1777 as a merchant to work for the American cause. A friend of Henry Laurens and the Lees, he was bound to be implicated in the controversy involving the Lees and Silas Deane (see Digges to Arthur Lee, Aug. 30, 1778).

[2] Richard Penn (1736–1811), grandson of Pennsylvania's founder. Penn had borne a petition to the king and Parliament from citizens of Pennsylvania in 1775 expressing a wish to avoid forceful resistance to the British government and recommending concessions that would promote conciliation. Now a respected resident in England and an acquaintance of Digges's, he was helpful in providing Digges, Franklin, and John Adams with information.

[3] Richard Champion (1743–1791) had married John Lloyd's sister in 1764 and was a friend of Edmund Burke (1729–1797).

[4] The phrase "a certain great event" is enclosed in quotation marks in the VHS copy.

[5] John Thornton (see Digges to Thornton, Dec. 1, 1777).

Oath of Allegiance

Passy, May 3, 1779

I Thomas Diggs, of Wharburton in the State of Maryland, do acknowledge the thirteen United States of America, namely Newhampshire, Massachusetts Bay, Rhode-island, Connecticut, New York, New Jersey, Pennsylvania, Delaware, Maryland Virginia North Carolina, South Carolina and Georgia, to be free, independent & sovereign States, and declare that the People thereof owe no Allegiance or Obedience to George the third King of Great Britain; and I renounce refuse and abjure any Allegiance or Obedience to him. And I do swear that I will to the utmost of my Power support maintain and defend the said United States against the said George the third, his Heirs and Successors & his and their Abettors, Assistants and Adherents.

So help me God
Thomas Digges

Sworn before me at Passy,
near Paris, this 3d Day of May 1779
B. Franklin

Minister Plenipotentiary at the
Court of France—

APS: Franklin Papers, 57:27. The signature is Digges's; the rest is in a different hand.

To Benjamin Franklin

Hotel de Yorke [Paris] 4th May/79

SIR

I am very sorry to be troublesome to You, but I find great difficulty in procuring my pass, & am not likely to get one without You will indulge me so far as to write a line to the Lieutenant de Police to grant me one. I have taken Dr. Bencrofts advice about it and He advises me to send the inclosd out to You either for alteration or to get a note to the Lieutenant de Police. I am fearful If I do not get it some time in the forenoon tomorrow I shall be prevented setting out in time to meet the next sailing Packet at Calais.

I shall wait on You early in the morning, as You last appointed, provided I receive from You in answer to this no intimation that You will not be ready by that time to dispatch me. You know my object, and may assure yourself I shall have the highest satisfaction in attending patiently to those or any other of Your Commands.

I am with the Highest esteem

Your very obligd & Obt. Serv.
Tho. Digges

The Honbe. Dr. B. Franklin
   Passy

HSP: Franklin Papers, 5:60.

To Benjamin Franklin

London 12. May 1779

Dear Sir

My journey hither[1] was a favourable one & I am in hopes will turn out to good account; I have not yet however been able to deliver *all* Your letters—those for the environs of London are yet in my possession, as I preferrd keeping them a day or two to *make a personal* delivery of them, to the risqueing them by penny post. I this day deliverd Miss Shipleys—His Lordship was not at home to join in the general satisfaction & joy expressd by the whole Female part of the Family on hearing from Yourself that you were well & happy[2]—I got a share of consequence by being Your messenger, and was rogue enough to wish (when I saw a hasty kiss given to B F at the foot of Your Letter) to have the biatitude transferrd to me—It is a shame for you to be so great a monopoliser of Hearts.

I understood from the Family that a french Gentleman (I believe the Ecuyer to the Count D'Artois[3]) sets out in the morning for Paris, & I am to send this to the Bishops for forwardance by Him.

Our matter goes on seemingly very well; on a meeting between Mr. H. and a certain great man, the later seemd to catch with avidity at Mr. H.'s application for an audience, & this night at nine oClock is the hour appointed for a parley:[4] I fear it will not be in my power to forward you the result of that parley by this conveyance, as I am under injunctions from Your Ruby-lipd Correspondant to send my letter this evening; I will however keep it to the last, and at any rate risque sending another letter to the Bishops in the morning. I write You from our friend Mr. H.'s where I am waiting his return from Westminster Hall & for his Roast beef.

Every thing seems working well for our Country & its cause; I hope no civil discord or nasty cabals will cast a cloud over the promisd fair & serene Western Sky. Arbuthnots Squadron is not yet saild from Torbay but will go with the first fair wind;[5] If a few Ships of War and nearly four thousand Recruits (which is the force going with him) can do America any further injury, I am confidant She has my friend Govr. Johnstone solely to thank for it; for He stands alone as to opinion that every exertion against America is now necessary for the Safety of this Country.

Ministry seem to speak out dispondingly of their affairs in America & particularly for the Southern army. The exposition of the correspondince between them & their Commanders in America has servd to open the Eyes of the people a little, and the Examination into the affairs of the Howes by the evidence which have already been given at the bar of the House of Commons, is likely to damn them compleatly; It now appears, that instead of vagabonds & poltroons the Americans are a vigilent, well disciplind, and a respectable Enemy. In the House of Lords yesterday, Ld. Rockingham gave a very melancholly picture of the state of things in Ireland.[6] It would seem to me that the period is not very distant when that oppressd people will seek relief to their distress from Congress's & assosiations of their own. In the debate on this matter the disunion among both parties, Whigs, & Tories, was a good picture of the distraction of the times. Lord Rockingham makes a motion for the state of Ireland to be laid before the House—Lord Weymouth opposes it with the previous question—The Duke of Chandos & Lord Townsend support Lord Rockingham—The Duke of Grafton[7] & Lord Shelburne oppose Him; & it all ends with giving the Marquis his motion He cutting off part of His preamble.

The leaders of the Bedford party have veerd about very much of late, & are from all appearances going over to opposition.[8] The quarrels among the Ministry has been the probable cause of this. Lord N. and Lord G. G. are at cat & dog if not at open rupture.[9] Lord N.'s language is, that Lord G. G. is such a blundering ass & so great a fool, that it is impossible to act with Him; The other says that North is so treacherous as *never* to support his friends when in need and always leaves them in the Dark.—When rogues quarrel, it is to be hoped honest men will get at their right.—

There has been some accounts from N. York to Ministry by way of Corke that have not been good enough to give to the publick in a Gazette, consequently they were bad. The talk is that the accounts from Byron in the West Indies are but indifferent—These, together with the reports which reignd very currently about ten days ago that overtures for Peace were negotiating, having ceasd, has causd the Stocks to fall two & a half pr. Ct. lately & the City gentry are rather in the dumps. Hopeing to have an oppertunity given me to write in the morning by the same conveyance with this I shall not add further at present than that I am with very great esteem Dr. Sir

      Your very obligd and Obedient Servant
      Tho. Digges[10]

HSP: Franklin Papers, 5:61.

[1] Digges had just returned to London from his visit to Franklin in Passy.

[2] Jonathan Shipley (1714–1788), bishop of St. Asaph, had become acquainted with Franklin some ten or eleven years earlier and, perhaps as a consequence of their increasing friendship, was soon an outspoken opponent of the North ministry's American policies, supporting the rights of both the colonists and the British dissenters. Of his five daughters, Georgiana (1756–1806) was the most sparkling and talented. She had studied classics with her father, was fluent in modern languages, studied painting at Sir Joshua Reynolds's (1723–1792) studio, and appears to have been a fine conversationalist. For eight years, possibly longer, Franklin had been sending her books out of his regard for what he called her philosophic genius. Mrs. Shipley was Anna Maria Mordaunt (d. 1803), niece of Charles Mordaunt, third earl of Peterborough (1698–1778), a leader among those then known as Tories.

[3] Charles Philippe, comte d'Artois (1757–1836), later Charles X, king of France (1824–1830).

[4] David Hartley and Lord North had been conferring about problems that ranged from facilitating the exchange of prisoners to offering concessions to Americans that would end the war. At this time North was willing to consider eventually granting independence, but, not prepared to take an official stand, he preferred to carry on negotiations through Hartley as a private person.

⁵Admiral Marriot Arbuthnot (ca. 1711–1794), carrying 3,400 troops to reinforce Clinton's forces in New York, had been delayed in his departure, first by storms, then by a need to assist the Channel Fleet against the French near Jersey, and finally by a decision to wait until the Channel Fleet could sail with his squadron in convoy from the bay on the east coast of Devon to safe clearance in the West. He did not manage to leave Torbay until May 24.

⁶Charles Watson-Wentworth, second marquis of Rockingham (1730–1782), a former first lord of the treasury (1765–1766), leader of the "New Whigs," the strongest opposition party (1770–1782), was with the support of Lord Shelburne to form the ministry after North's fall in 1782. The Irish, finding British regulation of their trade repressive, openly sympathetic with the American cause, and aware of the actions of the colonists, had at a large meeting in Dublin decided on the nonimportation of British goods that could be manufactured at home.

⁷Thomas Thynne, third Viscount Weymouth (1734–1796), was secretary of state of both southern and northern departments. James Brydges, third duke of Chandos (1731–1789), privy councillor since 1775, generally voted with the North ministry but was soon to move into opposition. Thomas Townshend (1733–1800), sharply critical of the North ministry, would become secretary of war under Rockingham in 1782. Augustus Henry Fitzroy, third duke of Grafton (1735–1811), had resigned his post in the North ministry in 1775, after serving more than four years, because of disagreement with its rigid American policies. When Rockingham and Shelburne assumed power in 1782, he became lord privy seal.

⁸The Bedford party, primarily a political faction named after its first leader, John Russell, fourth duke of Bedford (1710–1771), and now nominally headed by Bedford's brother-in-law, Granville Leveson-Gower, the second Earl Gower (1721–1803), had helped form the ministry over which North presided. But when North resisted their attempts to dominate his government, some of the group resigned their posts in order to undermine North and precipitate his fall.

⁹Lord George Germain, né Sackville, secretary of state for the colonies since 1775 and the most inflexible of advocates of "firmness" toward the Americans, was becoming a political burden for North. Germain had lost the confidence of the leading generals, served increasingly as the focus of the Whig opposition, and since Burgoyne's surrender at Saratoga, been associated with the various blunders attending the prosecution of the war.

¹⁰This letter was delayed in reaching Franklin; for on May 30, in a letter to Digges, he stated that it had not yet come to hand (LC: Franklin Papers, Series 1, 2:175–76).

To Benjamin Franklin

Londo. 14. May [1779]

DEAR SIR

The reason why you could not find out W. Peters by your letters was that they were directed to Nottingham instead of Liverpoole.¹—I have done the needful towards Your request & make no doubt of soon hearing from him for *He is in want.*

I gave you a few lines by private conveyance the 12th Int. since which nothing conclusive has been done on the matter I then wrote upon.[2] The begining of the Business & the stage it is now in promises well, but I am too apt perhaps to doubt of real sincerity. It has been opend by one to three or four others & will from them go to another one to night or tomorrow. In such situation You may easily guess how little I have to say & where the doubt hangs. I am in tolerable spirits about it & hope soon to say more to you.

I Am very truly Your Respectful & Ob. Sert.
Arthur Hamilton

HSP: Franklin Papers, 5:62.

[1] Richard Peters (1744–1828), Philadelphian, secretary of the Continental Board of War, had been trying for more than a year to locate his father, William Peters, in England through Franklin (and now in turn Digges). William Peters had originally emigrated from England and bought some land in 1742 on the west bank of the Schuylkill that he had named Belmont and established as the family seat, with a mansion and an annex for his library. He was now back in England and thought to be living in Nottingham.

[2] Franklin had not received the letter of May 12 by as late as May 30; thus this reference might have seemed cryptic.

To Benjamin Franklin

—18 May —79

DEAR SIR

Mine of the 12th & 14th Inst. have I suppose got safe to hand[1]— The last would give you some idea how matters stood at the parting of our friend with another personage in regard to a certain matter: The opening was auspicious & the parting favourable to our wish—Since that period till yesterday the affair remaind in embrio; *others* I apprehend were consulted upon the occasion of the first parley, and those others recommended it should be laid before a principal or cheif Phisician, which I suppose was done on Sunday last.² As I apprehended the business alluded to ought to be pushd forward or Settled with as much expedition as possible for fear of any other interposition, I urgd my friend to look to another consultation—He did so very lately, & the answer was "I will speak to You soon. I am not yet ready for You". In this situation it now rests—appearances tell me the Phisick is working powerfully—You know what a heavy dose it is.

Gen. Howes evidence is yet before the House, & from the vast strength of proofs as to improbability of success in America it would appear that Ministry will give up the idea of subjugation—Howe has 10 or 12 more Officers to call in proof thereof, and their weight of evidence is to be ballancd by about as many Mac's from the Highlands and twenty or thirty American Torey refugees now in England with Joe Galloway at their head.³ The fleet for N. York & Georgia is still at Torbay,⁴ & likely to be there while these western storms prevail—Sr. J. Wright has returnd to London a little down in the mouth.⁵

I am very truly & wth. much Esteem

Yrs. V. J. D[rouillar]d

[Addressed:] A Monsieur/Monsieur B. F./Passy

UP: Franklin Papers, 3 : 16.

¹But see Digges to Franklin, May 12, 1779, n. 10, and May 14, n. 2.
²The parley referred to was between Hartley and North; the "cheif Phisician" may therefore have been George III. In direct communication with Hartley himself, Franklin must have understood the specific allusion.
³Sir William Howe, recalled from his command in America, had reached London in July 1778 and demanded that he be given a hearing to enable him to justify his conduct of the war. After he was joined by his brother Richard in Oct. and assisted by attacks on Germain by Burgoyne that had provoked Germain to make accusations in reply, Parliament acceded to an inquiry, now under way (see Digges to Franklin, Feb. 7, 1779, n. 8).
⁴A reference to Arbuthnot's squadron (see Digges to Franklin, May 12, 1779, n. 5).
⁵As royal governor of Georgia in 1761–1766 and 1773–1776, Sir James Wright (1716–1785), an advocate of restrictive measures, had proved highly unpopular. Taken prisoner in Jan. 1776. he had managed to make his way to England only by breaking parole. Upon the British recapture of the colony in Dec. 1778, he was directed to re-

turn to reorganize its government, a task for which he manifestly had little appetite. He would sail in time to reach Savannah on June 14, 1779.

To Benjamin Franklin

21 May 79

DEAR SIR

I was in hopes to have given you some tidings as to the bargain I was about to make for the House but as yet I am little advancd. My Brother[1] this day slightly urgd the necessity of another meeting &ca. on the business, but it was *"a serious matter deserving contemplation & should be attended to"*—

I have done the needful as to Mr. W[illiam] P[eter]s but have not yet got his answer as to what He wants &ca.; I am told he is very poor. Should he want a small supply I have wrote him I will assist him as to negotiating the Bill. It is not unlikely He may draw upon me for a small sum on the account & I suppose it will not be disagreeable to you for me to repay myself by drawing on you. If you will allow me to include in such bill the sum I advancd J. Brehon & four others[2] (i.e. £20—for which You have seen a bill & promisd a friend of Yours You would pay) it will be a help to me & lighten in some measure a heavy debt I have for similar services; for I can assure You I am not at present cursd with a great deal of ready Cash.—

I was favord this Evening with a sight of the letter which coverd the underwritten note & am desired to give ⟨it⟩ to you with Compliments &ca. &ca.

The Commission for Sick & hurt Seamen &ca. present their Compliments to Mr. ———, and return him thanks for the communication in his note to Mr. Bell relative to the Milford transport which saild with the American Prisoners;[3] And as by the orders the Commissioners at present are under, further numbers will be sent as long as there are any English Prisoners taken by Americans to be returnd in Exchange for them, they would be obligd to Mr. ——— for any information he may be able to give them, or for procuring such as may be relied upon, as to the number of such Prisoners on the other side the water, as well as for giving such intimations there, as may be the means of having the number of Prisoners to be returnd for the next hundred that will go from hence, at hand to be embarkd without detaining the vessel unnecessarily—By Mr. ——— not mentioning any thing relating to Morlaix, the board concludes he has not receivd any answer upon that point, & should be glad, if He thinks proper, that it might be mentiond again, as it would be a much more convenient port.[4]

[Added later:]
The Cartel Vessel is not yet returnd & every party concernd wonders very much at her delay as the winds have been fair.

———

A Packet from Jamaica is arrivd & brings no news that is yet let out consequently none good. She saild the 4 Apr. & might have brought accounts from St. Kitts to the 25 March—

The following illustrious names are summond to give evidence to the House of Commons as to the expedience of the prosecution of the American War & to over throw the testimonies of Lord Cornwallis Genl. Grey, Coll. Montresor, Capt. Hammond &ca. &ca. &ca.—: Jno. Maxwell Esr. Jos. Galloway Esq.—Andw. Allen Esq.—Jno. Patterson Theos. [Theoe.] Morris—Enock Storey—& Jebas Fisher—I think they should have added James Delancy.[5]

[Addressed:] A Monsieur Monsr. Franklin

HSP: Franklin Papers, 5:63.

[1] David Hartley.
[2] On behalf of the American commission, Franklin was providing funds for the relief of American prisoners. Dr. James Brehon and the others had been in Forton (see Digges to Thornton, Dec. 1, 1777).
[3] The Commission (later the Board) for Sick and Hurt Seamen was responsible for superintending not only the care of sick and wounded British seamen, but also the treatment of naval prisoners of war. Although they derived their authority from the commissioners of the admiralty, they operated with considerable autonomy, favored prisoner exchanges (to lighten the costs of imprisonment), and in Mar., as a result of David Hartley's efforts, had agreed to send to Nantes aboard the *Milford* some hundred

men from Mill Prison, to be followed by approximately the same number from Forton in July. John Bell was first commissioner.

⁴The British were pressing for designating Morlaix instead of Nantes as the port of exchange, but the French were opposed to the belligerents' using a port only thirty-four miles from their important station at Brest. The issue would be finally resolved in Oct. when Franklin got from the French a safe-conduct passport for the British cartel at Morlaix.

⁵Howe had been blamed for delaying his attack on Philadelphia so long in 1777 that the capture of the city came too late to release help for Burgoyne. Cornwallis and Grey both testified that the delay had been necessary to permit the ground to be greened with forage for the army's animals; moreover, they explained, the traditional tactics of the British, based on tight organization and inflexible formations, had made their forces so dependent on slow-moving baggage trains that they could not effectively pursue a nimble enemy over rough terrain. Col. John Montresor (1736–1788?), appointed chief engineer of the British army in America in Dec. 1775 and participant in the battles of Bunker Hill, Long Island, and Philadelphia, along with Sir Andrew Hamond (1738–1828), who had served under Lord Howe in the naval action near the mouth of the Delaware during the last half of 1777, provided further vindication of the Howes' command. Those cited here as expected to offer contrary testimony had had little or no military experience and were, like Galloway and DeLancey, loyalists who had become increasingly fervent after the Declaration of Independence and considered renegades by the Americans. Andrew Allen (1740–1825), for example, once a leading Whig and member of the Continental Congress from Pennsylvania, had in 1776 hastened to put himself under Howe's protection at Trenton and later returned with him to Philadelphia before making his way to England; Enoch Story, Galloway's deputy inspector of prohibited goods in Philadelphia, Sept. 1777–June 1778, had been attainted of treason by the government of Pennsylvania when his allegiance to the crown had become firm; and Jabez Maud Fisher (d. 1779), another Philadelphia Tory, had fled to England to join Galloway, John Patterson of New York, and nearly a hundred other refugees from the colonies in forming the Loyalist Association, which undertook to convince Germain and the king that it was not the colonists' disloyalty that was to blame for British setbacks, but, rather, the failure of the British generals to provide the loyal inhabitants with protection sufficient to enable them to display their commitment. Although Galloway, as the most outspoken of the exiles and a vigorous contributor to the pamphlet war that kept the controversy alive, was examined by the House, most of the others alluded to by Digges were not called before the inquiry.

To Benjamin Franklin

25th. May [⟨1779⟩]

Dear Sir

On the business of the purchase which I have wrote you about by every post *save the last* for four or five back, I have nothing now to say, as nothing new has arose: There has been another item from the person who has it in contemplation, 'that the affair was properly attended to, that it requird deliberation, and the answer should be given as soon as possible'—nothing therefore can be further urgd by my friend until an opening is given by the person with whom he has to deal. I have every reason to beleive it was taken so seriously, that a messenger was dispatchd to a quarter where You are very conversant, in order to probe to the bottom what might appear dark, or palliate offensive parts of the proposition. This is not unlikely from the length of time taken to give an answer, and a seeming disinclination not to give one, or to throw any cloud over the matter, for a few days to come, when in all probability the answer may be returnd. If my surmises have any foundation, I make no doubt but You have discoverd or had a hint of what has been attempted.

We have no news here that is good save the arrival of the Wt. India fleet with the loss only of *one* ship which founderd[1]—this has given us vast spirits & contradicts the reports of the Brest fleet being out to intercept them. The report so current some days ago that D'Estaign had been beaten by Byron & lost 14 Ships is now totally discredited;[2] but a similar ridiculous storey even told as coming from N. York will be again beleivd & swallowd. It is yet asserted as a fact that LaMotte Picquets Squadron is dispersd & many of the American Ships lost.[3]

There was nothing material at New York the 10th Feby. nor no appearances of any active exertion on either side. The plan there now, I find, is to procure a revolt in the Jerseys. For this purpose there had been sundry Torey Gentlemen let to go freely into that Country. Jeb Fisher is one of those and after being twice there is at length arrivd in London and is much with the Ministerial People evincing the probability of still succeeding by such a maneuvre—Eden & Gov. Johnstone lean to the same opinion, & it has got out from one of them that Govr. Franklin is to be the chief Engine for the business[4]—He is to go into the Jerseys, insinuate himself into the good graces of some of the leading people & then to be supported by the Army when he sees proper to hoist the Kings Standard.—Wild as all this may appear to You, I am nevertheless of opinion there is one branch of the Administration that will encourage its being put into execution.—The

Examination to come on before the House this week of the Torey Refugees—Galloway, Allen, Fisher &ca. &ca. will probably throw some new light on this matter. It does not appear that the Ministry are yet tired of murder & devastation, but I think it high time for them to be warnd against the errors they have frequently been led into by hungry Governors & discontented Toreys driven from their freinds & Country by their wicked & insidious conduct. No accounts yet of the sailing of the fleet from Torbay.

I am &c.&c.
Allen Hamilton

I should be glad You will not forget Your promise to help me to a drawing from a certain picture I spoke to you & Mr. F[rankli]n about.[5]

HSP: Franklin Papers, 5:133.

[1] A fleet from Jamaica had reached Falmouth on May 22; one ship had burned and sunk on the way.
[2] No engagement between the two had taken place since the beginning of the year.
[3] Toussaint-Guillaume, Comte Picquet de la Motte (1720–1791), best known as La Motte Picquet, had sailed from Brest with five ships to reinforce the French fleet in the West Indies, where Byron would try to intercept him but because of other demands on his ships would have to abandon the effort.
[4] William Franklin (1731–1813), last of the royal governors of New Jersey and, though Benjamin Franklin's son, a confirmed loyalist, had been arrested at the outbreak of warfare, kept prisoner until his exchange in 1778, and become president of the Board of Associated Loyalists in New York.
[5] William Temple Franklin (1760–1823), son of the former royal governor, was his grandfather's secretary.

To Benjamin Franklin

Londn. May 31. 1779

Dear Sir

I have wrote You from time to time since I had the pleasure of seeing You, about a matter we conversd upon, and my last was by post the 25 Int.; since which time nothing material has transpird, nor any circumstance appeard to cast a damp upon the business I wish so ardently to be brought forward; on the contrary we have reason rather to be elated, for altho there has been delays in giving answers that might be expected, these very delays indicate to me a serious consideration of the matter by the partys most concernd.

I have just heard of a Mr. Panchaud returning to Paris and solicited his care of this letter. The Inclosd was written a few days back & intended for a private conveyance, but it came to my hand too late; I dare say my friend has explaind Himself to You in that letter.[1]

I mentiond in a former letter to You[2] the probability of having found Mr. W. Peters's proper direction, which Mr. Penn[3] told me was at *Liverpoole* instead of Nottingham as You directed to Him, but I have been disapointed. I took care to mark on my letter that it should be returnd to me if Mr. Peters could not be found, and it was this day returnd to me markd "Mr. Peters is not to be found in Liverpoole". I acquainted Mr. Penn of this, & solicited his further assistance among his Phila. friends to find Mr. Peters out, but he is fearful he must be dead, because Mr. Peters wrote to Him about four months ago from the same direction in Liverpoole, & mentiond that He was old & very infirm. I intend to try another letter to Mrs. Roberts at whose house he lodgd, & shall do what you request provided he can possibly be found.

I mentiond this oppertunity of writing, to Mr. Penn last night & he said he would send me a letter for you or to be forwarded by you to Philadelphia. I do not recollect which, but if it comes in time you shall have it enclosd in this.

I have a letter forwarded me by J. Johnson of Nantes, which from its contents must have been brought from Maryland by my Younger Brother about the first Feby. in a Ship to Bilboa, to which place He was bound for the recovery of his health in a consumptive case. I am fearful from Johnsons not mentioning how it got to his hands, & my Brother not accompanying it with a line from himself that He may have died upon the passage; but if this should not be the case, & he may think proper to travel quietly on to Paris (which he probably may do to inform You how matters stand in America) I am to beg a share of Your usual civility & attention to Him. He is a young Man brought up to Phisic, has had an excellent Education, & is very clever; His politics & conduct will I am sure do him Credit with You.[4]

The letter forwarded Me was from my Brother whom you knew at Paris⁵ but contains nothing but what you must be apprisd of, as there have been one or two arrivals from that quarter to France since I saw you.

There has been rather a gloom over the faces in the City and at Loyds since the late dispatch's from Byron and it has not been lessend by the Mediterranean advices, those from N. York by way of Corke or by the more domestic movements in Ireland & Scotland. Spain, tho more likely than ever to be upon the back of this Country in a few months, is not now talkd of.⁶

The chit chat of the day is the probable inexpediency of prosecuting the War in America, for since the American Enquiry before the House of Commons, some parts of the Administration hold this kind of language. If they had been wise they would have made these kind of enquirys before they fought & became disgracd.

It is said the Bedford party shew visible discontent as to continuing the War in America, & I beleive Lord N. is heartily sick of it. Ministry do not seemingly pull well together; fattend with the spoil it is likely they are becoming restive, & I live in hopes they may soon kick up some good. I shall keep this letter open till I go in the City to see Mr. Pinchaud to inclose you any thing that may be new at Loyds. I am with the highest esteem Dr. Sir

Yr. very obligd & ob. Ser.
V. J. D[rouillar]d

1st June—please to turn over

A meeting (which carrys the appearance of more meaning than any preceeding one) is appointed for tomorrow.

There is much conversation to day about a probable speedy rupture with Spain & it has found its effects on the Stocks.

You may perhaps think me (as a person totally unconnected or concernd the least for America) a little impertinent by wishing so ardently for peace or throwing out any probable terms that *may be listend* to but you must allow me to intrude upon you a few propositions. A hint in the common way of conveyance under a direction you are possessd of may find its effect. As prelimenarys only suppose—first. Commissioners to be appointed to treat subject to ratification of Parliament. 2d a Truce for 10 or 12 years (to commence immediately) *uti Possidetis*. Third all acts of Parliament specially regarding America (excepting such articles as relate to Dutys on import & thereby effecting the Revenue) to be suspended during the term of the truce. 4th a truce for ten or twelve years (to commence immediately) *uti Possidetis* between Gt. Britain & France. 5th upon these preliminaries a negotiation to be opend as soon as conveniently may be. What say you to this?[7]

I am going to Mr. P[anchau]d, and it is not unlikely I may give him a bill on you for the twenty Pound formerly mentioned to You for supplys to J. Brehen, Dr. Sims[8] & three others. On receiving it from you he may transmit me an order to receive a similar sum from a french House he is connected with here, which will be a much better mode than any common negotiation.

Mr. R. P——n has not sent the letter & I begin to be more fearful from what I hear, that Mr. Peters is dead.

HSP: Franklin Papers, 5:64.

[1] The enclosure was probably a letter from David Hartley. Isaac Panchaud (1726–1789), a banker, had served as courier to Franklin on at least one earlier occasion.
[2] May 14, 1779.
[3] Richard Penn.
[4] Dr. Joseph Digges (1747–1780), the younger of Thomas's two surviving brothers, died on the island of Teneriffe in Feb. of the following year.
[5] George Digges.
[6] Actually a formal declaration of war by Spain was close at hand. On May 18 the Spanish government had informed the Americans that Spain would declare war on June 21.
[7] These proposals came from David Hartley.
[8] No such name is among those listed by various individuals who were accounting for the Forton prisoners. Digges may have intended to refer to Dr. Clement Smith, mentioned in his letter to Thornton, Dec. 1, 1777.

To Benjamin Franklin

On May 30, with a postscript dated the next day, Franklin had acknowledged Digges's letters of May 14, 18, 21, and 24 [25] and noted that the one of May

12 had not reached him. On the subjects of David Hartley's efforts to promote conciliation, the expediting of the exchange of prisoners, and the House inquiry into the conduct of the war he had stated: *"I never had nor have I now the least Expectation that any Good can come of the Propositions made to certain Persons. Whatever is reasonable and prudent for them to do, seems to be out of their sphere: for hitherto they have constantly rejected the best Measures and chosen the worst. . . .*

"Mr. [Jean-Daniel] Schweighauser [American commercial agent at Nantes] has undertaken to write to the Commissioners for Sick and Hurt sea men and give them the Information they desire relating to the Prisoners here. I have mention'd Morlaix again and have found the Ministers of the Marine not unwilling to permit the Cartel's using that Port. But as I know some others of the Council are strongly against it, I do not expect to obtain any Change. The old Pass will be allow'd good as long as the Exchange continues.

"I shall be glad to see the Examinations of those Americans Worth your mention. If they have Judgment and hope ever to return to their Country, they will join with Cornwallis, Grey, &c. in the Opinion of Impracticability—If they strive to support the contrary Oppinion, they inevitably fix their Ruin."

He had gone on to request that Digges *"procure from Mr. [John] Almon [the bookseller (1737–1805)] the remembrancers Debates in Parliament Since the American Disputes and all Such other Pamphlets as may be of use to an Historian, who proposes to write the late Revolution,"* directing the package to the banking house of Horneca, Grand & Co. in Amsterdam. He had concluded: *". . . yours of the 24th . . . confirms me more in my Opinion that your friend ought to expect nothing from his Laudable Endeavors with those People. They are expert in little Parliamentary Craft, but have none of that true Wisdom which comprehends the extensive and great Interest of their Country Domestick and Foreign, present and Future"* (LC: Franklin Papers, Series 1, 2:175–76).

London 11 June 1779

DEAR SIR

I receivd Your favour of the 30th ulo. & find by it only one of my letters have miscaryd. By mentioning the dates of my letters I did not mean to draw You into answering any of them but meerly to ascertain their safety; I well know how much better Your time is employd than by answering letters of little import, never mind me, but when You have any thing to do which You may think proper to require of me to transact. I have never yet found any letters have miscarryd under Your last direction, but this will not do for such Towns as have french Prisoners in the neighbourhood, because there is a rule to open them in order to find out if the letters are not for prisoners; In London it will do well, but as I am going to Bristol for a few weeks having some goods to Ship on Spanish bottoms expected & now there I should be glad to receive any commands of Yours under direction *Mr. William Singleton Church Post Office Bristol.*

I have made every application in my power about Mr. Peters, & shall continue my endeavours to find him out & do what you require; I have wrote to Mrs. Roberts at Liverpoole, the house he lodgd in, to find out from her when he left that place, where gone &ca. but as yet I have no answer.

I wrote to you by Mr. Panchaud who went by the packet of the 1st Int. and as you had mentiond to me you would pay the bill on Brehon when it again appeard, I took the liberty to draw one for 20£ to Mr. Panchaud, which on Receipt He was to remit to his friend here. As You mention in Your last you had paid Brehons Bill, this will of course be cancelld & returnd to me.

I shewd D. H. that part of Your letter which relates to the Cartel of Prisoners & the mention of the Port of Morlaix in preference to Nantes &ca. He spoke to Mr. Stephens[1] about it before me, who did not seem at all averse to letting the whole remaining prisoners go in the next voyage, but about this, Lord Sandwich was to be consulted: They are, both at the Admiralty & Board of Sick & hurt, very much surprisd that there is as yet no accounts whatever from the transport which carried over the first hundred, & say She must be either lost or detaind for want [of] a like number of British Sailors to return for those who were sent. Much surprisd also to hear that there are prisoners in Spain.

The Books You order to be forwarded to Messrs. Horneca Grand & Co. of Amsterdam are now in the packing up, & will be sent in a Ship to sail in about ten days calld the Anna Maria Christiaan Roeloffs Master. They will be put in as small a deal box as possible and markd

B F directed also on a card to Horneca & Grand, so that you may give the necessary orders to Amsterdam about them. I have got some friends trying to collect annecdotes & matter to help Dr. Gordon in his work.[2] General Washington two years ago wrote to me to forward him some books, & give what assistance I could. I was with Dr. Price to day & mentiond such a work to him as well as our valuable Bishop In whose family, thanks to you, I have been more than once very happy.[3] They all went into Hampshire on tuesdy. & I beleive Yours was the last name mentiond in the town House by Miss Georgiana. Wilkes also promisd me some annecdotes, and Mrs. MaCaulay to use her pen, but the former is so busied in rectifying the errors of Christianity & putting all Religions upon the level of the haram, that I have little hopes from him; and I guess Madam is too much engagd as yet in the joys of new wedded Love and envelopd in the embraces of Her young highlander to take up her pen.[4]

I gave you from time to time, as often as any new occurrence arose, the progress of the business I have lately been upon, & which I had most seriously at heart, and as I was well convincd it was taken up seriously & properly by the parties most interested in it I gave it *all* my attention & constantly held it in view. I wish I knew all the actors as thoroughly as you know them, but I have attended long enough to their moves to discover they are very expert in little dirty parliamentary craft, but have none of that true wisdom which comprehends the extensive and great interests of their Country. I am sorry our friend got so little by his laudable endeavours to serve both Countries. There was a decisive negative to the first & leading proposition of a ten years truce, because it was in fact giving Independence. This is the sum total & I dare say I need not enter into particulars. The plan of Ministry is to try another years work in America. The idle scheme of Govr. F. which I mentiond in my last to you,[5] however ridiculous & absurd it may appear, is to be adopted; much expectation is formd from it, from dissentions & cabal in Congress, disunion & distress among the people &ca. &ca. Whatever Negotiations the Ministry at present have in view are certainly intended to be offerd thro Sr. H. Clinton who will probably be armd with a new Commission & fuller powers.[6]—Something similar to this & very great offers for the Georgians are gone over to Prevost.[7]

There will be some conversation to day in the house on a motion of Sir W. Merediths for Ministry to declare what they intend to do;[8] Our friend will hold forth on this occasion, & probably tomorrow will open some new lights.

The Evidence of the Torey Worthies who are calld in by Lord G. G. to overweigh the evidence of Lord Cornwallis Genl. Grey &ca. &ca. has not yet extended further than to Genl. Robertson, who has been three intire days at the bar giving as dull a narrative as was ever heard in that house.[9] It is thought Galloways will come next, and so on down to the worthy little Jebas. Many are of opinion parliament will rise on thursday & cut short this enquiry, & deprive these Gentlemen of an oppertunity to clinch the nail of their ruin in America; for I cannot help thinking if they controvert the evidence of Cornwallis Grey &ca. and aim at establishing an opinion of the practicability of carrying on the war and subjugating America they will innevitably fix their ruin in both Countries. Gen. Robinsons [Robertson's] evidence was generally much ridiculd & laughd at; It tended to exculpate Lord G. G. of any inattention to the necessary supplies of Men Ships &ca. &ca., to the crimination of Genl. Howe, and to prove to all the world (except those who are already well informd of the state of facts) that Washington with twelve or fifteen thousand Men (never *more*) has baffled every effort of the British and mercenary armies of upwards of 40,000 men commanded by Sr. W. Howe and aided by a fleet of 80 to 90 Sail of Men of War; But his Evidence more than all clearly serves to prove that this wise & good ministry have projected and carryd on the war by the advise & recommendation of Fools, and they now bring these very fools to prove it.

An Express armd vessel is arrivd from N. York the 4th May. The accounts nearest the truth & which are beleivd at Loyds are as follows. A Detatchd Army of 7 Regiments under Erskine about 2,500 Men was on the point of sailing to the So.ward on some expedition, said in N. York to be sent as a Reenforcement to Prevost, but more probably from Mrs. Tryons account to be bound to Chesepeak Bay, either to support some discontents on the Eastern Shore ot to act on the Virga. side as a divertion in favor of the Georgia Army which if report speaks truth, has receivd two checks from Lincoln & was obligd to retire nearer to their head quarters at Sav⟨annah⟩.[10]

Seven Sail of Vict⟨ualling⟩ transports under convoy of the Jason frigate bound from N. York to Georgia with supplys for the army in the South, were taken convoy & all by three American Cruisers on the Coasts of Carolina.¹¹

The Revenge Capt. Cunningham after taking in all about forty sail of prizes, was himself taken by an English frigate near Bermudas & carried into New York.¹²

No appearances of any active exertions of the British Army from New York, but there was a current talk that Gov. F. with a body of American Loyalists & a few troops were going into the Jerseys from which quarter there was strong desertions & every confirmation of the disunion & distress of the People.

Since I wrote to You about my Brother, a Cozen of mine Dr. Stewarts Son of Annapolis has been with me; he saild in the same vessel with my Brother the Doctor & was taken & carryd into N. York.¹³ I have a full detail of the state of things in that quarter of America. Their greatest evil is the failure for now two years of the Crop of Wheat. Mr. Stewart being a Scotsmans Son got interest to come to Europe gratis, but my Brothers politics being well known & his having been much about the person of Genl. Washington for the last two or three years, he could not obtain permission to die at Sea & was left a prisoner in N. York very near wore down in a Consumption.

If any thing new transpires to day I will give you a line by common post to night. This is intended for the Spanish bag. I am with great truth & the highest esteem Dr. Sir

        Yr. very obligd & Obt. Servt.
        T. D——

HSP: Franklin Papers, 5:67.

¹ Philip Stephens (1723–1809), member of Parliament and secretary to the admiralty board.

² William Gordon (1728–1807), an independent minister from Hertfordshire who in 1762 had published an abridgment of Jonathan Edwards's (1703–1758) *Treatise Concerning Religious Affections*, had removed to America in 1770, become a pastor in Roxbury, Mass., later chaplain of the Massachusetts provincial congress, and, while private secretary to George Washington, begun to prepare the four-volume work that he would publish in London in 1788, two years after returning to England: *The History of the Rise,*

Progress, and Establishment, of the Independence of the U.S.A.: Including an Account of the Late War; and of the Thirteen Colonies, from Their Origin to That Period.

³ Dr. Richard Price (1723–1791), a British nonconformist minister who wrote on moral and political subjects and vigorously supported American independence, was a close friend of Franklin's of some thirteen years' standing. The Shipley family is first mentioned by Digges in his letter to Franklin of May 12, 1779.

⁴ John Wilkes (1725–1797), a politician known for his extravagant habits, his offensively sharp and satirical attacks on the leaders of government and fellow members of the House of Commons who favored coercive measures against the Americans, and his advocacy of numerous reforms, especially parliamentary ones, demanded by middle-class radicals, was a committed advocate of religious liberty. Mrs. Macaulay, whose works Digges had told Jonathan Loring Austin in Aug. 1778 he had forwarded to Franklin, had in Dec., after being widowed for more than thirteen years, married William Graham, a man nearly twenty-seven years her junior.

⁵ The reference is actually to his letter of May 25, not May 31.

⁶ Clinton was then in New York. The commission being talked of did not materialize until summer, after favorable news from South Carolina, when Clinton was designated sole commissioner to replace the earl of Carlisle and his friends and, advised by a council of civil and military members, was authorized to grant pardons, restore the royal authority, and explore areas for negotiation with the Americans.

⁷ Maj. Gen. Augustine Prevost (1723–1786), commander of all British forces in the South, had established headquarters in Savannah at the beginning of the year, when Georgia had come completely under British control.

⁸ Sir William Meredith (ca. 1725–1790) had entered Parliament as a Tory in 1754, but on a number of issues supported the Whig opposition. In 1774 he had become a privy councillor and comptroller of the king's household and been considered a supporter of North's policies; but by 1777 he had changed his position: he had resigned his comptrollership and in 1778 had voted to repeal the Declaratory Act of 1766. The motion alluded to by Digges was that the king be directed to bring the American war to an immediate conclusion.

⁹ Maj. Gen. James Robertson (1720?–1788), who had been in America since 1756, been in command of the royal troops raised in America, and also been barracks master at New York, had returned home for the winter months and in May been designated civil governor of New York. He believed that the Americans generally supported the British and that the region around New York at least was ripe for reclamation.

¹⁰ Sir William Erskine (1728–1795), quartermaster general to Howe and Clinton and commander of a detachment quartered on Long Island, appears to have remained in the New York area to attend to his administrative duties until ill health led him to return to England in Sept. Otherwise, the account reaching Digges was accurate: Maj. Gen. Benjamin Lincoln (1733–1810) had some weeks earlier forced Prevost to abandon Augusta and then provided sufficient reinforcements for Charleston to dissuade Prevost from attacking it.

¹¹ The *Jason* and the other prizes were part of a fleet of nine that the three American cruisers, Capt. John Burroughs Hopkins (1742–1796), commodore, had captured in Apr. off Cape Henry.

¹² The treatment of Capt. Gustavus Conyngham, whose notable successes had begun

in May 1777, was now to become one of Digges's and Franklin's preoccupations (see Digges to Franklin, Sept. 4, 1779).

[13]Dr. George Stewart (d. 1784), a native of Scotland descended from Kennett II, had been educated at the University of Edinburgh and emigrated to America in 1721, to settle in Annapolis. There, with an interest in the official life of the colony, he had held various government positions, including the prominent one of the judge in the Land Office, where he had served for more than twenty years before returning home in 1775, always loyal to the crown but not required to leave, to claim the estates of Argaty and Ballachallan that he had inherited from his brother. Digges's cousin is Dr. Stewart's third son, David (1751–1814), register of the Land Office in Annapolis, 1774–1777, after which he had lost his position because of repeated refusals to "associate," muster, and take oaths of allegiance to the United States. He had attempted to sail for England in the fall of 1778 and in Feb. of 1779, but had either been denied permission or been taken from the ship and brought back to New York. It was from New York that he had now come.

To Benjamin Franklin

June 18. 1779

Dear Sir

My letters under the dates of the 11th & 15th Int.[1] will inform You very fully of the final conclusion of the business I was lately upon, and I make no doubt but the rejection has been lamented by another party concernd fully as much as by me & my friends.

The Books you orderd are already Shipd on board the Dutch Ship Anna Maria Captn. Christiaan Roeloffs which will sail for Amsterdam in six or seven days. There is a mark on the box in which they are packd thus ⬛W⬛ and a card is also naild upon it directed thus (Books) For Messrs. Horneca Grand & Co. Merchs. Amsterdam. I will accompany it with a line or two to them [these] Gentlemen giving information that the books are forwarded to their care by your order, as by so doing it may save a Custom house search of the box & the unpacking the Books. I have not yet got the bill of the exact contents of the box or the amount of the Cost &ca., but I shall do it soon and repay myself as you direct—In this way or whatever other You may please to command Me I shall be ever ready and willing to serve You or Yours.

As your letter of the 30th May informs me You had paid Brehons Bill, I am in expectation that the other drawn in favor of Mr. Panchaud will be soon returnd to me. The want of the usual intercourse as to negotiation of bills, inducd me (from your mentioning you would pay the money advancd to Brehon & others) to get Mr. P. to carry the bill to Paris & to remit me the 20 £ to his friend in London, & I unluckily gave him the bill but a very few days before I found from Your letter that you had paid it.

We are all in an uproar here about the late maneuvere of Spain, & the word perfidious is now transferd from the Court of Versailles to that of Madrid.[2] The notification was given to the House of Commons last Wedy. with a smiling face from our Primier who was pretty severely handled for treating lightly so momentous a matter. It was read yesterday to the Commons, & long, tho not very spirited or interesting debates ensued thereon; the house of Lords treated it in a higher stile & there has been much commendation on the speeches of Lord Shelburne and the Duke of Richmond.[3] In both houses many hints were thrown out about the propriety of withdrawing the Army from America in order that the whole force might act directly against the house of Bourbon. It will be a sad effort for this Ministry to abandon intirely the prospect of subduing America, but nevertheless there was a hint from the Treasury bench (from W. Ellis[4]) that the withdrawing the army might be adopted as a future measure and that the Independence of America was *no very improbable event.* It appears to me that one of the Ports of N. York or R. Island will be soon evacuated not unlikely the former as the later being an Island may be longer tenable. I have no doubt this would have been a measure some time ago adopted had not fresh proofs of disunion & discontents in America given ministry some hopes of subduing the Country—they are now seeking these proofs, to the eternal disgrace of this Country, by the evidence of Torey Refugees who never again can go to America. I suppose Galloways evidence will finish this night. Lord S. has been finely baited for not having the fleet out (28 sail of the line & 6 frigates) before yesterday.[5] I understand two of them are put back. It is said here that the Spanish fleet saild twelve of the line & frigates &ca. on the 27th May and 20 sail of the line &ca. on the 2d June. The Brest fleet of 28 sail of the line & several frigates on the 3d June. This is generally beleivd, & the consequence of such apparent superiority causes much discontent & a general gloom upon the faces of every one. The ministry are yet haughty & carry it with a high hand, & talk of being equal to all this force even if joind by Holland & Portugal.

It appears pretty clear that the 2000 Men which Saild from N.Y. the 5 May, are gone to Chesepeak said to be in support of a party of discontents to the Congress measures on the Eastern Shore of Maryland. There appears to be no line of battle ship in America & but few frigates, there was but three of the line went with Arbuthnot, and four of Byrons fleet unfit for active service are now on their way home.

Much alarm as to an invasion of Ireland, but the most general receivd opinion as to the Brest fleet is, that it is gone Southward to join the Spaniards.[6]

Mr. Hartley gave notice yesterday he would make a motion to bring in a bill to lead to some terms to be offerd America. It was to be debated upon to day, but put off till Monday on account of Lord N.['s] non attendance on account of his having lost an infant Son. He read to the house some articles for pacification or negotiation six in number, which he mentiond as terms he thought probable America would not totally reject, & of which the Minister had had some confidential information about & had rejected. This Gentleman is indefaticable in his laudable endeavours to do good, but from the present lethargic disposition of all ranks of men there seems little prospect of success.

I am in hopes the late movements in Spanish affairs here will induce some of my acquaintance's near You to take a journey soon; I am the more anxious for it, as I am certain You Sir will be left more at ease and to your wish, setting aside the public Good.[7] I cordially wish you happiness & Success and am with great truth and sincerity

Your obligd & Obt. Servant
W. P——

HSP: Franklin Papers, 5:76.

[1] The letter of June 15 has not been found.
[2] For more than a year Spain had tried to recover Gibraltar by making England's ces-

sion of the fortress the price for Spanish neutrality in the present war. Repeatedly thwarted, Spain had moved toward the use of force. In early Apr. it had given London an ultimatum thinly disguised as an offer to mediate the disputes between the British on the one hand and France and the colonists on the other, proposing an indefinite suspension of arms between England and France and treating the colonists as de facto independent. But the British had sought to postpone discussions, and Spain and France had soon drawn up and ratified a secret convention binding the two powers to assist each other in wresting from the British various possessions and rights to which they had been laying claim. With the Spanish fleet already collaborating with the French and a declaration of war against England ready for June 21, Spain on June 16 presented the British government with a manifesto: inasmuch as the Spanish dominions in America were being threatened, and Spanish sovereignty in Central America was being violated, and Spain's various complaints were answered with no reparations, the king of Spain, Carlos III (1716–1788), now found "himself under the disagreeable necessity of making use of all the means which the Almighty has intrusted him with, to obtain that justice which he has solicited in so many ways without being able to acquire it."

[3] Shelburne and Charles Lennox, third duke of Richmond (1735–1806), argued for a change in the system and the measures that had embroiled their country in difficulties in both America and Ireland. Shelburne singled out Germain for particular attack, and Richmond moved to withdraw troops from America.

[4] Welbore Ellis (1713–1802), treasurer of the navy, 1777–1782.

[5] A motion to remove Sandwich as first lord of the admiralty had failed, 39–78, on Apr. 23, but criticism of him had continued.

[6] The French, under Adm. Louis Guillouet, comte d'Orvilliers (1708–1792), had on June 10 already made a rendezvous with the Spanish ships near Corunna.

[7] Doubtless a reference to the possibility that Arthur Lee, the commissioner in closest contact with Spain's diplomats, might go to Spain to represent the colonies there. His resentment and suspicion of Franklin had made friendly association impossible.

To Benjamin Franklin

25th June 1779

I am happy to inform You that I have found out Mr. Peters after I had given over hopes of Him & supposing Him dead. He desires of me to place the remittance intended for him in the hands of Messrs. Fuller & Co. Bankers in London to whom I have applyd to accept my bill on You for the one hundred pound you limit Me to go to, but they being unusd to negotiate French Bills desird me to look out among the French Merchants to get the Bill negotiated & the amount paid to Fuller & Co. for Mr. Peters's use. I think of looking after this business before the next packet sails & if it can be done I will draw the Bill on You payable at the House of Monr. Grand & advice You thereof by next packet.

The box of books were sent as you directed and I shall by first oppertunity send you the Bill of Parcells which amount to £9:19:6 the Charges of Cocket &ca. &ca. two or three shillings more, so that I shall make my draft on You an equal ten pounds: It will be better I include this sum in Peters's Bill & make it one hundred & ten pounds but I shall inform You in the course of Post if this mode is adopted. Mr. Peters writes me he is old & rather infirm and lives near Nottingham. My two former letters to that quarter miscarryd by being directed to Mrs. Roberts's, but I have wrote to him to find them out.

I am &ca. &ca. &ca.

Dr. *Franklin*

[Addressed:] A Monsieur Monsr. F———n/Passy.

HSP: Franklin Papers, 5:78.

To Benjamin Franklin

London 19 [⟨26⟩] June 1779

Dear Sir

I wrote you a few lines by last post on the subject of drawing a bill on You for Mr. Peters's supply; I have not yet drawn the Bill, & the Regular packets being now stopt, I took advice as to the mode of doing it. I am advisd to draw at 10 days sight not on you but on Mosr. G[ran]d for an equivalent of liveres to the pounds Sterg. as the Exchange may govern here.

Mr. Peters being apparantly anxious for the remittance, & from what I learn in want of it, I think by the next packet I will draw a bill in livres equivalent to one hundred and ten pounds at ten days sight regularly on Mosr. G———d markd as on account of Dr. F[ranklin]. You will therefore be pleasd to give the necessary direction about it. I think it will be payable to Messrs. French & Hobson, and as soon as advice is receivd of its payment the amount i.e. one hundred pounds shall be lodgd where Mr. Peters directs at the House of Messrs. Fuller & Co. Bankers. I could not get them to take the French bill as they have no connexion in the bill way at Paris. If any other bills or remittances are wanted it will be necessary to give me proper directions how to write & direct to Ostend for the immediate conveyance is now no more. Every countenance here is sad, and carrys the appearance of serious and distructive War; I am among the foremost advocates for peace & I hope it will not be long before we are blessd with it.

I am Yr. very Respectful & Obedient Servt.
V. J. D[rouillar]d

HSP: Franklin Papers, 5:77. The date must be a week later than the one Digges provides, inasmuch as the first paragraph's reference is unmistakably to the letter of June 25.

To Benjamin Franklin

London 6 July 1779

DEAR SIR

I make use of the oppertunity by the under Spanish Secretary (who takes his departure today with the remaining domestiques of the Ambassador) to forward You this; in which I take the liberty to inclose one for Mr. Johnson at Nantes under a French direction & I am to beg the favor of you to cause it to be put into the common post as soon as may be. I also forward in my packet a letter from our friend,[1] to which I refer [you] for particulars. He, as well as myself, have nothing now left but hopes; but we would not have You loose sight intirely of what we have been lately aiming at, and what may on some more fortunate day, be brought about. The cloud is thickening apace, & if appearances speak truth, almost every discription of Men among the thinking & great seem afraid it will soon burst with violence on this Country. In consequence of the impending mischeifs, there has been very great exertions in the Naval department & many Seamen impressd, so that eight sail of the line *more* will be ready in about a fortnight to join the thirty one now cruising a few leagues west of Scilly.

I have got an answer from Mr. Peters pressing me to draw on You, that He may get the much wanted supply. I wrote you a few days ago that I shoud draw a bill on You payable at Grand's; I am advisd by the conversant in these matters to direct it to Grand himself marking it to be presented at Passy and so it will go by next mail—i.e. for Livres equivalent by the then Exchange to one hundred & ten pounds, payable at ten days sight to Messrs. French & Hopson. You understand the ten pounds is for another account, and as soon as there is accounts of the bill being paid Mr. Peters shall have his £100 lodgd where he requested & the proper receipts forwarded to you. You will please to give the necessary orders about the bill when it may appear at Monsr. Grands.[2]

I expect in a packet or two to forward You the whole printed Evidence of Cornwallis Grey & others officers respecting America; and also the very curious Evidence brought to counteract the others by Lord G. G. of his now friend & new ally Mr. Galloway. This Gentleman has provd too much, & has compleatly done for himself in the opinion of all honest Men even of his own Torey principles. He was treated as he deservd by some of the minority Speakers, & by attempting to prove the practicability of the American War, has innevitably fixd his ruin at home.

I begin to get more & more sick of these kind of Gentry and heartily tired of the Country. My business will lead me in a few months to Lisbon, but you shall have timely notice of my move; and I hope for Your aid & recommendations when ever the day comes that any thing may be done in that Country favorable to my own. Your mentioning me even in a common way to those You write to at home will I am confidant be highly servicable. It may seem odd that I have rejected three offers to attend Gentlemen whom You may guess at, as Secy.; & by such rejection appear cool in the cause they are engaged in.[3] This is by no means the case; I was engagd in matters here, that I could not leave; & to speak truly I was afraid of joining intimately & cordially those who were engagd in disputes & quarrels which I ever disaprovd & carefully endeavourd to shun. I am sure no good can come of disunion, & that I have no prospect of comfort or satisfaction by living with a Man or Men who are apt to quarrel. I love quiet, & have no doubt I shall find it where I am going, because I am well known & a little respected there. It will be a great additional happiness to me to have Your approbation & freindship, for there is no one who esteems You more or wishes You better.

I am happy to inform You the Milford Cartel Ship is again saild from Portsmouth with 119 Prisoners for Nantes, & will I hope be forwarded quickly back to Plymouth for the remainder there. There were 17 Officers & 102 Men, among the Officers Captns. Harris, Tew, Lunt, White, &ca.[4] They behaved very quietly & properly as they passd to the Ship, & by the joy & gifts of the people as they passd thro Gosport, there were strong indications that if Peace & accomodation could be brought about between this Country and America, the affections of Brethen and fellow Citizens would soon return. Leiut. Knox, who commands the Milford Cartel Ship is a very humane good Man, & gave a passage to a poor crippled American woman, & to some other dischargd prisoners who had been in Haslar Hospital for cure.[5] The general language of the lower class of People as the American Prisoners passt thro Gosport to embark was "they are fine fellows, God Bless them, & send them safe home".

I have thought it better to put the Nantes Letter into the Common post & therefore shall not trouble you with it. I am with great regard Dr. Sir

Yr. Obligd & Obt. Servt.
V[incent] J[acques] D[rouillar]d

[Addressed:] To Doctor Franklin

HSP: Franklin Papers, 5:82.

[1] David Hartley.
[2] Franklin replied on July 12 that the bill would be paid. He went on to decline to comment on the various peace proposals Digges had forwarded: "I find it an Endless and fruitless Business to consider and give Opinions upon Propositions of Peace, drawn up by Persons who have no authority to treat. I hope You will therefore excuse my Silence on yours" (LC: Franklin Papers, Series 1, 2:220).
[3] Both Arthur and William Lee were corresponding with Digges and with each other about him.

⁴See Digges to Franklin, May 21, 1779. Capt. John Harris and Lt. Thomas White were American officers in Forton Prison whom Digges had named in his letter to John Thornton, Dec. 1, 1777. Other documents show that James Tew, captain of marines on the *Swallow*, had been in Forton since Jan. 23, 1778, and Lt. Joseph Lunt of the *Rising States* since June 14, 1777.

⁵Haslar Royal Hospital, built during 1746–1762 through Sandwich's efforts, was located approximately a mile south of Gosport (which faced Portsmouth across the harbor) and was designed to accommodate some two thousand wounded or sick sailors and marines.

To Benjamin Franklin

July 14. 1779–

DEAR SIR

Having the promise of getting this safe into a Post Office on the other side of the water I have stept into a Coffee House to inclose to you the Satys. and yesterdays Gazettes of the American News. Much joy was expressd on the receipt of the first which came remarkably quick from N. York, but was as most Gazettes are looked upon as nothing the day after. There were accounts of a later date via Corke, which mentiond that Provosts Army had been defeated & routed in their attempt to possess Chas. Town; The *dates* of this affair do not seem to confirm this important news, but most people here who wish to establish the falsity of it seem to beleive it true. If it should prove so, the Southern parts of America will be left tolerably free from similar invasions.¹

Our grand fleet is probably saild again from Torbay by this day with an additional three ships, & not a word has been yet heard about the Combind fleet, but there are high fears of its not being far off, and nothing now talkd of but invasions.²

I have had a letter from Peters since I drew the bill on you for £100—& seemingly pacified his fears of being again disapointed of remittances from home. My Bill on You A Monr. Grands for 100£ was remitted the 9th Int. As soon as there are accounts of its acceptance the money will be paid to Mr. Peters order. I am to observe to you that the box of books did not amount *wholly* to ten pounds but the diffi-

[⟨31⟩ JULY 1779]

ciency shall be accounted for to you. I have not the exact shop bill now with me, or I would inclose it. There was a mistake in the first bill which occasiond the error in me and which I did not discover until minutely examining it some days after. I wrote You twice lately by private conveyance, & should be glad to have some name given me at Ostend to address Letters to for forwardance &c. as it will be soon very difficult to forward in the usual way. I expect to have another private conveyance in about 10 days till which time I do not expect any material occurence in this quarter.

> I am with very Great regard
> Yr. mo. Obedt. & oblig. H. Ser.
> V. J[acques] D.

[Addressed:] A Monsieur/Monsieur B. F——/ a Passy

HSP: Franklin Papers, 5:85.

[1] Prevost had invaded South Carolina in late Apr. and advanced sufficiently to enable him to call for Charleston's surrender on May 12. When the defenders had offered neutralization of the colony as a condition for British withdrawal, Prevost had declined the offer. But in early June, with Gen. Lincoln bringing up reinforcements for the American troops, Prevost had realized he lacked the strength to take the town and retired to the islands in the south of the harbor. In turn he had then repulsed an attack by Lincoln and returned to his base in Savannah.
[2] The Spanish and French had joined naval forces and threatened an invasion of England.

To David Hartley

Saty. 1/2 past 11 at night [July ⟨31⟩, 1779]

[*preceding missing*] put back on seeing them and run for safety into Lagos—this account comes by letters by the Lisbon Mail dated the 7th July, & proves the Spanish fleet was Stearing north most certainly to join the Brest fleet & that of Ferrol[1] which were also seen on the 24th cruising off Cape Finestre consisting of 41 of the Line & 8 frigates. Two French men of war are watching the port of Oporto for the fleet expected from thence to England; & four Spanish & as many French are watching the Strts. of Gibralter probably to keep that Garrison from getting any fresh meat. 9 of the Line were ready in Cadiz for Sea & only wanting men. It appears that the 32 sail went out on the 23d June.

Many long faces at Loyds for the fate of the expected homeward bound Wt. Inda. Fleet of upwards of 300 Sail,[2] and the accounts from Byron and St. Lucia are not the most favourable.[3] You see by what gradual steps the Enemies of this Country are possessing themselves of the Dominion of the Seas, & yet our lethargic Citizens & Rulers seem totally negligent about it.

I shall miss the post if I do not conclude. Pray write me what to Do about Cunninghame for I realy think they mean to try him.[4]

Yrs. &c. &c.
T. D.

[Addressed:] David Hartley Esqr. M. P./ at T. Cookes Esqr. Holcomb/ In/ Norfolk

BRO: Hartley-Russell Papers, D/EHy 039/23 b-c.

[1] A division of the Spanish fleet consisting of eight ships.
[2] The fear was that the British would fall afoul of the combined French and Spanish fleets.
[3] Early in July Byron had left his anchorage at St. Lucia to protect a convoy bound homeward from St. Kitts. While he was so engaged, the French had sailed by St. Lucia to seize St. Vincent.
[4] Digges had informed Franklin of Capt. Gustavus Conyngham's capture in his letter of June 11. On Aug. 20 Franklin asked Digges to provide whatever assistance was necessary (see Digges to Franklin, Sept. 4, 1779).

To Benjamin Franklin

Lond. 10 Augt. 1779

DEAR SIR

The last mail brought the needful for Your Friend Mr. W. P[e-te]rs's remittance, & I immediately placd it to His Credit in the Bank he requested, taking the proper receipts &ca. The Exchange being rather unfavorable he lost seven shillings by the Bill; but, from his late letters, I make no doubt the remittance will be highly acceptable to Him. From there being a mistake in the original shop bill for the books, I am something in your debt, which shall be settled hereafter or discounted in some future account when you may find it convenient to command me. I dare say I need not repeat my offer of service or give any fresh assurances of my readiness to do anything you may command me.

We have had many ups and downs of joy lately. The arrival of the whole Leeward Island fleet, 270 sail, not a ship missing, gave us great satisfaction on the saturday week last, and on the tuesday following, we were as much depressd on the news of the loss of St. Vincents and the probability of Granada falling a day or two after; as well as that D'Estaign has been so considerably rienforcd as to give a decided majority of *French ships only* in the West Indies, and that Byron in his folly of quitting St. Lucia to conduct the Leeward Island fleet a small part of the voyage (they say to the Island of St. Thomas) had thereby fell so much to Leeward as to make it a work of some weeks to get back to the protection of St. Lucia, St. Kitts Antigua &ca.—They begin to talk very freely of him here, & like *all the rest*, I dare say he will return to England a disgracd officer. We got accounts on the 8th that the Jamaica Fleet was also arrivd safe 106 sail; but again comes a black tuesday, & we are told that a certain Mr. Hopkins picked up three of them on the banks, & that He has probably taken the twelve that are missing.[1] Also that *certain* accounts are come thro France that Prevost had been beaten in two battles on the 11th and 14th June, & that He surrenderd the 26th. This is rather a sad affair, and more than usual Credit given to it from its probability, and that it is no ways contradicted by the generals which arrivd in Town the 7th at night from N. York which place they left on the 6th July. Gen. Jones, Sr. W. Erskine, *some say* Sr. J. Baird, Coll. West, & two or three others were landed out of an armd transport which put into Milford.[2] Altho they are three nights & two days in Town, nothing has been given out to raise our spirits—probably the Gazette of this Evening may do it. When asked the news at New York, these Gentlemen are remarkably silent— nothing material has been done—the Army is in good health & spirits plentifully supplyd &ca.—but not a word as to any intended active expeditions or opperations; and it would seem that the game there is nearly up. We however do not quite despair, as we continue still to get assurances from Ministry that all is well & in a fairer way than ever. You would be astonishd to see how uniformly our leaders pursue the old game of deceiving the People, & how admirably the bait takes. Our friend H. has been some weeks out of Town, & has I beleive lost all patience with them. We are dayly amusd with their wranglings & dissention but no apparent good comes out of it. I am promisd to have this put safe into a foreign Post Office and mean to keep it open as long as possible to add any thing that I may pick up this evening. Wishing You every success & happiness I remain

very truly Yrs.—
V. J. Drouilard

(afternoon Tuesdy.)

The news of Prevost's repulse before Chas. Town is confirmd by a vessel to Glasgow with official accounts from N. York of the 4th July. I suppose it will be kept snug from the public as long as possible. The late arrivd Generals must have known it, & had political prudence enough not to let so great a national calamity come forth to the public sooner than was absolutely necessary. It is however, like all other disagreeable news, much molifyd. "Prevost got very near to Chs. Town, & was about to summon the town to terms, when Pulaski arrivd with succour & assistance.[3] Finding this, Prevost thought proper to take better ground on St. Johns Island 16 miles from Chs. Town, where he now waits for rienforcements"—If He was not Burgoind before the 26th June I think He will have had very good luck.

[Addressed:] Monsieur—B. F——, Passy

HSP: Franklin Papers, 5 : 91.

[1] Capt. John Burroughs Hopkins, commodore of the three cruisers that had captured the *Jason* and other ships in Apr. (see Digges to Franklin, June 11, 1779), is doubtless the man Digges means. But the records show that, although two of the same cruisers were among the three that this time captured eleven of the Jamaica fleet (three of them to be later recaptured), Hopkins had been suspended from his command in May for

violating orders: he had returned to port when he should have continued on his cruise and had failed to send to the nearest port those prizes he had taken.

²Maj. Gen. Daniel Jones had for many months considered continuance of the war futile. Sir William Erskine, quartermaster general for Clinton and Howe in New York, had returned because of ill health. Sir James Gardiner Baird (ca. 1752–1830), lieutenant colonel of the Twenty-eighth Light Dragoons, would continue to serve in America.

³Count Casimir Pulaski (ca. 1748–1779), the Polish cavalry officer who had volunteered his services, had been allowed to enlist an independent mounted unit and was popularly given credit for precipitating Prevost's withdrawal.

To Benjamin Franklin

Londo. 13. July [August] 1779

DEAR SIR

I wrote You the 1st Int. by common conveyance of post a Ostend, and also by the last packet the 10th, which I had a promise should be put into the post office at Ostend, the bearer of it being bound to Brussels. In my last I acquainted You that the needful had been properly done as to Mr. P[ete]rs Remittance—His money has been placd in the bank he requested me to pay it into & I have the necessary receipts. I am in Your debt something, on account of the first shop bill for the Books being erroniously made out. The house to whom you desird me to forward them, have informd me by letter they got safe &ca.

Having now a safe oppertunity to Ostend I inclose you a letter from Raspe.¹ It has been some days in my possession, but a late journey to Birmingham & my not always having my papers about me, put it out of my power to forward it so soon after Mr. Raspes delivery of it as I could wish.

I write You in great haste, having accidently met at an Inn the friend who bears this abroad, & who is on his way to the Packet. I wrote You in my last *doubtfully* about Prevost. We have now our doubts cleard up by arrivals from N. York to Glasgow, St. Augustine to London, & a vessel quicker than either from Bermudas to the River. By this last it appears He was attackd by Lincoln at his post on St. Johns Island 18 miles from Chas. Town, & with the loss of about 100 Men obligd to get southward into a warmer Climate; & it is beleivd here he got to Beaufort with his army & is there waiting rienforcements. It does not appear He has capitulated or surrenderd, but this must be soon the case.

The grand fleets have yet done nothing. Our Commander is very unpopular in the Navy as is his Employers on shore, & the talk of the day is, that Lord Howe is to have the command.[2] It would take more than his skill to save this Country, and the people begin now to think so. The accounts from N. York by the lately arrivd Generals are that Washingtons army had been strongly rienforcd by the neighbouring militia—That he had crossd the Hudson River with 10,000 Men & got nearer to New York—This was a movement *after* Genl. Clinton had returnd from his Expedition up the No. River. There was an expedition about to depart from N. York on the 6th July—two small ships of war, several transports, and about 1500 Men among them a Corps of respectable Refugees. It was said to be meant for New London. The accounts from Canada by the only vessel come home this year & which saild the 18 June are very bad[:] a universal disposition in the native Canadians to revolt & provision flour & bread remarkably scarce. They had particular accounts there that the Govr. of Detroit (Capt. Hammilton who used Mr. Jno. Dodge so remarkably ill as stated in the last number of the Remembrancer) having venturd too far into the habitable parts of America in one of his Indian scalping Expeditions, had been made prisoner with about 200 Indians & English, and that the Americans soon after got the Fort.[3] I see many of your friends often, and you have their best wishes among numberless complaints that the communication is so obstructed & that letter writing is so dangerous in these times of alarm from immediate invasion &ca.

I have been made a little uneasy of late by some secret insinuating whispers from *two Brothers* whom You have some reason to know[4]— implying that I was cool & backward to a certain cause, had rejected offers of employ to serve those I wish best, & similar tittle tattle calumny; which I feel the less from knowing my own feelings & inability to serve more than I have done. It is true, from private, rather secret offers of their own, I might have found bed & board in their habitations; & however irksome such a situation might be to me, I would willingly have submitted, even to the prejudice of my private views or interests, provided I had been properly desird to do so. But why need I trouble you, who have had enough from that quarter already. I shall write whenever an oppertunity offers, & always be made happy by hearing of Your welfare & success.

I am very respectfully

Yr. obligd & Ob. Sert.
A. Mc Pherson

There is a small fleet arrivd at Corke from N. York which saild the 10th July & before their sailing an express had arrivd there with the account of Prevosts being 'retreating'.

I am sorry to find by the returns from Sweighauser that there were only 92 English Prisoners in France so that the American Cartel will stop on the return of the Transport to England.[3] Now about 140 at Portsmo. & 160 at Plymo. and in other places about sixty—

[Addressed:] A Monsieur/Monsieur B. F——/ A—— ——Passey

HSP: Franklin Papers, 5:84. Digges misdated the letter July.

[1] Rudolf Erich Raspe (1737–1794), German amateur geologist and antiquarian whose writings about the origins of earthquakes, volcanoes, and even continents had gained him a fellowship in the Royal Society, had been an occasional correspondent of Franklin's for more than a decade. He had escaped from Germany in 1775 after being arrested for pawning the landgrave's coins and medals in order to satisfy creditors and had settled in London, where, although expelled for his action from the Royal Society, he still had entree into some social circles. At this time he had not yet written the work for which he would be best known, *Baron Munchausen's Narrative of His Marvellous Travels and Campaigns in Russia* (Oxford, 1786). Digges had probably met Raspe in May when Franklin apparently had asked Digges to deliver a letter to him. Raspe's letter enclosed here is dated July 27, 1779 (APS: Franklin Papers, 99, no. 3, 130–31).

[2] Sir Charles Hardy (1716–1780) had in the late spring been called from inactive duty to assume the position of commander of the Channel Fleet after several flag officers had declined to serve under Sandwich, first lord of the admiralty.

[3] Lt. Gov. Henry Hamilton (d. 1796) was to become widely regarded as a cruel, base, and arbitrary man, given to granting the Indians bounty for enemy scalps and to taking pleasure in the suffering of imprisoned rebels, largely on the basis of the account to which Digges refers: "A Narrative of the capture and treatment of John Dodge, by the

English at Detroit," *Remembrancer; or, Impartial Repository of Public Events. For the Year 1779*, 6 (London: J. Almon, 1779): 73–81. Dodge, a Connecticut-born trader, had settled in Sandusky in 1770, befriended the Indians and been trusted by them to act as interpreter during their treating with the Americans, and been made captive in Jan. 1776 to begin what he had reported as six months of wretched treatment, characterized by cold dungeons, threats of execution, and the spectacle of officially subsidized savagery. Hamilton, considered responsible for such activities, had been finally captured at Vincennes by Lt. Col. George Rogers Clark (1752–1818) on Feb. 25, 1779, and at Jefferson's direction marched with his cohorts to Williamsburg, Va., where in retaliation for his practices he was held without trial for nineteen months, after which he was allowed to return to England. Recent scholarship has tended to modify the harsh judgment of Hamilton in the light of what others regarded as acceptable conduct at the time, what the Indians themselves initiated, and what Clark in turn proved capable of perpetrating without any inhibitions.

[4] Arthur and William Lee.

[5] Jean-Daniel Schweighauser (d. 1781?), the Americans' commercial agent at Nantes, was continuing to monitor the exchange of prisoners from France (see Digges to Franklin, June 11, 1779, headnote), where the number of captured Englishmen was now insufficient to secure the release of all the Americans held in the British prisons.

To Benjamin Franklin

Saty. morng. 4 Sepr. 1779

DEAR SIR

I have risqued two letters to You very lately, and having an oppertunity by private conveyance I repeat to You the substance of them. Mr. Peters's affair has been settled to His wish as You will see by his inclosd Letter. I am rather surprisd that my bill forwarded the 9th July had not appeard on the 20th Augt.—but suppose it is at the Bankers unknown to You. There was every care and attention paid to Capn. Cu[nningha]m immediately on its being known He was in England; He was wrote to three or four times with offers of service but by means of his being shifted about, I fear some of the letters did not reach him, & he might think himself neglected. He was movd from F[almou]th by strong Solicitation to P[lymout]h among the rest,[1] but during the late alarm,[2] I heard they were movd inland—I hourly expect a line in answer to mine pointing out what necessarys he may want, & You may be assurd they shall be freely & carefully given him.

You will by this time have read that Capn. Hutchins was taken up last Sunday at a friends house near Leatherhead, his papers all seizd, has had three or four close examinations as to accomplices, & himself a close prisoner in New Prison Clerkenwell. His accusation is treasonable correspondencies with Dr. Franklin Mr. S. Wharton & other Americans—a Mr. Beasley & a Mr. Bundy are said to be his accomplices—it appears the former has been a carrier for him, & it looks as if he had betrayd H——s.[3]

Since these examinations others have been taken up & their papers seizd & examind, particularly a Miss Stafford, and a Clerk of Mr. Neaves who it is said lately came from Paris; all Neaves books and papers have been searchd,[4] & they seem to be going on to the seizure of all papers of Persons who appear by the above correspondencies to have any connexion or intercourse with the partys, so that every person may suffer whose names have been imprudently used. Two friends of S. W. in Wimpole & Marybon [Marylebone] street may have their papers searchd,[5] from meerly having their names (I mean the former) imprudently mentiond in these correspondencies, which I suppose will turn out to be a meer friendly correspondence between Cap. H. and Mr. W. as Countrymen; for in these times I cannot suppose any person imprudent enough to enter into politics, or by mentioning the sailing of fleets, movements of armys, or panicks given at the apprehension of invasion, thereby be supposd to be given information.

I understand Capn. H—— gives himself up as a lost Man & desponds very much of being acquitted, He being in the Service & in all likelyhood to be tryd by Court Martial. It is said He has confessd to every thing that gives the least appearance upon paper against him— not unlikely from his little acquaintance in these matters and a natural timidity he may have acknowlegd too much, & thereby helpd his own condemnation. By every account his examination & papers have not led to that depth of information by the convicting others, that His prosecutors seem to be aiming to obtain. A little blood may be wanting to stop the popular clamour against our Leader[s] and turn the public conversation from the present gloomy state of affairs in this once great & flourishing Country. It may be necessary for You to give immidiate information of this to W., to whom a letter directed in the usual way has no chance whatever of reaching him. I should be very glad to know a proper person at Ostend to direct to, and it would be useful to have your proper address when I inclose to Monr. Grand. From the situation of the two grand fleets (which are now said to be both within sight of St. Helens) a grand naval combat may be hourly expected, & the Empire of the Sea decided in favor of one or the other. It is a critical hour for us Englishmen. If there is not a material rumpus or convulsion to prevent it, I will write you by a friend via Holland in a very few days. I am very truly

& sincerely Yours—
V. J. Bertrand

APS: Franklin Papers, 15:167.

[1] On Aug. 20 Franklin had written Digges about Conyngham: "I desire you would take care to supply him with Necessaries that a brave Man may not suffer for want of assistance in his Distress" (LC: Franklin Papers, Series 1, 2:233). For Digges's account of his own role in getting Conyngham transferred from Pendennis Castle at Falmouth to Mill Prison at Plymouth, see his letters to Franklin, Sept. 20 and Oct. 26 and 30, 1779.

[2] At this time the British repeatedly feared invasion (see Digges to Franklin, June 18 and July 14, 1779).

[3] Thomas Hutchins (1730–1789), born in New Jersey, had served in the Pennsylvania militia and then with the British troops during the French and Indian wars; he had kept journals of his travels, illustrated them with maps, and been elected in 1772 to the American Philosophical Society for his scientific work. When the war had broken out, he had been in England and, because he had not wished to fight against his countrymen, had asked leave to sell his captaincy. He had been refused, been offered a position in a new regiment, which he had rejected, and shortly after, as Digges says, been arrested for high treason. James "Beasley", correctly called Peisley in Digges's letters to Franklin of Sept. 6 and 20, kept a lottery office near the Strand and had been apprehended by a Capt. Grant of the Prince of Wales's American regiment because of his boasting of having access to state secrets; Bundy (actually Thomas Burdy, whose name Digges must have misread in the newspapers) was clerk to a merchant on the French coast.

On Oct. 7, after receiving Digges's next letter, of Sept. 6, Franklin replied: "I am Sorry to hear any innocent Men Should suffer on suspicion of holding a criminal Correspondence with me. The Truth is, that I do not know *that* Capt. Hutchins, and never had a Correspondence with him of any kind, directly nor indirectly. Nor have I ever understood that Mr. Warton received any Intelligence from England but what the News papers afforded" (LC: Franklin Papers, Series 1, 2:271).

[4] Richard Neave & Son, London merchants, were the financial backers for the firm in which Samuel Wharton was a senior partner.

5. One of these friends was R. Ellison, whose name had appeared among the donors to the fund for the relief of American prisoners, *London Evening Post*, Jan. 1–3, 1778.

To Benjamin Franklin

Sept. 6. 1779

DEAR SIR

I ventured to try the fate of two letters to you very lately by common post, cheifly to give information to you & others of a late publick arrest;[1] as also that Mr. Peters's remittance has been settled to His wish, and that every necessary step has been taken to give Capt. C[o]n[yngha]m information that I was ready to help Him to money or any other necessarys he might want: on account of His removal from Pendennis to Mill Prison, and from thence (on account of the late alarm at Plymouth) to an inland Prison of Devonshire, I have not yet been able to get an Answer to any one of four letters conveyd by different modes to Him, but am in hourly expectation of one. I had taken these steps before Your letter of the 20th Augt. came to my hands,[2] and by the help of a common friend who forwarded that letter to me, we had obtaind his removal from Pendennis and got him among his friends in Mill Prison, in order to take his rotine of Exchange; and altho there is at present no promising aspect from the Cartel, I am in hopes He will soon get out.

I wrote You on the 4th by the Chaplain to your Russian Embassay, and put my letter under the usual cover. I could wish you would give me a *proper name* for direction of those Letters put under cover to Monr. G. for their may be less risque in so doing.[3] My last was principally to recite the former parts of this letter, and to give further information of Captain Hutchins being apprehended for supposd treasonable correspondence with you and Mr. J. W[harto]n.[4] He has since his commitment undergone three or four close examinations before Sr. Jno. Feilding, Lord G. G. Mr. De Grey & Mr. Knox;[5] is committed a close prisoner to N. Prison, Clerkenwell & will likely be tryed for his life at the old Baily in 10 or 12 days. Some say, as an Officer, He will have a Court Martial, but I hope not. Mr. Peisley (who is generally suspected to have turnd informer) has been dischargd on condition of appearing an [as] Evidence against him, and Mr. Bundy yet remains a prisoner. As the papers of these three mentiond other names, some other people have been taken up, their papers seizd & examind &c.[6] Mr. Neaves book[s] & papers have undergone this fate; and *it is said* a Clerk of his just returnd from France has been apprehended & committed. There was a Miss Stafford also examind and Her papers taken; She was releasd but her papers held. It appears but too clearly that these worthy Examinants are bent upon all the mischief they can towards American People and their abettors, & most likely with an aim to get some publick Execution and raise a clamour against the friends of America, in order to turn the minds & conversation of the populace from the present very gloomy situation of publick affairs. As I obtaind a communication with Capt. H. and the Lady, I find the principal aim & bent of the Examinants were to pin crimes upon others; and there were particular questions asked about Mr. E[lli]s, Mr. D[igge]s, Mr. E[lliso]n and others. Mr. J. W. (whom it may be essentially necessary to inform of these particulars in order to prevent his further writing) can inform You who these people are. It is more serious against the former than any of the rest; but if I can judge right, it is not mischeviously so, & the others are not afraid. Poor Capt. H—— disponds exceedingly, says he is a markd victim, is sure no mercy will be shewn him, and hopes his friends will not forsake Him. Every thing will be done for Him that can; and I am strongly of opinion He disponds too much; for I well know His Enemies have been much disapointed that more has not come out. The *Good* Mr. Knox has been closer upon Him than any of the rest. He said, "You now see Capt. H——, by *your own confession* your life is in our power, but it may be spard by your openly declaring every thing & discovering Your accomplices and the other secret traitors who are ruining this Country." I fear very much that Capt. H., being a timid man, has answerd questions put to Him, which He has was in no ways obligd to reply to.

I come now to the principal point for which I write You this letter & indeed for which the Bearer purposely takes a trip to Paris. He is a little known to You, but the person who is principally engagd with Him is not. Mr. C——y [Cyprian] Sterry is from R. Island, & I beg leave to recommend Him to you. The other Gentleman (who is ill at present or would also wait on you) is Mr. W. Smith of Baltimore Brother to my friend Collo. S. Smith who defended Mud Fort.[7] The two Gentlemen have a considerable quantity of Blankets, and Coarse Cloths, and other articles much wanted in a certain Army; and for which Mr. S. principally came from Maryland to supply. There is *one* risque, much lighter than the usual one to Holland St. Eustatia & so on to the Continent; by purchasing a vessel here, getting a crew of their own, & clearing for N. Y. and taking an opportunity to slip into the Delaware or some other port. But a cover is wanted to shew that the vessel & Cargoe is orriginally meant for the use of the States, for fear she may be taken & claimd by American Privateers or cruisers going in. As I know the extreem want our people are in for winter Cloathing, and that these two Gentlemen can throw in several thousand pounds worth at a critical season of the year, I have encouraged their trying to get a certificate from You, that the ship was orriginally meant for some port of the northern Colonies, & the Cargoe meant to be offerd to the States at the current price. I have no doubt it will be of great public good should they succeed; and as to the propriety of the measure You are the best judge of. I think I can justify my strong recommendation of them & their scheme to You. Mr. Sterry will talk further upon it.

There has been a man here, & who left London 8 days ago to return to Paris, that I think worth mentioning to You, tho among the race of Sad Dogs. I suspect as he loung'd pretty much about Almons[8] & tryd to put himself into Company of our friends, & for some other reasons, that He is rather a spy upon your friends. It is Sr. H. Ecklyn, who has resided many years at Paris, rather a fugitive from this Country.[9] He passd here by the name of Loyd, & when he went away gave out to *his intimates* He should return from Paris in 10 or 12 days, in order to publish some secrets, relative to underhand offers made to the Court of France by Lord M[an]s[fiel]d[10] and other great men here, if they would give up America. He is a thin genteel dark man about 45.

There is also another person here from France whom I have reason to beleive has been with the Minister. Passes by the name of Monr.

Belson, is from Britany, lives in a stile, & keeps a Carriage, a genteel dark man, & like most Frenchmen, apt to brag of his importance and being in the secrets of the French ministry.

Poor Raspe has been often with me lately and is much down in the mouth at the treatment He has lately receivd by a Russian nobleman by whom He is likely to loose some money. I forwarded a letter from him some weeks ago & by this post send you another.[11]

I shall keep this open until I go into the City to hear the news of this Evening for we are all in such consternation & tremor that every hour may bring some alarming account from Portsmo. in which port it is now reported our grand fleet is blockd up by a far superior one of the Enemy. I am with the greatest truth & sincerity Dr. Sir

                Yr. very obedt. Servant
                V. J. Drouillard

      [Fragment filed with letter]

Jno. Stephenson[12] Commander of the Brig Sally taken the 1st July by a lugger-Riggd Privateer of Bretange named the Hawke Capt. Heden de Polly of six one pounders, 8 swivils & 38 men who carryd Him into Brest & He is now confind at Velse in Britagne.

The other application is for Alexander Currie late Commander of the Merchant Ship Henry. He was taken the 31st Octor. 1778 by the Vengeance Man of War, carried into Brest, removd to Samur [Saumur] and Ploermeet [⟨Ploërmel⟩] but is now at Tours. His ship belongd to Mr. Samuel Hartley.[13]

HSP: Franklin Papers, 5:92.

[1] The arrest of Capt. Thomas Hutchins mentioned in Digges to Franklin, Sept. 4, 1779.

[2] See ibid., n. 1.

[3] On Oct. 7 Franklin replied: "When you have occasion to write to Mr. Grand he tells me you may direct your Letters to the Care of Messrs. Fr. Romberg and Comp. at Ostend" (LC: Franklin Papers, Series 1, 2:271).

[4] Although Digges refers to Joseph Wharton throughout this letter, the earlier and later references are to Samuel, the more likely correspondent. Both brothers, though, were in France.

[5] Sir John Fielding (d. 1780), a magistrate known for his efforts to break up gangs of robbers, rescue deserted girls, and send unfortunate boys into the navy; Germain;

Thomas DeGrey (1748–1818) and William Knox, joint undersecretaries of state for America.

[6] Peisley, "Bundy" [Burdy], and others below are first mentioned in Digges to Franklin, Sept. 4, 1779.

[7] Lt. Col. Samuel Smith (1752–1839), born in Carlisle, Pa., and resident of Maryland since the age of eight, had been sent by Washington to command the forces defending Fort Mifflin on Mud Island in the Delaware in Sept. 1777; wounded after a gallant but hopeless defense in Nov., he was later honored by the Congress. His brother is probably John Smith, Jr.; it is in that name and Sterry's that Franklin's covering passport was issued on Sept. 24 (APS: Franklin Papers, 74:87).

[8] John Almon, the London journalist, bookseller, and publisher.

[9] Probably Henry Echlin, who had written a note to Franklin in Jan. 1777 from the Prison of Abbaie St. Germain introducing himself as a lover of liberty and enemy of oppression.

[10] William Murray, Baron Mansfield (1705–1793), chief justice of the King's Bench, privy councillor, and king's sergeant at law, was a nominal Whig whose caution made him a consistent supporter of the court and an advocate of coercion to compel the colonies to recognize Parliament's sovereignty over them.

[11] Raspe, Sept. 4, 1779, was writing Franklin for leave to visit him in order to secure support in France that would enable him to do research in the Royal Library (APS: Franklin Papers, 99: no. 3, 131).

[12] John Stephenson was also owner of the ship and a burgess of Hull. He was released in Feb. 1780 as a result of Franklin's efforts.

[13] A London merchant and cousin of David Hartley's with whom Digges had business transactions (see Digges to Philip Barton Key, May 28, 1808).

To Benjamin Franklin

Sept. 20, 1779

Dear Sir

I have written you the 3d Int. by Post,[1] the 4th by the Chaplain of the Russian Ambassador at Paris, & the 6th Int. by a person who purposely went to You on some business, & whom I am now in hourly expectation of hearing from. Since writing these sundry letters, I have found means to communicate with Capt. C. whom You desire in Your last letter of the 10 Augt. I may give some help and assistance to.[2] I have had three letters from him & the treatment He speaks of & describes is realy shocking. He was brought over all the way in Irons, & put into the first Prison (amidst the scoffs hisses threats & insults of a Mob, at which he *cryd* with rage and indignation) with only a common sailors thin jacket, one check shirt Trowsers, & pair of Shoes. As soon as I heard he was at F[almout]h, I got a friend to petition for his removal to Mill Prison which was granted,[3] & where he has receivd my two last letters, after having verbally describd his wants to a friend of mine who supplyd him with some Cloaths when he was shippd from Falo. I have informd him of Your request to give him help, & he is extreemly thankful for it. He writes me that the Cloaths he stands in need of, his common maintainance, (for our subscription fund has now got very low) and a few guineas to serve as occasion may offer, will make the sum he may want forty pounds or upwards, of which He has sufficient to repay in the hands of people in Nantes & Cadiz. I have given orders to a very worthy man of Plymo.[4] to look towards the proper supply to him of Cloaths and a little money, & he is now well off for the present. I shall draw as I last did on You for that sum, & remit his order on me for so doing when he forwards it; which I expect He will by next post. You will please to give orders to Mr. Grand to be attentive to the bill, which will be drawn by me on Him without mentioning Your name, for the more safe negotiation of it here.

The last Cartel arrivd at Plyo. some days ago, & Interest is now making to let the whole 190 Prisoners now there go in the next trip, in order to save a second voyage to that port; but I am fearful it will not do; as they say at the Office, there are no more prisoners for this Exchange in France. There is 140 odd at Forton, and about 30 at Pembroke.

I have left Mr. W[harto]ns *direction*, with my papers in a safe & distant quarter, or I would write to Him by this Conveyance about his friend Capt. Hutchins.[5] It is too dangerous to do it by post, or I would have wrote to both of you more frequently & explicit. Since my last of the 6th Int. The junto who sit as Examiners Judges &ca. &ca. i.e. Sr. J. F., Lord G. G., Mr. De Grey, & Mr. Knox, have found means, thro the assistance of a person who lodgd in the same house with Capt. H., and Capt. Grant & Peisley who betrayd Him, to get at an Iron Chest which Mr. W———n left under care of Hutchins, and which was broke open before the junto & the papers strictly examind. Wherever those papers or Capn. H———s's had references to other names, the papers of those other persons have been examind or the holders of them strictly enquird about. The papers & books of Mr. Neave have been taken; two young men I beleive formerly his Clerks were taken up; also a Mr. Bundy who was confind a night or two & is releasd. Mrs. Carr a Milliner in Covent Garden was before the junto & dischargd after many questions about Mr. W——n, Mr. E[lli]s, Capt. H., Miss Stafford &ca. &ca. Miss Stafford (who had time to secret *some* papers) was in prison *one* night; her house strictly searchd, & very scrutinous enquirys of what She knew? of Mr. W——n, Mr. E——s, Mr. Ell[iso]n, Mr. D[igge]s, & others. Mr. W—— to Whom I beg you will communicate this, can inform you of these connexions. The Evidence has turnd out much to the disapointment of the junto; for they fully expected to criminate some others, & get a publick Execution of some *Miscreants* as they are pleasd to call all those who are averse to their measures. I do beleive the proofs against Capt. H. are not sufficient to authorise his being tried, *for the key to the Cypher in which he wrote*, has been destroyd. There is no knowing what degree of mischief may attend him if brought to a Court martial. Mr. E——s and Mr. E——n are naturally uneasy & if they were ever wrote to by Mr. W——n, he should now be cautious how he writes.

I wish to have some name given me to direct to you under, for tho I always inclose to Monr. G[ran]d, I am obligd to express to him for whom the letter is, & this may be a risque in the Post Office. I requested this favor in my last letter of the 6th by Mr. S[terr]y, and if he bears not the answer to me, it may be done by common post in a single letter, wrote in any hand, for I shall know from whence it comes, and directd A Monr. Monr. Wm. Singleton Church Nando's Coffee House Londn.—A careful hand at Ostend to put letters under cover to, may also be very useful. At Amsterdam I use the Gentlemen Whom I forwarded the box of books to.[6] If you know of any means by which I can be useful, I hope You will not spare me, & you may depend upon my attention to any thing You may request.

We have not a word of news from the West Indies since the late Gazette. Since the two grand fleets in Europe have got into their respective ports, there is nothing talkd of but the miserable situation of our affairs in the West Indies;[7] and America is now of too trifling consequence even to be ever mentiond. I beleive the prospect from the

Continent is full as gloomy as that from the Islands, but nothing authentic is given us from authority altho ships arrive frequently at Corke from N. York. It is said Ministry have accounts from thence to the 17th Augt. and that the Garrison was inactive, had done nothing, & were anxiously expecting the arrival of Adl. Arbuthnot with his 4 ships of the line and 3180 Recruits. This fleet was spoke with in the neighbourhood of Bermudas the 6th Augt. & they were in extreem want of water. Notwithstanding this miserable picture in the West, bad accounts from the East, and a still more gloomy prospect at home, the Stocks are getting up, on account of a general Report that has got abroad of a serious mediation in Your quarter from Russia & Holland for Peace, on the terms of American Independence.

It was in every ones mouth last week that the Cabinet had determind to withdraw the Army from N. York & Rhode Island, & send them to the Wt. Indies. It is now said the Army from R. Island *only* is to be sent. A Frigate was dispatchd a day or two ago to that quarter, not improbably (I think) with an order for its evacuation. It has been long the language of Ministerialists that this post was of no consequence, & that 3000 men have been kept there doing nothing for this two or three years.

Our homeward fleet seems to be snugg in harbour for at least some weeks, if not the winter. That under Adml. Ross may be soon heard of on the Coasts of France, or probably in Ireland, to conduct safe home the Eight India Men & a rich Manilla Ship carryd into Ireland. It consists of 3 of the Line, 3 fiftys, and Eight frigates. Paul Jones has given much alarm to the Coasts of that Country, but as yet has done no mischeif; *here* he is lookd upon as already taken by Ross's Squadron.[8]

          I am Yr. very obedt. & obligd Sert.
          V. J. Drouillard

  I expect this will be put safe into a foreign Post Office by a young Gentleman who having finishd His Education here is pushing to his native home via Holland & St. Eustatia. He bears a paper parcel (from a friend in Mincing Lane[9]) for you & which He will contrive to forward by some private hand from Amsterdam to Paris, in case he finds none, it will be left with Messrs. Grand & Co. of Amsterdam to be forwarded to You.

Since writing the Inclosd, I have got a letter from Mr. W[re]n which informs me that the Cartel Ship has been at Portso. above a fortnight & that there has been no step taken towards her resailing with a Cargoe of Prisoners. The Captn. of this vessel says there are *no more* American-capturd Prisoners in France in or near the Ports of the Ocean, but that there are several in St. Maloes Havre, & Dunkirk. The Agent at Nantes says there are no more in any Ports of France, but that there are considerable numbers at Bilboa St. Andero [Santander] and Corunna, but there Exchange would require a Spanish passport.

If your multiplicity of business will allow You to look towards procuring such a pass-port I wish most cordially Sir You would do it; for I am certain it would have a most happy effect: You can scarcely immagine the distress another winters confinement may bring on these unhappy people, for our subscription is very nearly expended, & in the present state of things it is hardly to be expected we can get more money by opening the subscription. The money raisd, never extended, & consequently could not be applyd, to any but those in actual confinement; The consequence of this is, that any American sailors in distress, hiding from the press gangs, or who have found means to liberate themselves, generally fly to me, and drain me exceedingly of Cash: I should not think this a hardship, could I possibly get money from home or borrow it here on easy terms. I have spent larger sums on these & other purposes than may be strictly prudent, and the fear of being still further distressd by them, & to try to get them releasd by Cartel, is my principal motive for now troubling You. There shall be nothing wanted on this side to expedite the Exchange or to help them.

HSP: Franklin Papers, 5:93.

[1] The letter has not been found.
[2] Franklin's letter to Digges about Capt. Conyngham is dated Aug. 20, 1779 (see Digges to Franklin, Sept. 4, 1779, n. 1).

³ David Hartley.

⁴ Probably the Rev. Robert Heath, a Presbyterian minister in Plymouth who visited the American prisoners of war to distribute allowances in Franklin's behalf and otherwise to contribute to their material comforts.

⁵ See Digges to Franklin, Sept. 4 and 6, 1779.

⁶ Messrs. Horneca, Grand & Co.

⁷ Probably the weakened position of Byron's fleet following the loss of St. Vincent (see Digges to Franklin, Aug. 10, 1779).

⁸ John Lockhart Ross (1721–1790), rear admiral since Mar. and throughout the summer fourth in command in the Channel, had on Sept. 18 been sent to look for John Paul Jones in the North Sea; but on Sept. 25, two days after the celebrated encounter between the *Bonhomme Richard* and the *Serapis* off Flamborough Head, Jones and his convoy eluded his pursuers by sailing for the coast of Holland, the one direction the British had not expected him to go.

⁹ Benjamin Vaughan, son of a West Indies planter and merchant, had settled in Mincing Lane, London. A friend and supporter of Shelburne, occasionally employed as his private secretary, he sympathized with the American revolutionaries, as he later also did with the Irish and French, and was on good terms with Franklin, the first collected edition of whose works he edited in 1779: *Political, Miscellaneous, and Philosophical Pieces* (London: J. Johnson, 1779). The bearer was Gabriel Manigault (1758–1809), a South Carolinian who had since 1775 been studying abroad, first in Geneva and then in London, where he had entered Lincoln's Inn to read law. Early in 1780 he would return home and, though suspected of being a loyalist, later be elected to the state House of Representatives and chosen as a delegate to the convention assembled to ratify the American Constitution.

To Benjamin Franklin

London Octor. 8. 1779

DEAR SIR

The Bearer of this Letter, Mr. Peter Robert Luard is calld to Paris on Business of great importance to Himself in consequence of the late capture of Grenada,¹ as well as on some private matters of His own; in which Your advice and assistance will be essentially servicable: Altho Mr. Luard is not intimately known to Me, I am not a stranger to His worth; and cannot but comply with the request of some worthy and deserving Freinds to be the means of procuring Him an introduction to You. I wish you, my Good Sir, to extend Your usual civility and attention towards Him; and to beleive me on all occasions, to be, with the highest regard

       Your very obliged and Obedient Servant.
       Tho. Digges

HSP: Franklin Papers, 5 : 95.

[1] Peter Robert Luard (1727–1802) had married the daughter of a wealthy West Indian proprietor with estates in Grenada and St. Kitts, as well as in county Lincoln, Eng.

To Benjamin Franklin

       [London], 8th Octor. 1779

DEAR SIR
 I have taken the liberty to give the bearer hereof, Mr. Luard, an introductory line to You; and to get him to bear a few of the latest news Papers, as well as a packet from Mr. V[augha]n which I expect to deliver Him with this letter: He is among the capital sufferers at Grenada & goes to Paris to secure if possible his property on that Island.

 Mr. Sterry having taken the route of Amsterdam & not yet returnd, I have not got the Answer to my last letter on the subject for which He went to Paris, but by a letter from Him to the party concernd here (Mr. Smith) I have some reason to beleive it will do & Mr. S. is preparing a large Cargoe of Woolens & Linins for our friends; among his articles there will be 1600 £s worth of Blankets & a great quantity of the right colourd Cloathing—He is to push for head quarters. Altho I am totally unconnected with this or any similar adventures, I cannot help wishing they were more frequent, for by such means I am certain our friends can be very much releivd, & the unfair monopolys now practising in America may be very much broken.[1]

 I have done every thing in my power for Capt. C[onyngha]me & he is very grateful to You. He has been cloathd (for he went in nearly naked to Prison) & takes a regular small supply of money from a friend of mine near Him, He drawing on me for the amount and for which I shall have my riembursement in the bill forwarded to Monr. G. £50 dated Sept. 24 & payment at ten days sight which by a line to Mr. G. by post I desird might be presented to you. There is also in the prison with him & who deserves some little help for His services, *James Adams* Master of the Providence sloop of war in the service of the States of America & who was taken some months ago & put equally naked into Prison, & probably for a like reason to that of C———m— because He behavd well.[2] You will see in one of the papers sent you, the St. Jas. Chronicle, the Letter from the Secretary of Congress to Sr. Geo. Collier about Capn. C———m, together with Colliers impertinent answer.[3] There are also in another paper some resolves of Congress relative to the recall of Mr. Izard and Mr. W. Lee. We are so far behind hand here in American news papers or intelligence, & there are things in them so deserving of publication here that I am led to ask You for any of the Papers since May, which You may have thrown by; & which Mr. Luard will take the trouble of bringing on his return a few weeks hence.

Captn. H[utchi]ns has now got over all fears as to punishment that can effect his life, there being not a tittle of *proof* against him. He might get out by insisting on bail being taken for him, claiming the habeas corpus &ca. but we are unwilling to give the least offence *for the present*, hoping by his remaining quiet a little longer, that a promise made him of being allowd to sell his commission will be complyd with, & which will make 1500 Guins. difference to Him. He will not be many days in England after he gets out of Prison.

Mr. D. H[artle]y has done the necessary as to laying the Receipt taken for the 190 men capturd at Sea by the Miflin before the board of Sick & hurt; no answer could be given to it there, & it will be before the Admiralty & perhaps the ministry before it will be granted. The Cartel is now waiting for your answer and the proper passport for going to some other port with the next Cargoe.[4] I did expect before this to get a letter from Mr. H———y to forward to You, which is meant to contain a copy of one to You dated the 29 June, which I forwarded & we have some reason to think by your late letters has never got to hand—It related to the finishing a certain business with the Minister which I communicated with you upon. As I am obligd to keep my papers distant from myself, I cannot at present tell how or by whom that letter was sent.

I begin to get fearful the cartell will stop, & God knows what latitude of sufferings our prisoners may experience in another winters imprisonment, as the money is very near expended & no hopes of raising more. There seems a strange detention of the Ship in every voyage; and Mr. H——y being in the Country & not sticking close to the agents here, I fear helps on this detention. There is not above 135 in Forton and 190 at Plyo. & we are endeavouring that the ship may instead of the exact *one hundred* be orderd to take the whole from each prison when she sails next; which will make a difference of two voyages. On the return of the Ship to Port last voyage, it was universally given out that there were no more prisoners in France American-Captured, but this cannot well be an argument now, for Mr. Paul Jones has, in the two Men of War got 350 seamen besides the Crews of thirty odd vessels which He took & destroyd on his late cruise. Above twenty ships of war was dispatchd after Him; but after throwing the northern parts of England into full as much panick as the combined Fleets did the western, He has apparently got away with much booty & no little credit to himself.[5]

Whenever You want any thing done here I hope you will make no ceremony in commanding me. I find my letters from Nantes, Spain, & Holland, come regularly safe to me under the common direction & without cover thus *Mr. Wm. Singleton Church Nandos Coffee House London.* Yours need not be dated from any place but simply the day of the month, and without signature.

There has been much dispondance since the arrival of Genl. Vaughan[6] & the publication of the last Gazettes. People here begin to fear the Americans have alterd their mode of defensive war into an offensive one. The Genl. like all other returning officers from that quarter comes home discontentd, and keeps his mouth shut; when He ventures to open it, He does not speak very favourably of the British prospects in America. I find that there will be a push made to get to Chas. Town this winter; the burning of that Town & distressing the Colony more, are matters of great object, and there will be a detatchment from N. York to effect this purpose, and most probably such a force sent as will insure it. Twelve thousand Hessians are confidently talkd of for the American service in the Spring, but this Country seems to forget that She has lost the bridge over which these troops must be sent. The conversation about Invasion is again revivd, & this together with the gloomy appearances from the W. Indies & the improbability of doing any thing in America causes a universal depression & a more than usual abuse of our wise Rulers.

I wish you health & success and am with great truth & sincerity
Yr. obligd & obt. Servt.
T. D.

[Addressed:] His Excelly. Docr. Franklin

HSP: Franklin Papers, 5:94.

[1] See Digges to Franklin, Sept. 6, 1779.

[2] James Adams of Boston, taken when the British recaptured a prize of the sloop *Providence*, had been committed to Mill Prison on May 10, 1779, perhaps earlier, and suffered months of hardships before managing to escape on June 15, 1781.

[3] On July 17, 1779, the Congress had directed the secretary "to inform you [Sir George Collier (1735–1795), commander in chief] that they have received evidence that Gustavus Conyngham a citizen of America, late commander of an armed vessel in the Service of said states, and taken on board a private armed cutter, has been treated in a manner contrary to the dictates of humanity and the practice of Christian civilized nations. I am ordered in the name of Congress to demand that good and sufficient reasons be given for this conduct or that the said Gustavus Conyngham be immediately released from his present rigorous and ignominious confinement." If a satisfactory reply was not received by Aug. 1 the Marine Committee would confine "in safe and close custody such, and so many persons as they may think proper in order to abide the fate of the said Gustavus Conyngham."

On July 24 Collier's secretary had replied: ". . . I have it in command from the Commodore to say, that, not holding himself accountable for his conduct to any of his Majesty's subjects in this country [America], he is still less inclined to answer demands when they are made in the uncivil way they appear to him in your letter of the 17th instant. He however is pleased to bid me inform you, that no prisoners are ever treated (to his knowledge) by the King's Officers contrary to the dictates of humanity; and as it is the practice of civilized nations to punish criminals in the usual course of justice, Gustavus Conyngham, whom you enquire after, stands in this predicament, and is therefore sent to England to receive that punishment from his injured country, which his crimes shall be found to deserve."

First printed in Rivington's *New-York Royal Gazette*, July 28, 1779, it was reprinted Aug. 4 in the *Pennsylvania Gazette* before appearing in the London press (see Robert

Wilden Neeser, *Letters and Papers Relating to the Cruises of Gustavus Conyngham, A Captain of the Continental Navy, 1777–1779* [New York: Naval History Society, 1915], pp. 180–83). On Nov. 3 Conyngham managed to escape with thirty-two others and to meet Digges in London.

[4] The question, mentioned by Digges in the letter to Franklin of May 21, 1779, was whether Franklin could persuade the French to let the cartel use Morlaix instead of Nantes as the port of exchange.

[5] Digges had alluded to Jones's success in his letter to Franklin, Sept. 20, 1779.

[6] Maj. Gen. John Vaughan (ca. 1731–1795), second in command to Clinton in the expedition up the Hudson to relieve Burgoyne in 1777, Burgoyne's successor as governor of Fort William (in western Virginia), 1779–1780, and in command at the Leeward Islands, 1779–1782.

To Benjamin Franklin

Octo. 12. 79

DEAR SIR

I wrote you by the same conveyance with this on the 8th Int., and the detention the bearer has met with gives me an oppertunity to forward a few more news papers; as well as to inform you that I have got things in such a way with Capn. C[onyngha]m as to render his situation much more comfortable and easy to himself. I wish I had it in my power to say as much for His 193 Companions, who are become more than usually uneasy at their scanty allowance (which from having a more griping Agent[1] than that at Portso.) has been rather hard on them lately. The detention of the Cartel too makes them despond, and I fear it is but too true if Capn. C——m had not been among them several would have been prevaild upon to Enter on board the ships of their Enemy. Leiut. Wm. Picket[2] & Adams whom I lately mentiond to you as deserving some little aid, drew up a petition in the name of the whole, to You, & sent it me for forwardance. It is meerly a prayer for some little pecuniary aid, & it is not necessary to forward it. Adams & Picket were both taken in men of war belonging to the United States.

Your friend Mr. B[ridgen] was with me since I wrote You last. He wishes You much good &ca. &ca. & is looking out for an answer to His

Letter wherein He mentions a proposition to You about some blank Copper Meddals.³

I have also a strong solicitation from our friend D[avid] H[artley] to describe to You the situation of a man whom He has, in a letter to You lately, solicited Your aid to get releasd a man whom He is interested in the welfare of.—Mr. John Stephenson a Younger Brother of the Trinity House at Hull, a Freeman of Hull, and Master of the Brig Sally; He was taken on the 1st July 1779 by a luggar riggd Privateer of Bretagne named the Hawke Capn. Heden Le Polly of six one pounders, Eight Swivels & 38 Men, & He was carryd into Brest, and now confined at Velse in Bretagne. It will answer a very good purpose to our friend if You can help towards the getting this man releasd.⁴

There is no news yet from America. Adml. Byron is arrivd in a single Ship & *report* says that D'Estaign has left his Station for St. Domingo from whence He is to go to America—much fears about Jamaica & Adml. Byron is quite close mouthd about the disagreeable state of affairs in the West Indies.

The Quebec Frigate 32 Guns Capt. Fermor⁵ is blown up & only 17 Men of the Crew savd. It happend in an Engagement with a french frigate in the Channel.

I am with the highest esteem Dr. Sir
Yr. obligd & Ob. Ser.
T. D.

[Addressed:] A Monsieur / Monsieur B. Franklin / Passy

HSP: Franklin Papers, 5:96.

¹ The keeper and agent at Mill Prison was William Cowdry.
² Pickett, taken on the brig *Fancy* of Newburyport, Aug. 7, 1777, was from Marblehead, Mass.
³ Edward Bridgen, first mentioned by Digges in his letter to Franklin, Apr. 9, 1779, had on Sept. 17 sent Franklin two samples of copper to try to interest Franklin in ordering a supply for the Americans to strike coins and medals. Franklin's reply of Oct. 2, 1779, had apparently not yet arrived.
⁴ See Digges to Franklin, Sept. 6, 1779. Hull was Hartley's constituency.
⁵ In the engagement of Oct. 6, about fifteen leagues to the southwest of Ushant, Capt. George Farmer had refused to abandon his ship and crew until the very last when, se-

verely wounded, he had thrown himself into the sea, where, weakened by loss of blood, he could not stay afloat long enough to be rescued.

To Benjamin Franklin

Forwarding a letter from David Hartley to Franklin, October 26, 1779, concerning the use of Morlaix for the cartel and the plight of Captain Stephenson, Digges appended this note.

[October 26, 1779]

P.S. According to Your request I send You the particulars of Capn. C[onyngha]ms situation.[1] He was taken by an Engs. Frigate near Bermudas in May, kept in Irons on board Her, for some weeks at Sea & in the port of N. York, then put on board the Grantham Packet & brought in Her *all the way Irond* to Falmo. about the 9 July removd from this Packet to Pendennis Castle where He was kept in Irons & deprivd any open converse but with the Goaler. As soon as this was known here, a friend of Yours informd the Board of Sick & hurt of His Situation & bad treatment, & petitiond for His removal to Mill Prison there to wait the common fate of His Countrymen. The petition was granted & a Sloop of War carryd Him to Plymo. where His Irons were taken off, and where he still is in the same situation with others. As He was exceedingly nay shamefully, bare of Cloaths during His voyage to & from N. York, as soon as things could be got into Prison to Him he was comfortably clad, & in this respect, as well as small supplys of a few Guineas at a time to procure him tolerable food (for the Prison allowance is very scanty) He is now tolerably well off & has a communication with his friends; He being allowd to talk to them at the Grate of the Prison. He was harshly treated on board the Man of War & the packet, & very ill used while at N. York; but as his situation is now much better & rather more comfortable, I think it is but right it should be made known in America; In order that the three

[26 October 1779]

officers confind in the Goal of Philaa. *'to abide His fate'*[2] may also meet with better treatment from their keepers. There is no knowing to what lengths of mischief acts of retaliation may be carryd—there seems a disposition at present in this Country, to treat Prisoners better than heretofore; and I am given to beleive there will be no unfair proceeding against any individual taken in War and brought *here*, that will authorise retaliation in America.—

APS: Franklin Papers, 45 : 71 ½

[1] Digges had furnished some of this information on Sept. 20, 1779.
[2] The quotation closely approximates the words used in the Congress's statement to Sir George Collier (see Digges to Franklin, Oct. 8, 1779, n. 3).

To Benjamin Franklin

Octor. 30. 1779

DEAR SIR

Since I wrote You by Mr. Luard the 8 & 12th Int. (and in these letters took the liberty to introduce Mr. Luard to You) I gave You a line by common post the 20th past,[1] giving an account that an American Privateer calld the Gen. Glover was taken by the frigate which brought over Adml. Byron from Antigua about the 20th Sept.; This vessel soon after her sailing from No. Carolina fell in with D'Estaigns fleet & was with the fleet the 13. 14. & 15 Sept. off the Coasts of No. Carolina, 24 Ships of the line frigates &c.—they had a fair wind, & were steering No.Ward. Byron is much blamd for not sending this prize Express to New York with advices that D'Estaign was on the Coast & steering No.Ward. It seems that his appearance there will be a great surprize to Clintons Army. The latest accounts from that quarter is the 17th Sept. There were then 4,000 Men ready for an Expedition So.ward. The intelligent here say that 2,000 of them were going to Quebec, and one to garrison Pensacola against the Spaniards. Notwithstanding D'Estaigns move of situation we are much in fear for Jamaica. Two Regiments of the new raisd Corps will be sent there on board the fleet which sails about the 12 or 15 next month. Rodney[2] with 4 or 5 Ships of the line & about 30 Merchantmen will compose this fleet, & the troops are to be put on board the common merchant Ships.

Mr. S[terr]y who was lately with you was detaind sometime on his way & only arrivd last week. He will go in a few days with a large Cargoe.

By this conveyance there will be forwarded some duplicates of letters from our friend D. H. which He supposes have not got regularly to hand, at least those which are the most material & which relate to the Exchange of Prisoners[3]—The crew of the Gen. Glover Privateer has added 60 to the numbers in Forton which make them 206 there and 193 at Plymo. As yet there is no appearance of the Cartel moving, & the Agents say she is only stopt for want of the French Passport—Mr. H. and myself are in dayly hopes it will soon arrive; I am very much plagued with their solicitations, & in keeping them quiet. I believe had it not been for Capt. C[onyngha]m, many of those in Mill prison would have enterd into the service of the navy here, to which they have had strong temptation from want & the large bountys offerd them.

I have forwarded & got supplyd to Capt. C——m thirty odd pounds. I wrote you before[4] that I had drawn on G[ran]d for fifty Pounds the 27th last month for the purpose of help to Capt. C——m. —G——d (altho I wrote him to present the bill to You) writes to the person who negotiated it here, that it was not paid or presented for want of advice; and I am yet uninformed whether it is paid or not & consequently without the money. I remitted a second to the same bill about a fortnight ago, and wrote him as I had before done that my bills on You, were by *Your order*; and desird they might be presented to You before any Answer might be given as to protest or acceptance &ca.—this I thought was advice enough, but he does not seem to think so.

I now inclose You two American Loan Office Bills, the property of a man who is in want in Mill prison. One is for 80 the other 36 Dollars making in the whole four hundred & Eighty Livres. If they are good, be pleasd to mention so to me in a common letter directed

Mr. Wm. Singleton Church Nandos Coffee House; and Mr. Luard will bear the amount of them to me provided He has not left Paris—or I dare say Mr. W[a]lp[ol]e will take the trouble of it when He may return.[5] By any such oppertunity I should be glad of a name to direct to you under cover to Monr. G———d, which may be safer than Your own—there are many little trifling occurrances here that may be useful to You to know, & which I can communicate safely by that means, but when sent immidiately to *You* they will be stopt in the Post office where letters *lately* have undergone a stricter scrutiny than heretofore.

I should be very thankful for a line by common post as soon as this gets to hand, to know whether the poor Prisoners bills herewith inclosd are good or not. Your letter may be directed A Monr. Monr. Wm. Singleton Church, Nandos Coffee House.

I find by Yours of the 7th (receivd since I sat down to write this letter) that some of my letters have miscarryd; for I think I have in two or three mentiond the particular situation and present treatment of Capt. C———m.[6]—He was taken in May by an English Frigate, sent to & kept in Irons on board the said frigate at N. York till put on board the Grantham Packet which arrivd at Falmo. the 8th July in a passage of only 17 days.—He was sent directly (*Irond*) to Pendennis Castle & denied pen & Ink or to speak to any one but the Goaler. As a Mr. Milligan from Maryld. was a passenger in the packet, I very soon heard of Capt. C——— situation, & wrote four or five times to a freind of mine in Falmo. to give him every necessary help, but this could not be done there, as no one was allowd to speak to him; & my friend being fearful to trust the Goaler, & not on the spot while he was removing, He was put on board a Sloop of war much in want of Cloaths & refreshment. As soon as I was certain of His confinement & situation, I got a friend to solicit the Board of Sick & hurt to have his Irons taken of[f] & get him removd to Mill Prison; the request was granted, tho in such a manner as left me at a loss to know if he was gone [on] a cruise in the Ship from falmouth, or impressd as a Seamen; however he got a letter from me the 20th of Augt. since which He has been as comfortably situated as his place of confinement will admit, & I have had many letters full of thanks from him, & the last very expressive of gratitude to You for Your offer of assistance, which has been got to him by little & little to above thirty pounds, & for which you shall hereafter have his receipts. As it has been principally laid out by a friend of mine in Plymo. in purchasing Him Cloaths (of which He was *extreemly* bare) and other comforts, I have not yet receivd the accounts, & indeed shall not until I hear his wants have been amply satisfyd. He deserves this & much more from me, & I most cordially wish I had it more in my power to comply with the frequent solicitations I have from that and another quarter. I have spent so much that I really *must* stop; This is the case with some others here, and as our Subscription is in the last fifty, God knows what will become of these poor fellows when it is gone & if the Cartel should be stopt. The last five receipts and your intimation are before the Board of Sick & hurt, & we are hopeing dayly for an Answer. I wish the Texel scheme may be accepted, but altho humanity to the suffering Prisoners there may point it out, I have little Expectation it will; because the pride of these Gentry may prevent it.[7]

I gave your message to Mr. R[as]pe & He was extreemly thankful.[8] I did not observe by his manner that he meant soon to take a journey. By his recommendation a Mr. D. Williams sent me two books of His Lectures, which He requested might be forwarded to You.[9] They are gone by a like conveyance to the two paper parcels I lately forwarded to Mr. Grand at Amsterdam (who acknowleges the Receipt of them to me) I mean those from Mr. V[augha]n. When You get them, it will be a satisfaction to Mr. V—— to hear they are got safe,[10] & I shall be glad to hear of the safe arrival of the books.

I find by a letter from Mr. I[zar]d He is now at Amsterdam ready to embark for America I suppose in consequence of some late resolves. I am sorry for the motive or purposes for which He is going to America; that Country has enough to do without entering into further & fatal broils—Some folks seem to like living in hot water.[11]

His friend J. T[empl]e is still here; I see him now & then, but can make nothing out as to what he is about. I beleive he brought over something like a whisper, and is now seemingly much displeasd at the manner it has been treated. Our friend D. H. says he is perfectly honest and right, but in these times of peril & false appearances I keep a distance & live but among a few; one of these is honest little B[rid]g[e]n who is in some expectation of hearing from You I beleive on the subject of some copper meddals. I wish you all success & happiness & am with the highest esteem

Yr. very obligd & Ob. Sert.
Alexr. Hammilton

[Addressed:] A Monsieur Monsieur B. Franklin/ Passy

HSP: Franklin Papers, 5:99.

[1] The letter has not been found. Inasmuch as Franklin never acknowledged it, it appears not to have reached him.

[2] Adm. Lord George Brydges Rodney (1719–1792), who had distinguished himself as a naval officer before the outbreak of the American Revolution, then fallen into debt and gone to Paris to escape his creditors, had only in 1778 returned to service in Britain, having been called back to duty and made an admiral with subsequent command of the waters of the West Indies.

[3] David Hartley's covering note of Oct. 26, 1779, and texts of letters dated Sept. 1 and 18 and Oct. 11, 1779, are copied in Digges's hand and concluded by Digges's own statement: "There is another application for the release of Capn. Alexr. Currie late Commander of the Merchant Ship the Henry. He was taken the 31st Octor. 1778 by the Vengeanc[e] Man of War & carried into Brest removd from thence to Samur [Saumur] and Ploermet [Ploërmel] but is now at Tours—He was Captain of a ship belonging to Mr. Saml. Hartley. Copy of what was forwarded by Post 29h Octo."

Whether what was forwarded on Oct. 29 was a set of Hartley's copies or simply the paragraph about Capt. Currie is not certain. The first application for Currie's release was enclosed by Digges in his letter to Franklin of Sept. 6, 1779.

[4] Oct. 8, 1779.

[5] Thomas Walpole, a member of Parliament and associated with Franklin in the Vandalia land scheme, had financial problems that required him to spend time in France trying to recover money owed him.

[6] Franklin's letter of Oct. 7, commenting mainly on the plight of William Peters and the case of Capt. Hutchins, was silent about Conyngham (LC: Franklin Papers, Series 1, 2:271).

[7] When, after the battle between the *Bonhomme Richard* and the *Serapis*, John Paul Jones sailed with his prisoners into the Texel, the Dutch island roadstead in the North Sea, he was, though flying the American flag, under French orders, accompanied by a squadron mainly French, and expected to convoy naval supplies to France. At the same time he hoped to repair and replenish his ships, exchange his British prisoners for Americans, and operate as he would have in an allied port. But the Dutch were neutrals; the British insisted that Jones be treated as an outlawed pirate because in their view Americans were mere rebellious provincials, entitled to no belligerent rights; and the French, wanting to keep the Dutch out of the war because of the dangers of British retaliation, tried vainly to persuade Jones to accept a French commission as a way of

regularizing relations. Eventually Jones agreed to give custody of the prisoners over to the duc de La Vauguyon (Paul-François de Quélen de Stuer de Caussade, 1746–1828), the French ambassador at The Hague, who promised Franklin he would effect the exchange, something he failed to do. The immediate question addressed by Digges was whether the British would agree to the prisoner exchange.

[8] In answer to letters from Raspe that Digges had forwarded on Aug. 13 and Sept. 6, 1779, Franklin had written Digges on Oct. 7: "please to Let Mr. Raspe know, that if he comes here he will be welcome to live with me the two Months he mentions, and that I shall be glad of his Company" (LC: Franklin Papers, Series 1, 2:271).

[9] David Williams (1738–1816), creator of the Royal Literary Fund, proponent of Rational Religion, founder of a Rationalist church in London, and author of essays and lectures on religious and political subjects, had to rescue himself from the financial ruin threatened by his church's need by getting subscribers for his two-volume *Lectures on the Universal Principles and Duties of Religion and Morality* (London, 1779), a collection of lectures he had given at his church during 1776–1777, the first year of its existence.

[10] Digges first alluded to Benjamin Vaughan as "a friend in Mincing Lane" in the postscript of his letter to Franklin, Sept. 20, 1779.

[11] Because of his controversy with Franklin, Ralph Izard had been recalled, eventually to be vindicated by the Congress.

[12] John Temple (ca. 1735–1800), a Bostonian, must have appeared to be a person of undefined loyalties. He had in 1760 been surveyor general of customs in North America and by 1767 been commissioned to collect colonial duties more effectively. After marrying the daughter of a Massachusetts patriot (James Bowdoin) he had returned to England, become surveyor general of customs there in 1772, and six years later accompanied the Carlisle commission to America to help achieve reconciliation or reunion. In America he had then declared himself an American supporter, apparently aware only then that independence was necessary, and returned to England by way of Holland in July 1779, carrying letters of introduction from various American rebels. At the same time he managed to retain sufficient standing among the British to become, in 1785, British consul general to the American states.

To Benjamin Franklin

Novr. 9. 1779

The person whom You lately wrote to me to supply with necessarys for releiving his distresses in confinement, was servd as well as He could be by Agents on the spot & much to his satisfaction & wish. He got away with others of his Company (among them the owner of two bills for 60 and 36 Ds. lately forwarded to you for acceptance by a private hand) on Wedy. last, and is to all appearance clear. It is more than probable he will be with you in a day or two after this reaches

You.¹ As yet I hear nothing of the 50£ bill, which is rather a disapointment as frequent calls leaves me very poor. I cannot for some days render you any account. I know as yet but of thirty guins. being paid. This was the last sum & the other small advances I have no regular account of. By appearances and manner, I think the Gentleman may be soon in a way to riemburse his freinds and do the good he seems most to wish.

I am Yr. very obt. Sert.
Alexr. Hammilton

R[o]tt[e]r[da]m & Dun[kir]ke²
No arrivals from the Wt.ward.

HSP: Franklin Papers, 5: 102.

¹On Nov. 18 Conyngham wrote Franklin from Amsterdam: "I came by the way of London, it being the safest. At London we meet with our good friend Mr. Digges, who did everything in his power to serve me and all his countrymen that chance to fall in his way. Happy we to have such a man among that set of tyrants they have in that country" (Edward E. Hale and Edward E. Hale, Jr., *Franklin in France* [Boston: Roberts Bros., 1887], 1:347). Conyngham's companion who owned the two bills is identified in Digges's letter to Franklin, Nov. 15, as John Calif (properly spelled Calef), who was in command of the Newburyport schooner *Hawk*, a privateer, when he was taken on Feb. 24, to be committed to Mill Prison on May 10.

²Apparently a notation about Conyngham's destination, explained in Digges's next letter to Franklin, Nov. 10.

To Benjamin Franklin

Novr. 10 1779

DEAR SIR

I am in hopes this will be either handed You or put into some foreign post by Capt. C[onyngha]m, who not liking his late lodgings, left them with three others & came to me a day or two ago. I have done every thing in my power for him both at the former place & here, & He will be off this nights tide to R[otterda]m in a Dutch vessel. His plan is to push for D[u]n[kir]k & there wait Your orders or recommendation; This, as well as the state of his finances (reducd much lower by the aiding three others) will be best explaind in a letter which He is to write You immidiately on landing. One of his Companions is the owner and indorser of two C[ontinenta]l Bills Exchange for sixty & 36 Ds. I lately inclosd You for acceptance. In the present state of his fears & my hurry in getting them passages, Capt. C—— has not explaind to me the exact sum he has been supplyd with by my friend at P[lymout]h.[1] Some trifling sums of money have been paid into Him, Cloaths made & furnishd him &ca. &ca. for which I have yet no account as his departure was as sudden as unexpected by me. My friend writes me by this post that thirty Guins. has been added to the former sums—but what these sums are as I said before I know not but you shall be informd in time.—Poor fellow has been obligd to spend more on account of three others attaching themselves much to him & looking up to him as a saviour or deliverer—Those He left behind would be most happy to embark with him in any adventure & he holds a future eye to them.

We are at length informd that the Cartel Ship will be soon on float again the new passport for Morlaix having arrivd. I hope to God they will clear both prisons in a trip from each, & not make more for some time. I cannot describe to You the trouble I have with these people; and the expence is so heavy on me at times that even with my curtaild and oeconimic mode of living I am put to extreem difficulties. It is not trifles that will do for men who come naked by dozens & half dozens, & it is harder still to turn ones back upon them.

I gave You a few lines under this date meerly to inform you in the gross what is mentiond above of Capt. C——. I do not know how my letters fare which are put under cover to Monr. G[rand] and just marked as for You. We have *yet* no answer from him whether the bill for 50£ 24th Sept. is paid or not; Some days after it was forwarded He wrote to the negotiator here that he had no advice of it; altho before I drew it (as I had done with the former one for 100£) I desird him to present it to You for advice what to do, it being a risque here to me to explain why I drew it. Thus it stands now & it may be unsafe for me to explain it.

Capn. H[utchins] has not yet decidedly done any thing with his Enemys, nor has he yet got a promise to sell. He is using every prudent step to do so & to obtain Mr. W[harto]ns papers which are yet kept back tho his own are all restord. It is feard most Letters via Amsterdam or Ostend are opend before they go hence but there is no appearance of it to those from these places. No news from America yet the fears for Jamaica have a little blown over or rather been transmitted to N. York & for the Army & fleet there. D'Estaign being in that quarter gives much uneasiness here, & the wise ones who govern are caballing full as much themselves as about 12 Months ago they wishd to make the people believe was the case in Congress. I wish you every success & happiness & am very truly & sincerely Yrs.

V. J. D[rouillar]d

Since I wrote the above, I have understood from a very worthy Irish Merchant in the City that a Mr. Johnston formerly bred to the Sea & from the No. of Ireland is now with You on a certain matter of business relative to His going out with other friends to settle in America.[2]—I think Johnsons scheme & jaunt was hastily taken up & likely to turn out unsuccessful to Him. He is so well recommended to me (& I believe known to the bearer of this letter) that I cannot help mentioning him as worthy some attention.

HSP: Franklin Papers, 5:103.

[1] The Rev. Robert Heath.
[2] This is one William Johnston who took the oath of allegiance to the United States on Nov. 15, 1779, in Passy and ten days later received from Franklin for his signature a bond to the president of the Congress of the United States pledging the safe delivery in the United States of the cargo of the brigantine *Harrier* of London.

To Benjamin Franklin

London 15 Novr. 1779

Dear Sir

The Bearer of this Letter, Mr. Fabroni, has obligingly given Me an oppertunity to send the inclosd to You.—He is a young Gentleman of distinguishd worth from Italy, and has been some time travelling with His ingenious Friend & Companion Mr. Fontana. They mean to spend a few days at Paris on their return home, and as they stand distinguishd in the learned world, and have very liberal political opinions, I should be happy in bringing them acquainted with You— Their merit will be their best recommendation—I thus introduce them to Your usual civility and attention and am with the highest esteem

Dr. Sir
Your very Obligd and Obedt: Servant
T. Digges

[Addressed:] His Excellency/ Benjamin Franklin Esq.

UP: Franklin Papers, 3:31.

[Enclosure]

To Benjamin Franklin

Novr. 15. 1779

Dear Sir

I did myself the honor to write You by Mr. Hawkins of So. Carolina[1] the 1st Int., & inclosd two Loan Office Bills for 60 and 36 Ds. the property of Mr. Jno. Calif, in order to know if they were good,—Mr. H. was bound to Holland, & promisd to put the letter into the post Office there.[2] Since that, on the 11th Int.,[3] I had an oppertunity by Capt. C[onyngha]m & the afforesaid Mr. Calif to write You again; As they have to all appearance got safe to the other side, I make no doubt but the letter will get to you in due course. It was cheifly to explain how Capt. C——m and others got out of confinement. I understand 32 got away; but have yet no letter from my Revd. & good friend at Plymo.[4] as to what supplys he gave Capt. C——m, but this will come all in time.—I am led to beleive from Capt. C——s friendship in assisting others He has added more than I expected to the sum orderd to be advancd Him. I hope before *this* gets to Your hand all the affair will be explained to You by letter from Him, as He promisd to write & place himself at Your command or direction as to future opperation—for this purpose He will wait at D[u]n[kir]k till he gets your answer.

I have an oppertunity to forward this by two Tuscan Gentlemen who will pass thro Paris, and as men of literature & philosophic knowlege, have a strong desire to be made known to You. They travel at the Expence of the Grand Duke, & are under his patronage & Esteem; Their political sentiments & opinions seemd to be of the right sort, and as they have been known to some of Your good friends here, & have a strong desire to be known to You, I could not resist their solicitation for a common introduction. I some time ago got one of them, Signr. Fabroni, to bear a parcel from our friend Mr. V[augha]n; but his companion Signr. Fontana having been taken ill, their journey has been postpond for some days. I some time ago forwarded to Monr. Grand at Amsterdam another parcel from Mr. V———n, by Mr. Manigault of So. Caroa.,[5] which Monr. Grand acknowleges the Receipt of but I do not know that it ever reachd You—I hope it has, as Mr. V———n seems anxious about it, & wishes to know its fate.

I am very glad to find the Cartel is again on float, & that in consequence of the arrival of the fresh passport for the Vessel to go to Morlaix instead of Nantes, orders are gone down for the Vessel to take another Cargoe on board; I hope they will sweep the hundred & seventy odd at Plymo. and soon return for *near* the 200 that is at Portsmo.—The delays of Office are so great here that I fear another squad may be inducd to break Prison before they can be convincd that the Cartel will go on again—These breaking outs, are not only disagreeable, but at times highly distressing & dangerous to me and they seem to fly to me as one who was obligd whether it was convenient or not, to supply them.

We have two Ships from Halifax the 16 Octor. both with accounts from N. York to the 3d of Octor., but they differ so materially that one says there were no accounts receivd from N. York at Halifax about D'Estaigne on the 3d Octor.; The other says He was before N. York with a fleet of 22 sail of the line 10 frigates &ca.

15 NOVEMBER 1779

Rodney will sail in a very few days with 4 of the line, one 44, two frigates, & two 20 Gun Ships with a fleet of 40 or 50 Sail and about 2,500 Men. They go to Antia. [Antigua] and there join the We. India fleet (8 or 9 of which are unfit to act as Men of War at Sea & are coming home) and so proceed on towards Jamaica the fears for which are a little revivd lately. A few trading vessels for N. York will attend Rodneys fleet part of the way, & take a frigate or two to convoy them— They carry nothing like Soldiers or recruits, & I dare swear the Idea of sending more to that quarter is now given up. The town tho has been much amusd of late with the distress's of America. Her incapability of supporting her Independence, the surety of success in subjugating Her the next Campaign, & a variety of such stuf as they swallowd from Galloway[6] last Winter. This all comes from a little Irish Bishop who boasts an intimacy & confidence with you,[7] & that He had such accounts from Your own mouth—Those who know You laugh at him, but he has so far gulld the ministry into attention to his tale, that there have been several meetings where he was admitted to relate it to the junto particularly one or two at Lord Spencers.[8] If our *wise* rulers are led to go on by such tales as these, they will prove themselves greater fools than ever I immagind them.

The Indiamen not arriving yet from the Shannon is now attributed to there being a small french Squadron watching their motions. Our grand fleet of 37 sail of the line & one or two fiftys, has not yet got further Westward than Torbay, & will probably move from thence to the Et.ward when thing [they] have a certain account of the French fleet being out. The people here seem to be getting a little more out of their apathy & are much more generally abusive of Ministers and measures, & there is likely to be very warm work in the next sessions. The Irish business will cut out more serious work for them than people at present seem to be aware of—These *rights of mankind* are sad things to be discussd even by people ruled by *omnipotent* Parliament. Ireland declares she *will* have a free trade, & be no longer imposd on by temporary expedients. If this free trade is not given, they are likely very soon to take it; and if it is given the mobs of Manchester, Bristol, Liverpoole Leeds &ca. may very soon disturb the spechifyers in Parliament. The Irish seem to have caught the contagion of reasoning from America; and if the same incapable Councils continue to distract this kingdom, their reasoning will conclude (as Americas has concluded) in Independence—many here look upon this period as not very distant. The blundering Rulers of this Country seem to have made a most material slip when they drove America into the dangerous discussion of the ground of her duty to England, as well as to the reason & to the extent of Her obedience.—Once forcd to reason, She reasond herself into Resistance, & has now foresworn all allegiance; and this Oath of *forswearing* is of a nature less likely to be broken, than any possitive oath Lord Mansfield could frame for unconditional submission. Ireland seems to be following her footsteps and example exactly, only they seem to speak plainer, than America did until July 1775, for Independencey; for such the avowd authoritative claim of that Country must be allowd. If the powers of Government continue intrusted to the present incapable wicked set, His Majesty, whom the Irish now zealously stile their Sovereign, as America did in the begining of the quarrel, will find his Irish Title as effectually wiped out of his Escutcheon as his American Sovereignty is now.

 I forgot to tell You that the Little Irish Bishop has brought over with him, the Copys of the written accounts of the *State of things in America*, brought over by the Marquiss Fayatte, Genl. Conway and another.[9] These Statements were given says the Bishop from these officers to their several Patrons. He found means to get at them. They are filld with the disorders, calamities & distresses of America, & as such, have I dare say been read with great pleasure by the junto to whom He has divulgd all these *important* secrets. I am with very great esteem Dr. Sir

         Yr. very obligd & Ob. Serv.
         V. J. Drouillard

 Please to turn over.
 You will oblige me by telling Mr. W[harto]n, we have not yet been able to recover his papers from the Philistines. His Sick friend has got

well and is going on tolerably well in his affair at least He thinks so.[10] He receivd Mr. W——ns letter of the 26th Octor. & has nothing material to say. I am also thankful to him for two, the last of Octor. 31 coverd a point which I much wanted.—The same direction will do for any thing He has to say in common, & his books will be forwarded in a few days to O[sten]d, to the direction that the Sick Gentleman will give me.

[Addressed:] Dr. Franklin

HSP: Franklin Papers, 5:105.

[1] John Hawkins, a friend of Henry Laurens's, had become a prominent London linen draper.
[2] This letter has not been found and probably never reached Franklin.
[3] He may be referring to his letter dated Nov. 10, yet it lacks the explanation he alludes to. No letter dated Nov. 11 has been found.
[4] Robert Heath.
[5] See Digges to Franklin, Sept. 20, 1779.
[6] Joseph Galloway.
[7] Although he did not become a bishop until 1795, Thomas Hussey (1746–1803) may be the Irish cleric referred to. Hussey had been born in Ireland, educated at the Irish College in Salamanca, and admitted as a member of the penitential monastery at La Trappe until ordered by the pope to enter the service of the king of Spain. Then, toward 1767, he had served as chaplain to the Spanish ambassador in London and rector of the Spanish church there and in the early summer of 1779 had become head of the Spanish intelligence service in England. In Aug. he had visited Paris and in Nov. developed high ministerial contacts in London by offering to go to Spain as a go-between who could help in detaching Spain from her French ally. The British government knew about Hussey's official role, but hoped he could be useful to them anyway.
[8] Lord Charles Spencer (1740–1820) had served on the admiralty board during 1768–1778, resigned from it in protest against Sandwich's handling of the Palliser-Keppel quarrel, and as compensation been appointed treasurer of the chamber. He was a fairly consistent supporter of the North ministry and a member of the Bedford junto.
[9] The accounts attributed to the marquis de Lafayette (1757–1834) and Gen. Thomas Conway (1733–1800?) had supposedly been brought back to France when the two men returned home from service in America. Lafayette had reached Paris in Feb. 1779. Conway may have arrived earlier. Born in Ireland but a resident of France since the age of six, Conway had served in the French army for thirty years and become a high-ranking officer before joining Washington's army in 1776 and then a year later been appointed a brigadier general by the Congress. Critical of Washington, ambitious for a separate command, and refused a promotion, he had resigned his commission in Apr.

1778, taken ship for France, and in July 1779 been named aide major general of the army in Flanders.

10. Samuel Wharton's "sick friend" is surely Capt. Thomas Hutchins.

To Benjamin Franklin

26th No. 79

DEAR SIR

I risque a letter in the common post in order to forward You the King's speech—I wish it had been couchd in terms more likely to produce the blessings of Peace.

His Majesty's speech &ca. Novr. 25 79: My Lords & Gentlemen[:] I meet You in Parliament at a time when we are calld upon by every principle of Duty, and every consideration of Interest to exert Our united efforts in the support & defence of Our Country, attackd by an unjust and unprovokd war, and contending with one of the most dangerous Confederacies that ever was formd against the Crown & People of *Great Britain.*

The Designs and attempts of Our Enemies to invade this Kingdom, have, by the blessing of Providence, been hitherto frustrated & disapointed. They still menace Us with great Armaments & Preparations; But We are, I trust, on our Part, well prepard to meet every attack, & repel every insult. I know the Character of my brave People: The Menaces of their Enemies, & the approach of Danger, have no other effects on their minds, but to animate their Courage, and to call forth that national spirit, which has so often checked, and defeated, the Projects of Ambition and Injustice, and enabled the *British* Fleets & Armies to protect their Own Country, to vindicate their own rights, and at the same time, to uphold & preserve, the Liberties of *Europe*, from the ruthless & encroaching Power of the House of *Bourbon.*

In the midst of my care & solicitude for the safety & welfare of this Country, I have not been innatentive to the State of my Loyal and Faithful Kingdom of *Ireland.* I have in consequence of Your Address's, presented to me in the last session, orderd such papers to be collected and laid before You, as may assist Your Deliberations, on this important Business; and I recommend it to You to consider what further Benefits and advantages may be extended to that Kingdom, by such regulations, and such Methods, as may most effectually, promote the common strength, wealth, & Interests of all my Dominions.

Gentlemen of the House Commons[:] The proper Estimates shall, in due time, be laid before You. I see with extreem concern, that the necessary Establishments of my Naval & Military Forces, and the varoius services and Operations of the ensuing year, must innevitably be attended with great & heavy Expences; but I rely on Your Wisdom & publick Spirit for such supplies, as the circumstances & Exegencies of Our Affairs shall be found to require.

——My Lords & Gentlemen[:] I have great satisfaction in renewing the assurances of my intire approbation of the good Conduct and Discipline of the Militia, & of their steady Perseverance in their Duty; and I return my Cordial thanks to all ranks of my loyal Subjects who have stood forth in this arduous Conjuncture, & by their zeal, their Influence, & their personal service, have given confidence as well as strength to the national Defence. Trusting in the Divine Providence & in the justice of my Cause, I am firmly resolvd to prosecute the war with vigour, & to make every exertion, in order to compel our Enemies to listen to equitable Terms of Peace and accomodation—

This finishing part needs no comment from me—Our wicked Rulers seem to be determind to risque the *last stake*, and if this Country does not become a bankrupt by prosecuting so impolitic a War, it will have more luck than it seemingly deserves; & nothing will make them give up the American War but some decisive blow against their Armys in N. York or Rd. Island. The Debates in both Houses on the Amendment,[1] were, on the part of oposition, more bold and argumentative than I have before heard, and I think the Court party cut a more despicable figure even in argument than I ever before heard; They however carryd it according to Custom, 90 to 41 in the Lords, and 233 to 134 in the Commons. No further changes in the Ministry than from bad to worse. Lord Gower & Weymouth out in Disgust, and succeeded by Lord Bathurst & Hillsborough[2]—Lord Stormont in Lord Suffolks place, & the Chancellor Thurlow so crabid and churlish as to give items He will be soon out;³ to make it compleat they should put Your old friend Wed[derbur]n at the head of the Law.⁴

I got Mr. H[odgso]n to write You lately the State of the Cartel, now stopd for the specification of numbers, places where, &ca., & the agents name; as every thing is done by Contract & *per month* no wonder if it is delayd much longer.⁵

I find that the man whom You desird me to supply & who has since left his Lodgings, has exceeded what I expected. The Gentleman whom I desird to help him at P[lymouth], writes me, he has done it to the amount of 51 : 7 : 6 and He had in money, & other expences here, between twenty-eight & 29 Guineas of me.⁶ I shall write to Him to riemburse You & forward the account very soon: The overplus sum I shall draw for as usual, and include therein the amount of the things I am collecting for Mr. W. T. F. which He writes me he has Your orders may be placd to His account.⁷ As there are a great number in his order, & by sundry Authors, they are not yet collected but will be soon got & shippd as He desird—please to mention this to Him. You will also oblige me very much by mentioning to Mr. S. W[harton] that I receivd his orders for the books & that they will go in a day or two directed to Mr. Bowers [Bowens] at Ostend.⁸ I keep them back for the last number of the Remembrancer⁹ which I shall get to day. I am very Truly Yrs. mo. Respectfully

V. J. Drouillard

[Addressed:] Monsieur B. F——

HSP: Franklin Papers, 5 : 107.

¹The amendment moved in each House was to an address of thanks to the king; it noted the decline of the nation's fortunes since the opening of His Majesty's reign and asserted: "if any thing can prevent the consummation of public ruin, it can only be new councils and new counsellors, without further loss of time, a real change, from a sincere conviction of past errors, and not a mere palliation, which must prove fruitless" (Hansard's *The Parliamentary History of England from the Earliest Period to the Year 1803* [London: T. C. Hansard, 1814], 20 : 1034, 1098).

²Granville Leveson-Gower had been lord president of the Council; Viscount Weymouth, secretary of state of both the southern and northern department. Both were leading members of the Bedford party. Henry Bathurst, second earl of Bathurst (1714–1794), had broken with North in June 1778, partly because of disagreement over American policies, partly because of a feeling of being slighted; Wills Hill, earl of

Hillsborough (1718–1793), had been first secretary of state for the colonies during 1768–1772, had resigned his office because of a disagreement with Gower over the grant of land involved in the Vandalia scheme, and had maintained connections with the government, despite the king's opposition to him, through friendship with North.

[3] David Murray, the seventh Viscount Stormont (1727–1796), had served as attaché in the embassy in Paris, been an envoy to Saxony, Warsaw, Vienna, and Paris, and occupied the position of privy councillor. Henry Howard, twelfth earl of Suffolk (1739–1779), had been secretary of state for the northern department when he died in Mar. 1779. North had once hoped to replace him with Lord Howe, who had set impossible conditions, then with Hillsborough, whom the Bedford faction had opposed. Edward Thurlow (1731–1806), privy councillor and lord chancellor, actually retained his post until 1783.

[4] An ironic reference. Alexander Wedderburn (1733–1805), known for the ruthlessness of his political ambition and his virulent verbal excesses, had exceeded himself when, as solicitor general, he had vented an abusive harangue of Franklin before the Lords Committee of His Majesty's Privy Council for Plantation Affairs assembled in Jan. 1774 to hear the petition of the Massachusetts Assembly for the removal of Thomas Hutchinson and Andrew Oliver (1706–1774) as governor and lieutenant governor, respectively. Franklin's alleged crime was having stolen and made public private letters written by Hutchinson and Oliver.

[5] William Hodgson, who was collaborating with David Hartley in furthering Franklin's efforts to provide relief for Americans imprisoned in England and who was serving as an intermediary between Franklin and the Commission of Sick and Hurt Seamen, had sent a letter to Franklin on Nov. 23, 1779, explaining that the admiralty had no intention as rumored of clearing Forton and Old Mill of Americans but would continue to release them for exchange in units of one hundred from each prison alternately.

[6] Digges is referring to Robert Heath's assistance to Capt. Conyngham.

[7] William Temple Franklin had asked Digges to send him a number of maps and books (see Digges to William Temple Franklin, Dec. 20, 1779). The maps were intended for Lafayette, who had requested W. T. Franklin to get them for him, Oct. 29, 1779 (APS: Franklin Papers, 61 : 108).

[8] François Bowens, a Dutch negotiant, frequently forwarded Digges's correspondence.

[9] *Remembrancer; or Impartial Repository of Public Events for the Year 1779* (London: J. Almon, 1779). Edited by Almon, 1775–1784, the magazine was issued in monthly installments.

To Benjamin Franklin

St. James's[1] London Novr. 30 79

DEAR SIR

I gave You a manuscript Copy of the Kings Speech & the debates on the amendment thereon, by last frydays post; Since which I think the general conversation about a vigorous prosecution of the War is very much abated, & the topic now is that the American War must be given up. It is the general opinion, if it is carryd on further, that it will be meerly defensive, from the inability in this Country to send over more troops or spare more ships. It appears that some 8 or 10 Ships are preparing for the relief of Gibraltar—probably after throwing in some supplys to that Garrison to proceed on to the West Indies. I hear of none going to N. York. Sir Geo. Collier arrivd yesterday from that place. He left it the begining of Novr. and tho His Accounts are not authentically givn to the public they are nearly as follows—That the Expedition to the So.ward 2,000 Men under Ld. Cornwallis was laid aside on account of D'Estaign being on the Coast—this Expedition was meant against Chas. Town. That Rhode Island is evacuated and the troops got safe to N. York. That Sr. Jas. Wallace in the Experiment was taken by D'Estaigns Fleet, and that all the out posts save those of the Narrows on Statten Island, at Kings Bridge were calld in, & that the City of N. York was put in a perfect state of Defence.

Altho Sir Geo. saild so late as the 4th Novr. there was nothing certain as to *where* D'Estagnes fleet was. The last probable account of it is from the Crew of the Genl. Glover privateer now confind in Portsmo. who was with the fleet the 14. 15. & 16th Sept. in Latte. 39—and Long: 64—This privateer was taken the 20th by the frigate which brought over Adml. Byron.

I have seen some Pensa. Papers by the Packet but find nothing materially worth mentioning but what you have below. Under an article from Chas. Town So. Caroa. it appears that D'Estaigns fleet 26 sail [of the] Line, 20 frigates, & 3 Corvettes, were at anchor the 2d off Tybee. A Frigate had been sent to the Town with advices of this & pilots were sent to D'Estaign—The Article says there were High Winds on the 4th which woud probably oblige the fleet to stand off to Sea— There is also an account of the Death of Wm. H. Drayton.[2]

A Vessel arrivd at Bedford in N. England also gives accounts that she saild with D'Estaigns fleet as above from St. Domingo & left him in Latt. 25, Long. 70 & that He was bound to Georgia & So. Carolina & thence to the No.ward.

An Article from Chatham Octor. 5 says that Gen. Phillips & Gen. Reidsell and their suit arrivd there the 30 Sept.—They had been as

30 NOVEMBER 1779   117

far as Eliza. Town on Parole, but were orderd to Chatham by Congress there to wait further Orders.³ By this it would seem an Exchange had begun or was likely to open. Another article says His Excelly. J. Jay, late Prest. of Congress is appointed Plenipotentiary to the Court of Spain in the Room of Arr. Lee Esqr. recalld;⁴ and that Wm. Carmichael Esqr. is Secretary to the Commission.

Octor. 3. Monsieur Gerrard, accompanyd by Silas Deane Esqr., passd thro Morris Town on His way to Boston, where He intends to embark for France.⁵—Two Proclamations from Gov. Tryon & one from Arbuthnot, relative to the Spanish Declaration & to induce the people to fit out armd vessels against the trade of Spain &ca. &ca.⁶ It appears by Arbuthnots that they are in want of Seamen.—Nothing material has been yet done in Parliament. Lord Shelburn is to make a motion on Wedny. relative to Ireland & the state of things in the Wt. Indies. Yesterday there was no business done in consequence of a Duel between Mr. Fox & Mr. Adam on account of some expressions in debate from the former to the latter.⁷ Mr. Fox is slightly wounded in the Belly only a scratch, & the other man seems to be much blamd.

The above mentiond Gentlemen Mr. J—— and Mr. C——l will⁸ naturally be with you prior to their setting down at the port of their destination. I would esteem it a favor in You to mention me to them & to give Mr. C——l my direction. I have frequently written to him both before & since he left Europe, & am very ready & willing to do them any services here. I am well acquainted in the Country they are going to, & have some transactions of import in the merchantile way as well for a certain public body as for private individuals where they come from, in which they may be assisting—

        I am with Gt. truth & sincerity
        Yr. very obligd & Ob. St.
        Willm. Ross

[Addressed:] Monsieur / Monsieur B. F——

HSP: Franklin Papers, 5:108.

[1] Probably St. James's Park.
[2] William Henry Drayton (1742–1779), a South Carolinian educated at Westminster and Oxford, had been appointed judge in 1771, become president of the Provincial

Congress, been made chief justice in 1776, and come to be known as the author of various pamphlets favoring the American cause. A leading member of the South Carolina Assembly, he had been a delegate to the Continental Congress from 1778 until his death in Sept. 1779 and was a signer of the Articles of Confederation.

³ Maj. Gen. William Phillips (1731?–1781), an officer in Britain's army that surrendered at Saratoga, and Baron Friedrich Adolph von Riedesel (1738–1800), lieutenant general in command of the Brunswick contingent of German troops supporting Burgoyne at Saratoga, were to remain on parole until exchanged on Oct. 13, 1780.

⁴ John Jay had been appointed on Sept. 25, 1779.

⁵ Conrad Alexandre Gérard (1729–1790?) had been France's minister to the U.S. since July 1778. He, Jay, and Carmichael sailed from Philadelphia to France in late Oct. aboard the Continental frigate *Confederacy*.

⁶ Vice-Adm. Arbuthnot had succeeded to Collier's command; William Tryon (1725–1788), civil governor of New York, enjoyed only nominal authority.

⁷ The duel between Charles James Fox (1749–1806), a sharp critic of the ministry, and William Adam (1751–1839), a supporter of it, had been occasioned by what the newspapers had reported of the debate over the king's address in the Commons, Nov. 25. Adam asserted that the report recorded Fox as impugning his character. Fox, assuring Adam that he considered the press's account incorrect, nonetheless refused to contradict it publicly because he had not authorized the account. Adam had required more satisfaction than that.

To Benjamin Franklin

Acknowledging Digges's letter of October 30, Franklin on November 17 had written that he was surprised that the passport for the cartel had not yet been received: "But let not the Miscarriage of that Paper prevent her sailing for assuredly no advantage will be taken from the Want of it, the same having been regularly issued, signed by the king and the High Admiral, &c. Supposing that it must arrive, I have not applyed for another." He had stated that he had approved Digges's drafts on Grand, that he had not received the account for the books sent to Holland, and that he thought there was due him a sum of some twenty or twenty-five pounds "on Account of a Bill of Yours paid twice." In addition he had enclosed a copy of the letter written to Edward Bridgen that Bridgen had apparently not received. Finally, he had remarked: "I know nothing of Mr. I[zar]d's Intention in going to America. He Leaves his family here. If you please you may mention in your next what you hear of it. I wonder my friend Mr. T[emple] has never written me a Line Since his arrival in Europe, nor communicated to me a Syllable of the Whisper he brought over. I take this a Little amiss, Please to tell him so. I Sent him a Letter from his Lady by Mr. Luard, who said he would Endeavour to find him. . . .

"Tell Mr. H[artley] I will carefully consider his of June 29. of which I have now receiv'd a Copy; & send an Answer next Post" (LC: Franklin Papers, Series 1, 2:301−2).

Stepney 3d Der. 79

DEAR SIR

I have seen Your letter of the 17th. Nov. & have communicated the Contents to Mr. H., but I fear nothing will be done as to the sailing of the Vessel until specifications of numbers are receivd, about which You were last week wrote to by Mr. H[artley], & who at the same time acknowlegd the Receipt of the pass. Mr. H[odgso]n also wrote You on that Subject.

The draft on G[rand] has been properly paid & settled; but the Gentleman You meant to help & whom You mention in Your last has far exceeded my limit of 50£. His freinds Bill in the West is more than that Sum & I added between 27 & 28 Guineas to it here besides paying some other little trifles here; I have not yet heard from Him altho He promisd me to write & direct where to send an Account of the whole that it might be riembursd You.[1]

As to the bill for 20£ you mention to pay twice, I cannot recollect that I had it but once, at least by all my Memorandums & accounts. It was originally left in the hands of Josha. J[ohnso]n but not being *directed* it was never presented. Mr. R[idle]ys Clerk left it with Joa. J——, & He is so regular a Man, that I think if He had ever receivd it, He would have informd me & placd the Amount to my Credit.[2] I find by the account for the Books sent to Holland never having reachd You, that some of my letters have miscarryd for I remember well to have sent the Account by private hand to Amsterdam inclosd in a letter which was there to be put into the Post Office.—Mr. B[ridgen] has got your letter since I wrote You about it. As soon as I see Mr. T[emple] I will certainly tell him what You desire; I ever thought it odd, there was no Communication between You & Him, & this, entre nous, made me a little shy of Him; but hearing from very worthy friends that He stood perfectly fair, I assosiated with Him & have reason to think well of Him. I always avoid as much as possible the meddling with other mens affairs, which has been the reason I never askd him fully what He was upon, which is not for *self only*, but on account of others.

Since my visit in May, both Mr. I[zard] and L[ee] have been cool to me, not unlikely from my communicating so little with them, & refusing to listen to every circumstance that related to private quarrel, of which there was a seeming intention to draw me in some measure into. I have had one cool letter from L. since on a subject that I before mentiond to You, and I have had several from I—— cheifly to forward Him news books, papers &ca. but not a word as to what He means by a jaunt. I guess it is upon the uphill work of criminating those He quarrelld with in P[ari]s & to acquit Himself—I have a high opinion of his honor, honesty, & worth, but I fear He wants a little coolness & prudence. I reprobated the dispute from the first, because I am sure it must hurt the cause I wish best, & my open avowal of these sentiments to both of them has lost me their confidence & former open intercourse. He writes me that He will sail about the 10th & return to Europe in Eight or ten months.

We have yet no Accounts from America about D'Estaign that can be lookd upon as certain. People seem elated at the report of his being blown off the Coast, but they are by no means easy as to the situation & state of Affairs in America. The Accounts by Collier from N. York the 1st Novr. are talkd of thus but the Gazette gives no Accounts. Rhode Island Evacuated & the Troops got safe to N. York—*All* the out posts of the British drawn into New York but that of Paulus Hook, the Narrows, and the point of Long Island next to N. York—A revolt of the people on that Island[3] & a refusal to muster & aid the Army particularly about the County of Suffolk &ca. The dispersion & probable loss of 13 transports in a Storm. They were carrying 2,000 Troops to Quebec requird to be sent there by the Govr. of that province who seems fearful from an odd disposition in the native Canadians of loosing the City of Quebec; five of these ships put back to N. York after being 3 weeks out & terribly shatterd, two have been taken with 150 troops on board and carryd into Philaa. the other 13 unaccounted for.

The talk about a vigorous prosecution of the American War is greatly abated, tho if we may judge from Lord N.'s speeches of this day, He means not to relax in the least towards America—They have a terrible bone to pick in Ireland—most thinking people look upon that Country as lost—They have an open trade from the Western parts to America & laugh at the former Custom House regulations in Dublin as to the prohibition of clearing outwards their own woolens &ca. &ca.—all this is attributed here to the wicked machination of Doctor Franklin, & it [is] asserted that thro Him there is a very good understanding between the Rebel Congress & the people of Ireland.

I see by the papers from N. York, J. Jay is appointed Minister to Madrid & Mr. Carmichael Secy. to the Embassay. Pray let me know when they arrive & if You should see them, as by *chance* You may, give them my direction & let me have theirs.

I am Yr. very Affec. Nephew
Donald Forbes

[Addressed:] Monsieur / Monsieur F——

UP: Franklin Papers, 3:34.

[1] References, respectively, to Gustavus Conyngham and Robert Heath.
[2] Joshua Johnson, still in Nantes providing financial assistance for fellow Americans, was now associated with Matthew Ridley in some business ventures.
[3] The "revolt" was simply organized plundering by the rebels in response to the plundering conducted by a group of loyalists called the Honorable Board of Associated Loyalists.

To Benjamin Franklin

Saty. 4th Decr. 79
3d Dr.   17th Novr. 1779

DEAR SIR

Altho I wrote You by last nights post, I cannot omit so good an oppertunity as that of a fu[gitiv]e Countryman making the best of His way to some friends at the Texel[1] (and where He promises to put it into the post office) of writing to You. I observe in Yours of the 17

Novr. receivd a few days ago, Your suspicions about miscarriage of letters: To satisfy both Yourself & me of this circumstance, suppose you in future put at the top of any letter You may have occasion to write, *the date of Your last written letter*, as well as the date of the one You last receivd from Me; which to explain I have done above. I could wish any other name than that of Your own to direct to You, (suppose it Mr. B: Forbes) for such when under cover to Monr. G[rand] as heretofore, cannot be dangerous to me if discoverd, but directing in propria persona may—if you will take the trouble to direct Monr. G—— to forward all letters under the above direction to You, I will use it in my next & in future. I am told *franking* is not essential to or from Paris.[2]

Your relations Letter of the 9th Novr. came safe to hand by Mr. L[uar]d, and I shall pay due attention to what He requests as to the purchase & forwarding of the Maps & the Book[s].[3] I have lodgd a copy of the order with a Map Seller to collect the whole: As it is a large order & the Maps by several authors they are not easily collected; and I fear some are not to be had, at least Dury[4] tells me so. I have been confined with a Cold for some days past & as soon as I get out the order shall be forwarded together with the last requird Trios of Austogar,[5] and also two Books of an acquaintance of Yours A Methodist Docr. Williams who sent them Me for forwardance, & as they contain specimens of His outre Doctrines of Faith He seems particularly anxious to get them to You.[6]

The last bill on G——d which You mention, has been properly settld; It was owing to some neglect in Grands Clerk that it was not settled in due course.—I shall get the money due on the two Congress Bills from Tessier the first time I go in the City.[7] I have already settld it according to Capt. Califfs order to me before we parted.

I do not apprehend the bill for 20 or 25£ which You mention has been paid twice by You. The original one was drawn by Brehon for aid to Himself and others rather unknown to me.[8] It was sent abroad by Ridlys Clerk but the bill never having been *directed* it was not presented, & it was left with J. Johnson at Nantes till renewd—Johnson is so regular a Man, that I think He would have remitted me the money had the Bill ever been paid; but it shall be enquird into & properly cleard up to You.

The account of the Books sent to Amsterdam was inclosd from me to You in a letter by private hand to Amsterdam, I think the amount was about 9£; If such account never reachd You, it is a proof of miscarriage of some letters; but this I could never ascertain, as I do not write from the motive to procure an Answer. I am not at present in reach of my papers or I would send another copy of the Bill of Parcells for the Books.

As You mention Capt. C[onyngha]ms arrival, You must eer this have seen or heard where He is, as He promisd faithfully to write & offer Himself to You. I have not heard as yet from Him which I wonder at, as He promisd to direct me where to forward the particulars of His account in order that He might riemburse You. His friendship & desire to serve others inducd Him to exceed the limit of supply I desird a friend to give Him—That persons account in the lump is above fifty £s & He had twenty, 27 or 28 Guins. from me here indeed a little more when I include passage money Board &ca. &ca. for the five. Eight more besides the Bearer have gone the same route, & continue to press me, notwithstanding I use every means to inform them How near they are to an Exchange. These continued drains do not answer well with my present finances. I shall make out an Exact account against Capt. C—— when my friend sends me His particulars, & riemburse Myself on You for the Ballance over the fifty pounds already drawn for; He Has money in france & can repay you.

Mr. B[ridge]n got your letter very safe in a short time after I wrote You he was anxious to hear from you—He has lately wrote by an Italian Gentleman whom I took the liberty to introduce to You.[9]

I find by a late letter from Mr. I[zar]d that He will embark for America about the 15h Int. I am not in the secret of His plan; I have a good opinion of his heart, & hope the visit may turn out for the good of His Country, but as I guess it is on the score of criminating Deane & his party, I am in much fear it may produce fresh feuds & animosities in Congress; where I wish to see the utmost unanimity & concord, for we are not yet out of the bush. The quarrel already has done more mischief to the Cause of America, than the whole British Army could affect in the last two Campaigns. I lost much of the confidence both of Him and Mr. L. During a visit in May, since which, altho

I livd in terms of freindship & intimacy with them before, I have only receivd one cool letter from L.,[10] and a very few from I—— on the subject only of forwarding Him books news papers & other trifles— They neither of them likd the freedom with which I gave my sentiments about the quarrel when they attempted to explain it all to me & which I would not hear. I calld on T[emp]le since I receivd Your letter but did not see Him, I shall communicate what He replys in answer to You. I think his political sentiments upright & just towards His Country or I would not communicate with Him as I do, & He has ever spoke feelingly respectfully of You.

Mr. H[artley] has been informd of what You say as to writing Him soon, & He joins with me in opinion that the Cartel will not be allowd to sail without specification of numbers. The names of the prisoners are making out, & every other appearance of their being orderd to embark as soon as such specification comes. I wish most earnestly they were gone, as I am informd they will sweep both Prisons.

There has been another vessel since Sr. Geo. Collier from N. York. She saild about the 8 Nov. but nothing is let out from Ministry, nor a word in this nights Gazette as to the State of things in that quarter, altho it is pretty generally got forth that things are as bad as possible they can be allowing that D'Estaign is blown off, which now every body seems to agree to, & that after leaving a 50 & 2 frigates to aid Lincoln in Savanah He is gone to Porto Rico. This last vessel seems to have been hastily dispatchd with some important papers taken in a Spanish packet from or to the Havanah, which is said to discover all the intentions of Spain towards America & their intended opperations.[11]

I see by the American Papers Jay is appointed to Madrid & Mr. Carmichael His Secy. I should be much obligd to you to give them my direction when they arrive at Paris (particularly the latter for I do not know Jay). They are going to a Country that I know well & where by writing to them I may be servicable. It appears by the papers that *all* the out Posts from N. York are drawn in, save the point of Long Island & the narrows; the Post of Paulus hook seems to have been forcd as Stoney point fort was, and Major Lee of Virga. has got great Credit in the affair.[12] There has been a revolt of the People on Long Island which causes much trouble to the New York Garrison. A fleet of 12 Ships is arrived half Laden from Canada. The disturbances on the upper waters of that Country occasiond by parties of Americans & Canadians & Indians in the Service or Interest of America prevented the produce going as usual to Quebec. Genl. Haldimand made a requisition of 2000 Men to guard that province during the winter & they saild in 20 transports.[13] After being out 3 weeks *five* of these vessels put back in a shatterd situation, two were taken loaded with provision & Soldiers & carryd into Philaa. & the rest are unaccounted for, & are feard to have sufferd in a storm. It does not seem absolutely certain that Rhode Island is evacuated altho it is beleivd by every one.[14]

I am yr. very Ob. Sert.
Wm. Forbes

[Addressed:] Monsieur Monsieur B. F—— / Passy—

HSP: Franklin Papers, 5:106.

[1] The Dutch island was a place to which escaping Americans frequently fled.

[2] On Nov. 17 Franklin had said of letters he had written: "I suspect that several of mine to you and Mr. H[artley] have been stopped in the Post-Office here since the mail ceased going by Calais, for want of Being frank'd here, which I did not till lately know was necessary" (LC: Franklin Papers, Series 1, 2:301).

[3] William Temple Franklin had requested Digges to get him certain maps and books (see Digges to Benjamin Franklin, Nov. 26, 1779, and to William Temple Franklin, Dec. 20, 1779).

[4] A map maker.

[5] Probably *Six Sonatas for two German flutes or two violins and a bass* . . . op. III, recently published by their obscure composer, Giovanni Oliviero Astorga (b. 1750) (Wayne D. Shirley, reference librarian, Music Division, Library of Congress, Mar. 8, 1977).

[6] See Digges to Franklin, Oct. 30, 1779, n. 9.

[7] Franklin had told Digges in the letter of Nov. 17 that he had sent to Mr. L[ouis] Tessier, Old Broad Street, London, an order from Mr. Grand to pay Digges the money owed on the two Loan Office Bills that Digges had mentioned to Franklin, Nov. 10, 1779.

[8] See Digges to Franklin, May 21, 1779.

[9] Mr. Fabroni, Nov. 15, 1779.

[10] Perhaps a letter that Arthur Lee had written Digges, June 14, 1779, asking him to keep an eye on Dr. Edward Bancroft. A draft of the letter is among the Papers of the Continental Congress (NA: Microfilm M247, Roll 128, 3:57). William Lee continued to

correspond with Digges; his letterbooks (VHS) show he wrote to Digges, Aug. 19, Sept. 2, Oct. 7, 1779, Apr. 14, July 31, Oct. 27, 1780.

[11] The incident had been reported in the *Daily Advertiser*, Dec. 3, 1779.

[12] Henry ("Light Horse Harry") Lee (1756–1818), the Continental cavalry leader who had been made a major commandant in Apr. and given charge of one of the elite units, had commanded the successful raid on Aug. 19.

[13] Gen. Frederick Haldimand (1718–1791), the British general in Canada, had asked Clinton for reinforcements in Aug. They were now on the way.

[14] Indecision among the British commanders beclouded the fact that the British had in fact evacuated in late Oct.

To Benjamin Franklin

Putney 17th Decr. [1779]
4th by priv. Hand & *11*th Post[1]   14th Novr.

DEAR SIR

I am afraid the Commission for the purchase of the Books &ca. will take me so much time as to make you suppose I neglect it, but they are old & by so many Authors that I find it difficult to collect them—they shall be forwarded as soon as possible[2]—The Account against Capt. Gustas. [Conyngham] was forwarded the 11th Int.

I mentiond to T[empl]e what You requested[3]—He got the letter safe which You forwarded from His wife. He speaks in the most exalted terms of respect for You & indeed he has ever done so in our frequent interviews—His not writing to You *or any* person on the Continent, is meerly from prudential reasons here, & for his personal safety. This will be fully cleard up to You in a little time when he expects to see you on his way out—I have every reason to believe He is perfectly right in his politics.

A vessel is arrivd in a remote port of the West from Boston—she saild the 12th Novr. with 90 British Prisoners sent home in her as a Cartel to produce the exchange of alike number here—She belongs to New England & what will be given in answer to the propositions by her is yet not known as it is only by this days post that accounts are brought of such a vessel—The Crew passengers & Capn. of a Packet taken & carryd into Boston are among the number, & it strikes me as not unlikely instead of a Cartel She may be only a vessel purchasd to bring home a set of men permitted to come away—It is very clear that a passenger arrivd in London & which came in Her, says that there was not a word of news to the No.Ward about Destaign the 12 Novr.— no Ships of his at Boston & not a word of a storm having ruind his Fleet—Report sayd that the Small aid of Ships He gave Lincoln to the Southward, enabled Him to oblige Prevost to Capitulate—Rhode Island was certainly evacuated & taken possession of By Gates[4] with an army of 1500 Men—most of the heavy Cannon was left behind & many Stores, & the British did not destroy things as heretofore but left Houses & other property tolerably decently. There is also a frigate announcd to be just arrivd from Jamaica. The news by Her is not yet out but it is said She is come with some accounts of D'Estaign—I write You in great haste in order to save the post.

I am Yr. very obt.
Robt. Sinclair

HSP: Franklin Papers, 5 : 104.

[1] No letter dated Dec. 11 has been found.
[2] See Digges to Franklin, Nov. 26, 1779, and to William Temple Franklin, Dec. 20, 1779, and Jan. 10, 1780.
[3] See Digges to Franklin, Dec. 3, 1779, headnote.
[4] Maj. Gen. Horatio Gates (1728–1806), victor at Saratoga and since June 1778 commander of the southern department.

To William Temple Franklin

London 20 Decr. 1779

DEAR SIR

Having accomplishd Your order for the maps, & which I can assure You cost me no little trouble in the collection, they being by so many authors, some of old standing, & most of them in different

Shops, I am going this day to the Custom House with them in order to get them on board the first Dutch Ship which sails to Amsterdam. This will be inclosd in the box, which I direct according to your order to Messrs. Fizeau Grand & Co.; & I shall annex the price to each map on the other side & hereafter send You a regular bill thereof by some safe conveyance. I shall take my riembursement as you desire by placing it to the Docrs. Account. I have not been able to get the peice of musick you desire,[1] nor the Book calld the Gentlemans accomptant; this cannot be bought in the Shops, but a Gentleman promises me to give me one, & which I hope to forward together with the musick by a Mr. K[no]x who was with You about two or three months ago.[2] When You receive all these things pray give me a line—To the direction which the Doctor last wrote me under by post, & a common single letter (which need not be signd) will come very safe. I shall be very happy to render you any services in my power & I hope you will command them.

      I am very truly & sincere'y Yours &ca. &ca.
      T. D——

 Under the same box with your maps I have put two Books written by the Revd. David Williams.[3] They are a present from the author to the Doctor.

   Copy of Mr. B: T: Franklins Order Nov 9, 1779

Maps

County of

Cornwall in 10 or 12 Sheets by T. Martin (this is out of print). . . .		
Devonshire . .	12 Sheets by Down	£2. 2.0
Somerset on Several Sheets (not to be had) yet unfinishd		
Glocester	six Sheets by Taylor.	1. 5.0
Wiltshire	19 sheets by Andrews.	2.12.6
Sussex	6 Sheets-------------------------------------	10.6
Dorset—	6 Sheets by Taylor.	1. 5.0
Hampshire . .	6 Do. . . . . Do.	1. 5–
Surry	9 Sheets by Roque.	2. 2.0
Kent	27 Sheets by Dury & Andrews	3.13.6

Berkshire ...	18 Sheets by Rocque.................	2.12.6
Middlesex...	4 Sheets by Do.....................	1. 1.0
Oxford	4 Sheets by Jefferys................	1. 1.0
Cumberland.	6 Sheets by Donold................	1.11.6
Lancashire ..	not yet finishd	
The Country 90 Miles Round London by Dury...........		10.6
The Environs of London 16 Sheets by Rocque...........		2. 2.0
England one sheet..		0. 2.6
Do. . . . four Sheets.....................................		0. 6.0
Environs of Dublin four Sheets by Rocque		1. 1.0
Plan of Corke...		5.0
Packing Case..		3.6
		Stg.£25.12.0
Porterage, Boat hire, Cocket & Shipping Charges ...		6.6
		Stg.£25.18.6

[Addressed:] B. Temple F——k——n Esq.[4]/ at Passy near/Paris

APS: Franklin Papers, 101 : 153.

[1] Astorga's *Six Sonatas* (see Digges to Benjamin Franklin, Dec. 4, 1779, n. 5).
[2] Youngest brother of Col. (later Maj. Gen.) Henry Knox (1750–1806), whom Washington had placed in charge of the Continental army artillery, William Knox (1756–ca. 1797) had been devoting himself for the past two years to his family's financial interests in Boston and was now traveling in France and the Netherlands to establish business connections in the mercantile centers. During Sept. or Oct. he had been to Passy and, doubtless trying to get the same sort of pass that Sterry had gotten, was apparently about to cross the Channel again.
[3] See Digges to Franklin, Oct. 30, 1779, n. 9.
[4] Digges consistently addressed his letters to Franklin's grandson under this name.

To David Hartley

London 21 Decr. 1779

DEAR SIR

The Town was too much in a hub bub last night for me to find a quiet half hour to write to you—The Clamor in the Coffee Houses,

The park & Tower Guns, The illuminations, The Crackers & huzzas of the Street were as troublesome to my head as they were matters of wonder to my mind. You have read the Gazette & I need not comment upon it; a confirmation from Prevost is said [to] be arrivd this day.[1] It is said D'Estaign has got to France in one of His frigates & brought with Him the Experiment with Sr. J. Wallace on board[2]—The next mail must bring the French account of that affair. It appears now that The French Fleet have not been in any storm & were still doing nothing on the Coasts of America when the last accounts came away.

I sit down now principally to ask You what is to be done about the vessel & Passengers lately arrivd at Falmo. from Boston. The Captains, Crews, & Passengers of two Packetts taken between Jamaica & Falmo. & carryd into Boston, were permitted to buy a vessel & come away to the number of 90 odd, on Condition that they releasd an equal number of American Prisoners out of the Goals here. Captains Hill & Boulderson[3] of the Packets & and other Gentlemen & officers on board this vessel are willing to prove this Compact & give every aid to release a like number of American Prisoners at Plymo. or Portso. but I know not how to put forward the work. Pray let me know what you think of it, & whether you have heard of any thing about the Cartel Ship.

The minds of the People are a little subsided since last night, & since reading the Gazette, they begin (as has generally been the case when news of a like nature has come from America) to think it not *so great* as was blazond forth. If they were wise they would lament the era when a French army landed in America to drive out the expiring interests of Great Britain on that Continent.

I am yr. very Obligd & Obt. Sert.
Tho. Digges

BRO: Hartley-Russell Papers, D/EHy 040/14 a-c.

[1] D'Estaing, assisted by Lincoln, had early in Oct. attempted to take Savannah, where Prevost had recently reestablished his troops. The assault had been a failure, costing many lives. During the assault d'Estaing had left Lincoln unsupported, concerned himself mainly with his ships, and finally been blamed for a costly defeat.

[2] Sir James Wallace (1731–1803), captain of the *Experiment*, had been en route from

New York to Savannah in Sept. with supplies and money for the British troops in Georgia when he had had to surrender.
[3] Peter Hill and John Boulderson.

To Benjamin Franklin

24th Dec. 79
9th[1] & 17th Decr. 1779   *14th Nov.*

DEAR SIR

I have not yet been able to get the order for Books You some time ago sent me, so fully compleated as I wish; the Bookseller is busey in compleating it & gives me fair promises it shall be done by Monday, at least all those that are not out of print. I will then forward it as you direct & draw for the amount together with the overplus of Capt. C[onyngham]s account on whom I shall inclose you a bill for the payment of that Ballance. There is yet nothing done about the Cartel, which is seemingly owing to the want of specification of numbers from Your side.

Last week a Flag of Truce with 90 British prisoners arrivd from Boston at Pensance; She said the 12th Novr. There is a brig also to Bristol very lately arrivd which left Boston the 25th Novr. also a Flag of truce with 45 Prisoners. The Passengers of these vessels are cheifly Gentlemen & Ladys who were capturd in the Jamaica June fleet (9 of which it seems were taken off Newfoundland & carryd into Boston) and the Captains Hill & Boulderson of two Falmo. Packets & their Crews; The Condition of their parole is, to return an equal number of American Prisoners confind in England, in these vessels either to France or America, otherways these Parole passengers are to return to Boston in six months. The arrival of some of the leaders bound by this agreement, is so recent, that nothing conclusive has yet been done; & the application has not yet been regularly made to the Admiralty or Board of Sick & hurt, who are alone competent to say whether or no the agreement shall be complyd with: One of the Gentlemen most active to have it so, has been with Lord North,[2] & *he* promises very fairly it shall be done. The accounts by these vessels are that Fort Stanwix was taken by Butler[3] by surprize—That Jay & Monr. Gerard had saild from Philadelphia in the Confederacy Frigate—and that J. Adams, and F. Dana His Secy., had saild in a French Frigate from Boston about the 24th Novr.[4] The American Papers say that Adams is appointed *sole* Plenipotentiary to Europe to talk upon *Peace only* with the Powers at War; As we hear they are all arrivd in France, you know better than any one else what their errand is. I hope J. Adams errand may be successful, but it strikes me that He is only appointed to prevent those delays in a parley, that must necessarily take place in sending messages across the Atlantic—In case any confidential messenger is wanted in such a negotiation the Gentleman who went to you from hence in Apr. last (Mr. V. Jacques D[rouillar]d) freely offers Himself, and will obey any call for that purpose. His intention in so doing is meerly to serve so good a cause & from no sinister motive whatever.

As you get the Papers regularly I need not animadvert upon the two late Gazetts. Every one here says that the Compte ought to be hangd for his misconduct in that affair. The People of Boston were a little clamorous against Him & His Country for his demanding a surrender of the Garrison to the King of F[rance]. The numbers in killd & wounded are sunken already from 1500 to 300 & I beleive the last is near the truth.[5] We talk much now of prosecuting the American War, so that I fear this glimmering of success at Savanah, will lead us on to deeper mischiefs. It is in every ones mouth that the Dutch fleet now in the Texel loaded with naval stores for France, together with their Convoy, be it what it will, is to be attackd as they pass the Channel & if possible brought into England. The West Inda. fleet of 5 of the line & about 40 merchant Ships are still detain by Contrary winds; sixteen or 18 sail of the line are said [to] be going a part of the way with them, & then to the releif of Gibraltar. I expect to hear from you by Mr. W———[6] & am with great regard Yrs.

Wm. Ferguson

Monsr. B. F———

HSP: Franklin Papers, 5:109.

¹No letter dated Dec. 9 has been found, nor is it mentioned in Digges to Franklin, Dec. 17, 1779, as one of Digges's two preceding letters.
²John Jackson, a lawyer, passenger on the cartel ship *Polly*, under the command of Henry Mitchell (see Digges to Franklin, Jan. 10 (second letter) and Mar. 3, 1780).
³Col. John Butler (1728–1796), but the report was false.
⁴The Congress's appointment of John Jay as minister plenipotentiary to Spain and of John Adams (1735–1826) as peace commissioner to treat with Great Britain, with Francis Dana (1743–1811) as his secretary and chargé d'affaires, was the consequence of various political considerations, including the recognition in the wake of the Deane-Lee controversy that men of public spirit had to supersede those with personal ambitions.
⁵The inadequacy of d'Estaing's support of Lincoln in the attack on Savannah added to continuing recrimination between the allies, bitter as far back as the fall of 1778, when d'Estaing's crews had faced hostility in Boston for failing the Americans at Rhode Island. Inasmuch as the British wounded and killed totaled only fifty-five, the allied losses were judged excessive.
⁶Unidentified.

To David Hartley

1/2 past 11 oClk. [December ⟨24⟩, 1779]

Since I wrote you this Evening I have had a communication with the Gentlemen who came from Bristol out of the Flag of Truce arrivd there to speak to Lord North on the subject of having the terms of their parole complyd with. Lord N. was all complaisance & seemingly willing that the exchange should be complyd with—I can give you a fuller account of this tomorrow as it is now just at the period for giving the letter to the Bell man. I have letters from Philadelphia by this vessel; by which I find your old *friend* J. Adams is appointed *sole* Commissioner Plentipotentiary to speak to the powers at war, for *Peace*. Frs. Dana is His Secy., & I understand they are arrivd in France.

I know not what to make of this, but it would seem that Congress are of the same opinion with I[zar]d, that Dr. F[ranklin] has had it in his power to make Peace but *will not*.—This however I never will beleive; from my acquaintance & correspondence with the old man, I am sure it would be the delight of His soul to obtain Peace. Adams—stands totally unconnected with Him, & He with Adams. This may be a wise step for you know Adams went out Hostile to Franklin & in the interests of Lee & I——d—

It seems to be a slap at the old man.

Yrs. in haste
T. D.

BRO: Hartley-Russell Papers, D/EHy 039/26 a-b.

To David Hartley

11 oClk. 28th [December 1779] at night

DEAR SIR

I have been dining in a large Xmass circle & have but this moment got your letter & parcel by the Coach. I receivd them both at the same time from my having been absent from home ever since 1 oCk. I have answerd that part relative to the Cartel in a letter wrote you a few days ago. It is needless to push matters either with the Admiralty or Board of Sick & hurt, The passengers on parole who came over in these ships are doing every thing in their power to have their agreement complyd with, & I find from dayly experience nothing is to be done in this gothic Country but thro the old rules of office.

I observe what you say about Adams's appointment; you may rely that measure was agreed on in Congress as early as the 20 Augt. and at a period when every thinking man in America & almost all England thought the Army in New York intirely in the power of D'Estaigne and Washington. Adams saild from Boston 8 days before the last Cartel Ship which left it the 24th & the Disaster at Savanah was not known till after Adams got to Boston. His arriving now in Europe as a Peace Maker will be unfairly construed in England—it is now generally given out by the runners of ministry that Adams would never have been sent to make Peace had not America been beaten & made incapable of carrying on a war. This is the language of Downing Street & Pall Mall, & instead of improving on so favorable an event, Genr. Faucit set out 3 days ago to Germany to hire 15,000 more two legged Cattle.[1] I have seen so much of this sort of work, that, I begin to loose

[1779–1780]   135

all hopes & trust only to fortune & future Events. I do not however loose sight for a moment of the desirable object Peace—I like your opinion exceedingly, & would sacrafice every thing I possess to be even instrumental in bringing one about; My time or the Expence of going is no sort of object, but as the partys are not arrivd & I have not yet got the true ground on which He comes an immediate journey would be premature.

—By the post of this day week, & by private hand the day after, I have made an ample offer of services should a messenger to & fro be necessary.[2] I have letters of the 19th both from Fr[anklin] and L[ee], & there was no accounts then of His arrival. I am pretty certain He brings over no terms of Peace whatever, but I think prudence will dictate to Him to mention by some means or other to the Leaders here, that He is arrivd in France armd with powers to receive or assent to propositions & that He is willing & ready to receive any. If once an opening is made I have no kind of doubt but some good will come of it. I will examine your letters more minutely tomorrow & then give you a line if any thing occurs. At present the bell-man waits & I must conclude.

Your Mo. Obd. & Obt. Sert.
[Signature crossed out]

BRO: Hartley-Russell Papers, D/EHy 039/27 a-c.

[1] Maj. Gen. William Fawcett, or Faucitt (1728–1804), had already during 1775–1776 succeeded in recruiting Hessians and Brunswickers to serve against the Americans.

[2] To and from Adams. Correspondence between Digges and Adams prior to Mar. 1780 has not been found.

To David Hartley

Saty. morning [1779–1780]

I know of a safe conveyance to Nantz and I think it may be well to send half a dozen or a dozen of your books to Johnson[1] to be forwarded on by him to America. The Bearer will bring them.

I understand [*some words illegibly crossed out*]² in London the night before last, & I have been upon the tramp to find him but to no purpose—If you should hear of him pray let me know. As He will probably wish to continue a few days in cog you had better not mention his name—it was Almons³ servant that met him yesterday. If He comes with his former opinions & honesty He can give us the best account of the disposition of America towards peace—I am rather fearful of him, & am the more so because if He came thro' France & was honest, my friends there would certainly have trusted him with letters for me. I am very busy or would call on you but hope to do it in the Evening.

I am yrs. &ca. &ca.
T. D.

[Addressed:] David Hartley Esqr./ Golden Square

BRO: Hartley-Russell Papers, D/EHy 039/47 a-b.

¹Joshua Johnson at Nantes. Inasmuch as Hartley had not published as many as a dozen books, Digges is probably contemplating sending several copies of but one or two of Hartley's published speeches critical of the American war—*Letters on the American War*, for example, which on Nov. 26, 1778, Digges had written Hartley he was sending to America.
²The concealment of this individual continues to be successful.
³John Almon, the journalist and bookseller.

To David Hartley

Thursday morning [1779–1780]

DEAR SIR

I am too ill with a pain in my Ear to stir out this morning or I would call to hear what the old man says in his letter to you. As I have got one since that of the 20th Novr. I suppose you have by the same conveyance got the promisd answer to yours of the 29 July.

I hope you will hold in your remembrance the solicitation to Mr. Bell¹ about the poor man who wants to go in the Cartel. I suppose

Her sailing is nearer at hand than it was some days ago. Have you a letter for Fairfax to be forwarded?

I am yr. Ob. Ser.
T. Digges

BRO: Hartley-Russell Papers, D/EHy 040/27 a.

[1] John Bell, British commissioner for the exchange of prisoners and first commissioner of the Board of Sick and Hurt.

To Benjamin Franklin

London 9. Jany. 1780

DEAR SIR

I am without any of Your favors since that by Mr. Luard, & my last to You are of the 9th and 17th Decr.[1] I wish to have some other name than that of Franklin to direct to, & put under cover to Monsr. Grand; as it will pass better in the Post Office, & be more secure in point of my personal safety—in one of my late letters I mentiond that of *B: Forbes*,[2] as a name which might be usd whenever I had any thing to say by Common post: As Capn. H[utchi]ns arrest brought on me much trouble, I am warnd by that, & other hostile appearances here, to be as cautious as possible. I have never yet faild in getting safely any Letter directed as the last from Mr. Franklin Jnr. *Mr. W. Singleton Church Nandos Coffee House London*, where I get a friend to take them up as Mr. Church; if made up in the common small manner the better.

This will be given you by Mr. ——— Barber, who will return to Londn. in a very few days & bear any thing safely from You. He is concernd with Mr. Saml. Hartley in the African & Wt. Inda. Trade, & goes to Paris on some secret merchantile Business, which will be handed to Monsieur Sartine,[3] & which will be best explaind by himself. S. Hartley, is the Relation of & in close connexion with our honest freind David; He is a deserving man, & I hope from the circuitous trade He is upon with France & their West Indies, He will be a useful one to our Country; I therefore give Mr. Barber a seperate introductory Letter to You, for any aid that you may have in your power to give to his scheme.

I have wrote to D. H. (now at his Country House)[4] that Mr. Barber was going and as He has lately expressd a wish to write to You by some safe conveyance, I think I shall have a letter for You in time for Mr. Barber to carry. If not, in a very few days there will be one equally good by a Countryman, Mr. K[no]x, who will go to You on similar business with that of Mr. Sterry in Novr. last, & which is in the fairest way of being propitious—Mr. K——x was with You at P[ari]s, at the same time that Sterry was there.

I am sorry to tell You, that no one step is yet taken for the Cartel going another trip. The sailing is delayd by the board of sick & hurt on the former stale account "the want of specification of numbers." This is the harder on me as they are dayly breaking out & flying here for assistance & what is worse, many of the privates are entering into the Kings Service.

I have helpt on board Ship (a Dutchman to Amsterdam) no less than six to day & yesterday, i.e. Capn. Ruggles of a privateer, Capn. Coffin of Do., & the Captains White, Tracey, Bartlett & Clarke, all of New England.[5] As each man must be supplyd with some few Guineas, these burthens (so very frequent on me) are almost intolerable, & all my perswasions for the men not to break prison are inneffectual. There are two Cartel Ships from Boston, the terms on which they come away You will have on a seperate peice of Paper—as yet nothing is done towards releasing an equal number of American prisoners here, nor I beleive will there.

I annex You the Price of the maps lately shippd for Amsterdam. Their amount is £25:18:6. That of the books has been before drawn for in Peter's Bill[6] which was made *110£* instead of the even hundred, so that I owe You some shillings thereon. You will see by Conynghams account with Me, herewith sent, that His Ballance is 33:4:2d. due me over & above the fifty pound bill I drew on You; this added to the account of the maps make £*59:2:8*, which I shall draw on you for in the usual way on Monsr: Grand, & which I should be obligd to You to order Mr. Grand to pay attention to.

I do not apprehend you have paid a Bill of Jas. Brehons (a surgeon in one of the Continental Ships) *twice over*; altho it may be so, for this man & others after escaping once with my aid, was taken on his passage out, and again got away with four others from Forton—This can be cleard up when I get at my papers & made satisfactory to You.

If I have time I will inclose You a letter for Mr. Carmichael. I hope when Mr. Jay & Adams arrives, You will mention me as a person extreemly ready, & at their command, to do any Services to the cause, they are employd in. The latter appointment has causd much animadversion among the thick heads of this Country. I hope they may all arrive safe & to good purpose. I am with the highest esteem Dr. Sir

Yr. Obligd & Obt. Sert.

T. D—

Maps Bought Decr. 1779 according to the order from Mr. W: T. F[rankli]n & shippd on board the Ship Lady Elizabeth Captain Claas Doorn bound to Amsterdam. The Box markd BTF & directed For Messrs. Fizeau & Grand Merts. Amsterdam.[7]

Survey of Devonshire......	12 Sheets by Donn	£ 2. 2.0
---------- Glocestershire ...	6 Sheets by Taylor	1. 5.0
Wiltshire........	19 Sheets by Andrews	2.12.6
Sussex	6 Sheets ----------------------------------	-10.6
Kent............	27 Sheets by Dury & Andrews......	3.13.6
Dorset	6 Sheets by Taylor	1. 5.0
Hampshire......	6 Sheets idem	1. 5.0
Surrey	9 Sheets by Rocque..............	2. 2.0
Berkshire	18 Sheets idem	2.12.6
Middlesex.......	4 Sheets idem	1. 1.0
Oxford	4 Sheets by Jefferys	1. 1.0
Cumberland....	6 Sheets by Donald..............	1.11.6
The Country 90 Miles Round London by Dury		10.6
Environs of London	16 Sheets by Rocque..............	2. 2.0
England in one Sheet		2.6
Ditto in four Sheets		6.0
Environs of Dublin	4 Sheets by Rocque..............	1. 1.0
Plan of Corke		5–
Packing Case		3.6
		£25.12.0
Porterage, Boat-hire & Shipping Charges		6.6
		£25.18.6

The Survey of Cornwall is out of Print & cannot be had.
Somerset and Lancashire are not yet finishd.

As I find by Your last Letter the account of Books never got to hand, I am convincd some of my letters have miscarryd. I am pretty certain the letter which coverd the Bill of Parcels for them was sent, soon after the box was shippd in June last, by way of Amsterm. and was to be put into the post office there by a friend of mine who took charge of the letter that far. This is the more extraordinary as the letter escapd the philistine hands of the Londo. Post Office. I herewith annex another bill; but you are to observe, the whole numbers mentiond below, were not sent in the box, sixteen or eighteen numbers (suppose *18* which being shillings each is 18/–) are to be deducted therefrom. The *exact account* of this, is with my papers, purposely securd many miles from this on account of the trouble Hutchins's affair brought on me; so that I cannot make out the *exact* account at present, but it shall be hereafter settled to Your satisfaction.

Books sent in a box to Amsterdam June 1779 directed for Messrs. Fizeau Grand & Co.

Remembrancer eight vols: & eight numbers	
Parliamentary Register 10 vols: and 12 numbers................	£4:12:0
American Charters,[8] & two Political tracts.....................	– 7.6
Annual Register for 1774 & 1775[9]	–11–
Considerations on the French & American War.[10]	
Narrative of Lord Howes fleet in America[11]	
Examination &ca. Adml. Keppels defence.[12] West India Mercht,[13] Henleys tryal.[14] Valens Letters[15] &ca. & box	16.6
Annual Register 76 and 1777................................	11 –0
Parliamentary Register in numbers 6 to 28 & 35 to 72 ⎫ Remembrancer in do. for 78 & Nos. 42 to 49 & 50 ⎭	3:⟨1⟩:0[16]
	£9:19:0

APS: Franklin Papers, 61:109.

[1] A curious omission of the letter he had dated Dec. 24.

[2] See Digges to Franklin, Dec. 4, 1779.

[3] Antoine Raymond Jean Gualbert Gabriel de Sartine, comte d'Alby (1729–1801), a supporter of the Franco-American alliance, was serving as minister of marine.

[4] David Hartley's country address was Sodbury, Gloucestershire.

⁵Escapes had become frequent. Possibly the most recent were by Nicholas Bartlett and Christopher Clark, a carpenter on the *Rising States* who had been taken June 14, 1777; they had broken out of Forton on Dec. 31, 1779. By Nov. 22, 1780, the Board of Sick and Hurt could report to the admiralty that 229 Americans had escaped from Mill and Forton prisons, 118 of them since Jan.

⁶The same William Peters about whose plight Digges had written Franklin, May 14–Sept. 6, 1779.

⁷Bankers with close connections with Ferdinand Grand in Paris, whose brother George was a partner in the Dutch firm.

⁸*The Charters of the British Colonies in America* (London: J. Almon, [1774?, 1775]).

⁹The volumes of the *Register* were edited at this time by Edmund Burke (London: R. Dodsley).

¹⁰*Considerations upon the French and American War. In a Letter to a Member of Parliament* (London: J. Almon, 1779).

¹¹[Thomas Lewis O'Beirne, bishop of Meath (1748?–1823)], *Candid and Impartial Narrative of the Transactions of the Fleet under the Command of Lord Howe, from the Arrival of the Toulon Squadron, on the Coast of America, to the Time of His Lordship's Departure for England . . .* (London: J. Almon, 1779).

¹²Which of the several books about Keppel's trial Digges means by the *Examination* remains uncertain. The second title is obviously *The Defence of Admiral Keppel (before the Court-Martial, Jan 30, 1779)* (London: J. Almon, 1779).

¹³ *The West India Merchant. Being a series of Papers Originally Printed under That Signature in the London Evening Post [1776]. With Corrections and Notes. By the Author* (London: J. Almon, 1778).

¹⁴*Proceedings of a Court-Marial, Held at Cambridge, by Order of Major General Heath, Commanding the American Troops for the Northern District, for the Trial of Colonel David Henley, Accused by General Burgoyne, of Ill Treatment of the British Soldiers, &c. Taken in Short Hand by an Officer, Who Was Present* (London: J. Almon, 1778).

¹⁵ *The Letters of Valens [pseud.], Which Originally Appeared in the London Evening Post. With Corrections, Explanatory Notes, and a Preface by the Author* [William Burke, assisted by Edmund and Richard Burke] (London: J. Almon, 1777).

¹⁶Whether this amount is "3:1:0" or 3:2:0" is uncertain. In the second column one of those numerals has been heavily inked over the other, but we cannot determine which is the correction. Of course, if the "2" is the revised figure, then Digges failed to reflect that correction in his addition.

To Benjamin Franklin

London 10 Jany. 1780

DEAR SIR

My Friend Mr. Barber, the Bearer hereof, has obligingly taken charge of a letter & small parcel from myself, and also a letter from our Friend D. H—— for You. He takes a journey to Paris on some

Commercial Business, in which He is connected with Mr. Saml. Hartley (a particular Friend & relation to D. H———) and which must lead to the atten[d]ance on some Men in power at Your Court—This business will be best explaind by Himself; and I am a supplicant to You Sir for what aid and assistance You can give Mr. Barber in the prosecution of His plan.

His political sentiments, as well as those of Mr. Sam. Hartley, will not displease You; I have experiencd on many occasions Their willingness to oblige *Us*, and I am sure any scheme They may be upon will not be unbeneficial to Our Country; I therefore beg leave to recommend Mr. Barber to Your usual civility and attention, & to be esteemd

Your very Obligd and Obedt: Servant
T. Digges

[Addressed:] His Excellency/Benjamin Franklin Esq./at Passy/near/Paris

HSP: Franklin Papers, 5:112.

To Benjamin Franklin

[January ⟨10⟩, 1780]

At Plymouth Jany. 1. 1780 the Prisoners stood thus—

Exchanged by the Cartel Ship	97
Escaped in all ——————	72
Enterd into the Navy –	63
Dead –	15
	257 [*sic*]
Remaining in Prison –	183

The State at Portsmouth the same day, & since which 3 or four have escaped

In Prison – ———————— 227

[⟨10⟩ JANUARY 1780]

Sixty of these are Officers of inferior rank. Upwards of one hundred officers have escapd since 15th June 1777. The Cartel from thence 2d July 79 carryd *120* Men. Those dead, & enterd into the Service of England, & the number of the Whole that has been committed is not exactly stated to me.

The Cartel, or flag of Truce, Ship to Falmouth, saild from Boston the 12th Novr. 79. The vessel was purchasd by the Passengers allowd to come away on condition they releasd an equal number of Americans in England. The Passengers are principally the Captains, Passengers, & Crews of the two Packets taken & carryd into Boston: I have not their exact number but it is said to be *ninety* in all.

The Cartel Ship, Polly, Heny. Mitchell Commr. (who is an Irish man marryd in & belonging to Boston, & who owns the Ship) saild the 25th Novr. from Boston & brings 35 Passengers in all. They are cheifly West India Gentlemen taken on their passage Home in the June fleet out of which seven sail was conducted into Boston. The following is the Copy of their written parole, & I dare say the Passengers to Falmo. are under a like agreement.

"State of Massachusets Bay—Boston Nov 20th 1779

"Whereas the Honble. Council of the afforesaid State, Hath permitted Us the Subscribers prisoners of War To depart from this to England, upon our Paroles, in the Cartel Ship Polly Henry Mitchell Commr.; We Engage for our Selves &ca. &ca. (here follows the names & discriptions) That upon our arrival in England, we will procure the liberty of as many American Prisoners in England of equal rank with ourselves, & cause them to be sent over to France, addressd to the Honble. Benj: Franklin Esq. Plenipotentiary for the United States of America. We further promise, that in case of failure, that each of Us will return to this State in Six Months from the Date—Further that we will not do or say any thing prejudicial to the afforesaid States of America until duly exchangd & dischargd—As witness our hands &ca.

     John Jackson,   Jerea. Cochlan
     Edd. Barry   John Read Robinson
     Jno. Lawrance   John Smith
     Robert Leake—["]

The first namd Mr. Jackson has been twice with Lord N., and *promisd every thing very fairly.* But this not being the quarter to do the Business, I perswaded Him to try the Admiralty—They wanted to throw cold water on his application; but on His speaking out, & demanding it as a right not as a favor and threatening to have it mentiond in the House Commons, He was somewhat listen to by Mr. Stephens, & a slight promise obtaind that it should be attended to. I have no hopes myself, that it will; for just such a promise was obtaind towards procuring the release for *the Receipts* you forwarded D. H., and to the accomplishment of which *nothing yet* has been done and D. H[artley] is unluckily (as he too often is) out of Town. To obviate this inconvenience of His absence, & at times, inattention; I some time ago got Mr. Wm. Hodgson of Coleman Stt. to write You; I think any request from You to that Gentleman will be attended to, & he could then go with a good face to the board of Sick & Hurt to push forward the Cartel; and which, as an American, I cannot do.

Mr. Jackson was the first person who informd Lord N[orth] of Mr. Adams's appointment to Europe as a Negotiator for Peace, and that He saild from Boston the 22d Novr. in a French Frigate—Lord N——s expression on this occasion was a little curious—"I wish Mr. Adams had had confidence enough to come directly hither in the Ship with You". It is wonderful how the people here have been gulld by the Runners of Administration industriously giving it out as a fact that Mr. Adams was certainly coming to London with *very humiliating* propositions from Congress. It servd to raise the Stocks 2 pr. Ct.! and the period of its being talkd of here was a little unlucky for America, for the people never gave themselves time to think that the appointment of that Gentleman was at a time when America expected to make prisoners the whole British army in New York.

The Bearer[1] will carry you a seperate large packet which my friend Mr. Magellan requested me to forward;[2] There is two letters in it from our friend in Mincing Lane,[3] and one from Mr. L[uar]d. Any answers you may trust safely to the Bearer. He also carrys the Letter from our friend D. H——. The Bearer is an intelligent clever man & will give You the news of the Day. Much expectation is formd from the Fleet under Sr. J. Ross, It is gone either to the releif of Gibraltar or to destroy the Shipping in the Bay of Cadiz⁴—The Wt. Inda. fleet carryd out but two thousand Men & about 4 Sail of the Line will attend them.

All is *up* again about the Conquest of America. D'Estaigns shameful behaviour has with two much reason raisd the Spirits of the People, and I see no redemption for South Carolina as an Army from N. York of 3,000 Men is certainly gone against it. All the officers from Georgia, declare openly the place would have surrenderd if terms had been offerd to the Garrison. There were but 2,400 Men in the place in the total, & it was impossible say they to throw up works from the lightness of the sand. It seems that no one but D'Estaign could have lost it. I am very certain if he had only hoverd on the coasts with his fleet & blockd up the River the place would have surrenderd to Lincoln.

I suppose Mr. I[zar]d saild from Holland in the last St. Eustatia Fleet. I am sorry to find He goes out extreemly hostile to You. The L[ee]s I have not heard from for a long time; I am apprehensive from my formerly refusing (for I had it not in my power to do it) to go as second with them they may suppose & represent me as luke-warm in the cause of my Country—My uniform endeavours to steer clear of all disputes & to do good in the little way I had in my power, may encrease that supposition in them of me; but I trust there are many who know my heart & have been witness's to what I have risqued & done. J. T[empl]e, is still here & speaks in the highest terms of respect for You & hopes to see You soon. We condole with each other on the present gloomy prospects & folly of this Country & tho our hopes are in *peace* we can see no likelyhood of it at present.

I am &ca. &ca.

HSP: Franklin Papers, 5 : 1 1 2

[1] Apparently Mr. Barber, bearer of Digges's letter of Jan. 9.
[2] Jean-Hyacinthe de Magalhaens, or Magellan (1723–1790), a descendant of the famous explorer, had been born in Lisbon, for a while been an Augustinian monk, and for the past few years been settled in London, where he pursued interests in physics, astronomy, and mechanics and wrote several treatises on the use of various scientific instruments. A fellow of the Royal Society, he was among Franklin's correspondents.
[3] Benjamin Vaughan (see Digges to Franklin, Sept. 20, 1779).

⁴ Ross's fleet was part of Rodney's expedition to relieve Gibraltar; on the way they seized a number of merchantmen and defeated a Spanish squadron under the command of Adm. Don Juan de Langara.

To William Temple Franklin

London 10 Jany. 178[0]

DEAR SIR

I was sorry to be so long executing Your order for the maps, but they being of various Editions & by sundry authors, and not to be had but by hunting thro many Shops, I could not compleat the order till about the 20th last month; when they were boxd up and forwarded to Messrs. Fizeau & Grand of Amsterdam as You requested: They were shippd on board the Lady Elizabeth Capn. Klaas Doorn the box markd BTF and the Captains Receipt was inclosd to Messrs. Fizeau & Grand. I also sent in the same box two books from the author The Revd. David Williams to Dr. Franklin, a present, which I have long wishd to convey with safety. I have not been able yet to get the peice of musick & the Gentleman Accomptant which you wrote for,¹ but hope to do it, & forward them by a Countryman whom I expect will soon go to Paris for a few days. I have inclosd in the box of maps a Letter to You with the Bill of Parcels, a Copy of which I have also inclosd this Day to Dr. Franklin. They amount to £26:18.6² and are perfectly to Your order, save that of Cornwall which is out of print, and Lancashire & Somersetshire which are yet unfinishd. I shall be very glad to oblige You or my friends in any thing in my power, & I beg You will make no appology for troubling me. When You write make up Your letters in the small common way (suppose like this) and you need not sign them; direct as You did the last & they will probably come safe for I have yet missd none under that direction. For my *trouble* in forwarding your Commission I will claim of you a line of information when Mr. J[a]y & Car[michae]l and Mr. Adams arrives & any current American News you may have.

Pray offer my best wishes to Mr. C—r—m—l and give Him my direction with an offer to render him any services here & attend to whatever He may have occasion to write to me about. We have no arrivals lately from America nor a word of publick news worth communicating but what You will read in the papers.

Our friend L[uar]d is well & still here, as is Your God Father whom I find to be a very honest worthy Man & one of the right sort. I wish You all success & Happiness & am very truly Sir

Your Affect. Frd. & Obt. Servt.
T. D.

I some time ago left with You some printed proposals for a Print the Engraving of which is now very nearly finishd. I hope You will help me to a few names as subscribers to it—The Docrs. will much honour the subscription & please the honest little patriotic Printer who designs the original picture as a present to the publick Hall of the first Assembly in Your Country.

You should try to get me all the American names for the subscription that are about You, it will do Credit to them, & the picture is a flattering subject to Our Country.

Pray send me any news papers you may have to spare

Yrs. &

APS: Franklin Papers, 104:4.

[1] See Digges to William Temple Franklin, Dec. 20, 1779.
[2] The amount was £25.18.6 (see Digges to Benjamin Franklin, Jan. 9, 1780).

To Benjamin Franklin

Jany. 11, 1780

DEAR SIR

Mr. Barber the Bearer of this & several other letters to You which was given Him yesterday, has been good enough to wait a day, for the good tidings I expected to forward relative to the Compliance of the Admiralty with the terms of the two Cartel Ships which came lately from Boston. These terms are made known to You in my letter of yesterday. Some of the Gentlemen under Parole, waited on the Lords of the Admiralty, & were advisd to draw up a memorial stating their case, & praying that the terms of their agreement should be complied with; They had promises from the Admiralty their prayer should be heard, & an answer given this day. One of the Gentlemen has been with me with the tidings, that they receivd fair promises, but that the answer could not be given for some days. Altho I have little hopes from the promises of great men, I am not without expectation I may have it in my power in a few days to inform you the terms are in some measure complied with.

If you have it in your power, it would very much oblige our friend Mr. Hartley,[1] to get releasd or put into forwardance for the first Exchange by Cartel; a Captain and mate of His taken & carryd into Brest by the Renommé French Frigate. They are probably at Dinant & their description are Capt. Colley of the Brigantine David & His Leiut. Mr. Powel. Mr. Barber can more particularly describe them to You.

I am Sir Yr. very Obt. Serv.
Tho. Digges

[Addressed:] His Excellency/Benjamin Franklin Esq./Passy/ near/ Paris

HSP: Franklin Papers, 5:113.

[1] Samuel Hartley.

To David Hartley

Jany. 26. 1780

DEAR SIR

I will call on my way to the City upon Mr. Hammond & Hartley[1] & shew them the Petition.—I like the three concluding paragraphs very much, but cannot say so much for the first; for it may be fairly implied, that whoever signs to that paragraph, is sorry for the French interferance in the American dispute, *only* because by such interferance England was prevented from carrying into execution Her avowd plan (which is not even now given up) of bringing America to unconditional submission.

The second paragraph is complimentary to the French in the view of general Policy.

I speak thus openly to you because I know you like plain dealing, & my opinion shall not go further than to you.

I have another complaining letter from the Docr. about the shameful delay of the Cartel, after America having hundreds before hand in point of numbers. He seems to think, what indeed is much my opinion from observation, that the business will sink from not being attended to here: *I* cannot possibly appear in it, & your business puts it much out of your power to go to the office of sick & hurt, (for the going to Mr. Bell alone is of little avail) and I think this may be remedied, by your writing a few lines intimating that the Bearer of the Letter Mr. Wm. Hodgson Merchant Coleman Street waits on the board to know if the Cartel is to go or not.

The American Subscription being out, we propose opening a new one,² and expressing in the advertisement that the Cartel of American Prisoners is stopt altho there are a greater number of English Prisoners (American-Capturd) to stand against them in France; & besides that, Jones's prisoners about 280, 303 releasd at Sea by Receipts, & 134 lately permitted to come from Boston to England in two Cartel Ships have been all given up to no effect. If you will only write a line to Mr. Hodgson expressing your desire to him to ask the Board if the Cartel is to go, *before* He opens another Subscription with such an advertisement [, and] inclose to Him a line to Mr. Bell similar in purport to what I before mentiond, I am very certain the Board would attend to Him & the business be expidited. I am ashamd of troubling you so often on this score, & am not a little hurt that the old man should think me negligent of the business here. We have not a word of news but what you read but much talk about a Dutch war.

       I am yr. very Ob. Ser.
       T. D.

If any thing material comes to hand to be forwarded, it shall go the way you direct. I expect a person from P[aris] every day & have an oppertunity to write by one going to day to return here in 14 days.

Adams—nor none of the rest was arrivd the 12th Int. I am rather surprizd you should think that Mr. I[zar]d could possibly do any thing or speak to Sr. J. Y.³ on the terms of Peace. The patent I mentiond to have been sent to Sr. J. Y. was (*as was reported*) only to empower Him to speak to any Commissioners from America for Peace; not to any private individual which Mr. I——d now is.

[Addressed:] David Hartley Esqr. M. P. / Sodbury / Glocestershire

BRO: Hartley-Russell Papers, D/EHy 040/15 a-c.

¹ Possibly Winchcombe Henry Hartley (1740?–1794), David's half-brother, who represented Berkshire and shared his views; possibly Samuel Hartley (see Digges to David Hartley, Feb. 7, 1780).
² A second subscription to relieve the distresses of imprisoned Americans. Franklin had assumed that the prisoner exchange would be completed by now and so had not provided additional funding for relief.
³ Sir Joseph Yorke (1724–1792), British ambassador to The Hague.

To Benjamin Franklin

28 Jany. 1780

DEAR SIR

I wrote You under dates the 11. 12. & 14th¹ by a friend Mr. B[arbe]r, whom I am now under dayly expectation of seeing. The Bearer of this is an honest Captain of a Ship from my own neighbourhood, & one of a respectable & numerous family.² He has a ship & means to push homewards with Her, & from my recommendation is inducd to be a supplicant to You for such aid as You lately gave to Mr. Sterry & Mr. Smith. The vessel is the Brigantine Brighton, 100 Tonns, British Built, 8 Guns, & mannd with 10 or 11 Seamen: The Bearer is owner & Capt. of Her, but as others of our Countrymen are concernd it would be well for the —— to run thus[:] Capt. Walter Belt, Captain Aron Sheffield, & others Citizens & subjects of —— &ca.³ This vessell will certainly take out above ten thousand pounds worth of useful & necessary articles; This is my motive for helping the matter forward, &

28 JANUARY 1780   151

for the serving & putting in the right situation six or eight *good friends*. It will be a great obligation to Me Sir if You can be servicable in the matter to the Bearer Capt. Belt.

We are yet in a state of uncertainty about the American Cartel—The seeing a regular one Establishd between France & Engld. & the having been so often put off with hopes, makes the Prisoners very turbulent, often to break Goal & come distressd to the Capital, & to induce severals to enter on board the navy,[4] The Subscription is quite expended, But I got a few days ago a supply from the overplus of Mr. Wilkes's subscription to his Election for Chamberlain of fifty pounds;[5] this I fear will be soon gone, & there have been 20 added to the number since I last wrote.—Those at Millford to the amount of 32, liberated themselves last week, made off with a vessel loaded with flour & goods & got safe away. No steps are yet taken or likely to be taken for liberating an equal number of Americans to those permitted to come from Boston in the Ship Bob Capt. Dukin[6] to Falmo. with 95, and the Polly Capt. Mitchel to Bristol with 35. Nor are those releasd by Receipts at Sea the least attended to. The constant answer of the board of sick & hurt when enquird of about the detention of the Cartel, is that she is detaind for the want of specification of numbers from Your side—however the real reason is the fear of these Prisoners getting quickly on board Paul Jones's Squadron. Capt. Manley formerly of the Hancock & since Commander of a Continental Ship is now a prisoner at Plymo. & very poor & distressd;[7] I would help him but I am really so distressd on account of what I have already advancd those unhappy people that it is out of my power to give him aids of money. The Bearer will give you 8 or 10 News papers by which you will learn the current news of the day—12,000 Ton of Shipping is engagd to carry 5,000 of Faucits Cattle to America in the Spring, & we talk big of carrying every thing before us in that quarter.

The loss of the Posts on the Mississippi, & of Pensacola, are thought lightly of here,[8] all is lost in the grand naval success against the french victuallers in the West Indies, & of the capture of six Spanish Men of War & 18 Transports near the Bay Biscay this month, & we are quite sure Rodney will raise the seige of Gibraltar & do mischeif to Cadiz.

I understand that Mr. I[zar]d has lost his passage from Amsterdam to the Wt. Indies, & is at a loss at present what to do towards getting out. The Bearer will take care of any thing You may have to send here.

I am wth. very gt. regards
Sir Yr. Obt. Ser.
J. V. Drouillard

D. H. is so much out of Town & out of the way of personal application to the board of Sick & hurt, that I have pressd him by letter to get Mr. Hodgson (who some time ago wrote to you but has yet had no answer) to act as a go-between which will give Mr. Hodgson an oppertunity of now & then speaking to some good purpose towards the expediting the Cartel.[9]

Since writing the foregoing relative to the arrival from N. York, a friend of mine has it at second hand from the Capn. arrivd, that the fleet for the Southern Expedition was certainly to sail the day after the homeward bound fleet which saild upwards of 100 in number the 23d Dec.

5,000 Men are the Numbers sent to the So.ward & six men of war. 3 days after the sailing the homeward bound fleet was dispersd totally by a severe storm, which the arrivd Captain, thinks must have dispersd or driven off the Coasts the Men of War & transports carrying the Troops. It was generally given out that Chas. Town was their destination.

[Addressed:] A Monsieur/Monsieur B—— Franklin / Passy

HSP: Franklin Papers, 5:116.

[1] Apparently references to his letters dated Jan. 9, ⟨10⟩, and 11, 1780.
[2] Capt. Walter Belt, of Prince George's County, Md.
[3] The document was a bond whose text finally ran thus:

> Know all Men by these Presents, That I Walter Belt, of Prince Georges County in Maryland, Mariner, am held and firmly bound to the President of the Congress of the United States of America, for the time being; in the Sum of Three thousand Pounds Stterling, to be paid to the said President of Congress or his Order, in trust for the Use of the said United States. To which Payment well and truely to be done, I do bind myself, my Heirs, Executors, and Administrators, jointly and severally, firmly by these Presents, Sealed with my Seal, dated the 11th Day of Feby. 1780—

The Condition of this Obligation is such, that if the above bounden Walter Belt, who with Capt. Aron Sheffield & others, are owners of the Brigantine Brighton of about one hundred Tons, bound from London to America, with a Cargo of coarse Woolens, Linnens & other Clothing, shall land the Goods mentioned in their Passport (a Copy whereof is hereunto annex'd) in some Port of the United States, not in Possession of the British Troops, the Dangers of the Seas excepted. Then this Obligation shall be void, or else to be, & remain in full force and virtue.

         Walter Belt

Sealed & deliver'd in the
 Presence of
  B. Franklin
  L'air DeLamotte   (APS: Franklin Papers, 74:54)

[4] Between the French failure to implement the agreement relating to the prisoners that John Paul Jones had given into their custody in Holland and the British decision not to empty its prisons of Americans lest they make their way to enlist under Jones, the exchange appeared stalled.

[5] John Wilkes had succeeded, after his fourth attempt, in becoming chamberlain of the City of London.

[6] Edmund Dunkin. The conditions of parole agreed to by the passengers on his and Mitchell's ships had been explained by Digges to Franklin, Dec. 24, 1779.

[7] John Manley (1733–1793), of Massachusetts, now in Old Mill Prison, had commanded the *Hancock* early in 1777, taken a prize ship, been captured by Sir George Collier, and kept aboard prison ships before being exchanged in Mar. 1778. He had then assumed command of the privateer *Cumberland*, which had been captured in Jan. 1779 and taken to Barbadoes. Escaping and returning safely, he had got command of the *Jason* and cruised successfully until Nov., when he had become a captive once more. He had now been in Mill since Dec. 15.

[8] In Oct., after Spain had entered the war, her troops had seized the inadequately defended posts along the Mississippi and been able to threaten Pensacola, which, however, was well fortified and did not have to surrender until May 1781.

[9] See Digges to Hartley, Jan. 26, 1780.

To Benjamin Franklin

                London 4th Feby. 1780

Dear Sir

 I wrote you a few lines by Capn. B[elt] the 28th ultio., & hope to have it in my power in a few days to forward the Contents of this by another friend for fear it may be lost by the common conveyance of Post.

 The Royal Society at their last meeting, came to a resolution to have a certain number of Gold, Silver & Copper medals struck of Captain Cooke;[1] & that those of the Gold ones should be presented to the Societys abroad, to the King, to the Empress of Russia; King of France &ca. &ca.—these last, in testimony of the humane and liberal orders those potentates gave to their Navy Officers and Cruizers for the protection & safety of Captain Cooke. At the time such orders were issued in France, we were informd here, that they were procurd thro Your solicitation or recommendation; and that similar Orders were given by Congress, thro' You, to the Ships of War of the United States of America, or at least to some of them on distant stations from America. My particular friends Mr. Jones & Mr. Paradise[2] (two Gentlemen well known among the literati & who were with You in Paris last summer or spring) were present when this Resolve passd in the Royal Society, and they spoke in favor of a medal being given to the Congress & to Yourself in consequence of the attention shewn from that quarter to the welfare of Captain Cooke:[3] The proposition was well receivd by the Society, & the President declard the medal or medals should be so given provided proofs could be obtaind *within a month* that such orders were ever given by the Congress or You to any Ship or Cruizer belonging to America. As I am given to beleive such orders were given, I do not let a post pass over without informing You of the Resolution & declaration of the Society in order that the proofs may be obtaind for the right to ask the medal. My friends before mentiond, as well as many others of that society particularly known to You will give their aid towards getting it, & I should be made very happy by Your Commands as to forwarding the proofs or any other assistance in my power. I wish you every happiness and am with the highest esteem

Dr. Sir. Yr. obligd & Obt. Servt.
W: S: Church

[Addressed:] His Excellency / Benjamin Franklin / Passy

HSP: Franklin Papers, 5:117.

[1] Capt. James Cook (1728–1779), British explorer and scientist, who had been killed by Hawaiian natives on Feb. 14, 1779. A mariner since 1755, he had become known for

his contributions to science and natural history after he had charted the coasts of Newfoundland and Labrador during 1762–1767, published notes on a solar eclipse he had observed in 1766, observed the transit of Venus in 1769, explored the Society Islands, surveyed the coasts of New Zealand, proved that Australia was an island continent—all before 1771—then on two later voyages substantiated the value of lime juice in treating scurvy and explored new areas that ranged from the Antarctic Circle to the Pacific coast of North America.

[2] Sir William Jones (1746–1794), a jurist and orientalist, and John Paradise (1743–1795), a linguist and a friend to Samuel Johnson (1709–1784), were both fellows of the Royal Society and visited Franklin several times in the course of the Revolution.

[3] On Mar. 10, 1779, unaware that Cook was already dead, Franklin had addressed a letter to the commanders of armed ships commissioned by the Congress asking them not to molest Cook on his return from his Pacific voyage.

To David Hartley

Londo. Mony. night
7th Feby. 1780

DEAR SIR

Mr. Burkes motion[1] comes on on fryday, so that I have hopes to see you by that day especially as the Subject of it relates closely to a matter you some time ago movd for in Parliament. I want you in Town for another reason. I find the Cartel business—that is, of the two lately arrivd Ships from Boston will come before Parliament in both Houses; by Ld. Rockingham in one & Burke in the other. The Admiralty not only declare that the terms cannot be complyd with & that the Passengers must return to Captivity, *they not being on a footing with Rebels here who can only be releasd by Pardons &ca.* but they have publickly denyd under Mr. Stephens's own hand writing "that no Cartel exists or ever did Exist between this Country & America for the Exchange of American Prisoners here, against Englishmen capturd by American Cruisers & confind in France".[2] This must appear odd to you who fixd that Cartel, & know that two Cargoes have gone & that the Cartel still subsists.—I cannot account for Mr. Stephens's false assertion, especially as the order for the vessels sailing with the two Cargoes of American Prisoners was from under his own hand & cannot have been forgotton by Him. It hurts me to trouble you so often about these prisoners, & I should be very sorry to draw you from any thing you would regret to leave; but I think it necessary to inform you what is likely to be done in Parliament, where it is more than probable the whole matter relative to the settling that Cartel (& which yourself had the doing) will be fully canvassd. I have tryd to delay the bringing it on till you come to Town, but the suffering Gentlemen who are likely all to be obligd to return to Boston on Parole are uneasy under their situation, & have applyd to Lord R——m & Mr. Burke to bring their case before Parliament. I wish, for the Credit it would do you in America, & with those Americans acting in Europe, that you had brought it on. I need not add more on this score.

I have had the communication you wishd me on the subject of the Petition, your Letter to Sawbridge[3] &c. &c.—and I agree with you that it will be better for the City of London to mention in the Petition[4] a desire of Peace with America. They may do it, & still keep in view the Spirit of the York Petition which I do not approve of on the whole particularly the begining part, yet I think it well calculated to draw in people of all descriptions in Politicks. I have very freely given my advice to W. H.,[5] Mr. H[ammon]d and S. H[artley], that they neither shew Sawbridge Your Letter, nor on any account whatever, suffer it to be publishd as it now stands; for most assuredly it will hurt you in the Eyes of Dr. F[rankli]n & J. Adams. In your Letter, you state as a fact *"that the Americans have no alliance with Spain at all, neither is there supposd to be much cordiality or union of interests between them, or any prospect of close alliance in future."* I took upon the *fact* to be quite the reverse: There has been a Spanish Plenipotentiary resident in Philadelphia long before the Spanish rescript was given in here; that Plenipotentiary negotiated a Loan of money from Spain to America; & there has been a strict union of interests *in commercial intercourses* for more than two years. You again say *"the unusual alacrity Spain lately exerted in seizing upon West florida, carrys a jealous appearance on their part, as preparing a frontier to the Spanish Settlements in that part of the world* AGAINST THE AMERICANS."

I believe it has been settled between America & Spain, that the latter should again have the Settlement of Pensacola, for it is most assuredly the interest of America to have the Spaniards there in order to open an easy intercourse of commerce with So. America. If you will but recollect you must remember that more than 3 months ago I told you that my letters from America mentiond that the Congress had settled a plan with Spain for retaking the English Posts in Wt. Florida. From this, as well as my own observations & knowlege of the Country, I am sure that America either pland or aided in putting Spain in Possession of Pensacola.[6] The Posts on the Mississippi first taken by Spain are long eer this in possession of the Americans—What you mention as to alacrity in seizing on West Florida, is only the act of Spain & America begining first, & they have some little share of Credit for acting so politically. Altho I have no certainty of it, it is more than probable Adams is now settling a second loan at Madrid; this cannot be done without some alliance between Spain & America; such alliance not being known here is no proof to me that it is not so—The Commercial Alliance with France was not known in this Country for months after it was settled & signd. Therefore taking these premises, I would by no means have you assert in a publishd letter what "*is not,*" when you know *it may be*. I think if that Letter is read by Dr. F. or Mr. Adams, it will mar our scheme for your talking to them on any public matter hereafter.

I like all your arguments in the other part of the Letter very much—the political motives of France are very easily seen thro—they surely mean to prolong the war for by so doing they effectually prevent both this Country & mine from being able to contend with Her in a future war at least for some years to come. I cannot think as you "*that France has been scanty in her favors to America or done as little for their allys as was possible to do to preserve appearances*"—If the Fleet from Toulon had not had an uncommonly long voyage, it would by arriving a few days sooner (& even without fighting) have shaken this Empire to its very center; and the aid of 25 sail of the line & 5,000 men under any Commander except D'Estaign, would have effected the same purpose in 1779.

I shall miss the post if I do not conclude hastily.
       Yrs. &c. &c.
       T. Digges

BRO: Hartley-Russell Papers, D/EHy 040/16a-d

¹Edmund Burke (1729–1797), one of the advocates of a movement to reform Parliament by reducing government expenditures, needless positions and pensions, and the crown's influence, had framed a bill that would reorganize the king's household, strengthen public accountability, and eliminate places that provided ex officio seats in the House of Commons.
²Philip Stephens wrote as the admiralty board's secretary.
³John Sawbridge (1732–1795), a wealthy radical, supporter of Wilkes, formerly lord mayor of London, and now an M.P. for London, was one of the strong opponents of the North ministry.
⁴A petition signed at York, Dec. 30, 1779, by some six hundred men of influence and property advocating fiscal and parliamentary reforms that would reduce the crown's influence. Although the petition was a product of the Yorkshire Association, which attempted to remain free of political ties, it soon required the political support that Rockingham and Burke could provide.
⁵Probably William Hodgson.
⁶Pensacola was still in British hands (see Digges to Franklin, Jan. 28, 1780, n. 8).

To Benjamin Franklin

Peckam Feby. 10. 1780

DEAR SIR

I wrote You on a matter of business by Capt. B[el]t the 28th ulo. & hope as the interest of himself & five or six other Countrymen is nearly concernd, the prayer of his petition has been complyd with. I have many applications of a similar nature; & I rather encourage them, from seeing the advantages that must arrise to the Country for which they are meant, as well as the getting home the effects & property of some useful citizens who might be lost from remaining too long here. Whenever there is an appearance of discouraging such adventure from the other side, I am to hope You will give me an item thereof; in order that I may save the expences of some who may hereafter risque a trip to P[ari]s for such a help—It is most likely there will be one or two others very shortley.

This will be given You by a friend whom I have a particular regard & esteem for; I need not mention his name or worth to You, & his whole story will be best explaind by himself; I am sure Your aid will not be wanting to Him, & my trouble, if any there has been, in helping him away, will be amply repaid in the thoughts of the future services He may do where He is bound.

I am sorry that nothing is yet done further about the Cartel— The office of Sick & Hurt, parrys every application for the vessels sailing, with a reply that she is only detaind for want of the necessary specification of numbers from You. Many have enterd into the navy & I am seldom without half a dozen on my hands here; for no sooner does one set get away, but another arrives. Mr. Hodgson has wrote to You twice on this head partly by solicitation from me to do so: I think more might be done thro Him than by D. H., (at least at the Office on Tower Hill), for, with the best intentions & wishes to do good, that Gentleman is so much out of Town & employd in other Parliamentary matters, that the necessary business for the Prisoners cannot be duly attended to by Him.

The passengers on parole (particularly some of those by the Ship to Bristol the Polly Cap. Mitchell, for the others have been rather idle or negligent towards getting the terms of their release complyd with) have been active in their applications to the Admiralty, but they are not likely to succeed. They are told that the terms cannot be complied with; that they should not have made such an agreement with Rebels; and that they are not on a footing with the Rebel prisoners here who can only be releasd by a form of act of Pardon &ca.; nay, they have gone so far as to deny from under Mr. Stephens's own hand, that a Cartel ever existed between this Country & the American Agents in France for the Exchange of American Prisoners here against those carryd into France by American Cruisers. They have behavd so shamefully on the whole that the suffering parties have concluded on bringing the matter before the House of Commons, & most likely it will be movd next week by Burke & Hartley in one house & Lord R[ockingha]m in the other.

Mitchells ship is seizd as a Scotch prize, & lost to Him intirely; it has however been intimated to Him at the Admiralty that the worth of Her shall be paid to Him; this is most likely meant to stop his mouth & get him out of the way.—The Partys are to meet Mr. H—— & Mr. B.[1] at my rooms tomorrow in order to fix how the matter is to be stated.

I have sent some news papers by the Bearer as well as Burgoynes narrative & the plans of his different movements & maneauvres prior to his saratoga convention[2]—The Book may be of service in America altho there is no likelyhood of another British Army ever getting to that spot again. I hope the box via Amsterm. has got safe.[3] I drew a bill for the ballance of that & Capt. C[onyngham]s account, some time ago, but have not heard about it, as I have not seen the person in the City who negotiated it for many days. I wish You health & happiness and am with the greatest regard

Dr. Sir Your obligd & Obt. Ser.
W. S. C[hurch]

Our friend D.H—— is apprehensive that some letters between You & Him *have fallen into philistine hands.*

Since writing the above I am informd by a note from Mr. Hodgson that He has receivd a line from You & wishes to see me in the morning.

[Addressed:] A Monsieur/ Monsieur B. F——/ Passy

HSP: Franklin Papers, 5:118.

[1] David Hartley and Edmund Burke.
[2] Lt. Gen. John Burgoyne, *A State of the Expedition from Canada as laid before the House of Commons* (London: J. Almon, 1780).
[3] Probably the maps and books he had mentioned in his letters to Franklin, Jan. 9, 1780, and to William Temple Franklin, Jan. 10, 1780.

To John Adams

London 3 Mar. 1780

SIR

In a letter from Mr. L. of the 16th Feby. I find He was good enough to mention me to You & that You gave direction for any letters I might have occasion to write to be forwarded a Monr. Monr. Fernando Raymond San,[1] Negot. chez Monsr. Hocherau Libraire

Pont Neuf Paris. I shall be very happy in giving You any information of movements here that may come to my knowlege because in doing so I am certain I may in some degree serve the cause of my country.

I have never missd as yet any letter from Paris by Common Post directed for Mr. Wm. Singleton Church Nandoes Coffee House Temple Bar London. I dont mention my direction with a view to draw You in for answering anything I may have to write, but meerly to serve You in any thing you may require of me—that direction under cover to Mr. Edd. Bridgen Mert. Pater Nostre Row will also find me. I am thus explanitory at the onset, because it might not be safe to mention so much by common post, and that I have a safe oppertunity of conveying this to You by a Capn. Carpenter of the late Cartel Ship to Bristol from Boston who goes on business to Passy, & will return in 10 or 12 days:[2] If in the course of that time You chuse any other direction You may mention it to me by a line by Capn. Carpenter. I send by Him the news papers of four or five days back from which you will gather every thing doing here. The friends to Ministry & their measures are hoping every hour to hear that Clinton (who embarkd only 7,000 Effective Men, tho they are said to be *ten*, in the latter end of Decr.) is in possession of Chs. Town. That Detachment consisted of the Light Infantry & Grenadiers of the 7th, 23d, 33d, 42d, 63d & 64th British Regiments; a legion of Horse, the New York volunteers; Fergusons Corps;[3] Yagers;[4] four Battalions Hessian Grenadiers; one Hessian Regiment; & a detachment of the 71st British Regiment. Many are of opinion a part of this army was intended for the Windward Islands, & that they embarkd & saild the 26th Decr. & was much hurt by a Storm after sailing; but this does not seem probable, as there are no accounts from N. York later than the 23d Decr.—& the most intelligent accounts *then*, said they were not to sail till the 12 or 15 Jany.[5] 2,000 under Lord Cornwallis was said to be intended for the Chesapeak to burn two or 3 french Men of War then in Jas. River, and to serve as a Diversion in favour of the other five going against Chs. Town.

The toreys & others of the friends to Ministry do not at all seem to be in spirits about the picture of affairs in America & the West Indies; nor do they rejoice so much as I have seen them, on much less trivial occasions, for the success of Rodney over the Spaniards—They now begin to fear that the fleet at Gibraltar will be blocked up by the Cadiz fleet under Gaston which has many ships superior to Rodneys;[6] They also fear much for the French getting a majority in the West Indies, from whence some late accounts are come of vast sickness & disorder on board the Eng. Ships—The naval War will seemingly be removd for the next summer to that quarter. Rodney was to sail about the 20 or 25th Feby. with *four* ships for the Wt. Indies, & Walsingham will not take more than that number as a Convoy to about 100 Wt. Indiamen which will sail between the 15 & 20th Int.[7] More Ships of War will probably conduct this fleet off the land. It is most likely the N. York and Quebec trade about 50 more will sail at or near the same time. I dont hear of any troops or Ships of War going to that station; but there is a talk going about that Wallace will have a small squadron & carry 4 or 5 thousand men out but I don't beleive it in the later instance.

You will find by the papers sent to Dr. F. that the Ministry have been hard run in several parliamentary questions lately. Their party is loosing ground dayly & the County Petitions for reforms &ca. seems to be a heavy weight round their necks—these meetings & Associations are very similar to former movements in America & it strikes me in the end there will be a serious rumpus if reforms do not take place—The Committees of each County have already appointed 3 Deputies to meet & act for the whole. This is exactly a Congress & it will likely be stiled eer it is long. I dont know whether these movements at home or the Disturbances in Ireland chagrin & depress the ministry most—It appears that the Sovereignty of this Country over that, will not be of many months duration. The armd Associations of Ireland amount to near 64,000 Men, who from appearances seem determind to free themselves from every restriction laid on them by this Country. Their parliament are going to put an end to all appeals to England—to render the judges of that Country independant of the Crown, they at present holding their offices *durante bene placito* and not quam diu *se bene gesserent* as in England—To have a Habeas Corpus act—to repeal Poinings Law which enacts that all Bills shall originate in the Council & not in the Commons[8]—to confine the new supplys to the apportionment of new dutys only—to give bounties on their own Manufactures—and to have a mutiny Bill which last goes immidiately to the grant point of Jurisdiction, &ca.—this is all making for America but would have come better & more servicable to Us a Year or two ago. Even with all the present appearances against this Country, & the certainty of America succeeding to Her wish, I do not discover among what we term the Patriots in Parliament many men that go straight forward in their wish for American Independence. Those whom I intimately connect myself with are clearly & decidedly for it—vizt. Lds. Camden, Effingham, Coventry & Bp. of St. Asaph; Sr. G. Savile Dd. Hartley[9] & but a few others in the Commons—the rest whom I converse with, are all for Independence on some provisos; such as England to remain with a feather of Sovereignty, for America to give up the French Alliance, foederal alliance with England &ca. &ca. I wish they saw the Interests & exact state of both countries in a clearer view.

If you take in any of the English morning papers I think you will do well to fix a mode for getting regularly that calld the London Courant publishd by Almon in Piccadilly. The real state of Ship news, dispatches, sailing of Fleets &ca. are as regularly & justly put into that paper as can be. The Courier de Le Europe also in them [⟨those⟩] points is pretty chaste.

        I am Sir Yr. very Obt. Sert.
        T. D[unda]s[10]

[Addressed:] A Monsieur Monsieur J. A——ms Paris

MHS: Adams Papers, Reel 351.

[1] Hereafter Digges addressed Adams in this way. Mr. L. is probably Peter Luard.
[2] Capt. Benjamin Carpenter had accompanied Capt. Henry Mitchell on the *Polly* and was on his way to ask Franklin for a pass that would enable him to command the brigantine *Adventure* with cloth and other supplies for the United States (see Digges to Franklin, Mar. 3, 1780).
[3] Patrick Ferguson (1744–1780), wounded in 1777 while serving under Howe in a major battle against Washington, had recovered and was with Clinton at the siege of Charleston.
[4] A company of Germans—jägers—commanded by Capt. George Hanger.

⁵The army did in fact sail on Dec. 26 and encounter a troublesome storm, but they were headed for Charleston, not the Windward Islands.

⁶Rodney, having broken Spain's blockade of Gibraltar, had already sailed for the West Indies, leaving only one of his ships behind. Commodore Don Manuel Gastón, with more than twenty ships under his command, arrived too late to engage him.

⁷Robert Walsingham (1736–1780), whose votes in the House of Commons showed that only on naval affairs and the American war did he consistently support the ministry, had commanded a ship in Keppel's fleet during the battle off Ushant in July 1778. He now, however, was windbound at Torbay and so could not sail at the time Digges predicted: he did not leave until June.

⁸Poynings' Act of 1494, supplemented by later acts, was the work of the Irish Parliament. It effectively prohibited the convening of any Irish Parliament until acts intended to be submitted to it and likely to pass had first been approved by the king. The British Parliament in 1719 had passed a Declaratory Act binding the Irish even more securely to dependency by terminating the appellate authority of the Irish House of Lords.

⁹Charles Pratt, first earl of Camden (1714–1794), dismissed as lord chancellor in 1770 because of open disagreements with North's ministers, was a consistent opponent of the government in the House of Commons; Thomas Howard, third earl of Effingham (1747–1791), had resigned a commission in the army rather than fight the Americans and signed numerous protests against majority votes in the House of Lords; George William Coventry, sixth earl of Coventry (1722–1809), had as far back as 1776 spoken in favor of suspending hostilities in America and since 1778 supported the Whigs' opposition to North's measures; Jonathan Shipley, bishop of St. Asaph, was well known to Digges and Franklin as an outspoken critic of the government (see Digges to Franklin, May 12, 1779, n. 2); George Savile (1726–1784), a friend of David Hartley's, was known as a Rockingham Whig, an advocate of reforms, and supporter of motions to end the American war.

¹⁰Adams's endorsement attributes the letter to T. Dundas, a name Digges used again on Mar. 7.

To Benjamin Franklin

London 3d Mar. 1780

DEAR SIR

I receivd Your favours of the 2d & 9th Feby. very safely,¹ and by a Countryman (Capn. Ben. Carpenter of the Cartel Ship lately from Boston to Bristol) I take the oppertunity to forward you a letter from Mr. D. H. which will explain the state of the Cartel; I am in hopes before I seal my letter to also get one from Mr. Hodgson; & not unlikely one from Mr. Banks about the medal,² and also a line from Mr. B. Vaughan.

Captain Carpenter goes on the same errand with Belt, who is arrivd safe, & will go soon. It may be necessary to inform You that the Vessel in which Capt. Carpenter came from Boston has been seizd as a prize, & it is yet doubtful whether the owner of Her Capt. Hy. Mitchell who is also an inhabitant of Boston, & came in His vessel for the purpose of getting over Rigging Cordage & Stores for two vessels He has building in Boston, will get any gratuity made Him for His Ship, which He values at £2000.—Capn. Carpenter will be a supplicant to You for a pass for the Brigantine Adventure, Himself Commander, of about 160 Tonns & men answerable, which Mr. Mitchell will immidiately push forward from Ireland to Boston with the above mentiond articles, sail Duck, Tent Canvass, Useful Stores, & Provisions. Mr. Mitchells friends and Connexions in Ireland will enable him quickly to do this; and as His schemes bear a manifest tendency to do good for America, & that He may be in some measure riembursd his loss's on the Cartel business, I back His Solicitations & request to You, that another pass may be given for the Ship in which He will go himself. He would personally apply to You for it & go thro the necessary forms, but his attendance at the Admiralty every day with His Lawyer & in some hopes of getting a gratuity for the loss of the vessel, prevents Him. If the pass could express this last *an armd* vessel, it will be the better, & he might do something on his way from Corke. The Vessel is calld the *ship* James, Heny. Mitchell Commander about 200 Tons Burthen & would be found & fitted as a letter of Marque, *provided it is proper*, and a Commission can be given by You for Capt. Mitchell to act as such. If it can be done I see some good may arrise from the scheme to Our Country. I have been much with Capt. Mitchell on the Business of the Cartel &ca. and also with Captain Carpenter, & I find them persons every way qualified to be trusted & whom I would wish to serve. Capt. Carpenter will immidiately return to me in London & proceed on to Ireland, & will take charge of any thing You may have to send.

Capt. B[el]t got back near the same period with Mr. B[a]r[be]r, the latter of whom I have not yet seen tho he carefully calld & left Your Letters. He is an intelligent good sort of Man, but so buried in Ship Business in the City that It may be some time before I can get a sight of Him. As yet I am not acquainted by Mr. H[artle]y[3] whether or not he was successful in the persuit He went upon, & which indeed was so complicated that I did not clearly understand. In B———ts adventure you may rely there is none but Americans & those of the right sort, concernd. They are chiefly indeed all of them placd in this Country at present by the accidents of war; some prisoners—some left out of Bread by the stoppage of the Fishery &ca. &ca. but being six or seven in number & not without friends to lend them money, they will carry out full 10,000£ worth of Goods.

 I have receivd & placed to Your Credit the 100£ remitted me. Some days before I got it I had written to my freind at Plyo. to supply Capt. Ma[nle]y, to the amount of 16 or 18 Guins. that he might bribe some individual to give up his place to Him in the next Cartel. I think this or something else may be effected for Him & he never has, nor shall he want my aid. The 28. 1. 10 was paid to Brown & Collison & you have a Receipt inclosd.[4] I have also bought the Dictionary & Grammar Cost 36/6 & they will go in a box with other books from Mr. Vaughan to Ostend. They are directed to the Care of Monsr. Francois Bowens (Mr. Whartons friend) & He has orders to forward them on to you. I employd my friend Mrs. Vaughan to procure the peice of Irish Stuff calld independence, at least as much as would make a Ladys suit.[5] I fear by her not sending it to me to day that it cannot be had in London (but must be orderd from Ireland); but if it comes this Evening Capt. Carpenter will take charge of it to You. If not, I will send it in an Ostend trader to Mr. Bowens for forwardance. There will also go with the ps/s [of] Stuff the six trios of Augustar, which Mr. B. T. F. wrote to me some time ago for.[6]

 I am sorry I cannot give You a better account about the contract for Exchange of Prisoners by the two Cartel Ships to Falmo. & Bristol. Two of the Passengers in them made some little stir at first but their mouths seem to have been since shut. The two Capns. of the Packets Hill, & Boulderson, did what they could with the board of Sick & hurt, but it seems the Exchange as agreed on by the Prisoners could not be complyd with because it was *unusual* & *unofficial*, & because a Cartel for that purpose actually existed between Boston & New York. But I beleive this answer will not satisfy the Yankees if ever any of the Prisoners are again catchd in America. The Bearer will carry You a list of names & the written agreement instead of complying with which only *partial* releas[e]s are given to four or five out of the 130 which came in the two Ships—the releases are simply thus a letter to the Commander in cheif at N. York to release one person or Gentleman, for Mr. Jno. Jackson; (this Mr. Jackson is a talking sort of a forward lawyer who came in Mitchell) and also other similar letters to a Mr. Barry (an under secy. to Govr. Dalling)[7] & to the Capns. Hill & Boulderson. These last are appointed again to Packets and are Kings Commissiond Officers, & Barry very soon after his arrival was sent back with Dispatches to Govr. Dalling. The rest are all following their avocations & seem to be quite easy, nor do I find the Admiralty have ever thought it requisite to write to New York that an equal number for them should be releasd there. This shall be properly enquird into & You shall know the issue.

I have sent you 10 or a dozen News papers by which You will gather the present news & disposition in Parliament. Lord N. does not seem to hold the majority he used to do in his divisions of that House. The people do not seem at all elated with the success's & present state of Rodneys fleet. They think it at risque from Don Gastons Squadron. I find only 4 of his Ships are to proceed on to the Wt. Indies, & but 3 or four to go with Walsingham as Convoy to the Wt. Inda. fleet which will sail about the 15th or 20th but probably 8 or 10 others will see them some distance from the Lands end. There are many fears too about the French having the majority of Ships in the Wt. Indies next summer & fears are revivd about the safety of Jamaica. The Assosiations get more & more seriously formidable every day & the ministry are hurt exceedingly with them.[8] If there is not a general reform gone into I make no doubt but there will be soon some capital Rumpus. The Irish are farther than ever from being satisfyd & their parliament seem resolvd to Repeal Poinings Law—to put an end to all appeals to England—to render their judges independant of the Crown—to have a habeas Corpus act—to confine their votes for Supplys to the apportionment of new Dutys only—to give bountys on their own manufactures—to have a mutiny Bill &ca. &ca.—all which is very clever for us & must in the end hurt poor old England as She is now generally calld, very much.

Mr. Jones being on a Circuit Mr. Paradise deliverd Your Certificate about the orders to American Cruisers not to molest Capt. Cooke, to Mr. Banks who quibbled & shuffled all he could—by saying it was not an act of Congress, but meerly from Your own humanity that it was granted, that it expressd but one Ship when there was two, that it was dated a year after the order issued by France &ca. &ca.[9] He has promisd Mr. Paradise a letter for You which I expect this Evening & said that a Silver Medal should be certainly given You (gold ones only being given to Sovereigns) & that could there be proof that such orders were the deed of Congress they should have a gold medal.

I do not hear or discover the least signs of any troops meant to be sent to America. There are some going & gone to the Wt. Indies the amount not more than 5,000. It is thought Wallace will command a small squadron of frigates and conduct the trade to N. York & Quebec which will likely sail together about the 20th Int. not unlikely with the Wt. India Ships. I wish You a large share of health & happiness & am with very high Esteem Dr. Sir Yr. obligd & Obt. Sert.

T. D.

I send you also a Letter from Mr. Taylor of Bath.[10]

Since writing the within, I have seen Capt. Mitchells Letter to You as well as one to the Council of the State of Massachusets, and they are so explanatory of His business that I need not add a word on that head.

The Letter I expected from Mr. Banks, Mr. Hodgson, or Mr. Vaughan has not come to hand, but I have Receivd from Mrs. V. the peice of Stuff (Durant) as near the pattern as could possibly be got. It Cost 40/– and the ShopKeeper who brought it me says He could not cut the peice which Contains 30 yds.

I do not recollect I have any thing further to say than that I am with the greatest regard Dr. Sir Yrs. &ca. &ca.

The Dictionary & Grammar goes via Ostend with other books

from Mr. V———n. I shall write to Mr. Bowens by the Bearer & if they are arrivd at Ostend & can be forwarded by the bearer they will be sent by Him in the Carriage or Dilligence.

[Addressed:] His Excelly./Benjamin Franklin/Passy   pr.favr./Cap. Carpenter

HSP: Franklin Papers, 5:119.

[1] In those letters Franklin had acknowledged Digges's of Jan. 9, 10, and 11, mentioned that neither Carmichael nor Adams had yet arrived, informed him of letters he had written Hartley and Hodgson about the cartel, and provided him with money to assist prisoners, especially Capt. Manley.
[2] Sir Joseph Banks (1743–1820), a naturalist, was president of the Royal Society, then considering the medal to be awarded to Franklin for his efforts to assist Capt. Cook.
[3] Samuel Hartley.
[4] In his letter of Feb. 9 Franklin had written: "I am concern'd for Capt. Manley, who is a brave and useful Officer, and desire you to supply him with Necessaries to the amount of 25 Guineas. Inclos'd I send you a Bill for 100£; out of which I request you to pay Messrs. Brown, Collinson, and Triton the Sum of [28.1.10] which I owe them, and take their Receipt in full, and keep the rest in your hands to assist poor Prisoners. I hope they will all be now soon off your hands and at liberty."
[5] In his letter of Feb. 9 Franklin had requested a favor: "A Lady here has seen a kind of Irish Stuff which she understands is called *Independence*. She desires a Piece of it to make a suit, she has given me the enclos'd Sample. I must beg the favour of you to procure it for me and send it by some good Opportunity as soon as you can" (LC: Franklin Papers, Series 1, 4:10–11, 21–22).
[6] See Digges to Franklin, Dec. 4, 1779, and to William Temple Franklin, Dec. 20, 1779, and Jan. 10, 1780.
[7] Edward Barry, secretary to Sir John Dalling (d. 1798), governor of Jamaica, had been one of the six Jamaicans to sign the parole agreement before the commissary of prisoners in Boston, Nov. 20, 1779 (see Digges to Franklin, Jan. ⟨10⟩, 1780).
[8] Petitions for fiscal and parliamentary reforms had, following the lead of the Yorkshire Association's, been drawn up by a mounting number of associations in other counties (see Digges to Hartley, Feb. 7, 1780, and n. 4).
[9] On Feb. 15 Franklin had written Digges: "In Answer to yours relating to Capt. Cook [Feb. 4, 1780], this may inform you that I sent Copies of the Enclos'd to all the American Cruisers then in the Ports of france and spain with orders to our Agents to communicate them to others that might touch there. I also sent it to holland to be printed in the Dutch Papers, as a means of making it more generally known to our cruisers at sea, who might find it in those Papers in their Examination of neutral Vessels. It was accordingly printed there. I cannot now readily find one of Those Papers.
"I think I Saw it also in some of the English Papers" (LC: Franklin Papers, Series 1, 4:26).

[10] John Taylor, who had left America in 1762 and settled in Bath, had written Franklin on Feb. 2 for advice about how to proceed in claiming a tract of land in Chester County, Pa., for which he had the warrant (APS: Franklin Papers, 17:56).

To John Adams

7th Mar./80

SIR

Since my letter of the 3d a Gazette Extraordinary, has announcd the arrival of dispatches from Adl. Digby, who is returnd with the fleet & Spanish prizes from Gibraltar, and brought in with him a french 64 Gun Man of War & three Store Ships bound under Her Convoy from L'Orient to the East Indies[1]—The french & Spaniards seem lately to have been totally unadvisd as to the movements of English fleets or Ships, & to have placd their Convoys in tracks to be taken. This Man of War has 60,000£ in specie on board & was most fortunately for Digby met with on the 23d Feby. Rodney saild from Gibraltar with the fleet the 14th & parted with it the 18th taking four Ships of the line only with Him to the Wt. Indies. A like number will probably go under Walsingham about the 20th or 25th Int. with the fleet to the West Indies. Arbuthnot has left his American station & taken the heavy ships 4 of the line with him to the Wt. Ins. Some say that He carryd some troops with Him. By every appearance there are no more troops going to No. America & it looks as if Ministry meant not to continue the American War but to let it dwindle & die away. News from the Southern Expedition from N. York is dayly expected—a transport with upwards of 200 Hessians on board & which was driven off in a storm is arrivd at St. Ives—She saild with the Expedition from N. York the 26 Decr. & a few days after receivd considerable damage in a severe gale which it is thought seperated & dispersd the Fleet[2]—We have no exact accounts from this vessel yet, but from what can be collected it appears the storm will save Chas. Town for some little time further, & not unlikely baffle every future attempt. These uncommon instances of good fortune at Sea at least to Rodney's fleet have raisd the spirits of the people very much, but you find but very few even in their moments of exultation who wish a continuance of the American War.

I am Yr. obt. Sert.
T. Dundas

[Addressed:] A Monsieur Monsieur Ferdinando Raymond/ San,/Chez Monsr. Hocherau/Libraire Pont Neuf Paris

MHS: Adams Papers, Reel 351.

¹ Adm. Robert Digby (1732–1815), next in command to Rodney at Gibraltar, had taken the ships while headed home following the success in breaking the Spanish blockade.
² As a consequence of the storm that had dispersed the fleet, one dismasted transport drifted for eleven weeks with provisions for only four and ended up at St. Ives in Cornwall.

To Benjamin Franklin

London 7 Mar. 1780

Dear Sir

I am to beg the favour of You to inform me by first post, If the following American bills of Exchange are good ones; They are lodgd in my hands by a Countryman who waits to know their fate; that is, whether others of the same tenor & date have, or have not been paid. A letter sent to the former direction by Post, W. S. C[hurch] at N[and]os Coffee House with such information will greatly oblige Sr.

Your Most Obt. Servant
W. S. C.

No. 27—For 30 Dolls. dated feby. 23d 1779—payable to Jona. Warner countersignd Nicholas Gilman for State of N. Hampshire¹—

               26—For 30 Dolls. dated, payable, & Countersignd, as above
               25—For 30 Dolls.   Do.—   —Do.—   —Do.—
              166—For 24 Dollars dated Feby. 15, 1779—payable to
                    Jonan. Warner,
                    Countersignd Nat. Appleton Massachusts.[2]
                    N. B. the above are all seconds—
   No. 173   For 24 Dollars dated Feby. 23 1779 payable to Peter
                    Boilston Adams,[3]
                    Countersigned by Natl. Appleton Massachusets
                    bay.
                    N. B. this is a first bill.

              138 Drs.

[Addressed:] Monsieur/Monsieur B. Franklin/Passy

HSP: Franklin Papers, 5:120.

[1] In the left margin, next to a brace reaching from No. 27 to No. 166, "Paid" is written in a hand other than Digges's. Gilman (1731–1783), a shipbuilder, merchant, and one of the chief members of the Committee of Safety, was a councillor of the state and its treasurer.
[2] A prominent Boston Whig and member of various legislative bodies, Appleton (1731–1794) was commissioner of the Continental loan office.
[3] Peter Boylston Adams (b. 1738) was John Adams's younger brother.

To John Adams

Mar. 10. 1780

DEAR SIR

A Packet boat is arrivd from Jamaica which saild from thence the 29th Jany. with accounts of Fort Omoa being again in the possession of Spain[1] & that one of our Men of War has taken a Spanish Ship of War bound to that quarter of So. America with stores—She was peircd for 64 Guns but carryd only 52—The Jamaica fleet saild the 24th Inst. Convoyd rather slightly only with a force of about two fiftys and as many frigates—about forty Merchantmen in all. Nothing yet from America but it is generally surmisd & beleivd that a storm has seperated & dispersd Clintons fleet intended for the southern Expedition

I am with gt. regard
Yours

[Addressed:] A Monsieur/ Monsr. Ferdinando Raymond San/ Negote./Chez Monsr. Hocherau, Libraire/ Pont Neuf/ a Paris

MHS: Adams Papers, Reel 351. Adams's endorsement identifies the sender as T. Dundas. His notation on the face of the letter shows that he received it on March 19.

[1] The British had taken the fort in Spain's port in Honduras in Oct. 1779, seizing there some three million pesetas; but because the defenses were inadequate, the Spanish had succeeded in retaking it in Nov.

To Benjamin Franklin

10 Mar. 1780

Dear Sir

Your favour of the 26th ulo. got safe to hand,[1] & I have consulted with Mr. H[odgson] on the mode of distributing your benefactions to some unhappy sufferers[2]—a Vessel saild from Plyo. with 100 on the 5th Int. There remains there but 86 and what is rather singular there is pardons lodgd for 68 of that number against the return of the vessel. Means are taking to get the remaining 18 (of which M[a]n[le]y is one) to have pardons also, that there may remain none in that prison after another Embarkation takes place; but the Lord knows when this will take place, as the next Cargoe by the rotine must go from Portso. I have done the requisite for Capt. M., and had aided him at least wrote to my friend to do so above a month ago. The Revd. Mr. Heath —has been a second Wren to those people.[3]

My two friends who first movd the affair in the Royal Society,[4] will do the necessary business as to the medal for the Governor of Picardy.

No news yet from America but it is generally reported Clintons Southern Expedition has been renderd abortive on account of a violent gale which seperated his fleet & has driven one of the transports with Hessians on board to St. Ives. A packet is arrivd from Jamaica which saild 29 Jany. The homeward bound fleet of about 40 Vessels saild from thence the 24th with a Convoy of about 2 fifty Gun Ships & as many frigates—The treasure taken at Omoa comes in that fleet. That fort has been retaken by the Spaniards who have lost a man of war bound thither with Stores, peircd for 60 Guns but had only 50 mounted.

I am Yr. very Obt. Sert.
Alexr. McKinLock

[Addressed:] A Monsieur Monsr. B. F——n/ Passy

HSP: Franklin Papers, 5:121.

[1] Franklin had stated that he had complied with Digges's recent requests for assistance (passes) for various individuals, lamented the British refusal to honor the paroles, committed himself to send over English prisoners for all Americans brought to France, and recommended that Emanuel, duc de Croy (1718–1784), governor of Calais and Picardy, be given a medal for his zeal in disseminating orders not to molest Capt. Cook, even if he, Franklin, were not (LC: Franklin Papers, Series 1, 4:33–34).

[2] On Mar. 26 Franklin had also written Hodgson about relief for the prisoners and requested that he consult with Digges about the distribution (Francis Wharton, ed., *The Revolutionary Diplomatic Correspondence of the United States* [Washington, D.C.: Government Printing Office, 1889], 3:522–23).

[3] Both Heath at Mill and Wren at Forton were continuing to distribute supplies to the American prisoners of war.

[4] Sir William Jones and John Paradise.

To Benjamin Franklin

London 15 Mar. 1780

Dear Sir

I expect this will be handed to You, in the course of a few weeks, by a particular Friend of mine, Mr. Willm. Burn of the house of Messieurs Burn & Sons of Lisbon: He is the Gentleman, whom in two late letters[1] I solicited the favour of You to procure a Passport for (to be sent under cover to Messrs. Freres Aubert Tollot & Co. Turin) that would enable Him to travel in France & stay a short time in Paris; which place He is desirous of seeing before He finishes a Tour He has been some months upon.

As I have mentiond Mr. Burn to You in my former letters, I need only at present recommend Him to Your usual civility and attention. You will find Him a good friend to the Liberties of Mankind in general, & a well wisher to the cause of America;—In some instances He has been servicable to that Country, and in a particular manner friendly to those Citizens of it, who have accidentally visited Lisbon; among whom I am a grateful example.

       I am with great regard
       Dr. Sir Your obligd & Obt. Servant
       Tho. Digges

[Addressed:] His Excellency / Benjamin Franklin / at Passy / near / Paris

HSP: Franklin Papers, 5:122.

[1] These letters have not been found.

To Benjamin Franklin

                17 Mar. 1780

DEAR SIR

This will be handed You by a Capn. Jno. Snelling a native of Boston tho for many Years past He has been employd in the Streights Trade to & from London. He is well recommended to me as an honest American meaning to push out to his Home thro France, & as he wishes to take Your advice about proceeding to Nantes &ca. I have given him a seperate introductory line to You.—He knows nothing of former plans.

Since Capt. C[arpente]r left me, I have wrote You a few lines by post the 7th & 10th Ints. & am in dayly expectations of Capt. C——rs return; His Employer Mr. M[itche]ll is gone to Ireland & has done nothing.

As far as I have recommended the granting some late favors from You, I have not the least doubt the transactions are *bona fide* intended for the purposes mentiond—i.e. getting home property.[1] I dont mean by saying this, that *some* of the partys did not carry more than they had property to purchase. In the two instances which I lately recommended they were various persons (*every one natives & Citizens of America*) concernd. I would not on any account be aiding to any other set of men to obtain similar advantages for illicit trade. I never had, nor ever shall have, (without I am reducd to such necessity for getting out myself) the least concern directly or indirectly in these adventures, but meerly recommended them to benefit some deserving Americans who could not easily get out otherways, & from thinking such measures rather beneficial than otherways to my Country. They were people whom I had proofs were honest, & having a few hundreds of their own got credit for a few hundreds more, & so pushd out four or five in a Ship. Mr. L——th[2] of Bale. [Baltimore] was an exception to this. He came purposely to Europe to recover a debt of upwards of 3,000£ due his Father—He got it & carryd out double that Sum from having an extensive Credit. You know the circumstances of the *last* recommendations; If it succeeds there will go two or three honest men out with Capt. C——r, & these will be all that I know any thing of, for I beleive there will be then left here none others who deserve such oppertunitys.

I hope the box of books forwarded about a fortnight ago has got safe. They were seemingly well packd & forwarded to order. An acquaintance Snor. Ma[ge]ll[a]n took that oppertunity of forwarding to you a brown paper parcel which also containd books.

If You have not already done it please to answer my letter of the 7th Int. on the subject of the Bills of Exchange as I want to know whether or not they are good before I forward them on. A line by Common post to Mr. Wm. S. C[hurc]h (as You once before directed or if under cover to Mr. H[od]gs[o]n) will oblige me. Their tenor & dates are as follow

17 March 1780

No. 25—23d Feby. 79	a first bill³ to Jonn. Warner Esqr.	30 Dollars
	Countersignd Nichs. Gilman for New Hampshire	
No. 26—do.—	[a first bill] to [Jonn. Warner Esqr.]	30 —
	[Countersignd Nichs. Gilman for New Hampshire]	
No. 27—do.—	second bill to [Jonn. Warner Esqr.]	30 —
	[Countersignd Nichs. Gilman for New Hampshire]	
No. 166 15 Feby. 79	second bill to [Jonn. Warner Esqr.]	24
	Countersignd Natl. Appleton Massachuts.	
No. 173 23d Feby. 79—first bill to Petr. Boilston Adams		24 Dolls.
	[Countersignd Natl. Appleton Massachuts.]	

                                                                138 Dollars

I wish to know if these bills are good or not as they are left with me by a poor man for that purpose.

Nothing new since the Cartel saild the 5 relative to the Prisoners. There are 86 left at Plyo. 68 of whom have pardons ready against the return of the Ship to that place & by that time the pardons for the 18 others (among whom Capt. M[anle]y is one) will be forwarded down.

I have nothing yet decided about the medal for the Duke de Croy. My friends Mr. Jones is on a circuit & Mr. Paradise is sick & has no answer since the affair was stated to Mr. Banks.⁴

Those Gentlemen who came over on Parole in the two last Cartels seem quite easy under their breach of that parole, & seemingly now give themselves not the least trouble about procuring or abiding by the terms of their agreement. It is singular with what ease & facility an Englishman can break his parole to Americans, & how lavish they are of the words scoundrells & villains, when there is the least appearance (which I beleive there never has been) of Americans doing the like by them. Surely those lately returnd parole Prisoners, 139 in number, should be in some measure calld upon to abide By their parole Agreement, which was a written one & cannot be misunderstood; I think the mode of requiring by publick Advertisement, the People so releasd, to render themselves to you accordingly, would not be an improper one.⁵

The two Capns. of the Packets (*the Kings Officers*) and the Mr. Barry a Secy. to Govr. Dalling are long since returnd to their occupations the latter gone to Jamaica & the two Capns. got other packets for that Station. Should the *Yankies* once more take them, I think their chance would be but a shabby one. I am on all occasions

        Yr. very Affece. & Obt. Servt.
        P. Drouillard

 If you can with propriety oblige me in procuring a French Passport for Mr. Wm. Burn of Lisbon, now on a tour in Italy, & who wishes to see some parts of France & Paris, *meerly as a Traveller*; It woud be a very singular obligation to Him & me. He does not want to go to any Sea Ports, or where he may be suspected, but, I beleive, meerly the common route from Turin to Paris or any other capital Town worth visiting. The Pass to be inclosd in a letter to Him, and put under Cover A *Messrs. Messrs. Freres Aubert Tollot & Co. Turin*, where Mr. Burn will be in the course of a fortnight or 3 weeks.

 Mr. Burn is a principal in the House of Messrs. Burn & Sons at Lisbon, & is taking that tour meerly for his pleasure. He is a very worthy Man whom I intimately know. He has done much business with Messrs. Willing & Morris,[6] Cunningham & Nesbin [Nesbitt],[7] J. Wharton, and others of the principal people in Philadelphia & other parts of America—Is a *good* friend to the cause of that Country & the *only* house in Lisbon which has, since the disputes, openly acted in favour of America. In one instance, to my solicitation, He sent some Cargoes of Salt at the period it was most essentially requisite. He will be on any other occasions servicable to Us, and as He deserves much from me & my Country, I have not only askd this favour of you but given him a seperate line of introduction should he obtain his wish of being permitted *as an Englishman* to visit Paris. If such pass can be got, I should be obligd to You for forward[ing] it on as soon as is convenient by Post as his stay in Turin will not be very Long. The House of Messrs. Burn & Sons is a well establishd & very substancial one in Lisbon; should You or any friend want to make use of one in that place I know of none more fit.

 Please to forward the inclosd to Capn. H[utchi]ns, as it may be very satisfactory to him to hear What has been transacted since his departure & that his baggage is *all* arrivd safe at Ostend.

17 MARCH 1780   179

Since writing the inclosd, Mr. Paradise has been with me; He says Mr. Banks on receiving the paragraph of Your Letter relative to a medal being given to the Duke de Croy, said He could not possibly recommend the giving one to that Gentleman, as it would lead to a variety of similar requests &ca. Mr. B—— read to Mr. Paradise a letter which I am to receive in a day or two & forward to You. He has couchd it in very handsome & liberal terms to You, & speaks properly of the Congress, but persists in his old opinion that a gold medal cannot be given to that body without additional proofs, that it was by their order or Recommendation that orders were given to the American Cruisers to shew favor to Cap. Cook &ca. &ca. You will be a better judge when You receive Mr. Banks's Letter which I hope will be in a few days, if not by this conveyance.

[Addressed:] Monsieur Monsieur / B. F——n / Passy

HSP: Franklin Papers, 5:124.

[1] On Feb. 26 Franklin had written: "I comply'd readily with your late Recommendations, placing faith in the Declaration of the Parties, that the Transaction was bonafide intended, for the Purpose mentioned, getting home their Property. If this should be extended to cover an illicit Trade, it will when discovered effectually put a Stop to such Operations. I see by something in a late paper from that Country, that they begin to suspect them" (LC: Franklin Papers, Series 1, 4:33–34).
[2] Unidentified.
[3] In his letter to Franklin of Mar. 7 Digges stated that numbers 25 and 26, as well as 27 and 166, were seconds.
[4] See Digges to Franklin, Mar. 3, 1780.
[5] On Feb. 26 Franklin had also written: "The not complying with The Paroles is doubly provoking, not only by the refusal of what is Just, but by so long delaying the Refusal and keeping the matter in suspense. This however I put into a Bag I keep for small Accounts that may or may not some time or other be ballanced. We have so many greater Injuries to complain of that such little ones may at present without much Inconvenience pass unnotic'd.—So I urge that point no more, but shall send over English Prisoners for all the Americans Brought hither, I have Thoughts, though, of requiring by a public advertisement the People releas'd upon their parole, to render themselves here accordingly, as many of Them engag'd to do in failure of Sending Americans in their Places. But I do not flatter myself that a Single Englishman will have Honour enough to comply with the Requisition. So corrupt are become the Morals of that once generous and virtuous Nation."
[6] One of the best known mercantile houses in America, Willing & Morris, founded in the mid-1750s by Thomas Willing (1731–1781) and Robert Morris (1734–1806), Con-

tinental superintendent of finance during the early 1780s, "the financier of the Revolution," carried on an extensive trade and consistently provided support for the American cause.

[7] A shipping house founded in 1751 by Redmond Conyngham, with John Maxwell Nesbitt (b. 1730) as junior partner. After Conyngham's death and a period when the firm was known as J. M. Nesbitt & Co., David H. Conyngham (1750–1834), Redmond's son, had joined the firm and revived the original name.

To Benjamin Franklin

London Mar. 20. 1780

DEAR SIR

Captain Jno. Snelling, who will take charge of this & an inclosd Letter, and also a few News papers for You, meaning to push from this Country towards America by way of Nantes or some other Sea Port in France, and being without any friend to assist Him in that Country with advice, I take the liberty to introduce Him to You for Your advice to Him how to proceed.

I am not acquainted with Capn. Snelling, but He is so well recommended to me, that I cannot refuse giving Him an oppertunity of speaking to You & of thus recommending Him.

He is a native of Boston, but has been many Years from that Country employd as a Levant trader from London to the Medeterranean. He has sold his effects here & means to move homewards as above mentiond; But does not seem unwilling to engage in any way for the service of his Country that may offer favourable to Him in the line of His profession; and I make no doubt but He may be useful in the Medeteranean. He tells me He is acquainted with Your relation Mr. Williams.[1]

> I am with very great Esteem Dr. Sir
> Yr. obligd & Obt. Sert.
> T: D——

[Addressed:] His Excellency/Benjamin Franklin/at Passy/near/*Paris*

HSP: Franklin Papers, 5:123.

1. Jonathan Williams, Jr., son of Franklin's niece Grace (Harris) Williams and at one time a clerk in John Adams's law office in Boston, had been with Franklin in London to complete his education and form business contacts. Accompanying Franklin to France, he had been employed as the commissioners' agent at Nantes, been superseded by William Lee, and become involved in the Silas Deane–Arthur Lee controversy, during which he had been accused of having used his public position for private profit. Thereafter he devoted himself to private business ventures until he returned to America with Franklin, won Jefferson's favor, and was appointed first superintendent of West Point.

To John Adams

In two letters dated March 14 Adams had acknowledged, in order, receipt of Digges's of March 7 and 3. He was skeptical of reports that the British were bringing troops back from New York, so fixed was the nation on continuing the war, yet he did not see how they could find the resources to maintain their forces in America much longer. He had also communicated news of ship movements, wondered about the refusal to exchange prisoners, and questioned whether the economic interests of the leaders of the Committees of Correspondence in England and Ireland might not in the long run be at odds with those of the United States.

London 28 Mar. '80

SIR.

I am obligd to You for a letter the 14th Int. My writing to You is from the motive of making You acquainted from time to time with any material movement or particular news from this quarter, which may be interesting or serving in any way the business You are engagd in; Your particular situation must put it out of your power to write when ever you may wish to do so, & I by no means expect regular answers to Letters I send you. I should be happy to render you any services here, & if You can spare but a few minutes when any thing favorable from America reaches Paris, (for bad news flies quick enough) to inform me thereof, it is all I can expect from You.

We have got accounts here from the Windwd. Islands so late as the 20th Feby. and from Jamaica the 4th Feby. Nothing material from the last mentiond place, save that the former accounts we had of the

Spaniards possessing Pensacoa. seem not to be true at least that place was not taken the 3d Jany.

The fleet which saild the 26 Decr. for Barbados was arrivd. Genl. Vaughan and about 4,000 Men was with it & were preparing about the middle of Feby. for an Expedition against Grenada. A secret Expedition saild from Jamaica about the last Jany. 800 Men, one Man of War & 5 or Six armd ships, supposd for the Coasts of So. America nearest to Guatimala.

A Passenger by the last Ship from Barbadoes, says, that two transports of Clintons Expedition had been blown to the Wt. Indies (Antigua), but this is not publickly known or put forth by Gazette Authority; If it is true, that expedition must have faild in its purpose against Chas. Town.

There are strong reports that Ministry having receivd intelligence very lately that a Squadron of 5 or 6 Ships were going directly from France to No. America, have orderd six Men of War under Adml. Greaves to the New York Station.[1] The West Inda. fleet which have been some time at Portso. are still detaind: as well on account of the winds, as the waiting for some additional Men of War to see them safe & out of the reach of the Brest fleet. They will sail with about 20 Ships of War, only 3 or four to proceed on to the Wt. Indies, which it is said will make the summer West Inda. Fleet about 32 sail of the Line.

Altho we have so recent accounts from the Wt. Indies & many quick voyages from thence, there is not a little from N. York or America since the 26 Decr.

I am very respectfully Yrs.
W: C[hurch]

[Addressed:] A Monsieur/Monsr. Ferdinando Raymond San./Negotiant chez Monsr. Hocherau Libraire/ Pont Neuf/ a Paris

MHS: Adams Papers, Reel 351.

---

[1] Digges appears to be referring to expected sailings. Commodore Charles Louis d'Arsac, chevalier de Ternay (1722–1780), did not leave Brest until May 2 with seven

sail of the line. When the British concluded that his destination was neither the West Indies nor Canada but New York, they then dispatched Rear Adm. Thomas Graves (1725–1802) to try to intercept him.

To John Adams

London April 6. 1780

DEAR SIR

I have wrote you by Common post the 20th[1] & 28th of last month, & Capn. Cozeneau, whom you know something of, & who goes to Dr. F. on the business of the Cartel which He conducted from Boston to Pensance gives me an oppertunity of sending this letter, to gether with the news papers of the day & some pamphlets & papers which may open to you a little of the state of politicks here.[2] I wish your attention to the Pamphlet entitled "A Memorial to the Sovereigns of Europe on the state of Affairs between the old & New World." It is the production of Govr. Pownall who with many specious appearances too frequently acts & writes under the all-powerful sunshine of Ministry.[3] I have directed the parcell to Dr. F. and desird Him to send them to you after perusal—my present confind circumstances induces me to be thus oeconomical or I would send you duplicates.[4]

The movements among the people of this Country as to Associations Committees of Correspondence, meeting of the Deputys &ca. &ca. still continue & go on with Spirit, but I do not discover any common principle of union left in the minds of the People, which can be made a *foundation of Union*, & bind them together against the terrors and allurements of the Court.[5] The People in general seem bent upon a reform in the Constitution & representation, and so great a majority seem to speak for *triennial*, that I do not think there will be another septennial parliament in England. These movements and the critical state of affairs in Ireland embarrass ministry & the Torey party very much, & I think it cannot fail of being in a great measure servicable to Us; for 'tho the pride & haughtiness of many of the active leaders of the popular party may be averse to or displeasd with the declard &

absolute Independence of America there are very many worthy & high Characters among them who wish it most cordially; and I am sure there is a universal wish among the People for giving up the American War, and for withdrawing the Army on any terms however humiliating. I believe Ministry themselves Have thoughts of getting away the army, but it will be a difficult point to accomplish, & the leaving totally abandond in that Country those Americans who call themselves *friends* to Gt. Britain weighs very much—Experience might point out to them that the Expence of keeping the British Army three months in America, would give these unhappy traitors to the cause of their Country a handsome subsistence for life.

Even yet there is no news arrivd of Clintons Expedition tho the *lye* of the day is, that He made a Landing the 17 Feby. in Georgia. The Wt. India fleet is yet detaind for a fair wind—There are upwards of 200 Merchantmen to be convoyd by Commoe. Walsingham with *four* of the Line, one frigate, one twenty Gun Ship, and two or three fire Ships.—When this fleet & those of France arrive in the West Indies it is supposd the fleets for the Summers Campaign will stand 30 or 31 English against 35 french exclusive of Spanh.

There are strong rumours here that the last Brest fleet with troops &ca. is bound to Hallifax (some say to Quebec). The Courtiers talk of that place as their destination, & in consequence thereof Adml. Graves will be sent with six or seven ships (not sooner than 15 or 20 days hence) to the No. American Station.[6]

There is not the least likelyhood that any more troops not even recruits are going there & that there will be *no offensive* opperations to the *No. Ward.*

If you have any late News papers which contain matter worthy of publication in the Remembrancer or Newspapers I should be glad to have them by return of Capn. Cozeneau—sometimes American publications are very useful to be reprinted here.

I refer you to the Bearer and the Papers sent for any domestic news & am with the greatest esteem Dr. Sir

      Your Obedt. Servant
      T. D.

I should be much obligd to you to put the inclosd Letter in the post for Nantes.

MHS: Adams Papers, Reel 351.

¹ This letter never reached Adams and has not been found.

² Isaac Cazneau, like Capt. Carpenter a recent commander of one of the cartel ships that brought to England the prisoners that the Americans had paroled, was seeking Franklin's bond to assure him of safe passage with a cargo back to America (see Digges to Franklin, Apr. 6, 1780).

³ Thomas Pownall (1722–1805) had first gone to America in 1753 as secretary to Sir Danvers Osborn, governor of New York, become lieutenant governor of New Jersey for a year in 1755 and of Massachusetts Bay Colony for two years beginning in 1757, been appointed as governor of South Carolina in 1760 because the authorities in Boston found him too willing to defend the colonists' views, but soon resigned his position, and eventually in 1767 won a seat in the House of Commons. He wrote extensively on Britain's colonial rule, including *The Administration of the Colonies* (London: J. Wilkie, 1764) and the pamphlet cited by Digges, *A Memorial, Most Humbly Addressed to the Sovereigns of Europe, on the Present State of Affairs, between the Old and New World* (London: J. Almon, 1780), which Digges commented upon further in his letter to Franklin of Apr. 6, 1780.

⁴ On Apr. 15 Adams, obviously finding this arrangement unsatisfactory, requested that Digges supply him with duplicates whenever he sent anything to Franklin and guaranteed payment (MHS: Adams Papers, Reel 96).

⁵ In his letter of Mar. 14 acknowledging Digges's letter of Mar. 3 Adams had written: "I believe with you that the Committees of Correspondence in England and Ireland must embarrass the Ministry: but will they be of any Use to Us. If the Persons who take the lead in those Correspondences associations and Congress, should prevail and get into Power, will not their Œconomical Projects rather injure than Serve our Cause, by enabling them to command more Money, and make greater Exertions. But is there any common Principle of Union left in the Minds of the People which can be made a Foundation of Union and bind them together, against both the Terrors and the Allurements of the Court?" (MHS: Adams Papers, Reel 96).

⁶ See Digges to Adams, Mar. 28, 1780, n. 1.

To Benjamin Franklin

London 6 April   1780

DEAR SIR

I wrote You a few days ago by Capt. Snelling, and sent a few News papers & books. I now embrace the oppertunity by Capn. Cozeneau to send You the news papers of the day & a few political publications, which tho in the lump may not be worth Your reading, will in some measure shew the disposition of the times, which seem to be galloping fast on to some serious rumpus among the People—many go so far as to talk of a Revolution—a great majority of the People seem bent upon a reform in the Constitution, to reduce the power of the Crown, to have a better Representation, & to alter the duration of Parliaments to triennial; I do not apprehend there will be another septennial Parliament in this Country.

Among the Pamphlets I send, you will see "A Memorial addressd to the Sovereigns of Europe on the State of Affairs between the old & new World." I wish You to look at it, & should be glad to be at Your elbow during the reading, because it is the work of Pownall, who I am very sure frequently acts & writes under the beaming influence of Ministry—tho it has a specious appearance of being written to favour America, I do not like the manner he draws the attention of the Sovereigns of Europe (particular[l]y the Dutch when talking of the Spice Islands) towards my Country.[1] The other things are all on the score of Plans for Assosiations—Resolves of Committes Reports of the Deputation which may be calld the Congress, &ca. &ca. They will convince You of the destracted state of this Country, but to what good end these movements among the People may lead cannot at present be assertaind. They cannot fail however of doing good for America, however biasd the minds of the leaders may be (from pride, resentment, or former follys) against the giving America Independence or doing what is honorable & just towards Her. I am sorry to say it, but there does not appear among the People, those Assosiators, or Committees, any common principle of Union which can be made the foundation of Union, & bind them together against both the terrors & allurements of the Court.

The Petitions now before Parliament are to be read to day & it is supposd a considerable concourse of People will attend the avenues to the House. If these petitions & the clamours of the People who attend them operate in the manner which many foretell England is still a free Country; if not—then may we pronounce that spirit to be evaporated, by which alone the sacred flame of liberty can be nursd.

6 April 1780

The papers sent, & the Bearer of them (who is known to you) will give You all the publick news—We have yet nothing from America or Genl. Clinton since the 26. Decr.; but the *report* or rather the *lye* of yesterday was that He had arrivd with about 1/3d of His fleet & had made a landing in Georgia. There is to be no troops or even Recruits sent to America & it may be satisfactory to that Country to know there will be no offensive Campaign this year to the *No.Ward.* Discovery having been very lately made, that a fleet & army are going or gone from Brest, for Canada or Halifax, six sail of the line or seven are getting ready with all speed to go under the Command of Graves to America. 15 to 20 days will be the soonest they can sail. The West Inda. fleet is still detaind by contrary winds upwards of 200 Sail of Ships convoyd by Comme. Walsingham whose squadron consists of four of the line, one frigate, one twenty, and three fire Ships. Most likely they will sail as to day. When this fleet gets out to the Wt. Indies, it is supposd the force of the fleets for the Summers work will stand as 30 or 31 of the line English to 35 french exclusive of Spanish.

Captain Jos: Cozeneau[2] is the Captain of the Cartel from Boston to Cornwall. His vessel is *now* calld the Penelope and has got round to Liverpool from whence She is meant to proceed homewards with some useful Articles. Mr. [Edmund][3] Dunkin the owner of Her & a Citizen & resident of Boston will write You the particular state of the vessel and of those parole Prisoners whom He brought over. He with Capt. Cozeneau is a supplicant to You for a pass to convey their property in Safety. They are good Men & true, & I hope it will be in Your power to grant what they request. Capt. Cozeneau will explain every thing to You, and as He is personally known to You, I need not here add any thing in His favour.

I am to offer You Mr. T[empl]es Compliments & best wishes—We often drink Your health, & as we wish for a prolongation of Your Eye sight, we are to beg You will send over by the Bearer a Spectacle glass that will sute Your sight—A Gentleman here is possessd of a remarkable bright Cristal which was found in the Cherokee Country & He wishes to make You a present of a pair of Spectacles from it.

Inclosd You have Mr. Banks answer to you about the medal for Capt. Cook. I do not like his letter very much. He can never convince me that He is a friend to the Liberties of Mankind or that his mind is not biasd by political opinion. I wish much to contrive the getting a gold Medal for Congress, & will lend my aid here for doing so in any mode or manner You may point out. He has in answer to Your Letter to me about getting a medal for the Duke De Croy, said that it could not with propriety be given as it woud open a door to various other applications for similar presents.

I have taken the liberty to inclose You a letter for Mr. Carmichael which I am to beg a forwardance of.

When you have read the News papers & pamphlets you will oblige me to let Mr. J. Adams see them which may save me an expence of sending duplicates—my present finances obliges me to be thus œconomical.

I am with the highest esteem Dr. Sir.

Yr. obligd & Obt. Servant
T. D.

I should be thankful for any American News papers or intelligences that may be worth publishing in the Remembrancer or News Papers.

I hope the Box of Books & ps/s of Stuff has got safe to hand.[4]

I forward to You under another Cover two Letters from Mr. D. H. to the Chairman of the York Committee which He begs me to forward to You—the Enclosd has been some days in my possession.

[Addressed:] His Excellency/Benjamin Franklin Esq./Passy

HSP: Franklin Papers, 5:125.

[1] Cited in Digges to Adams, Apr. 6, 1780, n. 3. The 135-page pamphlet appeared anonymously, but only thinly disguised its authorship. The preface is in the form of an address from Paris to the publisher, Mr. Almon, and affects to be by the editor of "The Memorial . . . written by a Friend of mine, who is lately dead" and who, according to a footnote later, was living in the Azores while writing the essay. The "Memorial" itself begins with quotations from Pownall's *the Administration of the Colonies* (1764), argues that the European maritime powers should face actuality—America is by virtue of its agriculture, population growth, political spirit, and commerce de facto an independent power—and should recall that progress for nations had always come by negotiation rather than war, and proposes that they therefore convene a General Council to estab-

lish a system of universal commerce with guarantees of freedom of the seas, just administration of admiralty law, and mutually beneficial taxation of buyers rather than sellers.
² Isaac Cazneau.
³ Digges had either forgotten or did not know Dunkin's first name and so left a blank space.
⁴ See Digges to Franklin, Mar. 3, 1780.

To John Adams

14th Apl. 1780

DEAR SIR

I am obligd to You for the Book forwarded me by Mr. L[o]g[a]n,[1] but unfortunately there is a sheet wanting in the most material part of it, that of the description & powers of the Senate. From Page 16 to 25 the leaves are wanting or rather page 17 to 24 inclusive. This however is of no material consequence as the book is but the *report* & not the Establishd new Constitution of the Massachusetts—When such should get to your hands I should be extreemly glad of it for other reasons than those of meerly making myself acquainted with the Constitution of the different States of our Country—*Monsr. Francois Bowens* Negot. Ostend will forward such to me or any other parcells you may have to send, & thro him I can contrive to get you any publications from hence. The way to get News Papers in the safest way is to agree for them at the Post Officers in Paris who have a means of getting them from the same office here.

A Ship from St. Kitts the 5 March brings no other accounts than that La Mothe Picquets Squadron (which was here currently reported to be *blockd* up in Guadaloupe by Adl. Parker) has saild from thence[2] & made a junction with the other Ships at Martinico where the numbers were 14 of the line the 1st of March, so that when Monr. Guichens Squadron gets out & the other small squadron the number of French will be 36 to about 31 English.

The Wt. Inda. fleet saild the 8th & Greaves Ships after a very serious mutiny on board some of them are gone to sea (said to be for America) the 11th Int. No Man of War was intended for that Station but those were hastily got ready in consequence of hearing a fleet was soon to go from Brest with troops on board for No. America. Most people here suppose that fleet bound to Quebec or Hallifax.

Every day seems to produce more advocates or wishers for withdrawing the troops from America or giving up an offensive war in that Country.

A Motion was to have been made this day in the Commons relative to the State of the War in that Country & to push the Ministry for the giving up the principles of the War & to go seriously to some accomodation. The voice of the majority of the People are decidedly for some such accomodation, but there is no one who can devise the means by which it can be done; tho most of my parliamentary acquaintance are for giving the Independence none of them seem bold enough to stand forth & move it in the house—The time is certainly not yet arrivd when it would go down there but I do not think it very distant, and I am sure had the topic been debated to day there would have appeard a manifest disposition in the House to abandon the principles of the War in America, & it seems as if Ministry wishd to feel the pulses of the House upon that subject. A new & unexpected matter put off the whole affair; The Speaker without appearing to be very *ill*, stood up & declard a wish to resign from not being Able thro *illness* to go on with the Business of the House. It appeard as much a political as a real illness and I dare say some new movements perhaps in the Administration may be the consequence. He has not however resignd & the House is adjournd for the benefit of his health till next Monday week; perhaps it may be then too late to renew the intended motion about America or the State of the War there. The possession of Chs. Town if but for a week or the taking two or three Men of War from their Enemys may make these wise-heads think their arms invincible & that they may have some better success by prosecuting the War a little further.

There is with me a Mr. Jonn. Loring A[u]s[ti]n[3] who left Boston the 29th Jany. & was taken in Zephir Packet in the Bay. He leaves me to day & will soon be nearer you; He expects some letters to your or rather Mr. D[an]as care by the Protector, which vessel would sail about the 1st March.

There is a second Paul Jones alarm near the Coast of Hull—an Express has arrivd to day that four or five ships of the Enemy have got to that quarter & taken 3 or 4 prizes. They appear to be french frigates & the Hull people can spy *very clearly* the Countess of Scarborough (which once belongd to that port[)] to be one of the Squadron. I wish you every success & happiness & am with very great regard

Your Obedt. Servant
Wm. S. C[hurch]

[Addressed:] Monsieur/Monsr. Ferdinando Raymond San/negot. chez Monr. Hocherau/ Pont Neuf/ Paris

MHS: Adams Papers, Reel 351.

[1] George Logan (1753–1821) had studied medicine at the University of Edinburgh, graduating in 1779. Settling in Paris to study anatomy, he soon formed a close friendship with Franklin. He was now returning to Philadelphia by way of London.

[2] Rear Adm. Sir Hyde Parker (1714–1782) had left Guadaloupe to protect St. Lucia from an enlarged French fleet.

[3] Jonathan Loring Austin, to whom Digges had written in France in Aug. 1778, had returned to his home in Massachusetts later that year. In Jan. 1780 Massachusetts again dispatched him abroad to negotiate a loan. Captured, he had been released through effort of English friends and was now proceeding to the Continent.

To Benjamin Franklin

London 14 Apl. 1780

DEAR SIR

Since my last to You I have receivd a few lines from your Relation[1] by the hands of Mr. L[o]g[a]n, & am very much surprisd to hear that the maps &ca. forwarded to Amsterdam have not yet got to hand. They went very early in Jany. by the Ship Lady Elizabeth Klaas Doorn Commandr., the box markd B F and a Card naild to it with the Direction For Messrs. Fizeau Grand & Co. Amsterdam. I shippd it myself & long ago forwarded the Capts. Receipt and the bill Parcells for it—I think it may be better got at by Mr. F. writing a line to Mr. Grand at Amm. about it.

We have an arrival from St. Kitts the 5 March. An Expedition (of about 4,000 Men) was then talkd of as nearly ready to rendevous at St. Lucie from the quarter of Antigua. That part of the French fleet which was reported to be *blockd up* in Guardaloupe very easily found its way to Martinico & after the junction the latter end of Apr. found a fleet of 14 sail of the line &ca. We are given to understand here that when Monr. Guichens Squadron gets there, & the other five which went before him, the French will have 36 sail;[2] There is not much boasting of superiority & I beleive there will not be more than 31 English of the Line.

The Wt. Inda. Fleet saild the 8th 200 Sail of merchantmen under convoy of 4 of the line, one frigate, one 20, & 3 fire Ships. Adml. Graves (whose destination is generally said to be to America) was to have gone with 7 Ships but the Crews of several of them mutinyd, and one ship the Invincible remains so refractory as to have cut away all her boats & the Crew have confind their officers to their Cabins. Most likely by this day it is all right, & the Ship on Her voyage—This fleet was hastily got ready in consequence of some advices that a fleet with troops on board was going from Brest to America some say to Canada. We have yet no accounts of Clinton & Co. The general opinion is, that He has got to the Coasts of Georgia (some say to Beaufort) but the storms have left him in such a situation as to make it very improbable He can succeed against Chas. Town—The Ship from St. Kitts brings an account of another of His fleet being wreckd on the Rocks of Bermudas. That vessel had foreign troops & some horses on board. Mr. Jonn. Loring A[u]s[ti]n has been with me a few days.—He left B[osto]n the 24th Jany. & was unlucky on His voyage to F[rance] in a small unarmed vessel The Zephir. There was nothing particular in the news way when He left that place. You will hear more of him soon. The New Protector was to take Her departure about the 1st Mar. & will likely bring Mr. A——s——n a packet to Your care. Another packet would sail in about 3 weeks or a month after the Zephyr.

Mr. H[odgso]n is rather anxious to hear from You he not having a letter since the arrival of the Cartel without any passengers.[3] This causes much murmuring at Forton & severals have forced their way out since the vessel returnd & continue flying up to L[ondo]n. On the 13th Int. the numbers were 227 at Fort—n and about 85 at P[ly-mout]h—Mr. Drouillard wrote to his friend at that place to supply Capt. M[anle]y with the sum some time ago orderd. Whether this has Enabled him to take a journey or not I cannot yet learn but I apprehend it has, for silence is always the Answer to letters when things go well.[4]

I fear Capt. C[onyngha]m is again taken with 4 others. The Capn. of the Privateer who took the vessel from F. writes "she was a small vessel loaded with salt wine &ca. On board her were five Passengers among them the celebrated Capt. C——". The Passengers are kept on board the Privateer still on a cruise, but the Prize is arrivd.

This Day in the Commons the Petitions of the People are to be debated. Some of the late Petitions & all the subsequent Resolves at the adjournd meetings, declare the mischief done the Country by the war is intollerable & the people do not seem inclind to bear it longer. Most of them declare openly that the evil is in the prosecution of the War in America & pray it may be given up. Mr. D. H. moves the house this day on that theme, & many people think the debate of to day will evince a disposition in the House *even on the treasury side of it*, to give up the principles of the American War. The voice out of doors is universally for accomodation with America & many of those who were violent a Year or two ago for the prosecution of it with severity & vigour now go so far as to openly wish peace with America on the terms of avowd & declard Independence. I am with the highest esteem Dr. Sir

Your very Obt. Serv.
W. Ross—

I will keep this open as long as I can in order to give You any news that may come out from the quarter of the House of Commons. J. T[emple] often desires me to mention Him to You & I think it will not be long before you see him.

The Speaker was taken ill & all business of course stopt to day. Many say it was a political illness & that some moves in Administration will be the consequence—By his speech, it would seem He wishd to resign & most likely He will not be speaker very long—The House wishd to have an adjournment for some days, & Monday week they are to meet again.

[Addressed:] A Monsr. Monsr. B. F——/Passy

HSP: Franklin Papers, 5:127.

[1] William Temple Franklin.
[2] Adm. Luc Urbain de Bouëxic, comte de Guichen (1712–1790), was succeeding d'Estaing in the West Indies, where he managed to protect France's possessions until his return to Brest in Sept.
[3] The French had used John Paul Jones's prisoners, entrusted to them in Holland, to effect the release of Frenchmen held in England and had not in turn released Englishmen they held to exchange for Americans in British prisons. The British in Mar. had sent 119 Americans to Morlaix and found awaiting them no English prisoners to complete the exchange. Hodgson had good reason to be anxious (see Digges to Franklin, May 24, 1780, n. 4).
[4] Digges misread the silence. Manley was unsuccessful in this and later attempts to escape from Mill Prison and had to wait until Dec. 1781 to be released through an exchange.

To Benjamin Franklin

London Apr 17. 1780

DEAR SIR

Dr. J. Harvey Pierce, and Mr. William Sprague will hand You this. They are two professional & good Men who mean to quit this Country for a better, & will I make no doubt carry over knowlege & political opinions which will be beneficial to any part of Our Country where they may fix for life. Their particular intentions will be best explaind to You by themselves. They propose travelling thro France to Nantes and take their passage from that or some adjacent port for America. In the doing this Your advice & help will be very beneficial to them, and I beg leave to ask it for them.

I am with great truth & Respect

Dr. Sir Your Obedt. Servt.
Th. Digges

P. S.—I gave you a line by Post the 14th since which there is nothing new or any arrivals from the Wt.ward.

HSP: Franklin Papers, 5 : 129.

To Benjamin Franklin

London Apr. 17. 1780
[Deposition not in Digges's hand]

The Town of Falmouth } to wit

The voluntary examination and disposition of Nathaniel Harris late Master or Commander of the Ship or Vessel the Behmus of and belonging to Newberry Port in the Province of Massachusetts Bay in north America,[1] Taken on Oath this first day of April in the [year] of our Lord One thousand seven hundred and eighty. Before the Worshipful Joseph Hocken Gentleman Mayor and one of his Majestys Justices of the Peace of and for the said Town.

Who upon his Oath saith that on the twentieth day of December last past he together with the rest of the said Vessels Company Sat Sail and departed in her from Cape Nicola Mole in the Island of Hispaniola being bound for Newberry port afresaid with a Cargo consisting of Sugar Molasses Coffee and Lignum Vita the said Ship being then tight staunch and sound and in every respect well found and fit for the Sea and the Said intended Voyage on which said Voyage they proceeded with the wind at East and moderate weather untill the second day of January last past when being in the lattitude of about forty Degrees North they met with a Violent Gale of Wind at West variable to the North which obligd them to ly too untill the fifth day of February last pa[s]t at which time being in the Lattitude of about forty six degrees North the Wind increased in violence and the Ship being much loaded with Ice and very leaky and in a danger of foundering by reason of her violent labouring in the Seas which were very tempestuous they in Order to lighten the said Ship and to prevent her from sinking in the seas were obliged to throw overboard her Guns and part of her Cargo. But being much in want of provisions and water of which they had a Very small quantity remaining on board and had been at very short Allowance for some time the Gale not at all Ceasing and the Rudder Irons worked loose, this Deponent and the other Persons on board judged it absolutely necessary for the preservation of the Ship, the remainder of her Cargo—and their lives to bear away for Flores one of the Azores or Western Islands and they accordingly bore away for that Island and on the first day of March last past had sight of that Island and on the fourth day of that Month being got with the Ship near the Island this deponent went on shore at Flores aforesaid. Mr. Samuel Bailey having previously gone on shore there in order to procure some provisions and[2] other necessaries as were wanted to enable them to prose[ed] onto the remainder of their said Voyage but whilst this Deponent and the said Mr. Bailey were on shore this Deponent discoverd a Cutter rigged Vessel bearing down on the Behmus which was standing of[f] and on the Island of Flores and soon afterwards the Cutter ran along side of the Behmus, Whereupon this Deponent and the Said Mr. Samuel Bailey went on board the Said Cutter which they found to be an English armed Vessel and that she had Seized this Deponents Vessel as prize, and this Deponent further Saith that he together with Mr. Samuel Bailey and several Other persons were put on board the said Armd Ship which was called the Achilles and commanded by Capn. William Yawkins who carried them to Falmouth aforesaid and he has Since heard that the said ship the Behmus is arrivd at Cork in the Kingdom of Ireland—

> Sworn at the town of Falmouth
> aforesaid the first Day of april
> in the year of our Lord 1780   Nathaniel Harris—
>   Before me
>   Joseph Hocken Mayor

N.B. the Ship had taken a pilot onboard the night before but came to Anchor in so much Water that they were Oblidgd to Slip their Cable on account of the Wind blowing on Shore and stood of[f] at Sea untill the next morning when being Chased close in with the Land seventeen of my Men took the Ships boat and went on Shore to the Island of Flores and their we left them—

DEAR SIR

Mr. Samu. Bailey (of Newberry Port) has been with me & I am trying to get him out in a direct road to his home. He has related His singular storey to me. It appears manifest to me that the Privateer who took him had no right to commit such an act of hostility so near the shore of a Neutral Country; The People of Flores, particularly the Goverr. or Commandant, were Openly hostile to the Americans & appeard to have given information to the English Privateer (calld the Achilles Capt. Wm. Yawkins belon[g]ing to London) to come round from another part of the Island of Flores to seize the American Ship. Just before the period of their striking to the Cutter, seventeen of the Men belonging to the Bemus made their Escape in the boat to the Island and are left there in a miserable situation. Their names & discription are below. Can any means be usd to get them away? There is no trade to the Island of Flores save in the summer time[⟨.⟩] Just after ⟨the⟩ Harvest a few ships goes from Lisbon for the *only* produce of the Island *Wheat*.

I am Yr. very Obt. Ser.
T. D.

Captain—Pettice of Middle Town Connecticut
John Lewis Boatswain of the Ship Behmus
Danl. Ely Cooper to make the HHds. for the molasses
Thos. Merrell ⎫
Saml. Foot   ⎬   Seamen, all of Newberry Port
Saml. Long   ⎭
———Dorrington Seaman, an Englishman
    Forgoson an Englishman
Enock Rolf—Newberry
two Boys
———Young—Newberry Port
and five others names forgot

HSP: Franklin Papers, 5:128.

¹ The *Behemus*, a letter of marque, was owned by Moses Little, Joseph Moulton, and others of Newburyport, Mass., and carried eight guns and a complement of twenty men.

² Here Digges provides a marginal notation: "When the Vessel was taken She was within one quarter of a mile of the Shore on the Western part of the Island & near one of the two small villages of the Island.

"N.B. there is only two villages like Whigwams on the Island one to the Et. & the other to the Wt."

To Benjamin Franklin

London Apl. 22d 1780

DEAR SIR

I beg leave to recommend to Your usual civility and attention the Bearer of this my friend Docr. Plunkett, who means to take a journey in a few days to Holland & France; and should He return from Paris directly hither He will obligingly take charge of any thing You may have to send to this quarter. You will find him a good friend to the rights of mankind, & particularly attachd to the cause of Our Country, in the Armies of which, He has had a Brother who has very honourably distinguishd Himself.

I am with very great regard
Dr. Sir Yr. Obligd & Obt. Servant
Th. Digges

HSP: Franklin Papers, 5:130.

To John Adams

On April 15, acknowledging Digges's letters of March 28 and April 6, Adams had written: "Let me beg of you to send me duplicates, of Pamphlets, as they come out, when you send setts to another Gentleman—any Banker in London who will draw upon, Me or Mr. Grand the Banker for the Expense of them, shall be pucntually paid, or I will get Mr. Grand to desire some Banker of his Correspondence to pay you, or the Book seller if any one, will undertake to send them to me. Political Pamphlets I mean respecting the present War, and the actual State of Things.—It is of much Importance to me, and perhaps to others, that I should have all these Things as soon as possible and that they should be my Property that I may have the Use of them to myself as long as I please, and send them where, and as soon as I please" (MHS: Adams Papers, Reel 96). *He had then asked for some specific newspapers and magazines, mentioned having heard about Clinton's plight during a storm, and concluded by saying he wished to know "the Effect in England of another Storm from the North."*

Dulwitch 28 Apr. 1780

DEAR SIR

I attend to what You mention by Capt. C[azneau] the 15th Int. and have in consequence, some days ago shippd for Ostend, in a box markd A, with a card direction to *Monr. Frs. Bowens Mert. there*, sundry pamphlets & papers as you require; & have written to Mr. B. to forward it on in the manner He may think safest, & to hereafter attend to any other parcell I may send in the same way. It may be better you write to Him & point out the mode of conveyance from Ostend to Paris which you may think best. This will be by much the best way for Books or Pamphlets when private oppertunitys (which are very rare) do not offer; but it will not do so well for News papers as the ordering them immidiately Yourself from the Post masters at Paris, who, having an understanding with the Post office here, can get any papers by post which you may want. The morning Papers you mention, & the one I have lately sent, will be sufficient, and those of the Evening, *two* will answer Your purpose; they come out alternate, The Londn. Evening Post, & the London Packet. I could get a friend who is concernd in the neutral vessels & who lives near the tower, to send You a packet of these papers of every 8 or 10 days, as the vessels may sail, directed as the Box is to Mr. Bowens, if You think this a better mode, at any rate I will do it (in order that you may be supplyd with the Papers) until I get your answer to this letter, or the fixing on any other mode. I will continue to You the Courant, because it shows every movement of the People here relative to Petitions associations the proceedings of the Deputies &ca. &ca. For this reason I sent you a bound parcell compleat the 25 Novr. to the 18 Apr. & a few loose ones to the 26th which I had done up for the purpose of sending to a more distant quarter. I will make up another parcell of Pamphlets in a few days & forward them as the last were sent. I am obligd to you for the Pamphlet by Dr. L. When it comes to your hands *revisd*, & as the Establishd Law, I pray you send it to me together with any papers that are worth publishing here,[1] if the parcell is too heavy for post, send them to Mr. Bowens who will forward them by neutral vessels to the person near the Tower who will send you the papers & shipps most of my packages. By such a channell as this, (which I have long been wishing for) many useful publications may come to light. I will keep an account open for the Expence of so doing, & will apply to Mr. Louis Tessier (whom I have applyd to on former occasions) for my riembursement; better that Monr. G[ran]d should write a line to Him, for me to deliver, to pay me these sums as they are calld for. You will have annexd a list of what I have already sent you.

We have at length got news of Genl. Clinton, which came by a packet from N. York which saild from thence the 30th March. It appears (tho there are no official dispatches from Clinton Himself) that the fleet after being much buffetted about by the Storm & with the loss of four or five transports, got to Tybee about the begining of Feby. and that the body of the fleet got to the Barr of Chs. Town the 9 or 10th March, & were nearly landed the 12th when the Russell man of war saild from thence to N. York with the account. It appears they have occupied some posts 8 or 10 miles from Cs. Town particularly that of Stono ferry, but have neither attackd James fort nor fort Sullivan—by the Ministerial reports we are informd Lincolns army was between 5 & 6,000 men well posted *out* of the Town & that some strong works had been thrown up on the neck & to defend the Town. The Army of Clinton, when it saild consisted of 7,500 Men & he took a Regiment with him from Georgia; every account says He will not have more than 5,500 men *effectives* to opperate with, & I think from the feeble flat manner the whole storey is told in the New York papers & from the accounts I have gatherd since the packets arrival that his force is not equal to the possessing Chas. Town. He has but one ship of the line & 4 or 5 lesser Men of War to act against the Forts & Town;

there are 5 or 6 American & french frigates within the harbour, & if Fort Sullivan is as strong as it was in 1776, I think with the united Naval Force it will be able to give the British Ships of War a second drubbing. It cannot be many days before we have accounts here of the decided fate of the place. There are many particulars in the News papers, which You will have as soon as this, but the above is the substance of what I hear.

The late Russian Memorial for Neutrality is not at all relishd by the Ministerealists here, 'tho they attempt to palliate it by saying it is only a manoeuvere of that Court for arming their Ships, which when armd, are to join England,[2] this is too bad to be related, but such is the conversation of some who are determind to go on blindfolded to distruction. It appears that Holland has acceded to the wish of Russia in the substance of that memorial for neutrality & they are seemingly determind to defend their ships at sea against English Cruisers. If some better understanding does not soon take place between this Court & the States, it is more than probable there will soon be a dutch war.[3] How the northern powers of Sweden & Denmark stand, You are better informd than I can be—Portugal most likely will acceed to it, for they seem bent upon neutrality if such a desirable state will be allowd them.

The Parliament of Ireland on the two late great national questions, has produced a majority of 39 in favour of the Court, tho directly contrary to the wishes of a great majority of the People—The Commons have been touchd with English gold or English paper, & have provd themselves as corrupt as another parliament nearer me. It is most likely the disputes will not stop there but that the People will right themselves.

Every body hereabouts seems sick of the American War, but how to get rid of it is the question. The State of that war will be probably canvassd next Tuesday, when Genl. Conway is to make a motion relative to accomodation with America.[4] Much secrecy is observd as to the substance of his intended motion, but some folks think He will move for some profers to be made to America on the preliminary of a truce; but then the sending this profer over to America puts at so remote a period in point of time, as to make some friends speak discourageingly of the proposition or motion—most likely *some* Members of that House such as Gen. C——y & Govr. P[ownal]l, are urgd by Ministry to bring forth such conversations in the House in order to feel the pulses of its members upon that topic. If they could well do it, I beleive they would try to get the opinion of Mr. J. A[dams] (whom I understand is at Paris a Commissioner to Speak upon peace) upon the mode of making profers to America for tho our ministers try to make people beleive they know not the nature of Mr. A——ms's Commission yet I cannot suppose them so blind & ignorant not to know something of the nature of it. I am Your very

        Obt. Servt.
        Wm. Ross

[Addressed:] A Monsieur/Monsr. Ferdinando Raymond San/&ca. &ca./Paris

MHS: Adams Papers, Reel 351.

[1] One of Digges's functions was to arrange to have inserted in the London papers news and comments helpful to the American cause.

[2] On Apr. 1 the Russian ambassador had presented a declaration of neutral rights whose acceptance by Sweden, Denmark, and especially Holland would pose a threat to Britain's blockade of ports where Americans might be supplied. The three northern powers were about to form the League of Armed Neutrality to pry open Spanish and French ports for the naval stores of the Baltic fleets, but it was the more significant shipping of the Dutch that primarily concerned England.

[3] The British were refusing to allow Dutch naval stores to pass through the Channel in Dutch bottoms, were suspending the Dutch from commercial treaty privileges, were seizing ships, and were blockading Dutch ports.

[4] The motion was postponed (see Digges to Adams, May 2, 1780).

To Benjamin Franklin

Londo. 28 April 1780

We have at length got some accounts from Clinton. A packet which left N. York the 30th Mar. is arrivd. There are no official dispatches from Clinton himself, but it appears from what I can gather at all quarters, His fleet after much buffiting about & the loss of four or five transports, got to Tybee the begining of Feby. there took in one Regiment Refreshments &ca. & got to the Bar of Chs. Town about the 10th or 11th Mar. The Russell Man of War & a packet left the Army & fleet there the 12 or 13th, when they had chiefly landed all the troops & took post on James's Island, but at some distance from the Town. One part of the Army was at Stono ferry, but they had not taken or attempted to possess any posts or forts of the Americans—By accounts from the quarter of ministry I am informd Lincolns army was between 5 & 6,000 well posted without the Town, that the neck of Land had been seperated by a Ditch from the Town, & that in it there were cross canals cut so as to prevent fire & to form barriers. When Clinton saild from N.Y. he had but 7,500 men upon paper, so that after his losses, & the Storm it is not likely he can act with more than 5,000 men effectives. I think from the feeble flat manner the whole story is told with in the New York papers, and as it is represented here, that this force is not equal to the reduction of Chas. Town.[1] One ship of the line & some transports are said to be lost on the Bar; If so he has but one other of the line & about 5 frigates to act against the forts Sullivan & James; There were five or six American & french Frigates within the port, & if Fort Sullivan is as Strong as it was in 1776 surely with the additional aid of the ships they may be able to give the English Men of War a second dressing. There are many particulars in the papers which I shall refer You to because they will reach you as soon as this Letter can.

The House of Commons of Ireland, has on the two late important national questions produced a mojority in favour of the court of 39, but it appears directly contrary to the wishes of a great majority of the People—The members of that House have been manifestly touchd by English Cash & they have proved themselves as corrupt as ours in this Country. The affairs of Ireland do not seem to rest upon the hinge of a Parliamentary vote, for the people seem quite ripe to right themselves. Both in that quarter & this every person seems heartily sick of the American War & cordially wish it was given up.— The State of that war will be enterd into on tuesday next, when Genl.

Conway is to move the House about it, & intends as I learn to go into the non expediency of it & to make some proposals of getting accomodation with America. They are too secret for me to get at the terms on which such motion is to be founded or what lengths He means to go in his proposals for accomodation, but some say it is on the old score the preliminary to be a truce for a certain time. D. H. and the Genl. tho they do not frequently commune have I believe had some conversations about it, but I am not very sanguine as to expectations of good to arise therefrom.

I have not had any information that Capn. C[onyngham] is again taken & hope it is not true.[2] Capt. M[anle]y after making his escape, has been taken & reconfind. No news about the Cartel & little appearances of her again getting afloat. The Cartel to B[ristol] which was seizd[3] is likely to be paid for, but there is not the leas[t] stir or hope about the rel[e]ase of the equal number of Americans for those 130 which came over in the two vessels from Boston. D. H[artley] and Mr. E[dwar]d B[ridge]n often express an inclination to hear from You; the latter about the meddals.[4] Pray what is to be done further about the meddal I wrote to You upon, for since the forwarding Mr. B[an]ks's letter to You I have not had a line from You about it, nor do I know if the letter got safe, tho I think it was by Cap. C———z———n [Cazneau] that I sent it.[5]

                        I am with great Esteem
                        Yours
                        Wm. S. C.

[Addressed:] Monsieur Monsr. B.F———/ Passy

HSP: Franklin Papers, 5:131.

[1] Digges's optimism was unjustified. Reinforcements from Georgia enabled Clinton to attack Charleston on Apr. 10 and compel surrender on May 12.
[2] Digges's letter to Franklin of Apr. 14 was accurate. Conyngham was once again a prisoner. Taken by the privateer *Admiral Edwards*, he had been delivered to Mill very ill.
[3] See Digges's certificate, May 10, 1780.
[4] In Sept. 1779 Bridgen had sent Franklin two samples of copper to consider purchasing for medals and coinage. At that time Franklin had been without authorization to spend the money, and he had so informed Bridgen.

⁵ Digges had sent it on Apr. 6. Franklin finally acknowledged it on June 25: "I received yours inclosing a very obliging Letter from Mr. President Banks. The Congress cannot be said to have ordered the Instructions I gave, tho' they would no doubt have done it, if such a Thing had been mentioned to them. It is therefore not proper to use any farther Endeavors to procure a Medal for them. I do not indeed perceive that one is intended for me as you imagined, and tho' it would certainly give me Pleasure if voluntarily order'd I would not have it obtain'd by Sollicitation" (LC: Franklin Papers, Series 1, 4:162).

To John Adams

Wandsworth 2d May 80

DEAR SIR

You will have read, before this can reach you, the Gazette account of the Chas. Town Expedition; which is universally esteemd here rather a disagreeable account for Government, and plainly indicative of very great doubts if Clinton will succeed or not. I am perswaded by all I can hear He will be a second time disgracd and baffled in his attempts on that place.

A parcell containing Pamphlets & papers to the amount of 3. 5. 9d. was lately forwarded to you via Ostend directed to Mr. Frs. Bowens Mercht. there, who has orders to forward them on in the safest & best manner he can. He is made acquainted with the contents of the box, & has direction to forward in like manner to you any other parcell which may reach his hands (with or without any accompanying letter) markd **A** It may be not improper for you to write Him a line *how* & by what conveyance He is to forward You any thing else in future. My motive for sending You the whole of the *Courants* is because *that paper* contains every petition, address, Remonstrance, County meetings &ca. &ca. that are agitated in this Country, & is of itself a history of all the movements of the people as to obtain a reform in the Constitution.

—The Evening Papers i.e. the Londn. Evening [Post] & London Packet, will be sent on with the Courant in future until I have Your orders to stop them, which, You had better do when you can fix a mode with the Paris post office how to get them *by Post*. A small paper parcell of other Pamphlets & the News papers will be forwarded You about this day week.

There are accounts in the City today that the Jason Man of War & her Convoy about 15 Sail transports (which is given out were bound up the North Seas to bring the Hessian recruits *said to be 1500 Men* to England) have been met by two french frigates and dispersd, several of the Transports are put into Scarborough, the others & the Man of War still missing & supposd to be taken.

Genl. Conways motion relative to America was put off today for some future period, Hartleys stands for fryday the substance of which you will have in the General Advertiser of the 1st of May.[1] Some deviltry has got into Conway's head for He seems to think there is yet a door open for Peace with America short of Independence than which nothing can be so falacious & absurd. How the Devil he can imbibe such notions I cannot think, but I am told He is much in the circle of a Scotch acquaintance & some times talks to Refugees such as Mr. Galloway, Allen &ca. I cannot account for it otherways than that He is looking up to the Command of the Army.

I should be glad, when you see & read the Debates upon those motions to know what you think thereof.[2] I am on all occasions

        Your obedt. Servant.
        Wm. Russell

[Addressed:] *Flanders* A Monsieur/Monsieur Ferdinando Raymond San/Negotiant/ Chez Monsr. Hocherau Libraire Pont Neuf/ *Paris*

MHS: Adams Papers, Reel 351.

[1] Hartley had actually given notice of three motions that he intended to bring before the House: (1) "That it appears to this house to be unadvisable and inexpedient to carry on an offensive War in America; assigning among other Reasons, that it prevents the Employment of the great military and naval Force, against the natural Enemies of this country"; (2) "That an Address be presented to his Majesty on this Subject"; (3) "That an Address be presented to his Majesty to appoint Commissioners to open a Negociation for Peace with America; and that the Basis of the Negociation be a Truce of ten

years" (*Public Advertiser*, May 2, 1780). But, as the record of the debates shows, it was Henry Seymour Conway (1721–1795), not Hartley, whose motion would be taken up on Friday (May 5). Conway's proposal was "An Act for quieting the Troubles now reigning in the British colonies in America, and for enabling his Majesty to appoint Commissioners, with full powers to treat and conclude upon terms of conciliation with the said Colonies." Stopping short of recognizing American independence on the one hand and of insisting that Americans acknowledge Britain's sovereignty on the other, it sought to produce reconciliation by having the king concede to the colonies the various rights, immunities, and privileges demanded in their petitions to the king and the two Houses of Parliament prior to the outbreak of war. The objective was to enable England to concentrate on her war with France. Conway was known for arguing that the war was both cruel and unnecessary, but he was at the same time not prepared, even as late as Apr. 27, 1780, to delay granting supplies to troops overseas. Criticism of his present motion came mainly from those who felt that failure to recognize America's de facto independence reduced the measure to a futile exercise. Put to a vote, it lost, 123–81.

[2] Adams replied on May 13 criticizing both the government and the opposition: "I have seen the paper and read the debate.—Tis the scene of the Goddess in the Dunciad reading Blackmore to her Children.—The Commons are yawning, while the Ministry and Clinton, are cementing the Union of America, by the blood of every Province, and binding all to their allies, by compelling them to shed theirs.—All is well that ends well.—These wise folk are giving F. and S. a Consideration in Europe too, that they had not—and are throwing away their own as nothing worth. . . . The Minority means only to try if they can make peace with America separately, in order to revenge themselves, as they think they can upon F. and S.—but this is as wrong and as absurd, and impracticable as the plans of the ministry.—All schemes for reconciliation with America short of Independence, and all plans for Peace with America, allowing her Independence, separate from her allies, are visionary, and delusive, disingenuous, corrupt and wicked. America has taken her equal status, and she will behave with as much honour, as any of the nations of the Earth.—To say that the Americans are upon the Poise, are ballancing, and will return to their allegiance to the King of England, is as wild as bedlam" (MHS: Adams Papers, Reel 96).

Certificate

When Captain Benjamin Carpenter had visited Franklin early in March, he had secured the documents needed to enable him to take his and Henry Mitchell's property and effects back to the United States. On March 14 he had, through Franklin, given his bond to the president of the Congress for the safe delivery of their cargo in the brigantine Adventure *and the ship* James; *on March 15 he had taken the oath of allegiance to the United States; and at the same time he had received from Franklin the passport inside which Digges's certificate was now affixed.*

May 10, 1780

I, Thomas Digges of Warburton in Maryland and a Subject of the United States of America (tho at present Resident in England, for reasons which, in prudence, cannot be herein explained) DO by these Presents Certify unto All and every Person whom it may Concern; That I was principally aiding to & assisting in the procuring the annexd Passport for the Brigantine Adventure, from His Excellency Benjamin Franklin; And which Passport was obtaind for the sole purpose of removing from hence, or from Ireland, to the United States of America, the Property & Effects of Mr. Henry Mitchell, Merchant of Boston (who in December last came from America in the Cartel Ship—calld the Polly to England, & which said Cartel Ship was lost to the said Henry Mitchell by a regular seizure at Bristol) and of Captain Benjamin Carpenter who was Commander of the afforesaid Cartel. I Do also Certify that the said Brigantine Adventure, as well as the Stores & Effects on board Her, appears to me to be principally the property of the said Henry Mitchell, altho it is expressd in the annexd passport to be that of Captain Carpenter; whose name was necessarily inserted by His Excellency Benj. Franklin, as Himself was the personal applicant for the Pass, Mr. Mitchell being then in a process of Law to recover His said seizd Cartel Ship, & not having it in His power to go to Dr. Franklin Himself. Mr. H. Mitchell having now got His Effects from Ireland to London, means to push out directly for Boston or some port within the Laws & jurisdiction of the United States of America, & not to touch in Ireland, as was his first intention when the annexd Passport was obtaind. And in order the more effectually to secure His said voyage, and for the better cover of His purpose in case He should be met with and examind by any British Cruisers on the voyage, He has armd His said vessell the Brigantine Adventure, with fourteen Carriage Guns, (six Pounders) other necessary Stores, mannd Her with about thirty men, & procurd for Her an English Letter of Marque Commission.

I Do hereby further Certify, that I am neither directly nor indirectly concernd in the said Brigantine, Her Cargoe, outfit, or future purposes, nor no ways concernd in trade with the said Henry Mitchell. In Witness Whereof I have hereunto Set my hand and Seal in London this 10th day of May A. D. 1780—

Thomas Digges

Commonwealth of Massachusetts: Massachusetts Archives, 171:200.

To Benjamin Franklin

London 24 May 1780

Dear Sir

I took the liberty, in a letter of the 9th Int. to solicit the favour of You to help me to a full length portrait of Yourself.[1] It is to oblige a deserving and ingenious Engraver who means to employ his present time in producing a good print therefrom, & to take the plate with Him to a Country where his prospects for future happiness & success are greater than he can promise himself by staying here—He hopes too by handing with him a good full length print of a person whom America looks up to as Her first Citizen, that it will pave his way to future employment & to a good settlement. We have several good bust & half-length likenesses of you in England but none at full length—What we want is one of these either setting or standing, with such ornaments and emblems to the portrait as You may chuse. The size of the Print is meant to be about two feet by 18 Inchs. more or less as the decorations may require. The nearer the drawing or picture is made to that size the better for my friend the artist. If you can possibly give up but a few hours to this my request, it would be a very great obligation to me, besides the pleasure I shall receive in holding forever in my possession the likeness of the man to whom my Country owes the first & most extensive obligations. If the favour could be done me, the drawing, painting, or Craons would find its way safely & expeditiously to me, if it could be forwarded from You to Monsieur Francois

Bowens Negt. at Ostend.² I shall forward to that Gentleman on Saturday next a small deal box which contains a portrait of a Divine who is much respected by Yourself & every person of His acquaintance,³ & what will make it more valuable to You, it is done by the fair hand of his amiable Daughter Miss Georgiana, in return for a present from You which I frequently hear commended and very much prizd. I know of no private oppertunity to send it; I can get it safe to Mr. Bowens, & shall charge him not to forward it but by a very safe conveyance from Ostend.

We have been long impatiently waiting a line from You relative to the Captives in this quarter, as by what you last wrote Mr. H[odgso]n we had reason to expect another letter in a few days; neither him nor Mr. H[artle]y can do any thing with a certain board until another letter is receivd from You.⁴ In the mean time nothing is expected nor even is another cartel talkd of, but many of the prisoners have been lucky lately in getting themselves liberated. As Mr. H———n wrote you the 12th Int., & my letter of the 9th also mentiond these circumstances we are in hopes another post or two will bring one of us a letter.

We are still without authentic news from America, but every day produces a new report about the Fate of Clinton; many people here are wicked enough to hope the present one (which comes from France) to be true, & which says He has been repulsd at Chs. Town & flying towards Georgia. A Ship is arrivd at Cork which saild from N. York the 6th of April with the Reenforcement for Clinton 20 *transports with 3,000 men under convoy of the Rainbow only*—this ship left them on the 12th not far on their way, but steering South with a fair wind.

Our Wt. Inda. fleet of near 250 Sail is still detaind at Torbay for a fair wind. The N. York will probably sail (50 or 60 ships) about the middle June. I hear of no troops or ships of considerable force going with them. Sr. C. Hardy is dead & Adml. Geary got the Channel fleet which we are told is to be 25 sail & to be ready in June.⁵ There are accounts to day from the West, that the Ardent Man of War is retaken in the Bay Biscay by two fiftys—This appears to have been on a cruise by herself, & we rejoice exceedingly at getting our old Ship again.

I formerly took the liberty to mention a Mr. Burn of Lisbon to you & to ask Your interest to him to procure a passport from Turin to Paris; I expect He is by this time in Paris & will probably make use of my Name (or an introductory Letter I had lodgd for Him at Paris) with you. He is a very deserving Young Man & in several instances been servicable to Your Country, & I beleive the only well wisher to its cause that can be found among the British factory at Lisbon. I am to beg Your usual civility may be extended to Him, & You may safely trust any letters or parcells to him which You may have occasion to send hither.

I am Sir Yr. mo. Obligd & Obt. Sert.
W. S. C.

[Addressed:] Monsieur Monsieur B. F——/ Passy

HSP: Franklin Papers, 5 : 132.

[1] Along with his letter of the same date to Adams, this letter of Digges's was thrown overboard when the packet was seized by the British (see Digges to Adams, June 8, 1780, and to Franklin, June 10, 1780).
[2] On June 25 Franklin declined: "I have at the request of friends sat so much and so often to painters and Statuaries, that I am perfectly sick of it. I know of nothing so tedious as sitting Hours in one fix'd Posture. I would nevertheless do it once more to oblige you if it was necessary, but there are already so many good Likenesses of the face, that if the best of them is copied it will probably be better than a new one, and the Body is only that of a lusty man which need not be drawn from the Life: any Artist can add such a Body to the face" (LC: Franklin Papers, Series 1, 4 : 162–63).
[3] Jonathan Shipley, bishop of St. Asaph.
[4] The exchange of prisoners had effectively stopped after the British in Mar. had sent 119 prisoners to Morlaix and found none of their men ready in exchange (see Digges to Franklin, Apr. 14, 1780, n. 3), for they then discontinued serious discussion of further cartels.
[5] Francis Geary (1710?–1796), already frail, was to serve only a few months before resigning as successor to Sir Charles Hardy.

To John Adams

26 M⟨ay 178⟩0

DEAR SIR
I expected when I gave You the last West Inda. accounts the 9th Int.[1] that my next would be some thing about America but we have

yet not a tittle from that quarter which bears the face of authenticity. The Inclosd Gazette account from Rodney is all we have new, & we *Englishmen* who think rightly are by no means pleasd with the account altho the writer has stiled it a *defeat* of the French fleet. I am longing for a line to know if you approve my plan of sending forward the News Papers & pamphlets.² If you can make any agreement with the post office (as I before advisd) I think it would be better, because you may get the papers more expeditiously; if not, the present mode may be persued, for there is no great trouble in it, & every 8 or 9 days a neutral vessel is sailing for Ostend. Tomorrow will be forwarded the third parcell I have sent—it will contain news *papers only*, as there are no new political publications worth sending. I shall be made happy by a line when any good news arrives from Chs. Town—the bad flies quick enough. Almost every body here thinks Clinton will not succeed & many pray most cordially this may be the case.

 The Wt. Inda. fleet is yet in Torbay & most likely will now stay for the N. York, Quebec, & Inda. fleet. I am most respectfuly Yrs.,

W. S. C.

MHS: Adams Papers, Reel 351.

¹ The letter was lost (see Digges to Adams, June 8, 1780).
² See Digges's suggestion, Apr. 28, 1780. Adams finally replied on June 6: "Pray drop all the Papers.—I will get the Courant the same way that I have the General Advertiser and Morning post" (MHS: Adams Papers, Reel 96).

To Benjamin Franklin

London 29 May 1780

Dear Sir

 A friend of mine, Mr. Renny of Philadelphia, promising to put this into the post office at Ostend, I sit down to mention what I omitted to do in my two last letters the 24 & 26th¹ inst., which was only to offer You from Mr. Sam. Hartley some more good Jamaica Rum (which He has laying at Dunkirke) and of which You once before had a little. If any is wanted, we can with Your assistance & direction contrive to get a small Cask from Dunkirqu to Paris.[2]

We are yet without any letters from You relative to the further proceedings in the Cartel matter, & we are anxious for such letter from You, as every thing for want of it is stopd at the Office of Sick & hurt.[3]

I expect Mr. Wm. Burn of Lisbon, whom I formerly recommended to Your attention & askd a passport for from Turin to Paris, is now at Paris, & will soon move this way on his way back to Lisbon. He will take particular care of any thing You may have to send to your friends here, & be assurd He merits Your usual civility & attention.

We have no news yet from Clinton, but every body seems to give up his Expedition as a lost one & I believe a great majority of this Country would be glad to hear a certainty of it.

I forwarded to Monr. F. Bowens a few days ago a small box containing a picture of Her Father from Miss Georgiana. I hope it will reach You in safety. It will make me happy to have a request in my last for a *full length* Drawing of Yourself complied with. My friend waits. I have only time to add that I am with the highest Esteem
      Dr. Sir Yrs. &ca. &ca.
      W. S. C.

(please to turn)
The Inclosd is a Letter sent to me by Dr. Logan from Liverpoole from which port I expect he saild in a *direct* voyage to His home on Wedny. last. I was pleasd to have it in my power to get him forwarded by so desirable a conveyance.

[Addressed:] Monsieur/Monsieur B. Franklyn/Passy

HSP: Franklin Papers, 5:134.

[1] This letter has not been found.
[2] On June 25 Franklin replied: "I thank Mr. Hartley much for his kind offer of more Jamaica Rum. But as I have Still a great deal left of what he was before so obliging as to send me, a fresh Quantity is unnecessary. I wish you would hint to me how I could make him some acceptable Return" (LC: Franklin Papers, Series 1, 4:162).
[3] See Digges to Franklin, May 24, 1780, n. 4. The admiralty had instructed the com-

missioners to accept in exchange for Americans only those Englishmen who had been captured by Americans; Englishmen captured by the French would not do.

To Benjamin Franklin

London May 30th 1780

DEAR SIR

I am very sorry to be so frequently troublesome and repeatedly asking favours of You; But when I reflect on your readiness to do good, & that my present application is to help a deserving Man, I flatter myself I shall stand forgiven.

Dr. Upton Scott of Annapolis in Maryland[1] is necessiatd to seek His way back to His Country, Family & Home, by the same route (probably in the same ship) with our friend Mr. L[loy]d[2] in the next New York fleet. He is solicitous to Me to aid Him in asking the favour of You (to whom He formerly had the honour to be known) to procure Him if possible some written Instrument which may save His Baggage & Effects from seizure should the vessel on which He Embarks fall into the hands of an American Cruiser; in which case, tho the Doctor is a good friend to His Country, He may loose his Baggage, from the People who takes him not knowing any thing about Him or His worth.

Dr. Scott is an old & respected Citizen of Annapolis where He practisd Phisick with reputation for many years, and left that Country about four years ago with the approbation & good wishes of the Province, in order to look after a paternal inheritance in Ireland, from which Country He has lately returnd to seek a mode for getting home, & which He thinks He can easiest accomplish by getting past the lines of New York. The fleet for that quarter will most likely sail in 3 weeks tho the Convoy is not yet nominated; and if such an instrument of writing as I now solicit can be got without any impropriety or inconvenience to You I should esteem it a very great favour to have it forwarded by *the first post* to Me. The letter may be directed to me in propria persona and inclosd in a cover to Messrs. Wm. Hodgson &

Co. or Messrs. French & Hopson Brokers, which last may be probably more safe than the former; tho I beleive He has never yet missd any of Yours.

I have the honor to be with very great Esteem Dr. Sir
Yr. obligd & Obt. Ser.
T. D.

[Addressed:] Monsieur/Monsieur B. F——n/Passy

APS: Franklin Papers, 44:40.

[1] Dr. Scott (1722–1814) had originally removed to Maryland as personal physician to the royal governor, Horatio Sharpe, and remained until Tories had been outlawed, when as Digges's letter goes on to explain, he had hastened to Ireland. His wife was a great-aunt of Francis Scott Key (1779–1843), who would live with the Scotts while attending St. John's College, 1793–1796.
[2] John Lloyd had been settled at Nantes as a merchant working for the American cause (see Digges to Arthur Lee, Apr. 18, 1779). He was returning to South Carolina, where he would become a senator the following year.

To John Adams

London June 8 1780

DEAR SIR

My letters of the 9th, 26th, & 29th ulto. have not, I fear, all got safe to hand; that of the former date was probably lost when the packet was taken. I continue to forward You Pamphlets & News Papers via Ostend as Neutral vessells sail, & shall do so until I have some orders to the contrary. Mr. F. Bowens at Ostend receives & forwards them to the Hotel Vallois to You; I mentioned some time ago to him that You would give him a line in order to direct them more properly should You see fit; at any rate a line from You to Him may not be amiss, for it may insure more attention to parcels thus forwarded.

I mentiond to you there was a mode of getting papers abroad by means of agreement with the Post offices: If you find that way more eligible than the present you have only to write me to put a stop to sending them by way of Ostend—They can be conveniently forwarded every 9 or 10 days as heretofore, provided You do not dislike the delays consequent to merchantile vessels sailing;—The trouble is little or none to me, for I get a Friend near the Tower to purchase & ship them for the profits of first reading: I should be glad of a line to know Your determination on this point, & whether parcells have got safe sent on the following days—Apr. 25—May 6—May 16th—May 27th—and the present day. I will annex if I have time the particular books & papers sent by each conveyance in order that you may prove if any have been lost.[1]

I have passed to Your Credit four Louis De ors receivd by Capt. Cazneau, & Mr. T[essie]r told me a few days ago he had orders from Mr. Grand to pay me any demands (as far as 20 or 25 Guins.) I might make on Him. The City is in such a ferment on Account of the mob,[2] & the house's of all Papists (of which discription most likely Monsr. T——rs is one) that I shall take up twenty Guineas from him the first time I go into the City, most likely this afternoon; & I will account with You therefor. Most likely Mr. Jas. Barnet, the Bearer of this, will have twelve guineas to pay You on my account. He was Captain of a vessel part ownd by Monr. Rey De Chamont on whom he has given me a bill for 12 Guis. which I was necessiated to advance him to get him forward, & if this bill should not be paid (which I am not certain it will[)] Mr. Barnet promises to pay the money to You as well as any further small sum he may have occasion to take up at Ostend.

You must recollect every circumstance relative to the non acceptance of the two Cartels from Boston to Engd. in Decr. last. The vessel which C——z——au was master of will come off considerably sufferer by the voyage. She went to Ireland & is on her way to *N.Y.* Mr. Mitchell of Boston who ownd the other had his ship seizd at Bristol as a prize formerly taken on a voyage from Glasgow to N. York. His perseverance & petitions for redress on account of the Cartel not being complyd with, has got him payment for His Ship & all Expences, for last week the Ministry or rather Admiralty listend to his suit, and payd him £2918:0:0 Stg. which is near 1000£ more than was expected; but when an account was to be made out, that was supposd would be dockd, there was no harm in making out an exhorbitant one. I firmly beleive they payd it principally thro *fear*. Mitchell is 8 or 10 days on his way back, & will most probably be the first to state the whole transactions to the board & Council who Commissiond him to come to Europe in the Cartel. I wish the other vessel had fared as well. The non complyance with the Cartel in point of releasing an equal number of American Prisoners here, will naturally be much resented in America, & will I suppose, cause some stoppage to be made in the Cartels between Boston & N. York, if not lead to an act of just retaliation.

The American Cartel from hence to France seems totally at a stand for some months back & the prisoners are in consequence very discontented & numbers entering into the English service; There remains about 250 or 60 in all.

You will see by the inclosd part of a news paper the Camp & Position of the Protestant Petitioners on fryday last. The papers herewith sent will inform You of all the riotous & alarming proceedings since. *Martial Law* was proclaimd or rather read at the Parade of St. Jas. on Wednesy. & it still continues over all parts of the Metropolis—a great reenforcement of horse & foot being calld in in Consequence thereof, the mob were in a great measure dispersd & got under last night (i.e. *Thursday* for I have now got to the 9th) & a Camp of 6,000 Men is formd in Hyde park instead of going to Plymouth where they were intended. The mischeif done by fire & plunder both to private & publick property is incredible & nothing can throw greater disgrace upon the civil authority, or on the Government for want of energy, than that a very few hundreds Rioters & plunderers did such compleat mischief, alarmd the whole City for many nights, & intirely put an end to all police & government for several days. The bent of all seemd leveled at the Catholics—nothing of politics seemd to actuate the mob— Patriots as well as Toreys & ministerialists seemd to be indiscriminately the objects of wrath, tho in the latter part of the Riot the bent seemd to be leveled at the Court side of the question. The Words No Popery, No Papists, down with the Papists, &ca. &ca. &ca. were writ up on almost every House & wall. Strange it is to tell but those bigotted Petitioners seemd to have forgot all the innovations on their rights as Englishmen, for 15 years past, & now for a trifling phantom, a fear for Popery getting in, they rise in multitudes & by conflagration & Theft ruin hundreds of innocent people, While the principal authors of the mischief go unpunishd. The mob reveled in Theft, drunkenness, & distruction to property for several nights without hardly an appearance to put a stop to it by Magistrates or military. There were no prisons to confine in, no magistrates to commit, no Constables to apprehend, nor no soldiery to protect. About 100 daring fellows, cheifly boys, compleatly destroyd New Gate (the Strongest prison in Europe) & in one hour from the first onset releasd upwards of 300 Prisoners; They could with much more ease & facility & in less time too have compleatly destroyd the Bank of England, which they threatend the same Evening, but some over zealous patriot diverted their purpose by a harangue & desiring them to follow him to Lord Mansfields in Bloomsbury & defer the Business of the Bank till next night—at this very next night, so little was the protection given to the City, that the Country might have been put totally afloat by the destruction of the Bank, had not some other persuit diverted the attention of the mob & drew them off.

That quarter of the City is now guarded by several pieces of artillery, by different Troops of Horse & foot, & no sort of Business has been done for tuesdy. wedy. & thursday; for in stead of plodding Merchants in the Exchange the Horse & foot have been quarterd & parading within. The K[in]g I dare answer for it is now the happiest Monarch in Europe; He is now at the head of every thing & I beleive at the summit of his wish. This is the Country this is the People & power which are to bring America to unconditional Submission!!!

Not a word yet *authentic* from Chas. Town; report is current that ministry have accounts that Clinton was repulsd or gave up his purpose the 28th April.

I hope for a line (if but a line) when any satisfactory accounts arrive from thence to your quarter. We are all in the Dumps about the state of naval affairs in the Wt. Indies[3] & think Jamaica will fall an easy prey to the Spanish fleet which lately saild from Cadiz.

        I am with the greatest regard Dr.
        Sir Yr. obt. Servant
        Alexr. Brett

Fryday 9th late at night. Lord Geo. Gordon was taken up this Evening at 5 by a party of Soldiery aided with a Secy. States warrant. He was some hours under Examination at the Horse-Guards & was committed to the Tower for *High Treason* about 10 at night. This will breed a great disturbance among his Party, & it is generally lookd upon as an impolitic act, for the discontents in Country Towns & *in Scotland* are such as would indicate a rising among the people.—

[Enclosure]
Sent *Apr.* 25 a box markd J A
£1:15.9
A parcell of News Papers bound up 128 & 7 loose
   5/6   2/6
Prior Documents 1 vol.[4]—Administration Dissected[5]—
2/–   1/6   2/6
Facts—Burke's Speech[6]—The Peoples barrier against Corruption[7]
   5/–   2/6
—2 Epistles to Washington[8]—Memorial to the Sovereigns of Europe[9]
   2/–   6d.
Hartleys Letters to his Constituents[10]—Do. to the York Committee[11]—
      1/–
Considerations on the intended modification of Poinings Law[12]
   1/–   1/–
—Watsons sermon on the fast[13]—Observations on the Manifesto
      6s.
Letters from Ld. Carisfort to the Huntingdon Committee[14]
      6d.
—List of voters on Dunnings motion.[15]

May 6, 1780 in a bro[wn] paper parcell markd as above

London Courant—London Packet—& Londn. Evening Post from May 1 to the 6th inclusive and 3 other loose papers—making in all 18 Papers.

May 16—Sent the Londn. Courant—Londn. Evening Post—& London Packet from the 6th to 16th May inclusive making in all 16 papers. Also the following Pamphlets

1/— 1/—
Constitutionalists Letter to the People[16]—History of Opposition—
2/— 2/—
Dr. Price on the Population of England & in answer to Eden[17]—
2/— 1/—
Letters of Papinian[18]—Remarks on Burgoines Expedition[19]—
1/—
Dispationate Thoughts on the Amern. War by Galloway[20]—
2/—
Letters to a Nobleman on Do. by Do.—History of the
3/—
Rise & progress of the American Rebellion by Do.—Thoughts
1/—
on the Consequences of American Independence by Do.—
1/—
Letters to Lord Howe by Do.[21]—Examination of
2/—
J. Galloway before the House Commons.[22]

May 27th Sent a Continuation of the above mentioned News papers down to the 27th May in all 20 Papers.

---

turn over

June 10—Sent a Continuation of the news papers mentiond before down to this day in all Papers. Also the following Books and Pamphlets—

6/—
History of the War in America supposd to be written by the Revd. Mr. Boucher[23]
6/—

Burgoine's State of the Canada Expedition with maps[24]
The out of Door Parliament[25] 1/– C [sic]
    6d.
Account of the Rise & progress of the American war[26]
Map of the harbour & opperations at Chs. Town[27] 18d.

[Addressed:] Monsr. Monsr. Ferdinando Raymond San/Paris

MHS: Adams Papers, Reel 352.

[1] On June 22 Adams acknowledged receipt of all that Digges had sent (MHS: Adams Papers, Reel 96).
[2] Here and below Digges is referring to the so-called Gordon riots. In 1778 Parliament had repealed some restrictions in existing laws designed to prevent "the growth of Popery," thereby enabling Catholics who renounced the pope's temporal power to buy and inherit land. Lord George Gordon (1751–1793) had subsequently formed the Protestant Association, which by June 1780 had been able to capitalize upon mounting anti-Catholic feeling. On June 2, carrying a petition with some 120,000 signatures protesting the relief of Roman Catholics for even minor disabilities, Gordon and more than 20,000 of the petitioners had marched on Parliament. The mob had swarmed through the Houses, intimidated the members, and when the House of Commons had rejected the petition, moved into areas of the city frequented by Catholics, later into other areas, producing for a few days the confusion and damage Digges reports. Arrested, Gordon was eventually acquitted of treasonable intent.
[3] Britain's precarious position was made the more uncertain by illness among the troops, especially in Jamaica.
[4] An uncertain reference. On June [6] Adams had asked for "that volume of the Remembrancer, the Prior documents, which contains the History of the rise and progress of the present disputes with America. The Volume you sent me is not the right [one]" (MHS: Adams Papers, Reel 96). Perhaps Adams wanted the *Remembrancer . . . for the Year 1779*, which had reprinted in its entirety (8:1–72) *Observations on the American Revolution. Published According to a Resolution of Congress, by Their Committee, for the Consideration of Those Who Are Desirous of Comparing the Conduct of the Opposed Parties, and the Several Consequences Which Have Flowed from It*, a pamphlet first published in Philadelphia earlier that year. Whatever volume Digges had sent in Apr. was probably not that.
[5] *Administration Dissected. In Which the Grand National Culprits, Are Laid Open for Public Inspection* (London: J. Barker, 1779).
[6] Probably *Speech of Edmund Burke, Esq., Member of Parliament for the City of Bristol, on Presenting to the House of Commons (on the 11th of Feb. 1780) a Plan for the Better Security of the Independence of Parliament and the Œconomical Reformation of the Civil and Other Establishments* (London: J. Dodsley, 1780).
[7] Possibly an early edition or version of *The People's Barrier against Undue Influence* (London, 1783).

[8] *A Poetical Epistle to His Excellency George Washington, Esq. Commander in Chief of the Armies of The United States of America, from an Inhabitant of the State of Maryland. To Which Is Annexed a Short Sketch of General Washington's Life and Character* . . . , first printed by Frederick Green in Annapolis in 1779, was widely reprinted in 1780 in England (by J. Almon in London, T. and J. Merrill in Cambridge, R. Cruttwell in Bath, and T. Becket in Bristol, among others). Whether Digges sent two copies of this work or sent this and some other "epistle"—or even two different publications—remains uncertain.

[9] The pamphlet by Thomas Pownall to which Digges had referred in his letter to Adams, Apr. 6, 1780.

[10] Hartley's *Letters on the American War*, reprinted several times since their first appearance in pamphlet form in 1778 (see Digges to Hartley, Nov. 26, 1778).

[11] *Two Letters from D. Hartley, Esq., M.P., Addressed to the Committee of the County of York* (London: J. Almon, 1780).

[12] Hervey Redmond Morres, second Viscount Mountmorres (1746?–1796), *Considerations on the Intended Modification of Poyning's Law* (London: J. Almon, 1780). Morres was a member of the Irish Parliament.

[13] Richard Watson, *A Sermon [on Isaiah ii, 4] Preached before the University of Cambridge, Feb. 4, 1780, Being the Day Appointed for a General Fast* (Cambridge: [several editions under different imprints], 1780). Regius Professor of Divinity at the University of Cambridge, later bishop of Llandaff, Watson (1737–1816) was known as an outspoken opponent of the North ministry.

[14] John Joshua Proby, first earl of Carysfort (1751–1828), *A Letter from the Right Honourable Lord Carysfort to the Huntingdonshire Committee* (London: J. Almon, 1780), for fiscal and political reforms like those advocated by the Yorkshire Association.

[15] A motion by John Dunning (1731–1783), who as a staunch Whig and consistent opponent of North's policies had offered a resolution in the House of Commons on Apr. 6 stating "that the influence of the Crown has increased, is increasing, and ought to be diminished."

[16] Constitutionalis[t], *Letters to the Electors & People of England, Preparatory to the Approaching General Election* (London: J. Almon and W. Flexney, 1780).

[17] Richard Price, *An Essay on the Population of England, from the Revolution to the Present Time. With an Appendix, Containing Remarks on the Account of the Population, Trade, and Resources of the Kingdom, in Mr. Eden's Letter to Lord Carlisle* (London: T. Cadell, 1780).

[18] [Charles Inglis, 1734–1816], *Letters of Papinian: in Which the Conduct, Present State, and Prospects of the American Congress Are Examined* (London: J. Wilkie, 1779), five letters, the first and last of which are addressed to John Jay, the others "To the People of North America." Born in Ireland, for a while a minister in the middle colonies, Inglis was a consistent loyalist.

[19] *An Enquiry into, and Remarks upon, the Conduct of Lieut.-Gen. Burgoyne* (London: J. Mathews, 1780).

[20] *Dispassionate Thoughts on the American War, Addressed to the Moderate of All Parties* (London: J. Wilkie, 1780) should have been attributed to Josiah Tucker, dean of Gloucester (1712–1799).

[21] Joseph Galloway was correctly identified as the anonymous author of *Letters to a Nobleman, on the Conduct of the War in the Middle Colonies* (London: J. Wilkie, 1779); *Historical and Political Reflections on the Rise and Progress of the American Rebellion* (London: G. Wilkie, 1780); *Cool Thoughts on the Consequences to Great Britain of American Indepen-*

dence (London: J. Wilkie, 1780); and *Letter to the Right Honourable Lord Viscount H———e on His Naval Conduct in the American War* (London: J. Wilkie, 1779).

[22] *The Examination of Joseph Galloway, Esq., Late Speaker of the House of Assembly of Pennsylvania before the House of Commons, in a Committee on the American Papers* (London: J. Wilkie, 1779).

[23] A loyalist Anglican clergyman, Jonathan Boucher (1738–1804) had spent time between 1762 and 1775 in Virginia and Maryland and established himself in Annapolis until his views at the outbreak of the war had made his continued residence there unwelcome and led him to return home. Among his various writings the National Union Catalog includes the pseudonymous *The American Times: A Satire in Three Parts, in Which are Delineated the Characters of the Leaders of the American Rebellion[;] amongst the Principal are Franklin, Laurens, Adams, Hancock, Jay, Duer, Duane, Wilson, Pulaski, Witherspoon, Reed, M'Kea, Washington, Roberdeau, Morris, Chase, etc., by Camillo Querno, Poet-Laureat to the Congress* (London: Printed for the Author and Sold by William Richardson, 1780). But Thomas R. Adams, in *The American Controversy: A Bibliographic Study of the British Pamphlets about the American Disputes, 1764–1783* (Providence: Brown University Press, 1980), attributes the pamphlet to George Cockings (d. 1802), of whose satire it would have been characteristic. Whether this is the volume listed is uncertain, but on June [6], Adams had written Digges: "I wish to have a Poem that is advertised, in which some American Characters are Said to be drawn.–Good or bad, let it come—" (MHS: Adams Papers, Reel 96). To send *The American Times* would have been the appropriate response.

[24] Lt.-Gen. John Burgoyne, *A State of the Expedition from Canada as Laid before the House of Commons* (London: J. Almon, 1780).

[25] *The Out-of-door Parliament. By a Gentleman, of the Middle Temple* (London: J. Almon, 1780).

[26] [Joseph Galloway], *An Account of the Rise and Progress of the American War. Extracted from a Late Author* (London, 1780).

[27] Possibly, despite the date printed on it, *A Sketch of the Operations before Charlestown the Capital of South Carolina* ([London:] J. E. W. Des Barres, 17 June 1780), a map printed after the surrender of the city, focusing on the harbor area and showing the positions of fortifications, ships, encampments, and the like.

To Benjamin Franklin

Camberwell 10th June 1780

DEAR SIR

I find my letter to You of the 9th ulo. was lost by the Packets being taken & the mails thrown overboard. Those of the 24th advising of the Bishops picture being sent you via Ostend to the care of Mr. Bowens, that of the 26 by Post inclosing the Gazette, & that of the 29th offering you from Mr. S[amuel] H[ar]tl[e]y any part of some Good

Rum that he has lying at Dunkirque, I could not yet in course hear had got safe to Your hands. I should be glad of a line to the former direction (*W. S. Church*) when the picture gets in safety for the partys are anxious about it. I should also be very glad to know the fate of my application for *another picture* which I have very much at heart.

I am much with Mr. H[odg]s[o]n, & D. H[artley], & we have been many week in Expectation of a line (as promisd in Your last to Mr. H——s——n) relative to the Cartel, about which no one step has been yet taken here owing to the Expectation by every post of getting an explanatory letter from you, & which is also wishd for by the Board who seem inclinable to let another Cargoe go.—There is not now above 260 in all.

Not a syllable lately from the Westward, & from the late very alarming tumults & insurrections in & about London, there is no more talk about Clinton or America than if no such Country existed. The Bearer of this is a Young Man taken lately in a ship of Mons. Chamonts,[1] and I have sent by him 8 or 10 News papers, which, with his own account of what He saw, will more fully explain than I can do in sheets of Paper the late disturbances, Riots, insurrections, & Conflagrations, which have happend. I inclose You a news-paper plan of the ground which about 100,000 People took on the 2d Int., from which time until yesterday all Law, Police, or Government, seemd totally at a stand, & the whole City & Suberbs were in the hands of a set of People revelling in distruction to private Property as well as the publick Goals, in riot, drunkenness & disorder. The *Bank of England* was in the most imminent danger; for had not some zealous patriot led the mob from the Flames of New-gate to Lord Mansfields house in Bloomsbury, in one hour the Bank might have been put in flames & the whole funds & Country set compleatly afloat. *All* the Civil as well as Military force (which in all did not amount to 5,000 Men) were placed to protect the Western parts of the Town, so that about 50 resolute fellows were left uninterruptedly to destroy New Gate & many other Edifices. In one hour & a half the Strongest prison in Europe was forcibly enterd & the whole Edifice in flames—half that period would have done for the Bank of England, & the danger it was then in & has been since by the threats of the Mob, causd a considerable run thereon *Tuesday* & *Wedy.* last. The Riot seems now compleatly over. The Bank is guarded very strong, but even till yesterday the Exchange was more a Barrack for Troops of Horse & foot Soldiery than the walk of Merchants—never was a City in such confusion—It would be impossible to describe it to You without filling pages. The privy Council on Wedy. issued a proclamation for Martial Law, or rather to give power to the Soldiery to act as majistrates & punish with immediate Death all disorderly Persons in consequence of which a great number have been killd & wounded.—This Martial Law still subsists & in consequence of it neither house of Parliament can sit nor Courts of justice do Business.—The head quarter of justice *now* is at the Horse Guards, & the Commander of the Army is Lord Chief Justice—The cat is let out of the bag, & if there is one Sovereign in Europe more happy than another at this present moment it is the Defender of the Faith—now at the head of his *Respectable* military. By His mandate aided by a party of horse as well as foot—Lord G. Gordon was yesterday at 5 oCk. taken up, underwent some artful Examination at *the Horse Guards*, & was committed to the Tower in the night for High Treason. How this may opperate the Lord knows, but there seems a flame among the People even in distant parts of the realm not to lett the matter rest quiet, & I should not be surprizd to hear of 40,000 Protestants from the North rising to demand His release. Your predictions have all come right about this Country—surely there never was an instance of *Greatness* getting so rapiddly down to insignificance & contempt;[2] but *the People*, even yet, do not Seem to understand the cause of it all. This is the Country, the mighty & all powerful people who were to bring America to unconditional submission!!!—adieu my Good Sir, may Heaven favour all Your undertakings & turn the hearts & minds of men to what is right & fit—

Yrs. mo. truly
Alexr. Brett

I forgot to mention to you that the Cartel which was seizd at Bristol has been paid for to Mr. Mitchell her owner by the Admiralty 2918:8:8[3] after his dancing attendance 4 or 5 months. However it is an *ample* sum for the vessel & loss of time to the concernd.

I wrote you the 30th ulo. for a pass for Dr. Upton Scotts Baggage in case of his being taken by an American privateer on his way to N. York—He goes I beleive in the same Ship with Loyd—He has been formerly known to You as a phisical man in Annapolis, has been some years from there after some property in Ireland & is a good man respected by the Country & came away with full approbation of the People. If it can be given please to inclose it to me under cover to Messrs. W. Hodgson & Co. or Messrs. French & Hopson.

HSP: Franklin Papers, 5:135.

[1] James Barnet, mentioned in Digges to Adams, June 8 and 29, as well as to Franklin, June 29, Aug. 18, and Aug. 25, 1780.
[2] See Franklin's remarks of Feb. 26, quoted in Digges to Franklin, Mar. 17, 1780, n. 5.
[3] An amount slightly different from what he had told Adams on June 6.

To John Adams

London June 29. 1780

DEAR SIR

Since my letter by Mr. Barnet (who was Capn. & SuperCargoe of a Ship of Chamonts taken & carryd into Ireland) of the 8th Int., I have put in the common conveyance two letters for you the 10th & 23d Int. which I hope reachd your hands.[1] A freind going to Holland promises to put this in the first Post Office abroad. Since my last, there has been nothing whatever from America nor any other quarter save the account of a second brush between the French & English fleets in the Wt. Indies. A packet is arrivd from St. Kitts the 25 May. By which there is advices that on the 13th May, Martinico bearing W. by N. twelve degrees, Rodney descried the french fleet turning to windward to get into Martinico; after much manoeuvreing on both sides, the rear of the English fleet got up with the van of the Enemy & engagd— They got very roughly handled (tho not disabled so much as to be obligd to quit the Seas) before the body of the Fleet could assist them. The van consisted of six, cheifly the Copper Bottomd & best sailers—

They have lost it is said 220 Men in *killd* & three ships the Cornwall, Conqueror & another are very much pepperd. Rodney however prevented their purpose of getting into Martinique. Every other instance of this brush is spoken of as being very much against the English,[2] & stocks sunk thereon about ¾ p. Ct.—Altho there has been a packet, Government give the public no account of it, which carrys the face of its being a worse account than we hear. The Gentry at Loyds Coffee House rather shake their heads for fear of their Wt. India ships, if not Islands; but the friends to Ministry are trying every art to make it appear an action favorable to the English fleet, That Rodney remaind master of the Seas, that the French fleet fled back into Guadaloupe, that they can be effectually prevented from joining the other division in Martinique &ca. &ca.

By many private letters & the accounts from Passengers in the Man of War with Despatches of the Surrender of Chas. Town, there are very melancholly accounts of the state of things in the Country distant from Chas. Town, cheifly in respect to the negroes, where there are at least 8 or 10 for one white. These accounts say, that as soon as they had heard of the surrender of the Town to the English all bond of them towards their masters were broke & that the civil powers could not prevent their liberating themselves; They collected in bodies of one two & 300 each, quitted all sorts of work or controul whatever, took what they could carry & plunder from their masters, & were moving about the Country bending rather Westward when the last accounts were had of them. From these accounts as well as what I hear from the quarter of the Torey Carola. Merchants in the City, it is not possible for that Country to be in a worse situation than it now is. The last Crop of Rice & Corn had faild almost universally, The people during the invasion of the Country in the planting months of April & May could not attend to Agriculture, a scarcity of Cattle & hogs, & this more deplorable than all the other evils the blacks going at large and doing much mischief, together with the cheif of the principal Gentry being either prisoners in the Town or out of the Country, makes the whole a very melancholly picture indeed.—Their prospects too are bad from their Western neighbours & from the still greater Savages the back settlers of No. Carolina, whither it is said Cornwallis with about 1100 Men had certainly gone. The brutes in this Country, (who I am very sorry to say seems to be a majority of the People) seem to exult at all this, because in their opinion it leads to a sure reduction of all the Southern Colonies, & gives, as they term it, a death blow to rebellion. This is not the language of the common, but of the better sort of People, & of almost every man in power or of consequence—I cannot help damning them all together. I have been bouyed up lately with some hopes, that the Ministry would look a little further towards the Interest of the Country than the narrow circle of St. James, & have made some profers of terms—even the parley for which could not be disadvantageous to America & might at least have led to a cessation of hostilities for a small time. Every one must know, & I beleive they see themselves, that terms excluding France & Spain would not do. I am now fully perswaded that they are determind either England or America shall be totally ruind in the trial. The last days debate on Hartleys & Sr. Geoe. Savilles motion (which you will read in the papers) convinces me that my opinion is not ill founded.[3] You may depend upon it, the Ministry have no sort of idea of Peace or accomodation with America, & that they mean to send more troops & push another Campaign for the subjugation of it. It is impossible to explain to You why they are at this juncture prepossessd with an opinion, nay declare publickly, "that in all human probability they will succeed"— Many men of worth who thought other ways till lately, seem now, from the present account of the state of things in America which too many are infatuated to beleive, have fallen into an opinion that England should push the Contest further & risque much on another Campaign. Gen. Conway (tho I do not mention him as a pattern either of judgement or honesty, for sure I am he has been long under the sunshine of Ministry) in the House Commons the day of Hartleys motion, declard that another ten, another 20,000 Men, should be sent to America rather than offer terms of Independence *now*. If I were to write pages I could only mention such instances of folly & infatuation as these—I wish to impress upon Your mind that the intention in this quarter is still to prosecute the war vigorously against America, &

every nerve will be straind to send men & Ships to that Station. They will effect it too, if France & Spain, do not act more vigorusly at Sea & go *to work* instead of making a parade. Five Ships of the line on any of the Southern Coasts of America in the months of March, Apr. or May would have effectually securd Chas. Town, & capturd a British Army— The very same mischiefs will happen in Virga. if the Coasts are not guarded & protected by Men of War this summer; & the people finding it the woeful fact will become discontented with their allies, & naturally suppose the intentions of them are not to risque any thing but protract the war to the imminent ruin of that as well as of this Country. At present time there is no standing against the torrent of folly expressd in all Companys about the certainty of subjugating America. I have seen frequently these people as much depressd and as often in the lower appartments of the House, as they are now elated & dancing about in the Garrets; perhaps, before reason gives them time to think quietly in the middle story, some news may arrive that will put them all in the cellars. If one may draw a conclusion about the fate of this Country, from the general face of things in Europe as well as in America & the West Indies, one would be led to suppose that in a few weeks, if not days, some news would arrive far more depressing than the late accounts from America have been elating to the unthinking inhabitants of it—God send some that may bring them to reason & to think that the wisest measure they can adopt for the Salvation of the Country is peace and accomodation with America. I am wishing to hear of the safe arrival of the Books, papers &ca. I hope you did not put a stop to my forwarding them from any supposition that it was troublesome to me to execute Your Commissions, for I can assure you it was none, and that next to serving my Country, that of assisting its Servants abroad is my principal wish & desire. I beg you will not spare me whenever you think I can be servicable and that you will believe me to be with great Esteem Dr. Sir

         Your obet. Hum.Sert.
         T. D.

MHS: Adams Papers, Reel 352.

[1] There is no evidence that they reached Adams.
[2] Compare this account with the one sent to Franklin on the same day.
[3] Hartley had proposed that the crown appoint commissioners empowered to proclaim the cessation of hostilities in America and that for a term of ten years all acts of Parliament that had been designed to restrain intercourse with the colonies be suspended. He was supported by Burke and Fox, as well as Savile. The motion lost, 93–28.

To Benjamin Franklin

London 29. June 1780

DEAR SIR

Since my letter of the 8th Int. by Mr. Barnet, I have wrote you the 10th & 23d Insts.;[1] and hearing that my Lisbon friend Mr. B., whom I took the liberty to introduce to You,[2] is about this period to Leave Paris, I am in some hopes of getting by him a line from you, which may answer three or four requests I have made in late letters: I mean in respect to Dr. Upton Scotts Pass *for His Baggage* in case He is taken by an American Privateer on the voyage to N. York He meaning to push out in the next fleet to that place in order to get to Annapolis, which pass I took the liberty to apply to You for by Post the 30th of last month;—For a Spectacle glass that would sute your sight in order to oblige a Gentleman who means to present You with a pair made of Cherokee Cristal; To know what I am to expect relative to a request for a full length drawing or picture of Your self which is wanted for the purpose of getting a good print; and also to know what hopes of release remain to our captive Brethren &ca.[3]

I advanced Mr. Jas. Barnet £12:12:0 on a bill He gave me on Monsr. Rey De Chamont, & I find from my friend Mr. Bowins at Ostend, He made further use of my introduction and took up a few guineas more of Mr. B. on a similar bill. I should be obligd to you to give Mr. Barnet a hint to have these two Bills taken care of, for I am not in circumstances to bear well the protest of them. I am led to give this hint to Him from having lately experiencd inconveniences of protests on four bills, amounting to upwards of 60£, given me by Americans in a similar situation to Barnet, on people in Nantes & Bilboa; as well as one lately given me by an acquaintance of Barnets who drew for 10 Guineas on his unkle in Scotland, & who declard He would pay the bill of no R*e*ebel.

Nothing of any consequence has come to my knowlege from the West since my last, save an account from the West Indies of a second Brush between the French & English fleet, in which the English Ships sufferd most tho they remaind *as is the boast here* Masters of the Sea. A Packet from St. Kitts the 25th May, brings accounts, which from collecting the whole, stands pretty nearly thus. On the 13th of May Rodney descried the French fleet to windward of Him & not far distant, when Martinique bore W. by No. 12 Leagues; The french apparantly meaning to ply to windward & to get into Martinique. After much manoeuvring the Van of the English fleet (*six* Ships the best Sailers from being copperd) got up with & attackd the Rear of Monsr. Guichens Squadron. The other part of Rodneys fleet being rather distant on account of light winds could not get up, till the English Ships were pretty roughly handled, particularly the Conqueror the Cornwall & another, who were mauld considerably, tho not so disabled as to be obligd to quit the Seas:—on the getting up of the other ships of Rodneys fleet, *it is said* the French retreated back to Guadae. [Guadaloupe] leaving Rodney, as they express it in the City, Lord Paramount of the Seas.[4] The accounts go to no further particulars than that the English lost in the engagement 220 Men *killd*. Every person but the immediate dependants & runners of ministry look upon the account as a very bad one, and one strong suspicion of it is, that the Government give the public no Gazette accounts of the action altho the packet brought dispatches. The Gents at Loyds look a little black upon it, & visibly seem to fear for the Islands as well as the Ships on their way out. This news, as well as the present situation of things in consequence of the late curious Insurrection, would have thrown a deadly damp upon the spirits of the whole Country, had it not been for the oppertune arrival of what they call *good news* from South Carolina.[5] It is impossible for me to describe to You how much the minds of the people are elated at it, & how universal the opinion now is,

That America must in consequence be subdued; That the whole southern Colonies must fall; That [it] is a certain fact that [⟨the people⟩] of No. Carolina have submitted; That the Congress are routed by an Insurrection at Phila.; The french Minister obligd to fly &ca. &ca. &ca.—These reports, all aided by the Assertions of Ministry, and even hinted by them in the House of Commons as *Facts*, have had an effect on the minds of the people which you may better guess at from knowing their folly, than I can describe. They have Servd to raise the Stocks above three pr. Ct. and to bring over a number of people, who thought rationally before, to an opinion, that the game is totally up with America, That *Rebellion* there has got its death blow, & that one years vigorous war more will assuredly bring that Country to the unconditional submission to this. You cannot think Sir, how generally this opinion now possess's even the better & more thinking sort of people as well as the Houses of Parliament. In the Debates on Hartleys last motion for terms to be offerd America the ministry were more impudent than ever; & did in very plain terms persuade the House, that all which I have before stated about the distressd situation of America were facts.—Genl. Conway (whom I do not mean to mention as a virtuous or good Character) did as much as declare that the last farthing of this Country ought to be tryd against America & that if ten would not do send 20,000 Men more to reduce it rather than offer Independence *now*.

You may depend upon it (and I wish to impress it upon Your mind) that every remaining exertion in the power of this Country will be sent forth against America—Fleets & Armys will be sent to ruin if they cannot subdue it, provided fleets & Armys can be got; and they will effect in a great measure the ruin of other places in America, provided france & Spain do not act more vigorously at Sea, and go *to work* instead of making a Parade. I fear much from the discontents in America with regard to non assistance of Ships from their allies. Five ships of the Line cruising on the Coasts South of Philadelphia in the months of March, April, or May, would have effectually securd Chas. Town & capturd a British army—The very same mischeifs will happen in No. Caroa. & Virga. if those Coasts are not guarded & protected this summer. *One* English Line of Battleship (which has been for months lying up at Hallifax) and six or eight of the size of 44 Guns & frigates, have been *all* the Force of England in America since the month of Feby. & with this trifling naval guard, they are conducting small armys to Quebec, Hallifax, & other parts of the Coast.[6] Adml. Graves with 8 of the line may be expected to arrive at N. York about this period, & his intention is to watch the movements of Tierneys Squadron.[7] Our Idea here is that when Walsinghams fleet of six Ships gets to the Wt. Indies the English will be superior to the french by 3 Ships.

You, who have often laughd at the follys of this Country would wonder now at the infatuation that seemingly possess's every one— The Exultation about Chas. Town & the supposd excellent state of their affairs in America surpasses all belief, in short they are as much upon Hobby as ever they were since I had any knowlege of them. If one may judge rightly from the actual state of things against this Country as well in America & the West Indies as in Europe in general, one would be apt to think that before many weeks are elapsd they would be flung from this hobby & be as much in the dumps as Englishmen are used to be on the receiving bad news. I wish You every blessing & am with the most sincere regard Sir

Yr. very Ob. Sert.

P. S. a friend is to put this in the Post Office at Amsterdam.

HSP: Franklin Papers, 5 : 136.

[1] The letter of June 23 has not been found.
[2] See Digges's letter of introduction for William Burn, Mar. 15, 1780.
[3] Franklin's declination of June 25 (see Digges to Franklin, May 24, 1780, n. 2) had not reached Digges. In that letter Franklin had gone on to say of the prisoners: "As the Board after receiving the 500 English Prisoners we carry'd into Holland, in Exchange for frenchmen, refus'd to take other frenchmen (which the Government here had promised me) in Exchange for Americans, I gave over all Thoughts or Expectations of continuing the Cartel. I have however wrote to Mr. Hodgson about it by the Opportunity. We are much obliged to that good Man for the Pains he has taken in that affair. Finding that the Prisoners are like to be longer detain'd, I desire they may be paid from me the little comfort I can afford them of Six pence per week each. I will answer your Drafts for the Sums necessary" (LC: Franklin Papers, Series 1, 4 : 163).
[4] Compare this account with the one sent to Adams on the same date.

⁵Contrary to reports Digges had been passing along to Franklin, Clinton had suffered no setbacks and had occupied Charleston on May 12.

⁶Contemporary accounts confirm Digges's general estimate. The British naval force along the Quebec coast consisted of two armed brigs from the provincial naval force, a 10-gun and a 24-gun ship, and a 24-gun privateer.

⁷Ternay had embarked from Brest at the beginning of May with seven sail of the line to convoy French troops under Jean Baptiste Donatien de Vimeur, comte de Rochambeau (1725–1807), to Rhode Island. Graves, sent in pursuit too late, could not overtake him, and Arbuthnot, hoping to destroy the squadron at sea, never sighted him.

To John Adams

Londn. 12 July '80

DEAR SIR

I put on board a vessel which saild yesterday, the Books mentiond in the margin.¹ I thought the *Treaties* might be servicable to You, & I mention the other particular pamphlets that you may prove whether all I send by that conveyance will come to hand. I have not heard from You since the letter ordering me to stop the sending the Papers via Ostend.² There has been nothing material in the news way to inform You of since I inclosd a Gazette of the Chs. Town business. If I were to attempt to describe the folly & torrent of exultation about the taking that place, it would fill pages; You, who do not know this Country & the folly of its people, can have no Idea of it. The language of 1775 about unconditional submission is nothing to what you now hear.— The people are absolutely mad with Exultation, & look upon America as much theirs as they do the Isles of Guernsey & Jersey. There is no standing against the Torrent; all reasonings upon the matter are vain:—The Language comes from the Court, & gets thro the Nobles & better people, down to the lower, & so on to the City; where the folly is not less obvious. Stocks have risen in consequence of it about five perCent and every body is buying. The universal cry is, that America is again ours; We have beat the French fleet & remain masters of the *Seas* in the West Indies; (I wonder they do not claim dominion over the *air*) Rodney is certainly to intercept & take the Spanish Squadron; Monr. De Terneys fleet is thought an easy & sure prey to that of Adml. Graves; The Channel fleet is to continue blocking up the port of Brest, & prevent any junction of Ships from Cadiz &ca. &ca.—Turning towards America, they now say that No. Carolina will be certainly theirs a body of Troops with arms & amunition for 2000 of the back Settlers having been sent there by invitation of the People; That Virga. will also be theirs having sent Deputies to Chs. Town from the Back Settlements praying to be aided by the British Soldiery. If this is effected a fig say they for the northern Colonies, tho they even boast too of having a considerable body of the Connecticut People in the Interest of Government. News of the taking Mobille came this day thro the Spanish papers but this is reckond nothing; The junction of the French & Spanish fleets in the Wt. Indies would be reckond nothing; The taking Antigua, St. Kitts or other Islands, nay even beating the invincible fleet of Rodney, would all be reckond nothing; since we have got (*as they express it*) all the Southern Colonies. Such folly was never seen, the joy of the King & Court is visible to every one, & I do realy beleive they had rather hear of such another massacre as that of Tarltons against the Virginians on the borders of North Carolina[3] or the hearing that Colony had submitted, than the distruction of the whole french & Spanish fleet in the West Indies. It is inconceivable how implacably bent the first man here seems to be, for the reduction of America. You may depend that every nerve will be straind to get more Men & to send more Ships to America. Nothing but some disastrous news to put them again in the Dumps will prevent the ministry acting vigorously as they possibly can do against America.—Every thing will be risqued to carry on that war; & without France does assist Her Allies, with a small fleet to continue on the Coast, & thereby prevent the easy transportation of British Soldiers from Place to place, that much mischief will be done. They brag here of more troops being engagd in Germany by General Faucit & that 4,000 are to be sent out the 1st of Augt. next or between that & the 20th with 4 sail of the Line & some frigates. The N. York fleet is yet detaind about 60 sail, & notwithstanding all their bragging of Graves's superiority over De Terney, I beleive they will not let it sail till they hear on a certainty where Terney is gone—they certainly apprehend He is gone towards N. York.[4]

A fleet of 20 or 30 Wt. Inda. Men are also ready to sail & a few Et. Indiamen. Most likely the whole may go together soon after the return of the Channel Fleet which is now expected dayly to return to Torbay. News is come today that the Channel fleet is spread so as to extend a considerable way to intercept a homeward bound french St. Domingo fleet, three of which have been already taken by Adml. Geary & sent to Plymouth. Much has been put forth & very industriously too about a secret negotiation with Spain by a Mr. Cumberland & an Irish friar of the name of Hussy[5]—both of whom I know. I beleive nothing of it; as Cumberland took his family abroad for the purpose of cutting a little in his Expences, He being supposd much behind hand in the world. The Fryar was One of the Household to the late Spanish Ambassador & has been once to Madrid & back hither since the Ambassador took his leave.[6] This storey has helpd to raise the Stocks; but I beleive some late maneuvres of Sr. Jo. Yorke with the Dutch, has helpt them up more either than that or the late news from America. We are all anxious here to know whether the Dutch & Russians will act spiritedly or otherways in the protection of their Commerce. The line of conduct of Portugal most likely will be guided by these powers. I know every Corner of that Country well & am not unacquainted at its Court from having resided there three or four years. Should affairs so turn out that any person, I do not mean in a capital but subordinate way, should be wanted I am ready & willing to go there, for I am sure I could do it to the material service of my Country, either by encouraging adventure from thence or in other more substancial services—There is not a Merchantile man of any eminence in the Country that I do not personally know. I am with the highest Esteem

        Sir Yr. obedt. Servt.
        W. S. C[hurc]h

 P. S.
  Books Sent
  The 2 Vols. of Treaties from 1688 to 1771. Westminr. Magazine for June 1780—

Remembrancer containing an Account of the Riots[7]—2 Sermons on a fast day during the late War

Legal mode for suppressing Riots—Considerations on the late Disturbances (by Burke)[8]

Tumulte De Londres—also three small Pamphlets publishd gratis.

[Addressed:] A Monsieur./Monsr: Ferdinando Raymond San/Negote./Chez Monsieur Hocherau, Libraire/Pont Neuf/ Paris

NA: Record Group 360, Papers of the Continental Congress (Microfilm M247, Roll 93, Item 78), 5:487.

[1] The foot of the last page.

[2] A letter of June 22, 1780, had apparently gone astray. It is the only one to Digges copied into Adams's letterbook that followed a note of June 6 or 7 about stopping mailings (MHS: Adams Papers, Reel 96).

[3] On May 29 Lt. Col. Banastre Tarleton (1754–1833) had led 270 dragoons into an engagement with some 350 Virginia Continentals under Col. Abraham Buford (1749–1833), who had been withdrawing from South Carolina toward the north. Buford, believing himself outnumbered, had surrendered; but the British, alleging that some shots had been fired after the surrender, had then massacred all but a few of the Americans.

[4] The British had earlier supposed that the French fleet was headed for the West Indies; then, that it was bound for Canada.

[5] See Digges to Franklin, Nov. 15, 1779, n. 7. Richard Cumberland (1732–1811), a playwright and actor, had entered politics in 1775 as secretary to the Board of Trade through the influence of Germain.

[6] With the fall of Charleston the British hoped that Spain's links with the Americans could be broken, and Cumberland at first had reason to suppose they might, since he was told that the Spanish government wished for the total submission of the Americans. But the Spanish were cautious. They wanted control of navigation on the Mississippi and therefore had to make continuing aid to the Americans a possibility. Eventually, it turned out, neither the British nor the Spanish wanted peace too quickly. Success in South Carolina had emboldened the British to believe Spain's role was not critical enough to require the demanded concession of yielding Gibraltar; and Spanish interception of a rich British armada bound for the West Indies showed the Spaniards that continuing belligerency was profitable. Amid mutual suspicions and calculated delays and silences, the Hussey-Cumberland mission could only fail.

[7] "An Account of the Late Disturbances in London," *Remembrancer* 10 (1780): Part 2, 1–16.

[8] Edmund Burke had written *Thoughts on the Causes of the Present Discontents* (London: J. Dodsley, 1770), but it concerned public disaffection, political malaise, party conflict. More likely, Digges means the pamphlet by Thomas Lewis O'Beirne, *Considerations on the Late Disturbances* (London: J. Almon, 1780).

To Benjamin Franklin

12 July 1780

DEAR SIR

I got Your obliging favor of the 25th June by Mr. Burn & am very thankful for your attention & civility to Him. He is a very excellent young Man & may be useful to You or Yours hereafter, in case You should have anything to do at Lisbon, for which place He will set out in a month or two & where He is the head of a Merchantile House inferior to no other English one in that Country.

I mentiond to Mr. S. H[artle]y your thanks for a second offer of some Jamaica Rum, & your readiness to make him some acceptable return.[1] I put in as from you a hint for the release of Captain C[onyngha]m, who has been again taken & about this period is expected to arrive at Dartmo. in a privateer which Mr. H——y partly owns. I told Him one good turn deserves another & that You had by my recommendation got releasd from a french Goal one of His own Captains about a year ago & for which He was very thankful.[2] If Mr. H——ys letter gets to Dartmo. in time for the Captain of the Privateer before Capn. C——m is committed, I hope he will be releasd in consequence, but I fear if it gets to hand after Committment, there will be no hopes of liberating Him his name being so offensive.[3]

I observe what you say about the medal & have hinted to Dr. P[ri]ce, Mr. Paradise & Mr. Jones that no further applications are to be made.[4] I rather wonder that the Portrait of the Bishop had not reachd You before the 25th ulo. I think it was many weeks before that, that Mr. Bowens of Ostend acknowlegd the safe receipt of it & that it should be forwarded on. I have got our friend Mr. W[righ]t to promise the undertaking another portrait I solicited You for.[5] I think by what we have got, & the picture in Miss Georgianas possession we may make something out of it.

Mr. Hodgson has informd you about the answer of the Board. On seeing M. Sartines Letter they desird Mr. H. to draw up a memorial stating the circumstances of the Case & we are not without hopes, tho faint ones, that the Cartel may again go.[6]

Our friend David is quite desponding, & feels much for the want of wisdom in our Rulers here for not adopting any one measure that will lead to accomodation with America; He has been incessantly upon this, & I beleive American Independence would be the summit of His wish. So far from our wise heads thinking about, nothing but the extreem reverse is now talkd of. Since the affair of Chs. Town nothing but unconditional submission is talkd of. I do assure you Sir the great folks here look as much now upon America being in their power as they did the first day General Gage was sent to Boston. Nothing can exceed the infatuation. They look upon No. Caroa. & Virga. as already theirs, that Maryland must follow, & they give out with confidence they have a considerable body of the people in Connecticut, now in Arms for England. Since the quelling of the late Riots & Insurrections, & restord a little peace and order to a Capital that was for five whole days in possession of a Mob, they Think they can subdue the whole world. They Brag still of being masters of the Sea in the West Indies, (I dare say they will next claim a dominion over the air) That Rodney will infallably intercept & ruin The Spanish fleet, that Tearney's Squadron is a sure & easy prey to Adml. Graves, & that the Channel fleet is to shut up the port of Brest & keep the Spanish fleet from again joining &ca. &ca. This is not only the language, but seemingly the firm belief of the Court, the Ministry, & their out Runners; The flame has spread in the City, & many thinking people are led to a beleif of it & are actually purchasing pell-mell in the Stocks which have risen upwards of five pr. Cent lately. There is no standing against the present torrent of folly & I lean towards it in order to make my exultation the greater when some future day of gloom & sorrow may turn up. We may expect great & important news both from America & the Wt. Indies in a few days; If it does not turn up different from what is generally, nay almost universally expected here

I shall be very much deceivd. There is no arrivals or news from any part of America since the Despatches from Chas. Town, to keep us the more in the dark as to the state of things in that Country, not one private Letter was receivd by the last packet.

It seems as if the New York fleet, which was ready about 2 months ago, will not be permitted to sail till we hear the actual destination of Monsr. Teirnay; about 60 Ships compose it, & twenty or 30 others are intended for the West Indies by a Convoy very soon.

I am Sir Your Obt. Servt.
John Thompson

HSP: Franklin Papers, 5:137.

[1] Quoted above, Digges to Franklin, May 29, 1780, n. 2.
[2] See Digges to Franklin, Jan. 11, 1780. Hartley's ship was the *Admiral Edwards*.
[3] The diffculty failed (see Digges to Franklin, Aug. 18, 1780).
[4] Quoted above, Digges to Franklin, Apr. 28, 1780, n. 5.
[5] Joseph Wright (1756–1793), born and brought up in Bordentown, N.J., and the son of Patience Lovell Wright (1725–1786), celebrated as an artist and a revolutionary spy, had followed his mother to England in 1772 to begin a career as a portrait painter.
[6] The diffculty that Franklin faced was in producing a number of prisoners sufficient to equal those released by the British at Morlaix in Mar. (see Digges to Franklin, Apr. 14, 1780, n. 3, and May 24, 1780, n. 4). De Sartine had been the one expected to make sure the Americans were compensated for the prisoners Jones had had to relinquish in Holland by turning over to the Americans those Englishmen the French had captured. But de Sartine did not make good on the French commitment—there were not enough Englishmen to turn over; the king's authorization was first needed—and Franklin could not make up the deficit. De Sartine's explanation of how the initial complications had evolved is contained in a letter to Franklin, Apr. 24, 1780 (LC: Franklin Papers, Series 1, 1:51v–52v).

To William Temple Franklin

12 July [1780]

DEAR SIR

My friend Mr. Burn is with me & desires His best Respects as well as that I do inform You the parcel for Mrs. H[artle]y[1] was seizd, He not knowing what it containd & leaving it with other things in His trunk when sent to the Custom House at Margate. If you had mentiond to Him what the parcel containd it might have been savd. I shall inform Mrs. H—— of this. Mr. B. is uneasy about it, thinking You might suppose He did not take due care of it; which does not appear to be the case for He has tryd much to get the gloves restord altho He was first threatend with the penalty of 100£ for attempting to run them. He was obligd to leave His baggage behind Him at Margate on account of the seizure of that parcel.

I am on all occasions Yrs.
in very great haste
T. Digges

[Addressed:] B: T: Franklin / Passy

APS: Franklin Papers, 102:83.

1. Samuel Hartley's wife.

To John Adams

Mondy. 17th July 1780

DEAR SIR

Since my letter of the 12th we have no arrivals from America or any thing new but what will be mentiond below. I am anxious to know if my letter to You of the 8th or 7th of last month got to Your hands. The Behaviour of the Bearer of it to Ostend, who has been some days idling about London gives me strong suspicion that He did not do with the letter what He promisd me. I am uneasy about Him having had proofs He is a most notorious lyar and not to be depended on; & I have wrote to Passy about Him.[1]

There is a mail just now arrivd at the Post Office brought by a Packet from Jamaica in 37 days. Just before the sailing of this packet (which was with a fleet of upwards of 200 Merchantmen bound to Engd. under escort of 3 Men of War, & which fleet the packet left safe after passing the Windward Passage) an English frigate arrivd at Jamaica with the flag of the Fort of St. Juan situated on a river of that name not far from Cape Gracios a Dios and in the quarter of Nicarauga. It seems the Jamaica Expedition which saild in March last bent its course on a Buccaneering Expedition to that part of the Main; That they found no opposition till they got before this fort some miles up the River and before which they were near three weeks before its surrender. During this time, *it is said*, an offer of four Million Piasters was made to save the Fort & Town from Plunder & which was refusd for fear the Ransom would not be paid: (a Piaster at 3/4d. Stg. each makes this sum 666,000 £Stg., much more I think than the fee simple of that whole Settlement could be worth[)]. The fort afterwards capitulated about the 1st June or latter end of May. This is spoke of here in the most exalted terms—as a thing of infinitely more import than Omoa[2]—nothing but joy expressd upon the occasion.—Perhaps in a few hours it may be thought nothing of & of no national consequence. The same packet brings an account that the Natives & Spaniards had surprisd & taken the English Post & Settlement on the Black River in the Bay of Campeachy & that most of the English had fled to the Island of Rattan.[3] Another mail from Chs. Town arrivd at same time but no letters will be out till tomorrow; Genl. Clintons last Gazette Despatches are I think the 5 or 6 June & it is said this second packet saild with Genl. Prevost but a very few days after, so that the news by Her cannot be very material; *All* the City however will have it that No. Carolina has submitted to the terms proposd by Genl. Clinton & that Virga. *would certainly* accept the Same—there is no reasoning on this Torrent of nonsense so I give it you just as it is.

A Gentleman going hence immediately to Ostend with a fair wind gives me hopes this will be put into the post office there tomorrow morning which will be a day or two at least before our regular tuesdays mail sets out[4]—I forward by same oppertunity a letter from one of the two Gentlemen lately come from Your quarters a letter to Mr. D[an]a—I am on all occasions &ca. &ca.
W. S. C.

My friend D. H. told me a day or two ago He would write You a few lines—He is a very honest Man & means well & right for our cause.

[Addressed:] A Monsieur/Monsr. Ferdinando Raymond San/Negott./ Chez Monsieur Hocherau, Libraire,/Pont Neuf./Paris

MHS: Adams Papers, Reel 352.

[1] See Digges to Franklin, July 17, 1780.
[2] See Digges to Adams, Mar. 10, 1780.
[3] The Spanish attack had occurred in mid-Sept. 1779, but news from Central America traveled slowly. Digges misplaces the island of Rattan (or Roatán). It lies in the Gulf of Honduras, east of the Yucatan peninsula, northeast of Omoa, and northwest of the Black River (Rio Negro) settlement. The Bay of Campeche is to the west of Yucatan, a bay in the southernmost part of the Gulf of Mexico.
[4] Despite the time Digges hoped to save, this letter, according to the endorsement, was not received until Sept. 4, after Adams was settled in Amsterdam.

To Benjamin Franklin

Monday July 17. 1780

DEAR SIR

Since my letter to you of the 12th I have seen Jas. Garnet [Barnet] who is loungeing & going so idly about the streets, & whom I have detected in so many lies, that I think it necessary to apprise You of Him in order that Monr. Chamont may be warnd not to pay too implicit faith to what Garnet may write. He told me [he] had drawn two Bills on Him before He gave me the one for 12 Guins. about the 8th of last month: As he told me he was taken in a Ship of Mr. Chamonts & carryd into Ireld. & that He was sure of getting the command of another vessel of Mr. Chamonts now fitting out, I readily lent him the money to get away, without which He seemingly could not have movd. At Ostend He took up eight Guis. more in my name of Mr. Bowens, went as He tells me from thence to Dunkirke, then post to Nantes, & so back via Ostend to London, which He had not possibly time to do. When I taxd him home he prevaricated & lyed most abominably, but persisted He returnd on account of your sending Him an order to embark on board P. Jones, whom He said He did not like well enough to go to sea with. I wrote to You & Mr. A. by Him under date the 8th June or 7th I do not recollect which. I am much afraid He sacrificd my letters, & when You have an oppertunity should be glad to know whether Yours got to hand or not. I fear I shall be 20 Guins. out of pocket by Him, but prudence obliges me to keep up an outward civility, as yet I have not heard whether His bill on Monr. Chamont was paid or not. It will be no new matter to me to get it protested, for accept [except] the one you paid me drawn by a Dr. Jas. Brehon I have never had a bill paid, nor any remittance from any one of my Countrymen pushing home.

In my letter of the 12th I mentiond the mode I had used towards helping Capt. C[onyngha]m; We have no answers yet, but not destitute of hopes but we may succeed. Capt. M[anle]y has also had fresh hints given Him.

I have good reason to think this will be put into the Post Office at Ostend tomorrow morning (Tuesday) and by that means will most likely inform You sooner than advices by the Regular post from London that a mail in 37 days from Jamaica gives an account that The Expedition from that Island to the Spanish Main Commanded by Kemble, but generally calld Dallings Expedition had succeeded so far to take Fort St. Juan on a River of that name not far from Carthagena or rather in the quarter of Nicarauga Lake.[1] No particulars are yet transpird, but the clamour which is usual on every slight success is gone forth to a greater degree than for the fort Omoa. It appears the Expedition got an easy footing near Cape Gracios a Dios towards the 20th April, & from thence proceeded up the River St. Juan to the Fort, before which they were near three weeks. Report says the Garrison offerd the sum of 4, Million of Piasters as a ransom to the Place; (at 3/4d. each is 660,000 £ Stng.) I dont believe the fee simple of the whole settlement was worth so much. However, nothing less than millions are talkd of or will be beleivd—perhaps a few hours may paint the expedition but as of trifling consequence. The same packet brings accounts that the Spaniards & Indians have broke up the settlement of English on the Black River in the Bay of Campeachy, & driven all the English to the Island of Rattan. This Jamaica Packet appears to have saild the begining of June, had only 37 days passage, came thro the Windward passage with the whole Jamaica fleet, *upwards of two hundred Sail*, & left them in safety from the Cruisers in those Seas.

This fleet is expected to arrive in a week or ten days, and in a little time after, one from the Leward Islands of about 120 Sail.

There is also a Packet from Chas. Town with a multitude of Letters, none of which are yet out, but this packet cannot bring any material news, having saild but three days after the last publishd accounts from Genl. Clinton; But the cry is that No. Carolina has submitted to Engd. & that Virga. will certainly do the like.

I am Yrs. &ca. &ca.
W. S. C.

HSP: Franklin Papers, 5 : 138.

[1] Dalling, a general as well as the governor of Jamaica, was directing military expeditions from the island, but it was Col. Stephen Kemble (ca. 1730–1822) who was actually in command of the expedition to the San Juan River.

To John Adams

Hammersmith 25 July 80

DEAR SIR

I wrote You half a dozen lines the last post the 21st Inst.[1] to inform you of the junction of the Spanish with the French fleet in the Wt. Indies which took place the 16th ulo. at Dominique. This news was brought to England by a frigate & Cutter which had but a passage of 20 odd days, they haveing left St. Lucie the 22d June. The alarm & consternation here was great on receipt of this news, & there are yet very great fears for St. Kitts Antigua & other Islands.—Jamaica is *supposd* to be safe, as is Rodney's fleet; which was left at Barbadoes & woud there probably wait the junction of the Squadron under Walsingham. The Report now is that only seven of the Spanish Ships remaind with Guichen, the other 5 having gone down to Leeward with the Trade. This seven however gives such a decided majority over Rodney that we are all much in the dumps, & would be exceedingly so, were it not for several pieces of *good* News of yesterday & today. A Large Baltic fleet which had been thought in great danger from several late Captures being made in the No. Seas, have got safe into the River & sundry other ports. The Jamaica Fleet *upwards of 150 Sail*, are all arrivd without the Loss of a Ship. And this day An Express arrivd from India with the account of the taking of Punah the Capital of the Marrattas, in which there was considerable Riches.[2] Thus England is loosing in the West what she seems getting but a small compensation for in the East Indies; however our thick-heads seem satisfied with the Exchange, and I am sure the Enemys of England ought to be so, for no line of comparison can be drawn as to the comparative value of the one over the other Conquests when taken in a political national view; but here every wish & thought is for plunder, & those Expeditions to the *Richest* must of course be the most *substancially best.* Not a word from America & the furor about other Colonies *coming in*, seems much abated. The N. York Fleet is yet detaind & will be so till the distination of Monsr. Tierneys Squadron is more exactly known.

I am Yrs. &ca. &ca.
T. Williamson

[Addressed:] A Monsieur/ Monsr. Ferdinando Raymond San/ Negott./ Chez Monsr. Hocherau Libraire/ Pont Neuf/ Paris[3]

MHS: Adams Papers, Reel 352.

[1] This letter has not been found.
[2] Although the British had won battles in the area near Poona, there is no evidence that the capital of the Mahratta Confederacy was actually taken.
[3] When this letter reached Paris (July 31), Adams was in Brussels en route to lodgings in Amsterdam.

To John Adams

Camberwell 28th July 1780

DEAR SIR

A Vessel from N. York to Liverpoole which saild the 24th June, brings advice that Clinton had got back to that quarter and gone up the No. River with 10,000 Men & several small boats. About a month ago an intimate friend shewd letters from that General mentioning that his intention was to try if Washington's lines were forcible; I make no doubt this is the scheme he is upon—He will most likely look, and come back, which was the case with Him before.

The same Vessel brings an account of a smart action between the Trumbull frigate Cap. Nicholson & a Liverpoole Letter of Marque which got off.[1]

A Passenger in a Ship from St. Eustatia to Holland who landed at the Downs & whom I saw this day at Loyds, told me He saild the 8th of June; on the 25th He was brought too by Adml. Graves's fleet of 7 *sail of the Line* in Latte. 34—Longe. 52—about 70 Leagues N. E. of Bermudas. This fleet saild the 18th June in search of Terneys Squadron after which Graves enquird very eagerly.

It appears there were no accounts of that Squadron on the American Coasts at least near N. York, on the 24th of June.

I am Your Most Ob. Ser.
Alexr. Williamson

[Addressed:] A Monsieur/ Monsr. Ferdinando Raymond San/ Negott./ Chez Monsr. Hocherau, Libraire/ Pont Neuf/ a Paris

MHS: Adams Papers, Reel 352.

[1] James Nicholson, senior captain in the Continental navy since 1778, had commanded the *Trumbull* since Sept. 1779. The action was with the *Watt*, Capt. Coulthard.

To Benjamin Franklin

London Augt. 18. 1780

DEAR SIR

I recivd Your letter of the 30th ulo.[1] & forwarded Mr. Peters Letter thro the means of His Bankers Messrs. Fuller, Son & Co. The Spectacle glass has also been deliverd by our friend J. T[em]p[l]e who was the person that applyd for it. He talks of pushing homewards very soon via Holland. A particular friend of mine, left for me about 3 weeks ago, both with Mr. Bowens of Ostend & M. De Neufville of Amsterdam² a small parcell which were to be forwarded to You in my name. They contain porcelane representations of Washington & Yourself. I beleive the artist faild in doing yours or it was broke in the carriage so that I cannot say whether that will be forwarded on or not.

That Irish theif Jas. Barnet is still in London, & most likely will be soon taken on some high way robberry. I never was so deceivd & cheatd by a man in my life; cheifly owing to Mrs. W[righ]t & a worthy man from So. Caroa. (Mr. Ch[a]n[ni]ng) whom He also took in.³ As my letters both to Yourself & Mr. J. A., nor those to Josa. J[ohnso]n from Mr. Ch———n———g, never got to hand, I am fearful He has made some improper use of them. What vexes me most is, that the scoundrel went from hence to Ostend purposely to take Mr. Bowens in for 8 Guins. on the strength of a common recommendatory Letter from me to Him, & which I shall be under an obligation to make good.

This will be carryd abroad & put in the Post at Ostend by Mr. Saml. H[ar]tl[e]y whom I wrote you relative to Capt. C[onyngha]m & who offerd You the Jamaica Spirit. He is a considerable Merchant of this place & a uniform friend to the cause of our Country. He goes to Holland & thence to Paris on similar business to that Mr. Barber was some time ago upon.⁴ He takes Mrs. H———y abroad with Him & they will wait upon You if they visit Paris.

I had laid a scheme conjointly with Mr. H. (who owns part of the Ship which took Capn. C———m) to get Capt. C. releasd in consequence of Your having got two of Mr. H———ys Captains liberated in France. The proper letters were written to the other owners at Dartmo., but it was Capn. C———ms fate to be recommitted & put in the Black hole before our letters could get to hand. Since that period nothing could be done for Him towards getting his release. My freind at Plymo. got early orders to supply all his wants & writes me he has done so & keeps an eye to his future intentions.⁵ His health has been very bad, but he is now better. He was I understand 40 days in the black-hole & all the letters sent to Him were stopt & sent up to the Admiralty as was the case with some former ones I wrote to his now companion Capt. M[a]n[le]y. This person would have effected his Escape had he been prudent & took advice of not coming out of Goal but singly; instead of this three or four others were taken with Him & carryd back. My friend has also orders to supply Him with the necessarys He may want. We are not quite so well off in point of assiduity & cleverness in our Plymo. friend as we are in that of Portso.[6] but intentions are equally good. I beleive numbers stand now about 180 in one & 68 in the other prison. The board of Sick & Hurt have given a direct refusal to any exchange but immidiately man for man between this & france. It is a pity the American Cruizers do not hold more Prisoners & pay less attention to Ransoms. Your Donation of six pence a week to each man was very gratefully & thankfully receivd. It has commencd near four weeks & my friends regularly pay it in. The Dispondence among the men from the appearance of never getting exchangd is our greatest evil, & much argument is necessary to diswade them from Entering, which too many have done.

I have read Your inclosures about Capt. C——m & the treatment of others carryd into Lisbon. For the present nothing can be done about it, & I lay up these complaints in a little bag to open on a future occasion.[7] One of the most abominable practices of all is the robbing of almost every neutral Ship which is seen in the Channel by English privateers *under American Colours* and committing acts of insult & thefts that would disgrace Pirates. I have published many of these cases lately & continue to do so whenever I can get at *names*.[8]

I cannot pass by the mention of Lisbon without informing you that a Mr. ——— Dohrman has on many occasions shewn extraordinary civility & attention to many Americans who were carryd in Prisoners there some of whom I have seen in England.[9] Mr. Dohrman is a Nephew to the Dutch Consul Mr. Gildermester.[10] I am sorry to say it out of the whole British Factory, near a hundred of whom I know got very handsome Consignments & profits from America, not one (Mr. Burn excepted) that have shewn the Americans any quarter. Nay they are openly hostile against them, at a time too that I am very sure it is the wish of that Court to see the American Ships enter & trade unmolested. I know that Country & People very well, & I wish a proof could be drawn of their acceptance of American ships by some one or other unarmd Merchantmen going from America there for a market.

As you must have receivd accounts by the fleet lately arrivd in France from Chesapeak to as late dates as the 10–15th June I can send you nothing new from that quarter. Clintons arrival from the So.Ward at N. York is the latest accounts we have had from America. A Ship is arrivd at Whitehaven which left Hallifax the *11th July* & brings no accounts whatever from thence, the quarter of N. York, or more south, nor any the least tidings of Monsr. Ternays or Greaves's Fleet. The folly of all the Southern parts of America "coming in" as it was set forth with such industry, begins to abate considerably. The affair *now* they say must be decided in the West Indies, & most likely it is before this day. Nothing talkd of but the Russian bears and the northern league,[11] Six sail still in the Downs & others they say are gone down Channel with their trade. Many attempts are made to laugh at this armd neutrality & ridicule it as nothing; but serious people look upon it to be wearing a solid & consistant face, by which the Dutch & other maratime powers will get what they have been long aiming at 'That free Ships shall make free goods.' When this is establishd it will go near to annihilate the claim of Britain for the sole sovereign Dominion of the Sea. What measures will be adopted by our wise Ministry in respect to this northern Confedracy cannot easily be discovered. They will hardly embroil themselves by stopping and searching these neutral combind fleets; nor does it appear they will totally acquiesce at least without the appearance of resistance to that hostile confederacy: I am informd They are going on in their usual way of littleness, & have given such ambiguous & equivocal orders to the Captns. of Men of War that they will not know how to act under them—Thus they hope to preserve Engld. from a northern war without tarnishing the British Flag.

The N. York fleet has at last saild, about 40 Ships under Convoy of one Frigate & they go directly for the Hook. There are no troops on board it tho the Papers say there are.[12] I dont find any *civil* officer has saild or is going to their stations in So. Carolina; It therefore appears to me that this Country does not expect to hold that very long,

18 August 1780

& that a military is the best Government for a Conquerd People. I dont find the War is meant to be pushd from thence towards No. Carola. or Virginia. I beleive no plan is fixd on for opperations in that quarter; They seem to trust intirely to the Depradations of detatchd partys of the Troops, & to the exigencies of the day. I am with the highest respect

Dr. Sir Your Mo. Obligd & Obt. Servt.
W. S. C.

His Excelly. B. F——

HSP: Franklin Papers, 5 : 139.

[1] Franklin had enclosed a letter to Peters for Digges to forward to the right address, supplied the lens for the spectacles mentioned by Digges to Franklin, Apr. 6, 1780, reported additional rascalities by Barnet, and, confirming stories of Conyngham's mistreatment, recommended him "to your kind assistance in supplying him with what may be necessary" (LC: Franklin Papers, Series 1, 4 : 199–200).
[2] Jean de Neufville, senior partner of the Amsterdam firm that had the year before outfitted John Paul Jones's squadron and was developing close ties with John Adams.
[3] The victims were probably Patience Lovell Wright and John Channing, a friend of Henry Laurens's living in London.
[4] See Digges to Franklin, Jan. 9 and 10, 1780.
[5] See Digges to Franklin, July 12, 1780. The friend at Plymouth was Robert Heath.
[6] Where Thomas Wren was based.
[7] Digges is echoing Franklin's comment of Feb. 26, 1780 (see Digges to Franklin, Mar. 17, 1780, n. 5).
[8] See, for example, the *London Courant*, July 24, 1780.
[9] Arnold Henry Dohrman (d. 1813), a well-to-do Lisbon merchant of Dutch nationality, had been active for at least two years in providing relief and shelter for captured American seamen. Since June 1780 he had been serving as an unsalaried agent of the Continental Congress. When a few years later his business failed, he moved to New York and, as a result of his petition, was reimbursed for expenses in cash and land beyond the Ohio.
[10] Jan Gildemeester (1743?–1799), also a Lisbon merchant, was agent and consul general for the Batavian Republic.
[11] The League of Armed Neutrality, mentioned by Digges to Adams, Apr. 28, 1780. Digges's comments in this paragraph concerning the threat to Britain's dominion of the seas follows almost verbatim a statement in the *London Courant*, Aug. 5.
[12] The *London Courant*, Aug. 18, was not one of those alluded to. It noted that there were no troops on board, that the fleet's destination was Sandy Hook (N.J.), and that the date of sailing was Aug. 13.

To John Adams

London 24th [⟨22nd⟩]¹ Augt. 1780

DEAR SIR

I wrote You a few lines on the 18th & 22nd Insts. cheifly to inform you the news of those days, but as they were forwarded by the usual conveyance of Post (my not knowing You were then in Holland) I suppose they will not get to hand earlier than this letter; which is born by a particular friend Mr. Saml. Hartley a relation of D. Hartleys. He is a considerable Merchant of this place and goes abroad on some commercial business to Holland (I beleive in the neutral flag way) which will also lead Him to Paris.

He has ever shewn himself an open friend to the cause of our Country, & as I dare say He would be glad to express it to any of our publickly employd Men abroad, I beg leave to recommend Him to Your notice should chance bring you together either in Holland or France. As. Mr. Hartley is perfectly well acquainted with the publick movements of this Country & well informd as to the news of the day & the beating of the pulses of the people generally, I take the liberty to refer You to Him for particulars. The late news of the Capture of a whole outward bound East & West Inda. Fleet by the combind fleet of France & Spain, has thrown a gloom upon the minds of the people which you can much more easily guess than I can describe. It has been a black week at Loyds, & well it may, for one half of the underwriters that walk that Coffee House, will likely be ruind by such a vas[t] & unexpected Capture. The general uneasiness among all ranks, is not a little heightend by the dark prospect of things in the West Indies, & the flying reports of Rodney's defeat with the loss of several ships. The accounts from Amera. too are not the most favorable for the accomplishment of the desird object unconditional Submission. The Expedition into the Jerseys under Neiphausen² has been repulsd & was nearly surrounded; & that check it is said prevented Clinton from trying any thing up the No. River.

The Ministerial runners however still give out with a degree of impudence & falseness that is astonishing, that they are shure of No.

Carolina, Virga. & Maryland "comeing in" as they term it to the feet of this Country. The torrent of folly which reignd ever since the capture of Chs. Town on the subject of this "comeing in" of All southern America, has subsided very generally among the thinking people within this week or two. There are those among the great however who still keep it up & exult exceedingly about the State of Affairs in America, but I never suffer myself to be dejected by the triumphs of a People so easily & suddenly elated. God Governs, and I trust the second "hour of their Insolence["] will be of as short duration as the first.[3]

> I am with the highest esteem
> Dr. Sir
> Yr. Obligd & Obt. Ser.
> W. S. C.

MHS: Adams Papers, Reel 352.

[1] The dating is puzzling because this appears to be the letter of Aug. 22 to which Digges refers in writing Adams, Aug. 25, 1780. Yet if it is actually a letter of Aug. 22, then the first sentence here is equally curious. Neither of the two letters sent by the regular post has been found (never acknowledged, they were doubtless never received), and accurate dating of the sequence must remain speculative.

[2] Baron Wilhelm von Knyphausen (1716–1800), lieutenant general in command of the German troops in America.

[3] In his letter to Digges of July 30, a reply to Digges's of June 29 and July 12, Franklin had written: "Don't be discouraged by the present Triumph of a People who are so easily elated. God governs, and the Second Hour of their Insolence may be as short as the first" (LC: Franklin Papers, Series 1, 4:200).

To John Adams

London 25th Augt. 1780

DEAR SIR

Since I wrote You the 22d (by a friend Mr. S. H[art]l[e]y) nothing material has transpired And the arrival of news by a small vessel from Boston to Bristol has not removd in any measure the gloom on the generality of countenances here in consequence of the late disaster to the outward bound East & West India Fleet. Tho I have seen J. T[emple] we have no exact accounts by this vessel to Bristol. She appears to have been purchasd by Mr. R. Temple to bring to Europe His Family, He meaning to settle in Ireland for His Health,[1] She had 32 days passage which brings the day of Her Sailing to about the 21st or 22d July. The accounts by Her are that Monsr. Ternays Squadron had arrivd safe at Rhode Island where he had debarkd His troops & sent them on the Continent. Three of the Transports had Seperated & put into Boston but the troops had been immediately marchd over land to Providence.

There was no accounts of the arrival of Adml. Greaves or the least item of any Expedition up the No. River under Clinton. No other passengers but Temples Family & the above is all I can gather about the vessel or the news she brings. If any occurs You shall have it by next post.

I am with very great Esteem
Dr. Sir Yr. Ob. Ser.
W. S. C.

The vessel arrivd at Bristol the 23d.

MHS: Adams Papers, Reel 352.

[1] Robert Temple (1728–1782), older brother of John, was a loyalist whose sentiments had subjected him to threats and arrest. Finally, suffering from ill health, he had decided to leave home, sailing in a brig that the Massachusetts Council had authorized him to charter, with four prisoners paroled to the American authorities (see Digges to Franklin, Sept. 8 and 12, 1780).

To Benjamin Franklin

London 25 Augt. 1780

DEAR SIR

I did not receive Your letter of the 18th handed me by Mr. H. time enough for the Office Hours to make enquiry of or about Mr. G[oddar]d;[1] But I calld there this Evening & went to Mr. G———s Lodgings, where neither His Landlady or the Servant could give me further accounts of Him than that He had been near three weeks in the Country but *where* they could not tell. I shall call at the office again in the morning & get his direction, with which I can make the necessary enquiry as to his accepted Bill; but I fear it will be a post or two before I can inform You further; You may depend however no time shall be lost on my part. As Mr. G—— seems to turn out but an underhand Gentleman I am rather afraid for Your Bill.

I wrote You twice very lately. Since which there is nothing new save the arrival of a small Brig from Boston to Bristol which arrivd the 23d after a passage of 32 days so that She saild about the 21 or 22d July. She appears to be purchasd by Mr. J. Temples Brother in order to move Himself & Family to settle in Ireland He being ill in a Consumption.[2] We have no regular accounts as yet by this vessel nor can I immediately find J. T. to inform myself whether He has any. The publick receivd account by this vessel is, That Monr. Ternay arrivd safe at Rhode Island & had landed His men about 6,000 which had gone from the Island to the Continent. Three of the transports of His fleet had seperated from Him on the Coast of America & put into Boston. The troops on board them were immediately marchd for Providence. When this vessel saild there were no accounts in Boston of Adml. Greaves's arrival on the Coast nor any sort of news from N. York as to Clintons Expedition up the North River. In the rough as it was told this day at Change the news is not lookd upon as favorable, but rather the reverse, & will add to the gloom still very conspicuous for the loss of a whole Fleet lately taken by the Combind fleet. I dare say when it comes to be given in detail, it will still cast a deeper gloom.

I find my friend Barnet has been playing similar tricks in Bruselles to those he playd me. He there went by the name of Billinger.

Dr. S[co]tt receivd with great thankfulness the pass[por]t you sent for His Baggage. He went out in the N. York fleet which saild the 10th & much fears are expressd for this fleet. Mr. John Bowman of the State of Georgia (where He has a Considerable property in Land & blacks) Desires me to supplicate a similar pass for His Baggage. He means to go out in a running Ship to Savanah in a fortnight or 3 weeks. I meet Him frequently at our freinds in Mincing Lane (Mr. V[aughan]s) and have been enough in the habits of intimacy with Him for two Years back to know Him to be perfectly right in politicks

& principles with regard to His Country. He was at Paris & known to You about two or 3 years ago. If you can oblige Him be pleasd to cover the pass To *Messrs.* Wm. Hodgson & Co., better *Messrs.* than Mr. & the sooner forwarded the better.

Our Reverend friend Mr. W[ren] has been some days with me & we have put Your welcome donation to the Prisoners on a good footing. It commencd the 18th ulo. at F[orto]n to 152 Privates & 43 Officers 6d. per week to Each. The numbers are not exactly known at M. P[rison]. Mr. W——n will be in Town again in 6 or 8 days when I will settle the exact advance on this Charity & draw a bill on You as heretofore for the amount to that day. I am with the highest Esteem

Dr. Sir Yr. obligd & Ob. Ser.
W. S: C.

[Addressed:] A Monsr. Monsr. B. F——/ Passy

HSP: Franklin Papers, 5 : 140.

[1] A Mr. Jones had borrowed thirty guineas from Franklin and promised repayment as soon as he reached Bordeaux. Jones, though, never went to Bordeaux but made off for London, where Franklin thought Digges might locate him and recover the sum to use on Franklin's account. Jones had given Franklin as security a bill payable by J. Goddard in London, and Franklin was now seeking payment of that bill (see Digges to Franklin, Oct. 24, 1780). Which Mr. H. handed Digges Franklin's letter remains uncertain.

[2] The same information appeared next day in the *London Courant*. Whether Digges was the source of the *Courant's* report, or whether both relied on a common source, cannot be determined.

To John Adams

On August 17 Adams had written Digges from Amsterdam giving him his new address and asking a series of questions: "Pray what do the Politicians on your side the water think of the Plan of Russia, Sweden and Denmark! Do they think the dutch will acceed to it? These last have contended over 100 years, for the Principle of free ships free goods, is it thought they will refuse it now? Do they find much comfort in the news from America? Are the People ripe to declare for England? is the capture of Charlestown the Conquest of the States? Is the American mind wholly subdued? have they lost sight of the Pleasure of Self-

government? do they begin to despise a free Trade? do they begin to think the ministry, just, honest, wise and good? The Parliament uncorrupt? the nation virtuous? the national Debt no Burthen? the French alliance a Calamity? how is all this? To my Lord Norths proposal with his ways and means, for next winter? how many millions are proposed to be borrowed next? what Interest is to be given? Are the Israelites all ready? how is Gibraltar to be supplied next? how are the Grenadas and Floridas to be got back again? do the Politicians see their way, clear out of the Labyrinth? Is the American Trade quite annihilated with France Spain, Holland, Denmark, Sweden, the West Indies? how fare the Fisheries this year? which gets most the English or Americans? Does the nation still adore the Administration for their Wisdom their sublime plans and their wonderful success?" (MHS: Adams Papers, Reel 102).

London 29 August 1780

DEAR SIR

I am much obligd to You for a letter & some news papers by a friend. I have not yet seen the principal person concernd in the Flag to Bristol, he not having yet got to Town but hourly expected. A Townsman of Yours also a passenger in that vessel Has been with me, & mentioning to him that I was about to write to You, & asking if he had any news or letters from Your particular freinds, He answerd me He had not; that all things were well in the quarter of Boston, & indeed in every part north of Carolina, & likely to stand so. The picture he gave me of things generally was very comforting. His name is Br[o]mf[iel]d[1] & he is on his way to Holld. He says He saw Your Daughter a day or two before He saild (the 21st July) & that She was very well as were all Your friends. No other passengers in this ship save the Capn. & Supercargo of a Ship lately taken bound from Corke to N. York. The Flag has hitherto been respected, and present prospects indicate that the vessel will be in no way stopt. The Capn. means to return with Her to Boston. It is wonderful how Government have relaxd lately in their persecutions & conversations against Americans. They certainly begin to see that it is all over with them in America, & the more open the communication & intercourse between the two Countries the better for them—If ships under this discription are allowd to pass, they will soon be better informd of the actual state of things in America. There are many American violent Torey Refugees at Bristol, all from about Boston, those Gentry soon informd themselves how affairs stood in that quarter, & some of them have written up to their *worthy* Brethren here, That affairs certainly stand differently in America to what has been industriously put forth by Ministry & their runners ever since the capture of Chas. Town; some of them go as far as to say that America must & will be Independant. They begin to find that the American *mind* cannot be subdued, & that our people are not so tired of the *Tyranny* of Congress as they had reason to hope. Authentic News was yesterday Brought to Loyds that the outward bound Quebec fleet had been met near new found land the 12th July by an American frigate (supposd the Confederacy) & two Brig Privateers, & that they had capturd twelve of the remaining sixteen— This fleet was attackd soon after they left Corke about six weeks ago by three French men of war who only snapt up two & those were retaken soon after—Well done Yankee say I. The news coming immidiately upon the back of the important Capture of a Whole outward Bound East & Wt. Inda. Fleet,[2] cast a damp upon the phizes in the City which I have not discoverd heretofore. These accounts together with the general ones receivd by a N. York packet which saild the 11th July, put the whole Merchantile race, & every torey news monger, more into the dumps than you can immagine; for a little while the cry was all is over with us now in America, when the paltry cruizers of that Country, & their Gallic Allies, capture our fleets & repulse our Armies. This day we are again in spirits at Loyds—The Leeward Island fleet, The Oporto Fleet, & two India men are reported to be all safe arrivd at Falmouth. Therefore we are yet Lords paramont at Sea, & Rodney is superior in the Wt. Indies or these fleets could not sail. Such is the conversation tho not a word of intelligence authentic has been receivd from either of these fleets. This however is encouragement enough for a universal wish that England would immidiately declare war against Russia, Denmark Sweden, & Holland,—which last they accuse as being at the bottom of all the northern mischeif[3]—*Free ships* shall not be allowd to make *free goods* or England will be undone—this is our language & the Ministry have been accusd of pusilanimity for not seizing the 13 Russian Men of War which lately anchord in the Downs, tho there were not so many English Ships of War to do this job *then* in the Channel.

There has been much conversation since the arrival of the N. York packet about a letter said to be written by Sr. H. Clinton to some of his Friends, about the state of things in America—some people go so far as to say that He expressd the same in his publick Letter to Lord G. G[ermain]e. That it is full, intelligent, & explicit on the State of Enlish Affairs in America & very highly disagreeable to the Cabinet Council before whom it was read. It is said to give an account of the repulse with considerable loss of Genl. Knephausen's party of 5,000 Men who went into the jerseys to route Master Washington[;] That Genl. Clinton himself had lookd at the American Army from another quarter, & after several reconnoitering plans had returnd to N. York & given His opinion that He could not effect any thing *with the Army He now has*, against such formidable lines & so strong a position: That many skirmishes on foraging partys had happend, and none of them provd successfull; That on the arrival upon the Coast of America of Ternay's Squadron (which was first heard of in N. York the 5th July) He had drawn in some of His outposts, & was in hopes Adml. Greaves would arrive to protect the port &ca. &ca.

All these accounts, in some measure corroborated by private people, as well as the N. York papers down to the 11th July, give much uneasiness to the friends of Government here, & might if they would but apply it right be a good lesson to them to try to make some accomodation or Peace with America; but the fates have seemingly decreed that the war shall go on still further & that a nation of unthinking people shall be further blinded & led into deeper ruin.

I am with the highest Esteem Dr. Sir

Your obligd & Obt. Serv.
W. S. C[hurch]

[Addressed:] Outside address inked out: ⟨Monsieur/ . . . / . . . / Amsterdam⟩

MHS: Adams Papers, Reel 352.

[1] Apparently Henry Bromfield (1751–1837), eldest son of a Boston merchant whose interests in London needed attention. The younger Bromfield was on his way to Paris.
[2] Sixty-one of a convoy of sixty-four ships had on Aug. 9 been captured off St. Vincent, one of the Cape Verde Islands, by the combined French and Spanish fleets. Some three thousand prisoners were taken; the value of the loss in merchandise was variously

estimated, accounts ranging from little more than one hundred twenty thousand pounds to a million and a half.

³The League of Armed Neutrality.

To Benjamin Franklin

29 Augt. 1780

DEAR SIR

I receivd your letter of the 18 Int. & answerd it, as far I could do so, by frydays post. Since that period I have been twice to the office where Mr. G[oddar]d is a Clerk, & the answers to my questions about Him were rather extraordinary. I could find out nothing but that He had been 3 or 4 weeks in the Country (neither his Brother Clerks nor his Landlady at His Lodgings could tell *where* in the Country) but that if I left a line at the office it would be deliverd to Himself. I have wrote Him a line just to ask if such a bill (*copying* it *exactly from* Yours) was a good bill & requesting His Answer as soon as He conveniently could. I am afraid by what I could discover that You have been flung out of 30 Guineas. The moment I get any information about Him You shall certainly have it.

I mentiond to You on Fryday that a Flag of Truce brought by Mr. R. Temple had arrivd at Bristol. He is not yet come to Town but is to be here tomorrow—There are no passengers, but a Mr. Bromfield whom I have seen, and a Master & Super Cargoe of a Ship richly laden & lately taken going from Corke to N. York & carryd into Boston. I need not recapitulate to You any particular news receivd from Mr. B——mf——d. It is in substance extreemly pleasing to me & very different to what has been put forth with such assiduity by ministry & their runners ever since the news arrivd of the Capture of Chas. Town. This account has been rather confirmd to me since the arrival of the last packet from N. York, where it appeard on the 11th July the Garrison was aiming rather at securing themselves than making any excursions against the American Army, declard now on all hands to be too well posted for Mr. Clinton to attempt an assault. Bromfield says they had heard of a fleet of English Men of War arriving at Hallifax about the 8th July which must be Greaves's fleet. We suppose here from the various accounts lately receivd that it is intended by Genl. Washington & Monsr. Ternay to make an attack on N. York. Accounts are this day receivd at Loyds that the outward bound Quebec fleet had been met near the Island of N. Foundland on the 12th July by the Confederacy American Frigate & 2 small privateers who made an easy capture of twelve out of sixteen Ships—The other four escapd & told the dismal tale at St. Johns N. Foundland from whence the account comes to Bristol & it is authentic. Well done Yankee say I. This fleet was met by 3 french Men of War about 5 weeks ago soon after they saild from Corke. These Men of War then took but two of the fleet which were afterwards retaken.

We were much in the dumps here on this & the late Capture near Cape St. Vincents,[1] and very much so at the news by the New York Packet which *only* substantially informd us that Clintons Army was far too weak to effect any offensive opperation—We are however today got *up* again. The Leeward Island, the Oporto, & two of the Et. India homward bound ships are reported to be all safe arrivd at Falmouth, & in consequence of this immence great news, we are *now* mighty enough to war with all the world. The cry is that Ministry ought to be hangd if they do not immidiately declare war against Russia, Holland, Denmark & Sweeden for their late perfidy in forming an offensive league against the commerce of this Country.

I am with the highest regard
Dr. Sir Yr. Obligd & Ob. Ser.
W. S. C.

HSP: Franklin Papers, 5:141.

[1] See Digges to Adams, Aug. 29, 1780, n. 2.

To Benjamin Franklin

London 1st Sept. 80

DEAR SIR

I calld again this day at the office where a Bill given you was made payable & I could learn no intelligence of Mr. J. G[oddar]d more than

I had before—He was in the Country but *where* or when He returnd no one could tell. I have no Answer to the letter wrote to him (& left at the office) which containd only an enquiry whether the Bill was good or not. Dr. F[othergi]ll being down in Cheshire for some days I could not make the necessary Enquiry whether Mr. Jones the drawer of the Bill on Mr. G——d, was known to Him or not.¹ I will do every thing in this business that can be done & give you the earliest information—at present I have no hopes to give You that the bill is a good one.

We have no news since the last post by which I wrote You, save that a *general* opinion prevails that the Parliament was this day dissolvd. There is much bustle in consequence of it, & by every appearance the Ministry will get as many if not more Corrupt ⟨L[or]ds⟩ into the next as they have had in the late Parliament.

Adml. G[ear]y has resignd the Command of the Channel fleet, and Darby has retird,² both said to be in disgust at Palissers appointment to Greenwich Hospital.³ Digby with thirteen Ships saild on tuesday last supposd on a Short Cruise in the Channel. It will be lucky for Him if He does not fall in with the Combind fleet now hourly expected.

I have seen Mr. Robt. T[emp]le who came in the Cartel from Boston to Bristol, and the accounts of the state of things which I receive from Him are in the lump, & I may say totally, very pleasing. No fears of the Yankies *"coming in"* as the term & expectation here. He is in very bad health & brings away three handsome Daughters, comely & full grown, & which must be a loss to any young Country.

He seems to have taken his final leave; but His passport from the States is worded in handsome terms to himself, & expressive that He may return whenever He pleases.⁴ He sold his Whole Property to one of the Traceys⁵ who supplyd Him with the Ship (in which came 7 or 8 passengers bound or obligated as those by Mitchell & Dunken were in Decr. last to release a like number of Americans here) on condition & penalty of 3,000 £ Stg. He should see the ship safe to a port of France or Spain. This cannot possibly be done here, for they will not admit her as a Cartel or allow any Exchange of Prisoners, 'tho the most remarkable civility has been shewn to Mr. T—— & the vessel at Bristol, & Mr. Stephens of the Admiralty has given orders She shall not be seizd but permitted to return. This return means to Boston *empty*, but to no other place. Mr. T—— obligation is to put the Vessel in a port of

France or Spain so that He must stand the risque of running Her to F. or Spain at any rate. This makes Him uneasy, & I dare say You will hear more of the case as it opens more. I wish this Country would do the handsome thing, & allow this vessel to carry a Cargoe to Morlaix. They may do worse. I am calld upon by the post & am in a hurry.

Yrs. wth. very grt. Esteem
W. S. C.

[Addressed:] Monsr. Monsr. B. F./ Passy

HSP: Franklin Papers, 5:142.

[1] Franklin thought that his friend Dr. John Fothergill (1712–1780), a physician with interests in science and philanthropy and with numerous American connections, might know of Jones's whereabouts. He mentioned this to Digges later (see Digges to Franklin, Oct. 24, 1780, headnote), but may have done so earlier as well.

[2] Vice-Adm. George Darby (ca. 1720–1790) had succeeded Geary and appears to have remained at his post for two years.

[3] Palliser had been appointed by the ministry as governor of Greenwich Hospital. Intended to compensate him for the loss in honor and income that had followed the controversy over his role during the battle off Ushant in 1778 (see Digges to Franklin, Dec. 19, 1778, n. 8), the appointment provided North's opponents with an occasion to revive old arguments and demand the ministry's resignation.

[4] See Digges to Franklin, Sept. 8, 1780.

[5] John or Nathaniel Tracy, Newburyport merchants (see Digges to Ridley, Nov. 20, 1777, n. 7).

To Benjamin Franklin

London 8 Sept. 1780

(copy)

State of Masss. Bay } Council Chamber July 3d 1780

On the Petition of Robert Temple Esqr. praying for Leave to hire a suitable Vessel to be protected as a Flag of Truce,

To Carry, himself, His Wife, & three Daughters to Ireland; with Liberty to return whenever He shall think proper

Orderd, That the prayer of the Petition be granted, & that the said Robert Temple Esqr. Be and he is hereby Permitted to Charter a

Ship or Vessel, for the purpose of transporting himself, Wife & three Daughters with two or more Servants from hence to Ireland—And not to carry with Him any more Seamen than sufficient to Navigate said vessel, or receive on board more provisions than necessary for the voyage; And that said Temple with His Family have Liberty to return to this State again whenever His affairs will admit of it. Said Temple is further directed to carry with Him such and so many Prisoners as shall be convenient for Him, provided that such Prisoners shall give to the Continental Commissary of Prisoners their Parole That they will in one month after their arrival in Ireland procure the Liberation of an equal number of Americans being prisoners of War of equal Condition with themselves, if such Americans there are there, if not, of such other Americans as shall be prisoners of War in Great Britain. And that they will cause such American Prisoners as shall be Liberated as aforesaid to be sent to some Convenient port in France, There to be deliverd to the Honourable Benjamin Franklin Esqr. Minister Plenipotentiary of the United States of America, or to His order. And in case of failure of Exchange, that said Prisoners shall hold themselves as Prisoners of War to the United States, and that they will return again in six months from the time of their arrival in Great Britain—And That the Said Vessel have the Protection of a Flag of Truce for the greater safety of said Temple and His Family.

                True Copy
                Attest.
                John Avery Dept. Secy.

In Consequence of this passport Mr. Robt. Temple Charterd The Brig Temple 120 Tonns, no Guns, Capt. Jno. Fletcher; 11 Seamen From Mr. Tracey at Newberry Port, & binds Himself to Tracey that the Vessel shall be put in safety into a French or Spanish Port—which Mr. Temple thought could be effected as a Flag of Truce. This has been refusd Him by Lord G. Germain, the Admiralty, & the board of Sick & Hurts. The papers of the vessel has been seizd & lodgd with the Commissioners of the Customs but the Admiralty have given *an order for their restoration & that the Ship shall not be stopd or molested but permitted to depart.* But where She is to depart to no one can tell at present. A few British Seamen was permitted to Navigate this Vessel home on Condition a like number of Americans here were releasd—These

Seamen have been pressd on board Men of War. There are only three persons left on board, & as *British* Seamen will engage to go in her either to America or a port of France & Spain. As She is *allowd to depart*, I think the best way to clear Her *empty* for one port & go into another. We want to get Her to Bilboa, & if She is taken by a French or Spanish Cruizer, Going there, I suppose You will be troubled to get Her releasd—Her flag papers & the vessels being known will secure Her from American Privateers & the English Clearance from all British Cruizers—most likely the vessel will go & trust to these risques.

None of the English Parole Prisoners Passengers in Her, can obtain the terms for "releasing here Americans of equal rank or return to Boston in six months" of the People in office here. They have been assiduous to do it but meet with flat refusals at the Secys. Office, the admiralty, & the board of Sick & hurt. Either the Capn. or one of our friends who came in Her will be with You soon & state the whole case.

You have been informd of the State of Mitchells case (the Cartel to Bristol in Decemr. last). He obtaind a gratuity for his loss of time, & the price of his Ship which was seizd, 2900£. This was paid Him by acceptances of his own bills of Mr. J. Jackson a Secy. of Lord Sandwichs at the Bank of Engd. 3 months after Date. I was obligd to indorse two of 500£ each to help him away. When these bills became deue the 29th Augt. they were noted for non Payment & are still unpaid tho the acceptor is amply able & *must* discharge them—I guess the money being just at this period useful to his Electioneering Schemes at Huntingdon is the cause of delay, but they are fairly promisd for payment the 14th.[1]

You will see by the inclosures what has been done about Your matter between Jones & Mr. Goddard. Both in his letters to me & to Jones (which I forward You herewith) He acknowliges *the acceptance*[;] therefore *He is liable & must pay*. If You will indorse the bill to Me I think I can get it (at least as much as You have advancd thereon) but Your letter covering it must express that *value* has been given therefor. I can pass it as a Credit to Your account & this will be as *value* to me. Your name has never been mentiond or hinted at. Goddard can know nothing of me, & I wrote to Him about this bill as at the desire *of a friend* in France who had given money, on it. You will therefore act as You think fit in this matter.

It is a little extraordinary that Mr. Goddard can never be seen, & that they still say at the Office He is in the Country but they know not where. By these appearances, as well as from the tenor of His Letter to me & Mr. Jones I am apt to think it has been some jumble between Jones & Him to raise a little ready Cash & that it is not convenient now for Him to pay His acceptances, & which He can be obligd to do by Law provided He has effects. I think of giving him a line or two in answer to his Letter to Me (a Copy of which I annex) saying that I had forwarded Jones's Letter to my friend at Paris, who having advancd money on the Strength of His acceptance which is not denyd by Him, that He certainly would expect payment for such advance when the bill became due, & that it would be regularly presented & prosecuted for in case of failure. Expecting to hear from You further on this head by return of Post, I remain with great esteem Dr. Sir

      Yr. Obligd & Ob. Ser.
      W. S. C.

  [Digges's copy of letter from Goddard]
            Sepr. 5. 1780

SIR

Your favour of the 26 last month has been forwarded to me from the Office—In answer to which I am under the necessity of acquainting you, in justice to your friend to whom the bill you mention has been offerd, that it will not be paid by me, having been obtaind with some others, upon promises which have not been complyd with, either by Mr. Jones or His agents; And it is matter of much surprize to me to find Mr. Jones has presumd under the Circumstances attending it, to attempt to negotiate—I am much obligd for Your Civility in writing to me, & am Sir Yr. M. Obt. He. Ser.

      J. Goddard

P. S. As I have no other means of conveying a letter to Mr. Jones, may I request the favour of Your forwarding the enclosd for him to Your friend, & that You will be pleasd to put a wafer in it.

  Mr. ———

HSP: Franklin Papers, 5:143.

[1] George Jackson (1725–1822) had been secretary to the navy board in 1758 and judge advocate for the fleet in 1766, served in the courts-martial of Admirals Keppel and Palliser in 1779 and been second secretary of the admiralty board since 1766. In 1786 he became a member of Parliament. The *London Courant*, Sept. 1, 1780, reported the "remarkable transaction" in detail and concluded: "What can the Treasury, the Admiralty, or the *virtuous* patron of this Mr. Jackson, think of such trifling, shuffling, and improper conduct in one of their servants?"

To Benjamin Franklin

London 12th Sept. 1780

Sir

I have frequently been with three of the within signd Gentlemen, all natives of Ireland & seemingly very honourable men, and to my certain knowlege & observation they have (aided by Mr. Robert Temple[)] done every thing in their power here to comply with the terms of their parole agreement, both at the Admiralty, & Board of Sick & hurt Seamen, as well as that they have stated their case to the Secretary of State for the American Department & prayd for releif, but all to no effect.

I am with great regard & Esteem
Yr. Excellys. most Obt. Servt.
T. D——

[Enclosure, not in Digges's hand]
His Excellency Benjamin Franklin

London 10th Sept. 1780

Sir.

We the Undersigned Master, Surgeon, & Passengers late of the Ship Jane, but now Prisoners on our Parole to the United States of America; As We know not how to relieve Ourselves out of Our present disagreeable circumstances, Otherwise than by Applying to Your Excellency for Your Advice & Assistance, We therefore take the liberty of thus Addressing Ourselves to You, & Stating Our Case At large, in Order that from Your being fully informed of Our Scituation, We may learn by Your direction how to Act.—We Shoud be Verry thankful for an answer As Soon As is Convenient, directed Under Cover To Messrs. David Harvey & Company Merchts. in London: & if it is attended with A Certificate from You, that we the Undersigned have represented to Your Excellency, that every means in Our power have been Used to Obtain the release Of So many American Prisoners, Out of those confind in the English Prisons (which the Ministers & Men in Power will not hearken to) We Shall Esteem it the highest Obligation.

We Conolly M[c]Causland Master, Wm. Stewart Surgeon, James Campbel & Marcus M[c]Causland Passengers, were taken in the Ship Jane (bound from Cork to N: York loaded with provisions & dry goods) on the Coast of America, by, The Tracy Privateer Capt. Hopkins, & were Carried into Boston the Second of July last. We Are glad to have it in Our power to Say, that We were treated On board by Capt. Hopkins & his Officers with great kindness; Such indeed As we had little reason to Expect. When Arivd in Boston We recevd every indulgence we Coud wish from those in Power, except that of liberty to go when we woud, which no doubt Substantial reasons of State Sufficiently forbid. We allso Acknowlege Ourselves much indebted to many who were in a private Capacity. Mr. Robt. Temple having procurd from the Council A flagg of truce to bring himself & family to England, We Obtaind leave of the Council to come in the Above Vessel Upon Our Parole of honnour, that So Soon As we Arivd in Ireland Or England, we Shoud Effect Our exchange with American prisoners of equal description, & in case we Coud not obtain it, we Shoud returne to America & deliver Our Selves Prisoners of War when Calld Upon by the American Commissary.

We the Undernamed did Upon Our Arival in London, wait on the Commissioners of the Sick & hurt Seamen whose buissness it is to transact All buissness relative to Prisoners of War, and After Stating Our Case fully to them & praying A release of As many American Prisoners now Confind in the English prisons, We were told it coud not possibley by [be] complyed with; for the Americans here being Committed for Acts of Treason & Piracy, were held On the Score of rebelion & coud not be released but by Acts of pardon from his Majestie; that when So released they Coud Only be exchanged by Cartels going directly to France, & Against English Seamen Captured by American Vessels & carryed into France. We have Used every Argument we Coud Suggest; in particular Urged the good treatment which we recevd while in America & the readiness with which we recevd leave to come to Europe frome the Council & board of War: besides this we have made Application by A Friend of consequence & power; We have Allso made Application in writing to L: G: Germain; We have As yet had no Answer to the last, but judge of it as of the first that we Shall not be Exchanged—Our principle hopes Are in Your Excellency & if Your Certificate to Us can be So Expressed, As to Save us in Case Of being taken Again, from the treatment which those desearve that are Supposd to Breake their Parole Of honnour; or to Save Such Of Us as perhaps might not go to Sea Again, from being Obliged to go at the Commissarys instant Call, whatever might be the Scituation of Our affairs at that time. As we may All Separate in a Short time, if not too much trouble, we woud request A Certificate for each name, by which means we Shall consider Our Selves as throughly protected in every part of the world, & Shall Allways consider Our Selves as Under the greatest Obligations to Your Excellency.

We are Yr. Excellencys most Obedt. humb: Servts.
       Conolly McCausland Mr.
       William Stewart Surgn.
       James Campbell Passanger
       Marcus McCausland

HSP: Franklin Papers, 5 : 144.

To John Adams

London 15 Sepr. 1780

DEAR SIR

We are all so very busy in Election bustles that hardly anything political is talkd of. The Ministry seem to be going on swimmingly in getting in Creatures of their own so that their majority in the next will be more decided than in the last Parliament. The Poll has ended for the City & the members are Hayley, Kirkman, Bull, & Newnham.[1] The last tho a Torey beat *Sawbridge* by 79 votes. Rodney & Fox will get Westmr. & Burke & Cruger[2] will be thrown out by two toreys in Bristol. Whispers are going about from the high flighers of the Court Party, that the new Parliament will early go upon accomodation if not declaration of Independence to America; this is either put forth to serve Election purposes, or to help up the Stocks; for I do not think the ministers are yet grown wise enough to adopt such a politic measure. If misfortunes & the appearance of gloomy accounts arriving from all quarters, save that of the East, would be a means of bringing them to their sences, one would think they had enough of these.

The various accounts from America by the Cartel to Bristol which I lately wrote you about, and by two or three vessels lately taken, (part of a fleet of 11 Sail which left Chesapeak bay about the 1st of Augt. bound to Amsterdm.) have alterd the minds of the people wonderfully lately, & they now begin again to think that the affairs of Engd. in America are in a deplorable way. I find there are several passengers in this fleet but luckily none of them in the Ships that are taken, so that I have reason to think that by this time some of them have got to Amsterm. The names recited to me are all from Maryland vizt. Mr. Ridout of Annapolis, Mr. Cheston a merchant of do. & a Mr. Dorsey from Elk Ridge. I hope they will be able to give you satisfactory accounts of the State of things in the West.

The Boyne Man of War is arrivd in a very shatterd Condition at Plymouth, She with the Preston was convoy to the Leewd. Island 1st of Augt. Fleet about 80 Sail in all. On the 3d Int. the fleet was dispersd by a violent storm which lasted 3 days & it is feard many of the ships are lost as none came in with their Convoy or are since arrivd—three of this fleet arrivd some days ago but they lost the Convoy nine days before this storm happend. The West India accounts do not place the situation, Supplys & health of Rodney's fleet as in an enviable situation. Altho the late Gazette mentions nothing of ten of his ships being sent down to rienforce the Jamaica Squadron It is lookd upon here that they did go. We have yet no authentic news of Greaves's arrival out or any late accounts from N. York—The People here rather laugh at a Seige of N. York, & still persist Hallifax or Quebec is the object of the combind force of France & America. If Ternays object is to block up Sandy hook it is a hundred to one if the whole N. York fleet which saild about 5 weeks ago does not fall into His hands; at any rate that fleet is in much risque & may probably produce a third great blow to the underwriters at Loyds—the late losses among these Gentry will effectually prevent their 1781 Subscription of Millions to the Minister for carrying on the War.

The Cartel Ship to Bristol is yet detaind for want of getting the necessary protection for men to conduct Her to Bilboa—The Exchange of an equal number of American Prisoners is peremptorily refusd. It is astonishing to me that they knew no better in Boston than to expect an Exchange here—Mr. Dunkin & Mr. Mitchells vessels had both been refusd as Cartels in Decemr. last, one of the ships found its way back to Boston long ago, and Mitchell himself was in Boston four or five days before this vessel saild the 21st July. The former two vessels brought 90 Prisoners & this 11 so that upwards of an hundred men are lost to Us, & so will thousands be if the United States allow their prisoners thus to come away. To my great grief the capture of these two American vessels mentiond before will add near 80 more Prisoners to our list already amounting to 280 or 290. I have made a push to get a part of these sent over gratis in Temples Cartel to France *to stand in account*, but it was to no effect; These people seem determind to do nothing in good nature or what has a tendency to Conciliation. Their audacity & impudence in publick offices seem to encrease with their impotence.

I am Dr. Sir Yr. ob. Sert.
W. S. C.

MHS: Adams Papers, Reel 352.

[1] George Hayley (d. 1781), a wealthy London merchant; Frederick Bull (ca. 1714–1784), an associate of Wilkes's and supporter of Gordon's Protestant campaign; and John Kirkman (1741–1780), a London silk merchant and, like Bull, one of Wilkes's supporters, were allied with Sawbridge against the North ministry—though Kirkman would not serve because he died six hours before the closing of the polls. Nathaniel

Newnham (ca. 1741–1809), head of a large grocery business and bakery, was an opponent of the American war, but since he had sometimes sided with the ministry, they preferred him to Sawbridge.

[2] Henry Cruger (1739–1827), a New Yorker who had moved to England in 1757 to establish himself in Bristol as a merchant, had entered Parliament in 1774 and professed himself a radical, but drawn by conflicting loyalties to both America and England, he had refrained from joining North's critics and did not enjoy the confidence of Burke's followers in Bristol.

To Benjamin Franklin

London 18 Sept. 1780

DEAR SIR

As the bearer Mr. Jones[1] is known to You as well as his Companion Mr. Paradise I need not ask Your usual civility to be extended to them. They are two excellent Men & of the right sort to fix themselves in our Country where I am not without hopes of seeing them settled in a year or two. They will wait upon you immidiately on arrival at Paris & return hither in a fortnight after. I hope to hear from You by their return, & to receive any American news papers which may be laid aside as useless to You.

They frequently contain matter useful to publish in this Country, especially where such matter expresses the strength, fortitude & determind resolution of America to exert herself towards the extirpation of the British army. The minds of the people here are getting reconcild apace to the Independence of America & these publications help them on. The language now spreading abroad in the Western quarter of the Town is that the *New* Parliament will very early go upon the business of declaring American Independence, & getting the best terms with that Country that Circumstances will permit; but whether this is only an artful language, held out to serve Election purposes, or to raise the Stocks, or is really meant, I cannot determine. It is spoke of in Circles of the great folks perfectly attatchd to the Court. If our wise Rulers have a spark of Wisdom left they must soon go to some such work. The Country in general is earnestly wishing for Peace and how can this be got but by getting rid of the American War. People of all descriptions in Politicks are alarmd for the critical situation in which England now stands; even the Toreys and Court Runners have given up the late language of all the Southern Colonies *"coming in"*— that the People of America were all ripe to declare for England—that the Capture of Chas. Town was the conquest of the States—that the Americans & their allys were quarrelling—that they had nothing left to carry on the war &ca. &ca. &ca.

Some late captures and arrivals from America have opend their eyes to the actual state of things in that Country, & they have learnt that the American mind is not subdued[2]—that they have the means, & are carrying on an active offensive Campaign—that their allies have given them an effectual aid of Ships & Troops, & have been receivd most Cordially—that the People are not tired with the pleasures of self Government—that they do not despise a free trade, nor begin to think the Ministry just, honest, wise or good enough to place themselves at their feet. As America has been long lookd upon by a great majority of this Country to be lost to England, these appearances do not effect the minds of the people half so much as the state of things nearer home. Ireland, tho at present divided by partys brought on by the intrigues of the Court, is lookd on as lost, at least the absolute dominion of it, to this Country & that no further revenue or places can be got from thence but such as the People chuse to give. The northern armd Confederacy is a bitter pill, and is lookd upon as a direct hostile act to this Country—Since the two Russian Ships, (which were loaded with Naval stores from Petersburgh to France) have been given up, the peoples minds are easier as to a War with those powers, some blame the Ministry for their pusilanimity, others rather wish it so than get into a deeper War, but all say it will soon give the House of Bourbon a Superiority at Sea, & this will be a dreadful blow to the Sovereign Lords of the Ocean. The affairs in the West Indies are spoke of with dejection & chagrin. Tho not mentiond in the late gazette, it appears Rodney has sent 10 of his Ships down to succour the Jamaica Squadron, which Island is supposd in imminent danger. It is not at all improbable but the Spanish flag is this day waveing on some of its Forts.

The Capture of the whole outward bound July fleet will be a

dreadful blow to all the Islands & to Rodneys fleet in particular for there were in it 10 or 12 transports loaded with naval stores, masts, sparrs &ca. for that fleet besides Provision Ships. Two of the line of his fleet is lately arrivd in a shatterd Condition at Plymo. They were convoy to the 1st Augt. homeward bound Leeward Island fleet, but seperated from it in a violent Storm which happend the 3d Int. & continued for three days. As none of the trade came in with the Men of War & only 8 or 10 of eighty vessels are yet arrivd it is feard a great number has been lost. This, with the former extraordinary Capture, the taking of 12 out of the Quebec Ships on the banks N. foundland (which I am told are worth from 30 to 35,000 £ each) will be a death blow to the gentry at Loyds, & prevent some of their names from appearing to the Government loan of 1781 for the twenty or twenty two millions which the premier will want. I do not pity these chaps a bit, for it has been by the prayers and addresses & the conversation & opinions of these & such like, that the war has been prolongd.

There is yet no accounts of Greaves's arrival in America. The first arrivals from N. York must determine it—the expectations of the people are much up for accounts from that quarter. Many people think the Port of N. York must be blockd up or accounts must have been receivd. Others laugh at the idea that the French fleet can even alarm the place or that the united efforts of French & American Armys can endanger that garrison. Within this few days the Ministry have hinted forth their alarms for the safety of Hallifax. On enquiry from a pretty good line, I find that on the 14th at night an Express arrivd from Sr. Jo: Yorke with a discovery of his "that Ternays fleet & an army of American & french were actually meant against Hallifax before the close of the Season."

Mr. R. Temple has not yet finally succeeded as to getting a protection for the Cartel to depart for some port of Spain or France. The Vessel will be obligd to clear out for Oporto & so make her way to Bilboa at the risque of Mr. Temple. All idea of Exchanging an equal number of Americans in confinement here for those who came on Parole in that Cartel is at an end; The application was scouted, & the Parole Prisoners were told to go back to N. York & there give themselves up for an equal number of *Rebels* exchangable in that place only with British prisoners taken & carryd into America. The Insolence of People in Office here, & their inattention to the solicitations of their own subjects in cases of this sort, seem to encrease with the impotence of Government. They seem determind never to do a good natured or a conciliatory act.

There have been two Tobacco Ships from Balte. to Holland lately brought into the Thames. They saild as late as the 6 or 8th of Augt. from Hampton, as did one also from No. Carolina, yet we have no accounts or any kind of news by these Vessels—the papers & letters have been all seizd & sent to the Ministry. The Men (which will add 70 or 80 to our numbers in Forton) have been put on board Men of War to be sent thither, & the accounts from them being all in possession of the Torey Merchants & owners of these privateers, none are comeatable.—They cannot however be bad for America or they would be let out, & it does not indicate that Cornwallis has over run *all* No. Carolina & Virga.

I expected to have given You further accounts of Mr. Goddard & the Bills, but have not been able to see him. He is not visible. I sent you the 5th a Copy of his letter to me, acknowledging they were his acceptances (consequently he must pay the Bill) & am waiting Your answer.[3] I think You better send the bill to me indorsd & I will contrive to get it paid, at least as much as you have advanced on it.

I am anxious to hear if the Bishops picture got safe as well as the one sent you from Amsterdam by M. De Neufville, lodgd there by M. Champion of Bristol.[4] I would not have the Bishop lost in the carriage on any account. As that worthy family is in the Country, there is no knowing from them.

I expect to write You in 8 or 10 days by a *friend* who came in the Cartel & who has letters for You. One of the Instruments of writing You gave Capn. C[a]rp[ente]r in Apr. or May last, has not been used & shall be sent back (at least a part of it) to You by the above conveyance. Mitchell I understand has got safe into Boston, *by the fortune of War a prize to the Dean.* He had a fine useful Vessel of 18 Guns & carryd near twenty Captives with him hence. His business was well done, tho I am at present in a calamitous situation in consequence of my name being on 2 bills of 500 £ each, which were paid him by the Admiralty (thro an under Clerk of theirs Mr. J. Jackson⁵) for the Cartel vessel which was seizd from Him at Bristol. These bills were drawn by Mitchell on Jackson & accep[te]d to be paid at *the Bank of Engd.* the 29th Augt. When the day came they were noted for non payment & are yet unpaid but in a fair way to be recoverd.

I expect my Reverend & Good friend Mr. W[ren] here every day, when we will settle Your donation of 6d. per week to each prisoner. Most likely in a post or two, I shall draw for 30 or 35 £ the then advance—The Bill will be on Mr. Grand for account B. F. & I will give him a line of advice with it. You will please also to mention it to Him.

As there is no domestic occurrence but Which my friends the Bearers are acquainted with, I beg leave to refer You to them and to assure You that I am with the highest esteem

Dr. Sir Yr. obligd & Obt. Sert.
T. D.

(Please to forward the inclosd in safety to Mr. Carmichael.)

Mr. Petrie has been some days in England & has lately returnd to Town an unsuccessful Candidate for Cricklade⁶—a very extraordinary attempt. I do not know him personally so that we have not met tho He is frequently with two or three valuable acquaintances of mine.

HSP: Franklin Papers, 5:145.

[1] Not to be confused with the rascal who owed Franklin thirty guineas, this is Sir William Jones, the member of the Royal Society who, along with John Paradise, had tried to get a medal honoring Franklin for his help to Capt. Cook.

[2] Digges's comments in this paragraph reflect his reading of John Adams's letter to him of Aug. 17, 1780 (see Digges to Adams, Aug. 29, 1780, headnote).

[3] See Digges to Franklin, Sept. 8, 1780. Goddard's letter, not Digges's, is dated Sept. 5.

[4] The picture of Jonathan Shipley had not yet "got safe," nor was it in Franklin's hands as late as Dec. 5, when he was undertaking to trace it.

[5] George Jackson.

[6] Samuel Petrie, the son of a Scottish merchant in London and a friend of John Wilkes's, was a repeatedly unsuccessful candidate. His return to England was probably from Paris, where he had been living extravagantly for three years as a refugee from

bankruptcy. While there he had been some sort of retainer of Silas Deane's and become involved in the Deane-Lee controversy, earning a bad name among the Lees as a consequence.

To John Adams

London 20 Sepr. 1780

DEAR SIR

A Servant of Mr. De Neufvilles going to Amsterdam early in the morning gives me an oppertunity of sending a letter to You for Mr. Ridley in Maryland which I beg you to give to the first safe hand bound to America.[1]

We are still without any authentic accounts from N. York or the quarters of the British army tho the general Town report is that Ministry have been some days in possession of bad accounts from Sr. H. Clinton. Many people are possessd of an opinion that Ternays fleet with an Army of French & Americans are to opperate against Hallifax & this opinion arrises from an account said to be transmitted from Sr. Jo. Yorke about a week ago, which He discoverd by some Emissarys in France. I have had oppertunitys lately in doing the business for the Cartel to Bristol which brought over Mr. Temple to discover a little of the disposition in the office of Admiralty and board of Sick & Hurt, & I discover a wonderful alteration within this two months. They are much more civil than usual & discover many tokens to indicate they look upon their affairs in America in a very bad way indeed—*Last week*, they could not think of releasing on any account one or more *Rebels* from prison to stand against those parole prisoners who came over in the Flag to Bristol—*Today* on an application for Capn. Manlys release (to stand against a Capn. Scott of the Golden Eagle Privateer taken in June by the Pickering American Privateer & carryd into Bilboa) they say it certainly shall be granted & that orders shall be sent down for His discharge in a day or two, so that I hope you may see Him in a few days.[1]

We are still in the bustle of Elections—There is a more than usual cry out from *all* partys against the American War—some ministerial

Candidates have addressd their Electors on that score—this theme must be given them from the older hounds of the pack or they would hardly venture to nose it. The Cry however is very general "Our evils have all arisen from the American War. We shall be ruind if it is not put a stop to &ca. &ca." Many people are of opinion, & speak it out, that the Cabinet have determind to abandon it & get the Troops away as well as they can. Some folks, on the side of Ministry too, go so far as to say that they would give it up directly could they bargain with America to hold possession of the Ports of N. York, Chas. Town &ca. for a little while, a few Years only, & these ports to be equally open & free to America, in order that by holding them they might prevent the French & Spaniards from Possessing all the Wt. Inda. Islands, but this is only talk, and they better talk not about possessing Ports if they really mean to get peace with America. I may be sanguine, but I really think their fears have put them very near making some proffers for peace with America.

A Privateer is arrivd in a Short time from the mouth of the Tagus & has given an account that there was an Embargo laid there on all English vessels. The news is not relishd in the City at all as the affairs of Europe indicate that Portugal if she is obligd to declare at all will join the side of Bourbon. The Portugue Envoy set out yesterday for Lisbon but I beleive He only goes on his private affairs—The Envoy from His Court at the Hague is arrivd here to be in his place till his return to England.[2] This departure of the Envoy happening at the same period with the account of the Embargo is much talkd of & supposd by many to prognosticate a War between England & Portugal. I am obligd to break off hastily the person waiting for my letter.

I am with the highest regard
Yrs.
W. S. C[hurch]

Mr. Ap[p]l[eto]ns best Compliments.[3]

[Addressed:] Mr. J. A.—/to the care of Mr. De Neufville

MHS: Adams Papers, Reel 352.

[1] Digges, together with Robert Temple and William Hodgson, had on Sept. 1 asked to confer with the Board of Sick and Hurt about the cartel, and it is clear that Digges had, either alone or with others, discussed the matter again more recently. What his role was in promoting the exchange of Capt. Manley for Capt. Robert Scott is less clear. Scott's ship, the British schooner *Golden Eagle*, had been taken on June 2 and carried into Bilbao by the *General Pickering* of Salem, Capt. Jonathan Haraden, commander; on July 12 Scott's liberty had been granted on the condition that in return one Caleb Foote would be released from Forton; for some reason that condition had not been met and the Americans had raised the stakes, with Digges in some way providing assistance.

[2] Portugal's diplomatic activity as it emerged in the press appeared to involve more than an envoy's private affairs. The *London Chronicle*, for example, noting on Sept. 14 (48:250) that the Portuguese envoy to The Hague had been recalled in order to be sent to London, was able to report on his predecessor's return to London less than a month later (Oct. 12, p. 360): "Mr. De Pinto, late Ambassador from the Court of Lisbon, is returned to his house in Audley Street, from Falmouth; at which port he was to take shipping for Portugal. It is rumored he has been sent for express by Government on some important remonstrance, now on the tapis, to be sent by that nobleman to the Court of Portugal." De Pinto was Luís Pinto de Sousa Coutinho, visconde de Balsamão (1735–1804); the envoy to The Hague who served as his chargé d'affaires was Agosto Antonio de Souza Holstein (d. 1781).

[3] John Appleton (1758–1829), son of Nathaniel Appleton, had been in Paris during Aug. on a mercantile mission and then taken letters to Adams in Amsterdam before coming to London.

To Benjamin Franklin

London 20th Sept. 1780

DEAR SIR

The Inclosd will inform You fully of some applications made Mr. H.[1] for the release of some Prisoners now at St. Omers which seem to have passd Your notice. They are American Capturd & have lately petitiond the Admiralty to procure their release. The Capt. Scott mentiond also in the inclosd Letter, will I hope stand against Capt. Manly; The Board of Sick & hurt have promisd his r[e]lease & that an order shall be sent down for this Purpose to Plymo. in a day or two. A good word has been spoken for Capn. C[onyngha]m but he being a more recent offender, it was refusd; not however without some tokens of attention to the application.

The Board of Sick of [and] Hurt seem wonderfully civil of late, (indeed they have always been attentive to our applications) and I am led to think therefrom, that they begin to see how likely it is that America will succeed & how better it is for them to temporise & be civil. A small vessel from No. Carolina to France, which saild about the 6th of Augt., and two others from Baltimore to Holland, Tobacco loaded, which said in a fleet of 30 from Hampton the 8th Augt. have been taken by English Cruisers & brought in. The two latter into the Thames. All papers, Letters &ca. &ca. have been seizd & kept secret, and eight of the Crew of one of them put on board the Tender at the Tower for his Majestys Service. I do suppose that the accounts by these vessels are such as our great folks do not like, or they would have been let out—nay I think these very accounts have been the reason of so much civility in Office. I told You in a late letter that the Cartel Brigantine Temple had got permission *to return.* On Mr. H[odgson]s mentioning to day at the board of Sick & hurt, that it would be impossible for this vessel to return *without Seamen*, Mr. H. was desird to get Mr. Temple to petition for these 8 Seamen on board the Nightingale Tender at the Tower to be releasd & sent to Bristol to Navigate the Ship away. I shall draw up the Petition tomorrow & Mr. T. will give it into the Admiralty, where I have reason to think it will be granted. As these men are only pressd by the Gangs for this work, & have not yet been committed for Treason or Piracy, there can be no plea (as there was in the case of the Parole Prisoners by the Cartel) "that prisoners committed by a Magistrate for Treason &ca. cannot be releasd but by certain forms &ca."

I am expecting dayly a line from You about Goddards Bill as well as an answer to Mr. Bowmans supplication for a pass *for His necessary Baggage* in case the Ship He is goi[ng] in to Charles Town may be taken by an American Privateer.

No authentic news yet from N. York but much rumour is going about that the Ministers have for some days had possession of bad accounts from that quarter.

The General cry of all partys is that the American War is intollerable & so little to be born, that the new Parliament is speedily to go upon the business of accomodation if at the expence of the Declaration of Independence. I realy beleive the Cabinet have determind to abandon that war, & look to their affairs nearer home. A Privateer just arrivd from Lisbon says there was an Embargo laid there on all English Ships the morning that He slipt away.—This has causd some little alarm in the City.

The Portugue Envoy set out yesterday for Lisbon, but *apparently* only to bring to England a few months hence His Lady. The one coming so immidiately on the back of the other causes much conversation. The Lisbon Merchants tho apparently frightend say it is only some partial embargo to detect or take some State Prisoner or publick theif. A few days will shew the truth. I wrote you on the 18th by two friends going directly to P[ari]s. This will be put into the Post office in Ostend or Holland most likely before the next foreign mail gets across the Channel.

I am with the highest respect
Dr. Sir Yr. obligd & Ob. Ser.
W. S. Church

[Addressed:] Dr. Franklin/Passy

HSP: Franklin Papers, 5:146.

[1] William Hodgson.

To John Adams

London Sepr. 26. 1780

DEAR SIR

My friend Mr. B[romfield] will give You the news by the Cartel I some time ago mentiond to You to have arrivd from Boston at Bristol, as well as the proceedings here relative to that Cartel. I send you also by Him a Book and seven lately publishd Pamphlets. There has been a dearth of these sort of publications during the summer, but probably by the meeting of Parliament several political writers will put forth their works.

I mentiond to You in my late letters that the receivd opinion here was the Cabinet had determind to abandon the American War, for several days past the reports & conversations among a certain description of men seems to give weight to this opinion; most likely it is the general state of things in this Country and not their will which assents to such a measure. Some little alarm was given a few days ago by the arrival of a Privateer from Lisbon, which reported an Embargo had been laid on all English Ships in the ports of Portugal—this could not be accounted for here, consequently it was not beleivd. Today they are a little more alarmd and fearful for a general prevailing report, that a French Squadron had arrivd at Lisbon to *demand* of that court an acquiesence to the northern Confederacy or immediately declare which side they would take in the present war. People who are unwilling to beleive any thing say that the numerous insults offerd by Commode. Johnson to neutral Ships & the captures carryd into Lisbon may provoke some such desperate measure.[1] I do not know how it effected the Stocks or the wise acres about Loyds Coffee House coming so immidiately upon the back of what they all term unfavorable news from America. If Englishmen would speak candidly they should say England ought to trust as little as possible to the fidelity & firmness of a power situated as Portugal is, subject to the immidiate controul & even compulsion of arbitrary, powerful & daring Enemys—Most likely the account may be premature, yet there may be some foundation for it, from the Complexion of things between Spain & Portugal.

Every day produces some new instance of the wretched state both of the English army & navy in the Leeward Islands. The English fleet seems fixd to the quarter of St. Christophers *inactive* till some rienforcements are sent thither. Eight ships are preparing to go there with all expedition, & Sir Hugh Paliser is talkd of as the Commander —this fleet goes in consequence of intelligence being receivd that a like number of French were dispatchd there about 5 weeks ago.

The Virginia Frigate is arrivd express from N. York with Dispatches born by a Coll. Dalrymple,[2] & a Navy officer and is said to have brought passengers—Govr. Tryon,[3] Genl. Matthews[4] & others. The account only getting out this afternoon, there is no getting at the truth & probably we never shall for no *bad accounts* are now given to the publick in the Gazette. If there is one given to night Mr. B. will carry one. By every Torey phisiognomy & appearance The news is lookd upon as *bad*; & *reports* State it That the frigate saild the 30th Augt. & that an attack was expected upon N. York the next day, Washington with the French Army having possessd the heights of Brooklyne, the fleet of France off the hook & other movements from the quarters of Kings bridge & the Jerseys; also that they had certain intelligence the French fleet from the West Indies was hourly expected to join that of Ternay. This frigate is said to bring bad tidings also from Chas. Town—such as that a large body of Americans who had joind the British having taken an oppertunity had securd a number of Officers who commanded them & gone off to the side of their Country, that there was excessive want & sickness in the Town &ca. &ca.[5] There are innumerable other reports, all of which from their corroboration, & the remarkable silence on the part of the Kings friends & ministerial people is sufficient to indicate the news is bad, & I wish them their belly full of it.

There is a lad (son to a good friend Mr. Champion of Bristol) living at the House of Mr. Martins in Amsterm. who is finally meant to fix in America. The Father, who is a very valuable man, hearing you had two Sons about his age in Amsm., is anxious they should know each other & begs of me to be a means of making them acquainted, that *his* may hereafter find some acquaintance in America & imbibe some of the Political sentiments which He supposes *Your* boys to inherit from their Father. I submit this to You, and subscribe myself with the highest Esteem

Dr. Sir
Yr. obligd & Obt. Ser.
T. D.

MHS: Adams Papers, Reel 352.

[1] George Johnstone, previously referred to as "Governor" by Digges, had been rewarded by Sandwich in May 1779 for his political support with command of a small squadron off the Portuguese coast.

² Col. William Dalrymple (d. 1807) had taken dispatches from Germain to Clinton in May and become Clinton's quartermaster general; he was now returning as Clinton's emissary to Germain with a request that Arbuthnot be recalled as uncooperative—or that Clinton's resignation be accepted.

³ Tryon had enjoyed only nominal powers as civil governor of occupied New York and was resigning his post.

⁴ Edward Mathew (1729–1805) had served under Clinton in the early years of the Revolution and under Knyphausen during the raid in New Jersey during the spring. (His name was frequently misspelled.)

⁵ Digges is probably referring to rebel uprisings during the spring and summer when Cornwallis had been trying to consolidate his gains in South Carolina. News of victories by Cornwallis and Tarleton in mid-August had not yet arrived.

To Benjamin Franklin

London 26. Sept. 1780

DEAR SIR

My freind Mr. Bromfield can best explain to You the business He is going upon as well as give You every account of the proceedings relative to the Brigantine Temple (the Cartel) in which He came from Boston. As I forwarded five Seamen from among our friends to that vessel this day, I hope it will not be many days before She sails. There being nine Seamen, taken in a Ship of Ridleys bound from Baltime. to Holland now on board the Tender at the Tower for after Commitment to Forton, I got Mr. Temple to Petition the Admiralty that these men be allowd to Navigate the Cartel away; for every favour has been shewn towards the getting the vessel away but allowing Her American Seamen to navigate Her back. I am to have an answer tomorrow & from appearances hitherto I have reason to expect it will be granted, as there is not the old stale plea that Americans Committed for Treason cannot be releasd from Prison without tryal or pardon.

I begin now to expect Mr. Sam H[artle]ys return hither. I should be glad to get by Him Your passport for Mr. Jno. Bowmans baggage to Carolina, & to hear of the Picture sent by Miss Georgiana got safe, for she has once or twice applyd to me with anxiety about it. Mr. Bowens some time ago receivd it & wrote me it should be soon forwarded by a safe conveyance. I should be also glad to hear of the safe arrival of that from Amsterdam left by Mr. Champion.

I mentiond in my late letter to You, an appearance here that the Cabinet had seemingly abandond the American War; for several days past the reports & conversations among a certain description of men seem to give weight to this opinion—Most likely it is necessity & not the will that assents to the adoption of such a measure. The affairs at Home & in all the Dependencies of Britain were [wear] such a gloomy aspect as might frighten bolder men than those who compose the British Council.

Some flying reports from Portugal frighten them a little. A few days ago a privateer which had touchd at the Entrance of the Tagus brought accounts to England that an Embargo had been laid on all English ships at Lisbon & the report of the day is, that a French fleet has enterd the Tagus to demand of Portugal an acquiescence to the Neutral Confederacy or declare which side they will take in the War. The more thinking part of this Metropolis say that England ought to trust as little as possible to the fidelity & firmness of a power situated as Portugal is, subject to the immidiate controul & even compulsion of arbitrary, powerful, & daring Enemys—Most likely the account may be premature, yet there may be some foundation for it from the complexion of things between Spain & portugal.

Every day produces some new instance of the wretched state both of the English Army & navy in the Wt. Indies. Rodnys fleet seem fixd to the harbours of St. Christophers *inactive* till the herricane months drive Him away or until some succour is sent from hence. Eight Ships of the Line are preparing with all Expedition to go thither. This fleet is orderd out in consequence of ministry having receivd advice that a like number was dispatchd about five weeks ago from France to Martinico.

The Virginia frigate is arrivd express from N. York, but as the Bearer will not deliver this letter for many days to come & long after Your getting more authentic accounts of the news she brings, I need not mention particulars here—indeed we have nothing as yet but reports, & these are all spoken of as unfavorable to England. Every Countenance speak them *bad*. I am with very great respect

Your Obt. Ser.
T. D——

HSP: Franklin Papers, 5 : 147.

To John Adams

London 29. Sep. 1780

DEAR SIR

I hope my letter of the 26 By H[enr]y B[ro]m[fiel]d and a parcell of Books will get safe to Your hands. Since that period, the arrival of news from N. York by the Virginia Packet, which saild the 1st Int. has depressd the Spirits of the people & put them deeper into the dumps than they were ever before elated. Every thing here is in extreem. Nothing could exceed the folly of Exultation about the taking of Charles Town. I predicted the "hour of their Insolence" would not be of very long duration.[1] The general cry ever since Wedy. morning is that we are undone & ruind—all is over—We always had hopes till now—our army in N. York & Chas. Town will be Burgoind &ca. &ca. &ca. The affairs in N. York were in such a situation as to induce Genl. Clinton to send away a packet, *much out of time*, on the 28th Augt. which is not yet arrivd. A very few days after the Virginia Frigate was dispatchd at a very few hours notice, with other alarming intelligences & that Washingtons Army was approaching towards N. York. Her arrival has thrown a remarkable damp upon the spirits of the Court, the Ministry, their out Runners, & their advocates. The Substance of the news brought by this Vessel, which I have collected from the best quarters of information is, That Monsieur Ternays fleet arrivd on the 10 July & The French troops landed the 12th. This arrival not the landing was unknown to Clinton for nine days after—Admiral Greaves arrivd nearly about the period it reached New York, & His fleet was Cruising between Rhode Island & Sandy hook when this Dispatch Frigate saild. As soon as Clinton heard of the arrival he determind on an Expedition to attack the French at Rhode Island, and Embarkd a large portion of his Force on board transports at N. York. Admiral Arbuthnot (who is superior to Graves) did not think the measure prudent, for reasons that there was not provision enough to victual the transports (there being scarcely sufficient for six weeks at short allowance and no supplys soon expected) and that by such an Embarkation the Garrison might be so weakend that Genl. Washington might attack & take the City. This last reason only founded in speculation was soon realizd into Fact; for after the troops had been many days embarkd Genl. Washington passd the No. River and approachd by regular march towards N. York with 16,000 Men. The British Troops were in consequence all disembarkd & the Expedition laid aside; on hearing this Gen. W. halted a little & retreated some miles back—Dalrymple (who bears the dispatches[)] says that his Army consists of upwards of 20,000 effective men exclusive of French. The French Admiral[2] had issued a Proclamation in the name of the Congress & King of France, assuring the People they should receive every support, & that the King his Master had resolvd upon the Conquest of Canada & of ceeding that Province to the United States, & that He was in dayly expectation of considerable rienforcements: Before the Virga. Frigate saild Sir H. Clinton had receivd advices of a late date from Lord Cornwallis, informing that His detatched partys had had several Skirmishes with Detatchments from Gen. Gates's Army and had been repulsd in all of them; That the People of Carolina who had taken up arms in the royal Cause, had revolted & joind Gen. Gates, to whom they had given up all their officers. In consequence of these disasters, Lord Cornwallis had determind to abandon all the interior Country of So. Carolina & retire within the lines of Chas. Town; In which place, during Lord Cornwallis's absence, there had been an insurrection of the People against the Soldiery, which had been quelld at the Expence of 4 or 500 Americans killd & wounded & with the loss of 80 Soldiers.

A Sloop from the West Indies, which arrivd at N. York the day before the Virginia saild, brought accounts that Monsr. Guichens fleet had been seen the 28 July steering for Jamaica & not far from it—His fleet consisted of 32 of the line, several frigates & lesser vessels, making in the whole 76 sail & having 16,000 troops on board. There are various other intelligences by this vessel of lesser note, among them, that Monr. Rochambeau had entrenchd himself strongly on Rhode Island and that the June & July packets from England had been both taken by American Privateers very near to Sandy hook.

The Quebec spring fleet which saild in June from England were met on & near the Banks of New foundland by several American Privateers, which took *twenty-two* out of the 30 Sail. The list of twenty of them is markd on Loyds Book as arrivd in New England & the account is brought by London by a SuperCargoe on board one of them, who got permission to leave Boston to come to N. York & so on in the Virginia Frigate to England. This is a much greater blow *to Loyds* than the West India Capture, as more money was done in that Coffee House upon them, near 400,000 £ having been insurd there. I am told most of these Ships are worth from 30 to 35,000 £ & many of them considerably above forty. O Rare Yankee! Well done Yankee! A report is very prevalent to day that a similar fate has happend the Provision fleet for Quebec which saild from Cork the 1st July, as well as that seven homeward bound East Inda. men are capturd near the Entrance of the Channel—it cannot rain but it pours—

The cry is very much against ministry. I am pretty sure the Cabinet had a month ago abandond the principles of the American War & were fixd on making peace even at the Expence of Declaring America Independent. This news may accelerate it; I am sure if it does it will be good news for Great Britain, for all ranks & descriptions of men now begin to see the mischeifs to England from this wicked & unnatural war.

I am with the highest Esteem Dr. Sir
Yr. obligd & obt. Servant
W. S. C.

[Addressed:] A Monsieur/ Monsieur Ferdinando Raymond San/ Chez Monsieur Henqu. Shorns/ a/ Amsterdam

MHS: Adams Papers, Reel 352.

[1] See Digges to Adams, Aug. 24 [⟨22⟩], 1780.
[2] Adm. Guichen.

To Benjamin Franklin

[Sept. 29 1780]

DEAR SIR

You have intimated in a late letter to me, in answer to one wherein I attempted to describe the folly & infatuation of these people in their extraordinary exultations ever since the taking of Charles Town, "That the *second* 'hour of their insolence' might be of as short duration as the *first*".[1] This has been strictly veryfyd, & the whole City is as much chap fallen & in the dumps as they were ever elated. The general cry for two days past is that "we are undone & ruind"—all is over —We always had hopes till now—Our Army will be Burgoind &ca. &ca. The affairs of New York were in such a state as to induce Genl. Clinton to send away a packet *out of time* on the 28th of last month which is not yet arrivd; and in a very few days after the Virginia Frigate with other alarming intelligences & of the discovery of the approach of Washingtons Army towards New York. She saild the 1st Int. and her arrival has thrown an unusual damp upon the Spirits of the Court, its creatures & their out runners & advocates. The heads of the news brought by this vessel, which I have collected from the best quarter of information is, That Monr. Terney arrivd at Rhode Island the 10th & landed His Army the 12th. This arrival or landing was not known to Clinton for nine days after—Admiral Greaves arrivd at nearly the same period at N. York & his Fleet was cruizing between Rhode Island & N. York when the Virginia Frigate Saild. As soon as Clinton heard of the arrival he determind on an Expedition to attack the French army at Rhode Island, & embarkd a large force on board Transports at N. York. Adml. Arbuthnot (who Commands) did not think the measure prudent, for reasons that there was not provision enough to victual the Transports (there being scarcely sufficient for 2 months at short allowance and no supplys soon expected) and that by such an Embarkation the Garrison might be so weakend that Genl. Washington might attack & take the City. This last reason only founded in speculation was soon realizd into fact; for after the Troops had been many days embarkd Genl. Washington passd the No. River & approachd by regular march towards N. York with 16,000 Men. The

British Troops were in consequence all disembarkd, and on hearing it, Genl. W—— halted and retreated a few miles back. Dalrymple (who brings the dispatches) says that Washingtons Army is 20,000 Effective Men, exclusive of French. The French Admiral had issued a proclamation in the name of the Congress & King of France assuring the People they should receive every support, & that the King his Master had resolvd upon the Conquest of Canada & of ceeding that province to the United States, & that He was in dayly expectation of a considerable rienforcement. Before the Virga. Frigate Saild, Sir H. Clinton had receivd advices of a late date from Lord Cornwallis, informing that his detachd partys had had several Skirmishes with Detatchments from Gates's army, & had been repulsd in all of them; That the People of Carolina who had taken up arms in the Royal Cause, had revolted & joind Genl. Gates, to whom they had given up all their officers. In consequence of these disasters, Lord Cornwallis had determind to abandon all the interior Country of So. Carolina & retire within the lines of Charles Town, in which place during Lord Cornwallis absence, there had been an insurrection of the People against the Soldiery, which had been quelled at the Expence of 4 or five hundred Americans killd & wounded and near Eighty Soldiers.

A Sloop from the West Indies which arrivd at N. York the 30 Augt. brought an account of Monsr. Guichens Fleet being seen on the 28th July steering for Jamaica & not far from it—His fleet consisted of 32 Sail of the line several frigates & lesser Ships making in the whole 76 Sail & having 16,000 Troops on board. There are an hundred other accounts of lesser note, among them, that Monr. Rochambeau had strongly entrenchd himself on Rhode Island, & that the June & July packets from England had been both taken by American Privateers very near to Sandy hook.

The Quebec Spring fleet which Saild in June from Spithead were met on & near the banks of Newfoundland by some American Privateers which took twenty two out of the 30 Sail. The list of 20 of them is on Loyds book as arrivd in N. England brought by a passenger who was allowd to come immidiately from Boston to N. York & so home in the Virginia. This is a greater blow *to Loyds* that [than] the late capture of the West India Ships, near 400,000£ having been Insurd on them at that Coffee House. I am told most of these Ships are worth from 30 to 35,000£ & some of them above forty. O Rare Yankee! Well done Yankee!

A report is very prevalent & much Credited that seven homeward bound East India men are also Capturd.

I am with very high Esteem Dr. Sir
Yr. Obligd & Obt. Serv.
W. S. C.

I wrote you on tuesday last by Mr. B[rom]f[iel]d who will stop a day or two in Amsterdam. He can give You an account of the Cartel to B[risto]l &ca.

[Addressed:] A Monsieur/Monsieur B: F:——/Passy

HSP: Franklin Papers, 5:148.

¹See Digges to Adams, Aug. 24 [⟨22⟩], 1780, n. 3.

To John Adams

On September 3, on the Newfoundland banks, the unarmed Continental brig Mercury *(Captain William Pickles, commander), lacking a promised convoy, had been taken by the British frigate* Vestal, *commanded by Captain George Keppel. Aboard had been Henry Laurens, former president of the Continental Congress and representative of South Carolina in the Congress. Laurens had been en route to Holland to arrange a loan for aid to American troops and to discuss the details of a treaty of amity and commerce with the Netherlands that had been drafted by William Lee and Jean de Neufville, who had had the approval of Engelbert Van Berckel, grand pensionary of Amsterdam, a man without any authority from the Dutch government to approve anything. Laurens had managed immediately to burn or sink all obviously official documents but had not at first included among them personal papers. When his secretary,*

Major Moses Young, also the secretary to the commercial committee of the Congress and a man with legislative as well as military experience, had finally persuaded him to throw those overboard as well, it had been too late; the hastily weighted sack had filled with air and remained afloat, been retrieved by the captors, and disclosed to them, among other items, a confidential list of Dutch gentlemen friendly to the American cause and a draft of the Lee–Van Berckel treaty. The British naval authorities had perceived at once that the capture of Laurens and his papers had political significance. Admiral Richard Edwards, commanding the Newfoundland squadron, had promptly put Keppel in charge of the Vestal's *sister ship, the* Fairy, *and dispatched him with his prisoner to England. The vessel, as Digges reports, had then put in at Dartmouth, whence Laurens was being taken by chaise to London in the charge of a Lieutenant Norris of the* Fairy.

London Octor. 3 1780

Dear Sir

I am sorry to inform You that Mr. Henry Lawrens and two other American Gentlemen [are] Prisoners in England—They were taken up in a small packet on the banks of New foundland about 24 days ago & sent to St. Johns, where Admiral Edwards thought the capture so important as to immidiately dispatch the Vestal Frigate Capn. Keppell with them, & the mail which was also taken, to England.[1] Mr. Laurens being very much indisposd was put on Shore at Dartmouth & is now on his way to London, travelling slowly and guarded by the Leiutenant of the Ship. The frigate had but 14 days passage to England. The Ministers give out confidently they not only possess the mail, but all Mr. Laurens's papers (which is scarcely to be credited) and that they discover to them his business to Holland which was to get a loan for which France was to stand Guarantee. They also say that the mail discovers an Expedition from France was expected against Hallifax to arrive there between the 20th and a last day of Sepr. There is no appearance of exultation for the taking Mr. Laurens but they seem much pleasd with the discoverys his papers have lead to. I will take the earliest oppertunity to write You when I hear more. A second Man of War is arrivd from N.foundland Express upon the heels of the Vestal—She must bring news of some importance, & *not good* because it is not given to the publick. *Report* says She is dispatchd in consequence of discovering a small french fleet & armament near Newfoundland.

I am Yrs. mo. respectfully

W. S. C[hurch]

[Addressed:] A Monsieur/Monsieur Ferdinand Raymond San/Chez Monsr. Henge Shorn/Amsterdam

MHS: Adams Papers, Reel 353. Adams did not receive this until October 18 and wrote after his endorsement: "Where has this Letter been all this while."

[1] Digges's account corresponds with one in the *London Courant*, Oct. 3. But reports reaching Digges were less than accurate. Laurens's own well-known narrative of his capture later identified the ship in which he made the crossing as the *Fairy*, and other documents show that the "two other American Gentlemen" neither accompanied Laurens at the time nor were made prisoners later: Moses Young had been kept aboard the *Vestal*, to be commanded by Capt. Berkely (or Barclay), who had exchanged places with Capt. Keppel, and did not reach England until mid-November. Capt. Pickles had accompanied him, but the second American gentleman was not Pickles but Winslow Warren (1759–1791), son of Gen. James Warren (1726–1808) and Mercy Otis Warren (1728–1814) of Plymouth; he had originally set out for Europe in May, only to be captured and taken to Newfoundland, whence he had attempted to resume his journey on the ship carrying Laurens.

To Benjamin Franklin

London Octo. 3. 1780

DEAR SIR

I am very sorry to inform You that Capt. Keppel of the Vestal frigate arrivd here on Saty. Evening with an account of his having taken about 28 days ago on the Banks of Newfoundland a Packet calld the Congress bound from Philaa. to Holland on board which was Mr. Heny. Laurens, His Secy., and another American Gentleman. It appears that the Man of Wars boat took up the mail before they boarded the prize, it being a pitchd leather bag & too boyannt for the weights fixd to it. The friends to Ministry give out that Mr. Laurens's papers were also securd, but this I have no reason to beleive, and that they discover an intended Expedition against Hallifax which was expected to arrive in that quarter between the 20th Sept. & 1st Octor., also that a Small fleet was going from France to Chesapeak bay.

Mr. Laurens being much indisposd was put on shore at Dartmouth, where He yet is, but I learn He will soon be in London, probably put upon parole. There is not the least appearance of exultation on account of this capture, tho it appeard to Adml. Edwards of such consequence as to induce Him to dispatch a frigate immidiately from N. foun[d]land. No particular news from that quarter, save that the number of Yankee privateers this summer out upon the banks & Coasts of that Island, as to have in a manner totally ruind the fishery for this Season. Another Sloop of War arrivd Express from thence yesterday at Portsmouth. The news is not given to the publick, but must be of consequence from her being dispatchd so immidiately upon the heels of the Vestal Frigate—report says this latter vessel was dispatchd with an account of the discovery of a small french fleet in that quarter, supposd to have an intention to attack the Island.

The late news from N. York & So. Carolina, even garbled as it is [in] the last Gazettes is lookd upon as very bad & the cry still is "that we are all ruind in America". Yet there is an appearance of four Ships of the line intended to go soon to rienforce Adml. Graves, and eight are talkd of for the Leeward Island Station.

I am respectfully Dr. Sir
Yr. Obligd & Ob. Ser.
Wm. S. C.

[Addressed:] A Monsieur/ Monsieur B. F. / Passy

HSP: Franklin Papers, 5 : 149.

To John Adams

London Octor. 6. 1780

DEAR SIR

I am thankful for Your late favor & shall send you the Books desird by first oppertunity. Mr. Heny. Laurens was brought to Town last night, rather in better health. He was lodgd that night in the messengers House in Scotland Yard, & denyd all sort of communication with his friends or those who wishd to speak to Him. He was Examined at noon at Lord G. Germains & committed by a Warrant of Justice Addington[1] a close prisoner to the Tower—orders that no person whatever speaks to Him. These folks are so foolishly changable that most likely in a few days the severity of His confinement may be relaxd. At present two men are always in the same room with Him, & two soldiers without. You shall hear more from me by next post.

No news from the Westward of any sort. The general beleif is that the privy Council yesterday have determind to prosecute the war further in America with vigour—perhaps the fools have concluded that as they have catchd Mr. Laurens they can conquer America. I can see no other reason for their supposition of success in the further prosecution of that war.

I am Your mo. obt. Ser.
W. S. C.

[Addressed:] A Monsieur/ Monsr. Ferdinand Raymond San/ chez Monsieur Henri Shorn/ Amsterdam

MHS: Adams Papers, Reel 353.

[1] William Addington (1728?–1811), chief magistrate of the police in London.

To Benjamin Franklin

London Octo. 6. 1780
Fryday

DEAR SIR

Mr. Laurens has been so ill as to retard his journy up to London very much. He arrivd in rather better health on thursday night, & was this day examind at Lord G. Germaines office & committed to the Tower—The first night he was kept at the Messengers House in Scotland Yard, & taken from thence to Lord Ge. G.'s office about noon. He was watchd & kept very close, so that no one of His friends could even offer him any assistance. As those folks are ever in extreems, perhaps this rigour will be soon removd, & Mr. L. allowd to speak to his friends. They boast much of discoverys made from His papers *all* as they say being taken; but I beleive my share of this. Not a word of any other news.

I am with great Esteem
Sir Your Obedt. Ser.
Wm. C. C.

One report is that He is not to be sent to the Tower till tomorrow but, I have good reason to think He went this afternoon.

HSP: Franklin Papers, 5:151.

To John Adams

On September 25 Adams had asked for two or three copies of Pownall's Memorial, *mentioned by Digges in his letter to Adams, April 6, and one copy of Dr. Price's* Essay on the Population of England, *listed by Digges in his letter of June 8 as one of the many books and pamphlets he had sent Adams. It would not be until October 14 that he could comment on Digges's news about Laurens, who was now being questioned by the ministers and, in disregard of his claims to diplomatic immunity, kept a prisoner on suspicion of high treason. The Lee–Van Berckel treaty provided not only a partial pretext for this treatment but also a justification for Great Britain's declaring war on the Dutch as belligerents.*

London 10. Octor. 1780

DEAR SIR

Since my letter of the 6th there has been no material incident relative to Mr. H. L[auren]s Commitment; nor is the rigour of his confinement abated. No person whatever can speak to Him but in hearing & sight of the two attending messengers. It is said the Secy. of States order will produce admittance to his room, but nothing else. Some of his torey relations, and a Mr. Manning a Merchant of the City & a Correspondent of Mr. L——s,[1] have made attempts to speak to him but did not succeed. He is wise enough to be cautious who he speaks to. It is generally thought this rigour will be taken off in a few days, & that His friends, who are now backward for fear that any stir may be disadvantageous to Him, will have admittance. Almost every person here is crying out shame upon this sort of treatment of Mr. L——s. These people seem determind to act always in extreem & never to take the middle road. Nothing veryfys it so strongly as the present exultations for a defeat given to Genl. Gates's Army by Lord Cornwallis on the 16th Augt. An officer arrivd with the account yesterday & put the whole city in a ferment of joy. I inclose you the printed Gazette account. Last week, & indeed until yesterday every Torey face wore an uncommon gloom & the cry was "We are *all* undone, We have lost America—our army will be Burgoind—our fleets beaten["] &ca. &ca. *Now* it is directly the reverse. "The defeat of Gates gives us No. & So. Carolina certain—Virginia will come in—Washington will be able to do nothing at N. York. The french fleet will be blockd up—We shall conquer America yet["] &ca. &ca. This sort of nonsense makes me sick. It has been pretty confidantly talkd of lately that the Cabinet had determind to prosecute the War in America with vigour, & that 10 Ships of the line & 10,000 troops were to be sent out immidiately. There seems to be as thick heads *within* as without the Cabinet. There is an appearance of 4 Ships of the line and some troops being intended for America immidiately—most likely for the Southward; But this may be a politic measure in the ministers to give out even if they are determind to get rid of the American War. The people generally are in fears about Jamaica & for the other Islands no news from thence lately.

I am with great respect & Esteem
Your obligd & obt. Ser.
W. S. C.

MHS: Adams Papers, Reel 353.

¹William Coventry Manning (d. 1791), a well-to-do West India merchant in London through whom Laurens conducted business in England, a longtime friend of the Laurens family, and the father-in-law of Laurens's son John since 1776, was well placed socially, respected by both the court and London's bankers.

To Benjamin Franklin

London Octr. 10. 1780

DEAR SIR

Since I wrote you the 6th Int. no alteration has taken place with regard to Mr. Laurens confinement & treatment. No person whatever has been permitted to speak to Him, but it is said any person may who will apply for a Secy. of States order to do so.—I hear of none of his friends who have made any attempts to do so; I suppose from thinking any stir made to see Him may be disadvantageous to Mr. L——.

A torey Cozen or two, & his Correspondent in trade, Mr. Manning, have made unsuccessful attempts. It is thought this rigour will be relaxd in a few days, & most likely it will for these folks are ever acting in Extreems. Nothing can more strictly verify it than their behaviour at the present moment. Last week & indeed until last night the general cry was "we are undone—We can never do any thing in America—the War must be given up—our armys will be Burgoind—our fleets beaten" &ca. &ca. &ca. Yesterday an officer arrivd Express from Cornwallis with an account of a victory over Gates's Army at Cambden in So. Carolina, and now they are all in the Skies again—The whole Southern America is theirs—Virginia will "come in" on a certainty—the Rebels will be beat every where—a few thousand more regulars sent over directly will insure the subjugation of America—let us persue the war vigorously &ca. &ca. Their folly is enough to make one sick.

For several days before this arrival, it was the general talk that the Cabinet had absolutely determind in pushing the war in America with vigour & that 10 Ships of the line & as many thousand Men were to immidiately be sent.

If there are as great fools within as there are out of the Cabinet, most likely this measure will be adopted. There are appearances of four Ships of the line & some troops being intended for No. America but this may be a necessary measure even if it is determind to relinquish the American War.

I inclose you the gazettes account of Engagement in So. Carolina. A report is going about, that while Cornwallis was out, there was an insurrection in the Town which was quelld at the expence of near 400 lives of Americans & about 80 British, but the report does not gain much Credit.

> I am with the highest Esteem
> Dr. Sir Yr. obligd & Ob. Ser.
> W. S. C.

I expect the Revd. Mr. W. in Town soon to settle the amount of Your Donation weekly to our Captive friends.[1] I will draw a Bill on Monsr. Grand for its amount & give notice by the same post of the draft.

[Addressed:] A Monsieur/Monsieur B. F―― / Passy

HSP: Franklin Papers, 5:152.

[1] The Rev. Thomas Wren, Portsmouth, was continuing to make distributions among the American prisoners in Forton.

To John Adams

London 17 Octo. 1780

DEAR SIR

It was not until the 14th Int. that *any person whatever* was permitted to see Mr. Laurens in the Tower. On that day after repeated applications for admission, Mr. Manning, & Mr. Laurens Jur.[1] (a youth of 16 or 18 who has been some years at Warrington school) was permitted to see Him. An order went signd from the 3 Secretarys of State Hillsborough, Stormont, & Germain, to the Govr. of the Tower permitting the two Gentlemen above to visit Mr. Laurens for *half an hour*—the Warrant expressly intimating that their visit was to be limited to that time, & that they could not a second time see Him without a new order. The Govr. of the Tower sent a note to Mr. Mannings that he had receivd such an order from the Secy. of State, & He with young Laurens went accordingly last Saturday Morning. They found him very ill of a lax, much emaciated, but not low spirited, & bitterly invective against the people of England for their harsh treatment of Him. He spoke very handsomely of Capt. Keppel who took him & the Leiut. who accompanyd Him to London; but from the period of his putting his foot on shore He was treated with a brutality, which He could not even expect from Englishmen. His weakness from Sickness, & the agitation on seeing His son, took up the first *ten* of the *thirty* minutes allowd Him to converse with His friends—the rest was filld with bitter invectives against the authors of His harsh treatment. His outer room is but a very mean one, not more than twelve feet Square, a *dark* close bed room adjoining, both indifferently furnishd & a few books on his table. No pen & ink or news paper has been yet allowd him, but He has a pencil & memorandum book in which He occasionally notes things. The Warden of the Tower, and a Yeoman of the Guard is constantly at his elbow tho they make no attempts to Stop his Conversation. Mr. Manning & His Child being the first Visitors he has had, perhaps Mr. L——ns was led to say every thing He could about the Severity of his treatment, in order that it might be known abroad, & contradict the general report of his being exceedingly well treated. He has hitherto declind any phisical advice, or the visits of any of those Creatures near Him who may be put on with a view to pump. Mr. Penn is making application & will likely see him.[2] It is doubtful if the Son will again get leave. His harsh treatment being now pretty generally known, every one is crying out shame against it, & they accuse a great personage known by the name of White Eyes[3] as the immidiate author of it.

17 OCTOBER 1780　　　　　　　　　　　　　　　　301

You have read all the news I can give You. Since the late arrivals from So. Carolina, N. York, & Jamaica, every thing seems to have taken a different turn. The inactivity of the French in Europe, the West Inds., and in No. America indicates that the Campaign will end with thier doing nothing very effectual for America. This has seemingly induced the Cabinet to push the war in America vigourously another year. New Regiments are raising, 10 or 12,000 Men are preparing to go, & every transport Ship that can be got is actually engaging to carry troops either to No. America or the Wt. Indies.

　　　　　　　　　　I am Yrs. mo. Truly
　　　　　　　　　　W. S. C.——

[Addressed:] A Monsieur/Monsr. [Names inked out]/ Chez Monsieur Henri Shorn/ a/Amsterdam

MHS: Adams Papers, Reel 353.

[1] Henry Laurens, Jr. (1763–1821).
[2] Apparently the Richard Penn whose assistance Digges had sought in locating William Peters (see Digges to Franklin, May 31, 1779).
[3] Doubtless George III.

To Benjamin Franklin

　　　　　　　　　　　　　　　　London 17 Octo. 1780
DEAR SIR

It was not until the 14th inst. that *any person whatever* was permitted to see Mr. Laurens in the Tower—*Then* after repeated applications for admission Mr. Manning and Mr. L——ns Son, a Youth of 17 or 18 who has been some years at Warrington School got admission to Him. A permit was given them, signd by the Lds. Hillsborough, Stormont & Germain "for *half an hours* interview & that the permit did not extend to any future Visit." They found Him very ill of a lax, much emaciated, not low spirited, & bitterly invective against the people here for his harsh treatment. He spoke handsomely of his treatment while on board Ship, & of the Capn. (Keppel) & Leiut. Norris who attended him to London, but from the period of his landing He was treated with a brutality which He did not expect even from Englishmen. His weakness from sickness & the agitation on seeing his Son took up the first *ten* of the 30 minutes allowd him to converse with His friends;—the rest was filld with invective against the Authors of his harsh treatment. His outer room is but a mean one, not more than twelve feet Square, a *dark* close bed room adjoining, both indifferently furnishd, & a few books on his table. No pen and Ink has been yet allowd him, but He has a pencil & Memorandum book in which He occasionally notes things. The Warden of the Tower & a Yeoman constantly at his elbow tho they make no attempts to stop his conversation. Mr. Mannings being the first visit he has had, perhaps He said every thing He could about the severity of his treatment, in order that it might get out & contradict the general report of His being exceedingly well treated. He has hitherto declind any Phisical advice, or the visits of any of those Creatures about Him who may be set on to Pump. Mr. Penn is making application to see Him, & will likely get leave. It is doubtful if the Son will be able to get admission a second time. His treatment being *now* very generally known every person is crying out shame upon it & the authors thereof are very much abusd. It is a strange thing to go forth, but it is the general receivd opinion that the orders for such harsh treatment were in consequence of an intimation from the *first* Man in this Country, now generally known by the appellation of *White Eyes*.

Every appearance indicates that this Mr. White Eyes is determind on prosecuting the American War vigorously. New Regiments are raising—10 or 12,000 Men under orders to go & transports actually got & getting at unusual high prices. Nothing can exceed such folly but it actually appears the determind resolution of the Cabinet to risque every thing upon a last stake—The inactivity of the French in America & the West Indies, seems to be the bait of inducement for these folks to go on. About a month ago, before the arrivals from N. York & Carolina & Jamaica, there was every appearance of the Cabinet having given up the American War.

I am without any of Your favours lately. I wish to know if You got the picture of the Bishop safe. What is further to be done about Jones's Bill on Goddard. What answer to the Letter sent by the parole Prisoners who came over in the Temple Cartel to Bristol. & if Mr. B[o]w[ma]n may Expect a pass for his baggage.

I drew a Bill on Monsr. G[ran]d the 16th 10 days sight for 48£ payable to the person You write to frequently about the Prisoners.[1]

I am with Esteem &ca. &ca.
W. S. C.

[Addressed:] A Monsieur/Monsieur B. F——/Passy

HSP: Franklin Papers, 5:153.

[1] Communication was slow. Letters from Franklin of Sept. 18 and Oct. 9 were noted by Digges on Oct. 24, and answers to the questions posed here had to await Franklin's reply of Nov. 7, acknowledged in Digges's letter of Nov. 21. In the present instance the delay was probably occasioned by interception in the General Post Office, where a copy was made and its having been sent by Digges under cover to Mr. Grand noted (see B. F. Stevens, *Facsimiles*, no. 952).

To John Adams

London 20 Octor. 1780

DEAR SIR

The close confinement of our friend & the denyal of all visits the use of pen ink & Paper, as well as all newspapers, still continues with unabated rigour. No person but His Son accompanyd by Mr. Manning has yet found way to Him, & these have been peremptorily refusd a second visit. It now appears that Government find him nothing but His furnishd appartments, Mr. L. ordering his own dinner every day from the Coal Exchange Tavern in Thames Street, Government allow 5/- per day for sustenance to all State Prisoners, & He may claim this pittance or not just as He pleases at the end of His Confinement. It is a pity that His severe ill treatment is not known in America.

No news yet from America since the late Carolia. accounts. There are two ships arrivd in Scotland which left St. Kitts the 6th and 10th Septemr. No news transpires by them. If they brought any that was palatable to Scotsmen it would certainly have got out before this, so that from the silence I suppose there is none which can be reckond bonny.

I am your obt. Ser.
W. S. C.—

We have just heard of 8 or nine arrivals from America at Amsterdam. These vessels must bring some late American accounts. When You get the American account of the affair of Camden please to favor me with it.

[Addressed:] Mr. Ferdinand Raymond San/at Mr. Henry Shorns/ Amsterdam

MHS: Adams Papers, Reel 353.

To John Adams

London. Octor. 22d 1780

Dear Sir

I wrote You some time back[1] requesting you woud take notice of a Youth (son to Mr. Rhd. Champion of Bristol a very particular & valuable friend of mine) and that You would make Him acquainted with your boys at Amsterdam. I have reason to think this has already been done, but in case it is not, Mr. Champion Jur. will wait upon you with this and I beg leave to recommend Him to Your usual civility and attention.

I am with very great regard Dr. Sir
Your obligd & Obt. Servt.
Th. Digges

[Addressed:] The Honourable/John Adams Esqe./Amsterdam

MHS: Adams Papers, Reel 353.

¹Sept. 26, 1780.

To John Adams

Londn. Octo. 24 1780

DEAR SIR

The friend about whom I have lately wrote You is much in the same situation as heretofore, no person being allowd to see Him; I have the satisfaction however to inform You his health is restord & that He is now very well. I have got the means of communicating to Him 'tho no person is admitted as a visitor. I mention this circumstance that You may improve it to any advantage You may chuse. We have no news but what You know.

> I am with very great Respect
> Yr. obt. Servant
> W. S. C.

[Addressed:] A Monsieur/Monsr. Ferdinando Raymond San/Chez Monsieur/Henri Shorn/Amsterdam

MHS: Adams Papers, Reel 353.

To Benjamin Franklin

On September 18 Franklin had commented on the problems Digges was having recovering money owed Franklin: "I am sorry you have had so much trouble about Jones's affair. When he borrow'd of me the 30. Guineas, he gave me the enclosed Bill. . . . Thirty Days Sight of Such Bill, is in reality 30 Days date because he must have seen it when he wrote it—By enquiring at Dr. Fothergills perhaps you may find him & demand it of him. If you recover it, that will be so much in your Hands on my Account. I gave him a Receipt for the Bill of Mr. Goddard's Acceptance acknowledging that it was put into my hands as a Security for the 30 Guineas lent. I will deliver up the Bill on payment of the Money and return of the Receipt. He behav'd here very foolishly and fraudulously. I wish all American Fools & Knaves would stay at Home, for the Credit of their Country" (LC: Franklin Papers, Series 1, 4 : 257). Then on October 9, acknowledging Digges's letters of September 20 and 29, he had stated that he had not yet received the picture of "the good Bishop" (Jonathan Shipley), that he had already written about Goddard's bill, and that he had enjoyed visits "from your two friends" (Jones and Paradise, who had carried Digges's letter of September 18 to Franklin), by whom he was sending the present letter with an enclosure replying to the petition Digges had sent him on September 12 (LC: Franklin Papers, Series 1, 4 : 282–83).

Stepney 24 Octor. 1780

DEAR SIR

The letter of Sepr. 18 with an inclosd Bill reachd me but a very few days ago, & I immideately made the necessary enquirys about Mr. Jones. This Gentleman is not in England but I hear He is coming this way, & is at present in Amsterdam, where (I suppose) he is playing similar tricks to those He has imposd upon You. The good old Doctor of whom I made my enquirys after Jones, tells me that He drew upon him from Paris for Eight Guineas "to keep him out of a French Goal." This draft was followd a post or two after by another for 20£ "to enable him to get to America". Besides these Bills, he by imposing himself on Dr. F. as a Brother to Dr. Jones of N. York, obtaind several small sums of money, & the old Dr. knows nothing of him at present. I will be upon the watch for Him & therefore hold the Bill you inclosd me; but I think Your best & only remedy is on Goddard, Who having acknowledgd His acceptance of such a bill, is in consequence thereof liable to pay what has been advanced on it.

My two friends are arrivd & I receivd the news paper by them. I am uneasy about the picture; upwards of two I beleive *three* months ago Mr. F. Bowens at Ostend acknowlegd the save [safe] receival of it,

& said it should be forwarded properly. I will write to Him about it, & desire Him to address You on the Subject. Three of the four men whom You address a line to are gone to Ireland; but not till after (by the advice of Mr. H[odgso]n & myself) making the proper application for the Receipt for four men from the Sick & Hurt, to stand against as many confind Americans.[1] There are above an hundred people in their predicament in England, & most of them seemingly very easy under their situation; many have behavd well & done every thing in their power.

The Person whom I have lately wrote to You about the Confinement of, is in much better health, tho rigorously confind as usual. I have communicated with Him. This is mentiond for your Government in case You have a word to say to Him.

I am With the highest respect,
Your Obedt. Servant.
Wm. S. Ross

No Western news but appearances speak that Some Ships & troops are soon going to the Wt. Inds. & No. America.

A Bill on Monr. G[ran]d dated 16 Octor. for 48£ for account of Your Charity at F[orto]n.

HSP: Franklin Papers, 5:154.

[1] See Digges to Franklin, Sept. 12, 1780.

To John Adams

27 Octo. 80

DEAR SIR

Your last is of the 25 Sepr.[1]—Mr. W. S. C. lately got the annexd note[2]—it is sent for Your Government.—No news but what you will read in the papers as soon as this Letter—A *great portion* of the people here are hurt and as much astonishd as You can be at the treatment

Mr. L[aurens] has met with—the rigour is no ways abated.—This, with Lord Cornwallis's military Executions & cool butchery of defenceless people in South Carolina, irrevocably seals the perpetual disunion between Great Britain & America.—Tis to be lamented that present appearances speak peace to be far distant—come when it will, we may safely pronounce that it will be accompanyd with anguish & humiliation to the savage heart, that seems insatiate of human Gore & the principal actor for carrying on the war.

"Tho not personally known yet I am well acquainted with Your (W. S. C[hurch]s) Character & attatchments as well as with his connexions & correspondence *yonder* and I had letters for Him from ——— & ——— Happy to be informd the Bills are taken up—there will no more appear—had reprobated the premature & dangerous step of drawing—Shall be glad when possible to see you and L. De N[eufvill]e[3]—The present confinement is cruel—the mode & terms aggravate, but there is no abatement on this or any other consideration, of Spirits—These are calm & composd—had these faild, the flesh under the late malady would have sunk totally—Continue to keep these friends F[ranklin] and A[dams] informd, & communicate intelligence from them as speedily as possible—Should not Friends interpose for obtaining some enlargement on parole, by bail, or Exchange?—have no hint to communicate at this moment, except that those papers said to be taken, which were intended to be sunk, are of no importance or very little—A million of thanks to W. S. C.——— but a snatchd moment to write all this.—["]

I wish you all good & am with the highest respect
Yr. obedt. Servant
Wm. Fitzpatrick

[Addressed:] A Monsieur/Monsr. Ferdinando Raymond San/Chez Monsieur Henri Shorn/Amsterdam

MHS: Adams Papers, Reel 353.

[1] Acknowledged by Digges, Oct. 6, 1780. Beyond requesting books, Adams had inveighed against England's lack of any principle or system on which to rest opposition to the American cause.

² In his next paragraph Digges has copied a note received from Laurens.
³ Leendert de Neufville was the son of the Amsterdam merchant, Jean de Neufville, and at the time a London resident.

To Benjamin Franklin

[London: October 27, 1780]

DEAR SIR

I wrote you lately that Jones was not to be found here, consequently the Bill irrecoverable from Him. He is at Amsterdam playing his tricks as I understand. The person who accepted the Bill & acknowleges the acceptance, may be obligd by Law to pay what has been advancd on it.

I hear our *sick* friend is better—His disorder being contageous I am afraid to visit him—He is getting better & I hear from Him & he from me now & then.

There are many people here hurt & as much astonishd as You can be at Mr. L[auren]s treatment; which still continues rigorous to an extreem—This, with Lord Cornwallis's military Executions & cool butcheries of defenceless People in So. Carolina, irrevocably seals the perpetual disunion between Gt. Britain & America. Tis however to be lamented that Peace is so far-distant as appearances indicate, and come when it will, we may safely pronounce it will be accompanyd with anguish and humiliation to the Savage heart, that seems insatiable of human gore. No news but what the papers will inform You. The annexd note will explain itself. Mr. W. S. C. can do the needfull.

      I am with high respect
      Your Servant
      Wm. Fitzpatrick

    [Enclosure]
"'Tho not personally known, I am well acquainted with Your (*Mr. W. S. C.'s*) Character & attachments & with his connexions *yonder*, &

had letters to Him from —— and ——. I am happy to be informd the bills are taken up—there will no more appear—had reprobated the premature & dangerous step of drawing—should be glad were it possible to see You & the person concernd in taking up the Bills (*L. De N[eufvil]le*)—The present confinement is cruel, the mode & terms aggravate, but there is no abatement on this or any other consideration of Spirits—these are calm & composd—had these faild, the flesh under the late malady would have sunk totally—Continue to keep those friends F[ranklin] and A[dams] informd, & communicate intelligence from them as soon as possible—Should not friends interpose for obtaining some Enlargement on parole, by bail or Exchange?—have no hint to communicate at this moment, except that those papers said to be taken, which were intended to be Sunk, are of no importance—A million of thanks to W. S. C.—but a snatchd moment to write all this."—[1]

HSP: Franklin Papers, undated mss. (acquisition no. 10189). This document bears no date, endorsement, address, or cover. A slightly inaccurate copy, not in Digges's hand, of the letter, classified as intercepted, General Post Office, Public Record Office; France, v. 555 (PRO: SP 78/325), bears the endorsement: "London, October 27, 1780/Copy of a Letter from/William Singleton Church/to Dr. B. Franklin/ Recd. October 27, 1780." And it records as the address: "a Monsieur B. F. under cover/ To Mr. Grand Banker—Paris.—" But the similarity of this letter to the one Digges wrote Adams on October 27 and Digges's practice of often writing both Adams and Franklin nearly identical letters on the same day suggest that October 27 is the date on which Digges wrote the letter; the date of receipt in the endorsement is most likely the date of interception.

[1] See Digges to Adams, Oct. 27, 1780, n. 2.

To John Adams

On October 14 Adams had acknowledged Digges's letters of October 6 and 10 and continued: "Upon which Principle is it, that they confine Mr. L. as a Pris-

oner of State?—After so many Precedents as have been set.—Sullivan, Sterling, Lee Lovel, and many others have been exchanged as Prisoners of War.—

"*Mr. L. was in England when Hostilities commenced, I believe. He came into public, in America after the Declaration of Independence, after the Extinction of all civil authority under the Crown, and after the Formation of compleat new Government in every State.—To treat a Citizen of a State thus compleatly in Possession of Sovereignty de Facto, is very extraordinary.—Do they mean to exasperate America and drive them to Retaliation? Are these People governed by Reason at all, or by any Principle, or do they conduct according to any System; or do the[y] deliver themselves up entirely to the Government of their Passions, and their Caprice? . . . Pray inform me constantly, of every Thing relative to him, and let me know if any Thing can be done for him, by way of France, or any other.*

"*Cornwallis's and Tarleton's Gasconade serves only to diminish the Esteem of Mankind, for the People of England, by giving Fuel to their Passions, and making them throw off the Mask.—I dont believe that his advantage is half so great, nor the American Loss half so much as they represent.—Time you know is the Mother of Truth. Audi alteram Partem.—And wait the Consequences.—Fighting is the Thing—Fighting will do the Business.—Defeat, will pave the way to Victories.—Patience!—Patience! il ye en a beaucoup en Amerique*" (MHS: Adams Papers, Reel *102*).

Tuesday—Octor. 31, 1780

DEAR SIR

We have not the least news from the Wt.ward more than the publick papers will announce, but in hourly expectations of some from N. York. Our grand fleet passd Plymo. the 27th & these winds have probably put them on their intendd station for Cruizing. A small fleet has saild to N. York—a frigate or so with 10 or a dozen Store Ships & Merchantmen, but no troops or any thing like any. Four ships of the line are going soon to the Wt. Ins. They carry troops 3 to 5,000 & I guess these will be the last Expeditions or fleets in this year of our Lord 1780.

We are all anxiety for the Speech, which some say is not to [be] deliverd to day but tomorrow.[1] I shall keep this letter open to a late hour to inclose it or give you any cue of the tendency of it that may be in my power to gather.

Yours of the 14th got to hand after my letter of the 27th was forwarded. I have in my possession one from Mr. S[ear]le² to Mr. L[aurens] which I understand the substance of from the bearer of it Mr. J[o]nes.³ This shall find its way to Mr. L. tho the letter may not. Please to mention this to Mr. S——le with my best wishes &ca. &ca. Any thing flat & smally folded will duly find its way. I only observe a caution of not doing *Him* any hurt by what is written. The day will come when relaxation from present severity will take place, therefore any discoverys may make confinement longer. Any hint can be securely communicated. He is made easier, & better in health by them.—No one I beleive can tell upon what *principle* Mr. L. was committed upon[;] *principle* here, is not so much regarded as you immagine; It is generally the sudden impulse of the hour that lead our rulers in Error. I beleive they think themselves in an error already about the Committment & ill treatment of that man, and probably they will act with more lenity soon, & sink into the other extreem. Appearances however speak that His Confinement will be a long one. The Law for suspending the Habeas Corpus to those who have embarkd & been beyond Sea, which was passd in 1777 & is I *beleive* in force to Jany. 1. 1780,⁴ prevents Mr. L. getting releasd by Bail, & authorizes his Enemys to keep him in confinement as long as they think fit. I will get you the Law as well as the Arguments in Ebenezer Smith Platts case⁵ & send them You.

It is impossible to describe why or wherefore these people act as they do; every thing seems to indicate they mean to play away the last stake with America, to exasperate Your Countrymen all in their power, & drive them to acts of retaliation—They seem to deliver themselves up intirely to the Government of their passions & their Caprice, & conduct themselves according to no system whatever. This harsh treatment of Mr. Laurens, together with Lord Cornwallis's military Executions & cool butchery of defenseless people in So. Carolina, irrivocably seals the perpetual disunion between Great Britain & America. I cannot but lament that appearances speak Peace at a very great distance—Come when it will we may safely pronounce that it will be accompanyd with anguish & humiliation to the Savage Heart of "*White Eyes*," that seems insatiable of human gore.

I am with the Highest Esteem
Yr. Obedient Servant
W. S. C.

There was no Speech today but the jet of it is supposd for a Continuance of the War—that Cornwallis success shews what may be done by vigorous exertions—very Complimentary to that Genl.—assuring that the money which may be granted will be properly applyd &ca. &ca. &ca.

G. W. Cornwall chosen Speaker by a majority of 31 votes
for Cornwall.— 234
for Sr. Fletcher Norton—203
31 [6]

MHS: Adams Papers, Reel 353.

[1] The king had decided to defer his speech opening the first session of the fifteenth Parliament until the House of Commons should have elected a Speaker.

[2] James Searle (1733–1797), a Pennsylvanian elected to the Continental Congress in 1778, was now in Europe as Pennsylvania's special envoy to try to negotiate loans for the purchase of military supplies. After visiting Franklin, he had gone on to Amsterdam.

[3] Sir William Jones.

[4] He must mean 1781.

[5] Platt, an American merchant, had been charged with high treason in Georgia in Jan. 1776. He had then been transferred from one place of confinement to another, finally to England, in order to render invalid the various writs of habeas corpus secured by his friends, and had not been allowed to see witnesses against him or hear their affidavits read. On Feb. 17, 1777, in a speech against suspending the Habeas Corpus Act, John Wilkes had cited Platt's case as an instance of illegality and as evidence of the need to preserve English rights carefully.

[6] Although Sir Fletcher Norton (1716–1789) had for ten years been Speaker and a supporter of North's policies, he had in recent months evinced doubts and thereby impelled North to support Charles Wolfran Cornwall (1735–1789), who had had no doubts since joining North's camp in 1774. The vote, according to the record, was actually 203 to 134.

To Benjamin Franklin

[⟨London⟩ October 31, 1780]

DEAR SIR

The rigorous Confinement of Mr. L. yet Continues. I did hope eer this there would have been some abatement in it. There is no telling upon what principle it is they confine Him a *close* Prisoner of State after so many precedents have been set. Sullivan, Stirling, Lee, Lovell, & many others.[1] But why should we expect these folks to act upon any *principle*. To treat a Citizen of a State thus compleatly in possession of Sovereignty de facto, is very extraordinary. They apparently mean to exasperate America & drive them to acts of retaliation. They seem to govern without any reason or principle, & to conduct their affairs without System, delivering themselves up intirely to the Government of their Passions & their Caprice. This treatment of Mr. L., together with Lord Cornwallis's late Military Executions & cool butchery of defenceless People in So. Carolina will irrevocably seal the perpetual disunion between G. Britain and America. Cornwallis[']s & Tarletons late Gasconade serves to diminish the esteem of mankind for the People of England, by giving fuel to their passions, & making them throw off the masque. I dont beleive that His advantage is half so great or the American loss half so much as they represent. Time you know is the mother of Truth. Audi alteram partem, & wait the consequences.— Fighting is the thing—fighting will do the business—defeats will pave the way to victories. Patience! Patience! il y en a beaucoup en Amerique. Tis however to be lamented that peace is so far distant—at least appeerances speak it so—Come when it will, we may safely pronounce that it will be accompanyd with anguish & humiliation to the Savage Heart (of "White-Eyes") that seems insatiable of human gore.

I shall keep this open to give You the substance of the Speech now about dilivering in the House Lords. That Society of worthies will be added to by about a dozen new plumpers for Ministry. I dare say He will find His usual majority in the other stable, for there is a motley & a curious set got into it this sessions. It is not much to us who is out;—The Nation will go to the end of its Tether as your *friend*

[31 OCTOBER 1780]

Govr. Bernard did, let who will be in or out.—We know the worst of it—& are prepard, let it come. The weaker our Enemies before they make Peace the safer we shall be & the longer the Peace will last. As to Friendships of Great Britain towards America it is gone to all Eternity. She never can forgive Us the injuries She has done us.[2]

Not a word from the Wt.ward but what you have read in the news. The *talk* now of *10,000* Men going to America is reducd to *six*— most likely these are only meant for the Wt. Indies with the 4 Sail of the line going soon under Adl. Hood—a Small N. York fleet lately saild without any. Our Grand fleet passd Plymo. on a Cruize the 27th Int. 26 Ships.

The friend whom I have lately wrote to You about, *has his communications*, & very lately expressd an expectation of hearing from You.

I am with the highest respect
Yrs.
Wm. Fitzpatrick

There was no speech today—it is not to be given till tomorrow— the jet of it is said to be for a continuance of the American War—that the success of Lord Cornwallis justifys the continuance of the war provided it is carryd on with spirit—much praise is given to His Lordships gallantry & conduct—compliments & prayer as usual for more money—that it shall be prudently & faithfully applyd &ca. &ca. &ca.

Cornwall was proposd as Speaker
by Lord G. Germaine—he had votes 234
Sr. Fletcher Norton ------------------ 203
Cornwall carryd by a Majority— 31[3]

[Addressed:] Monsieur B. F. [Outside cover:] A Monsieur/Monsieur Grand/Banquiere/Paris

PRO: SP 37/27 no. 52; reproduced in B. F. Stevens, *Facsimiles*, no. 954. The date is derived from a copy in LC: Franklin Papers, Series 2, 19:621.

[1]Generals John Sullivan (1740–1795) and William Alexander (1726–1783), who claimed the unofficial title of the earl of Stirling, had been captured by the British dur-

[31 October 1780]

ing the battle of Long Island in Aug. 1776 and exchanged the following month; Gen. Charles Lee had been captured near Morristown in Dec. 1776 and exchanged in Apr. 1778; James Lovell (1737–1814), a member of the Continental Congress, had been arrested for spying in Mar. 1776 and taken to Halifax, where he had been confined until exchanged in Nov. of that year. Digges is throughout this paragraph appropriating the language of Adams's letter to him of Oct. 14 (see Digges to Adams, Oct. 31, 1780, headnote).

[2] In the concluding five sentences of this paragraph Digges is again appropriating Adams's language, this time contained in Adams's letter of Sept. 25, 1780, in which Adams had criticized the English want of principle: "But what is this to us, who is in, or who out? The Nation will go to the End of its Tether, as Governor Bernard did let who will be in or out. We know the worst of it, and are prepared. Let it come. The weaker our Ennemies before they make Peace, the safer we shall be, and the longer the Peace will last. As to the Friendship of Great Britain towards America, it is gone to all Eternity. She can never forgive us the Injuries she has done us" (MHS: Adams Papers, Reel 102).

[3] See Digges to Adams, Oct. 31, 1780, n. 6.

To John Adams

Novr. 3 1780

Dear Sir

I have receivd Your line with an inclosure the 24th ult., wrote to the partys & am now busey in putting forward four of the *Horses* requird by my new Correspondant. By the time limited, I hope to send Him a set that will compleat His Carriage. As 17 or 18 have been sent from me since the 6th of last month I hope a considerable part of them will answer & give a good temporary lift.[1] A Bundle of Books will go in a day or two coverd to Messrs. J. D. N. & Son.[2] I hope those sent the 10th Octr. have got safe.

No abatement whatever as to the person I lately wrote about —His health good, spirits better, & communications as usual. Mr. S[ear]les letter will be with Him tomorrow. He has had the contents of it before. The Youth[3] is totally forbid further admittance & no hopes of him or any friend seeing him for some time—when I do not write, you may assure yourself that nothing new since the last written letter has transpird.

You see the sum & substance of the Speech & debates &ca. &ca.[4] There was nevertheless no *strong* appearances in the House that the

American War would be vigorously carryd on—at present no appearances of troops going there.—Ten to 12,000 are likely to go in a month or two to the Wt. Inds. The Carolina fleet is to sail with that fleet, so that it is at present not easy to decide whether there are any going to Chas. Town, but I should rather suppose some were to be sent there.

Several Ships for a week or ten days past have continued to slide away seperately from Portso.—but whether meant, as is now reported, in order to form a part of a fleet going from the Channel Squadron to Gibraltar, or as was before given out, to rienforce the fleet in the Wt. Indies, is not easy to say. I rather think they are gone for the Wt. Indies, to which quarter Sr. Saml. Hood is to follow with 5 Sail of the line.[5] It is said troops are to go with Sr. Samuel (& I beleive some thousands are) but none appear moving towards the Seaports yet except a part of Fullartons ragged Regiment who are a sad disgrace to every thing like a Soldier.[6]

        I am with high esteem
        Yr. very obligd & ob. Sert.
        Alexr. Hamilton

MHS: Adams Papers, Reel 353.

[1] What Digges is alluding to here can only be conjectured. Just as he sought to insert in various British publications items favorable to the American cause, and for that purpose welcomed news from Franklin and Adams that he could have printed, so did Franklin and Adams attempt to disseminate American news on the Continent. The treatment of Laurens provided an excellent occasion for publicly calling British behavior into question, and Adams had close at hand at The Hague a man who had become an agent to promote American interests in that way. He was Charles Guillaume Frédéric Dumas (ca. 1725–1796), born in Germany of French parents, resident in the Dutch capital since 1756, and adept in many languages; he had been interested in America since the 1760s, when he had consulted Franklin about the possibilities of emigrating to New England or Virginia. At the outbreak of the Revolution, Franklin had secured his help in advancing American interests, and he was now serving as an adviser to the American delegates, a translator, a go-between among influential politicians, and an individual who had access to journalists willing to publish American news. Letters from Dumas to Adams, Nov. 7, 1780, and from Adams to Dumas, Nov. 9, make clear that Adams was forwarding to Dumas extracts from Digges's letters about Laurens for translation and publication (MHS: Adams Papers, Reels 353 and 102). It is possible, then, that it is for Dumas that Digges is preparing a sheaf of reports about Laurens.

[2] Jean de Neufville & Son, Amsterdam merchants.

³ Laurens's son, Henry, Jr.
⁴ The king's speech, mentioned on Oct. 31, 1780.
⁵ Adm. Hood (1724–1816) was being sent to the West Indies as second in command to Rodney.
⁶ A reference to the regiments (the Ninety-eighth and One Hundredth Foot) raised by two Scottish lairds, Thomas Mackenzie Humberston and William Fullarton, who earlier in the year had received permission from the ministry to enlist the troops, fit out warships, and cruise the Pacific to capture the Acapulco fleet. Humberston had been a soldier, but Fullarton had not and was therefore regarded as simply a political favorite. Amid a welter of dreams and shifting government policies, the expedition was delayed and its destination changed, with the result that it did not sail until Dec. for India.

To Benjamin Franklin

Nov. 3 1780

DEAR SIR

I hope e'er this that the picture of Your valuable friend has reachd You. I have been very uneasy about it & wrote to Mr. Bowens (who long ago acknowlegd the Receipt of it in safety & that it shoud be forwarded) to clear up to You where the stoppage was occasiond. I am almost afraid to pay Your valuable friend a visit till I hear it is in safety for the Young Lady has it much at heart.

The friend of whom I have lately wrote continues in the same situation—much rigour shewn him—his friends absolutely denyd any further admittance—yet *communications* are kept up.

You will have read the Speech & debates upon it in the House Lords—War! War! was the theme.—I was an attentive observer & tho it was full of big words, it did not strike me, nor did the conclusions of that day, that the *American* War would be pushd with vigour, if *that* war *could* be carryd on rigorously, I have no doubt but it *would*. The means are wanting. I see no likelihood of Troops going to the Continent tho some few may be intended for Chs. Town in the fleet now about to sail. 10 or 12,000 are I beleive going to the Wt. Indies but at present no appear[an]ces of any marching to the Sea Coasts, and there are none at Portsmo. save the Corps of Fullartons Raggamuffins, who are a disgrace to the name of Soldier.

Several Ships of the line have during the last 8 or 10 days slid away *seperately* from Portso., but whether they are intended, as is now reported, to form a part of a fleet going from the Channel Squadron to Gibraltar; or; as was before given out, to rienforce the fleet in the West Indies, is not easy to say. I rather think they are gone for the West Inds., to which quarter Sr. Sam. Hood is to follow with about 5 Ships. Troops are going with Sir Sam. but in what numbers cannot be told. As the Carolina fleet is to sail at the same time it will be difficult to say what part of them is intended for Chs. Town but the number talkd of for that quarter is 2,500. It is generally beleivd that Rodney has gone with his fleet from the Wt. Indies to N. York—

I am respectfully Yrs. &ca.
W. Hamilton

HSP: Franklin Papers, 5:155.

To John Adams

8 Nov. 80

DEAR SIR

Yours of the 17 with an inclosure to J.T.,[1] as well as one of the 27th both got safe which was particularly satisfactory, as a friend who is now a fellow Citizen of yours & who left me about the 24th Ultio. may have before now explaind. He could explain to You every thing that I for the present wish explaind. Things are not worse, but insults and aggravation increase.—Nothing can exceed the folly & infatuation of the day. To attempt to describe it would be impossible—they have got to the very paroxism of folly, aggravation, & resentment. An opinion *generally* goes forth thus—America is ours still; If a reasonable man does not willingly give into this opinion, He is insulted & contemnd. You may form some sense of this by the publications of the day, which I hope You get regularly. You may write to me as usual—I wish for a line to put to the test whether it gets safe, & tell me in it how the papers come to hand &ca. &ca.

J. T. got away the 2d Int. to O[sten]d & will I hope see you. On no account whatever risque his coming here again—he parted rather reluctantly & talkd strangely—more of this hereafter. I wish Your Countrymen kept all their fools &—more to themselves & not suffer them to expose others. Much is the mischief which has arrisen from that quarter. I will write you more particularly soon.

We Englishmen not only think we can war successfully with all the world, but we are now actually possessd of an opinion that America is ours again. Nothing now remains but a small force of men & ships to be sent in the spring are wanted & these are actually intended to be sent in the spring. The Virga. Expedition there is great expectation from—but more from defection of principal men in the American Army.

I am with great respt.
Yrs. &ca. &ca.
S. W. C.

MHS: Adams Papers, Reel 353.

[1] Adams's letter of Oct. 17 has not been found, but the initials appear to refer to John Temple, who was making his way home via Holland, as he had been talking of doing for nearly three months (see Digges to Franklin, Aug. 18, 1780).

To John Adams

London 10 Nov. 1780

DEAR SIR

Nothing material occurring, I did not write You on the last post day. Things were then in a train for other communications & I am in hopes to add something to this letter in the Evening, before I seal it, from our friend. Mr. S[ear]les letter & some late ones from home via Nantes got to Him.

Mr. L[aure]ns treatment remaind with usual & unabated rigour till the 8th Int.—His Son & Mr. Manning were *unexpectedly* on that day allowd to pay Him another half hours visit, which the Depy. Governor permitted to be extended to *one whole hour*; and the same day He got an order to be permitted to walk round the Tower whenever He chose to apply to the Depy. Governor to do so. His Son & friend were watchd as before by two Warders, as He will continue to be whenever He walks out. His health & spirits are good.—During the first part of His illness, & while He was very bad, He had a visit from the Lords Hillsborough & Stormont—a Jesuitical visit no doubt, & with a visible meaning to pump & get out of Him what they could. This circumstance without any *particulars* of the visit has got out to me the prisoner expressing the extreem *Complaisance* of His ministerial visitors, particularly in the point of the cringing Complimentary offers of services from Lord H——, in which I dare answer, the Scotchman was not behind hand. I cannot account for this sudden lenity towards the prisoner in no other way (for they very lately peremptorily & rudely refusd the son a second visit to His Father) but from a Whisper going about that the Opposition meant to take up the ill treatment shewn Mr. L., & to move Parliament for a mittigation of the Severity shewn him, that He be permitted parole on giving bail &ca. &ca.—This *was* in agitation, & getting to the ears of Ministers would be enough for them to give one lenitive order to Mr. L——, and the granting him to walk out for air in the Tower, might be brought in argument that He *is not* a Close Prisoner or rigorously treated. These wretches tho they seldom look further than their noses after great national concerns, are nevertheless clever enough at these *little* kind of tricks.

We have no news but what You will see in the papers. Our grand fleet when last heard of was some where about Scilly—The Carola. & Wt. Inda. fleet to sail in 10 or 12 days,—also one from Cork with transports to carry about 7 or 8,000 men, the portion of 2000 or 2,500 of which are intended for Chas. Town, & I see no likelyhood of any others going to other parts of the Continent.

I am with very gt. regard Yrs.
W[illiam] Fitzpatrick

[Addressed:] Mynheer/De Heer Ferdinand Raymond San/Ten Luyze van de Heer Hendrick Shorn/Amsterdam

MHS: Adams Papers, Reel 353.

To Benjamin Franklin

London 10 Novmr. 1780

DEAR SIR

I have seen Miss Georgiana[1] & sympathisd with Her for the present appearance of the picture She sent you in June or July last being stopt somewhere between Ostend & Paris.

It was carryd safely by my friend Mr. Champion of Bristol and lodgd with Mr. F. Bowens at Ostend for forwardance to You; that Gentleman was *then* in the habits of sending parcells of Pamphlets News papers &ca. &ca. forward to Paris for J. A[dams] almost weekly from me, & none of them having miscarryd I trusted the picture by a like conveyance would be safe also. He acknowlegd the safe Receipt of it a very few days after Mr. Champion left it in June or July, & has acknowlegd to me in two letters since, that He held it for a safer conveyance than the dilligence. I have also more than once wrote to Him to make You acquainted where it was, thinking you might point out a safe way of getting it, & from a long silence from both of You, I made sure it had got safe. Your letter of the 9th Octor. cleard up to me You had not receivd it. I cannot account for the delay & have lately wrote repeatedly to Mr. Bowens to give You a line about it. When it gets to hand I beg to be informd of it, that I may satisfy Miss Georgianas uneasiness's therefor.

I hear now & then from the friend I have lately mentiond in Letters to you, & he express's wishes to hear from others & to know what can be done in His case. His son is now with me.

Mr. L.'s confinement has been rigorous as usual till the 8th inst. His son & Mr. Manning were on that day allowd another half hours visit which was extended to one hour, & the same day He got an order to be permitted to walk round the Tower whenever he chose to apply to the Dep. Govr. for leave to do so. His health & spirits are good. During His illness he was honourd with a visit from Lord Hillsborough & Stormont, a jesuitical visit no doubt, & with a visible meaning to pump or get at some thing. This, without any *particulars*, has got out from his late Visitors, only by the Prisoners expressing the extreem complaisance of his two ministerial visitors, particularly in the point of the cringing complimentary offers of services from Lord H——— and I dare say the Scotsman was not behind hand.

I cannot account for this lenity towards the Prisoner in no Other way (for they very lately peremptorily & rudely refusd the Son a second visit) but from a whisper going about that a motion was to be made in Parliament for a relaxation in the Severity of treatment to Mr. L., & that He should be put upon Parole or baild—This *was* in agitation, & the now granting Mr. L. a walk out will be brought an argument that He is not a *close* prisoner or ill treated. As appearances speak our *wise* rulers are not well pleasd with the treatment they have shewn Mr. L., I doubt not but they will soon allow Him further favours & most likely give him parole.

We have no news yet from America or any other but what You read in the publick prints.

I am with very great respect
Yrs. &ca.

[Addressed:] A Monsieur Monsr. B. F./Passy

HSP: Franklin Papers, 5:156.

¹Georgiana Shipley.

To Benjamin Franklin

Novr. 13. 1780

DEAR SIR

The Bearer of this, Capn. Benjamin Joy, waits upon Your Excellency on a matter of Business which will be explaind by Himself to You. He is so well recommended and His attattchment & active services for the cause of His Country are so well known to me, that I cannot but back His solicitation to Your Excellency with my strongest wishes that you gratify Him.

His Business is on a similar nature with that I wishd Your Excellency to grant a Friend I recommended in a letter the 26th Septr.; and I am the more anxious for its completion, because the Adventure is meant for the State of Virginia now very much in want of Blue & Colourd Army Cloths, Blanketts, Coarse Woolens, Tent Linin, Sail-Duck &ca. &ca., which Captain Joy has been recommended to carry out at every risque by some of the distinguishd leaders of the People in that Quarter; particular[l]y James Barron Esqr. of the Board of War, Duncan Rose Esqr. of the board of Trade and General Weeden.[1]

For the accomplishment of His purpose, Captain Joy means to vest His property & effects in Europe in such articles as are specifyd above and to Conduct them to Virginia, on board His Vessell the Brigantine Swallow of about 150 Tons Burthen, mannd with fourteen or fifteen Seamen & carrying Six Carriage Guns four pounders—a Copper sheathd vessel of the Bermudian mould having a square tuck &ca.

If such vessel and Her intended Contents can be protected by Your Passport from any stoppage by the Cruisers of America or Her Allies, I am very sure the scheme will turn out of great publick benefit to my Country.

> I am very Respectfully Dr. Sir
> Yr. Obligd & Obt. Sert.
> T. Digges

His Excelly. B. Franklin Esqr.

[Addressed:] His Excellency/Benjn. Franklin Esq./*Passy*

HSP: Franklin Papers, 5:157.

[1] All three were Virginians. Brig. Gen. George Weeden (ca. 1730–1793), though, was no longer in active service but was helping organize military resistance to British raids.

To Benjamin Franklin

London 13 Nov. 1780

DEAR SIR

Since I wrote You last, on the 10 Int. I have had another letter from Mr. F. Bowens at Ostend relative to the picture, for the safe delivery of which I am so anxious as to be frequently troublesome to You. Mr. Bowens by letter the 4th Int. informs me He has wrote to the necessary stages about it, particularly to his friend at Lisle (to which place it got in safety) and He thinks it has been detaind at and may be found *at the Bureau des Diligences de Flandres a Paris.* If it has not got to hand, be pleasd to order your Servant to enquire at that Bureau for it; for it would give me, as well as the Young Lady who sent it, the greatest satisfaction to hear *by the Bearer* it had reachd You in safety.

Your two packages by Mr. Jones went thro my hands in safety to Mr. Hodgson—He will write You in case there is any new move relative to the Prisoners. At present all is at a stand with the board here, for want of hearing from You with the specification of numbers on hand in France, & which I fear very much you will not have in Your power to give while the American Cruizers continue the abominable & impolitic practice of not holding their Prisoners, but suffering them to go at large whenever they have oppertunity. Numbers have reducd lately at Forton, owing to the exemplary exertions of a very worthy little agent; numbers having found their way over to a certain *House* in Amsterdam. At Plymo. there are 135 the 2d Int. & their numbers woud have been greater had 15 or 16 remaind, who in a fit of dispair of getting Exchangd, lately enterd into the British service.[1] I cannot here omit the extraordinary conduct of one lately (of the name of Laurance, rather above the common level, a Yankee, well read & informd) who glancing over a Chapter of the bible that expressd "Eunucks had a better chance for the Kingdom of Heaven than man in perfect verility" immidiately with a sharp knife committed the operation on Himself, and is now perfectly recoverd. Man[le]y & Co[nyn]g[ha]m are still in their old quarters & have been very roughly treated & punishd for two attempts to elope. Your former charity of 25 £ to M——y, has been servicable to them both, & the 6d. per week to each man is a good help.

Every day here produces some new proofs of the inattention in the Captains of American Cruizers towards holding their Prisoners for Exchange. The Pilgrim Cap. Robinson[2] of Salem, 18.6 pounders & 150 Men, landed about a month ago six or seven Captns. & 53 Seamen near to Cape Clear in Ireland. Capt. Ferguson (one of the

Captns.) who relates this says that during the 15 days he was on board, The Pilgrim took 7 homeward bound Wt. Inda. Men (four of them from Monserrat out of the 5, the only ships which came from thence this year, & sent them all for Boston) and that His Ship was the 79th prize the Pilgrim had taken—The Pilgrim has only been 20 months off the Stocks.

Your letter in answer to that wrote by the parole Prisoners which came by Capt. Fletcher from Boston,[3] has been receivd; and they made the requisite application at the board of Sick & hurt *to be exchangd by receipt & stand in Account with You*, as You recommended; This has been refusd them as unprecedented, & Capt. McCausland[4] wrote You last post about it; praying to know if it was necessary for Him to go to Paris & surrender themselves to You. If you can favour them with an Answer by *the Bearer* it will be a great obligation on some good Men who seemingly wish to do every thing in thier power to comply with their parole agreement.

No new movement with respect to Mr. L[aure]ns since my late letters. It is the opinion of some, that there will be soon a further relaxation of sevirty towards him, & that there will be a probability of his getting out soon on Parole. The Papers which our Ministry took from Him & sent over to the States General, made thier appearance in the English news today, & causes much exultation, such as by the Message of the Statholder &ca. &ca. it is *apparant* Holland will stick to the Interest of England &ca. &ca. They boast the same way too of affairs in Portugal. Spain too is *certainly* (say they) listening to overtures lately sent over by the Priest Hussy; & the cry of many is, that our Ministry will do well to detach Spain from the American Interest at the expence of submitting to let Gibraltar be taken, to give the Dons East & Wt. Florida the whole of the Campechy Lod[Log]-Wood trade &ca. &ca. Time the Mother of Truth,[5] will discover what all this will come to; at present the fashion is to beleive that our wise Ministers will certainly seperate Spain from the Bourbon Compact ha! ha! ha!

I inclose You a Certificate which you formerly granted to Carpenter.[6] As I found the partys concernd in it, were not expressly going according to the tenor of that pass, (not that I mean they intended to go to an Enemys port) I refusd to give it to the partys, & they proceeded out in a Strong armd vessel & have got to B[osto]n; where every thing went well.

You recollect, Mitchells Cartel was after much trouble paid for by bills of 500 each on Jackson at the Admiralty who accepted them *payable at the Bank*. When the Bills became due they were refused payment & are still unpaid, & unfortunately for me (who had no other motive or benefits in them but to get them discounted) my name stands upon two, which has much distressd me.

Your last to me is of the 9th Octor. & I expected to hear further from You about Your bill from Jones on Goddard—If I can be any ways servicable You may freely command me—I have informd You how the same Jones took in Dr. Fothergill.

My late Dates have been the 3d Octor. giving an Account of H. L——ns capture. Also the 6th, 10th, 17th, 24th, 31st; and the 3d & 10th Int. I am rather curious to know whether *one* of these got safe— it containd an extract from a captive & is dated I think the *31st octor.*—The getting this information, as well as to have *a name* to direct to instead of the B. F. a Passy which I always cover to Grand will be servicable & safer to me.

The bearer will give you the current news of the day & carry a few News Papers. He is a Young Man who has renderd Services to the Cause particularly in the quarter of Virga. & on whom I have very good reasons for placing strict confidence & good opinion.

       I am with the highest Esteem
       Yr. Most Obedt. Sert.
       W: S: C.

    please turn over

Monday night

P. S. Since writing the foregoing, I find there is a Capt. St. George arrivd at the Secys. office with Dispatches from N. York of a late date—The Town is in a hub-bub to get at their *real* contents—accounts are so incoherent that it is impossible for me (before I am obligd to seal & deliver this to the Bearer) to obtain any thing like the true account; but this will be remedyd to You by the Bearer fulfilling his promise to carry the tomorrow mornings papers & add them to the few of today that I send You. It appears that Rodney with 11 Ships saild from the Wt. Indies the 24 Augt. & got to Rd. Island the 20th Sept. lookd into that port, did nothing, touchd at N. York, and returnd to His Wt. Indn. Station ⟨P[or]ts⟩ on the *26th*. One account (tho not a beleivd one) says his fleet remaind at N. York when this last packet saild. It is with concern I inform You that Arnold has turnd Traitor to His Country & got into N. York—It appears by the todays yet incorrect account He had obtaind some secondary Command under Washington near N. York, they say some Posts or Fort. He had prior to that made *his bargain* with an Emissary of Genl. Clintons to betray the American Army & direct the British where to Surprize it. On the day fixd for this acheivement, Clinton sent out a Major St. André to inform Arnold of His movement[7]—He went in the Character of a deserter valet de Chambre, was known on his landing, apprehended, detected & immidiately hangd—Drafts of the American Army, plan of its lines, & the plan fixd between Arnold & Clinton was found upon Him. Arnold immidiately fled & got by water into N. York. The accounts further say that Gen. Washington improvd this settled plan to his own advantage & strengthend a Post which Arnold had declard would be but faintly defended, & by that means routed the British army who went to possess it & had advancd too far before they heard of Major St. Andre's fate.

Altho these accounts have been bandied about ever since ten oClk. this morning, there is no exact recital given from the quarter of Authority—there, they are rather mute, do not exult in the least, & by every appearance the accounts are in the lump highly dissatisfactory.

HSP: Franklin Papers, 51 : 158.

[1] The Board of Sick and Hurt reported on Nov. 14 that there were 181 in Forton and 120 in Mill.
[2] Joseph Robinson.
[3] See Digges to Franklin, Sept. 8, 1780.
[4] See Digges to Franklin, Sept. 12, 1780.
[5] Adams's phrase (see Digges to Adams, Oct. 31, 1780, headnote).
[6] See Digges to Adams and to Franklin, Mar. 3, 1780.

[7] The story of Benedict Arnold (1741–1801) and Maj. John André (1751–1780) requires no retelling here, but Digges's reference to St. André may be of interest to biographers of André, some of whom have speculated about whether the major was related to a family with that other surname.

To John Adams

On October [28] Adams had asked Digges to send him the General Advertiser *and the* Morning Post, *the narratives by General Burgoyne and by General William Howe, and information about the condition of Captains Manley and Conyngham, to whom he offered help. On November 7 he had acknowledged Digges's letters of October 24, 27, and 31, stated that Laurens's note (enclosed with the letter of October 27) "is of much importance to me.—I wrote, sometime ago, to see if any Thing could be done by way of Exchange," and requested two books for his sons: [William] Lily's* Grammar *and Clark's* Latin Exercises *(MHS: Adams Papers, Reel 102).*

London 14 Nov. 1780

Dear Sir

Your favors of the 28th ulo. & 7th Int. came both to hand since mine of the 10th and I begun from yesterday to forward the two news papers as directed—You need not apologise for any trouble given me of this sort, for I shall be always glad to serve You. The Books you request in both these last letters will be forwarded by a Ship to Amsterdam to sail in a few days; there are other political Pamphlets put up with them, & I hope you got those parcells forwarded by Mr. Bromf[iel]d the 26 Sept. and by a Ship to Amsterdam, the Content Capt. Nanne Ibetts, which Saild the 10th or 12th of Octor. I shall continue to forward any thing politically new as it comes out & inform You when I want Cash.

Poor Manly & C[onyngha]m whom you enquire after & offer to help are still in a miserable situation in Mill Prison Plymo. & *very severely treatd.* A sum remitted them thro me from Dr. F. and the few guineas they get from me (which by the bye I can very ill afford) has been of material benifits to them & kept them in a manner from sinking under the severity of ill treatment.—I mean by *ill treatment* the Confinement of a dungeon & fed on bread & water only for 40 days, whenever the agent thinks fit to inflict this punishment—They have both undergone it twice, for threatening severe retaliation on the English whenever the chances of war puts it in their power—this is also a punishment for every attempt to break Goal.

I am glad to hear the note annexd to my letter of the 27th ulo. got safe to Your hands. Mr. L[auren]s confinement still continues as on the 10th Int. & nothing new since—better spirits on account of some late communications; & I hoped by this nights post to inform You what our friend wishd done with some letters mentiond by You, but I must wait till next oppertunity.

The papers will inform You of Genl. Arnolds apostacy & his attempts to ruin the American Army by treachery. The Toreys here do not exult at all at this acquisition, nor at the news brought by the late Dispatch vessels from N. York or the Wt. Indies. Adml. Rodney by every account arrivd the 10th Sept., lookd into Rhd. Island, did nothing—went into N. York & was to sail again for his station the day after the Dispatch frigate left N. York—Not a word about Monr. Guichens fleet or any rienforcement to Ternay—where the Devil these french & Spanish ships are no one knows—they seem to be doing nothing at the very time their superiority of numbers promises every thing—I wish they may not play the game of protraction too refinedly for the Interests of America.

You see what Lord G. Germaine expressd when calld upon to explain what He meant by saying this Country could treat with America whenever she pleasd on the footing of Indepen[den]cy—He gave up the idea of Conquering the Country, yet said the War must be prosecuted thro the sides of America to bring France to terms, & to accomplish this detatchments must be sent to carry destruction into different parts of America open to the sea such as Virginia &ca. &ca.—this diabolical scheme will be probably put in execution too if the Allies of America out of their abundance of Ships do not find means to stop these naval Expeditions.

I inclose You a letter from a valuable friend for Mr. Searle to whom, tho unknown, I beg my best wishes & respects.

> I am with great respect
> Your mo. Obet. Serv.
> W. S. C[hurch]

[Addressed:] Myn Heer/De Heer Ferdinando Raymond San/ten hyuze Van de Heer Hendrick/Schorn/a/*Amsterdam*

MHS: Adams Papers, Reel 353.

To John Adams

Nov. 17 80

DEAR SIR

I acknowlegd the Receipt of Yours the 28th Octo. & 7th Int. in my last letter of the 14th.—Since that day no material move with regard to our friend; but I am in consultations now & then to fix upon some mode by a motion in Parliament to have him put on parole or releasd by Bail. By the inclosd letter You will discover as much as I have *yet* been able to discover of the writer who appears to be Mr. L[auren]s Secy.[1]—The other papers alluded to in His letter are no where here abouts yet, but I will keep a look out for them knowing *some of the names mentiond in the inclosd.*[2] As the inclosd has but this moment come to hand & I am rather pinchd for time by this Post, I can not further add.

You will by this time have read & heard as much as I have relative to Arnolds apostacy—Ministry have been in possession of the plan of this plot above a month (ever since Gov. Trions arrival) & it has been the cause of their holding out such strong assurances of success from America, and of their confidant elation. They now brag very much of a considerable disunion in W[ashingto]ns army & that Knox, Skuyler, Howe & another Genl. have come over to their Interest.[3] I do not beleive any thing of this—it is meerly held out to cover the disgrace & ruin of their dearly purchasd plots.

It is said Rodney was not to Leave America till the 25th Octor. then to go to His old Station—By the packet & other arrivals from N. York subsequent to the Gazette accounts it appears the whole British fleet of 24 ships was blocking up Rhode Island, & no accounts whatever, in that or any other quarter of the French or Spanish fleets. How can You account for them?

The Books lately wrote for are shippd on board the [*left blank*] Captain [*left blank*] for Amsterdam, twelve or fourteen in all. The papers are sent regularly as directed. As I shall be uneasy about this inclosure please to acknowlege the Receipt of it.

The Expedition for Chesapeak is said to be saild from N. York. When you get any News from the Southern army or from Virga. give me a line.—What think you of the article in the inclosd mentioning the recapture of Gates's Baggage taking Lord Cornwallis &ca.

The writer of the within & the Captn. Pickles⁴ will most likely be sent into Prison with their Countrymen at Portsmo.—I do not know how to help them as yet, probably Mr. L——ns friend Mr. Manning, may be inducd to advance them a little money—Mr. Young is Mr. L——ns Secy.—and the papers said to be left with Mr. Shute were so orderd to be by Mr. L. probably to be forwarded from N. foundland to some part of America.

Your Pamphlets & 2 s[c]hool books, went yesterday or this morning (13 in all) in a paper parcell directed to Messrs. J. D[e Neufville] & Son—I cannot yet get the Ship or Captns. name.

MHS: Adams Papers, Reel 353.

¹The enclosure, in a hand other than Digges's, was a copy of a letter from Moses Young to Henry Laurens written aboard the *Vestal* off the Isle of Wight, Nov. 14, 1780, and carried to London from Spithead by Winslow Warren. Young informed Laurens that letters to his son Col. John Laurens and to the Committee for Foreign Affairs, along with their duplicates, were being forwarded by "Mr. Shute" (Robert Shute of St. John's Island), told him of the battle of Camden, S.C., whose disastrous outcome he had learned (with some inaccuracy in details) from Capt. Hugh Smith, commander of the brigantine *Fair American*, which the *Vestal* had taken during the crossing, and asked for

a sum of money to enable him "to appear & act as I know Col: Laurens wishes I should."

²Digges must mean Winslow Warren (see Digges to Adams, Oct. 3, 1780, n. 1), who was friendly with John Temple. In addition to Pickles and Shute, the only other individuals mentioned in the letter are wardroom personnel and officers who had participated in the battle of Camden.

³It is difficult to explain the bases for the British rumors. Henry Knox had played important roles in several major battles and was soon to be promoted from brigadier general to major general; it is curious that he should have been included in such a list. Philip Schuyler (1732–1804) had had a falling out with Gates in 1777, but was now a delegate to the Continental Congress from New York and appears scarcely to have favored British interests. Maj. Gen. Robert Howe (1732–1790), Arnold's predecessor as commander at West Point and a member of the board that had condemned André to be hanged, had fought with distinction in Georgia and continued to have significant responsibilities in New Jersey. The other general, probably (see Digges to Franklin, Nov. 17, 1780) Brig. Gen. William Maxwell (ca. 1733–1796), once accused of excessive drinking but acquitted, had served at the battle of Monmouth and was now retiring.

⁴The commander of the *Mercury*, on which Laurens had been a passenger when captured (see Digges to Adams, Oct. 3, 1780). He was sent to Forton and escaped on May 14, 1781.

To Benjamin Franklin

Novr. 17. 1780

Dear Sir

I wrote You by a friend the 14th Int.¹ which I suppose will reach you before or about the same time with [this]. I mentiond the defection & going over of Genl. Arnold to the British. For this noble action He had found many advocates here, & the Ministry are mightily elated therewith; putting it upon defection in the American Army, strong discontents &ca. &ca. They brag of four other Generals & several Officers being also in their Interest & gone over; nay they go as far as to mention the names of Knox, Skuyler, Maxwell, & another which I forget²—but this is all in their own way—meerly held out to these thick-heads (who believe every thing the Ministry tell them) in order to cover the disgrace & ignominy of the Transaction with Arnold, for whom no doubt they have given quite His worth in British Guineas. This has been an old plan, & Arnold was certainly got at before He left Philadelphia to take a Command nearer Washington—Tryon & Genl. Patterson[3] certainly brought over, a month ago, the whole outline of the plan, & ministers were so sure of its success, that I am confidant it has been this & this alone which has made them so unaccountably impudent of late & so prone to brag of a certainty they had of yet doing well in America—The Refugee cry now is—that if the plan had succeeded The American Army would have been cut up & the game woud have been ours—it is now all over, we must begin the work again, appearances are bad &ca. &ca. ha! ha! ha.

They are confident still that Ternays fleet is to be destroyd & Rhode Island retaken. Much expectation from the Southern Expedition which had saild from N. York before the last packet saild. If the accounts in the inclosd paper may be beleivd (and Capt. Smith the relater of them is a man of veracity)[4] this Expedition may probably arrive in Chesapeak after the Southern army has driven Cornwallis into Cha. Town, and then a fig for their Virginia Expdition.[5]

It may be necessary to inform You for Your better understanding the inclosd paper, that it is written by the Secy. to Mr. Hy. L——ns, who, with the Captain of the Ship in which Mr. L. was taken have left at St. Johns to come to England in Capt. Berkely.—Mr. Young writes to Mr. L——ns from Spithead supposing He was not a Close prisoner—the letter just now found its way to me & I thought a copy might be acceptable to You. No *new* move as to Mr. L——ns Confinement.

         I am very respectfully Yrs.
         W. ⟨M.⟩

[Addressed:] Monsr. B. F——/ Passy

HSP: Franklin papers, 5 : 159.

 [1] He must mean Nov. 13.
 [2] Robert Howe (see Digges to Adams, Nov. 17, 1780).
 [3] Apparently Brig. Gen. James Paterson, who had been in South Carolina with Clinton and who must have been among "the others" with Tryon mentioned by Digges to Adams, Sept. 26, 1780.
 [4] Digges had made a copy, not entirely exact, of the letter from Young to Laurens that he was sending Adams at the same time (see Digges to Adams, Nov. 17, 1780, n. 1).
 [5] According to Capt. Hugh Smith, as Young reports the information, several vessels

had reached North Carolina and Virginia with quantities of arms and military stores sufficient to provision the Americans in those two states for a considerable time, and the people were expecting Gates shortly to make prisoners of Cornwallis's army.

To Benjamin Franklin

On November 7 Franklin had written Digges that he would try to see whether a friend to whom he was writing might be able to procure "some Relaxation on Parole" for Henry Laurens and continued: "It may be some Satisfaction to him to know that a dirty Attempt to deprive him of some of his Property has not succeeded.—A Number of Bills of Exchange, some for considerable Sums drawn upon me in his Favour, others purchas'd by him in America have been presented to me for Acceptance. Their not being endors'd by him occasioned at first some Suspicion, & on Examination of the Bill Book, it was found that precisely the same Bills, endorsed by him to Veuve Babut & Co. at Nantes had already been accepted. On enquiry of the Dutch Banker here how he came by those Bills we learnt that they were sent to him by M[ess]rs. Hopes of Amsterdam, who are intimate Friends. It is said of Sir Joseph York, who probably had them from the Ministers, who found them among our Friends Papers—This may be but among the many other Instances of British Meaness, that tend to make one regret the generous Civilities we have Shown to their People, by delivering up to Passengers & Captains taken Prisoners every Pennyworth of Property they would claim as belonging to them Personally" (LC: Franklin Papers, Series 1, 4:300).

21 Novr. [1780]

DEAR SIR

Your suspicions relative to some Bills mentiond in Your last were well founded from the then appearances. I was satisfyd the transaction was a fraudulent one till I had it cleard up by the only person who coud clear it up i.e. the friend of the man whose property they were. They were slipt into his hand at a first & watchd interview by our friend, unindorsd I suppose, & the friend to the owner remitted them thro the Dutch House You mention, at a risque, & unindorsd, meerly to stop payment for others which might be unfairly obtaind & sent forward as lawful plunder from our friend. This matter has been cleard up to the Dutch House by the intimate of our friend, who is still in the same situation.

The heads of these people seem turnd topsy turvy since they have had a victory in So. Carolina & got an addition to their Army of *Brigadier Genl.* Arnold. The conquest & subjugation of America is as much as ever talkd of as a very probable event and 7/8ths of the people of England seem content & happy that another vigorous campaign should be pushd in America—Whether it produces benefits or not, they say the Country cannot be in a worse situation than it is, & there is almost a certainty of quarrel between America & Her allies. The Bill you remitted in Your last for 100 £ I am in the line of advice about, & think what you recommend the properest mode to be taken.

No foreign news, and all that is domestick which I hear, is that an American Gentleman whom I never heard of before of the name of Trumbull is taken up for Treason on the oath of two N. England men who knew him, He was Seizd on Sundy. night & is in close confinement & Irons.[1] I understand every person who occasionally visited him the next day Viz. Mr. Stewart a painter, Mr. Digs, Mr. D[e] Neufville a Dutch Merchant Mr. Laurens Jnr.[2] &ca. were all taken to a magistrate to declare what they knew of Him & a Mr. Tylor (who I understand has been many days gone from England) but that nothing was got out of the witness's. The oaths of His informants & his own papers, everybody says is sufficient to convict Him & the reason assignd for His now apprehension is that means are using to make retaliation for Major Andrés death. Mr. Trumbull being formerly they say an Adjut. General in the American Army is exactly of Andrés rank, and is therefore thought a proper person to retaliate upon. Good God what a degree of Wickedness folly & weakness are we Englishmen reducd to.

[Flourish]

[Addressed:] B. F——/Passy

UP: Franklin Papers, 4:64.

¹John Trumbull (1756–1843), son of the governor of Connecticut, Jonathan Trumbull (1710–1785), was a stranger to neither Digges nor Franklin, and Digges's affecting not to have heard of him was an act of prudence necessary at a time when mail risked interception and American associations were suspect. Trumbull, recently an officer in the American army, had embarked for England in May to study painting under Benjamin West (1738–1820), assured by British authorities that he would not be disturbed as long as he adhered to his peaceful pursuits. He had traveled by way of Nantes and Paris, where he had come to know both Franklin and his grandson. Apparently, his status as a tolerated rebel had irked the American loyalists in London, and two had made allegations of treasonable activities against him and another former American officer, Maj. John Steel Tyler, who had accompanied Trumbull on the voyage to England to settle some mercantile affairs of his late father and lodged at the same address. Winslow Warren, hearing by chance that a warrant had been issued against Tyler, had managed to warn Tyler in time to enable him to flee the country. Trumbull, though, not named in the warrant and not expecting difficulties, had been surprised in his rooms on the evening of Nov. 19 and been arrested when a search uncovered various papers in his possession that seemed to confirm the charges against him. Among those papers were letters addressed to Digges and one letter to Trumbull from "William White" that told of a proposed expedition abroad similar to those that Digges had been promoting with Franklin's assistance to take various materials and supplies to American ports with means provided in France. Subsequent investigation would identify White as William Brailsford, a Massachusetts merchant, and lead to his being taken up, along with Warren, in Jan. 1781. One of the accusers was undoubtedly John Grey, son of Harrison Grey, a refugee from Boston. The younger Grey, according to the *London Courant*, Jan. 19, 1781, was the informer on Maj. Tyler.

²Gilbert Stuart (1755–1828), Leendert de Neufville (the junior partner in his father's firm), Digges, and Henry Laurens, Jr.

To John Adams

22d Novr. 80

DEAR COZEN

I understood from seeing a letter lately from Paris there had appeard at a Dutch Bankers in that City sundry seconds of Bills for acceptance the firsts of which had been paid by regular indorsements to Vieve Babet & Co. Nantes, which seconds of Bills appeard to have been taken among Mr. L[auren]s papers & forwarded to Paris unindorsd for acceptance.¹ This causd some uneasiness at Paris; the Bills were tracd to a Dutch Bankers who had them in remittance from Messrs. Hopes. This transaction appearing rather too mean even for my Countrymen the English, I probd the matter to the bottom, & find it was all done for the best. A particular friend of a person who has frequently been the subject of my late letters, got the bills above alluded to, slipt into His hands during a first & watchd interview, & they were that way forwarded to prevent any unfair Method being usd of obtaining thier value in another way. This affair has been cleard up by the friend of our friend both in Yours & a neighbouring Country.

No news from abroad save a disagreeable account of the dispersion of the expected Jamaica fleet—I fear I shall *be ruind* by it for the produce of my valuable Estate in that Island is on its way uninsurd.

Since the news of Adjut. Genl. Andre's Execution in the Rebel Washingtons Camp nothing has been talkd of here but "making Examples" acts of retaliation &ca. &ca. A person of the name of Trumbull was taken up for high Treason on Sunday night & committed Irond to Prison—A search has been made after a Companion of His a Mr. Tylar who I am told got away some days ago. Many people were also carryd before the Magistrate who accidentally calld to visit either of these Gentlemen on Monday. Many names are talkd of in this last list Mr. De Neufville a Dutch Merchant, Mr. Digs, Mr. Stewart a Limner of Rhode Island, Mr. H. Laurens Jur., & sundry others, but nothing as I can learn was got out of them & it is impossible to say to what lengths they will go against Mr. Trumbull—report says that the affidavits of two Refugee N. England men & his own papers are quite sufficient to hang Him, & hang him they certainly will if they can, for my Countrymen seem to thirst after blood most exceedingly since Andre's execution.

Many others Americans are threatend, but as I know none of them having no connexion with that Country I realy forget their names. I can assure You Sir from present conversations & dispositions for revenge which is dayly expressd, my Country has become exceedingly disagreable to live in, & I heartily wish I could live among people fonder of Philosophy & philanthropy—

adieu
Yrs. Affecy. &ca.

[Addressed:] Myn Heer/De Heer Ferdinand Raymond San/Ten Huyze De Heer Hendrick Schorn/Amsterdam

MHS: Adams Papers, Reel 353.

[1] See Digges to Franklin, Nov 1, 1780.

To John Adams

12th Decr. [1780]

DEAR SIR

All your favours to the 27 ulo. and particularly that with a disagreeable inclosure came safe to hand,[1] & I should be glad to know the parcells I forward get safe. I have attended regularly to Your order, & they go by every post.

I have no news to relate to You. Were I to attempt to describe the present dispositions & folly of us Englishmen it would fill pages. The opinion that America is ours again is now so universally prevalent that a person almost gets insulted who indicates a doubt of it. The malevolent and insulting language now held by a very great majority of this Country towards honest Americans or those who avowedly espouse their Cause is beyond all beleif. Things here are getting fast to an extremity which philanthrophy could wish to avoid: but thus it ever was in similar cases. I had no notion that we Englishmen corrupted as we are, should so soon become a society of Devils—for literally we are little Better—I dayly pray it was in my power to quit it forever. Were it not direful necessity that keeps me here I would very soon quit it for a better clime. Every opinion is that You Hollanders will tuckle to, & do nothing hostile to the interests of this Country, & we look upon Your joining the northern leagued neutrality as nothing materially affecting the Interests of Great Britain. Give me a line as heretofore & intimate what is novel as to Your Provinces acting hostily or otherwise with regard to this Country.

I dont find the friend You lately wrote to me about possess's any other Commission than what was first intimated—some late manoeuveres has for a time shut out communication between us.² All friends are well as the present intemperate season will admit & join me in good wishes to You. Compliments to a late Traveller from hence—tell him some few things left behind in his Lodgings at Norfolk Street have been forwarded on by me.³ I wrote him a line last post, & should be glad to hear from Him.

I am with great Regard
Yours
S: C: W.

[Addressed:] A Monsieur/Monsr. Ferdinand Raymond San/Chez Monsr. Henri Schorn/Amsterdam.

MHS: Adams Papers, Reel 353.

¹ Adams's letters of Nov. 19 and 27, commenting on Benedict Arnold's defection and posing questions about England's attitude toward the Dutch and the League of Armed Neutrality, provide no clue to the enclosure (MHS: Adams Papers, Reel 102).

² On Nov. 19 Adams had asked: "Can you discover, whether Mr. [Laurens] had a Commission as Plenipotentiary or only to negotiate a Loan.—This is a Material Question" (MHS: Adams Papers, Reel 102).

³ Leendert de Neufville, whose association with Trumbull had prompted him to return to Amsterdam.

To John Adams

22d Dr. 80

DEAR SIR

I am thankful for Your favor & its inclosure of the 15th Int.¹ I hope my parcels go regularly for I never omit to put them in the common conveyance. Let me know if the present rupture will make any alteration. When You write Mr. W. S. C. you are requested not to *direct* but only mark the letter thus X on the seal part, & put it under a Cover directed to *Mr. Stockdale² Bookseller Piccadilly London*. The times are going very bad here & we Englishmen seem to feel we can war with all the world—we laugh at & hold You Dutchmen very Cheap— Orders are out for Reprisals & I dare say eer this some Ships are

26 December 1780   341

taken—We talk *big* about seizing immidiately every Dutch ship in our ports taking all Your East & West India Possessions &ca. &ca.

I am winding up matters so as to get into a Country less embroild. You will be timely acquainted with my motions for I intend to take the Tour of the North. I beg my Compliments to my friend Mr. D. N[eufvill]e & am thankfull for his present of news papers & letter. The times & temper of the People at present are against my getting an Answer from a friend whom I have lately wrote much about to the question you last put.

We begin to talk here now that Mr. L. bore a Commission of Plenipotentiary but this I think can be only known by himself. No news but what You will see in the papers.

I am yours &ca. &ca.

[Addressed:] Monsieur/Monsieur Ferdinand Raymond San/Chez Monsr. Hendrik Schorn/Amsterdam

MHS: Adams Papers, Reel 353.

[1] There is no record of a letter from Adams written to Digges on this date. On Dec. 17 he had written one, addressing it to Mr. Timothy D. Ross, but its contents give no clue to an enclosure. He had criticized the British and informed Digges that no books or pamphlets had reached him. (They had been stopped by officers at Margate three or four weeks earlier.) No other letter from Adams to Digges dated in Dec. has been uncovered.
[2] John Stockdale.

To John Adams

⟨Lond.⟩ Decr. 26 1780

DEAR SIR

I have had a sight of yours of the 15th, 17, & 18th Inst. and am thankful for thier inclosures.[1] Whenever any publications worth notice, come to Your hands, send them in like manner & they will find immediate insertion here. The *Courant* being now the most generally read paper for early American intelligence, I constantly give the American papers to the publisher of that paper, and at any time, missing of me, You may have occasion to send any thing worth republication You have only to cut out of the papers the articles & inclose them To *Mr. Cooper No. 134 Drury Lane London.* They will be very thankfully receivd & will be usefull to us folks here.

Before this reaches you, the accounts of our Cabinet proceedings with regard to Hostilities & War with Holland will be publickly known. We Englishmen seem in general to be much Elated at the rupture, & have already taken all the Dutch homeward bound fleets, their spice Islands, St. Eustatia &ca. &ca. &ca. The wise ones about the Ministry say there will be no war & that the Cabinet only act in this bullying manner to make the Mynheers tuckle to & cry piccavi. They boast much of disunion in Holland, that there will be an insurrection of the people, that the other Cities of Holland are divided from Amsterdam, one province from the other &ca. &ca. &ca.—This is the old American tune that they are playing, & will I guess have as little effect upon the Mynheers as upon the Yankees. If an insurrection is effected I guess the purpose will be to make a King of an insignificant Statholder.[2]

We have no news from the Continent of America. A Frigate is arrivd from Barbadoes with a most dismal account of losses sustaind in several of the Islands in the Wt. Indies in a storm which lasted from the 10 to 18th Octor. Barbadoes has sufferd most, 4,000 Inhabitants lost their lives the principal part of Bridge Town destroyd & all the vessels in that Harbour—Antigua sufferd little—St. Kitts considerably in the shipping & Craft as well as Stores near the Water.—Guadaloupe escapd tolerably well. Martinico very much, all the ships being blown out to Sea & several transports with Troops—St. Lucia—Dominica & Grenada (particularly the latter) felt a great share of distress. St. Eustatia sufferd exceedingly. As the dispatches are but just got to London no correct account can be given & you must be referrd to the papers of tomorrow.

I am Yours &ca. &ca. &ca.
W. C[hurch]

MHS: Adams Papers, Reel 353.

¹See Digges to Adams, Dec. 22, 1780, n. 1.
²The British government had declared war on Holland on Dec. 21. Digges is largely confirming Adams's comments of Dec. 17: "The Dutch hate War. They will not be aggressors, but your Ministry have War in their Hearts against Amsterdam, if not the whole Republick. The Ministry laboured to divide the People of Boston from their Leaders, the People of Massachusetts from Boston, and the other Colonies from Massachusetts, until they united all in one independent Sovereignty, which will be an Example in Arms, Arts, Liberty and Glory, for the Admiration and Envy of the rest of mankind. They are now labouring to divide the People of Amsterdam from the Regency, the other Cities of Holland from Amsterdam, and the other six provinces from Holland. That Ministry have no other Maxims of Government than Corruption and Division but they take their measures so awkwardly, every where but in England, that they produce Union. They will do so in this Case, and presently the 7 United Provinces will be as independent as the 13 United States of America" (MHS: Adams Papers, Reel 102).

To Benjamin Franklin

29 Decr. 80

DEAR SIR

I communicated what you desird in a letter of Octor. 18th to the freind who has of late been often the subject of my letters.¹ His reply was abundance of thanks to you, desiring His best wishes & respects &ca. &ca. I have been out of the line of communicating with Him since about the 25th of last month, but I often hear from him by message of a Friend.

His debts are heavy, & from examining His accounts I see no likelyhood of better days to Him than He at present experiences, at least for some time—It would seem to be a punishment to Him for late imprudencies. Another persons affairs are in a better train & likely soon to be adjusted.

I am as much concernd as You can be for the miscarriage of the picture.—Mr. B[owe]ns letters mentiond the tracing of it as far as Lisle. Out of twenty or thirty parcels that I forwarded in like manner, it is a little unlucky that this, which I had more at heart than any other, should have thus miscaryd. The Porcelain is meant for You; & is a proof of the skill of a Young artist here who may soon visit the person whose likeness it is.²

Mr. T[rumbu]ll before His misfortune, finishd an exceeding good picture of W[ashingto]n—full length & very much admird as a good painting. It is now Engraving by a masterly hand & the print will be out in a very few days.³—I am to have a Companion to that picture, full length also, of the hoary headed F[rankli]n; which will also be engravd. I am sure it will be an equal good one to that already done of W——n. I know neither of these illustrious personages, but I am sure I shall be happy in holding in view good likeness's of the two first Men of America.—I think the young Artist will be much helpt in the likeness for the later by the little meddalions, the miniature lately sent a young Lady in a snuf box, by former pictures in possession of Friends, & by the Artists recollection of the hoary head.

I am thankful for Your late attention to the business of a friend. My motive in that as in every prior application was for the publick good & Encouragement of the Arts. I never was or ever will be concernd in any pecuniary manner in these negotiations; unless I ask one for my sole use & purpose. You may rest assurd there has been no foul play, & that every one that I had any knowlege of succeeded properly, *and got safe*—The last but one will be laid aside for very good reasons.⁴

Your order for additional advance of pay to Your Servants have been complyd with & the account will be renderd thereof very soon—a great addition of numbers lately will make it come heavy. My own private account cannot be got at for some days without very great inconvenience, I being generally distant from all papers books &ca. but it shall be very soon forwarded.⁵

We have no news but what the publick news papers will inform You . . Sad devastation & havock in all the Wt. Indies. Things are getting to a crisis here that Philanthrophy would wish to avoid—War, War, is the cry, & no matter whether with all the world or not. We Englishmen seem to have lost all political reason or foresight & are apparently bent upon throwing for the last stake & to compleat the ruin of the Country. Come out of Her my People says a good old book, and tho an Englishman holding considerable property here would to god it were in my power to go forth.⁶—If I can be servicable to You or Yours, You have only to mention it & my Services shall be given.

           I am Yrs. mo. respectfully
           W. R.

HSP: Franklin Papers, 5 : 161.

¹ Franklin's letter has not been found. The two individuals whose difficulties Digges alludes to are probably Henry Laurens and John Trumbull.

² Franklin had inquired at the Bureau des Diligences about the portrait of Shipley, as Digges had suggested on Nov. 13, but had reported on Dec. 5 that he could learn nothing (LC: Franklin Papers, Series 1, 4:318–19). He had, however, received a china portrait of Washington before Oct. 9 (ibid., 282–83).

³ According to an advertisement in the *London Courant*, Dec. 16, 1780, the masterly hand was V. Green, "mezzotinto engraver to his Majesty, and to the Elector Palatine." He had been commissioned by the owner of Trumbull's painting, L. de Neufville.

⁴ On Dec. 5 Franklin had written about a pass he had recently issued: "I have done the Business for your Friend: But having never had the Satisfaction to hear of the arrival of one of these undertakers except Mitchel at Boston who was seized there, I begin to suspect unfair Dealing" (ibid., 319).

⁵ On Dec. 5 Franklin had also written: "The Bill you drew on me for Expenses on the Prisoners is accepted. Having mislaid some of your Letters I find myself at a Loss in some Parts of the Accounts between us; & some of the Things you have sent being for other People, I wish you would be so good as to send me out of you[r] Books, a Compleat Copy of your Account from the beginning, which will much oblige me. To add a Little to the relief of the unfortunate Americans still in Prison, I request you would from the time you receive this, & during the Months of Jany. Feby., March and April, give them double the allowance I formerly directed per Week: but manage it prudently, and order it so far as to do them in your Opinion the most Good." He had then, on Dec. 18, written Hodgson confirming the instructions for increasing the allowances (ibid., 324–25).

⁶ On Nov. 27 Adams had written Digges: "Things are coming to an Extremity, that Philanthropy would wish to avoid: but thus it ever was, in Similar Cases. A free Nation corrupted, becomes a Society of Devils.—Angels fallen, retain nothing but immortal Hate. Come out of her my people! says a good old Book.—" (MHS: Adams Papers, Reel 102).

To John Adams

5 Jany. 1780 [1781]

DEAR SIR

Altho hostilities, & seemingly rigourous ones, have commencd between your Country & mine, I see no reason why our former friendships may not be kept up & you and I communicate by letter as we were used to do. I got your favour of the 18th & hope eer this the two parcells of Books which were then missing have got to hand.¹ There were Receipts taken for them but as I have not been able since the Receipt of Your letter to see the person who dispatches things for me in the Custom House, & get the Receipts or names of the Ships & Captns. who carryd the parcells, I can not yet put you in the right road to find them. They were directed in an over bro[wn] Paper Cover to Messrs. N[eufville] & Son & I dare say were application made for them at the Custom House in Amsterdam they might be found—it frequently happens here that Captains do not properly attend to the delivery of parcells, but lodge them in a common room appropriated for these kind of things in the Custom House, till they are applyd for. I sent a day or two ago another parcell of Books directed as above, to Mr. De N——es friend in the City desiring him to forward them to Amsterdam by the first trader that is permitted to Sail. Hitherto we have stopt all Dutch vessells & 80 or 90 are said to be taken since the Manifesto was published,[2] about 20 of which are already condemnd in the Commons & disposd of—Thus You see our wise Ministry leave no door open to creep out of or put an end to the Hostilities in the case Holland should take fright & concede to the terms which Sr. Joseph[3] askd. For what purpose I know not (without it is the old one of deceiving the People) but the Ministry & their friends give out & assert pretty roundly that these Hostilitys will stop in a few days & that Holland will certainly do what England has demanded of them. As yet Sr. Joseph is not arrivd in Engld. & only one Dutch Ship of War taken. Nothing talkd of but the extreem distress & critical situation of the West Indies, The Accounts are enough to make humanity shudder, but I cannot help looking upon it as in some measure the punishment of divine vengeance for our manyfold Sins & wickedness's. It would seem that the distresses of the principal part of the Islands are so extensively calamitous that the opperations fixd on for next Campaign will be alterd, & most likely shifted to North America, where we cannot even yet give up the idea of subjugation & conquest —We still cry out that America is ours, & that the Dutch war cannot hurt us, not a Guinea more for the carrying on that war being necessary to be raisd—thus we argue & thus we go on to ruin. Eight or ten days ago there was a universal cry for a Dutch war—nothing could be more popular—we are now beginning to slaken very visibly in this opinion, & now many thinking folks say we may take hundreds of their shipping & craft, ruin their trade, take their distant possessions, cut their Dykes &ca. &ca. &ca. but ultimately it must be a mischevious war for England. I dare say in another month it will be thought as ill of as it was at first generally well Receivd. By Genl. Leslie's hasty moving from Virginia all hopes of that Colony *"coming in"* & submitting to English Government, is given over, & we begin to see Lord Cornwallis is not in the good situation & high road to conquests as when His Lordship last wrote Home. Leslie was certainly calld hastily from Virga. to his assistance & aid in consequence of his being "surrounded with Enemys" & his situation renderd dangerous from the defeat of Furgusons party, not one of which, out of a thousand that composd the party, but what were killd or made Prisoners.[4] We must have some accounts from that quarter of America very Soon. Nothing of any note from other quarters. I suppose you now & then mix with the Americans in Amsterdam, pray when you get any news from them give me a line—Mr. De *N——le has got the direction.*[5] Reports of the day are that Gibraltar was lost to England for want of Amunition & Provision the 3 Decr.—some folks have lookd upon it as lost for many months back. I am told there is very little hopes of the two Gentlemen confind for debt getting soon out as their debts are enormously great. Some recent transactions has effectualy cut for a time my communication with one of them.

I am placd very distant from all my papers & books so that I cannot tell how accounts stand between us. In a week or two the particulars shall be transmitted If the communication is not too much cut— When there is a favorable oppertunity a small Bill may be remitted me & which ever way it tells, it shall be accounted for.

      I am with very great Esteem
      Your obligd & ob. Ser.
      W. R.

MHS: Adams Papers, Reel 351, filed under the year 1780.

[1] Digges must be referring to Adams's letter of Dec. 17, 1780 (see Digges to Adams, Dec. 22, 1780, n. 1).

[2] Britain's declaration of war, issued over the king's name on Dec. 20 after four days of discussions with the ministers about its timing, had been accompanied by an order-in-council for reprisals against Dutch ships and cargoes. The pretexts for the war were

that Holland had secretly assisted England's enemies and the rebel colonies, had sought to incite enemies in the East Indies, and had concluded a secret treaty with rebel subjects (the Lee–Van Berckel treaty). The generally understood reason, though, was the Dutch decision to join the League of Armed Neutrality.

[3] Sir Joseph Yorke, British ambassador to The Hague since 1761.

[4] Maj. Gen. Alexander Leslie (ca. 1740–1794) had been sent by Clinton on an expedition into the Chesapeake Bay region to provide a diversion that would support Cornwallis in the Carolinas. But because Maj. Patrick Ferguson's contingent of loyalist rangers had been overwhelmed at Kings Mountain, N.C., in Oct., Cornwallis had required Leslie's assistance further south.

[5] Apparently the old address was no longer safe.

To John Adams

Tuesday night late [9 January 1781]
Londn. Gazette Ex[traordinar]y Jany. 9 1781

This day arrivd Lieut. Waugh of the Invalids, at Lord Hillsboroughs office, with Letters from Leiut. Govr. Irving. of Guernsey, inclosing a letter to Him from Lieut. Govr. Corbet, of the Island of Jersey dated Jersey Jany. 6 1781 of which the following is an Extract.

'I am now to acquaint You, that the French landed this morning about 2 oClk., between two posts, so distant that the Guards did not perceive them. They marchd across the roads, & were in the Market place by six this morning. I was taken prisoner about 7 oCk.; but was fortunately releasd by the very brave & steady behaviour of the Troops & militia; & the Commandant then informd me they had surrenderd prisoners of war: They were all taken killd or wounded. Poor Major Peirson exerting himself at the head of a brave troop of Followers, at the close of the affair was unfortunately killd.[1]

P. S. We have about five hundred Prisoners. Some hundreds are killd, & about one hundred wounded. The rest left their arms, & are fled into the Country, but I hope to have them all tomorrow.

Our loss may be 50 killd, & perhaps half that number wounded. My friend Mulcaster has as usual exerted himself. I am not hurt; but two shots thro my hat. I shall transmit Particulars tomorrow morning to England; but send this if You can.[']

The above is a Copy—We are all got up into the Sky for news also from Chs. Town about the 27th Novr.—the substance of which is that Tarlton on the Tyger River about 30 miles west of Camden came up with & defeated Sumpter a second time[2]—it is said to be a total rout of the Rebel Sumpters Corps which consisted of 1000 Men. Tarltons party are asserted to have been no more than 280 or 290 Horse & foot. Not a word from the head quarters of Cornwallis which we all very much fear has been rather on the retreat from No. towards the Capital of South Carolina.

It is supposd this last account will be publishd in the *or*dinary Gazette of this night, which will not be out in time for posts.

MHS: Adams Papers, Reel 354.

[1] Maj. Francis Peirson (1757?–1781) was killed the moment the surrender began.
[2] Tarleton had defeated the guerrilla forces led by Thomas Sumter (1734–1832) at Fishing Creek, S.C., Aug. 18, 1780, but the outcome at Tiger River was variously reported. Recent biographical accounts of Sumter credit him with having repulsed Tarleton.

To John Adams

Jany. 23–81

I am without any of your favours for some time—not a word of news to write about that concerns your Country—We English yet think that the Mynheers will tuckle to, and we are even so idle as to suppose Russia will be with us—four mails are due from Holland, and *we* are extreemly anxious for the answer to our Memorial—If it is possible to get it before it comes out in the foriegn news papers, pray inclose it to me. I am informd a warrant for apprehending Mr. W[a]rr[e]n is out & report says he is taken up for some improper correspondence with Mr. Ty[le]r their letters being intercepted & producd against W——n.¹

I am yrs. &ca. &ca.
W. S. C.

[Addressed:] A Monsieur/Monsr. Ferdinand Raymond San/Chez Monsr. Henri Schorn/Amsterdam

MHS: Adams Papers, Reel 354.

¹ Winslow Warren was apprehended on a warrant of high treason and, though eventually released, was continually watched and several weeks later, just before he left for Holland, was arrested again, at Margate, where he was detained four days.

To John Adams

Feby. 11. 1781

DEAR SIR

My long silence has not been owing to any want of regard or attention to you, but has been solely occasiond by the imprudence & folly of some Young Men, whose conduct has producd a general hunt after Americans, the stoppage of letters, seizure of baggage &ca. &ca. —and it seems as if it would never have an end. The last who went from here Mr. W[arren] may have explaind in part what has happend. I am sorry to say, entre nous, that the bad Refugee Company that He kept here was in great measure the cause of his trouble & he seemingly got what He deservd. His imprudence & that of Mr. B[rai]ls[for]ds will most likely be the cause of Trumbulls confinement many months longer than it otherways would, & I am very sorry for Him, because He is the only prudent & discreet American I have seen here for a long time back. I wish to God they were all either gone or taken up & that my Countrymen woud not permit their fools to come abroad.

The Bearer will explain his case & situation to You; He seems a clever deserving man & may stand in need of Your advice & recommendation how to act in the business He is upon which is the recovery of some debts due to Him in Holland. Please to mention Him to Mr. Jan Spuyt[1] to whom He may be of service.

He will explain the state of things here better than I can do in the short space I have to write. He is Captain G———r———sh[2] from your neighbourhood in this Kingdom. Please to appologise to Mr. Spuyt for my want of time to write Him. The *times* are too much against us yet to open the contraband commerce which we formerly dealt in successfully, & I do not yet know the charges of sending goods via Ostend.

I have lately forwarded You four or five parcells books by that rout—I send them to Mr. Frs. Bowens Mert. Ostend with an under cover For Messrs. De N[eufvil]le & Son which also covers another direction to Mr. Schorn. I some time ago forwarded a letter from Mr. Jones[3] to Mr. S[ea]rle. Pray enquire of Mr. S———le if He ever got it for having no answer, there is uneasiness about it.

I am yrs. mo. Respectfully
W. S. C.—

I sent yesterday a small parcell pamphlets to Ostend as above.

MHS: Adams Papers, Reel 354.

[1] Unidentified.
[2] Unidentified.
[3] Probably Sir William Jones.

To John Adams

8 Mar. 1781

DEAR SIR

It has been some weeks since I have heard from You & indeed near a month since I wrote myself. You may easily suppose the cause, & that I had nothing material to communicate.[1] In a former letter you mentiond to me your willingness to help Captains M[anle]y or C[on-yngha]m to some pecuniary aid should they need it[2]—The long confinement of these brave & unfortunate men makes every small donation welcome as it adds to their comfort: I have frequently aided them

& if you chuse to oblige them with a trifle only mention the Sum & it shall be done.—I can easily riemburse myself for that sum or any ballance that may be between us by a Bill on Mr. De N[eufvi]l[le], or, what is a better mode, He may give me the name of a House in London on whom I may call for the money on giving them my bill on Him. I am the more anxious for the Comforts of these two & other brave men (now near 600 in Prison) because the subscription money for their releif is on the last legs, nay by this time it must be exhausted. The public papers will give you every tittle of news that I know as I have been for six or 8 days & likely to be for as many more out of Town on some business at a great annual Cloth Fair. We seem all as blind as ever to our Interests, We laugh & ridicule away every peice of News that seems of serious import. We laugh at any mischeif the combind neutral league can do us—We laugh at any person who says Gibraltar is in danger, that Holland will go seriously to war against England, that the Combind fleets are nearly eaqual to ours, that we shall not be victorious in the West Inds. & North America, that Arnold will not conquer Virginia &ca. &ca. In short our folly seems to me more than ever unaccountable, & we are for the present more than commonly bouyd up by the prospects of pacification with Spain & Holland seperately from France & America.—I will write You immidiately on my return to Town which I expect will be in 8 or 9 days & am in the interim very truly

Yrs.

MHS: Adams Papers, Reel 354.

¹Digges had been away from London for several weeks. On Feb. 27 the *London Courant* had recorded his having arrived in Bath six days earlier; later he was reported in Bristol purchasing goods for Lisbon. Apparently Digges was in both places and buying goods not only for Portugal but also for the American army.
²A letter of Oct. [28], 1780 (see Digges to Adams, Nov. 14, 1780, headnote).

To John Adams

Word had reached the British ministers that John Adams's commission to negotiate a peace settlement had been enlarged to include Franklin and three others.

[20 March 1782]

Wanting confirmation in order to be able to discuss a truce, Lord North had, as Digges would explain in detail to Franklin in a letter of March 22, set in motion an inquiry that sent Digges to Amsterdam to find out. Digges had hesitated, but after consulting David Hartley, who was still out of Parliament but in touch with North, had agreed to undertake the mission and carried two letters from Hartley: one, a copy of a letter of February 19 asking Adams about Adams's and Laurens's respective commissions; the other, of March 11, vouching for both the government's sincerity and Digges's authority: "I understand that Mr. Jay Dr. Franklin Mr. Laurens and yourself are impowered by a special commission to treat. I hope the powers of that commission will soon be called forth into action and that success may attend. The public proceedings of parliament & the proposed bill to enable the Crown to conclude peace or truce with America are or will certainly be made known to you. The first object will be to procure a meeting of authorized persons and to consult upon the preliminaries of time place & manner, but the requisites above all others are mutual good dispositions to conciliate & to accommodate, in the confident hope that if the work of peace were once well begun it would soon become general. Permitt me to ask whether the four gentlemen above specified are impowered to conclude as well as to treat and whether jointly so or severally. The bill now depending in Parliament on the part of this Country is to conclude as well as to treat. As to other provisions of it I cannot speak positively but I understand (from the best authority) that the general scope of it is to remove the parliamentary obstructions now subsisting, which would frustrate the settlements which may be made at the termination of the war.—I heartily wish success to the cause of peace. . . .

"P.S. Mr. Digges who will deliver this to you will explain many things of great importance on the Subject of peace. I have been witness of the authority upon which they have been delivered to him. When the first application was made to him he consulted me as knowing that such topics had more than once passed thro my hands. I have recently had many conferences on my own part with the Ministry here relating to the mode of entering into negotiations of peace, & am fully informed of the subject of Mr. Digges's commission to you. You may therefore be assured that it comes to you from the highest authority" *(MHS: Adams Papers, Reel 356).*

Digges had earlier attempted to play a part in furthering diplomatic conversations that might lead to peace negotiations, but the attempt had come to nothing. A torn and largely illegible note that he had written Henry Laurens

[20 MARCH 1782]

on or shortly after January 9, 1782 (date established by C. James Taylor of The Papers of Henry Laurens), indicates that Digges at that time had undertaken to arrange a secret meeting between Laurens and the Swedish envoy to England, Baron Gustav Adam von Nolcken (1733–1812). The meeting had not taken place, though, because Laurens had objected to the proposed secrecy and in addition was ill (USC: Kendall Collection, Reel 31, where Digges's note is mistakenly attributed to James McHenry).

Hotel First Bible [Amsterdam] Wednesy. night 10 oClock
[20 March 1782]

SIR

I am just arrivd here from London, and instead of personally waiting upon You I make so free as to send a messenger with this & its inclosure together with a few late News Papers.

I have a matter of publick moment to mention to You; as well as to speak to a private affair of consequence to myself which will I think lead me in a very few days to Dr. F. at Paris. My present purpose is to beg for half an hours conversation with You. I am at present and shall be for tomorrow, totally unknown in the Hotel, A line directed for me, or any message *to the Gentleman who arrivd this night & lodges in the Room No. 10* will be duly attended to.

I am with Great Respect
Sir Your very Ob. Servt.
T. Digges

[Addressed:] John Adams Esqr.

MHS: Adams Papers, Reel 356.

To Benjamin Franklin

On March 21 Adams had replied to Digges's note of the night before: "Mr. Adams will stay, at home, for the Gentleman in No. 10, whom he will receive at ten OClock, this Day, Sans Ceremonie, provided the Gentleman is content the

Conversation Should pass in presence of Mr. [John] Thaxter [Jr.], Mr. Adams's Secretary.

"But Such is the Situation of Things here and elsewhere, that it is impossible for Mr. A. to have any Conversation with any Gentleman from England, without Witness. And indeed, Mr. Adams's Advice to the Gentleman is, to proceed forthwith to Paris, and communicate, whatever he has to Say to Dr. Franklin and [Charles Gravier] the Comte de Vergennes [(1718–1787)] in the first Place, without Seeing Mr. A. who will certainly think himself bound to communicate, whatever may be made known to him, without Loss of Time to those Ministers, as he has no Authority to treat, much less to conclude, but in Concert with them and others" (MHS: Adams Papers, Reel 356).

Rejecting Adams's advice, Digges had met with Adams on both March 21 and 22 and then written to Franklin, enclosing a letter to Franklin from Hartley of March 11 similar to the one that Hartley had written to Adams in Digges's behalf: "Mr. Digges who will deliver this to you informs me that having been applied to for the purpose of communicating with Mr. Adams on the subject of his commission for treating of peace, he is now setting out for Amsterdam, and that he intends afterwards to go to Paris to wait upon you. I understand the occasion to have arisen, by some mention having been made in parliament by General Conway of persons not far off having authority to treat of peace, which was supposed to allude to Mr. Adams, and some friends of his in London. Ministry were therefore induced to make some enquiries themselves. This is what I am informed of the matter. When the proposal was made to Mr. Digges he consulted me, I believe from motives of caution that he might know what ground he had to stand upon, but not in the least apprized that I had been in any degree in course of corresponding with you on the subject of negociation. As I had informed the ministry from you that other persons besides yourself were invested with powers of treating, I have nothing to say against their consulting the several respective parties. That is their own concern. I shall at all times content myself with observing the duties of my own conduct, attending to all circumstances with circumspection, and then leaving the conduct of others to their own reasons. I presume that ministry have only done what others would have done in their situation, to procure the most ample information that the case will admit. I rest content to act in my own sphere, and if my exertions can be applied to any public good, I shall always be ready to take my part with sincerity and zeal" (WTF, Memoirs, 2:286). Digges had not, though, dis-

patched his letter and its enclosure on March 22, but as the correspondence with Franklin and Adams makes clear, hesitated for four days before resolving to send them.

Doubtless one reason for Digges's hesitation arose from his knowing that Franklin had come to doubt his honesty. In January 1780 Digges had sought Franklin's help in enabling a friend, Captain Walter Belt of Maryland, along with some others, among them some Boston captains, to ship by the Brighton *more than £10,000 worth of "necessary and useful articles" to some part of the United States not in possession of British troops (see Digges to Franklin, Jan. 28, Feb. 4 and 10, and Mar. 3, 1780). The help sought, a pass that would protect the* Brighton *from American privateers, had been promptly given; on February 11 Belt had signed a bond in the amount of £3,000 for the performance of the agreement (see Digges to Franklin, Jan. 28, 1780, n. 3); and, with this special protection in Belt's possession, the* Brighton *had sailed soon after in an English convoy headed for New York City and its loyal merchants, carrying as part of its cargo eleven or twelve hundred guineas' worth of articles for the American army that Samuel Hartley had quietly consigned with a promise of sharing the profits with Digges for his aid in circumventing the intent of the pass, which Franklin had meant to benefit only Americans. The understanding had been that Belt would at an opportune moment slip away from the convoy and run into the Delaware or the Chesapeake to deliver the goods to Ridley & Pringle of Baltimore or Conyngham & Nesbitt of Philadelphia. Actually, pressed by the Boston captains, Belt had instead put into Boston, where the entire cargo, including goods shipped by unsuspecting English merchants, had been sold at a great profit to Hartley, Belt, and others aboard. Hartley had then denied Digges his promised share, even suing Digges for seventy or eighty pounds that Digges had once borrowed from him (see Digges to Philip Barton Key, May 28, 1808). Yet Digges's complicity in the scheme to have Belt slip away from the convoy, once become public, had been sufficient for William Hodgson, apparently ignorant of Samuel Hartley's involvement, to tell Franklin on March 20, 1781, that Digges was guilty of having contributed to a notorious breach of faith (APS: Franklin Papers, 21: 117): English merchants had sent cargoes insured by English insurers in an English convoy, they had been betrayed, and Belt and Digges had known in advance.*

Franklin had issued the pass to Belt as a way of getting needed supplies to

America and so could not have condemned the barratry. But the profiteering was another matter, and even worse had been Hodgson's conviction, stated in the same letter, that Digges had proved himself an embezzler of the money Franklin had designated for the prisoners. Instead of distributing the allowances that in January 1781 Franklin had authorized be doubled (see Digges to Franklin, Dec. 29, 1780, n. 5), Digges had, according to Hodgson's information, advanced not a single shilling and indeed had gone off to Bristol to purchase goods for Lisbon, his suspected destination. Franklin's response had been, on April 1: "If such a Fellow is not damn'd, it is not worth while to keep a Devil" (LC: Franklin Papers, Series 2, 19:717). Given wide currency, that statement had gravely injured Digges's reputation in both American and British diplomatic circles. It had, moreover, appeared to be substantiated by subsequent events. For on May 8 Hodgson had reported to Franklin that Digges, owing considerable debts in London, had been arrested in Bath (APS: Franklin Papers, 22:12); Digges had written Hodgson that he would go to Passy to justify himself (Hodgson to Franklin, June 29, 1781 [APS: Franklin Papers, 22:61]) but had never gone; and further allegations of Digges's chicanery had circulated (Hodgson to Franklin, July 20, 1781 [APS: Franklin Papers, 20:86]; Gustavus Conyngham to Franklin, June 21, 1781 [ibid., 22:53]; [⟨Ward Nicholas⟩] Boylston to John Adams, Aug. 31, 1781 [MHS: Adams Papers, Reel 355]; Mark Pringle to Matthew Ridley, Dec. 15, 1781 [MHS: Ridley Papers, Norton Gift, 8]). In addition, throughout those critical months Digges had seemed elusive. He had been observed in Bath. He had been in Bristol buying articles for the American army. Had he been seeking to escape creditors? He had returned to London by February 12, 1782, when he had dined with Ann Ridley's cousin John Hunt (Hunt to Matthew Ridley, Feb. 12, 1782 [MHS: Ridley Papers, Nichols Gift, 9]), and, it is clear, soon thereafter he had conferred with David Hartley. Although Hartley seems to have trusted Digges, no evidence has been found to indicate that Franklin's judgment had been modified. Digges's position was now, at the least, a delicate one.

Amsterdam, March 22, 1782

SIR,

I left England a few days back, and until my conversation and some consultations with Mr. Adams on a matter which will be mentioned to you by him, and more particularly explained in this letter, my determination was to have seen you, as well on that business as on a matter of much consequence to my private reputation.[1] I feel the disadvantages under which I labour when writing to you on a matter which cannot be explained or cleared up but by personal conversation. I do not give up my intended purpose of personally speaking to you, but it being found better and more convenient to my purpose to return immediately hence to England, and from thence to Paris, in preference of going first to Paris, it must be unavoidably delayed for some days.

It would take up more than the length of a letter to explain the whole opening and progression of a matter I am here upon, which was and is meant to be jointly communicated to you with Mr. Adams; I will therefore take the liberty to give you an abbreviation of it in as few words as I can.

About a fortnight ago a direct requisition from ministry, through Lord Beauchamp,[2] was made to Mr. R. Penn to know if he could ascertain *that any person or persons in Europe were commissioned by Congress to treat for peace, whether they were* NOW *willing to avail themselves of such commission, and of the present sincere disposition in ministry to treat, and whether they would receive an appointed commissioner to speak for a truce, and mention a place for the meeting, &c.*

Mr. Penn's referring Lord Beauchamp to me, as knowing the nature of Mr. Adams's former commission, was the sole cause of my being privy to or a party in the matter. I had various meetings with Lord Beauchamp in Company with Mr. Penn on the subject; the particular memorandums of which, and Lord B.'s statement of what the ministry wanted to obtain, together with every other circumstance relative to the matter, I regularly consulted Mr. Laurens and Mr. D. Hartley upon; and the result was my taking the journey hither, and to Paris in order to put the questions (as they are before stated from Lord B. to Mr. Penn) and to bring an answer thereto. I am well convinced by Lord Beauchamp's pledge of his personal honour, as well as from Mr. Hartley's telling me he knew the matter to come directly from Lord North (for he visited him more than once to ascertain the fact) that it is a serious and sincere requisition from ministry, and that they will immediately take some steps to open a treaty provided I go back with assurances that there is a power vested in Americans in Europe to treat and conclude, and that they are willing to avail themselves of such power when properly applied to.

I have stated the whole transaction to Mr. Adams, read every memorandum I had made, informed him of every circumstance I knew, and when I put the questions (as they are before stated from Lord B. to Mr. Penn) he replied, "that there were certainly commissioners in Europe, of which body he was one, who had powers to treat and conclude upon peace; that he believed them willing to enter into such a treaty, provided a proper offer was made; but that no questions now or to be made in future could be answered by him without previously consulting his colleagues, and afterwards acquainting the ministers of the belligerent powers thereof." Mr. Adams recommended that any future questions might be made directly to you, for that the present, as well as any subsequent propositions would be immediately communicated to you and Mons. de Vergennes.[3]

His answers to my questions were nearly what I foretold and expected, and is substantially what Lord Beauchamp seemed so anxious to procure. When I relate this answer to his Lordship my business will be finished in that quarter. I will here explain to you my only motive for being a messenger from him whom I had never known or been in company with before. It will enable me to say, I have done one favour for you, and I claim of you another, viz. to obtain a restoration of my papers from Lord Hillsborough's office, which were in a most illegal and unjustifiable manner seized from me near a twelvemonth ago, and are yet withheld notwithstanding the personal applications for them from Lord Coventry, Lord Nugent, and Mr. Jackson,[4] each of whom have explained the injury and very extraordinary mischief the want of my papers for so long a time has and is now doing me.

On my first conversation with Mr. Adams I had concluded to go to you, partly by his advice to do so; but as the expence of two journies where one may serve is of some import to me, and from supposing your answer would be substantially the same as that from Mr. Adams, I have thought it better to go back immediately to London, and then set out for Paris with the probability of being able to bear my papers.

I will take the liberty to trouble you with another letter if any

thing occurs on my arrival in London. I am to leave this with Mr. Adams for forwardance; and for the present I have only to beg a line acknowledging the receipt of it. If your letter is put under *a cover to Mr. Stockdale, Bookseller, Piccadilly, London*, it will the more readily get to hand. I am, with great respect, Sir, your very obedient servant,
        T. Digges

                Ostend, 26th March.

 On my last visit to Mr. Adams, Friday evening, to explain to him the substance of the foregoing letter, and ask his forwardance of it to you, we had some farther conversation on the matter, the ultimate conclusion of which was, that it was thought better I did not send the annexed letter to you, or mention my business with him until my going in person from England. Mr. Adams's reasons were these. That if I made the communication *then* he should be necessitated to state the matter in a long letter to you and others of his colleagues; that the matter as it then stood was not of such importance but he could save himself the trouble of the explanation; and that as he recommended any future questions or applications to be made directly to you, your situation making it more convenient sooner to inform the French court thereof, he thought my letter had better be postponed, and the substance of it given in person as soon as I could possibly get from London to Paris.[5] I acquiesced, though reluctantly, and having thought much on the matter on my journey hither, I have at length determined to forward the foregoing letter with this postscript, and at the same time to inform Mr. Adams of my exact feelings on the matter, viz. that my wishes and intentions when I left England were to see, and make known the matter to you; that through Mr. Hartley or some other channel you must hear that I had been at Amsterdam, and my seemingly turning my back upon you might be thought oddly of; and finally that I could not answer for carrying the inclosure from Mr. Hartley back to England, not knowing the consequence it might be of. I hope and think I have done right in this matter. The purpose of my moving in the business I went to Mr. A. upon, has, I own, been with a double view of serving myself in a matter of much consequence to me, for after delivering the explanations I carry, I can with some degree of right and a very great probability of success, claim as a gratuity for the trouble and expence I have been at, the restoration of my papers; the situation of which I have already explained to Lord Beauchamp, in order to get him to be a mover for them, and I have very little doubt that a few days will restore them to me, and give me an opportunity to speedily speak to you on a matter which gives me much uneasiness, vexation, and pain. Excuse the hurry in which I write, for I am very near the period of embarkation. Paul Wentworth embarked this day for England,⁶ I trod on his heels chief of the way from the Hague which he left suddenly. General Faucit is on his road hence to Hanover.

WTF, *Memoirs*, 2 : 290–93.

¹ What Digges intended to say can be only conjectured on the basis of a letter John Hunt had written Matthew Ridley, July 22, 1781. Referring to Digges as "a worthy Charactor," Hunt had given Digges's explanation of what had occurred: during John Trumbull's trial Digges's aliases had been revealed and his exculpatory letters to Franklin had been intercepted; four prisoners who had escaped from Forton to go to France and carried proofs of Digges's payments had been recaptured and the documents lost; Digges had paid the prisoners "but not by the common agents employed for that purpose," leaving Wren, Heath, and Franklin alike in ignorance of the transactions; and Digges had procured triplicate vouchers that he could show Franklin to put all doubts to rest (MHS: Ridley Papers, Nichols Gift, 7). But Digges never did make the journey to clear himself with Franklin.

² Francis Seymour Conway, Viscount Beauchamp (1743–1822), was a recent lord of the treasury, at present cofferer of the household, and a consistent supporter of North's policies.

³ Adams's own summary of his response is in a letter he wrote Franklin from The Hague on Mar. 26 relating the substance of the conversation with Digges: "I answered, that I came to Europe last with full Powers to make Peace: that those Powers had been announced to the Public upon my Arrival, and continued in force until last Summer, when Congress sent a new Commission, containing the same Powers to five Persons whom I named: that if the King of England were my Father, and I the Heir apparent to his Throne, I would not advise him ever to think of a Truce, because it would be but a real War under a simulated Appearance of Tranquility, and would end in another open and Bloody War, without doing any real Good to any of the Parties.

"He said that the Ministry would send some Person of Consequence over, perhaps General Conway, but they were apprehensive that he would be ill treated or exposed. I said that if they resolved upon such a Measure, I had rather they would send immediately to Dr. Franklin, because of his Situation near the French Court but there was no doubt, if they sent any respectable Personage properly authorized, who should come to treat honorably, he would be treated with great Respect: but that if he came to me, I would give him no Opinion upon any thing without consulting my Colleagues, and should reserve a Right of communicating every thing to my Colleagues, and to our Allies" (MHS: Adams Papers, Reel 102).

⁴They represent a variety of political views. George William Coventry (1722–1809) had supported the Grenville Whigs in opposition to the North ministry, spoken against declaring war on the Dutch, and come to conclusions that would lead him to support Burke's reform bill of July 3, 1782, and Shelburne's peace terms in 1783. Robert Nugent (1702?–1788), vice-treasurer of Ireland, had been a consistent supporter of North and of maintaining the influence of the crown, but on Dec. 14, after hearing about Cornwallis's capitulation to Washington at Yorktown, had been persuaded that American independence must follow, even while he continued to vote for the ministry's motions to carry on the war. George Jackson was secretary to the admiralty board under Lord Sandwich (see Digges to Franklin, Sept. 8, 1780, n. 1). Why Digges's papers had been seized so long after Trumbull's arrest remains obscure.

⁵Whatever Adams may have said to Digges about sparing himself the trouble of lengthy explanations to his colleagues, his letter to Franklin on Mar. 26, cited above in n. 3, must have been written in ignorance of the fact that Digges was writing to both him and Franklin the very same day from Ostend.

⁶Paul Wentworth (d. 1793), an American loyalist in England who had become one of the most effective of Eden's spies. It was he who had recruited and directed Dr. Edward Bancroft.

To John Adams

[⟨Ostend⟩, 26 March 1782]

DEAR SIR

I got here this day & am nearly about the hour to Embark. I find I passd Mr. Laurens Jnr. at Rotterdam as some questions were askd in the Hotel where I put up for a person answering my description from one who was at another Hotel who did not leave His name but answerd the description of Mr. Laurens.

I stopt at the Hotel Angleterre at the Hague & found that P. Wentworth had gone from thence for England rather suddenly the day before; He went from Antwerp for Brussells, & by the time Genl. Faucit went from hence, for Brussels also, I do suppose these Heroes in different line of action & for as little purpose (I hope) met at Brussels: Faucit is going to Hannover (as was said here) and P. W. embarkd in a purposely hird boat about 2 hours ago for England.

In the matter I lately visited You upon I have informd You of every step taken as well as my motives for acting, & shall keep nothing from You relative thereto.

Since our last conversation I have thought much on the subject of witholding from Dr. F. a letter I bore to Him from Mr. Hartley (which I know is partly on a publick matter in agitation between them) as well as informing the Doctr. that I had been in Holland; and upon much consideration I think I cannot acting fairly to Dr. F. either carry back Mr. Hartleys letter, or explain to Him my motives for being silent when I had got so much nearer Him & had matter of much private consequence to myself to explain & clear up, with [sic] by letter or personal appearance. Besides others, I have two motives for writing; the first is that of forwarding a letter which I know contains matters of business between Dr. F. & David Hartley & which would be rather unjustifiable in me to carry back to England, and the other is an explanation *why* I do not repair to Him while now abroad on the matter relative to myself. I cannot see another road for doing either without intimating to Him the Business I went on to You: I have mentiond my first intention to visit & explain it to you & the motives I had for altering that intention & going back as quick as possible to Engld. & then set out for Paris.—That You did not think the matter in the stage it then was of so much moment as to think it necessary to make it known to Your Colleagues, that my doing it soon & in person to Dr. F. would be the best mode; That all future movements must be made known to Dr. F. & Mr. Vergennes, and that You urgd strongly to have any future movements in the business made directly to Dr. F. whose residence made it more convenient to give the Communications to the French Minister. I am sorry in doing this that I have deviated from a purpose which I had rather fixd with You; but on much thinking I really think I have done the best; for Dr. F. would certainly here [hear] I was at Amsterdam and think rather odly of me that I had turnd my back upon Him & seemingly gone from a purpose of explaining a matter to Him which my reputation is at stake for.

I beg a thousand pardons for writing thus hastily & Desultorily to You. The Packet Boat is so near sailing I have not time to read over the letter & I am rather in the midst of hurry & noise. I will write You immediately on my arrival & if any thing occurs which You want done

[26 March 1782]

or to say to me a line under cover to Mr. Stockdale Bookseller Piccadilly London will get safe to

Sir Your very Obedient Hume. Servant
T. Digges

MHS: Adams Papers, Reel 356. Adams's endorsement indicates that he supposed Digges to be writing from Helvoet. But Digges's letter to Franklin, March 22 (with a postscript of March 26), a second one to Adams, March 26, and another to Adams, April 2, establish the place as Ostend.

To John Adams

Ostend 26 Mar. 1782

DEAR SIR

Since my letter to You of this date, I have accidently met here Mr. Jacob Sarley the Gentleman I mentiond to You at Amsterdam I Expected to meet there. He is from the State of N. York & fixd in Partnership in a very considerable House in Leeds. From some years acquaintance I have found Him a good & true American 'tho for the present a Resident in England. He wishes to pay You His respects while on His tour of Business and I beg leave to introduce Him to Your usual civility & attention.

I am with great respect
Sir Your very Obt. Servant
T. Digges

MHS: Adams Papers, Reel 356.

To David Hartley

Fryday noon [March 29, 1782]

I want to see You very much on a matter of consequence—I will dine at the Cannon Coffee House at four oClk. & should be glad You

[30 March 1782]

would take a Chop with me—If I should be gone from thence I will leave word where I am or be again there at 9 oClk. in the Evening.

I am truly Yours
T. Digges

[Addressed:] David Hartley Esq.

BRO: Hartley-Russell Papers, D/EHy F-90. Hartley's endorsement gives the date as March 31, but that was a Sunday. Perhaps, contrary to custom, Hartley was noting the date of receipt.

Memorandum for Lord Shelburne

A series of military defeats had followed Yorktown and led to the resignation of the North ministry on March 20, the day Digges had arrived in Amsterdam. The king had quickly turned to Shelburne to persuade him to occupy a central position in a coalition cabinet. Rockingham became first lord of the treasury and titular prime minister, but Shelburne, who had supported the concept of a vigorous monarch and still fancied that a peace could be agreed to without granting the Americans independence, became secretary of state for home, colonial, and Irish affairs, which gave him prime responsibility for devising a preliminary peace. It was, accordingly, to him that Digges reported about his mission to Adams.

[March 30, 1782]

Mr. Adams, Dr. Franklin, Mr. Jay, Mr. Laurens & Mr. Jefferson are The Commissioners in Europe to Treat for Peace.

Their Powers are to treat & *conclude* with the Ambassadors, Plenipotentiarys or Commissioners of the States with whom it may concern. Each of them are vested with equal powers relative to the Establishment of Peace and a majority of them, or any *one*, (the others not being able to attend) can treat & conclude.

Mr. Adams cannot speak to any proposition of a direct tendency to Truce or Peace from England without consulting His Colleagues, &

from them it must be expected to go to The French Minister; The other Belligerent powers having as yet no right to expect information about any propositions for Peace.

There may however questions be askd Mr. Adams & His Colleagues that they may not think essentially necessary to communicate to The French Court, and any proper messenger sent to ask such questions will be answerd with confidential Secrecy.[1]

Mr. Digges read over Mr. Adams's Commission; It is dated the 15th June 1781, and His Powers (which are exactly the same as the other four) are as full as possible, and go to *conclude* as well as treat for Peace.

Mr. Adams's first Commission appointed Him to the Court of Great Britain; & this was in force until about the beginning of Sep. 1781 when the above Commission conjointly with the other four was receivd in Europe; And it was so alterd by Congress for no other reason than some ill treatment of the Americans by the British Army in South Carolina and from the unfavorable treatment shewn Mr. Laurens in the Tower.

Mr. Digges has Mr. Adams's assurance that any questions put to Him as to further consulting upon the mode of opening a parley or entering into a treaty shall be confidentially & secretly answerd. And altho His, Mr. A.'s name, stands first in the Commission any direct propositions made to Dr. Franklin will be equally attended to.

Mr. Digges leaves these memorandums with Lord Shelburne for the purpose of His Lordships communicating them to any others of the present Administration whom Mr. D. has not the honor to know.

UM: Shelburne Papers, 72:17. Manuscript copies made by others exist in the Shelburne Papers (UM) and the Franklin Papers (LC), and a transcript in George III's hand is the basis for the text in *The Correspondence of King George the Third*, ed. the Hon. Sir John Fortescue, 6 vols. (London: Macmillan, 1927–28), 5:431–33.

[1] If this memorandum for Shelburne is one of those that Digges had told Franklin (letter of Mar. 22) he had read back to Adams during their interview, then this item requires explanation. It generalizes on Digges's understanding that Adams had not wanted to write his colleagues lengthy explanations about Digges's visit; it misrepresents Adams's long-standing aversion to all negotiations that would separate the Amer-

icans from their allies (see Digges to Adams, May 2, 1780, n. 2); and it was promptly denied by Adams, who had supposedly listened to Digges read the words to him. In fact, when Henry Laurens was paroled in mid-April to confer with Adams at Haarlem, carrying with him a copy of Digges's memorandum that Shelburne had given him, Adams denied more than this item. Of the third and sixth articles, as Laurens called them (apparently the fourth and seventh paragraphs), he told Laurens: "I said no such thing to Mr. Digges," and he added: "Part of the 5*th* is a misrepresentation or not fully represented, I said if the Ministers of Great Britain by whom you say you are sent mean any thing honorable let them release Mr. Laurens & communicate to him what they have to propose & he will join his Colleagues. In short I paid very little attention to Mr. Digges or to any thing he said. I have since he was in Holland received two letters from him but have thought it proper to return no answer" (NYPL: Miscellaneous Papers, Laurens Memorandum, Apr. 14, 1782). Possibly his decision to pay little attention to what Digges said accounts for the misunderstanding.

To John Adams

London Ap. 2. 1782

DEAR SIR

I wrote You from Ostend the 27th Ulo.[1] and stated what I had done with Dr. F. I arrivd here the last mail day but too late to look about me & to write so fully as I could have wishd. I found the intire kick up of the great ones to make much noise & to give universal pleasure. As the Parliament is not sitting no fixd measure of the new people is yet talkd of & the reports are various & vague. Mr. L. being out of town & still in the West of England I had not the oppertunity of making my *first* communications with Him or of mentioning anything from You.[2] As Genl. C[o]n[wa]y was privy to & at the bottom of my message to You, I was not many hours in Town before I communicated to Him the sum & substance of what I brought. From him I went to the man whose province it now is to act in any negotiations with America (Lord Shelburne). I am intimate with Him & he was pleasd with the Communication & matter of my Errand in every instance but that of the necessity of communicating any serious or direct profer going from hence, to the French Ministry.[3] I have had much conversation with Him & others of the new ministers on the matter; They all talk of Peace with America if it can be got by great &

direct offers, but what this great offer is I cannot learn for they rather draw back when a question is put is this the offer of Independence. Notwithstanding such shyness their insinuations go to that point; but I should be glad to be ascertaind of the real fact. I found all ranks of people delighted with the change of men. All & every visage speaks a general joy from the prospect of getting better times & Peace with America; but a quiet thinking American even in the midst of this clamor is apt to reason with himself & things, & to say to what point of good will all those changes tend? will my Country or those European friends who have helpt her be benifited by the new system and set of men; certainly no; without that new set of men go heartily to the work of Peace. Every declaration among the great & leading men is for Peace, but I suspend my opinion until I see some actual measures adopted for the attaining that desirable object—a Peace with America seperately from France seems universally scouted; & within a few days an opinion seems to go generally abroad that the Present Ministers are likely to detatch Holland from its present connections with the house of Bourbon—This I look upon as only a manoeuvre to help the Stocks; yet it is confidently said that the Marquis of Carmarthen will be sent forthwith to Holland, and that a Messenger is already gone to the two Imperial Courts to desire them to again open their intercessions for Peace.[4] There are vast exertions making in the Navy & no increase of Army—The new men have the wishes of the people very much with them & there is an appearance of unanimity which during my 8 or 9 years residence here I have never seen before. Lord Sh[el-bur]ne is the only new minister suspected of not wishing to go to the length of declaring American Independence; but I think his good sense & excellent information of things in America must make him think the measure a necessary one whatever He may hold out as his "intention".—He may be said to be prime minister for the *great work* is in his department, he having all the Southern district of Europe, the whole of home & Irish matters, the East & West Indies, & every thing relative to America. There seems a little disunion between him & the premier Lord R[ockingha]m, but I can not tell where the disunion lays. If the whole of them do not pull together it will not be long a popular ministry. My Communication & interest with Lord Sh——ne has procurd me a promise of a Chart blanche to look for any of my papers that may be transfered from Lord Hillsboroughs office to His, but this cannot be done till some consequent arrangements take place & indeed I am rather chagrind & [at] His telling me that it never happens that the whole of papers are turnd over from one to the other office when a minister retires for the Custom is to make a sweep of office as they term it & to destroy every paper that the retiring minister does not chuse to take away with Him. I fear in this way Mr. L——ns is likely to loose His or a chief part of them. Mr. Galloway had the Examination of them & not longer ago than 6 months, a considerable part of them & extracts of them were arrangd for publication for the *virtuous* & *honest* purpose to gull John Bull into a beleif that there yet remaind a chance from the vast numbers of friends to Government in America, their distress[']s, want of resources &ca. &ca. [which] gave every hope of success to his Majestys arms from another vigorous Campaign!!! Strange as this may appear, I had it from such authority as I cannot doubt. When Lord G. Germain walkd out of Office he took the most of Mr. L——ns's papers with Him.

I have been very busy for a day or two in the business of Capt. Luke Ryan and Captain MaCator both condemnd & likely to suffer[5]—There were some prisoners brought up from Mill Prison by Habeas Corpus as Evidence to prove American property & Commission in the last mentiond Ship, McCators, and I have obtaind from the new Admiralty a promise that these witness's shall not be remanded to prison but left on Parole. There is a young man soon going to his home by way of Amsterm. in one or some American vessel that may be going from thence provided He can obtain a passage, He has been a hostage & now set at large so that likely in a day or two I may give You a line by Him.

I am with very great respect Sir
Yr. obligd & ob. Servant
T. D.

[Addressed:] J. Adams Esqe.

MHS: Adams Papers, Reel 356.

¹ April 26, in fact.

² Laurens, suffering from severe gout, had been released on bond on Dec. 31, 1781, ostensibly to await trial but actually, as it turned out, to await his exchange for Cornwallis. He had promptly gone to Bath for his health, and although he had apparently then returned to London and in early March visited prisoners in Forton and Mill, he was possibly now once more in Bath. What Digges had in mind to mention to him is indicated in the letter Adams had written Franklin on Mar. 26 about the interview with Digges: "I desired him and he promised me not to mention Mr. Laurens to the Ministry, without his Consent, and without informing him that it was impossible he should say any thing in the Business, because he knew nothing of our Instructions; because altho' it was possible that his being in such a Commission might induce them to release him, yet it was also possible it might render them more difficult concerning his Exchange" (MHS: Adams Papers, Reel 102).

³ Digges is doubtless reporting Shelburne's reaction to the third paragraph of his memorandum of Mar. 30. But Shelburne was also interested in the statements that Adams was to call misrepresentations, for on Apr. 5 he reported to the king that on the preceding day he had talked at length with Laurens and found him "averse to France" and "ready to go to Mr. Adams, to ask those questions, which Mr. Digges says Mr. Adams is ready to answer confidentially without communicating with France" (*The Correspondence of King George the Third*, 5:442–43). The result was that Laurens was given leave to confer with Adams, showed him a copy of the Digges memorandum, and learned that Adams had been misrepresented (see Digges's Memorandum for Shelburne, Mar. 30, 1782, n. 1).

⁴ Despite doubts he may have been forming about Digges, Adams found it worth writing the French ambassador at The Hague, the duc de La Vauguyon, on Apr. 10 that he had received a letter from Digges "informing me that he had communicated what had passed between him and me to the Earl of Shelburne, who did not like the Circumstance that every thing must be communicated to our Allies. He says that Lord Carmaerthen is to be sent to the Hague to negotiate a separate Peace with Holland. But according to all appearances Holland as well as America will have too much Wit to enter into separate Negotiations" (MHS: Adams Papers, Reel 106). Carmarthen was Francis Godolphin Osborne (1751–1799).

⁵ Luke Ryan (1750?–1789) and Edward Macatter were daring Irish smugglers who had been among those commissioned by Franklin to command French-owned privateers in European waters. Their motives for becoming "American" captains had been profit and security: having captured one of His Majesty's revenue cutters in 1779, they could be convicted of piracy and condemned to be hanged, but if regarded as Americans, they could become simply prisoners of war. Franklin's motive in supporting their activities had been to enlarge the number of British prisoners who could be exchanged for Americans. When the arrangement had not produced the numbers Franklin had hoped for and jurisdiction over prizes brought into French ports had become tediously complicated, Franklin had discontinued the enterprise. But the smugglers, disregarding the personal risks of conducting their plunders under the French flag, had then accepted French commissions. In Apr. 1781 Ryan had been captured; in Oct., Macatter. Both had been tried before the High Court of Admiralty in the Old Bailey on Mar. 30, 1782, convicted of felony and piracy on the high seas, and sentenced to the gallows.

But, largely because of the change in the ministry after North's fall, the execution of the sentence had been delayed. Digges's involvement related in part to the predicament of two Americans called to give evidence at the trial, John Smith and Charles Collins, who had been brought to London from Mill Prison for that purpose and then sought to extend their stay in London but discovered that no legal security could be provided within the admiralty for their subsequent appearance, thus leaving them with only the prospect of a return to prison. Digges then stepped in and somehow himself gave security with a show of authority that was sufficient to secure their release in his custody.

To John Adams

London Ap. 9 1782

DEAR SIR

I have not yet been able to see Mr. L., he having left Town just before my return to it & not having got back till yesterday. Without my urging to Lord S[helbur]ne the propriety of immediately speaking to Mr. L. on the matter of my message to You & for releasing him from every tye here, I found His Lordship had concluded to make his approaches to that quarter, for most assuredly it is the right one, & I beleive He was purposely calld to Town about it.[1]—If they mean any thing sincere & direct that is the road & I hope they are about it. I could wish however I had it more in my power than I now have to say I had clearly discoverd the intentions of the new set, at least those I have conversd with viz. Lord S———ne, Lord C[am]d[e]n, Genl. Conway & Lord K[eppel] to be that of going to Peace with America on the avowd basis of Independence.[2] Every voice pronounces it to be their intention, but I like a little more open declaration for so doing. Time will shew what is meant, but I own appearances at present do not please me.

There is a universal conversation & opinion got forth for a seperate peace with Holland built intirely upon the re-opening the Empress[3] the mediation for Peace; & the new Ministers have got credit with the publick for the active manner they went to work to renew it. The whole of the Cabinet seem to be well likd by the People & much praises are forth for their vigorous exertions in the naval line in particular. America seems to be forgot, for one never hears now about Her, save when some blunderhead holds forth for *seperate* Peace with America & Holland and a hearty drubbing to the French.—John Bull will keep up this sort of language as long I beleive as He can roar out any thing.

I have had every indulgence shewn me towards the recovery of my papers; but altho I have a Chart Blanch to search in the office things are not yet so en train in the new offices as to have things in proper order for looking over.—Notwithstanding the savage practice of every Minister when he goes out of office making a sweep & taking all papers he likes with Him, I have yet the hopes of soon getting the material part of mine;[4] & if ever after that I am a supplicant for any favour in England I hope I shall be foild. I have been more than commonly lucky with the Admiralty Department for I have with very little or no trouble got the prisoners who were brought from Mill Prison by Habeas Corpus as evidences in the case of Luke Rian & Captain McCator releasd from going back to Confinement, & got passes for the two who were tryed for their Lives & acquitted.[5] These together with 7 or 8 arrivd to day from the West will shortly move over, & one of them will see You.

If there are any papers in the Request or Memorial way[6] come forth since I got the last, please to send them by a Young Man I recommended to You from Ostend[7]—They are all translating & will be put into the Remembrancer with any preface or other additions You may think fit. Any thing for news paper publication will be immidiately attended to if sent according to the direction left. I am with great respect

Yrs.
J. W.

MHS: Adams Papers, Reel 356.

[1] Laurens had arrived in Plymouth on Mar. 30 to visit the American prisoners but had been there only a day when he had received an express from London that had led to his immediate return.

[2] In the new government these critics of North had, along with Shelburne, positions

of influence. Camden (Charles Pratt) was lord president of the council; General Conway was commander in chief with a cabinet position; Admiral Keppel was first lord of the admiralty.

[3] Digges must mean "the Empress's reopening."
[4] For an account of Digges's success see Digges to Patton, Apr. 24, 1813.
[5] Nicholas Field and Edward Duffy, who had been indicted, along with Macatter, for piracy.
[6] These were official statements made by various governors, by governing bodies of towns and cities, and by Adams himself.
[7] Jacob Sarley.

To John Adams

London Apr. 16 1782

DEAR SIR

Since my last there has been no material occurrence but what will be announcd in the Papers save the arrival in Scotland of two vessels one from N. York the 5 Mar. & the other from Chas. Town the 24th Feby. The letters by the latter is not yet out nor is there any particular accounts given out but those of the old kind that the Garrison were chearful healthy & in no fears &ca. &ca. Those letters from N. York are full of complainings & uneasiness's, such as no trade nor bills or money to remit, constant uneasiness's between the Civil & military Comm[⟨ande⟩]rs & People, the garrison much harrassd in erecting new batterys & defences, and fears of a vigorous attack in the Spring. The winter has been remarkably mild, yet there was no depradatory Expeditions or any skirmishing between the Armys—The Garrison is about 8,000 Men & Washingtons quarters in the jerseys about 20 miles from N. York of which they had little information in N. York as to force & no kind of intercourse.

There has been a deputation of the Principal merchants in London trading to & having Effects in N. York to wait on the minister to know what was to become of their Property & Effects, if an Evacuation of that place was meant, and if the ministers woud encourage their sending out more goods provisions or Stores; & they got the answer which You may expect vizt. that their Effects would be taken as much care of as possible & that the Ministry could not advise the sending out more goods or stores.

Genl. Carlton saild 4 or 5 days ago & has certainly some direct profer to make to Congress;[1] similar I suppose to what is meant to be made to the Commissioners in Europe, & of which you are better informd than I can be, for communications will soon be (if not already) made thro Mr. L[aure]ns. I am sorry to say it, but appearances do not indicate to me that the new men mean to make any direct offer of Independence, & without it nothing can be done. A Treaty for Truce, sending Commissioners to You to treat, making profers to Holland & America for seperate Peace, and at any rate getting a seperate Peace with Holland, is very much the subject of present conversation, and the People seem mad in their expectations & quite forget the situation in which their own Country now stands. The cry still is that a seperate Peace with Holland will certainly take place; & a man who attempts to controvert the opinion from reason & observation on the political State of that Country with the other Belligerent Powers is lookd upon as a fool.

The New Rulers are popular yet, but not so much so as they were a week ago; John Bull seldom looks for a week together towards one point, & in his veerings about He is apt to go to the Extreems. There is certainly disunion among these new men as well on the score of America & what is to be offerd Her, as on the score of appointing friends to the Loaves & fishes: I know most of them & tho they formerly professd great predilection for America, its libertys & privileges, I see so great an alteration in conversations now that I dispondingly wait to see their actions & cannot take their words or pretences of those even who speak favourably for avowd Independence to America.—I wish they fully knew the situation of America & how little She cares about it.

The Prisoners are likely all to be Shippd off very Shortly. In consequence of the late Bill Ships are getting ready to take them away & I hope none will remain in a week or two.

The Requests & Memorials &ca. of the different Towns which I brought are translating & will be in the Remembrancer. They would cost too much to translate to make them servicable to a News Paper—I hope to see one from the States General soon and that the holding-out States of Groningen & Guilderland will soon acceed. I should be very glad to be instrumental in getting publishd, for the reading of this deluded People, any other Memorials or Requests; but I beleive nothing will open the Eyes of some men.

I am with very great Respect
Yr. Obligd & Ob. Servt.
J. W.

[Addressed:] His Excellency/John Adams Esqe. &ca. &ca./[also:] For Mr. J— ⟨ms⟩

MHS: Adams Papers, Reel 356.

[1] General Guy Carleton (1724–1808), appointed to command all British forces in America under the new ministry, was under instruction to inform the American Congress of the peaceful intentions of the British government.

To John Adams

London 23d Apl. 1782

DEAR SIR

Since the Sailing of Adml. Barrington there has been much surprise & speculation as to His destination, & an express just arrivd from Plymouth announces that a few days ago & not many leagues off Brest one of His look out frigates the Artois Capt. McBride fell in with an outward Bound India Fleet of 4 line of Battle Ships (two armd en flute) and about 20 sail of Transports, four of which were taken by Capt. McBride & brought into Plymo. and The fleet under Adml. Barrington left in chase in such a position as to make it morally certain He would capture the whole.[1] *Report* at first said it was the homeward bound Domingo fleet & that Adml. Barrington had taken 23 merchantmen & two Men of War; but the above seems to be the nearest account to truth. As this account came too late for the Gazette, without its publication is purposely kept back, I give it You in a hurry just at the period of the post setting out.

No other news. The idea of Peace with Holland or America seperately has pretty well blown over; & as a substitute in conversation the cry now is that Genl. Carlton carrys over such profers as will *assuredly* be accepted of. Mr. L[aurens] too is very shortly to return from the Continent with such an assent to the proposals He carryd to His Colleagues as will insure a *Peace*!!!

        I am with high Esteem Sir
        Your ob. H. Ser.
        W. R.

MHS: Adams Papers, Reel 356.

[1] Barrington, second in command of the Channel Fleet, was sailing westward from Spithead at noon on Apr. 20 when Capt. John McBride's *Artois* first detected the enemy.

To Lord Shelburne

        No. 10 Spring Gardens
        Fryday Morning [April 26, 1782]

 Mr. Digges presents His Respects to The Earl of Shelburne & calld to mention to His Lordship That the Report from Sir James Marriot[1] to His Majesty against Captains Ryan & MaCator is to be given in this day; and also to beg the favour of a few minutes conversation on those subjects when convenient to His Lordship, Mr. D. wishing to give some answer to the Solicitations from Paris about these Men.

 Since the delivery of the four Letters from Paris to Your Lordship, Lord Keppel, Coll. Barré[2] & Mr. Burke, Mr. Digges has receivd by a second Express another Letter to Sir Robert Harland[3] to intercede for these men, which letter was obtaind thro the solicitation of the Queen of France but Mr. D. does not know by whom it was written.

UM: Lacaita-Shelburne Papers. The endorsement dates the letter "25th. Apl." but that was a Thursday.

¹Sir James Marriott (ca. 1730–1803) was judge of the admiralty court. A supporter of the North ministry in the past, he was sufficiently prudent to support whatever ministry was in power.
²Isaac Barré (1726–1802), long opposed to North's policies and a friend of Shelburne's, was now treasurer of the navy.
³Admiral Harland (ca. 1715–1784) was a member of the admiralty board.

To John Green

Captain Green (1736–1796), a Pennsylvanian and an ardent patriot who had commanded ships on both mercantile and military missions for nearly twenty years, was in Mill Prison awaiting exchange. He had been employed by Robert Morris for the firm of Willing & Morris, Philadelphia, in 1764; after the outbreak of the Revolution he had sought a commission in France and, supported by a recommendation from Lambert Wickes, had been entrusted with sailing the Continental ship of war **Queen of France** *to Boston in 1777; he had then been furnished by Morris with a new ship bound for France. In May 1779, sailing the brigantine* **Nesbitt** *from Philadelphia, he had been captured by an English cruiser and taken to Falmouth, whence he had escaped to Bordeaux. Given command of another vessel, a privateer, he had been the victim of a pilot's carelessness—his ship had sunk—but soon thereafter had succeeded in acquiring another vessel in Nantes,* **Le Patriote,** *whose outfitting had, through the French owner's shiftiness, become largely his financial burden. Then on August 31, 1781, commanding the* **Lion,** *he had been recaptured and been in the prison several months when Digges wrote to him. In November 1781 Green had written Henry Laurens to express the sympathy of the American prisoners for Laurens's distressful situation in the Tower. In early March, when Laurens had been able to visit the prison, Green had given Laurens a list of all the Americans detained there (SCHS: Laurens Papers, Roll 16: Green to Laurens, Feb. 19 and Mar. 8, 1782), and in the following month had begun to correspond with Digges about the keeper's monstrousness, the repayment of £20 Digges had lent him, and the possibilities of release. Following an exchange of several letters Green had on June 7 offered to carry out any commands Digges might have for America (Thibault: John Green's Letter Book, 1781–1783: Green to Digges, Apr. 20, May 3, 16, 21, 26, 27, June 7 and 18, 1782).*

London June 11th 1782 Tuesday.
DEAR SIR
    I receivd Your last letter & note Your expectation of a Cartel being hourly expected—I make no doubt it is by this time arrivd & in order to loose no time I now embrace the oppertunity of sending You a few inclosures which I beg Your particular care of. They are from *good friends* or I would not trouble You with Them. I will (as one frank will not hold all the Letters I have to send) inclose You a few more tomorrow & a second to my Brother;[1] which I beg You to get on board a second ship in case of danger to one. I am to beg of You to give me a line of as late date as You can prior to Your Sailing & just mention to me the Cartels names, their Captains, & the numbers that embark on Each. I will make up a parcell of news papers & Pamphlets of reecent dates and forward them by Coach to Mr. Mentz[2]—They will not only be acceptable but informing to our friends in America. I have sent a small parcell by the Cartel from Portsmouth. I was askd at the Admiralty if The Prisoners did not mean to take the Cartels into France; I answerd I had no reason to beleive so.—I hope it will not enter the heads of anyone, for it would be very unfair after the handsome manner the new Ministry have permitted the Prisoners to get home. You cannot think the pleasure I feel that they are all going away.—The trouble I have had with them for five years back particularly with the fugitives who have thrown themselves on me (of which I can safely say there has not been less than 150 or 160) is more than You could beleive. There are seven now here who broke from Portsmouth after hearing Cartels were ready to take them in, & they are rather affronted with me for not giving them near 15 Guineas each on their Bills. Adieu God Bless You & success to You all. Mind if ever You go to Maryland to call at Warburton & see my home & friends.
                Yrs. &ca.
                T. D.

[Addressed:] Captain John Green/to the Care of Mr. Ben. Ments/Plymouth

Thibault: John Green Papers.

¹George Digges, at Warburton Manor.
²Benjamin Mends was the son of C. S. Mends, of Plymouth, who had largely at his own expense been providing relief for the prisoners for nearly five years. In Feb. the son had forwarded a petition from the prisoners to Adams and was apparently also doing what he could to alleviate their conditions (MHS: Adams Papers, Reel 357: C. S. Mends to Adams, May 2, 1782).

To Robert Traill

A Scotsman and at one time collector of customs at Piscataqua, Maine, Traill had left New England to associate himself with the American loyalists in London during the early days of the Revolution and joined forty-eight of them in the autumn of 1778 in signing a pledge to Germain to contribute to the public safety if England should be invaded. Since the summer of 1780 he had been collector of customs for the Bermudas. Digges did not know Traill but had begun a correspondence with him in November 1782 after becoming concerned with the plight of Traill's son, Robert, apparently American-born, who had suffered a mental breakdown in London and, in addition, been arrested for debts.

Robt. Traill Esqr.—
Third   Bermudas   London Mar. 3rd 1783—
SIR,
    I have written you at three different periods to make you Informd of Your Sons disagreeable Situation, & to explain the Necessity for, Your appointing some person to look after him, and Obtain from His attorney (Mr. Owsley Rowley of Staples Inn) the effects in Bonds Notes &ca. Which Appear to be Above £1200:—
    I forwarded these Several letters in Manner following Vizt. 1st Novr. 82, I inclosed one with a duplicate to a friend in New York by Packet, desiring him to forward them on by two Seperate Oppertunity's for Bermudas.—I also wrote the 23d Novr. a Simular letter to the first & put it under cover to Messieurs Powel & Hopton of Chas. Town, & my last was the 1st Febry. by the New York Mail directed to you at Bermudas—I was in hopes that in taking these various modes

of writing that Some One of the letters would Reach You; But as I have heard & experienced much of Irregular proceedings with regard to letters at New York, & not hearing a Syllable from You I begin to fear for Miscariages & now to remedy It I mean to Copy three or four of this letter & forward them by various ways the most likely to reach You. I shall leave two Copys with Mr. Jno. Brickwood (Clerk to Mr. Strettell Merchant in Lyme St.) & a Principal agent for Ships going to Bermudas—and send the others By the first Ships Going either to New York, or Chas. Town. I hope & trust Sir you will Answer them by the first Conveyance—If Inclosed to me at Mr. Samuel Hartleys Merchant London or directed to me at the Mount Coffee House London, they will meet me Either here or wherever I may be.

Before I proceed further, I beg leave to assure you that your Son is very much better in his State of mind, & perfectly well & Hearty in other respects. I have Strong hopes that another Month or two quiet living with the usual Care that I have Seen has been taken of him, will restore his Mind to quiet & Bring him Among his former friends.— To be Brief as I can be on a Subject that must very much affect you, & in which I am a Sincere Sympathiser, I have only to repeat to you that soon after he was let out of Mr. Strattons Private Mad House at Bethnal Green last Summer (His Confinement In which you Cannot be a Stranger to) He was Arrested for a Small Sum & put into the Kings Bench, where Other detainers were Lodged, against him ammounting in all to about 100 or 120£. This ill Treatment with other Irritations, Threw him back to the disorder For which he was sent to Mr. Strattens. I Know your Son but as a Coffee House Acquaintance, & as a Country man whose Sentiments with regard to American politicks I respected & who ever Behaved like a Gentleman & Man of Honour. I Knew Nothing of his Connections, His Circumstances, or his Situation in life; Nor that he had been Confind at Mr. Strattens, or was then in the Kings Bench, Until a friend of Mine Coll. Glover, about the Begining of Octr. told me he had Seen Mr. Trail in a Miserable & Deplorable Situation in the Kings Bench,—Coll. Glover Spoke to me about him in Consequence of Knowing I was Employd in this Country as agent for the American prisoners—Appointed by Congress, & Guessing Mr. Trail might Come Under the Discription of an American prisoner, & was An object of my Care I went immidiately to See him & Need Not add to your Uneasiness A Discription of the miserable Situation I found him in. It was as bad in point of distress & want as bad Could be; for Going to that prison without a friend or a penny about him, & No One Appearing even to ask after him, He had nothing but Straw Upon the bare flaggs (in an Outer lock-up Room) and Nothing to eat but the Scraps from the Keepers plates. I found Upon inquiry that the Martial of the Bench had made application to the Court of Kings Bench to Get Mr. Trail Removed by Habeus Corpus to an Hospital, but from the State of his mind, No Hospital would take him in, I Helped to Get all his creditors to forego their demands & Give him a Discharge which the Court of Kings Bench on a Motion Acceded to, And his State of mind being Such as to make it dangerous for him to go at large, I got him again into quiet & Comfort, at Mr. Strattens House at Bethnal Green. He was there from about the 20th Octr. to the 4th Jany. when he was admitted to St. Lukes. I have taken every Care & Caution to see he is well Used & accomodated there; it is a free & very excellent Charity, & he is every Whit as well off there as he Could be at Mr. Strattens, where the expence is above a Guinea a week. Had he been my Brother or Nearest friend I would have Acted the Same part by him, & you May assure yourself Sir, he is as well Treated as Can be, & is Geting better very fast, in So much That he is Now Nearly well enough to be let Out.—You may depend I should have Kept him on at Mr. Strettens, in preference to the Charity of St. Lukes had my finances been Such as to allow me to do So, But I have for the last Six years been Distressd Exceedingly for money, and in times as much in want as any American prisoner I had the care of. I have been fagging in their Service Now Upwards of Six years, without any Allowance or Stipend for doing So, and have Generally had on hand from 5 to—600, & at times 900 & a thousand—all of them in Want. I am from The State of Maryland myself, & tho in A More likely Channell than Any Other American in england, Tho Possessing exceeding Good property in Maryland & Virginia, Yet it has been Impossible to Get Any the least remittance from it during the War.

As I said before, Your Sons Debts, do not appear to be More than £120, and his attorney Mr. Rowley of Staples Inn (with whome Mr.

Trail Seems to have had a quarrell) Has in Bonds Notes &ca., Most of which Mr. Rowley told me were Good tho Not Imediately Recoverable, Ammounted to Upwards of £1200.—In my endeavours to serve him I tryd to find Out Some friend or Corospondent of yours who would take the Burden a little off my Shoulders (for I Can assure you I have otherwaise Much to do) But I Could find None altho applications were Mad[e] through Means of Mr. Rowley, to Mr. Tymmonds, Mr. Brickwood, & others. I Can assure you Sir it is not only inconvenient to me to look after your Son But at times Impracticable, for I have in the Course of the last Six Months and Pending the Negociation for peace been, three or four times to the Hague & to Paris on Publick business, & I am Not Certain but I may be Sett off for america before your Answer to this can arrive in England. It is therefore highly essential to you & for your Sons wellfare to appoint some person to look after him, & to get at the Money & effects he has in Mr. Rowleys hands—During the Span of time of his leaving Mr. Strattens, & Being put into the Kings bench He appears to have been plunder'd of his Wearing Appearl &ca. &ca. He had a Servant (Whom I have Never Been Able to Catch or I would punish) when he first went into the Bench, who Got at almost every thing he left in his Lodgings in Bond St. Under pretence that his master had Sent him for them, but he Never Carried a rag to him in prison. What few things were Save'd Mr. Rowley Had Got at his Chambers before I Knew Anything of him, & these have been all Sent to Mr. Strattens, Who has acknowledged the Receipt of them to me, & who will help Mr. Trail to them as they appear to him to be wanted. All that I have done for him, & all That appeard Necessary to do Hitherto, I have done, & this is only to pay for a Bed & Comfortable Dinner &ca. from the day I saw Him first in the Kings bench (about the 6th of Octr.) to his Going to Mr. Strattons (about 20th Novr.) & Supplying him with a New waist Coat Breeches, Stockings, Shoes &ca. For his theif of a Servant left Him, But two Blue frocks & Some washing Waist Coats & Breeches; & the Expence of washing was thought too much of at the Hospital.—I have Not yet Settled with Mr. Stratten the Charge of Keeping him from the 20th Novr. till he was Sent into St. Lukes the 3rd Jany. By the excellent Institution of that Hospital, He may be Kept for Twelve Months Gratis;

But I was obliged to give Bond with Security (Mr. Chas. Chapman of Leaden Hall Street. & Mr. Wm. Perkins Duke St. Adelphia) And 100 £ finally to take him out before the Expiration of the 12 month,— Longer than which No patient Whatever is allowd to Stay. This is also a Secondary Inducement for me to ask of you, to appoint as Soon as possible Some Person here to take Care of your Son for I would Not on any Account whatever have the two Securities Troubled or put to Any expence in Consequence of my Absence.

—Expecting Soon to hear from You I Remain Sir
—Your Very Obedt. Humbe. Servt.
Thos. Digges

15 Mar. 1783

I send this third Copy, to Mr. Strettel for forwardance hearing than [that] an oppertunity is likely soon to forward it.

I have seen Your Son this day & He continued quiet and rather mending. T. D.

[Addressed:] Robert Traill Esqr./Collector of the Island of/Bermudas third

[By Jennings:] Antigua. June 18. 1783 forwarded by/Your Most Obedt. Sert./Daniel Jennings

NLS: Steuart Papers, Ms. 5033, f. 76. The heading shows this to be the third copy, to which Digges's second paragraph and postscript make reference.

To William Carmichael

When in June 1782 John Jay had left Spain for Paris at Franklin's behest to participate in the formulation of the peace treaties, Carmichael, Jay's secretary for the preceding two years, had become acting chargé d'affaires of the United States. The position was a difficult one. Despite their having joined in a common war against the British, the belligerents could not immediately agree on terms during the preliminary talks, and Spain particularly had continued to resist acknowledging American independence, partly out of fear that such acknowledgment would strengthen the ability of the English and Americans together to stir up rebellion in Spanish territories. But Carmichael's friend Lafayette had arrived in Madrid, with the support of the American commissioners, to ease negotiations and succeeded in persuading the prime minister, José de Moñino y Redondo, conde de Florida-Blanca (1728–1808), to invite Carmichael to a diplomatic dinner in March, providing thereby public recognition of the new nation. Late in August Carmichael would be officially presented to the king and royal family.

London April 3d 1783

DEAR SIR

I am very happy at hearing from my Friend Mr. Edmund Jennings[1] that You have been lately Received publickly at Madrid, and this as well from the benefits which will naturally accrue to our Country from such a reception, as that a person so distinguishedly servicable to America as You have been has obtaind the appointment to that Court.

Except in the instance of two or three short trips to the Continent, I have been here and hereabouts ever since my last letter to You,[2] and fagging as heretofore at a sort of up-hill work, which I thank God I have got rid of ever since the Negociation of the Provisional articles at Paris. I would have continued to have written to You as any matter of consequence occurrd, but a variety of disagreeable and, in some instances, dangerous incidents made me decline it—Such as the capture & ill treatment of Mr. Laurens, the apprehending & confining Trumbull, The seizure of my papers, & the unfair accusations of my bribing Prisoners to Escape & take off Vessels[3] &ca. &ca. Mr. Laurens is still here and in better health than when He came from Paris—Mr. Jennings has been a few weeks here, and these, with Mr. Penn, are all the Americans of any note as yet in England & I frequently meet them—Mr. Silas Deane is said to be in London but I have not yet met Him, nor do I know Him.[4]

I have a good oppertunity of sending You this (or any thing else You may want from hence) thro the medium of a House in Lisbon in which I am connected (Messrs. Edwd. Burn & Sons,) and supposing from Your present situation and vicinity to Lisbon that You must hear something of or know whoever may be appointed by Congress to form a Commercial Treaty with the Court of Portugal, I mean to make so free as to suggest a few hints respecting the Commerce between our Country & that, with which, from some years residence in Lisbon, I made myself informd of.[5]

I am well enough acquainted with the Portuguese & the nature of their Government & Court, to know That much good may arise if in the *onset* of the Treaty of Commerce, The Negociator be instructed to obtain or ask for such regulations as to Port Duties, Entries inward & outward &ca. as the Portuguese would most likely assent to; but if *old forms* are allowd of much mischief may ensue, & such forms will be very difficult to get alterd when once in the rotine of office.

The Evils at present subsisting are

1st That *Guards* generally two at a heavy expence to the Ship, whether She has any Contraband Goods on board or not, are kept on board from the arrival to the final discharge of the vessel. They are paid by the Day & the charge might I think be lightend considerably if not done at the Expence of the King.

2d Ships calling in the Tagus to seek a Market or to get orders to proceed elsewhere, Should be allowed so many days, (suppose six or eight days) free of all Charges save that of the Fort, for they have no lights to Pay.

3d It is a common thing in the Tagus to take a Cargoe out of one Ship and put it into another, alongside of each other & without landing any thing; This act is calld *Baldiacam* & pays I think near 2 pr.Ct. upon the Cargoe so shippd or shifted.—This duty might I think be easily got off, & it may be highly beneficial to America to be easd from it, as it will much aid the Carrying Trade.

4th There is a duty of 4 pr.Ct. to the King, paid exclusive of other charges on any Cargoes that are landed & stored (not for Sale or consumption in the Country) but sometimes only from necessity of landing from a leaky or bad Ship, or intended for another market in a different bottom &ca. &ca. This duty woud be a good thing to get off or lightend to one pr.Ct. which is quite enough for warehouse Rent, even in the Kings Storehouses.

5th Ships going empty there for Sale (which is a very common thing) are subject to a duty on Tonnage—It will be a great benifit to

America to get this duty lightend or taken off, for many of the Ships in the Brazil Trade are bought from Foreigners and America will naturally look to the supplying that market with Ships.

Every Country to be sure has a right to lay such dutys or restrictions on their import & Export as they may chuse; but there appears a *particular hardship* on the Part of Portugal to America in their Restrictions & dutys upon Flour & Rice. Such Regulations have been made in Lisbon since the rupture between this Country & America (owing I suppose to some evil machinations from Men in power here) as make the introduction of *Flour* impracticable: It is now subject to a heavy duty, & besides this it can only be sold in the Corn market and there by *measure, and the sale is taken out of the Proprietors hands.*—Formerly it was as open as any other business, and this circumstance contributed greatly to the flourishing Commerce between America & that Country—for at times while I was there in 1770, 71, 72 & 73 it was no unusual thing to see near an hundred Sail of American Ships in the Tagus at a time:—This restriction is an ill advisd measure on the part of the Portuguese, as it is calculated only to serve partially the millers at the Expence of the publick.

Rice is prohibited in order to encourage the growth of that article in the Brazils, from whence large quantities (tho of an inferior quality to the Carolina) is imported.

I have from time to time communicated these matters, and others of less merchantile moment, to Merchants in Philadelphia, in Maryland, Virga. & So. Carolina, & explained them fully to Mr. Ridley and Mr. Johnson in France[6] whom I constantly write to; and most likely Congress are well apprisd of them, & will instruct their Negociator, should they find it expedient to form a Commercial Treaty with Portugal, to get these dutys & restrictions taken off, and to insist on the Sales *particularly of Flour* to be intirely free.

I before mentiond to You that I had a connection in the House of Messrs. Burn & Sons of Lisbon; And You may freely make use of it in any way You may think it can be servicable to You:—It is *second* to no English House in Portugal; has large Correspondencys in America (particularly in Philadelphia & Maryland) and has distinguishd itself during the War in befriending American Ships, wishing well to their Cause &ca. &ca.—On the slightest intimation that it is Your wish, they will inform You of every exact Port Regulation, Duty &ca. &ca. laid formerly & now existing against the American Ships. If You know or should hereafter know of any American Negociator at Lisbon a line of introduction to Messrs. Burn & Sons or rather (*Wm. Burn Esqr.* the Partner fixd there) it cannot fail of being servicable. If I can forward any of Your wishes in this place or in Ireland (where I am going soon on a two months tour) You have only to cover Letters for me to Messrs. Burn & Sons *Lisbon* or send them direct by post under cover to Messrs. Wallace, Johnson, & Muir Merchants London or to their care; for I am in constant correspondence with threi [their] Houses at Annapolis & Nantes & hope to see Johnson in a few days to open the same firm here; The House warehouses &ca. being already taken.[7]

If before American Consulages are regularly fixd, Ships should go either to Lisbon or Setuval (which last is the greatest European mart for Salt) The two English Vice Consuls, vizt. Mr. Clarke at Lisbon & Mr. Williamson at Setuval,[8] are *good* men & will give the Captains & vessels every advice & assistance in their power and this at very little or no expence.

The Publick news papers will inform You of what has been done in Parliament as to opening the Trade & intercourse with America.— Near six weeks has elapsd since Mr. Pitt brought into the Commons a Bill *"for The Provisional Establishment & regulation of Trade and Intercourse between Great Britain & America[*"*]*!! and the Commons are this day further off the passing such Bill than when it was first brought in.[9]—There never was such folly to be sure—They seem to think that America even yet is to be bound or in some measure implicitly accept of their Laws to regulate Trade. The debates in the Commons on this Bill (which I closely attended & latterly with Mr. Jennings) serves to convince me more strongly than ever, that the English House of Commons are very unequal judges of any commercial matter even for their own Country, and that they have not yet nearly learnt the probable state & situation of things in the United States of America.

I inclose You the *first*, and third Bill that was printed—The second I cannot lay my hands on, but it was so fritterd away & alterd from the orriginal that they hardly appeard the same Bill; & this *third*, which You have inclosd, and the Debates thereon shews the cloven foot of the Commons pretty plainly; and leaves out the word *recipro-*

cal, as well as the declaration of evincing a disposition to be on terms of *perfect amity* with the United States. The Bill has been four or [⟨five⟩] times in committee of the whole house, debated upon, & as often deferrd to a future day; It is now put off for another week, & it is my opinion they will throw it out all together, & do what they ought to have done in the first instance *repeal all Laws that prevent ships coming from or going to America*, and trust to future events or the effects of negociations for Commercial Treatys, for further benefits.

The Bill will damn itself in the point of reciprocity of Advantages. The word *Reciprocity* has been bandied about both in the Provisional Treaty & in debate here. These *wise* Debaters at least a majority of them, seem to think America bound to receive all the Manufactures of England, & to submit to import Dutys on Amern. produce here; yet none of the Manufactures of America are to be allowd to come to England; Where then is the reciprocity of advantage?

It is too bad to comment upon.—In the refind & mutilated Bill, they seem to forget that the American States are free sovereign & independant, and that She ought & must be treated as such. It is astonishing how much of the old torey leven of the House of Commons as to their rights to bind America, regulate Her trade &ca. &ca. was discoverd during the whole of this debate. The House shewd an inimical and uncandid turn of mind towards the United States of America and to evade the provisional articles of Peace; and this, when discoverd by my Countrymen will make them seek security in the friendship of the rest of Europe to the prejudice of the political & commercial Interests of Great Britain. Why at the time that the generality of Europe is seeking intercourse with America, did not this Country repeal all offensive Laws against America, and make a publick Parliamentary Declaration that She had a disposition to be on terms of perfect amity with the United States?—This would not have disgracd England or prejudiced the Nation, & would likely have producd similar declarations from our Side. But there seems a fate attending this Country & that some evil genius is for ever leading them wrong. Most likely as they have now arrangd a new ministry they will go to work on a commercial Treaty with America, as I suppose the Commissioners at Paris have powers to make one.

This Country has been in a state of confusion & in a manner without Government for near seven weeks & the strangest combinations among men professing different opinions in politicks have taken place that could be immagind—a motley Ministry is at length fixd & You have the arrangement below.[10] Without careing a fig who is in or who is out of place I cannot but be highly disgusted at the Politicks of the day—Every debate serves only to debase each party at St. Stephens in the eye of honesty and integrity, & to heighten the prospects of those, our Countrymen, who are likely to be governd no longer by such interested wickedness. The Political as well as moral depravity of this Country seems to have attaind its meridian; & I long & hope in 5 or 6 months to get out of it. The people deserve every thing for suffering themselves to be so miserably gulld by their unmaskd oppressors. As to the Establishment of Norths influence & power, it appears to be designd to keep open the breach with America—She must be greatly inclind to shake hands with a nation that still continues to cherish the bitterest of Her Enemies.

There is a great appearance of *vast* Emigration to America, & I encourage it all I can; hundreds of People *with money in their pockets* are moving.—They look to that Country as an Elezium, & seem certain it is *there* only where nature opens her broad lap to receive the perpetual accession of new comers, & to supply them with food. People seem tired out here with the party feuds & scramble among the great for places of profit.—The Country may truly be said to be in a doleful situation, & it strikes me that it will soon experience some publick commotion—A bankrupt Treasury, a mutinous army, a Seditious navy, insurrections at the high price of bread in the heart of the Country, numerous robberies of bandittis some even in the publick streets of London, and a distracted People, are disorders not easily allayd by the feeble hand that seems now to govern. I thank God most cordially that my Country by its own virtuous exertions is now placed out of the Reach of all mischief from this—She has *very few* in this quarter to thank for it; and I most sincerely hope & trust Her rise to power & greatness will be as uninterrupted & rapid as Her efforts to obtain it have been spirited & successfull.

I mean to set out in 8 or 10 days to see the northern manufactories & thence to Ireland & Scotland so as to be back here by the time a neutral vessel which I expect is by this time in Virga. returns either here or to Ostend & which Vessel I shall have at my Command on her return.

I take this tour principally to serve my Brother in Law Mr. Jno. Fitzgerrald settled in an extensive Commercial way in Alexandria,[11] as well as for some purposes of my business in Portugal. If I can any ways be servicable to You I hope You will command me. & Letters directed as before mentioned will always come regularly to hand. I wish You every success & happiness & am with great regard

Your very Obligd & Obt. Serv.
Ths. Digges

Duke Portland is 1st Lord of The Treasury.
Mr: Fox foreign } Secretarys of State—so that His Lord- }
                    ship must now ⟨have⟩ the negociation
Lord North home } with America—!!!   }
Lord Stormont presidt. of the Council
Lord Carlysle privy Seal
Lord Keppel—first Lord of the Admiralty
Lord Jno. Cavendish Chancellor of the Excheqr.
    These only are to compose the Cabinet Council.
Mr. Eden has got a vice Treasurer Ship in Ireland—
Mr. Burke—Paymaster—Coll. Fitzpatrick Secy. at War—
Lord Townshend—head of the Ordinance Richmond having resignd
Conway still Commandr. in Chief but that place to be abolishd
Treasurer of the Navy not yet fixd but said to be Lord Beauchamp
Lord Temple to be succeeded if He resigns by Lord Fitzwilliam
Chancellor to resign & the Seals to be held by Commission }
    by Lord Loughborough, Baron Ayre, & Baron Skinner   }
& about 15 new Lords to be made to give a majority of voices [in] the House of Lords—

NA: Record Group 233, HR 27A G7.4: Papers of the U. S. House of Representatives [Property of the House], Papers of William Carmichael, No. 77.

[1] Edmund Jenings of Annapolis (1731–1819), grandson of an early eighteenth-century acting governor of Virginia and son of the king's attorney, the secretary of Maryland, had been educated at Cambridge and the Middle Temple, practiced some law, and then during 1778–1783 traveled on the Continent, living most of the time in Brussels. He had early won the confidence of the Lees, to whom he was related and who had recommended him to Adams as being reliable, and Adams had indeed soon found him a valuable compatriot. Jenings had access to the London press and, like Digges, regularly could secure publication there for pro-American writings, whether by Adams, by himself, or by others. During 1782 Jenings and Laurens had had a quarrel over an anonymous letter charging Adams with misconduct, but the event had not shaken Adams's faith in Jenings or in any way affected the relationship between Jenings and his fellow Marylander, Digges.

[2] The date of Digges's last letter to Carmichael has not been established, but if it is Nov. 2, 1777, when Digges had sent Matthew Ridley a letter for forwardance (see Digges to Ridley, Nov. 20, 1777, n. 9), then there appear to have been only two trips to the Continent: one to Passy in 1779 during which he had taken the oath of allegiance to the U.S. (see document, May 3, 1779) and another to Amsterdam, Mar. 20, 1782, when he had taken Lord North's inquiries to John Adams.

[3] In alluding to these accusations, unmentioned earlier in his letters, Digges must be referring to reports other than those that Hodgson and Franklin had circulated in 1781 and after about Digges's apparent misuse of the prisoners' allowances and his alleged profiteering from the export of goods to America (see Digges to Franklin, Mar. 22, 1782).

[4] Nonetheless, there is evidence that for more than a year Digges had been corresponding with Deane (possibly through Edward Bancroft) and that the two men were at least known *to* each other. In seven letters from Deane in Ghent to Bancroft in London, written between Feb. 17, 1782, and Feb. 28, 1783, Deane mentions "W. F." Deane wants to hear from W. F. again, or he sends W. F. his compliments, or he asks how W. F. is, or— toward the last—he expresses suspicions about W. F.'s fidelity. In the index to *The Deane Papers (Collections of the New-York Historical Society for the Year 1890*, 23, New York, 1891) these initials are given as those of William Fitzpatrick, who is in turn identified as William Singleton Church, both names used by Digges in letters to Franklin and Adams (see *The Deane Papers*, 5:64, 67, 82, 84–85, 99, 130, 144).

[5] The substance of Digges's comments about trade with Portugal appears to have been sent by Digges to Ridley prior to Mar. 18, enabling Ridley on Mar. 24 to pass along the information to Robert Morris in Philadelphia (MHS: Ridley Papers, Letter Book, Feb. 16, 1782–June 16, 1783: Ridley to Digges, Mar. 18, 1783, and to Morris, Mar. 24, 1783).

[6] Matthew Ridley in Paris, Joshua Johnson in Nantes.

[7] Charles Wallace, Joshua Johnson, and John Muir had made this house one of the principal tobacco houses; through it merchants in Philadelphia and Baltimore conducted most of their business.

[8] Williamson's first name was William; Clarke's has eluded discovery.

[9] William Pitt the Younger (1759–1806) was at the time chancellor of the exchequer and in Feb. had prepared a bill that would modify restrictions on Anglo-American trade. First submitted to the law officers of the crown for revision, it had been considered from time to time during the Mar. debates in the House, subjected to amendments, but not brought to a final vote.

[10] Digges's list is only partial, but his roster of familiar names suffices to show the nature of the coalition that had been formed from a range of opposing factions to force Shelburne's resignation for proposing peace terms that contained too many unpalatable concessions, whether to the Americans asserting their right to trade as equals with British colonies or to allies struggling to consolidate their dominions overseas. Least familiar are those whom Digges had had no occasion to mention in earlier letters to Franklin or Adams: William Henry Cavendish-Bentinck, third duke of Portland, (1738–1809), titular head of the Rockingham Whigs but to a considerable extent simply a follower of Fox's direction; John Cavendish (1732–1796), also a member of the Rockingham party and critic of Shelburne; Col. Richard Fitzpatrick (1747–1813), an intimate of Fox's at one with both the opponents of North and the critics of Shelburne; George Nugent-Temple Grenville (1753–1813), since the age of ten teller of the exchequer, since 1779 the second Earl Temple and member of the House of Lords, since 1774 leading opponent of North, and since the fall of North privy councillor and lord lieutenant of Ireland; William Wentworth Fitzwilliam (1748–1833), a nephew of Rockingham's, a friend of Fox's, an opponent of North, and a critic of Shelburne. With respect to the commissioners for the custody of the Great Seal, Hansard's *Parliamentary History* shows that along with Baron Loughborough (a title that the vehement and energetic Alexander Wedderburn had been enjoying since June 1780) the commission included Sir William Henry Ashurst (1725–1807), judge of the King's Bench, and Sir Beaumont Hotham (1737–1814), baron of the exchequer.

[11] Fitzgerald (d. 1799), an ardent Catholic, was married to Jane Digges (b. 1755). He had been one of Washington's aides-de-camp, had been serving since 1781 as settlement agent for French contractors buying forage and supplies for the Yorktown campaign, and was established as an important dealer in wheat and tobacco in Alexandria, where he had settled in 1769 after emigrating from Ireland.

To Matthew Ridley

Ridley was still in Paris and, with Digges's collaboration, busy arranging for shipments of indentured servants and goods from the British Isles and the Continent to ports in Maryland, Virginia, and South Carolina. The two men had been corresponding about their common interest for more than three years. How recently Digges had heard from Ridley is uncertain, but an entry in Ridley's letterbook for February 25, 1783, doubtless embodies the substance of the correspondence: ". . . wrote him [Digges] that Passports have been granted by our Ministers for English Vessells.—That I furnished Mr. S. Hartley with a list of such articles as I think best to form a cargo.—If any good House in Ireland will send out a number of Indented servants consisting of Farmers & Tradesmen I will take one half Interest if they will send the Vessell to Baltimore to my House & will agree to remit them for our half by the return of the Vessell; allowing them a price from £3 Stg. per head & not exceeding five for the Passages of the People out exclusive of the expences of collecting them. I think the price of Passage out from Ireland . . . to be about four pounds sterling p. head. I cannot say how much they would fetch but I think they would answer if there was care used in the collecting them & at no place would they answer better than Baltimore.—As for the loading of the Vessell they might put in any thing they pleased provided she was double decked.—Irish linnens,—Liverpool & Bristol & in Bottles, cheese & a variety of Irish Manufactures the Vessell might bring back a load of flax seed & Barrell Staves" (MHS: Ridley Papers, Letter Book, February 16, 1782 – June 16, 1783).

Brighthelmstone,[1] Augt. 20. 1783

DEAR SIR

I have been here a few days getting away a small Brig for Virginia ownd and fitted out by the same man at Shoreham that Belts vessel the Brighton belonged to. She will sail on Sunday for Potomack & carrys out about 8 or 900£s worth of Goods & some 16 or 17 Indentures viz. 2 Black Smiths, 3 Ship wrights, a Sadler, a Shoemaker & Tanner of some property, and 10 or 12 excellent Husbandmen. It is uncertain if She goes to Richmond where the owners Brother wishes to settle or to Alexandria but I am in hopes to get Her to the later.

You will likely eer this reaches You see Mr. Bingham[2] who went from hence for Paris & Holland a day or two ago. Mr. Barklay[3] meaning to follow Him in this days packet, I cannot let Him depart without giving You a letter. I should have done it by Bingham but I had no idea He would have set out the day He Did. He has left his Lady (and a very pretty agreeable one She is) in this place until He returns; We have also here Mr. & Mrs. Penn, Mr. & Mrs. Ricketts &ca. and with these & 3 or 4 Lisbon Ladies whom I formerly knew abroad, I have spent a few days very agreeably—one of them *Mrs. Walpole* wife to the English Envoy at Lisbon & Brother to Mr. Walpole at Paris goes in the Packet with Mr. Barklay and deprives Brighton of what is generally thought the first beauty of the place.[4] I shall be here till the 26th & go hence to Portsmouth and Bristol so as to be in London by the 15th about which time there will be a vessel for Maryland by whom I shall have much to write & send to George.⁵ His last letters to me (altho they are near 3 months old) informd me of my Fathers death & disposal of His property; & altho He has left George the Chas. Town Estate with every thing thereon, and the Bladensbg. Estate &ca. (this last worth full 12,000 Guins.) & not less than 140 Slaves, yet He has the modesty to ask of me to sell one of the Virginia Estates (which with the Home Estate & appendages are mine) in order to raise a little money to discharge the debts which *He* by the Will is burthend with and amount to about 2,000£ Stg.—However this I will do & more to oblige Him & I shall send Him the proper powers of Attorney by the next Ship from Mr. Johnson.⁷

I am well pleasd to hear that two of the vessels I' directed out have got safe one to Cunningham & Nisbit at Philadelphia the other to Brailsford at Chas. Town.⁸ I gave these as well as some others introductory letters to several such as to Your House in case of going to Baltimore, Johnsons at Annapolis, Fitzgerralds to Virginia &ca. &ca. &ca. I have very late accounts from Cunninghame & Nisbit from Philadelphia & papers to the 5th July—(apropos, in none of these papers do I see the letter from Genl. Washington, by which I doubt its authenticity 'tho it is written much in his spirit & sentiment, pray clear up this doubt to me)—Cunningham gives me very pleasant accounts of things generally, and of the late tumult among the Soldiery particularly. The two ring leaders of the tumult are got to London & have cried picavi to Mr. Laurens in a proper sort of manner altho the act was not justifiable on any ground whatever.⁹ If You have any thing particular to say or wish me to do give me a line to the *Post Office Bristol* until about the 15 next month. There is a vessel going from thence about that period to Alexandria in which I mean to send some of the animal as well as human species. Mr. Davis who went out in April got safe to Philadelphia I find by Cunninghams letter & means to fix with his 8 or 9000£ Str. Stock in Alexa. [Alexandria] in the Tobacco manufactory line in which He was very considerable in Bristol. Many others are moving & going in the Spring to that quarter of America notwithstanding there is many ill naturd lies propogated & publishd here to discourage Emigrations. For my part I encourage it all I can but I always avoid advising the parties to risque much and by all means not to go to the considerable Towns of America which must at present be expensive; but to get into the quiet remote parts & become tillers & workers of the Earth.

Mr. Pitt—Dr. Jebb[10]—Dr. Price & two or three other particular friends of mine are now here & I am much with them—The former does not like the proceedings of ministry relative to the Commercial Regulations in the West Indies respecting the Carrying trade, yet He insists England cannot give up Her navigation Laws. I have some reason to beleive Mr. Fox was averse to the measure of the Proclamation in the Gazette & that orders are now gone out to permit or allow American vessels to carry to & from the Wt. Indies & the Continent, if not to every part of Europe save Gt. Britain; These people seem determind to keep on in their old way of doing wrong, redressing that wrong from necessity & not inclination, & thereby displease those who have no great predilection in their favour or care little about them. When You hear of the signing the definitive treaty, or that of Commerce between America & England, I should be much obligd to You for a line as it may concern some of my Lisbon negociations. I beg my best respects to Mrs. R. & little Essex & that she may soon bless You with another little one. I am on all occasions Dr. Sir

Your Obligd & Ob. Serv.
Th. Digges

MHS: Ridley Papers, Norton Gift, Box 2, f. 1783.

[1] More familiarly known as Brighton.
[2] William Bingham (1752–1804), who had served as British consul in Martinique before the Revolution and as Continental agent in the West Indies from 1776 to 1780, had married Anne Willing in Philadelphia in 1780 and with her father subsequently founded the Bank of North America. He was now in Europe for an extended stay.
[3] Thomas Barclay, who had come from America to take over Franklin's consular duties.
[4] Brighton's "first beauty" was Diana Grosett (d. 1784), daughter of a Scottish merchant in Lisbon, no doubt where she had met her future husband (m. 1780), Sir Robert Walpole (1736–1810), clerk of the privy council and envoy to Portugal (1771–1800). Fourth son of Horatio Walpole, Baron Walpole of Wolterton (1678–1757), Sir Robert had previously been secretary of the embassy at Madrid, secretary of the embassy at

Paris, and minister plenipotentiary at Paris. His brother Thomas, Horatio's second son, was a banker and for some months had been in Paris privately authorized to sound out all parties concerning the peace preliminaries. Both men were cousins of the more famous Horace Walpole (1717–1797), author of *The Castle of Otranto* and the *Memoirs*.

[5] Digges's brother.

[6] William Digges had died on Mar. 28, 1783.

[7] Joshua Johnson. For a discussion of the brothers' inheritance, see introduction.

[8] William Brailsford, member of a prominent mercantile family in Charleston, had established a partnership with Thomas Morris of Philadelphia.

[9] In June more than fifty (eighty, according to some accounts) members of a Lancaster (Pennsylvania) regiment, under the leadership of Capt. Henry Carbery and Lt. John Sullivan, had marched on Philadelphia, seized the barracks, and laid siege for a day to the Continental Congress because payment of the troops had been too long delayed. The problem had arisen more than a year earlier when decisions had been reached, first, to keep the army intact through the peace negotiations; then, to diminish the expense of that decision by pressing for voluntary retirements; then, to stop promotions, withhold commissions, and consider turning the burden of payments over to the separate states. Discussions had been prolonged and inconclusive. When finally troops had been furloughed without pay—only promises given—the men had taken action. Washington had then dismissively attributed the mutinous behavior to recent recruits who had not endured the heat and hardships of the war.

[10] The reference to Pitt is probably not to William Pitt but to his cousin Thomas (1737–1793), an independent in Parliament consistently supportive of motions against the American war. John Jebb (1737–1786), who had received his M.D. from St. Andrews in 1777 and practiced medicine in London during the following year, had also become an Oriental scholar, been elected to the Royal Society in 1779, and then given most of his energy to politics as a leader of the Yorkshire Association movement and a supporter of Fox and the efforts to reform Parliament.

To Charles Steuart

Steuart (1725–1797) was Robert Traill's cousin. Born in the Orkneys and educated at the University of Edinburgh, he had gone to Virginia as a storekeeper in 1741 and before the Revolution been successively surveyor general of customs for the eastern middle district of America and receiver general of customs in Boston. With the outbreak of fighting he had returned to England a loyalist and, now cashier of American customs, been given the responsibility for paying salaries from various funds to refugee officers. On July 4 Traill, enclosing a copy of Digges's letter of March 3, had written Steuart about his son's

29 August 1783

predicament and asked him to advance money to pay for young Robert's care and to reimburse Digges for whatever was owed him. At the same time he had written Digges and provided him with a letter of introduction to Steuart.

Brighthelmston 29 Aug. 83

Sir

I receivd a Letter from Mr. Trail of Bermudas with the inclosure a few days ago bearing date the 4th July, and which is the first letter I have receivd from Him in answer to the many I wrote Him last winter & early in the Spring giving Him an account of His Sons unhappy situation & of the Steps I had taken to help Him, of which I dare say You have been fully informd by Mr. Leonard or others.

I inclose You Mr. Trails letter for Your better information of His wishes as to the Effects of His Son, & You may return me the letter in the inclosd frank mentioning at the same time any particular point in which I can further help Him or inform You. I should be very happy to render Him any further services & assist You in any means in my power.

I am in advance for Him something above thirty pounds, but not having my papers with me I cannot assertain it precisely; but will give it You on my return to London which I expect will be in 10 or 12 days from the present time. In consequence of Mr. Trail's order to riemburse myself on You I will give an order in a day or two most likely tomorrow for thirty pounds payable at sight to Mr. Peter Clark or order on You, and I shall be obligd to You to pay attention thereto it being to help a person to that sum who will leave London for America the begining of next week.

I left orders with Mr. Dunstan the Secretary to St. Lukes Hospital to supply Mr. Trail with any trifles He might want, but Mr. Stratton (the Keeper of the mad House at Bethnal Green, who lives at Mare Street Hackney, & who has shewn Mr. Trail many civilities when formerly confined in His house) is my principal director in matters concerning Mr. Trail.

As I expect to hear from You I shall say no more for the present. I shall leave this place on Wedy. or thursday next & expect to be in

London the 14 or 15th when I will call on You & give any assistance in my power.

I am Sir Your Ob. Servt.
Ths. Digges

NLS: Steuart Papers (1783–1784), Ms. 5033, f. 109.

To Charles Steuart

Worcester 17 Novr. 1783

SIR

Since I last wrote You & drew a bill as by Mr. Trails request for the Supplys to His Son, I have Receivd two letters from Mr. Trail from Bermuda, the first of which I beleive was forwarded under Cover to You. I have wrote Him lately by a vessel from Liverpool & have now by me a duplicate to said Letter which I wish to send by any vessel going soon from London. I have wrote Mr. Traill very fully & inclosd Him a Memorandum of the money advancd to His Son amounting to £[*left blank*] as You will see by inclosd account; which is over and above what I last drew upon You for ten pounds 12/6d., and for which Ballance due me I have this day inclosd a bill made payable to my Landlord in London David Forsyth No. 28 South Molton Street, at Eight days Date which You will please to honor.

If there is any vessel going from London sooner than 15 days I should be obligd to You to inform me thereof by a line directed to me at the Post Office Worcester and I will forward You my duplicate to Mr. Trail, but if no oppertunity offers by that time I will take Your silence for my answer & wait upon You as soon as I get to London, which I think will be in 15 or 16 days from this date.

The Gentleman who prom[i]ses to deliver this or send it You in London waits for me so that I have only time to add

I am Sir
Your Obt. Hum. Servt.
Thos. Digges

I have not time to *copy* & inclose the Account.

[Addressed:] Charles Stewart Esqr./at Mr. Knights, Apothecary/ Pimlico/London

NLS: Steuart Papers (1783–1784), Ms. 5033, ff. 135–36.

To Thomas Trant

May 5th 1784

DEAR SIR

In answer to Your request to be informd of the probable benefits on a Cargoe of Indented Servants from hence to Virginia, I can in a word say I know of nothing that can be sent from this Country to greater prospect of success.

You know I am directing out the Washington[2] with 200 or 250 to the address of my Brother in Law Mr. Jno. Fitzgerrald at Alexandria on Potowmack River, from which place, or indeed from any part of Virginia or Maryland, there is a moral certainty of back Freight of Tobacco, Wheat, Flour, Lumber, Iron or other exports of these States.

I have many letters from Mr. Fitzgerrald (which I will shew You if You will take the trouble to call) dated in Novr., Decr., & Feby. last, in every one of which, He urges the sending out Indented Servants as the most certain beneficial Commerce from Ireland to that quarter, and I make no doubt they will do equally well in any other parts of Virginia, particularly to James River, York River, or Rappahannock.

You know the facility with which these Servants can be had from the numbers of poor now begging about. The term of *four* years is better than a shorter period, & the fewer you have under Redemption articles the better they will sell. There is already upwards of 130 Engaged for the Washington, & among them are 70 odd Tradesmen vizt. Ship wrights, House Carpenters, Joiners, Masons, mill & wheel wrights, Coopers & many other lower mechanicks—the more of these kinds you get the better, and send but few women and Boys—*Country* Labourers will also do well. You must calculate on the Expence of outfit about 3£ or 3 Guins. a man to Sea, and if they are decently clad the better they will sell. I have reason to beleive with a healthy voyage they will leave a profit in Virginia of about five Guineas for Common men, & from 15 to 25 Guineas for the tradesmen on the term of 4 Years.

As I hear You cannot sell or freight the Angelica, I guess it is for this vessel You are making the Enquiry the Captain having told me without such freight or sale He must proceed empty round to London —This would be a heavy charge on the owners who perhaps have no freight for Her when She gets to London, where ships I am told are plenty & cheap. As She is an American bottom She can take no freight from hence, & Her Expences will be double as to lights & some other charges to those on a British bottom.[3]

Were I Her owner or could direct the Ship, I should have no Sort of Doubt to immideately fit Her out with Indented Servants and push Her to Richmond on James River, which place in a great measure commands an extensive back Country, where Servants are wanted, as well as the Towns of Norfolk Suffolk, Hampton, Petersburgh, & many other places upon and near James River, and from whence *Tobacco* of the first quality can be got for the proceeds of the Cargoe or even for the Ship Herself, and where it is very likely to obtain for Her a Tobacco or Corn freight to some British or European Port.

There is a moral certainty that a Cargoe of Wheat, and Her twixt Decks filld with James River Tobacco back to Cork or any port in Ireland will answer capitally well in the autumn or fall. If She goes to Richmond I would advise You to address the vessel to Messrs. Ben: Harrison & Son, who is a Gentleman of the first distinction & consequence in Virginia,[4] & who, if advisd of Her coming beforehand, would lodge directions for the Captain at the Post Office of Hampton or Norfolk advising Him *where* & to what spot to proceed.

If She goes to Petersburg which is very near Richmond, the House of Messrs. Pleasants may be trusted with anything, but Her owners will naturally know these & many other Gentlemen in Virginia.

I am Yr. Obedt. Serv.
Tho. Digges

Thos. Trant Esqr.
[Addressed:] Thomas Trant Esqr.

NYPL: Miscellaneous Papers.

¹Trant was a resident of Cork. Digges was writing either from there or from Dublin.
²According to Lloyd's Register, the *Washington*, owned by a Mr. Harvey and in the charge of a Captain Stickney, sailed in May from Cork.
³The owners of the *Angelica* were Jeremiah Wadsworth (1743–1804) and John Barker Church (1750–1818), merchants of Hartford, who had entered into a partnership in 1780 to handle contracts they had secured with the French. Wadsworth, a native of the city, had been commissary general of purchases for the Continental army before 1779, when he had resigned his position, and also commissary for the French troops in America until 1783. It was in connection with French contracts that he and Church had come together. Church, born in England, had fled to the United States for personal reasons at the beginning of the war, assumed the alias "Carter," become commissioner of accounts for the Northern Army in 1776, eloped with Gen. Schuyler's daughter Angelica, and in association with Wadsworth established a firm that traded extensively in grains. In behalf of their enterprise Wadsworth in Mar. 1784 had traveled to England and Ireland to invest in merchandise that he could carry back home. Trant was apparently his agent and successful, for on Aug. 11 Fitzgerald was able to write Peter Colt (1744–1824), also a Hartford merchant, experienced as a commissary and intimate with Wadsworth, that some ten days earlier Wadsworth and Church had sent the *Angelica* (under Captain Timothy Parker) to his address with approximately a hundred servants (MHS: Miscellaneous Bound, 17). For additional details see Digges to Huntington, Sept. 13, 1788.
⁴Benjamin Harrison (1726?–1791), formerly a member of Virginia's Committee of Correspondence, a delegate to the Continental Congress, and a signer of the Declaration of Independence, was currently governor of his state.

To ———

The addressee of Digges's letter, unnamed and still unidentified, was doubtless a friend of Shelburne's, for this letter and its enclosures have survived among Shelburne's papers—as copies, not in either Digges's or Shelburne's hand, but, one must suppose, in the hand of someone who wished Shelburne to have them.

[Dublin, August 1786]

Immediately after the signing the Preliminarys for peace, (to which I was the first tho' humble messenger at the outset of Lord

Rockinghams administration) I quitted London & have since visited many Countries & Climes, & I have been some time here on a matter of publick Agency as well as private Law business of my own, & which has troubled me nearly as much as all my uphill troubles during my agency for American Prisoners in England; But I hope very soon to finish & get to my old walks in London & Bath, & spend some time among a people whom I have every reason to like better & esteem more than those I have of late been obliged to Cohabit with.[1]

I understand that just about the close of the last Sessions of Parliament some publick stir was made about the St. Eustatia seiz'd papers,[2] & that my name was handed about as *one* of the purloiners of these papers from the secretary of States Office.—I got intimation of this from London, & had Ld. Rodneys & Genl. Vaughans depositions before Parliament sent over to me, together with a paragraph or two taken from the London News papers rather pointing at me, one of which I now enclose you. I also got a letter from a Gentleman (I believe *yet in publick Office*, & whose name out of Delicacy I forbear to mention) requesting some information about these papers. As his letter and my answer will in a great measure explain the matter to you I send you a Copy of them, together with the paragraph which led to my being informed about the movements of those two Commanders. You will oblige me very much by informing me if you heard any thing about the movements in Parliament near the close of the last Sessions respecting these St. Eustatia seized Papers, & if it is likely that Ld. Rodney & Genl. Vaughan will make any further stir about them—*Entre nous* I do know something about these papers, & many are *yet attainable*, not a mile from where I direct this letter to you, & at *my command & disposal*, But Ld. R. or General *Eosopus*[3] shall not derive any benefit from them without paying very smartly therefore—They were obtained by me in a perfectly fair & justifiable manner, which I will hereafter in confidence explain & prove to you, & *I* can acquit Lord Shelburne or any other personage then in Office from the insinuations of Lord Rodney & Genl. Vaughan. This is enough for me to say at present, & as I think you a very likely person to have heard something about the papers, I thus presume upon our former intimacy to solicit you to inform me, as soon as your Business will admit, what you have heard about them.

My direction is to No. 30 Essex Street Dublin.

[Enclosures]
[To Thomas Digges]
(Copy)

London 24 July 1786

SIR

Presuming on but a very slender acquaintance between us, I make free to address you on a subject which is in some measure a public one, and in which as two very honorable and gallant Men are materially affected I am in hopes from your well known generosity & Liberality you will comply with my request & forgive this intrusion on you.

You can be no stranger to the late movements in this place against Lord Rodney & Genl. Vaughan respecting the Capture of St. Eustatia, particularly their affidavits given into the House of Lords respecting the Seized Papers sent from St. Eustatia to Lord George Germaine's office & which appears to have been obtained out of that Office by an order from the Marquess of Rockingham or Lord Shelburne soon after the dismission from public employ of Lord North & his party; the substantial proofs of which you will see has been produced by Ld. Rodney & Genl. Vaughan thro' Mr. Knox, Mr. Polluck, Mr. Nepean,[4] & others now in Office, together with strong assertions that the papers in question were given up in consequence of said order to Mr. Savage,[5] & the *American Agent* then in London, *meaning you*—Ld. Rodney & Genl. Vaughan meant to get a Parliamentary Summons for you in order that your Testimony before the Lords might be brought into effect respecting the St. Eustatia Bill,[6] & otherways avert any damage to them, but could not find out thro' Mr. Adams, or any other American Gentleman here, *where* to be found further than that you were in Ireland.—After much enquiry in the City I have learnt from Mr. Johnstone[7] you are at present in Dublin, & without any Authority or request from Lord Rodney or Genl. Vaughan to do so, I have thus made free to intrude myself upon you, and to ask as a very particular favor if you know any thing about the papers in question, & *if they are attainable* at least such of them as will come in aid to the Captors of St. Eustatia to avert the heavy damages which have & are likely to be given in the Courts of Westminster against the said Captors. Altho I have no Authority for saying so, I am very sure Sir that no expence within the line of moderation will be spared to get them, & every acknowledgement of the obligation will be made to you.

However different your opinion in Politics might have been, I trust as the War & the t[h]reats of Animosity are now over you will agree with every one that they were two honorable Active & vigilant Officers for this Country & if they were led into any severity to Individuals, their order from a Superior power Obliged them to do so. Expecting the favor of an Answer I remain with respect Sir

       Your very obedt. Humble Servt.

For Thomas Digges Esqr./of Maryland/now in Dublin

       Answered Dublin Augst. 2d. 86

SIR

Your Letter of the 24 last Month did not reach me untill this day, when it was sent to my lodgings (free of any postage) by one of the Castle Servants & I am prompted to give it an Immediate answer from suposing you to be the Mr. ——— whom I had the honor to be introduced to by my late valuable friend Sr. Geo. Saville at Rufford in the Summer 1779—at least I cannot recollect an acquaintance with any other Gentleman of your name.

I certainly have been informed of some of the late movements in London respecting Lord Rodneys & Genl. Vaughans suits in the Courts of Westminster in consequence of their unparallelled conduct at & after the Capture of St. Eustatia, & I should not write truth to you were I to insinuate otherwise than I receivd much pleasure on hearing that the Actions in the Courts went generally against them, *with heavy damages & Costs.*[8]

I never heard they intended to send me a Parliamentary Summons had there been time at the close of the last Sessions for doing so:—They did well to spare themselves that additional expence, for, not withstanding the Omnipotence of the British Parliament (which I believe has heretofore been the subject of a conversation between yourself & me) I should certainly not have obeyed their Summons; being not ameanable to it or any other European Mandate—Yet perhaps I might have taken the journey to London, *as then* as well as in my present circumstances & situation it would have been a convenience to me.—I dont know what *proofs*, Ld. Rodney or Genl. Vaughan procured respecting the St. Eustatia seized Papers having been obtained out of the Secretary of State's Office by Mr. Savage & myself; *all* I have heard lately about it is from the vague relation of that matter in the inclosed printed paragraph which was taken from a London Newspaper & sent me; & I am given to believe if those Commanders do not obtain more substantial proof than this Newspaper paragraph they will soon have more heavy damages & Costs to pay.

I can justify as well by written Testimony as by some of the Gentlemen themselves in *Office* that *all* the Papers which fell to my lot to obtain, *were fairly gotten*; & there are a quantity of them *yet attainable* in London without your being authorized by Ld. Rodney or Genl. Vaughan so to do. Your request to be informed about these papers appears to me to be an extraordinary one, for I know not in what manner either the loss or the attainment of them can affect you.— There are Gentlemen in the City of London & other parts of the World to whom these papers would be of very essential Service, & it is on their Accounts I mean yet to hold them. Whatever may be your attachment to or opinion about those two Commanders I stand under no sort of Compliment or gratitude to them. Lord Rodney if he will condescend to reflect, may perhaps recollect & acknowledge himself under some triffling obligations to me & two or three other Americans whom he at times conversed with at Paris during his Difficulties in that City[9]—His severe treatment of Mr. Saml. Curzon the Congress Agent at St. Eustatia (& my particular friend & intimate) whose health was ruined by being tether'd & kept upon the Cable Tier of the 64 Gun Ship which brought him a State Prisoner to England & the Cruelty of forceing the American Seamen whom he Captured in the West Indies to war in his own Ship against their Country are acts sufficient to prevent my being prone to do his Lordship any essential favour—much less claim has General Vaughan on me—His conduct at the new and populous Town of *Esopus* near new York where he forced Men, Women & Children naked & without food into the fields [⟨"⟩]spared not a single House from the flames"* is still recent in my memory & will not readily be for gotten by any true American.

I expect soon to be in London at my old quarters, where I will recieve any further communications from You & am in the mean time Sir

       Yr. Obedt. Servt.
       T. D.

(*Vide London Gazette)

  Copy of the London Paragraph alluded to in the Letter
"The affairs of giving up the St. Eustatia papers to a certain American Agent by his friend & patron the then Secretary of State is yet much the subject of conversation, & Ld. Rodney's well known spirit & attention to his Country's rights, will not let a matter rest which requires public investigation: All the discovery this Active Commander has yet been able to make is, that the papers were got out of the Secretary of State's Office, very soon after Ld. North's dismission by a Mr. Digges who had acted during the War as Agent under Congress for the American Prisoners in England, & had been employed as a first Messenger for Peace to Dr. Francklin & Mr. Adams; & who as a reward or bonus for his Services to the then Patriotick Administration, obtained from a noble Marquess a letter to the Secretarys Office to have all his Seized Papers restored to him—In seeking his own he found the papers of many others of his friends & Correspondents & by some means or other got all the papers of Mr. Curzon & Gouvernier the Congress Agents at St. Eustatia, & then State Prisoners for treason in England, also those of Mr. Laurens & Mr. Trumbull, then in the Tower, as well as some belonging to his London Acquaintances; & for want of which last Ld. Rodney & Genl. Vaughan

have lately been cast in the Courts of Westminster with very heavy damages & Costs.["]

UM: Shelburne Papers, 84, items 107 and 159.

---

[1] Among Digges's troubles was imprisonment for debt. On June 17, 1785, Jonathan Williams had written Franklin from Dublin: "You will not be much Surprised when I tell you, that Mr. Diggs, who has So much of our Prisoners money is in . . . Prison; He has been playing the Rogue in this Country, but like all other cunning Rogues Shewn himself to be a Fool also, and is now paying Severely for his Folly & Wickedness" (APS: Franklin Papers, 38:158).

In Oct. Digges had joined some "gentlemen of the Four Courts Marshalsea"—fellow prisoners—in testifying to the effective work of Doctor Wemys, who had "for a considerable time attended the poor prisoners in a malignant fever, attended with mortifications" and through "his care and method" enabled "the people . . . [to be] restored to a proper state of health" (*Dublin Journal*, Oct. 31, 1785). And in Dec. he, along with others, had signed a statement giving notice that they intended "to take the Benefit of an Act of Parliament passed last Sessions, intitled, *An Act for the Relief* of Insolvent Debtors, with Respect to the Imprisonment of their Persons" (*Dublin Gazette*, Dec. 3–6, 1785).

[2] Early in Feb. 1781 Adm. Rodney and Gen. Vaughan had taken possession of the Dutch island now consistently known as St. Eustatius (or, among the inhabitants, as Statia) and confiscated £3,000,000 worth of goods found there. Set up as a free port by the Dutch, St. Eustatius, with warehouses filled with all kinds of produce and products from both sides of the Atlantic, had offered an accessible trading center for neutrals and belligerents alike. Rodney, convinced that the Dutch had been enjoying the cooperation of British merchants willing to violate Britain's blockade for the sake of profit, had seized merchandise and stores possessed by Englishmen along with those possessed by the Dutch: any British merchant with property there, he had reasoned, must have been guilty of trading with England's enemies, supplying them with critical provisions, naval stores, ammunition, and weapons. To expose these treacherous compatriots, Rodney had then taken off their commercial letterbooks and ledgers, together with the papers of the two island agents of the Continental Congress, Samuel Curson and Isaac Gouverneur, whom he had made prisoners, arguing that they had enabled Dutch aid to reach America and should, British citizens still, be tried in London for high treason. To assure the safety of all these documents he had seen to it that they were given to Germain's care. But from the very start of his proceedings against the merchants Rodney had had to face protests, both from Englishmen on the island insistent on the legitimacy of their property and from members of Parliament critical of Rodney's and Vaughan's tactics and their having sold captured goods for personal profit. Now the two commanders were having to defend themselves in the admiralty court against suits for restitution. For their defense they wanted as supporting evidence the papers that had been consigned to Germain's care, but the papers had vanished. Shelburne, who as Germain's successor had been secretary of state when the papers had disappeared, was now out of office and apparently could provide no leads. Digges, though, was in some quarters suspected of knowing the papers' whereabouts.

³Digges's name for Vaughan because of Vaughan's actions at Esopus (Kingston, N.Y.) in 1777, mentioned in Digges's enclosed copy of his reply to an unnamed correspondent.

⁴William Knox, undersecretary to the colonial department at the time of the papers' disappearance; William Pollock, still first clerk in that office, and Evan Nepean (1751–1822), undersecretary of state in Shelburne's ministry and now undersecretary for the Home Office.

⁵Arthur Savage (ca. 1731–1801), an American loyalist from Boston and former comptroller of the customs at Falmouth, who had assisted in examining the seized papers. He had been living in England since 1776.

⁶"An Act for vesting in Trustees, the Stores, Effects, and Property, captured from the Enemy by His Majesty's Forces at or near the Islands of Saint Eustatius, Saint Martin, and Saba, and their Dependencies, in the Year One thousand and eighty-one, and for enabling said Trustees to place out Amount of said Property at Interest upon Government Security, for the Benefit of the several Persons intitled thereto, until the Claims made shall have been determined, and a just Distribution thereof can be made," introduced in the House of Lords, June 26, 1786.

⁷Which Mr. Johnstone this is remains uncertain.

⁸Sixty-four claims, heard individually, had been made against Rodney and Vaughan by June 17, 1783. The two lost repeatedly and were compelled to make restitution to the claimants, not according to the amount of the returns from sales but according to the original value of prime cost, with charges, freights, and insurance included.

⁹In 1775 Rodney, after four years in command of the Jamaica station, had contracted so many debts because of his known fascination with women and addiction to pleasure that he had gone to Paris to escape his creditors, remaining there until made an admiral in 1778.

To Thomas Jefferson

Dublin May 12, 1788—
No. 30 Essex Street

SIR¹

A Cotton manufactory having been lately set up in Virginia, not only patronizd by the State but encouragd by some of the leading Gentlemen in it,² some artists from England as well as this Country are wishing to get to it; And altho I have been a little hurt since my arrival in Ireland through my endeavours to get some useful mechanicks to my home near Alexandria,³ (two or three of whom are *now* under rigourous trial in the Courts here for attempting to ship themselves with their Tools implements &ca. &ca.) I cannot refrain from troubling Your Excellency with this letter—merely introductory of Mr. Henry Wild now the leading mover of the late Major Brookes's Cotton Manufactory at Prosperous near Naas in this County. This Gentleman about the year 1782 made an effort, thro' the direction & advice of Doctor Franklyn, to whom He is well known, (and in which he was somewhat aided by me) to move with His Family &ca. &ca. to Philadelphia; but on the point of his Embarkation he was forcibly & openly stoppd by an order from the Secretary of State, and Mr. Brookes above mentiond obtaind a large premium for getting Mr. Wild fixd at Prosperous as director & conductor of the principal & still most flourishing Cotton Manufactory in this Kingdom.[4]

Mr. Wild, who is not only at the head of His trade as an Artist but an excellent scholar & man of genius, has long & still ardently wishes to settle in a Country, which from his principles in politicks & love of liberty, He looks to as far above his own, has brought his affairs to nearly that Crisis as to enable him to move from Ireland; and stands only in need of that advice & proper direction in his attempt which I would wish ever honest & good Tradesman to possess before he wildly sets down in America.

You will oblige him very much Sir, and it will be rendering our State an acquisition to get such an able & accomplishd artist to settle in it, if You will favour myself, or Him, with a line mentioning what state the Cotton Manufactory is in—at what particular spot in Virginia it is fixd—what Engines or implements are most immediately necessary for him to take—The tradesmen such as Spinners or Weavers most wanted—who are the directors or patrons of the Work—where & to whom to apply on his landing—or any other directions which may strike You as most useful for Him. Mr. Wild is not only a perfect master, but can construct *every article of machinery* necessary for the Cotton Manufactory. I not only wish him success in it, but most ardently request You to add your advice & aid to Him in the further progress of His plan.

I am with the highest Esteem
Your Excellencys Most
Obedt. & very Hle. Servant
Thos. Digges

P. S. My direction is to *No. 30 Essex St. Dublin*, And Mr. Wild will add his at the foot of this Letter & mention any other matters He may want to communicate, for I am obligd to send this letter to Him at Naas some 15 or 20 miles from hence.[5] I woud recommend that what You write Him may be directed to me; for as a Citizen & tradesman He may be much injurd if the substance of this correspondence should become known.

I can give Mr. Wild introductory Letters to my neighbour Genl. Washington & many others at Alexandria & thereabouts but I guess the manufactory is at or near Richmond.

There is a Mr. Jno. Linton a Printer & dyer of Cottons a perfect Master of his Trade who would also attend Mr. Wild to America.

[Addressed:] For His Excellency/Thomas Jefferson,/Envoy &ca. &ca. from the United States of America at Paris

LC: Jefferson Papers, Series 1.

[1] Jefferson (1743–1826) was in Paris, having in 1785 succeeded Franklin as minister to France.

[2] In his reply of June 19 Jefferson said he was unaware of such a manufactory and argued that manufactures could not succeed in America, where the great demand was for agricultural workers and the price of factory labor was consequently high (LC: Jefferson Papers, Series 1 [Reel 9]).

[3] On Apr. 17, 1788, the *Dublin Evening Post* reported: "Friday last, the right hon. the Attorney General applied to the Court of Kings-bench, for an information against a Mr. D——, on a charge that he had seduced various artificers and mechanics to embark for America. The Court granted the rule, and it is a high misdemeanor to exercise such kidnapping practices."

[4] Henry Wyld had visited Franklin in Dec. 1781 to explain his plans to establish a cotton manufactory near Philadelphia. The manufactory of Robert Brooke (d. 1802?) that he now ran could be called "late" because of its recent misfortunes. Brooke had served and fought gallantly in Bengal in the interests of the East India Company from 1764 to 1775, rising from ensign to captain, and returned to the British Isles to establish the village of Prosperous in County Kildare with the object of developing cotton manufactures there. Digges was mistaken in locating it in Dublin County. Although he had perfected many of the manufacturing processes, he had not escaped debts, with the result that in 1787 he personally had had to give up his enterprise for the benefit of his creditors. In that year he had been appointed governor of St. Helena and served until illness forced him to return home in 1801.

[5] Wyld did not add anything to Digges's letter but preferred to write one of his own on May 20 and send it as an enclosure (MoHS. See *PTJ*, 13:183–84.)

To Samuel Huntington

Dublin Septemr. 13. 1788—

Having just heard that the Catharine Capt. Parker of and for New London is to sail tomorrow I have taken the liberty, tho personally unknown, to address Your Excellency[1] and forward some written proofs of the illicit and very unfair methods which the Magistracy of Dublin, & others concernd, have for the last few years practicd, and are still intent upon practicing, for the introduction of the Felons & Convicts of Ireland into the United States of America *as Indented Servants.*

I am well assurd I stand in no need of an appology to Your Excellency for this intrusion—my motive will be a plea for the trouble I put You to, and I trust these my hints may tend to prevent in future the admission of such vile miscreants (for of all people in the world the Irish Convicts are the wickedest) into our Country. I have before frequently written to Virginia and Maryland upon the subject, for my having a heavy Chancery Suit to look after in this Country has brought me often to it, & causd a frequent residence in it since 1784. So that I am a witness to three or four of the six instances mentiond in the inclosd paper and particularly so to the two Cargoes of them disposd of to Colo. Wm. Deakins at George Town,[2] & to my Brother in Law Colo. Jno. Fitzgerald at Alexandria; But as every Ship load takes a new destination, & goes to a distant part from where they dropt the last, it is very difficult to assertain in time for detection *where* they go. This was the Case with the 201 Shipd on board the Nancy Capt. Rob. Winthrop in June last—I was then on the spot, but could not after the most industrious enquiry assertain to what part of the Continent Capt. Winthrop meant to take them, and I little suspected that an *American,* with a respectable connection, & relations ranking among the first of his fellow Citizens, would commit so base an act upon his own neighbourhood or even at any distant part from it, as to plant such villainy & vices immidiately at his home,[3] for I understand He arrivd at New London the middle of July last and disposed of his *precious* Cargoe as Indented Servants from Ireland!! This has been the trick imposd upon our people every where, and if some stop is not put to it, or examples made of their Carriers, no one can tell to what depth the evil may extend. I send You now the clearest proof that one of Your own Citizens has so lately as July last imposd *201* Convicted Felons from Newgate in Dublin upon his unsuspecting Countrymen as *Indented. Servants from Ireland.* It is true they were indented to himself in the Goal of Newgate a few days before embarkation, in presence of the mayor of Dublin or His Secretary, thereby the better to cover the design, & it is the interest of the Culprits themselves to keep the Secret & pass for Indented Servants rather than be stigmatizd as Convicts.

The inhumanity and bad treatment given to some Cargoes in the instances I have stated in the inclosure (*which I think ought to be publishd in all the Papers of America*) is disgraceful to humanity, and I am sorry that Capt. R. Winthrop (of whom Capt. Parker & others have given me a good Character) should be the first *American* depraved enough to so vilely impose upon His fellow Citizens.

I could not believe the accounts in the News papers (which I send Your Excellency in a seperate parcell) of the arrival of this vessel at New London—the sailing of which with Her Cargoe of Convicts I had been witness to but so short a time back; and I went on board the Catharine & learnt from all Her Crew that She had arrivd, and was selling Her Cargoe as Indented Servants just before Capt. Parker saild. It was given out before Capt. Winthrop saild, & I had some reason to believe the account, that He was bound among His fellow Loyalists for Port Roseway, or Shelburne in Nova Scotia, but I suppose he had heard the account of the 4th vessel which Saild having touchd there and the people had unanimously & wisely rejected them.

I have reason to think that from my informations heretofore that the States of Virginia & Maryland have, or very soon will pass some Law against the admission of such Cargoes as Capt. Winthrops. The Ship carrying them should be made liable to Confiscation & no Servants of any kind admitted without strictly swearing the Captain & his officers as to their regular & fair indenture, and possitively to their not being Convicts.

Captain Parker himself in the year 1784 when I casually met him at Cork wanting a freight for his Ship Angelica, took out by my direction & advice a Cargoe of Indented Servants for 3, four, & five years, and consignd them to my Brother in Law Colo. Fitzgerald in Alexandria—another larger ship went at the same time & to the same place, and altho I had not a shilling concern in them I had the satisfaction of knowing they both made great voyages.[4]

I mention this because it brought Capt. Parker to my House & Estate *Warburton* near Alexandria, & fronting General Washingtons: He can inform You Sir who & what I am, that I have long been & am in the trust & confidence of my Country, having servd it during almost the whole of the last war as agent under Congress for American Prisoners in England, and that I would not intrude an account upon You that I could not veryfy as fact. Your Excellency may rest assurd that the account herewith sent is perfectly just in *substance* however it may be defficient in minute detail.

I shall be exceedingly obligd for a few lines in answer and for information in particular about Capt. Winthrops Sale of his passengers as *Indented Servants*; and I would not ask the favour of Your Excellency but that such information will tend to put a stop *even here* to the putting the Felons upon us; for I am at this present in the habit of frequently seeing & speaking to the Lord Lieutenant upon the matter who promises to get them properly sent abroad *as the law directs* in future. My direction is to the care of Messrs. Wallace, Johnson, & Muir Merchts. Tower Hill London, & if the letter is put on board any English Ship will come easily & safe to me. If the matter is publishd in the American papers (as I really am [of the] opinion it ought to be directly) I should be very thankful for a Paper that contains it, coverd to the direction above. I am with the highest Esteem & Respect

Your Excellencys
Most obt. & very Hle. Servt.
Thomas Digges

P.S. I send a small packet under the same direction with this Letter to Your Excellency which contains a few of the late news papers of Dublin & I have markd such paragraphs relating to the Convicts as I think should be republishd in America.

I also inclose Your Excellency a Letter from Joseph Harrington late mate of the Ship Baltimore bound to Baltimore (who with Thos. Philpot Super Cargoe of the Ship Golden Rule for Maryland) were taken out of their Ships in March last & condemnd to two years Confinement in New Gate & a thousand pounds Strg. fine, for enviegling away *artists* as Indented Servants to America—these *artists* as they are stiled were three ragged & starving beggars one a *Taylor*, the other a *thread maker*, & another a *Wire Drawer*. A printed account of the trial goes herewith, & should I think be publishd to guard the American Captains from being taken in by such infamous informers, for it was all a plan laid to share in the fine.

For His Excelly. Governor Huntingdon[5]

[Enclosure]

Dublin Septr. 13th 1788—

The Convict Ships which saild from Dublin since the War disposd of their Cargoes as follows[6]

The *first* Vessel—Was the Brigantine Nancy, said to be of N. York, Michael Cunnim Master, (who with his Brother who was Mate, were chief owners) saild from Dublin about 19th Nov. 84, took out of New Gate about 100 Convicts, and attempted to land them all on the Island of Farro [Ferro (Herrio)] (the News papers said the Island of Teneriffe). But after three boat loads were landed the crew revolted at carrying any more & a scuffle ensued between them & the Captain & Mate. For the want of a health visit, or Pratique, an indispensible rule in all the Spanish & Portugue Ports, these poor people to the number of about *forty six*, were surrounded by the Army & every one put to Death!! The vessel got away & went to the West Indies & was from the informations given against the Capt. taken & held by the Boreas frigate, The Captain was put in prison in St. Kitts but He got clear for want of Evidence & by saying the Crew mutinyd upon Him. He was in Dublin for a few days in Feby. 87 & would have been again taken up had He stayd.

The 2d was   The Snow Ann Mary Ann of Dublin Capt. Duncan Nev-

13 SEPTEMBER 1788   415

in (with one Shannon a Super Cargoe) saild from Dublin with *120* odd Felons the 20 Sepr. 1785, calld at Corke and took on board 50 more and saild from thence the 1st October. The felons were all previously sham indented in presence of the Mayor & his Secretary in New gate to Shannon the Super Cargoe—They were bound for Baltimore & consignd to the House of Stewart & Plunket Merchants there (who were concernd in the Cargoe) but the Ship was met off the Capes by a Pilot boat purposely sent by Stewart & Plunket and the Vessel orderd to George Town on Potowmack where they were all sold by Colonel Wm. Deakins & The Super Cargoe as *Indented Servants.*
- The *3d* Vessel was   The Dragon Brig belonging to Dublin Capt. Hamilton (with the same Shannon as Super Cargoe). She saild from Dublin about the 20 June 86 and took *145* Convicts having them also first sham Indented to Shannon as before & in presence of the Mayor of Dublin and His Secretary. This Vessel was to call at Corke for *45* more, and the whole was sold in a lump to Colonel John Fitzgerald in Alexandria Virginia in Augt. 1786 as Indented Servants from Ireland.
- The *4th* vessel   Was the Snow Dispatch of Yarmouth in England Captain Napper who saild from Dublin in June *87* and took 183 Convicts from New Gate. It was mentiond in the Dublin papers that they were all landed at port Roseway or Shelburne in Nova Scotia in Augt. 87, but the people there very wisely refusd to admit them on Shore or receive them in any way. The Captain was in Consequence Inducd to put them all on Shore in a remote & desolate part of Machias Bay, where many of them perishd & others beggd their way & dispersd themselves through parts of the United States under cover of their being Indented Servants from Ireland & put on shore by the Captain for want of Provisions & water.
- The 5th vessel   The Brig Chance Captain Stafford of Barmouth in Wales took about 120 Convicts from New Gate and landed them on the dessolate Island of Heneaga [Inagua] (one of the Bahamas) where they sufferd extreme hardships & want, and the *forty-*

nine Survivors were accidentally & providentially seen by an American Vessel passing nearer than usual to that Island, the Captain of which took them on board & after humanely supporting them landed them in some part of New England.

  Capn. Stafford is an Irishman from the County of Wicklow and has a Wife & family in Baltimore Maryland, but from this inhuman act has become a fugitive from both Countrys.

The 6th vessel was the Brigantine Nancy Captain Robert Winthrop of and from New London in Connecticut. He saild from Dublin in June 1788 and took from New Gate *201* Convicts they being previously indented to Him in New Gate for three years Service in presence of the Mayor and His Secretary. By the news paper Accounts This vessel arrivd at New London about the middle of July 1788—and after disposing of many in and about that place by selling them as Indented Irish Servants for three years Capt. Winthrop sent the remainder to the Southward for Sale.

A *seventh* Vessel was sought after & about to be hired in Dublin in Sepr. 1788 to take out another Cargoe of these miserable & wicked people, for it is notoriously & well know[n] that a Dublin Convict is generally the most villainous & depravedly wicked of any other of the Human Species.

Mr. H. W. Stockdale a Merchant of Dublin has hitherto been the Contractor for Convicts, and engaged most if not all the foregoing vessels to take them out.

  The Mayor of Dublin is now allowd *ten pounds* a head by Government for taking these Felons to a part of *British* America. He can easily contract with Merchants or Captains of Ships to take them for five or *six* pounds a head, so that in the first instance He pockets from four to five pounds a head, and must have got by Captain Winthrops *201* passengers at least 800 if not 1000 £. Captain Winthrops advancd frieght of five, or say *six* pounds Stg. per head, must amount to 1200 £, and if He sold them for even the reducd same sum in America, the Amount of profit, allowing 400 £ for their provision outward, must have exceeded 2000 £!! a very strong temptation to such a wicked, unfair, & nefarious trafic for the United States.

Dublin Septr. 13th, 1788—

SIR,

The foregoing account if not minutely true, You may rely is substantially so; And I take the liberty to address it to You in order to have it publishd in the American News papers, thereby to warn & guard the unsuspecting Citizens of the United States against any impositions of this sort in future.

To His Excellency Samuel Huntingdon } A Friend to America
    Governor of Connecticut

[Addressed:] For His Excellency/Governor Huntington

HEH: Ms. HM 47751 and HM 1613.

[1] A former member of the Continental Congress, a signer of the Declaration of Independence, and recently chief justice of Connecticut's Superior Court, Huntington (1731–1796) had become governor of his state in 1786 and was to be reelected to that office annually until his death.

[2] Deakins was one of the first directors of the Potomack Company, established in 1785 to open and promote navigation of the Potomac River.

[3] Robert Winthrop (1764–1832) was the great-great-great-grandson of the first governor of Massachusetts Bay, and his immediate family had long been settled in Norwich, Conn., near New London. Despite the respectability of his lineage, though, young Winthrop was no ardent patriot. His father had died before the Revolution, and his mother, a loyalist, had shortly after the outbreak of hostilities arranged with her brother, stationed with the British on Manhattan, to have Robert educated in England. There he had soon entered the British navy and in 1782, as a midshipman on Rodney's flagship, participated in the British victory over the French fleet off Dominica. At the conclusion of the peace he had sailed home to go into business with his half-brother William, a Norwich merchant, and at the time of Digges's letter was still engaged in the family's commercial ventures. But two years later he would return to England and resume his career in the Royal Navy.

[4] For an earlier reference to his dealings with Captain Timothy Parker, see Digges to Trant, May 5, 1784.

[5] Huntington's endorsement states that he replied on Dec. 15, but this letter has not been found.

[6] With only minor variations in details, none of them substantive, the account written by Digges appeared in the *Hibernian Journal*, Sept. 15, 1788, the *Dublin Evening Post* and the *Dublin Chronicle*, Sept. 16, 1788, and the *Dublin Journal*, Sept. 13–16, 1788 (with a Sept. 15 dateline). Digges was apparently responsible for the publication. Earlier Digges could have read brief reports of the voyages of the *Anne Mary Ann*, the *Dragon*, the *Dispatch*, and the *Nancy* in, respectively, *Faulkner's Dublin Journal*, Sept. 24–27, 1785,

and the *Volunteer's Journal*, Feb. 20, 1786; the *Freeman's Journal*, Mar. 27–29, 1787; ibid., Aug. 23–25, 1787; and the *Dublin Evening Post* and the *Dublin Chronicle*, Sept. 9, 1788.

To Theobald Wolfe Tone

Best known for his association with Thomas Russell (1767–1803) in organizing the United Irishmen in 1791 for the purpose of curbing England's influence in Irish politics and ultimately freeing the Irish from it completely, Tone (1763–1798) was at this earlier moment primarily concerned over a threatened war between Great Britain and Spain. In September 1790, reflecting upon the importance of the recent discovery of the Sandwich Islands, he had sent to the duke of Richmond and to Grenville a proposal for establishing a British military settlement there that would serve as an outpost in case of such a war and provide a valuable position for attacking Spain's commerce. When in October his proposal had been no more than politely acknowledged, he had considered it rejected. Yet now war with Spain had come closer, and Tone had decided to renew his efforts, this time by extending his proposal to include the subversion of Spain in South America. Russell, kept informed by Tone of all the proceedings, had gone to Belfast from Dublin and there met Digges, who, in turn, shown all Tone's correspondence with the ministers, had then written out some comments to assist Tone. Tone was particularly interested in the possibilities of encouraging uprisings against Spanish rule.

[Belfast, November or December 1790]

There have been several ineffectual attempts made by the Mexicans to revolt from Spain, but I have heard of none in the Peruvian quarter; yet this last strikes me as the most eligible situation for such an attempt, because there is a larger portion of the people native descendants of America, who keep up a jealousy for their old blood and color. The priests too are not so numerous nor richly stationed as in Mexico, where they have a vast power over the people; and, above all, there is a great part of Peru, particularly about Chili, and near the

[November/December 1790]   419

island of Chīloë that has never been conquered by Spain, and the natives hold them in dislike and defiance. I have been told this by two Spanish friars, who passed with difficulty from Mexico to Congress on a secret mission for revolution, and came to me during my agency for America in London, in 1779 or '80, as well as by an old jesuit by the name of Faulkner, an Englishman, who lived lately at Worcester, and spent twenty years of his life near the Rio de la Plata and Peru, as well as by some of my countrymen who have found their way to Mexico from New Orleans and Kentucky.

I am clearly of opinion that no predatory expedition, for the sake of plunder or territory, will do good. The churches must be held inviolable from insult, and the priests offered every thing. Indeed the priests should be the first objects to get at. Through them it may be easily communicated to the people that the expedition is not meant for conquest or plunder, nor to deprive any one of his property, but merely to shake off the Spanish yoke, and make the people their own masters.

In the year 1760, there was a very general tumult in Mexico. It was the people against the Government of Spain, that is, the governors, army, tax officers, who are very numerous, priests, &c. The dispute was about the king's quinta, or one-fifth of all saleable property, bullion, &c. It gave Spain more uneasiness than all the thunders of the memorable Pitt. In 1761, a deputation of respectable Mexicans, groaning under the galling yoke of ecclesiastical hierarchy and tyranny, empowered the Marquis De Auberade to offer Lord Shelburne, then in the Ministry, a large territory and a subsidy of £ 300,000 a year, for the assistance of two ships of war and a regiment of infantry, the expense of which was also to have been paid by those colonists; but this proposal, though very advantageous, was refused by the cabinet as tending to promote * * * * * * * *.[1] It came to London too, when some overtures had been made for a peace.

There was another attempt to revolt and surprise the king's troops at Mexico, in 1774. I could never get any accurate account of it, although it was currently talked of at Madrid, where I was that winter, and heard in confidence from the Marquis De Auberade, the story before recited. Indeed, it was dangerous at that time to speak about the affair. I was told by the king's librarian, that Dr. Robertson, the historian,[2] then collecting materials for his book, was in possession of the whole story.—The Doctor was too fond of royalty to state it fairly in his history. In 1785, there were risings of the people in great numbers, on account of the king's troops seizing upon some mines a little south of Mexico, but they were soon dispersed by the troops, and by the acts of the priests. The Governor of New Orleans,[3] where several North Americans reside and trade to, received an express over land, about September, 1789, of a serious insurrection of the people in the neighborhood of Mexico, owing to an attempt to seize some mines for the king's quinta. The people to the amount of 7 or 8,000 appeared before and menaced the capital, and had actually got possession of the king's magazine, which, by-the-by, was destitute of arms. They were here again checked by the priests.

During the war between England and America, and even at the period when Spain was an ally to the latter, several Spaniards from the northern stations of Mexico, and particularly four Spanish friars, two of whom were Jesuits, found their way to Congress, and actually produced a plan for the emancipation of New Spain. Congress had then formed offensive and defensive alliance with the Court of Madrid, and could not violate first faith. Indeed, to this day, it would be very difficult to get that body, and more particularly the President, to engage in any act of hostility against Spain; but the states individually, and particularly those of Maryland, Virginia, Carolina, and Georgia, would secretly give help, and numbers of gentlemen are ripe and ready to assist their southern brethren. Two of the above friars, with a certain Padre Heres Mendez, who was taken about the same time in a ship from Vera Cruz, and was often with the Ministry, and was to have gone out in Governor Johnson's squadron to the Rio de la Plata,[4] were frequently with me, the two former bringing introductions to me from some leading men in Maryland, and were very positive that the slightest aid in ships and troops would bring vast numbers to the standard of freedom, in any part of New Spain. They had a worse opinion of the Peruvian districts of South America, but their arguments never convinced me, for the people there being less under the yoke, may surely be easiest brought to revolt.

At that time two young Mexicans remained in Maryland, which is the most Catholic of the states, and went back since the peace. The consequence of this communication has been, that we have now four or five students at the college of Philadelphia, and Washington College, Maryland, from Lima, Mexico, and Santa Fe. This intercourse will, in the end, I am persuaded, lead to the completion of a most ardent and general wish throughout United America, the freedom and independence of Spanish America. I know there are plans and emissaries now in North America, in England, and in Old Spain, for even near the throne there are Spanish nobles who wish for it, trying to fix correspondences, and to get aid for the revolt. It may take years to accomplish it in this uphill way; but it surely would be accelerated by England now beginning hostilities with Spain, and despatching some small force of ships and men to act on either side of Mexico.

If, without warfare with the natives, England could make a military settlement in the Sandwich Isles, the temperature of the Pacific Ocean would admit of easy excursions into the coast of Mexico, and those places near the Isthmus of Darien, Panama, &c. At this last place the Spaniards are generally strongest in military and weakest in ships. Acapulco, in Mexico, is better guarded with ships, as the Manilla and Philippine riches flow more into Spain through this than any other part of South America. I fear England will never give up her heretofore constant practice of warring for dominion and plunder. How few wars has that country been engaged in for liberty or for freedom!

The subjects of Spain in Mexico, or those we may call royalists, are very few, but hold the whole weight of power. By every account that I have been able to collect, they do not form near the proportion to the other inhabitants, that our North American royalists did at the period of our revolt. One line of battle ship and a few frigates, with 3,000 soldiers, would insure the surrender of Lima or Valdivia, but they could never be held without aid, and a good understanding with the people. The going there or to any more insignificant port in Mexico, for the purpose of conquest or plunder, would certainly fail of success. Get a station in any spot, and make known that your intention is to free the country, and not injure the people in their rights, and it will insure a revolution.

Life of Theobald Wolfe Tone, ed. William Theobald Wolfe Tone, 2 vols. (Washington: Gales & Seaton, 1826), 1:539–42.

¹The date is probably a typographical error; otherwise Digges would be mistaken about either the year or Shelburne's position. Shelburne had succeeded to his father's earldom late in 1761 and then entered the House of Lords, but it was not until 1763, with his acceptance of the presidency of the Board of Trade and the position of privy councillor, that he became a member of the cabinet and not until 1766–1767 that he held the influential position of secretary of state, southern department. In fact, it was during 1766–1767 that Guillaume-Claude d'Aubarede (b. 1717), an adventurous French marquis with a record of distinguished military service in his own country and subsequent service in the Spanish infantry, became engaged in plotting the separation of New Spain (Mexico) and Louisiana from Spain. (Dr. Eric Beerman, Madrid, an authority on Spain's archives, has uncovered the foregoing elusive facts.) The unprintable word remains speculative; Professor Thomas Holloway, Cornell University, suggests that it may be "sedition" (the number of letters matches the asterisks), but the need for such circumspection is for others to explain.

²William Robertson, D.D. (1721–1793), was collecting materials for his *History of America* (London: W. Strahan and T. Cadell; and Edinburgh: J. Balfour, 1777); he was principal of the University of Edinburgh, historiographer to His Majesty for Scotland, and member of the Royal Academy of History at Madrid.

³Estevan Miró, more correctly called the governor of Louisiana.

⁴At an earlier date governor of West Florida and then member of the Carlisle peace commission (see Digges to Franklin, Dec. 19, 1778, n. 3), George Johnstone was also a sailor and in Mar. 1781, as commodore of a small squadron cruising off Portugal, had been assigned the task of taking the Cape of Good Hope from the Dutch. In what turned out to be an unsuccessful attempt to deceive the French, reports were circulated that Johnstone was bound for South America, a destination Digges appears to have still regarded as fact.

To Thomas Jefferson

Belfast 28 April 1791

Sir

I wrote You on the 24th Int. & am sorry to put You to the trouble of reading a second long Letter nearly upon the same Subject—It is of such importance to the Manufacturers of our Country as to insure me Your forgiveness. The artist Mr. Wm. Pearce, mentiond in my former Letter & whose works You will have describd at the End of this Letter, has finally determind to go for America with his Invention, & to fix there; And I have so little time before the Vessel sails to address The President & YourSelf on the subject of Pearce's & McCabe getting a Patent or premision for their work, that I hope You will excuse haste & inaccuracys.[1]

I before wrote You that a Box was forwarded to Mr. Geo. Woolsey Merchant of New York and a relation of McCabes, containing the materials & specifications for a new Invented double Loom, & so sent For the Inspection of the President & YourSelf as to obtain for the Inventors Pearce & McCabe a *Patent* or such exclusive Benefit as the Laws of America provide for Artists who furnish new & usefull Inventions.— At that time I had my Eye upon Pearce, & a strong hope of his going, but as His doing so much crashd with the present Interest of his Partner McCabe, I was necessiated to write to Yourself and the President in the stile I then did *as if Pearce was not to go.* He is now, very much to my satisfaction & pleasure, so engaged as not to be able to recede, without a forcible stop from the Government, who are making Laws & trying all possible means to stop the Emigration of Artists & their Tools—I need not tell You that it is not only Difficult to get such away, but highly dangerous to those concernd; Therefore the more secret it is kept the better. Pearce will bear this Letter to Yourself and a similar one to the President; together with the box before mentiond.[2] For fear of a miscarriage of my former Letter I will annex to this a duplicate of my discription of his Sundry Looms &ca., as also to inform You that the Box contains a pair of *double Temples* near 7 ft. in Length for spreading at the same time two ps/s of Linin or Callico on one Loom, also a set of *Headles*, Elbow, & Shuttle for Linin &ca. I have one satisfaction that should they miscarry, Pearce if He Lives can make every atom of them (which I beleive no other Man can do) and with Him goes two ingenious workmen Jameson, & Hall,[3] who can make most kinds of Machinery such as Spining Jennys, Billys, Mules, Carding Machines &ca. and they will be excellent *seconds* to Pearce who has been twice or thrice beset here by Emissarys from Manchester to invigle Him back to England, & I doubt not but they will follow him for like purposes to America.

He puts his trust in the President & in You to whom it is with alacrity I have given every testimonial in my power of his industry, sobriety, worth & Extraordinary [*several words torn off*] illiterate man. He is not rich 'tho an Independent Man having [*tear*] of money left in the hands of a friend in Manchester on whom He can draw (which He has done to me for the advance of getting him & the other two out & for passage money &ca.). He has a wife & Family in England who will soon follow him, & I trust his invitations will lead a number of Mechanic Artists to follow his fortunes. I have given Him introductory Letters to Mr. Seton of N. York,[4] Conyngham & Nesbit, Governor Dickinson,[5] my Brother at my home near Mt. Vernon, Colo. Fitzgerald &ca. but with Express orders that no one shall have access to the Box but the President & *YourSelf*, for the disclosure of it to an ingenious artist or good drawer might pirate from McCabe & Pearce their Invention. He wants nothing but health *water fall*, wood & Iron to carry him thro' any Manufactory & being delighted with my discription of our Rivers & Falls &ca. it is with my advice He will wait upon Mr. Dickinson & look at the Brandywine mills &ca. &ca.

I hope by tomorrow He will be at Sea & in safety—It gives me great pleasure to have been the means of getting so valuable an Artist to our Country, and I cannot too strongly recommend Him to Your patronage & every other aid He may want.

I am with great respect & Esteem
Yr. Obedt. & very Hle. Servt.
Thos. Digges

If I can in *any way* assist or help You, I hope You wont spare Your commands—I shall be in England till Sepr. next & my direction will be to care of Mr. Josa. Johnson American Consul London—tho my stay will be chiefly in Yorkshire & the Manufacturing Towns of England. I have wrote till I am nearly blind.

[Enclosure]

[*several words torn off* ⟨William Pearce . . .⟩][6] was induced to leave England [*several words torn off* ⟨about a year⟩] back & come to Ireland with

Mr. Thos. McCabe watchmaker of Belfast, and they are now jointly concernd & bound to each other in the line of making machinery for manufacture of Linin, Cotton, Callico, Checks, Thicksets &ca. and for the getting *Patents* or premiums for their inventions.

Pearce came last from Doncaster in Yorkshire, & is the artist who erected the famous Mills of Messrs. Cartwrights of that place,[7] which Dress the Wool, Spin and weaves it in to Broad Cloth by force of Water, Steam, or Horse (when I saw the works, they were forc'd by an Ox or Bull) and the Proprietors were making a fortune by it.

He also was the inventor of the Arkwrights Spining & weaving machinery at Manchest. but was robbd of his invention by Arkwright (then a hair dresser & since made a Baront. from His wealth) But Pearce and a Mr. Thos. Hayes, then a joint Artist in the work broke Arkwrights Patent 'tho not till after he acquird a large fortune by it.[8]

In Belfast, where I attended to & saw the whole process of his work, Mr. Pearce's *First* Loom was for weaving two webs of Callico at once (34 inchs. broad and about 20d. per yard in value) on which Loom he weaves 23 to 24 yds. per day of twelve hours with two shuttles, each thrown by the same stroke of the hand in the usual *fly* way. It is a simple cheap Loom with very easy movements, & has an ingenious *double Temple* which Spreads both peices at once—The two ps/s are fixd on the same bar at about a foot asunder, & when at work He sets between or rather behind the two, & never moves from his seat to alter any movements of the Loom.

His *second* Loom was nearly the same for weaving Yard wide Linin (the Linin was what is calld 1600 thread fine, which will be when bleachd 3/–Engh. per yard Cost). But as the *Selvages* are reckond a criterion for good Linin, tho not much regarded as Callico or Cotton, He had affixd to this Loom some machinery, chiefly wire, which playd at the stroke of each shuttle up to the Selvage, & which drew in the thread to make the Selvages *Sharp*—To the excellence of his work on this Loom He procurd affidavits of six of the first Linin buyers & Bleachers in this quarter (which is the first market for Yard wide fine Linin in Ireland) & of which Linin he makes 6 to 6½ yds. per day, & two yds. is reckond good work in the common way.

His *third* Loom was for Checks, two peices on the same bar as before, but workd with *four* shuttles, Vizt: two Shuttles for each Web, thrown in the usual *fly* way, two of which Shuttles with the white or blue thread dropping occasionally into a Socket at the extreme end of the bar as He might want the blue or the white thread to work—The sinking or raising of each Shuttle was effected by an easy movement of his left hand or with his foot. Of this Check which was of 800 fine & value of 16d. per yd. Cost He easily wove *two Yards per hour*! full three times as much as can be done in the common way.

His fourth Loom was for weaving three ps/s of Thickset or Corduroys at once, with an additional invention of a flat peice of Iron with *Cutters*, to cut the Thickset as He wove on (the Expence of Cutting Thickset is 1d.½ or 2d. per yard). I did not see the Cutters [*several words torn off* ⟨work, but the⟩] peices, which were all of Cotton about 900 fine, & nine yards per day [*tear* ⟨was easy⟩] work. This was his neatest & best looking Loom, But the Linin one is far more valuable to this Country, & his Check one the most ingenious.

Mr. Pearce has also an invention for Spining Flax thread (which I saw in a small brass miniature model that convincd me of the principle) But this was not exhibited here. By this machine He assures me He can spin Flax thread by water, steam, or other force to as many thousand threads as the force will carry, which is well known of Cotton & of Silk.

He has also an invention for Spining Yarn or Worsted; And another for Cotton without the use of the Spining Jenny, which invention is at work in England with manufacture of what is calld British Shirting, now getting into use among the Gentry—It is made of any finess, & by hard round spining, feels as firm as any Linin. He has also at my request made a small simple machine for working thread fit for *Sail Duck*—It is turnd & workd by a small boy or girl, walking backwards, and with facility spining two threads at once, Vizt, one in each hand.—The motion is producd by an endless rope fixd to their waste while Spining—This is gone forth to Mr. Thos. Russell of Boston[9] for the Sail Duck manufactury there.

He can also make machinery for the working. Twine fishing-nets of any size or marsh, either for the Herring or other fisherys—in short there are few or none his equal in the machinery way for Weaving or Spining. I saw and closely attended to his erecting & working his Looms, & You may rely there is nothing exaggerated in my Account.

The Intention of Messrs. Pearce & McCabe was to get a premium from the Irish Parliament for these vast improvements in manufacture, But after a long attendance & producing every possible & convincing proofs of their Utility, They were foild by a *party*; And by a trick of *Jobbing*. (for there is no publick work done in this Country without its becoming a *Job*) Ireland is likely to loose not only the invention but so ingenious an Artist as Pearce. He will I trust be a blessing to Our Country, where from the dearness & high price of mechanic wages, all manufacture must at first receive a Check; But by the aid of such Machinery & mill work as Pearce's He will make *Wood & Water* a vast substitute for manual Labour—

LC: Jefferson Papers, Series 1.

[1] No letter from Digges to Jefferson, now secretary of state, of Apr. 24, 1791, has been found, nor any to Washington earlier than July 1, 1791.

[2] As the letters to Washington, July 1 and Nov. 12, 1791, and to Alexander Hamilton, Apr. 6, 1792, make clear, Pearce did embark in May. But it appears that Thomas McCabe (d. 1827?) remained in Ireland, an opponent of the slave trade, an intimate of Theobald Wolfe Tone's, and a member of the United Irishmen.

[3] William Jameson's career has so far remained obscure. William Hall was to become superintendent of the calico-printing department of the Society for Establishing Useful Manufactures. See *PAH*, 11:245, n. 10.

[4] William Seton (1746–1798), a Scotsman who had emigrated to New York at an early age, had earned respect as a merchant engaged in shipping and importing before becoming a leading New York banker, occupying what was then the important position of cashier at the Bank of New York.

[5] John Dickinson (1732–1808), author of *Letters from a Farmer in Pennsylvania to the Inhabitants of the British Colonies* (1768), a former member of the Continental Congress, a recent leader of both Delaware and Pennsylvania governments, and one of the delegates to the convention that had framed the Constitution, had given up public office but remained prominent and influential in the region.

[6] The conjectured wording is drawn from the nearly identical enclosure in Digges to Washington, July 1, 1791.

[7] Although Major John Cartwright (1740–1824), known as a political reformer, and Charles Cartwright had a financial interest in the enterprise, their brother, the Rev. Edmund Cartwright (1743–1823), was the member of the family responsible for the Yorkshire mills. He had invented the power loom and developed a machine for the combing of wool and recently set up a steam engine to provide its power.

[8] Sir Richard Arkwright (1732–1792) had been embroiled for more than a decade in

suits challenging his ownership of patents for the machinery he had been successfully using. In one case before the courts in 1785 a principal witness had been the man Digges refers to as Hayes, who in various histories of cotton manufactures usually appears at Highs and in at least one account as Heyes.

⁹Russell (1740–1796), a director of the local branch of the Bank of the United States, was a businessman of considerable influence in the city.

To George Washington

In writing the president (1732–1799) Digges could presume on personal acquaintance. Warburton Manor was situated across the Potomac from Mount Vernon, and through the years the Diggeses and Washingtons had been rowed across the river to exchange visits.

Belfast 1 July 1791—

As I am writing to Mr. Fitzgerald I take the liberty under a Cover to Him to inclose Your Excellency a discription of Messrs. McCabe & Pearce's new invented double Loom for weaving two peices at the same time, & which description is annexd to the Report of a Committee of the Irish House of Commons upon the utility & benefit of such a Loom.¹

Since Mr. Wm. Pearces embarkation hence to New York in May last, in order to obtain a Patent from Congress for said Loom, His partner Mr. Thomas McCabe has taken no steps in this Country for a premium, But He is now in London endeavouring to obtain a Patent for [it] in Engld., where He will undoubtedly succeed.

It is necessary for me to mention to Your Excellency, That the drawings & spe[c]ifications commonly necessary for the obtaining a Patent went out in the Brig Endeavour Capt. Seward to N. York with Mr. Pearce and a working Artist Mr. Wm. Jameson who made the Looms, and together with a set of Temples & Headles, Elbow & Shuttles &ca. were boxd up, seald, and directed for Your Excellency to the care of Mr. Geo. Woolsey Merchant New York. Mr. McCabe as well as myself mentiond this in seperate Letters to Your Excelly:, and I gave

Mr. Pearce a seperate introductory Letter. He will be a most valuable acquisition in whatever quarter He may fix, & has I think eer this been at Alexandria & the Falls.

As I had it not in my power then to forward the printed Report of the Committee, I take this oppertunity of forwarding it, And am with the highest Esteem & veneration

Yr. Excellencys most Obedt. & very Hle. Serv.
Thos. Digges

[Enclosure]

Belfast July 1, 1791—

William Pearse, the Artist mentiond in the annexd Report of the House of Commons Ireland, was inducd to leave England about a year back by Mr. Thos. McCabe watchmaker of this place, And they are jointly Concernd & Bound to each other in the line of making *Machinery*, Looms, &ca. for the manufacture of Linin, Cotton, Callico, Checks, Thicksets or Corduroys &ca. &ca., and for the getting Pattents or Premiums for Thier inventions.

Pearce came last from Doncaster in Yorkshire, and is the Artist who erected The Mills of Messrs. Cartwrights, which dress's the Wool, spins, and *weaves* Broad Cloth by force of Water, steam, or by a Horse (when I saw it, it was workd by an Ox or a Bull) and the Proprietors were making a great deal of money by it. He also was the inventor of Arkwrights famous Spining & Weaving Machinery at Manchester, but was robbd of his invention by Mr. Arkwright (then a Hair Dresser of Manchester & since made a Baronet from his wealth & consequence) But Pearce and a Mr. Thos. Hays, a joint partner in his Work, broke Arkwrights Patent, 'tho not 'till after He had acquird a considerable fortune by it.

In Belfast, where I attend'd to & saw the whole process of the work, Pearces *first Loom* was for Weaving two Webs of Callicoe at once, (34 Inchs. broad and about 20d. per yard in value) on which Loom He wove 23 to twenty four yards per day of 12 hours, with two Shuttles, each thrown by the same Stroke of the hand in the usual *fly way*—It is a simple cheap Loom with very easy movements, and an ingenious double *temple* which spreads both webs at once: The two peices are fixd on the same bar, & when at Work He sits backward and between the two & never moves from His seat to alter any movement of the Loom.

His second Loom was nearly the same & for weaving *Linin* of yard wide, (the Linin was what is termd of 1600 fine, which would be when bleachd about 3/– Engh. per yard) But as the *Selvages* is the criterion of good Linin, 'tho not much regarded in Cotton or in Callico, He had affixd additional to this Loom some machinery, chiefly of wire, which playd at each stroke of the shuttle up to the Selvage & which drew in the thread to make the Selvage *Sharp*. : To the excellence of His work on this Loom He has procurd the Certificates of six of the first Linin Buyers & Bleachers in this quarter (which is the first station in Ireland for fine yard wide Linins) And of which He easily wove six & six and a half yards per day, & *two* yards is good work in the Common Way.

His third Loom was for Checks, two peices on the same bar as before but workd with *four* Shuttles, vizt. two for each piece thrown in the *usual fly* way; two of which Shuttles with the blue or the white thread dropping occasionally into a socket at the extreme end of the bar as He might want the blue or white thread to work—The sinking or rising of each Shuttle was effected by an easy movement of his foot or his left hand: Of this check, which was of about 800-fine & value of 16d. per yard Cost, He easily wove *two yards per hour!* full three times as much as can be done in the common way.

His Fourth Loom was for weaving three peices of Thicksets or Corduroys at once, with an additional invention (*which He had not compleated*) of a flat Iron Plate with *Cutters* so as to cut the Thickset as He weaves on (N.B.—The *Cutting* of thicksets is 1½d. to 2d. per yard). I did not see the cutting work, But the peices were all of Cotton of about 900 fine, & nine yards per day was easy work—This was his neatest and best looking Loom, But the Linin is far the most valuable to this Country, & His Check Loom the most ingenious.

He has also an invention for Spining Flax thread (which I saw in a miniature model that convincd me of the principle) but this was not exhibited here & held up as a great secret: By this machine He assures me He can spin flax thread by Water, steam, or other force to as many thousand threads at once as the force will carry which is well known in Cotton & in silk.

Mr. Pearce has also an invention for spining Yarn or Worsted, and another for Cotton without the use of the Spining Jenny, which invention is at work in England in the manufacture of what is calld British Shirting now getting into use among the Gentry—It is made to any finess, & by hard round spining feels is [as] firm as any Linin. He has also, at my request, made a small simple spining machine for working the thread fit for Sail Duck—It is turnd & workd by a small boy or Girl walking backwards & with facility & quickness spining two threads at once, one in each hand; the motion producd by an endless Rope fixd to their waste while spining—This is gone forward to Mr. Thos. Russell of Boston for the Sail Duck Manufactory there. He can also make machinery for the working or weaving Twine fishing nets of any size or finess of marsh either for Herring or other fisherys. In short there are few things in the Machinery Art that his ideas or His hands cannot go up to, & I look upon Him as the first of Artists in this way.

The intention of McCabe & Pearce was to get a premium from the Irish Parliament for those vast improvements in the Loom & in Manufacture, but after long attendance & producing every proof of their utility They have been foild by a party; and by a trick in *jobbing* (for there is no publick work done in this Country without its becoming a Job) Ireland is likely to loose for a time both the invention & so valuable an artist as *Pearce*. He would be a blessing to America, where, from the dearness & high price of Mechanic Labour, all manufacture must at first meet a check, But by the aid of such machinery as His; He will make *wood* & *water* a great substitute for Labour.

On Mr. Pearces disapointment here, & becoming vexd with the Rulers of this Country, I got Him with some difficulty, *and no little danger*, to Embark for America—An Express was sent from Dublin to stop Him, & the Vessell was twice board'd & stopd in which He went by two Cutters. I saw him safe away in the Brig Endeavour Capn. Seward belonging to Portsmouth N. H. & who saild from hence the 3d of May for New York. His wish is to Establish himself where a Water fall in the vicinity of any great town can be easily obtaind—He took out with Him the *working* artist who made his Looms (*Wm. Jameson*, who is Brother to Messrs. Jamesons Merchants Iron Monger Lane London) also one Jno. Hall[2] another artist; and He went recommended (his purpose being first to obtain a Patent in America) To The President, to Mr. Wm. Seton, N. York—Mr. Thos. Jefferson, Gover. Dickinson, Conyngham & Nesbit Philadelphia to Colo. Fitzgerald Alexa. [Alexandria] Geo. Digges &ca. &ca. and also to Mr. Thos. Russell Boston. His wish is to be near the Foedral Town, & He is bent upon looking at the Falls of Potowmack for His *Mill Station* before He fixes.

T. D.

[Addressed:] His Excellency/George Washington/President of the United States &ca. &ca./Mount Vernon near Alexandria

NA: Record Group 59, General Records of the Department of State, Miscellaneous Letters (April–July 1791), 104–7.

[1]The *Report* that Digges encloses consists of two printed pages; its author, John, first Viscount O'Neill (1740–1798) in the Irish peerage, was a member of the parliament of Ireland from Antrim and a Protestant who supported Catholic relief or emancipation:

REPORT

ON THE PETITION OF THOMAS MACABE AND WILLIAM PEARSCE.
*Reported to the Irish House of Commons, 14th February, 1791,
By the Right Honourable* JOHN O'NEILL

Mr. Speaker,
    Your Committee appointed to examine the matter of the Petition of Thomas Macabe and William Pearsce, having met according to order, and examined several witnesses relative to the subject-matter of the said Petition, directed me to report as follows:
    Mr. John Kelsey, an inspector of Linens in the County of Antrim, informed your Committee, that in December last Mr. Macabe called on him to look at two webs in a new-constructed loom; that he examined the cloth, found the fabrick good and well executed; that he afterwards saw a man weaving in it through a small opening in a door, and on examining the linen he wove, it appeared to be as good as that he first examined; that he conceives the weaving was more expeditiously performed by this than by a common loom, inasmuch as there were two webs weaving at the same time, and the operation of each of those was faster than that of one in the common mode; that the selvages of those webs were very well executed, and a good selvage is generally the test

of good cloth; that the weaver appeared to him to weave with less labour than in the common mode, as he sat in an erect posture; the quality of the linen he saw wove was about that of a sixteen hundred. Says that he apprehends the use of this machine would be an improvement to the linen manufacture.

Mr. Pearsce, one of the Petitioners, and the person whom Mr. Kelsey saw weaving, says, that he is not by profession a weaver; that he wove callico, linen and cheque in this loom; that he believes he worked twenty-three yards of a callico in a day in it; that he understands eight yards of callico is a fair day's work, and two yards and a half of linen; that he is convinced he could on this loom work double the quantity of linen that could be wove in a common loom, and that an experienced weaver could certainly weave much faster than he could.

Your Committee then called upon Mr. Thomas Russell, who informed them that he saw the piece of linen which Pearsce wove, and compared it with a pattern piece of Mr. Sinclaire's of Belfast, and the selvage of Pearsce's was by much the best; he also said that he had received a letter from Mr. Digges, stating that six of the principal linen-drapers of the neighbourhood of Belfast had examined a piece of linen of Pearsce's weaving, and compared it with one of Mr. Sinclaire's, and they were of opinion Pearsce's was equal in quality, if not superior, to any they ever had seen.

They then called upon Mr. John Russell, who has been for many years a very extensive dealer in linen; he said that he saw the linen in this new loom; that the quality of it, particularly the selvage, which he closely examined, appeared to him to be very good—he observed the two webs in the loom at the same time, and is convinced that linen could be wove much faster by it than by a common loom—says that this loom was in a loft, which is too dry a place to work a loom with advantage, and that he is of opinion it bids fair to be of great utility to the linen trade.

Mr. James Ferguson, another very extensive dealer in linens, informed them that he saw this loom, and that it appeared to him to be simple and plain in the construction—the two webs were in it, and beamed on the same beam, and it appeared to him to be an invention of great and general advantage—he observed that he never saw a loom but this in a loft, and till he saw it he thought it was not practicable to work one in such a situation, and that it was certainly wrought there to great disadvantage.

Both those gentlemen were of opinion that the universal use of this loom would work up all the yarn at present spun in this country, a vast quantity of which is now exported, and that their linens would rate much lower, which would enable them to contend with other markets much better than they can at present.

Your Committee then called upon the Rev. Dr. Young, a Senior Fellow of Trinity College, and Professor of Natural Philosophy, who said that he has examined the mechanical principles of this loom, and that it is evidently capable of working two webs at the same time; that the operation in weaving each web is more simple than in the common loom, and consequently more than double the quantity of linen can be wrought in the same time, and with less fatigue to the weaver; that the selvage must, from the nature of the machinery, be more exact than that of webs wove in the common loom; that the force with which the weft is shot can be adapted to the nature of the thread in the most simple manner; that the new part of the machinery is extremely simple and not subject to go out of repair, and from the nature of it must cost little; and from inspection it is evident the expence of this loom must be less than the expence of two common looms:

And on the whole he is of opinion, that the invention must be of great advantage to the linen manufacture.

The Rev. Mr. Stack, who was also present at this examination, declared that he was exactly of the same opinion with Dr. Young as to the construction and utility of this loom.

And your Committee came to the following Resolutions:

Resolved, That it appears to this Committee, that the Petitioners have invented a Loom applicable to the weaving of cotton and linen, by which two webs can be wove at the same time by one weaver, with more expedition, ease, and perfection, than one web is now wove in the common loom.

Resolved, That it appears to this Committee, that this loom is simple in its construction, easily kept in order, and will not cost double the price of a common loom.

Resolved, That it appears to this Committee, that this invention, when made public, must be highly advantageous to the linen and cotton manufactures of this kingdom.

[2] He means William Hall.

To George Washington

Belfast, Ireland, Novr. 12. 1791—

I hope Your Excellency will forgive my intrusion upon Your more important concerns when my purpose is solely to serve the Infant Manufactures of Our Country, and once more to mention a few words about Mr. Wm. Pearce the loom & machinery artist whom I inducd to go out to America last spring & took the liberty to introduce to You. He has I find met with the encouragement & patronage which He deserves, & I doubt not but with the assistance of Some English machinery or the getting to him *the hands which make such*, that He will very soon bring the Cotton manufactory to a favourable pitch of benefit to the United States. The two men who went with Him Jameson & Hall are good workmen in the line of making Spining Jennys, Slabbing Billys &ca. &ca. which are essential to the begining of the work and other matters for Coarse Spining, And I have very good hopes I shall be enabled to forward out by the next vessel (if He does not go with this) a most excellent white & black Smith who wishes to follow them. His name is McCormick, of the first note as a maker of brass & Iron Wheels, Spindles, Rollers & other movements essentially necessary for the finer spining by Mill work, or by Mules; This last (the

Mule which is movd by hand on a large scale & spins several hundred threds) is but little known out of England as yet, having been only obtaind in this Country since Pearce went away 'tho it is well known to Him, And it is only essential for spining the finest thred such as is used for Muslins and is of course of less utility in America *as yet* than the wheel machinery which is workd by water & spins the Cotton fit for Dimitys, pillow & plain fustains, Thicksets, Corduroys &ca.

Those mules are of such a size as not to be admissable in the hold of any common Ship, & are brought coverd upon the quarter deck, one on each side only; They might be got to America with a little address, & some risque both to the person shipping them & to the ship—The vessell must be *English* & she cannot clear out direct for America, but may clear for Cork or the Isle of Man & so proceed on— They stop no sorts of Machinery coming from Manchester or Liverpool to this Country which are not pattented or can be got from the Inventor. But they are so watchful in England as well as here for any going to America that upon the slightest suspicion they stop & search the Ship—This was the case with the Vessel that took out Pearce—a Cutter persued & searchd His Vessel twice for His double Loom & they would have brought him back had He not enterd & given in a different name—this was done in my sight & within a half hour after I had parted with him sailing out to Sea. The punishment for enveigling away an Artist is 500 £ fine & one Years imprisonment.

Jameson, who attended Pearce, did not behave perfectly Correct to his first Employer here, *Mr. Thos. McCabe* who is joint with Pearce; & they having employd him to make the heavy part of the Loom obligd him by an Oath & written articles not to divulge the Secret, but he broke or denyd the articles, threatend them with discovery here, & went away to America without divulging it. Hall, the other workman has a very good name. Mr. Jesse Taylor of Alexandria knows McCabe very well & his various efforts in bringing artists here in the Cotton & Glass line.[1]

It will not be difficult to get *necessary* machinery shippd at Liverpoole, but it would be a risque to get out Mules, as they are bulky & must be Exposd. Pearce knows perfectly well how to order them and to describe minutely the Sorts. The Getting out the artist who makes them is far the most eligible plan & the easiest done. I know Manchester well, & shall be there in Feby. & March, & shall have the highest gratification in being useful to Pearce's or any other Cotton manufactory in the United States, for I well know the utility of them, & dayly wonder at the fortunes they are giving in England & in this neighbourhood to adventuring individuals—Children of both sexes from five to 8 years old earn from two to five Shillings per week. Weavers are plenty & going in numbers by every Ship to America, but the ease with which they obtain Freeholds makes them quit the Loom for farming. This must be the case while Lands are so easy attainable & labour so high; But I have great hopes that in the circumstance of the Cotton manufactory, by improvd Mill Work, & the new invented machinery for Spining, that such high price of labour in America may be in some measure counteracted by those mechanical inventions. I have wrote to Pearce by this conveyance and offerd Him or His work any assistance in my power, & should any thing be wanted from Manchester I will with sedulous care try to forward it & attend to any orders directed for me at Mr. Joshua Johnsons our Consul in London.

I am with ardent prayers for Your Excellencys long & happy life
Yr. most devoted & obt. Servt.
Thos. Digges

NA: Record Group 59, General Records of the Department of State, Miscellaneous Letters (November–December 1791), 152–53.

[1] Taylor had probably known McCabe more than twenty years earlier in Belfast, where during 1778 and 1779 Taylor had written Franklin about plans for an expedition to America that would include himself, his family, and other men of standing and would serve to induce hundreds of his countrymen to follow.

To Alexander Hamilton

Belfast (Ireland) Apr. 6. 1792

SIR.

I stand in need of Your forgiveness for intruding myself upon You, but I hope that my motive for so doing (an ardent desire to promote manufactures in America) will in some measure appologize for me.[1] A Vessel sailing this day from hence from [for] Boston, and the oppertunity of inclosing this Letter to Mr. Tho' Russel of that place (who I am sure will forward it safe) induces me to write to You on the subject of Manufactures & Machinery, which I am happy to see begins now to be tookd up & pratonizd in our Country.

I have not the pleasure to be personally known to You, 'tho well acquainted with Your worth & the benefits our Country is likely to derive from Your assiduity & ability—my home & soil is at Digges's Landing on Potowmac nearly fronting the Presidents, to whom & many of the Gentlemen about Him & yourself I am known, and am but a casual Resident in this manufacturing quarter of Ireland in order to get over some Tennantry, and among them Artists, to fix on lands I possess both in Virginia & Maryland not far from the new Federal Town.

It was with much pleasure & attention I very lately read Your Report to Congress on the Subject of Manufactures, which I found publishd in the New York papers in Numbers compleated to the end—In this quarter American Books are very rarely to be met, & when sent as presents, little read & not attended to. This inducd me to take the liberty with your book of having it republished at my Expence 1000 Copys price 1/– by Byrne Book Sellers in Dublin[2] in order to distribute it with ease, & for disseminating its information among many Manufactoring Societys here as well as in England, (where I will take 3 or 400 Copys in a few days) and by so getting it read, induce artists to move towards a Country so likely to very soon give them ample employ & domestic ease. I hope You will not be offended with me for so doing, & I am confident the distribution of it, in the way I intend, will induce many to move towards the Manufactoring parts of America—sorry I am to say it that mine is still backward in the encouragement of manufactorys or artists, but I trust it will soon get better as the Slavery by blacks decreases & by Emigration from these Countrys we get betterd as to a free tennantry.

I was very lucky in being the means of sending Wm. Pearce to Philaa. last June, where I hope He has succeeded & been encouragd in obtaining a Pattent or Premium for His new invented *double loom*. I gave him recommendatory Letters to the President, to Mr. Jefferson, Goverr. Dickinson, Mr. Seton, Conyngham & Nesbit & others, & I am to hope He has made His way to You[3]—He is a Man deserving to be cherish[d] as an uncommon ingenious Artist in the fixing Mill Machinery, Looms, &ca. and before He went explained to me the principle of a Mill for weaving Cloth by force of steam or water, as well as one for spinning Flax thred nearly on the same plan of facility & numbers of threads that the Cotton Mules can spin, which is from 80–to 180 threads at once & attended by one man & two small children to each Mule. Mr. Thos. McCabe of this Town (to whom the introduction of Cotton fabricks in Ireland is much indebted) is a partner in the Loom scheme with Mr. Wm. Pearce, and has now in His possession the compleat drawings & specifications of a machine for Spinning the thread which I now inclose you (a description of which you have in the paper covering the thread)—It is the first effort in England & spoke highly of as to the benefits of reducing manual labor, for one man & a small boy tends the machine which Spins 80 threads at one throw of the machine. I have seen the work & got copys of the drawings, and I have Mr. McCabes possitive promise of sending it to You or the President by the first Passenger Ship which will be the Wilmington Cap. Jefferies for Philadelphia & She will sail in May.

I go from hence in a few days to spend the summer among manufacturers & artists in Lancashire & Yorkshire, a Country I have before known, & where many are ready to move for America, but the difficultys of so doing are very great—By the laws of England they can stop an artist from migration, & the smallest particle of machinery, tools &ca. will stop the Ship if informd against.—The person attempting to inviegle away an artist is subject not only to very rough treatment, but a fine of 510£ & 12 months imprisonment. In this Country they, are not so nice, & by some art, & very little expence I have been the means of sending 18 or 20 very valuable artists & machine makers in the course of last year—It subjects You however to unpleasant circumstances of jealousy from acquaintances, & private sensure.

There will be considerable emigration this Spring from this place, Derry & Newry, I dare say not less than 10,000 people, and in every family there are spinners & often weaver's—almost wholly a protestant body, sober & industrious & very different from the Southern & western Irish, where Manufactures have not yet found their way & the people in consequence, idle, distressd, & extremly poor. Such is the increasing commerce & manufactories of Antrim & Down (by far the fulest peopled Countys in Ireland) that in the Course of the last 12 months not less than 12 or 15,000£s worth of Machinery for spining Cotton only has been imported from Liverpool into this port—The Mules, Billys, Brush Rollers & all other of the machinery comes in the frame bulk nearly ready to work, & is of such bulk that very few vessels can admit them, particularly the *mules*, into the hold —of course, abstracted from the risque of shipping them direct from Engd. to America, the getting 'em across the atlantic would be attended with vast difficulty. The only way to counteract this will be to get over the two men who make each of these machines Vizt. the Brass, Clockwork movements of them, & the frame & wood-work makers.—I mean to make an attempt at this, and will trust to Yours & other patronage to such Men as may go to fix in America. The beauty & benefits of *machinery* is such, & has so much reducd the manufacture of various articles, by the reduction of manual labour, as to make it incredible to those who have not seen and contemplated machinery. You have now the man in America, *Wm. Pearce*, who invented first the famous wheel machinery for Sir R. Arkwrights famous spining mill in Manchester; and He also had a hand in the Mill at Doncaster, which by force of an ox *weaves* Broad Cloth by Machinery—He also knows the principle on which the thread which I now send You is so quickly & beneficially spun without going thro the usual form of the Finger— His double Loom, which I hope You have by this time seen at work is also an admirable piece of simple art, and without applying other force than the hand, which He can do to throw the Shuttle, weaves in proportion of three yards to one in the common way. I look upon Him somewhat like a second Archimedes—His pride, 'tho an ignorant & low bred man prompted Him to move from Hence on being disapointed, by an il-timed party in the House of Commons here, of getting the Sum that He & Mr. McCabe askd for the discovery of the loom. He has I understand quarrelld with Jameson, & Hall, (two working artists whom I sent out in the Ship with Him) and I am sure Jameson is in fault, for he *here* made a vile tho' feint attempt to discover Pearce's secret because He had been employd by Pearce to erect the Loom.

I am sure it woud have a tendency to good to have some plan fixd in America for the Encouragement of ingenious artists & manufacturers going there, something like a premium or reward—to be publickly advertisd & held out in the American Papers, & those papers carefully get distributed here & about Liverpool & Manchester, for in these Countrys they hardly ever will publish any favourable account of America or insert a Paragraph which may lead the people to Emigration. I think too a small bounty per head on every Emigrant landing (suppose only one Dollar per head for every one that goes in a Vessel carrying more than 100 adults[)]; and to exempt the vessel so carrying them from the Tonnage or other Fees for that voyage, may have a good tendency to induce more to go, for here a few Shillings makes a difference in the price of passage money, that retards many from going. Such are the wants of a people even in a very full peopled Country & possessing a most beneficial staple manufactory of Linin & rapidly rising in the Cotton one.

I hope You will excuse Sir the length of my letter & loose suggestions. I have much at heart & wish most earnestly to see manufactures *begin* even in my Country—I am very confidant our high price of labour will be no obstruction, when the facility & cheapness with which we can Errect mill work, & I trust machinery too, will be put in counterpoise to manual labour. Already there is a Mill in England which can twist from a small Cord, up to the largest Cable for a Ship by force of water, & by which in the making of a Cable the labour of about sixty persons is saved. At Manchester too a man who I well know (Mr. Grimshaw)[4] lately erected a mill at the Expence of 14,000£, which by force of steam wove some hundreds of ps./s of Cotton at once, under one roof & with but little attendance, of only dressing the Looms & loading the Shuttles, but the misguided multitude, fearing it would ruin the working weavers maliciously burnt down the mill after it had begun to work. From the increasing spirit of the English towards discovery of machinery in various ways, it is impossible to tell or guess what lengths the human genius may not go. I hope it will take a flight across the Atlantic, & by way of expediting it I shall be extremely happy for any hints from You, or from any Gentlemen Engaged in the promotion of American Manufactures, & who may have more leisure to write.

My stay in England will be a full twelvemonth from this period, and my direction is to the care of *Joshua Johnson Esqr. Consul Gen. for U. S. in London.* I shall be happy to execute any Commands for You & am with great esteem & respect

Sir Yr. Obt. Hle. Serv.
Thos. Digges

You will please to Excuse this hasty letter which in truth, as the Captn. is about to move, I have not time to read over—

LC: Hamilton Papers.

[1] Hamilton (1757–1804) as secretary of the treasury could be expected to be interested in this letter.
[2] *Report of the Secretary of the Treasury of the United States, On the Subject of Manufactures. Presented to The House of Representatives, December 5, 1791* (Dublin: Reprinted by P. Byrne, No. 108, Grafton-Street, 1792); cited in *PAH*, 11:242, n. 4.
[3] He had already done so. Receipts among Hamilton's papers show that on Aug. 20, 1791, Pearce had received from Hamilton in Philadelphia $100 to be used for preparing machines and models of machines for the Society for Establishing Useful Manufactures in New Jersey; then on Sept. 7 and 17 and Nov. 10 and 18 he had received, in installments ranging from $50 to $150, a total of an additional $300.
[4] Nicholas Grimshaw had in 1784, in Belfast, already constructed a mill to card and spin cotton. According to some accounts, the power loom in Manchester that he had constructed in 1790 had been burned before it had manufactured anything (see *PAH*, 11:246, n. 11).

To Thomas Jefferson

Birmingham 10 Mar. 1793

SIR

I send You this Letter in a Book of Medals & Coins (as numberd & markd) which were done at Mr. Boultons mint at Soho near this place[1]—Some of the trash of half-pence which are in local tho' current circulation in & about the Towns to which they appertain, are added to fill up the book; And as I know You have made the American Mint & Coinage much Your study, they may serve as assistant samples towards perfection, those of Mr. Boultons being of a very superior kind.

I am at present engagd in this central part of England trying to get Leasehold or annual Tennants for my Lands, fronting the Presidents on Potowmac, and adjoining the new Federal City & Bladensburgh, and I expect to Embark for America in May or June. Not knowing of a safe conveyance to You, I have made free to send the parcell to and ask the favour of Mr. Pinkney to forward it.[2] And, as I understood from Mr. Boulton He had made some application for a Die Sinker I have left open the book of Coins for his inspection.

Since my Letter to You by Wm. *Pearce* the double Loom maker,[3] and the original inventor of Arkwrights first weaving & spining Machinery, I have not had occasion to write, nor would I have likely done it before my Embarkation for America But am inducd now to do so from having accidentally seen a Birmingham production of one of the American *Cents*, the intended coin of America & the $\frac{1}{100}$th part of the Dollar. Knowing it had been determind in Congress to have all their money minted in the States,[4] I made it my business to seek out and inform myself all I could about this Cent coinage here and of the Artists & Merchants engaged about them.—I first applyd to Messrs. W. & Alexr. Walkers (who have a Partner Mr. Thos. Ketland in Philaa.,) and they shewd me the specimens No. 16 and No. 17 sent herewith & afterwards gave them to me—They said it was merely a *speculation* or trial to obtain the order for making the intended cents here which inducd them to the attempt in 1791 and that some hundred weight or so had been sent to America & given to the President & other public Gentlemen; But that on the determination of Congress to mint their own money, thier scheme here had fallen thro'. They were close & secret as to *who* the die sinker was, *where* coind &ca. but upon further Enquirys I found Messrs. Walkers had orderd them to be done at Mr. Obediah Westwoods (a considerable maker of these kinds of money[)], and that his die Sinker Mr. Jno. Gregory Hancock (one of the first in this place 'tho with the Character of a dissipated man)⁵ and a prentice Lad Jno. Jordan very Clever in that line, had executed them & still hold the dies. This Lad Jordan, has two years of His time to serve, wishes much to go to America, but I suppose his time would be worth 200£. The face likeness on both are the same die and a good likeness of the President tho the Eagles and motto are different—The likeness was taken from a large medal struck at Phila.

Those enquirys about the American *Cent*, and my intimacy with Mr. Boulton & Mr. Watt led me to look at and study more the apparatus & modes of Coining, the Expence attending a Copper Coinage, &ca. than I otherways should have done, and I suppose I need not inform You that Mr. Boulton is by far the neatest & best Coiner & has a more excellent apparatus for Coining than any in Europe.—It cost Him some thousands—The whole machine is moved by an improvd steam Engine which rolls the Copper, for halfpence *finer* than copper has before been rolld for the purpose of money—It works the Coupoirs or screw press's for cutting the particular peices of Copper & coins both the faces *& edges* of money at the same time, with such superior excellence & cheapness of workmanship, as well as with marks of such powerful machinery as must totally prevent counterfieting it. By his machinery four boys can strike thousands of Guineas in an hour—Eight presses works four ton of Copper per day—four or five presses two ton per day, and the machine by the Evolutions of the great wheel which is of cast Iron, keeps an unerring account of the number of peices struck. It is not workd in the old way but the mettal is put into a kind of hopper, & drops out into a bag nearly as smoothly as grain in a Mill.

The Excellence of His Coinage are

1st—The peices are perfectly round—2d They are all precisely Equal in Diameter.

3d The work is exactly concentric to the Edge.

4   An inscription or Ornament is put round the Edge, either indented, or in relief, or partly one & partly the other, and this inscription is Struck by the same blow that gives impression to the Faces, Whereas the common mode of making ornaments on the Edge, is by a seperate well known operation calld milling & which is much more easily immitated.

5. The ground of his Coin is smooth and of a light polish.
6 Much greater quantities of money with all these perfections may be coind in less time, with fewer persons, & with more exactness & ease by those employd than by any mode hitherto invented.

—

Memorandums: A Water Mill will work all the machinery as well as a steam Engine & will be better understood & managd in America—indeed the power of two or 3 horses might answer. [(]Mr. Boulton told me He would sell the whole apparatus, *exclusive of the Steam Engine*, (which is a considerable part of the Cost) & it might be got to America (I think) for 11 or 1200£).

The whole apparatus is this.

A *Rolling Mill*, which must be unconnected with the Coining Mill.

—

Mill work to work Coupoirs
Do. Do.———Coining
Do. Do. for Turning Laths & cleaning the Blanks.
Do. Do for Lettering the Edges.

—

The Arts necessary, & which might be easily learnt are
  Hardning & polishing Dies.
  Multiplying the Dies.
  Managing the Presses.
  Improvements in presses & Coupoirs
  In annealing so as to preserve the Polish

—

The *Matrasses* (which are the Adam & Eve for Casting medals or Coins) being obtaind, the *multiplication of dies*, and the hardening them, (a sort of secret) is to be learnt. The best artists in this line are said to be in Paris; But Mr. Boulton would lend His assistance in this, and give His instruction & direction to any confidential person sent from America for the purpose of looking after or superintending a Copper Coinage at His mint, which with the Dies &ca. &ca. He would afterwards sell for a fair price to America & on easy terms.

—

Sheet Copper from England being Cast or rolld *Hot*, & liable to stain at Sea will not do—It may be sent over a little thicker than the money & then put thro a Roller to make it of exact thickness.

—

Mr. Boultons prices for Coining Copper, not withstanding the superior beauty & Excellence to any in England, will be equally cheap.

The following is an Estimate given me by Mr. Obediah Westwood for Coining halfpence or Cents.

Suppose *a Cent*, made in pure Copper 29 ps/s in the lb. of Copper one ton would Contain 64,960 Cents, which is 649½ Dolls. at 4/6 is --- £146.19.9

    The Copper Cost—say 90 £ the ton
    Dies & Expence of Manufacturing—30– } ---------------- 120—

    Profit on the ton when paid out would be ------------------ £26.19.9

But Copper is now as high as £112– per ton. At this or the above price not a less order than for twenty ton would answer for Him in finding dies, Rolling the Copper, manufacturing into Cents, lapping in paper & Casking up &ca.

According to the greater or less number of peices made from the pound of Copper, so the Expence of Coinage would alter Vizt. *for work* only.

    For 40 ps/s in the lb. it would amount to --------- 42 £ suppose
        Copper at 100 £ the ton
    for 36 ps/s -- 34—
    for 32 ps/s which is ½ an Oz. each ps.------------- 32—so that in his order for half pence say of 40 ps. in the lb. the profit would be to the Emitter £45.13.4 on the ton, thus the ps./s amount to

                                         £187.13.4
        Cost of Copper ----------------------- 100—
                                           87.13.4
        Expence of Coining ------------------ 42
                                           45.13.4

The standard of the British half penny is three to one ounce of Copper which is 48 half pence to the lb. an Enormous profit to the Government on Emission!

If I can obtain any other information, or hear of a person likely [to] serve in this Business I will write You. I am in the interim With great regard Sir Yr. Ob. Hle. Serv.

Th. A. Digges

[Addressed:] Thomas Jefferson Esqr./Philadelphia

LC: Jefferson Papers, Series 1.

---

[1] Matthew Boulton (1728–1809), extending the business his father had established as silver stamper and piercer, had been so successful in perfecting both the workmanship and artistry of coinage that he had been soon confronted with demands that water power could not satisfy. In 1775 he had therefore gone into partnership with James Watt (1736–1819) to develop steam power for the Birmingham works, establishing the firm that became known as the firm of Boulton & Watt. As secretary of state, Jefferson was responsible for the mint that Congress had established.

[2] See Digges to Thomas Pinckney, Mar. 12 and 21, 1793. Pinckney (1750–1828), a South Carolinian who had served in the revolutionary army, been governor of his state and a member of its House of Representatives, was now the American minister to Great Britain.

[3] Apr. 28, 1791.

[4] On Mar. 1, 1791, the Congress, wishing to remove foreign coins from circulation, had resolved that a mint should be established and that the president should engage artists to work out implementation of the resolution. On Apr. 2, 1792, it had enacted an "Act establishing a Mint and regulating the coins of the United States."

[5] Obadiah Westwood had struck the medals that Hancock had designed. The coins appear to have been the 1791 large and small Washington eagle cents and a similar 1792 cent. The Philadelphia model, identified as "Washington before Boston" (1786), had, according to Don Taxay, in *The U.S. Mint and Coinage* (New York: Arco, 1966), actually been made in Paris and was not the exact prototype (p. 53, n. 18).

To Thomas Pinckney

Birmingham Mar. 12. 1793—

SIR

Without the pleasure of a personal acquaintance tho not a stranger to Your name & worth, I am at a loss to apologise for this intrusion, and the making so free as to forward to You *a Book of Medals & Coins* minted at my friend Mr. Boultons at Soho near this place. They are so nicely executed that I have been at some pains to obtain the specimens for forwardance to The American Mint, and I have to solicit the favour of You Sir to forward them to Mr. Jefferson as soon as a convenient oppertunity may offer. I have sent a similar Box to my friend Mr. Joshua Johnson meant for my illustrious neighbour The President.

I have added to them many other of the current halfpence of different Towns in England merely to fill up the Book; But as the jolting of the Coach may injure the box & Mr. Boultons finer specimens, and as it may be a gratification to see what can be done in minting, I have sent them unpackd—When the Book is forwarded to Mr. Jefferson They may be placed in it to thier seperate numbers—The key goes with them, & the box is opend & shut, with a spring lock, by slideing off endways the labelld back of the book. I have also left my Letter open to Mr. Jefferson for Your perusal, (& to save unnecessary repetitions) as upon some conversations with Mr. Boulton I find You have applyd to Him for a Dye Sinker for The American Mint. I refer to my Letter in the box upon that subject—If the young man *Jordan*, mentiond therein could be got I am of [the] opinion He would answer better there than any of those I have seen or spoken to here; for workmen in this line are *very few*, and often & [are] drunken & worthless in thier manners. I should be very glad to second Your views in obtaining a Man of this art for our Mint, but it is rather a service of delicacy & some danger, as they are become in this Country very tenacious of thier artists even Drunken & worthless as they are. Mr. Boulton is a liberal & worthy man, and His Partner Mr. Watt has hardly his equal in knowlege. Mr. B. has promisd to call on You when next in London, and if You can spare a week in the Spring it would be a gratification to You to visit Him & see his work, as well as the various mechanic industry of this & the neighbouring Towns, altho at present getting retrogade from an impolitic war (at which the generality of people are much displeasd) which has producd a slackend trade and general want of foriegn orders.—If it was not for the uncommon large orders from our Country, which have of late been the best, & are now the only ones, they might lay by 3/4th of thier Hammers. Many workmen and artists have in consequence gone into the army, & several making their way to America, lured by our uncommon high wages & ease of attaining property in Land—Some of the wealthy & discontented Protesters are also going—It is a bad wind which blows no body good.

 I have been in England some few months among the principal Graziers & Farmers of Yorkshire, Suffolk, & Leistershire (& lately at Mr. Bakewells the first Breeder of Cattle in the World)[1] principally to get some Lands I hold in Virginia, near Leesburg, sold, *or set* at Leases of 21 years to farming people, as Specified in the inclosd Advertisement. My home Estate is Warburton fronting the Presidents where I have more land, inclusive of a long tract adjoining the Federal district & Bladensburg, than I can properly till or occupy, and the recent death of an only and Younger Brother[2] now puts me into greater difficulty about them. I shall be here and at Lichfield about 15 Days, and after upon visiting Mr. Bakewell, where I have a yearling Bull, & Sheep, of peculiar value, I shall go towards Bristol & London, & proceed I think in the June or July Packet for N. York. I shall not be in this town longer than to get an answer from Mr. Josa. Johnson and to insert in these & other Country papers an advertisement about the New Federal City which the Commissioners have sent Him. I shall esteem a line in Answer, directed to me at *The Post Office Lichfield*, acknowleging the Receipt of the box, as an obligation. Not knowing Your London direction I sent it to a friend in the City for private conveyance to You. If I can render any service to You while in the Country I hope You will freely command Sir

Yr. Obt. Hle. Serv.
Thos. A. Digges

 I have made free to give Mr. Obediah Westwood (a considerable manufacturer of this place) a line of introduction to You as He wishd to speak upon the subject of a Copper Coinage &ca. when He goes to London in a week or two.

[Addressed:] Thomas Pinkney Esqr./Envoy & minister Plenipotentiary/from the United States / *London* [Stamped:] BIRMINGHAM

LC: Pinckney Family Papers, Series 3, Box 4.

¹ Robert Bakewell (1725–1795), having become manager of a 440-acre farm in Dishley, near Loughborough, was developing the new Leicestershire breed of sheep that would soon be found throughout the kingdom, Europe, and the United States and was also breeding what was known as the new Leicestershire longhorn cattle.
² George had died on Nov. 17, 1792.

To Thomas Pinckney

Birmingham Mar. 21. 1793

SIR

I forwarded a Book of medals & Coins, intended for Mr. Jefferson, by a Coach from hence to London the 13th Int., which by way of saving You trouble I directed to Mr. Chapman No. 80 Corn Hill¹ with orders to Him to send a porter with them to Your Hotel—By a letter from my friend Mr. Josa. Johnson, to whom I sent a parcel by same conveyance, I find they had not arrivd on the 13th. I have written to Mr. Chapman about the parcell & I hope You will get it by this day or tomorrow.

Mr. Boulton, with whom I frequently communicate, intends going to London tomorrow, and will likely call upon You. It may be as well that You do not mention to Him that I obtaind any of the halfpence minted by Mr. Obediah Westwood or that I mixd them in the same box with His Mr. B.'s so far superior Monies—I told Him I had made free to send the Box for Mr. Jefferson *open to You* supposing it would gratify You to see his neat & excellent coinage.

Without supposing our Rulers in America will either employ Him to mint the Copper Coinage, or to purchase his beautiful apparatus, it was on this theme I spoke to Him in order to find out the prices & information given in my open letter to Mr. Jefferson.—He is a liberal & very good kind of Man, but like other great artists, is a little close when applyd to for information about Men in the money diesinking line.

Since those communications with Mr. B., and my letter to You, I have found out a variety of money-coining practices here, disgraceful, I think, to the Country or its Laws, and in the one instance I shall mention likely to do mischief & injury to the vast circulation of spanish Dollars in the American States.² I have not only seen *pattern Cards* of Shillings, six pences, & half Crowns of base mettal (some of the Shillings for instance so bad as to be markd for sale at the rate of 28, 30, & 35 Shillings for the Guinea) but a mischevious mode of depreciating the Spanish Dollar by recoining & making it of *nine* pence less value each. Also dividing the pistereens thus with an Equal triangular bit taken out of the middle as no. 4. done by an Order from a West India House in London, with intent to pass the *three parts* no. 1, 2 & 3 each as a half pistereen in the West India Islands. The silver seems of nearly the same standard as that of the pistereen St[g]. quarter Dollar, the ps. is stampd here in the circular form, & after cutting out the triangular bit No. 4, which is again melted down, these 3 ps/s pass each as a half pistereen or bit!! These, I was told are an order for Barbadoes.

Dutch Ducats are also immitated thus—a ps. of pure soft Silver which like the Ducat is easily bent to & fro is cut to nearly its size & thickness, which before impression is thickly guilt with an amalgum of Gold & struck off to the exact marks of the real Ducket, which was shewn me & weighs nearly of pure Gold to the value of 10/– Engh.— The counterfeit, which is an amazing likeness is worth & can be made for about 1/6d. Each. This is some recent & secret order for assisting the good Belgian allies. I have also seen paper Assignats of ten and of two hundred Livres—The paper done in London, with the real water marks, & sent here in quires for engraving & impressions, and the partys were so indiscreet as to tell me there were at this very juncture several thousand pounds worth of it in London on its way to France. —This reminds me of *Boxes* filld with American forged paper which was taken in the War on the voyage from England to New York.

They are a little more secret about the Dollars—These however come here in *real* Spanish Dollars 10,000 in a Cask by waggons from London. They are recoind, copying as exactly as possible the old impressions (of which seven or 8 sorts & of different dates have been made) but mostly of the old impression & lank visage of His Catholic Majesty. They are all made of the same finess of silver as those sent, but with a diminution of *nine pence* in value on each dollar. Two pence half penny or 3d. on each, is *ample* pay to the minter here for dies, recoining, rolling &ca. &ca. & sending back to London.—Near six tons, I was confidently told, has been done here since last August; and upon close investigation no doubt remains on my mind but that they are so orderd & coind to be put in upon Us in the United States & the Wt. Indies as real Spanish money. The parties here were very secret as to names, but dropt to me upon being closely pushd that the work was done by them under a *Regular order* from a House in London much connected in the Et. India trade & that they were meant for India. By this villainous forgery the publick whereever this light recoinage is issued will be defrauded *nine pence* upon each Dollar of 4/6, and the enormous profit of seven pence or at least six pence, goes to the pockets of the Schemers in this vile trafic after paying the minter here two pence or three pence on each.

I mentiond in a Letter with the box I sent the name of one person here to Whom I had given a few lines to You in order to speak upon a matter therein explaind when He might hereafter go to London[3]— He has been concernd in some of the first mentiond transactions, but not as far as I can guess the least so as to the Dollar. The depravity of some men in these lines of trade & art is astonishing, & as the Laws take no cognizance of such crimes, or are at least dormant or look over them, they talk of doing these things, & coining the monies of other nations, without any kind of compunction or awe.

         I am with great regard Sir
         Yr. Ob. Hle. Ser.
         T.A. Digges

 They are also making here Dollars here of *Copper* well plated, & with a silver hoop edge, which will stand rubbing with a knife, Their value is not more than 1/6, & may be easily passd off among numbers.

[Addressed:] Thomas Pinckney Esqr./ Envoy from The United States
  of America/ London

LC: Jefferson Papers, Series 1.

[1] According to *A London Directory* (London: W. Lowndes, [1795]), Charles Chapman had a shoe warehouse at the given address.

[2] The Spanish piece of eight reales was the coin in greatest use in the United States, but Digges was mistaken in assuming that the mischief produced by counterfeits would come only from abroad, for an industrious group was already at work in Massachusetts using the techniques Digges describes.

[3] Obadiah Westwood.

To Thomas Pinckney

On March 22 Pinckney had written Digges from Great Cumberland Place, London: "I received your favor of the 12th a few days ago and that of the 21st with the Box with Medals last Evening. This shall be forwarded by the first Vessel sailing for Philadelphia but I shall be glad to know whether it is to be addressed to Mr. Jefferson or the Secretary of State as it is possible Mr. Jefferson may be no longer in Office when this Box shall reach America. I have to make my acknowledgements for the Information contained in your two Letters as well as for your Enquiries for Artists. None will now be necessary as in consequence of my last Letters from America I have desisted from endeavoring to procure them. I had however obtained Leave from the Secretary of States Office for sending out such as might be really intended for the service of our Mint so that the enquiry was attended with no Danger nor was it ever intended to be concealed.—Your Information concerning Counterfeits will be of utility by putting our people on their guard against them. I purpose forwarding this account by my next Letter" (SCHS: Thomas Pinckney Letter Book, November 29, 1791 – January 10, 1794, pp. 253–54).

Birmingham, 6th. Apr. 1793

SIR

Having been some days with an Archery & Fox hunting meeting near Coventry I did not get Your obliging Letter till yesterday, and have only to say in reply that the box of Medals & Coins was intended for Mr. Jefferson to whom I have before wrote on the subject of our Coinage, & who will make every communication of such specimens to the American Mint which can in any way assist the Artists engagd in it. I am very happy that no Artist, in the diesinking way, goes from this quarter, for the genius & wickedness of the place would soon lead to counterfeit the American moneys—I know of no preventative to the so doing but the coining with Mr. Boultons invented apparatus, which from its exactness, nicety & being done in the *Collar* way almost precludes the possibility of counterfiet immitation. He is now busied in a half penny Coinage for Bermudas with the Kings head, & a Ship or Sloop on the reverse, also with some for Antigua & Sierra Leone. His Sons illness has prevented his yet going to London. He will call on You, & perhaps upon Enquiry mention the *Exact* Sum He would take for His apparatus *exclusive of the Steam Engine*, for water work, or other force, will do equally well with Us, and the Engine is the principal Expence.

In the mention heretofore to You about counterfieting the money of other Countrys You are to understand Mr. Boulton stands clearly & honourably above all such vile proceedings, 'tho He must know some of the parties engagd in those practices. In Your conversation You need not drop a hint from *whom* You obtain the information as to Counterfiets, which I think is highly necessary to apprise America of—I therefore will here annex another account of these proceedings.

Since these my communications with Mr. B. and Mr. W., and my last letters to You, I have found out a variety of money coining practices here, highly disgraceful, I think, to the Parties, to the Country and its Laws; And in the instances I shall mention likely to do infinite mischiefs to the vast circulation of Spanish Silver in the United States.

As early as Mar. 1791 They began with the American Copper *Cent* only upon reading the resolve of Congress to have such a money and the getting over a print of the American Eagle.—There were three different sorts of those *Cents* made here (the samples of *two* of which I forwarded for your perusal in Mr. Jeffersons Book) all with the Presidents head, not a bad likeness, & tolerably well executed—I find however this was merely an attempt of some artists here to induce Congress to give Birmingham the order for Coinage of their copper money.

I have seen *pattern Cards*, of shillings, six pence's, & half Crowns so base as to be markd for Sale at the rate of 28, 30, & 36 shillings for the Guinea.

Quarter Dollars, & Pistereens, (but principally quarter Dollars, cut thus into three or rather four peices— an exact triangle taken out of the centre as No. 4.—The other three peic's No. 1. 2 & 3 of debased Silver, is nevertheless to be run off as halves of the quarter Dollar—The central peice No. 4 is again coind down, and is left rather plain in the dies (which were shewn to me with ps/s of the money) and the crescent formd peices No. 1. 2 & 3 struck off to nearly as possible the stamp of that part of a real spanish quarter Dollar— The pistereens were worse executed.

I have also seen Dutch Ducats, and Dollars which were done as follows—The Ducat was cut out of a pure peice of soft silver to the proper size & to be easily bendable in the finger as pure Ducats are— There is then a thick *amalgum* of Gold (which is made of quick-Silver & Gold & then squeezd thro' shammy leather) laid on this soft silver and then struck in the press to the exact size & marks of the Dutch Ducat of date *1752*. This order came thro' *English merchants* from Holland & London soon after the declard & open assistance given by England to their High & mighty allies the Dutch—The value of these forged Ducats is about one & sixpence Stg. workmanship & all—they weigh about 2 dwts.—5 grs. [⟨50⟩ grs.] and by weight the real Ducat would sell here for nearly ten Shillings, so that here rests a profit of Eight and sixpence on each peice.

Spanish milld Dollars are of three sorts, *two* only of which I have seen. The baser one is cut from a well silver-plated Sheet of Copper of due thickness, then hoopd around the Edge with a silver wire so thick as to not expose the Copper if scraped moderately on the edge with a knife (a common mode here to detect base Silver) and is then milld to the copied Dye, of which there are more than one sort—They are so well executed as to pass easily among others, and are in value workmanship & all about one and sixpence!.

The other & more pure Dollars the Artists are more close & secret about, as being a better thing—Those however come to Birmingham in real Spanish or Mexican Dollars bought at the Bank & other places, sent down by land Carriage about 10,000 at a time in a Cask, and they

6 APRIL 1793 455

are melted & recoind, copying as exactly the old impressions of which there are three or four sorts but mostly the lank visage of His most Catholic Majesty, *nine pence* of silver being taken from Each of the new Coinage, & these new ones want but little alloy to bring them to a proper thickness—2½ or *three* pence on Each peice is ample pay to the Artist here for dies, recoining, sending back to London & all other Expences so that the publick upon whom they are put loose nine pence in Every four & six pence and the Emitter has a clear benefit of six pence on Each. Upon close investigation *no doubt remains upon my mind,* but they are meant for the West Indies or for the United States. *Six tons* of them & of other silver have been so melted down since the begining of August last!—The Parties were very secret as to names but droppd to me upon being closely pushd, it was done by them under an order in a regular way from a House in London wholly in the *East* India line, & that those dollars were meant for the East; But this cannot be the case the people in that Country being very nice & scrupulous as to silver imported Coins. I have actually heard *professional* men (one in the Church & the other a Phisician) speak of knowing somewhat of this last coinage & having recommended an artist for the purpose of doing it!!

Assignats in quires, both stampd & signd, as well as in blank unstampd, with the proper paper and all the French words necessary in the *Water* marks, executed as I was told in London & sent hither for the Engravings printing & finishing strokes—The *head* of poor Louis however (which is done by a stamp the same as is on the Bills & notes here) appears now to be a want here & a loss to these schemers; one of whom told me, cursing & execrating the war, that He should have been ten thousand pounds richer if the declaration had been delayd a month or two longer—Those assignats which I saw were all for ten, twenty, & two hundred Livres Each.

In like manner in the wartime (and which I discoverd during my Agency under Congress for American Prisoners in England) did they forge & counterfeit *Boxes* full of our Continental paper money—In one vessel there was taken four or five Boxes of it, & others which got into America helpd much the depreciation in 1779. In this place such practices are held not criminal but a fair advantage over an Enemy, indeed hardly any thing Else short of murder is criminal among them for I never yet saw a people so totally devoid of principle, morality, & those lesser ties which bind & unite mankind.

I am with great regard & Esteem
Sir Yr. Obt. Humble Servt.
Thos. A. Digges

I direct my letters in a plain way, as I have known instances of freedoms being taken with Letters directed to public men.

LC: Jefferson Papers, Series 1.

To Joshua Johnson

Godlamin [Godalming] Mondy. forenoon—
March 10th [1794]

DEAR SIR

After writing to You yesterday about the Bearer Robert Owen an American Lad of 17 years old born at Lewis town in Pensylvania, I had the good luck by waiting on Admiral Affleck[1] to obtain His promise for the Boys immediate release from the Confinement He was unfairly thrown into; And by a mere accident in crossing the Country on my road for Kent[2] I over took the Boy this morning & gave a lift to Him on. He says He is bound to London & to get the Consul to help or direct Him to a birth out to His Country. I have just time enough to write You these few lines by Him, & have given Him a few shillings to help Him to London.

Yrs. in great haste
Thos. Digges

For Joshua Johnson Esq.
    American Consul London

[Addressed:] For Joshua Johnson/American Consul/No. 8 Coopers Row/Tower Hill/London

25 NOVEMBER [1797]

NA: Record Group 59, Consular Despatches, London, 6: Miscellaneous Letters to Joshua Johnson, 3: 1790–1797 (Microfilm T168, Roll 1).

¹Philip Affleck (1726–1799), who had served in the East India Company, had assisted Rodney in the West Indies in 1780, and was with him in the capture of St. Eustatius. In 1793 he had been appointed one of the lords of the admiralty under John Pitt, second earl of Chatham (1756–1835).

²Digges was on his way to visit Chilham Castle, the ancestral estate, with the intention, one may suppose, of looking into his chances for making good his claim on Chilham. There he would find extensive genealogical information about his family, both in books and in records kept by villagers, and fill a notebook with his discoveries (MdHS: Ms. 246).

To Rufus King

King (1755–1827), who after John Adams became president had succeeded to Pinckney's ambassadorship to Great Britain, was collecting information about the so-called Blount conspiracy. William Blount (1749–1800), governor of the territory of Tennessee in 1790 and Tennessee's senator when it had become a state six years later, had not been long a senator when financial difficulties had made him receptive to a plan devised by his Indian agent, a Scottish-born former British soldier named John D. Chisholme, to take Spain's possessions in the Floridas and Louisiana with a force consisting of Indians, frontiersmen, and British ships for the purpose of turning the settlements over to Great Britain. The scheme had soon been discovered, and Blount had been impeached and expelled from the Senate in July 1797; but meanwhile Chilsholme, having found himself increasingly ignored by Blount, had undertaken negotiations on his own. He had presented his plan to the British envoy to the United States, Robert Liston (1742–1836), waited for a response from the ministry, to which it had been forwarded, and then, impatient with a silence that gave no promise of being broken, secured Liston's consent, along with a handful of letters of introduction from him, to enable him to sail for London to deal directly with the government. Although tales were circulated alleging that Chisholme's intention was not to mount an actual attack but only to frighten the Spanish into paying him to prevent one, Chisholme's own professed purpose was to be rewarded by the British: the captors would divide the public money and personal property with the crown, and he would become the British superintendent of Indian affairs. In London, though, where the British were wary of disturbing American neutrality and of dealing with characters like Chisholme, he was proving no more successful than he had been overseas. Unable to get from British officials more than a pittance as reimbursement for the expenses he had incurred in behalf of the enterprise, even as the costs of a sybaritic life in London mounted, he had apparently agreed to give King information in the hope of extricating himself from his predicaments. King, who would cross-examine him at length on December 5, seems either to have enlisted or simply accepted Digges's assistance in investigating the conspiracy.

[London]
26 Red Lyon Str.
25th Novr. '96 ['97]

SIR

I calld in upon Mr. Chisholme yesterday evening in order to obtain from Him the *names* of the Persons in America who may have been implicated in the plan of surprizing the Spanish Posts &ca., and I took in with me Majr. Geo. Barnes, a native of Virginia now in London selling a large quantity of Georgia & Tennessee Lands, (about which I understand He had wrote to You) and from his being acquainted with Mr. Chisholme when He was at Philaa. with the party of Indians making the southern Indian Treaty, I think I am in a fair way, through Him, of obtaining most of the names implicated in [the] scheme from [for] wresting the Southern Territory from the Spaniards, & of which Mr. B. and Mr. C——spoke freely before me.—Mr. Chisholme has heretofore uniformly told me he would expose Every matter & plan relative to that transaction save the exposition of names, and hinted at several in N. York as well as Philadelphia who were concernd therein. He shewd me a letter receivd yesterday from Mr. Moore of Ld. G[renville]s office,[1] dry & guardedly written as if an answer to one from Chisholme asking for supplys or that He Mr. C——should be obligd to seek for aid & assistance through other Channels, meaning, as I conceivd, through You.

I went to him by appointment to be the bearer of a Letter, which states his Case & purposes, in some measure, together with a larger bundle of seald papers, which He said were colateral proofs &ca. as to the matter—I read the letter before he seald it but had no view of the other papers. I deliverd them to the Young Man Sutton[2] last night, & He will wait upon you to day about 12 oClk. with them. I think it best to apprize You of this by a messenger which I now send.

I will get Mr. Barnes to go in from time to time to Chisholme and doubt not but he will be able to get at *names* &ca. &ca.—Neither of the three parties know I have any communications or acquaintance with you, and so it had better remain for the present. I will attend to any request of Yours as to what queres or questions to put to Mr. C—— through the other two Gentlemen, for I was obligd during my conversations with him to co-incide in his opinion that the giving up *the names* of his friends & party would not be perfectly fair—He however told me last night He would do it, provided they were held back from the *Spaniards* in that quarter of the Country.

I am in haste & with Esteem
Sir Yr. Obt. Hble. Serv.
Thos. Digges

[Addressed:] Rufus King Esqr./&ca. &c. &c./ No. 1 Cumberland Circus/Oxford Road

NYHS: Rufus King Papers, 1797–1798, No. 36.

[1] William Wyndham Grenville (1759–1834), Baron Grenville of Wotton-under-Berenwood, was secretary of state for foreign affairs.
[2] D. J. Sutton, Jr. (see Digges to King, Nov. 27, 1797).

To Rufus King

Following Digges's conversation with Chisholme during the evening of November 25 Chisholme had—almost immediately, it would appear—written Digges:

Saturday Evening 25 N. 97

My Dear Sir

may I expect to see you Early Tomorrow morning—I am so Destressed—That I cannot Refrain Troubling you. I have thought of a mea-

sure that perhaps will serve me—if I can gitt it Done—perhaps You can have it Done for me.

*Believe me Sir Cencerley
Chisholme*

an answer if you please (NYHS: Rufus King Papers, 1797–1798, No. 48).

Digges enclosed the note with his letter to King.

[London]
26 Red Lyon Strt. 27th Nov. 97

SIR

Mr. Chisholme in many instances seems wild and incoherent, altho he has rather spoke out to Mr. B[arnes] (the Gentleman I mentiond in my last letter) respecting the names of some of His Colleagues. He wrote me the inclosd supposing from a slender acquaintance with the Duke of Portland, & in that office, I could solicit for him some appointment in Uppr. Canada, but this is totally out of the question. His plans & expectations must have been more developed to You by the letter & papers I took from Him to Mr. Sutton which I suppose You have seen. The following are the names I have discoverd of those persons concernd with Him, & which may lead to some queu for the discovery of others. Vizt.

At N. York a Captain Mitchell[1]—Captn. Stedman (who wrote The Expedition to Surinam)[2]—Doctor Romain (who enterd into the plan and made his Unkle Mr. Vandam of London acquainted therewith[)][3] —a Mr.———Morris then in N. York but formerly of Kingston Jamaica,[4] and another name which is blotted in my memorandum.

Governor Blount seems to have been the chief or main spring— also a Colol. Ore in the Tennessee[5]—a Colol. Wm. Whitley in Kentucky was promised him would join in the plan.[6]

N. B. he has promisd to give *the plan* in writing to Mr. Sutton, and you will of course see it.

At Philadelphia—a Mr. Nicolas (a Ship owner of Newhaven in Massachusets who would send armd vessels to Florida & orleans [)]—

From Philadelphia he wrote to Colol. Brandt,[7] and The Corn Planter[8] upon the business, & they came to Philaa. bringing with them a Mr. Street a member of The Assembly of Uppr. Canada—Captn. Johnson[9] and a Mr. Smith[10] an Indian Interpreter.—Chisholme sent for Captain Mitchell beforementiond to Philaa. and Mitchell there spoke to Major Craig of Pennsylvania,[11] and Mitchell was then sent by the party to The Mississippi to sound the people there & get plans &ca. of The Forts & posts—also saw & opend the matter to Capt. Collins[12] at Philadelphia but who resides in Marblehead—also a Mr. Blackburne of Richmd. in Virginia.[13] The plans were all concerted with & known to Mr. Liston[14] the English Envoy some time between 1st Nov. 96 and Mar. last, at which time Capt. Chisholme saild for England to concert measures here in Engd. and brought Introductory Letters to Lord Grenville, Mr. Dundass, Mr. Hammond[15] & others all close packd up in sheet Lead so as to be easily sunk if He was taken at Sea; and He had artificial Introductory Letters to Mr. Listons friends in Hambro. [Hamburgh] to cover him from detection if taken at Sea. I wonder much at the confidence placed in such a Man! but the plan seems to have been deep & well laid.

Mr. Chisholms seems to be poor, & abandond by His Ministerial Freinds at the Treasury, & is of course very anxious to get out of Prison. There is a mode of getting his *release*, & which is frequently & every Term done in the Courts here, which You may not be apprizd of:—It is by getting him Baild out by Jews, or men who openly do it for a certain perCentage of the Sum, & never after look for the person so baild, nor can he be troubled or run to Execution for some 3 or 4 terms after He is baild out—In this way I think He may be releasd for 9 or 10 £ advance to such Bail upon their producing His discharges. Whether he is worth this, or not, is the question.

Least some doubt may arise in Your mind respecting a passport for, or helping out another person to America (as expressd in Chisholms proposals) I think I can confidently assure you it is for *Mr. D. J. Sutton Jnr.* (the young man who has waited on You) and the reason is this—By extravagance, & some boyish indiscretions, He is an alien from His Fathers affections, & actually forbid appearing at his House No. 18 Great St. Helens—His Father is a respectable Quaker Mer-

27 NOVEMBER 1797

chant who lived many years in Alexandria (which is in sight of my Estate of Digges's-landing on the Potomack just fronting Mount Vernon & in sight of Washington City) where the Father now is collecting & remitting home Debts—His Son (the young man in question) was born there & was brought up in Virga. but for some 3 or 4 years back has been a Clerk to his Father in London, who unfortunately left him in too great a trust; & I know his wish is to get out to America with Chisholme or with any one rather than meet his Father, whom I expect dayly in London.—The way he got acquainted with Chisholme was by being put into the same prison for a Taylors Bill of 12 or 15 £ which I soon got compounded & procurd his discharge about 3 weeks ago, The Taylor willingly taking half the Sum.

        I am with great respect Sir
        Yr. most Obt. He. Serv.
        Thos. Digges

 I thought it better to send this information to You, as Young Sutton will probably call on You tomorrow forenoon with further communications from Mr. Chisholme.

NYHS: Rufus King Papers, 1797–1798, No. 37.

[1] John Mitchell was a surveyor and land speculator familiar with the western lands, especially the Spanish posts on the Mississippi.
[2] Captain Stedman was a Canadian, whom Digges mistakenly identifies as the author of *Narrative, of a Five Years' Expedition, against the Revolted Negroes of Surinam* . . . (London: J. Johnson, 1796). The author, Capt. John Gabriel Stedman (1744–1797), had never left England after returning there in the 1780s.
[3] Nicholas Romayne (1756–1817) was a New Yorker who had received his medical training in Edinburgh, returned to teach and practice in New York and New Jersey, failed in his professional arrangements and gone back to Europe, and then in 1797 supplanted Chisholme as Blount's principal associate.
[4] Robert Morris was a British subject who had moved to New York.
[5] James Ore (1762–1812), who had been born in Maryland, fought in the Revolution, moved to Tennessee, and served under Col. William Whitley (1749–1813) in 1794 in an expedition against the Cherokees, was a successful Indian trader, owner of a mill, and keeper of a tavern.
[6] Whitley had moved from Virginia to Kentucky in 1775 and was one of that state's distinguished settlers.
[7] Joseph Brant (1742–1807), the famous Mohawk chief who had fought against both

the French (in the French and Indian wars) and the Americans (during the Revolution), had failed to reach a settlement with the United States, led his people into Canada, receiving land and funds from the British as compensation for his revolutionary support, and then traveled to Philadelphia in 1797 to renew efforts to reach an agreement with the United States.

[8] Cornplanter, or Capt. John Abeel (ca. 1740–1836), a Seneca chief whose father was a Dutch trader and mother a Seneca, had been friendly toward the Americans throughout the 1790s, not concluding until 1810 that coexistence with whites was impossible.

[9] Possibly William Johnson (1775–1812), an officer in the British army whose father, Sir John Johnson (1742–1830), was a loyalist in New York and whose grandfather, Sir William Johnson (1714–1774), had been general superintendent of Indian affairs.

[10] Joseph Smith was employed by the United States as an Indian interpreter.

[11] Isaac Craig (1741–1826), a career officer who had fought on the American side in some of the major battles during the Revolution, had bought considerable tracts of land in western Pennsylvania and in 1797 joined in the building of the first glassworks in that region.

[12] Lewis Collins, whom Chisholme had met in Philadelphia, had planned to sail from Boston to the Floridas with men and provisions.

[13] Blackburne was a man Chisholme had met in a Philadelphia lodging house.

[14] Robert Liston had been appointed in Feb. 1796 as ambassador extraordinary and minister plenipotentiary.

[15] Henry Dundas (1742–1811) was secretary of war; George Hammond (1763–1853), secretary to David Hartley during the peace negotiations and recently minister to the United States, was undersecretary of state in the Foreign Office.

To George Washington

Mr. Rhd. Edmonds's
No. 96 Grace Church Street
London 10th Apr. 1798—

Mr. Digges presents His respectful complements and best wishes to General Washington and sends this in a small box of seeds, which accompanies a few Potatoes of a remarkably approved kind & productive Growth, which Mr. Rhd. Edmonds Seedsman No. 96 Grace Church Street London handsomely offerd to and pressd Mr. D. to present in His name to General Washington.

Mr. Chs. Pye, who has also purchasd some seeds of Mr. Edmonds with me, has promisd to take care of them, He being one of the passengers by the Mount Vernon Capt. Johnson bound to Alexandria.

The Potatoes and the Garden Seeds are obligd to be put in seperate parcels for fear of the yielding damp of the former hurting the seeds.

[P.S.] Mr. Digges has taken the liberty to send in the Box of seeds a few late News Papers—

[Addressed:] His Excellency/General Washington/at Mount Vernon, Virginia

LC: Papers of George Washington, 288: No. 9 (Series 4, Reel 112).

To Thomas Jefferson

Warburton (near Piscataway) Novr. 17. 1801

SIR

I am very unwilling to trespass upon Your time, but as my nephew Billy Carroll (a Clerk in the auditors Office)[1] is going hence to the City and will wait upon You with this, I am inducd to solicit Your reading the inclosd letter from Mr. Pinckney to me, and informing me whether You ever receivd the box and paper mentiond in His Letter.[2]

The Box containd some very fine specimens of Coins, medals, & provincial Copper money made at the famous Manufactory of Messrs. Boulton & Watt of Birmingham, which were obtaind by me for the purpose of presenting to You at the time when I understood You were at the head and engagd in establishing the Mint of this Country.

At that time I was at Birmingham & Sheffield engagd in the persuit & anxiously wishing to direct & get out to America some ten or a dozen Men of no small wealth & of celebrity in the Manufacture of Iron, founders, Nailers of the split cut sort, Smiths &ca. &ca.; and Mr.

Pinckney knowing what I was about solicited what information I could obtain as to Dye Sinkers and the value and prices of Copper, expences of Coinage &ca. &ca.

In these persuits I found out such a systematic villainy as to Forgerys & Coinages of base Money, that I added to the memoir or account given Mr. P. a full description of the mode & process used by those Artists in the making false money: for they had been at the American Loan Office Certificates as well as at Dutch Ducats Spanish Dollars, French Crowns, Pistereens &ca. &ca. &ca. making a variety of each of these moneys Vizt. some plated & rimmd with Silver, & others of base mettal similar to Silver and of various grades as to the value of each—for instance they had orders (chiefly from London) to make such & such Dollars at the value of 1/10d. each, some at 2/6d. & others as high as 3/- of actual value. I am sorry I have not now at hand the original descriptive account of this curious trafic or I would inclose it to You—The practice was not punishd in England though it was connivd at. In each of the three boxes I sent to Yourself, Genl. Washington and Mr. Pinkney I inclosd a Copy of my Memorandums and I had the pleasure of being informd by a letter from Colo. Fitzgerald that the information had arrivd in time to detect a large quantity shippd to Chas. town So. Carolina, as well as an attempt to put some into the Bank at Alexandria while Colonel Fitzgerald was then a Director: For I had also inclosd one to Him and to Mr. Josa. Johnson then Consul in London.

It is very well known that many Casks of this money coverd with nails & hardware were shippd to this Country and to the West Indies—The better sort of Dollrs. would deceive any one without close inspection.

       I am Sir with great esteem and truth
       Yr. Obt. Servt.
       Thos. Digges

MHS: Jefferson Papers.

[1] William (1782–1855) was the son of Digges's sister Elizabeth (1753–1843), who had married Daniel Carroll III of Rock Creek, Md. (1732–1790) in 1776.

²See Digges to Jefferson, Mar. 10, 1793, and to Pinckney, Mar. 12 and 21, 1793. On Nov. 19, 1801, Jefferson, now president, replied: "I believe I am not decieved in saying that a little before I went out of office in 1793 I did receive from you the specimens of coins you describe, with an account of the falsifications going on in England, and that I published in the news papers what related to the letter in order to guard the public." The coins themselves, he explained, he had of course left in the secretary of state's office, where he had also probably filed Digges's letter (LC: Jefferson Papers, Series 1 [Reel 25]).

To Thomas Jefferson

[Washington] Bookstore/Capitol Hill
28 Octo. [1803]

SIR.

The Bearer is Mr. Wm. Byrne an ornamental Stucco Worker & Plasterer whose good Conduct, sobriety, and rectitude I think I can answer for, having known Him as a respectable Tradesman in Ireland as well as in the City. If You have not engagd one for Monticello, I make no doubt but He will answer Your purpose and be full as reasonable in Charges, & perhaps more so, than others of His trade hereabouts.

I am in some hopes Mr. Latrobe may Employ him at the Capitol;¹ But this will be a job after what You have in Contemplation at Monticello.

I am with very great esteem & attachment Sir
Yr. Obt. Serv.
Thos. Digges

MHS: Jefferson Papers.

¹The architect and engineer, Benjamin Henry Latrobe (1764–1820), had emigrated from Yorkshire, England, in 1796 and been promptly given, among other assignments, those of improving navigation on the James River and of directing the installation of a new water supply for Philadelphia. On Mar. 6, 1803, Jefferson had appointed him surveyor of public buildings, with the immediate task that of building the south wing of the Capitol.

To John Carroll

Known as "Father of the American Church" because he was the first bishop in the United States, Carroll (1735–1815), a native of Upper Marlboro, Maryland, and a Jesuit, had been ordained to the priesthood in Belgium in 1769 after twenty-one years of study and teaching in Flanders and had been a resident of his native state since 1774, when he had returned home because of the suppression of his sect abroad. In 1784 he had been appointed superior of the Maryland mission and four years later named by the pope to be bishop of Baltimore. Although the tone and contents of Digges's letter suggest a history of close and cordial relations between the two men, those relations must have developed only after Digges's return from his long stay in England. For despite Carroll's relationship to the Digges family through the marriage of his niece, Catherine Brent (1772–1835), to George Digges, as late as 1792 he had not only never become acquainted with Thomas but also had formed only the most unfavorable of impressions of Thomas's integrity. On April 16 of that year he had written James Thomas Troy (1739–1823), archbishop of Dublin: "I understand . . . that a principal mover in the business of the North, and in coaliting Catholics with Presbyterians, is a person from this country of the name of Digges. With him I am not acquainted, but pretty well with his character, and I am induced, by a solicitous regard for the Catholics of Ireland, and for your Lordship in particular, to mention some circumstances relating to Mr. Digges, which need not be mentioned farther than you will find it necessary. He is of respectable family and connections in this country, no one more so; in his early youth he was guilty of misdemeanours here, indicating rooted depravity, but amazing address, but even this could not screen him, and his friends, to rescue him from the hands of justice, and themselves from dishonour, sent him out of the country. He went first to Lisbon, where fresh misconduct compelled him to seek refuge elsewhere. He arrived in England at the beginning of the American War, and with his wonted address and insinuating manners, engaged himself deeply into the familiarity of all the Americans in England, and the lords and commons who combated the ministry on the subject of the American War. He even wrote such good accounts of the designs of England to the American negotiators at Paris, that they conceived the highest confidence in his zeal for their cause, and entrusted him with the disposal of large sums of money for the relief of American prisoners languishing in England; but all this time, as it was afterwards known, he was a spy for Lord North, and employed by him in some important business. He never applied the money sent him. After the War he continued his malpractices, but has sufficient dexterity, by shifting his scenes of action, and displaying extraordinary abilities, to gain confidence for a time. You may easily conceive how dangerous it would be for such a man to obtain any degree of trust in the management of your concerns, which require such sound heads and hearts" (The John Carroll Papers, ed. Thomas O'Brien Hanley [Notre Dame, Ind.: University of Notre Dame Press, 1976], 2: 25– 26). *Editor's interpolations omitted. No correspondence between Digges and Carroll prior to the present letter has been found.*

Warburton 3d June 1804.
DEAR SIR
On my return home from Baltimore I found a letter from Mr. Rhd. O'Mara of Tipperary Ireland in answer to one I wrote Him about two years ago concerning the Irish Estate, to which You seem (barring alienship[)], to have a legal claim—I send You inclosd an extract of the letter so far as relates to the property in question, and the original with its philippicks, Politicks &ca. I yesterday sent up to Billy Carroll by his Brother George[1] whom I brought down with me in the chaise on Monday. It seems a great pity that a due attention and legal claim to this estate has been so long delayed, and I am not competant to judge whether the Acts of Limitation, penal Irish Acts, or that of alienship will shut You from a just claim to it.

Captain O'Mara with some naval officers of the Frigates, stoppd here yesterday on their way down—He says it is not at all unlikely but his Brother Rhard., my correspondant, will be soon in America—He seems perfectly well acquainted with the property.

Two of the frigates are between this & Belvoir and two laying off Alexa. waiting only for a wind.—I have every reason to believe they go out better officerd and under more *subordination* (which our youth on ship board stands somewhat in need of) than any Squadron heretofore sent, and the recent example of breaking Capt. Morris[2] may be a spur to future activity.

We got to Rock Creek[3] to an early dinner the day after leaving You, & not a little gratified to find a great portion of the Tobacco crop planted & well struck, (none being planted or the ground even prepared between that & Baltimore) the Wheat & clover fine & flourishing, and not in the least injurd by the hailstorm on Tuesday.

The ravages committed by the Hail Rain & wind on Tuesdy. were very conspicuous at and about Elk Ridge landing, leaving large boughs, some trees & abundance of Leaves in the Roads, but it did not extend downwards more than 3 miles from the Ferry. It has done immensity of mischief in the line from thence towards monokasy & Frederick in a breadth of six or 7 miles.

I just hit the moment for a second Brakefast on Mondy. with Mr. Merry[4]—heard all the *English* News (not so favourable as I could wish it, but far from being so bad as the *Baltimore Count*[5] detaild it to me) and was highly gratified with the gift of some dozens English Papers, Debates, &ca.&ca. [Father Fenwick[6] has been feasting on them for 3 or 4 days.]. Refusing an invitation to his Dinner from my saying I was obligd to push home after dining with Mrs. Young,[7] Your name came upon the tapis Mr. M. lamenting he had not seen You when He & Mrs. M. was at a dinner or visit to Your sister[8] &ca. He hopes to know when You are next in the City and expressd a strong desire to see You—You know says he how much I have lived with and respect those of the Cloth—and how often You & I have been with the then good old Bishop Butler of Cork, Doctor Moylan,[9] & others and that the Catholics was far the most agreeable Society he enjoyd at Cork—& You know what good dinners & wine Bishop Butler used to give us—what a good Cook he was—going into the Kitchen himself & tucking up his sleeves to make the good sauces &ca.&ca. And oh how he has disgracd himself, says Mr. M. by the two or three last acts of a doating life—first his abjuration. 2nd his vanity in probably doing it for *a peerage*, & thirdly taking a young wife when 70 years of age![10] From many coinciding circumstances & recollection of former scenes I cannot but entertain an opinion that *He* is one of our Sect—This is *entre nous*. There may be some *weighty* reasons however why He, as first a partner in an English protestant House in Malaga—then a vice Consul to one of that house—then the Consul at Malaga—then Consul-general of Spain—then Naval agent Victualler & Inspector of public Provisions at Cork—then a messenger of legation to Madrid—then minister of Legation to make the Commercial Treaty with Denmark—then minister at Paris—and now Envoy & Minister Plinipotentiary to America (in mostly all of which situations I knew Him) might not wish to keep his Faith in the back Ground. No man however able or amiable, avowing himself a Catholic, would be employd in any of these avocations under the British Government. I hope when You are next in the City that you may have an oppertunity to meet Mr. M. I am sure it is what he wishes, & it would highly gratify me to be one of the trio.

My remembrance to Dudley & Bob Brent[11]—I hope to see him *here* in the vacation, and wish, if *he can*, to be more attentive to his book, & less so to news papers and Politics—it is but a thorny path for Boys. I cannot help being pleased with his progress, and the eligible situation he is in. The annual outgoing however of 400$ is lamentably too high for such a Country as this.

I am Dr. Sir with the highest esteem & regard
Yr. Obt. Servt.
Thos. Digges

We have been nearly inundated here with Rain—very heavy showers almost every day for a fortnight—a field of Wheat of mine, I believe the best in the County (save Thomas's at Addisons Ferry) in full head has been leveled with the Earth for some days & every rain press's in the more—Tobacco mostly all planted, Indn. Corn very fine and no better clover in Maryland.

[Enclosure]

Extract of a Letter from Mr. Rhd. O'Mara to T. Digges (Recd. at Warburton 31 May 1804) dated Shally Feby. 1. 1804 . . . N.B. Shally is in the County of Tipperary Ireland near Nenagh the County Town, & not far from Cashell.

It is an answer to one wrote to him by T. Digges on the 15 of June 1802 to get information respecting an Estate in Ireland to which Wm. Carroll has some Claim as Heir at Law.

"I would have wrote to You on receipt of Your Letter had I got any information respecting the farm You mention calld Liscaruff, but no one in this neighbourhood that I applyd to could give any satisfactory account until I saw Mrs. O'Brien* of Carrigatoher, to whom You referrd me; and who was in a bad state this long time back, but has now almost establishd good health, And by the way, Her account is not as pleasing as I could wish. At present, I think her memory is treacherous, as I consider her in or near her dotage, but when the constitution is recoverd her memory may also. However all I could glean from her is nearly this.—Daniel Carroll of Ballycrenode, her great grand Father, & also great grand father to Bishop Carroll had three nephews, well informd but confined in Circumstances, to each of whom he gave an Estate. She is not decided in opinion whether these Estates were part of his own, or, whether at that time he purchasd them for the purpose of presenting his nephews with them; But this place in question fell to the lot of old John Carroll, known by the name of John of Liscariff, who had no lawfull Issue, which intitled Daniel Carroll (brother to the Bishop) to the Estate, being the next heir at Law: Mrs. O'Brien says He was in this Country after the death of John, and She does not know whether or not he made any agreement with James Carroll (who got into possession at Johns death[)] but She is rather inclind to think he did not. James was uncle to the now occupant, Josina, He concluded no bargain with James, as He Commisiond Richard Fitzgerald (an unkle of mine) when in America, to get possession of the Ground, and as I believe to make the best of it he could for Him—It rested there, and I know not nor heard any reason why—this happend about 28 years ago. The property lies in the direction You describe, and You passd through it on your way from Cashel to the Silver Mines, about 22 miles from the former and four from the latter. It contains 70 acres let out to Farm some years back for about 50£ a year, and would let at present for £1:0:0 an acre, and soon higher, as ground is looking up astonishingly in this kingdom: that is all improveable, and has the best manure on the premises, 'tis also in a good Corn Country.—["]

*This Mrs. OBrien lives at Carrigotogher 2 miles from Nenah, & [an] old Lady who claims relationship with Mr. Carroll of Annapolis & the Carrolls of Maryland.

T. D.

AB: Carroll Papers, 3C10.

¹George Attwood Carroll (1788–1844), a younger son of Digges's sister Elizabeth.
²Richard Valentine Morris (1768–1815) had been dismissed from his post in the fall of 1803 because as a commander of the Mediterranean squadron during the war against Tripoli he had failed to maintain a blockade against Tripoli and been judged by a court of inquiry to have lacked "the diligence or activity necessary to execute the important duties of his station."
³Elizabeth Digges's family lived there, as did some of the other Carrolls. Her husband, the late Daniel Carroll III, was a nephew of the bishop's.
⁴Anthony Merry, British minister to the United States, 1803–1806.
⁵The beneficiary of this sobriquet has not been identified.
⁶The Rev. John Ceslas Fenwick (ca. 1759–1815), a native of Maryland, had studied and become a Dominican in Belgium, returning to Maryland in 1800 to labor in the missions in the southern part of the state, mainly Charles County. The brackets are Digges's.
⁷Apparently Carroll's sister Mary, Mrs. Notley Young (1742–1815).
⁸Although Carroll had four sisters, the context again suggests Mary Young.
⁹Francis Moylan, bishop of Cork, had been educated in France, where he had served as curate from 1761 into the 1770s, when he had returned to Ireland, a proponent of the legislative union of Ireland with Great Britain and opponent of all government attempts to interfere with clerical appointments.
¹⁰The downfall of John Butler (d. 1800), at one time bishop of Cork, had been precipitated by his having inherited from a nephew property that entitled him to become the twelfth Baron Dunboyne. Hoping to perpetuate his name, he had sought a special dispensation from the pope to marry his cousin, a Protestant, and when his wait had been rewarded with silence, he had in 1785 married anyway, two years later reading his recantation of Catholic doctrines before the parish. A few days before his death, though, he had become reconciled to the church and bequeathed his estate to Maynooth College, whose purpose was to educate young men intended for the priesthood.
¹¹William Dudley Digges (1790–1830), son of George Digges and hence Thomas's nephew and Carroll's grand-nephew, is surely the "him" of the rest of the sentence. Robert Brent (1746–1819), Carroll's nephew—son of Carroll's sister Anne Brent (1733–1804)—had become Washington's first mayor, appointed to the office by Jefferson in 1802 and destined to be reappointed under both Jefferson and Madison until his death. Brother of George Digges's wife, Catherine, Brent was also Dudley's uncle and his guardian as well.

To Thomas Jefferson

Warburton (near Piscaty.[)] Decr. 13 1804

DEAR SIR

A long confinement to home with a Bileous & attack, & the approaching end of a Sister,¹ has prevented me the pleasure of paying my respects to You & receiving those civilities & attentions for which I am very much Your Debtor.

I wishd very much to have accompanied the bearer Wm. Mordaunt Esqr. to the City today, and to have gratified Him in a wish of personally introducing Him to You; But it is out of my power.

I make so free as to intrude this scrawl to You merely for such introduction. Mr. Mordaunt is a Gentleman of respectability & worth—a native of Portugal & whose Family I knew & highly respected when travelling in that Country many years ago. He has spent some years laterly in India, & came from thence in one of our Indiamen to New York—Is here to see & look at our rising Country & from his high opinion & respect for You I should be sorry He left the City without paying his respects to You.

I am with high esteem
Sir Yr. very Ob. Sert.
Thos. Digges

MHS: Jefferson Papers.

[1] Ann Digges (b. 1750) died on Dec. 28.

To Thomas Jefferson

Warburton (Near Piscataway) June 30 1806

DEAR SIR

I am much obligd in many instances by Your kind attentions, and particularly so for the present of Quarantine Corn, which I have carefully sown in good soil & put in according to Your instructions. The grain appears to me exactly that round, red-& yellow kind which the Spaniards & Portuguese with success (though in but small quantities comparatively to their wants) cultivated while I resided in those Countries, and where that kind of seed was much preferrd to our large *goardseed* sort:—If its produce is but two Crops the season (instead of four in Italy & three in Switzerland) it will be a valuable acquisition to the United States, and the Importer of it will deserve well of His Country.[1]

Altho I detest great crouds and their consequent *gapers*, I mean and hope to see You on the 4th.—Some of my acquaintance & colleagues, firm Republican Supporters of The Executive Government, & of considerable influence in the Forest part of this County,[2] entertaining an opinion that they should *now*, more than they have heretofore been prone to do, (from some late intemperate indecencies in Congress) shew thier attachment & regard for our Executive Rulers, have expressd a wish for my meeting them on the 4th for the purpose of Introduction to notice & to conversation &ca.—Mr. Levi Gant, Mr. O. Sprigg, Colo. Lyles, Dr. Kent &ca.[3]

I am to meet them at Stells at 11 oCk.—conversations in a croud are out of the question; but I should be very glad of a subsequent oppertunity for a little conversation (which, if they remain for the night, may be conveniently arrangd) And it cannot but be servicable to the cause We are unitedly engagd in, as well as contravene some Election machinations begining to shew itself from the soddend embers of an opponent Federal party in the County. Mr. Vanhorne (supposd to be a Deserter from the cause (though I am very unwilling to believe so) is to run for Congress against Covington, supported too with a considerable personal Interest about Bladensburgh, and the *Vansville* District, (which has heretofore been our sheet anchor against the Torey merchantile Interest of this division) And He is backd too by the Foederal phalanx altho thier execrations were violently open against him two years back—this smells a little of apostacy added to disapointment from our party nominating Covington in preference to Him, and I fear he stands a good chance of getting in.[4]—This is not worth the mention to You but may remain *entre nous.*

My boy passing to Geo. town will drop this as he goes thro Washington, and will call as He comes back about noon. I should be very much obligd for 2 or 3 cast by News papers (for by some unaccountable neglect in the printer or in the post I have receivd no paper for 10 days back, & wanted much to read Mr. Randolph's address to His Constituants, & having a strong hope that eer this some accounts have been had of the *Hornet* favourable to her errand[)].[5]

       With the highest esteem & regard
       I am Yr. Obt. Ser.
       Thos. Digges

LC: Jefferson Papers, Series 1.

[1] This small-eared strain of early corn, known in northern Spain as *Cuarantino* and in Italy, where it was planted late, as *Quarantino*, proved to be both too early and too low-growing to be suitable in the United States.

[2] No doubt the eastern part, where John Adams's Federalist friend, Uriah Forrest (1756–1805), who had served in the Third Congress, had dominated the politics.

[3] All were members of prominent Maryland families, and some had held elective office: Osborn Sprigg (d. 1815), uncle of Samuel Sprigg (1782–1855), who became governor in 1819 for a three-year term, had subscribed to the ratification of the Constitution at Maryland's ratifying convention; William Lyles, Jr. (ca. 1753–1815), whose military rank dated from 1780, became a candidate for elector for the state senate; and Joseph Kent (1779–1837), a surgeon in the militia, was to enter the U.S. House of Representatives in 1811 as a Federalist and later, as a Republican, to return to the House, serve as governor, and become a United States senator.

[4] Leonard Covington (1768–1820) was the incumbent, identified as a Democrat. Archibald Van Horne (d. 1817), Speaker of the state House of Delegates during 1805, did in fact win the election and become known as a Republican.

[5] Jefferson received Digges's letter the same day Digges wrote it and acknowledged it the following day: "Th: Jefferson salutes Mr. Digges with friendship & respect and sends him the newspapers recieved last night. He is sorry that only the latter part of the particular publication, which Mr. Digges wished to see, is in them. He will be happy to see Mr. Digges & his friends on the 4th of July, and to join in congratulations on the return of the day which divorced us from the follies & crimes of Europe, from a dollar in the pound at least of 600. millions sterling, & from all the ruin of Mr. Pitt's administration. We too shall encounter follies; but if great, they will be short, if long, they will be light: & the vigour of our country will get the better of them. Mr. Pitt's follies have been great, long, & inflicted on a body emaciated with age, exhausted by excesses beyond it's power to bear" (LC: Jefferson Papers, Series 1 [Reel 36]).

The "address" by Jefferson's son-in-law, Thomas Mann Randolph, Jr. (1768–1828), *Letter of Thomas M. Randolph, to His Constituents*, completed in Apr. and published in Washington as a pamphlet of twenty-three pages, had appeared serially in the *National Intelligencer*, June 13–16, 1806, and the *Richmond Enquirer*, June 20–24, 1806. It was a defense of Jefferson's policies concerning the West Florida boundary question. Randolph's wife was Jefferson's oldest daughter, Martha (1772–1836).

Jefferson's reply did not clarify the nature of the "errand" on which the diplomatic courier ship *Hornet* had been sent.

To Thomas Jefferson

Warburton near Piscaty. [19 or 20]th Sepr. 1806[1]
[received Sept. 25]

DEAR SIR

I am obligd to yield up what I had very much at heart, (a visit to Monticello) to my other riding avocations, and to the extreme heat for the last ten days, as well as the still continued severe & afflicting drought. The Eves of my old House has not dropt five minutes at a time since the 3d July—not a sprig of green grass, and scarcely any vegitation in the Tobacco: of which hereabouts we have not a fourth part of a Crop and scarcely Corn enough for the hog feeding—three or four miles of River shore servd my stock in water, or I should have had them to drive for miles. The upper & Eastern districts of the County are however better off: And in all its divisions our party in Politics have had no little consolation in the chagrin, disapointmend and, I may add, *defeat of the Feds*—as You will see by the Papers.

I have the favour to ask of Your again aiding me in a little seed of *The spanish broom*, the severe drowth having killd mostly all the stalks of what I had growing flourishingly from a little Seed You favourd me with in Sepr. 1804—It is of easy growth, takes kindly even in but indifferent soil, is a handsome evergreen for covering broken parts of pasture, and above all a very excellent food for Sheep.—I should be very much obligd by a little more of the Seed, and perhaps it may be attainable before You set out from Monticello and not much burthen Your Servants baggage. We are hoping to see You early in October.

I was at Annapolis on Mondy. last the day of meeting for Electors to chuse our next five years Senate, which is an all-important and influencial part of our State Constitution.[2] Mr. M[e]r[ce]r, my old acquaintance, is hid & in the dumps—very much & most deservedly down in public estimation, by his Quidisms and superficial manoeuvres being beat upon the poll for Elector (of which he had great confidence) by *some hundreds of votes*—It is not likely He will soon again get into any office.[3]

The Majority on our side far exceeded *my* Expectations, for I could not help entertaining fears of preponderance in our opponents, from knowing the late nearly equipoise of my County, from thier more than ever-before known vigilence assiduity and secret workings among thier party, thier private meeting and deep laid plans &ca. They hardly left a thing undone, and were so sanguine of success as to speak out very confidently just before the Election & even make bets they would have a Federal senate.—You may guess thier feelings and thier disapointments, thier ill-humour & vexations when they lost the appointments by a majority of nearly three to one!

From the 10 Western Shore Countys, with the two Boroughs of Annapolis & Baltimo. and the 8 Eastern Shore Counties, there were *in all* 38 out of which there could not be musterd but 11 Feds. two members doubtfull as Quids Vizt. Maxwell & Scott from Kent Coty.— and 1 decided Republican sick—so that it may be stated of decided Republicans present—26. And the 15 Senators Chosen were Jno. T. Mason (who had 28 votes) S. Ringold*—Shriver*—Christie* of Harford formerly in Congress & likely to be our next Governor—McCullogh* of Baltio.—McEldery Ditto—Thos. Ducket*—Wm. Thomas* St. Marys—Loyd Dorsey—Partridge*—Be[n]tton—Williams*—Gibson— Purnell—& Wheatly*—those markd with a * were former Senators and the Rest good men & true.

Some Federal Gentlemen were proposd by the minority as Carroll, Chapman—Shaaffe—Bowie of Montgomery—Dr. McHenry— Dennis—Goldsborough—Rhd. Potts—Gen. Ridgely—R. B. Taney of Frederick &ca. &ca. Carroll getting 13 votes & the rest from 8 to 10 votes.[4]

Mr. E: Calvert for the County (notwithstanding his 80 Healot Tenants) beat Lyles in this County but by one; But the Bladensburgh District Return was voted void & Mr. Calvert sent home: owing to his Brother Geo. Calvert perswading two of the Judges to re-open the Poll after the time had elapsd & the Tickets actually adding up, and polling five votes which He had brought in which put his Brother so many before Lyles: But the majority on the whole was so decided that he Lyles Did not urge his Seat, and the two Judges (Feds.) made but a very lame excuse.[5] Appearances markd them both corrupt & guilty.

It is a very satisfactory event to me & others, for it is a complete defeat to Mr. Calvert & his party—who stand no chance in the future for the County, provided our people can be got out, and the heads & Rulers of the Country continue as they hitherto have done to deserve well of the Country.

        With great regard & Esteem
        I am Yr. Obligd. & Obt. Serv.
        Thos. Digges

If your Relative Mr. Sam Carr is with or near You[6] it may please Him to hear of this result of Republican endeavours & on the ground too on which He was once a successful & able advocate—

Councellor Brodie[7] who is still an inmate with me begs his Respects to You. He has been up at Mr. Ringolds but did not like the flat low situation of the Lands offerd Him by Mr. Sam Ringold—He seems fixd for trying the Gennessee Country, but at times has a wish to see a place somewhere near You which You had mentiond to Him last winter.

Mr. Jefferson

LC: Jefferson Papers, Series 1.

 [1] In the light of the dates of the elections to which Digges refers, the inference to be drawn from his "Mondy. last" in the third paragraph, and the notation by Jefferson in his endorsement that the letter was received on Sept. 25, we are left with only Sept. 19 and 20 to which Digges's ordinal suffix can be affixed.
 [2] Actually, the meeting lasted beyond a single day. On Monday, Sept. 15, the electors, already chosen in county balloting, convened to submit their credentials. The next day the results were verified and the electors seated. Sessions were held on Sept. 17, and the following afternoon the senators themselves were chosen.
 [3] Digges's failure to spell out the name is surely shorthand rather than excessive caution. For he appears to be referring to John Francis Mercer (1759–1821), a Virginian at birth, an officer during the Revolution, a law student under Gov. Jefferson in 1779–1780, a member, in turn, of the Virginia House of Delegates, of the federal convention to ratify the Constitution (which he had voted against), of the Maryland House of Delegates, and of the U.S. House of Representatives before becoming governor of Maryland, 1801–1803, after which he had served for three years once again in the Maryland House of Delegates. A Republican in Maryland politics, he had joined the so-called Quids, a faction within the party that opposed the purchase of the Floridas and that

disagreed with the Jeffersonian handling of impending troubles with England. In the contest for electors for Anne Arundel County, concluded two weeks earlier, he had been fourth among four candidates for two positions: John Johnson had received 599 votes, Lloyd Dorsey, 590, Horatio Ridout, 345, Mercer, 323.

[4] The *Maryland Gazette*, Sept. 18, 1806, confirms Digges's report of the outcome with a single exception. Dr. John Maxwell and James Scott did represent Kent County. The senators chosen from the Western Shore were John Thomson Mason (b. 1764); Samuel Ringgold (1770–1829); David Shriver; Gabriel Christie (1755–1808), who, though, never became governor; James H. McCulloch (1756–1836); Thomas McElderry; Thomas Ducket; William Thomas; and Lloyd Dorsey; and those chosen from the Eastern Shore were John Partridge, Mark Benton, Thomas Williams, Jacob Gibson, Zadock Purnell, and William Whitely. The exception is in the names of the Federalists. Charles Carroll of Carrolton (1737–1823), a frequent member of both state and national legislative bodies before 1801; Henry H. Chapman; Arthur Shaaf; Dr. John Bowie; Dr. James McHenry (1753–1816), a student of medicine under Benjamin Rush (1745–1813), a surgeon in Washington's army, a member later of both state and national legislatures, and then secretary of war, 1796–1800; Robert Dennis; Robert Henry Goldsborough (1779–1836), a member of the state House of Delegates; Richard Potts; Roger Brooke Taney (1779–1864), the future chief justice of the U.S. Supreme Court—all are listed in the *Gazette*'s report. But General Charles Ridgeley (1760–1829), from Hampton, the wealthy future governor of Maryland, remains unmentioned.

[5] Col. William Lyles had challenged the results in the Prince George's County balloting, which had given Edward Henry Calvert the victory, 104–103. Lyle's memorial on the subject had been considered on the morning of Sept. 18.

[6] Samuel Carr, a nephew, was with or near him. When Jefferson's sister Martha Jefferson Carr had been widowed in 1773, Jefferson had taken her, her three sons, and her three daughters into his home and educated the children.

[7] Francis Brodie, an Englishman interested in buying a hundred or more acres of farmland in the region, had earlier visited and corresponded with Jefferson and was to stay at Warburton on more than one occasion during the next two years. In 1789 he had been living in Dublin, where, some evidence suggests, he may have been one of Digges's prison companions in the Four Courts Marshalsea four years earlier.

To Thomas Jefferson

Warburton Decr. th 1806 [received Dec. 23rd]

DEAR SIR

My friend and old acquaintance Dr. Hamilton, of very respectable connections at Waterford Ireland, and of late a neighbouring Phisician to me but about to fix in Baltimore, having intimated a desire to wait upon You, I most cheerfully give Him this Introductory line with a solicitation for Your usual kind attentions and civility. I knew Dr. Hamilton a practitioner in London, for some years after a resident in Alexandria, & for the last two or three years residing in sight of this—where the field is too circumscribd for Him.—In all situations I found Him a firm friend to this his adopted Country, a combatter against Toryism (to some effect) in Alexandria—an assistant to Us & our party hereabouts, and ever an admirer of Yours, altho mere chance has hitherto denied Him the pleasure of a personal interview or introduction.

He takes the City in a day or two on His way to Baltimore with a very amiable English Wife. He will, at my request call on You, if but for a few moments, with this. I have been confined *to Home* or would have waited on You.—I hope Mrs. Randolph & Her Dear little ones are fixd with You as heretofore & are all well,[1] for except a letter from my old acquaintance Dr. Logan inclosing Your Speech[2] (which is a highly satisfactory one to me) & the subsequent moves in Congress, I am a total stranger to the late movements in the City.

Many happy Years—May You go on my Good Sir continuing to do good & recieving the benefits of it.

I am with great regard & Esteem
Yr. obt. Hm. Servt.
Thos. Digges

LC: Jefferson Papers, Series 1.

[1] Although Thomas M. Randolph, Jr., was living in the presidential mansion while Congress was in session, Martha had decided to remain in their home at Albemarle.

[2] Jefferson's sixth annual message to the Congress, Dec. 2, 1806, in which he had concentrated on foreign affairs and on success in exploring the West. He had been optimistic about the progress of negotiations with Great Britain, uncertain about the outcome of negotiations with Spain, and pleased especially with the results of the expeditions undertaken by Meriwether Lewis (1774–1809) and William Clark (1770–1838) and by Zebulon Montgomery Pike (1779–1813). George Logan, a Democratic U.S. senator from Pennsylvania since 1801, had after passing through London in 1780 on the way to Philadelphia (see Digges to Adams, Apr. 14, 1780, n. 1) engaged in scientific farming, been elected to the Pennsylvania House of Representatives, become a Republican, and gone to France in 1798 unofficially to improve Franco-American relations (precipitating the so-called Logan Act that forbade private diplomacy).

To Thomas Jefferson

Warburton Near Piscaty. Feby. th 1807 [received Feb. 20th]
DEAR SIR

A long confinement to my chamber (with a Rhumatic & Pluracy complaint) will I hope plead my excuse for troubling You to read a latter [letter] in lieu of giving an answer by personal enquiry.

I have a very favourable oppertunity & mean shortly to send a relative of mine (a Lad of about 15 years old) *to Spain*:—there to fix him for 6 or 8 years in order to attain the Language and Merchantile advantages of that Country.—If my old acquaintance Mr. Young is still at Madrid, & likely to remain there a little longer, my wishes thereby would be half accomplishd: for I have known him ever since his being put on shore in England a State prisoner with Mr. Laurens, to whom He was private Secretary; and he owes to me the good luck of getting hastily from England to Dr. Franklyn at Paris instead of being put to prison with some hundreds American Prisoners then under my care. I ever knew Mr. Young a valuable, prudent & firm Republican, and it gave me great pleasure when You kindly reinstated Him to his post at Madrid some year or two past.[1]

All I want to know if he is yet in Spain under Your employ and likely to be there a little longer?

My boy passing will drop this, & call to know if any answer. I am quite in a nook here, and by some ill luck of the Post rider I have not seen a paper since that of the 6th, so that I have only to hope *all* is going on well to the westward, that the neck of the Conspiracy is broken, and that the perpetrators may meet their just reward.[2] With the best wishes for Your long preservation & personal happiness I remain with

    Sincere regard & esteem
    Dr. Sir. Yr. Obt. Hle. Sert.
    Thos. Digges

P.S. Accustomd as I have been to ask & to recieve favours from You I am sure I too boldly Step from one to another. The Solicitation

I made to You by letter to Monticello to assist me with the Postmaster Genl. "to get the Alexa[n]dria postmastership given, when vacant, to my nephew Jno. Fitzgerald" is likely to be tested in a very few days by the death of Mr. Washn. Craik—for I learn from his Phisician & friends he is nearly exhausted.[3] Dr. Logan with his usual goodness, personally assisted my nephews solicitation with Mr. Granger[4] about a month back; Who told the Doctor that my nephews recommendations stood very high, and altho there were many applicants, *one other* stood so equally well recommended & that he was so undecided, that he meant to submit the nomination to The President, after shewing the pretensions of each applicant.

If fate decides in his favour I am very confidant the office will be faithfully & well attended to.

MHS: Jefferson Papers.

[1] Moses Young, imprisoned in Forton on his arrival in London in 1780, had with bribes and disguises managed to escape to Ireland and then to France. Finding no opportunity there for government service, he had embarked on private ventures, largely unsuccessful, concluding in his managing in 1797 to become United States consul at Madrid, to which post Jefferson had reappointed him.
[2] Aaron Burr (1756–1836) had been charged with conspiracy to separate the western states from the others and create an independent confederacy.
[3] George Washington Craik, son of Dr. James Craik (1730–1814), who had been chief physician and surgeon in the Continental army and chief medical officer to George Washington, was farther from death than Digges surmised, for he is recorded as occupying his postmastership through 1808. Digges's earlier letter to Monticello has not been found.
[4] Gideon Granger (1767–1822), the postmaster general. Logan and Digges were in the same political camp (see Digges to Jefferson, Dec. 1806 [received Dec. 23]).

To Thomas Jefferson

Warburton Mar. 11 1807

DEAR SIR

My old acquaintance & neighbour Doctor Rhd. H. Courts who is now with me, & who has a plaint to make to You, (which from my confinement I cannot *personally* attend Him in,) will wait upon You with this.

The Doctor served faithfully & for several years in our Revolutionary War, has been ever a firm & uniform Republican (even in the worst of times), a constant supporter of the present Administration, and no small aid to our party in our County Election Combats altho living in the neighborhood of a phalanx of our hardy & direct opponents.

For His public services He has never Recieved any Compensation as will appear by Documents now in His possession—I chearfully acquiese in giving Him this introductory to You, and to solicit Your usual kindness & attention to Him. I have often wishd to give Dr. Courts a personal Introduction to You, But his avocations in Phisic & in Magistracy in His neighbourhood has prevented our meetings in the City.

The Doctor has been the first to inform me of my friend Mr. T. M. Randolphs illness,[1] He having visited Mr. R. in his sick chamber. I sincerely hope he has recoverd, & may long live a blessing to His charming & amiable Family.

With grt. regard affection & esteem
I am Dr. Sir
Yr. Obt. Hle. Serv.
Thos. Digges

MHS: Jefferson Papers.

[1] Randolph, who had recently voted with the Federalists on two resolutions concerning the handling of Burr's conspiracy, had come to believe that someone had said libelous things about him to his father-in-law. Feeling himself in disfavor and ignored, he had left the presidential mansion for a boarding house, where, suffering from melancholy and a severe fever, he had resisted Jefferson's appeals to return for better care and was now managing a recovery that would only enable him to travel home and abandon national politics.

To Thomas Jefferson

The Diggeses' Warburton Manor, part of which was situated on a promontory across the Potomac from Mount Vernon at the mouth of Piscataway Creek, had long been regarded as a strategic location for fortifications. It was there that the Indians in the early days had etablished the village of Piscataway, and it was there that Washington, who had explored the region extensively and discussed the matter with George Digges, had proposed in 1794 that fortifications be erected. Negotiations for the government's purchase of the required part of Warburton had apparently languished; for George had died in 1792, Thomas had remained abroad until the fall of 1798, and the heightening of concern for the capital's defenses had had to await an increasing of tensions with Great Britain.

Warburton near Piscataway 29 July 1807
DEAR SIR

In compliance with Your request I hastend all in my power to obtain an accurate Survey & Plot made of that part of my Warburton Farm *where* its extreme point (a high promontary) at the narrowest part of the Potomack hereabouts, and where the channel makes an angular bending close in with the shore, forms a seemingly favourable position for a Fort on its heights as well as a battery near the Shore. It is the spot designated by General Washington (and *was* recommended by Him) as the most favourable station on the Potok. River for annoying Vessels passing up or down: General Washington has often had foot on it, and I was told by the late Colonel Fitzgerald (my Brother in Law) That He once made a Survey of The premises in company with a French Engineer Officer of some celebrity.[1]

I lookd out, but to no effect, for a proper Draftsman in the City on the day I left You, and finally engaged Colo. Gilpin of Alexanda.[2] who is esteemd a very accurate draftsman & Surveyor. He got through the laborious part on the 24th & 25th Inst. after employing here Chain carriers, and three other men (*particularly well acquainted with the Channel*) to stake its edges on both sides for a mile or two above & below Warburton point; to which, and to conspicuous objects, He took from four or five favorable Stations, *the course & bearings of each*. I make no doubt (for I closely attended to Him myself) but that He is correct, and that his Draft (which has but just now got to my hands) will enable Yourself, The Secy. at War[3], and others, to designate the proper spot for a Fort or Battery, or both. The position is spoken of by some Military men, and all who have seen it, as a very favourable one—may it be effectually so if ever put to the test.

I hasten to send up the Draft of Colo. Gilpin by my Nephew John

Fitzgerald (who has promptly & heretofore made a profer of His Service in any way in which He can be useful to His Country or the Administration of it) and if, after examining the Plot, there may be any required additions I will attend particularly to Your instructions th[e]rein, And I not only hope for the pleasure of soon waiting upon You & the other Gentlemen You may bring to Warburton, but of personally paying my respects in the City a few days hence.

I am with great regard & Esteem
Dr. Sir
Yr. Obt. Hle. Servt.
Thos. Digges

His Excellency / President U.S.

HSP: Daniel Parker Papers.

[1] Maj. Pierre Charles L'Enfant (1754–1825), who had served in the American army and in 1791 been authorized to plan the capital. Jefferson, as well as Washington, had participated in the decision to commission L'Enfant to survey the ground and lay out the city.

[2] Col. George Gilpin (d. 1813), one of the first directors of the Potomac Navigation Company (est. 1785), a recent judge of the Orphans' Court of Alexandria, and soon to become the city's postmaster, was familiar with the problems of opening and maintaining the river as a navigable waterway and hence the problems an enemy would confront.

[3] Gen. Henry Dearborn (1751–1829), a former soldier and in the Third and Fourth Congresses a Republican representative from Massachusetts, had been appointed secretary when Jefferson had become president in 1801.

To Henry Dearborn

Warburton near Piscataway
Maryld.—Sept. 15. 1807.

My Good Sir.

I was unfortunately too late by a few hours of meeting You on the day of departure from Washington, and now unwillingly trespass upon Your home enjoyments by directing this Letter to Boston.

I have thought, and thought again, on Your request for being informd of "the *price* of the Site or Soil contemplated on for building a

Battery & Forts prior to any step being taken for their Erection"; and though I am no wanderer in the feilds of extravagance, but rather willing to yeild up a little for the aid of Government & good of my Country, Yet I am unable to fix a price. I trust a good deal to Your friendly openess and candor, & hope for Your advice Whether it is not better and the fairest mode for me to have the place viewd & the price submitted to any twelve Gentlemen living on & holding Lands and Fisherys on the Potomack say between the Eastern branch and Mount Vernon or to Crane Island. You may assure Yourself it is not the *earth* that I am anxious about, but the consequent evil of trespass, & of inroads to the intended Fortifications, the injury to domestic Comforts to the future possessors of Warburton, and the present pecuniary disadvantage it will be of to a valuable Fishery: for Sir a battery on the point close to the tide water (which You first viewd) will occupy all that narrow space on both shores of the point so as to prevent the Landing netts on either side of the Battery, as well as break up a road way along the shore to another fishing Landing nearly under the high promontary or bluff. For this point Landing I have refusd one thousand & fifty Dollrs. per Year Rent including the warehouse & two small Dwellings upon a Lease for Eleven years. I will either leave the price to the decision of the twelve Gentlemen to be so chosen between us, or submit, (as I am informd I may by Law be forcd to do) to take what an appointed Jury by Law may assess the value.

I have to solicit your friendly information as to a few following points.

> The primary one is to know at what time it may be likely that the Battery or Forts may be begun?
>
> Is it at the will of the Executive to make such Fortifications or to await the decision or assent of Congress?
>
> Whether much Timber may be wanted for such Battery or fort & how it is usually contracted for?
>
> Whether any and what terms for Digging or moving of Earth by Slave Labour? as I Would take from my Feild Labourers 15 or 16 hands to be so employd.

I am encroaching I fear too much upon Your time by such enquirys but it would be servicable, in the dispositions of my Farm now laying out for the next years Crop of Grain, to be so informd.

We continue to be tolerably healthy in these districts save only in the visitation of an Influenza seemingly progressing from Your northern quarters towards the So.westward—our militia progressing & volunteers turning out rather well considering old & former apathys— The minds of the people becoming more & more united, & thereby putting into oblivion if not annihilation that ugly prejudicd Anglo-Federal party which of late did some mischief; And I am truly happy to see that the Executive Adminustration of the Country is getting more & more popular.

I am hourly looking for more important News from the north of Europe altho the late accounts have been as importantly advantageous to us, as they must be awful & critical for Great Britain[1]—May it all be for the best.

I am with gt. regard & best wishes
Dr. Sir Yr. Obt. Sert.
Thos. Digges

[Addressed:] The Honble. Henry Dearborne/Secretary at War &ca./ Boston [*crossed out*] Washington City [*substituted in another hand*]

NA: Record Group 107, Letters Received by the Secretary of War, Registered Series, 1801–1860 (Microfilm M221, Roll 6), D-184.

[1] News of Napoleon's victory over the Russians at Friedland in June and of the treaty at Tilsit in July ending his successful war against the Russians and Prussians had reached the U.S. in Aug. and disclosed the extent of France's domination of Europe.

To Thomas Jefferson

Warburton Near Piscataway Sept. 15 1807

DEAR SIR

I have had an anxious desire, & at times nearly fixd on setting out on a visit to You at Monticello, but My Wheat & Hay harvest with other troubles have deprivd me of that felicity. I was anxious to do so by taking a lift downwards in Mr. Fosters carriage but could not accomplish my wish at that time. Soon after my Nephew Jno. Fitzgerald deliverd You the requested Survey & plat of the Site where the Battery & Forts are intended to be erected, (and which my lameness prevented my personally delivering) I had the pleasure of a visit from The Secy. at War, accompanied by some Naval & military Gentlemen to take a view of the Situation, its distances & bearings upon the passing vessels, the Elevation of the Ground, the depth & breadth of the channel &ca. &ca. towards which They seemd to express perfect satisfaction: And it appears to be the spot formerly viewd & surveyd by General Washington with two French Engineer Officers, one of them I am informd was Baron DeCalb.[1]

Nothing passd, material to the subject, between the Secretary at War and myself, but His expressing Himself "that before any steps to fortifications were begun it would be necessary to ascertain *the price* of the site & soil &ca. &ca.["] *I* am as much at a loss for equitably fixing the price, as I am unacquainted with the mode of legally taking it away by a Jury of Valuators as may be directed by the Government &ca.; And altho ever desirous to assist my Country by any reasonable sacrifices or Services, I stand much in need of advice whether it would not be the fairest mode to ascertain the value of what is wanted by leaving it to the decision of any twelve Gentlemen possessing Fishing Landings from the Eastern branch downwards as far as Mount Vernon or Crane Island, who are most likely to be the best & most impartial Judges of its worth.[2]

Exclusively of the Soil, the tresspass's, & other inconveniencys, I shall (provided the *Battery is fixd on the water edge of the point* as contemplated) Be deprivd of a Landing place for Nets on each side of that point & also of a roadway along the Shore, which will go far towards destroying a Shad & Herring Fishery, for which, together with a Warehouse & two small Dwelling Houses, I have been offerd 1050$ per year on Lease for eleven years.

We are healthy hereabouts save in the visitations of an influenza apparently progressing from North to South. I hope You Sir enjoy Your usual share of health, and that no political movement, evil, or fresh *outrage* may draw You from the comforts of Monticello until the alotted period for meeting at Washington. The Chesapeak outrage,[3] which (save in the instance only of National degradation) I was not displeasd at, has workd a heap of good in creating a wonderful unanimity in the People, adding Credit & weight to the Executive Government, and very effectually *silencd*, if not intirely broken a nasty anglo Federal party in this part of the Union which was doing all the ill-naturd harm it could effect—May You & Your Colleagues go on in doing good & recieve the benefit of it.

       With great truth & regard I remain
       Your Obt. Servt.
       Thos. Digges

The President of The United States at Monticello

MHS: Jefferson Papers.

[1] "Baron DeCalb" was probably Johann Kalb (1721–1780), the son of Bavarian peasants and a soldier in the French army before accompanying Lafayette to America in 1777 and becoming an American major general. He was killed at the battle of Camden, Aug. 1780. When he, L'Enfant (presumably the other French engineer officer), and Washington could have visited the Warburton site together has been impossible to establish.

[2] In an acknowledgment of Sept. 21 Jefferson wrote: "Your readiness in aiding our survey of the site for military works is duly estimated, and certainly our duty to the public as well as yourself requires that full justice shall be done you in the valuation. Whether the law requires absolutely a jury for valuation I do not know. If it does we may name the jurors mutually; if it does not, we can name arbiters mutually approved" (LC: Digges-L'Enfant-Morgan Papers, 3: 474).

[3] In June the U.S.S. *Chesapeake*, bound for the Mediterranean, had been hailed by the H.M.S. *Leopard* off Hampton Roads and ordered to submit to a search for British deserters believed to be aboard. The American commander had refused, whereupon the *Leopard* had crippled the frigate with repeated broadsides, killing three and wounding eighteen Americans, and the British had then taken off four men alleged to be the deserters sought. In fact, only one had proved to be a deserter; the other three had simply deserted from British impressment. But the national outrage lay in the Britons' implicit claim of a right to search another nation's vessels and to use force in the assertion of that right.

To Thomas Jefferson

      Rhodes's Hotel [Washington] Sundy. forenoon 14 Feby./8
DEAR SIR
  Supposing my business will oblige me from hence in the afternoon (while I can catch a spert of fair Weather) And that I may thereby not

have the pleasure of seeing You this trip, I make free to inclose You Mr. Brodies intimation, (*the only one I have yet been able to obtain!*) about the late military visit to Warburton—which unluckily happend while I was replacing a boundary stone & busy with a Surveyor on a part of my Farm rather distant from the House. I am vexd that the Gentlemen (whose names are yet unknown to me) neither got refreshment, or receivd any clue or guides to the Sites, the markd posts at the Channel, the course for ships to avoid the Virga. mud flatts &ca. &ca.

I am sorry to learn that Mr. Madison[1] as well as the Secy. at War are both confind by illness—of course I cannot wait upon the latter for usual communications.

I expect about Wedy. next a Swan or two up from Cob point (which is a little below Hoes ferry)—a resident there assurd me positively I should have them, & I have sent a messenger down to bring them up:—If they come I will send my Boy up with them, and can *then* get a return of Mr. Brodies inclosd & formally written note which He might not like to be freely made use of. I hope to obtain some further information about the visit when I reach the Capitol Hill or see General Wilkinson[2] whom I am going to call upon.

       With the highest esteem
       Yrs. &ca. &ca.
       Thos. Digges

I have not yet been able to obtain the Draft &ca. made by Genl. Washington, Baron DuCalb, and another French Engineer of the Site at Warburton—I believe the narrow minded & vile political enmity held by the Generals intimates & *Executors* is the cause of witholding it.—I hope the visiting Gentlemen may have found a more eligible spot for Fort &ca. as this would be a dreadful inroad upon my retirement in age—

MHS: Jefferson Papers.

[1] James Madison (1751–1836), secretary of state, was too ill to conduct business at his office, but did do so at his home.
[2] James Wilkinson (1757–1825), commanding officer of the U.S. Army, who, despite his implication in numerous devious, self-serving schemes had managed to retain Jeffer-

son's confidence. Born in Maryland, he had risen in rank during the Revolution and then intrigued against Washington. Allegedly motivated by greed, he had subsequently engaged in irregular business dealings. He had settled in Pennsylvania and in 1783 been elected to the state assembly. Moving west, he had worked to separate Kentucky from Virginia, to ingratiate himself with the Spanish, to gain the trust of Adams, Burr, and Jefferson; and with Jefferson's favor had shared the honor of taking possession of the Louisiana Purchase in 1803, succeeded in becoming Louisiana's appointed governor, and in 1807 escaped possible indictment in the Burr conspiracy largely by assuming the role of Burr's chief accuser. Although there was both popular and congressional resentment of his rewards and absolution, Jefferson let him continue in his army post, apparently content to stand by the man who had helped expose Burr.

To Thomas Jefferson

Warburton Feby. 23d 1808

DEAR SIR

My negro messenger to Cob point (which is a little below Hooes ferry) has just returnd, although He might have been back on tuesday last.—He has brought me two Swans, killd on fryday night—an *old one* which weighs in his Feathers &ca. 19½ lb. and a young one, much leaner which weighs 15 lb.—The old fellow will likely be a tough morsel, & I am sorry the young one is not fat which none of them are at this advancd Season of the year—Such as they are they are very much at Your Service.

My Boy is going on to my Sister Carrolls at Rock Creek,[1] and will call on his return back about *Wednesday noon*. I should be very thankful for any cast-off news papers, & particularly so for English ones; for the late wet weather & living in a retird nook for the last ten days makes me quite a recluse, my news papers coming but irregularly, & having seen no person since I left the City but my old guest Mr. Brodie. We have mutual hopes that the negociation is progressing smoothly and that the Embargo may be of short duration.

Pray is *our first American* Packet, Osage,[2] saild? or is it *yet* in time to forward a letter by Her for Lisbon?—ill-fated Lisbon![3] in which I have spent some of the happiest days of my life! May Yours Sir be lengthend to Your wish and still afford to our Country such benefits as every deserving Inhabitant of it will acknowlege he has experiencd under Your happy Administration.

With sincere regard & best wishes
I am Yrs. &ca. &ca. &ca.
Thos. Digges

P.S. I hope Mr. Madison and the Secy. at War have got better. As yet I have not been able to hear a tittle from the General, or any others, about the Military visit to my Landing; But if my hip lameness will permit I intend to the City on fryday or Satury. wanting to get a *sure* London Bill from Mr. Erskine[4] for Cash, & rather prefering one from The British Minister on His Treasury than from our speculating Merchants—

MHS: Jefferson Papers.

[1] Elizabeth Digges Carroll.
[2] Probably the ship owned by an American, J. McIver, that in Nov. had traveled between Dublin and New York. It was now scheduled to sail from New York to Lorient in early Mar. with official dispatches for American representatives in Paris and London.
[3] In Nov. 1807 part of Napoleon's army had invaded Portugal intent on punishing that country for its refusal to join in the war against England; by Feb. 1 the French had established themselves in Lisbon and announced that the house of Braganza no longer ruled.
[4] David Montagu Erskine (1776–1855), British minister to the United States, had first met Digges when the two had traveled from England to America in the fall of 1798. At that time Digges had been returning home after his prolonged stay abroad, and Erskine had been carrying certificates of transfer for his father to the British consul in Philadelphia. Erskine had remained in the country long enough to marry into the Cadwalader family of Philadelphia the following year before embarking for home, where in Feb. 1806 he had been elected to succeed his father in Parliament. Then in July of the same year he had obtained his appointment to his present position, which he would retain until 1809.

To Henry Dearborn

On March 5 the secretary had written: "It being desirable that your terms should be known, on which you will convey to the United States the proposed

11 MARCH 1808   493

site for fortifications at Digges' Point, I take the liberty of requesting you to state to this Department, the lowest sum you will accept as a consideration for the land per Acre. You will understand that this site is to be so located, as not materially to interfere with your fishery, and to embrace the ground where a battery was contemplated when I was with you the last summer, and to continue back, so as to include a site for a block house on the summit of the ridge, or avenue. Should your price appear reasonable, there will be no occasion for a reference; if otherwise, I am ready to agree mutually on three suitable disinterested characters, as referees, to decide on the value of the land. I presume however that you will set such a reasonable price, as will supersede the necessity of a reference. The probable quantity when surveyed will be from four to five acres" (MdHS: Ms. 246).

Washington March 11th 1808

SIR

It is impossible for me (with any degree of exactness) to fully reply to Your request for "the price *per Acre*" of my land at Warburton point contemplated for Fortifications—: for reason that it has never been Surveyd, save on the River-shore line by Colo. Gilpin; And altho' the direct line up to the summit or avenue from the water has been nearly ascertaind, yet neither Gilpins or the last Survey marks the length of its *cross line* eastward & westward from the begining stake near the persymmon Tree.

It is not by *acres* that this Site can be estimated, as at that spot either four or nine acres (in *point of produce of Soil*) is very unimportant—The narrow space of shore or beach for landing Nets, or passage way to the meadow Landing, is already an evil—A *wharf* too, which Colo. Williams[1] seems to think essential nearly at the point, may perhaps also narrow that passage way. Among many other circumstances, not now necessary to mention, the ultimate danger of injury to The Fisheries, from the proximity of the Site of the lower Battery to the landing-place of the Seins (where I am already too much pinchd for room between the tide way and the grass heights) is what I am most fearful & tenacious about.

Colonel Williams supposes that the whole of the ground wanted will not exceed nine acres:—Within the lines of which, to make the intire Site properly formidable, a great quantity of Earth will be to be dug and many thousands of cubic yards of Earth must be removd and sloped down each sides of the emminence—the doing which on *the River side* of the ridge must injure one of the Landing places.

The Colonel seems to promise me another visit when an expected Engineer Officer may arrive from the Northward, in order for a Survey to ascertain the Acres as well as for designating what was further to be done should the parties come to an agreement. This would certainly give better data to go upon: Yet, however unprepard, & as yet unwilling to answer Your request for Price, (and in no small degree actuated to give every reasonable aid to an Executive Government which I highly appriciate) I will forego the quiet comforts of a pleasant retreat, and alienate & fully convey to the United States, all that part of the ridge point of Warburton *westward* of the stake markd No. 7 markd as the Summit height in Colo. Gilpins Survey—the boundary *Eastward* to be a line crossing over the ridge & avenue to the meadow fence (touching this stake at No. 7) begining at a dirt bridge over a drain & hollow at the end of a No. 60° East 28 ps.-22 links Line from Gilpins 5th station (markd 5 in his plat) & near to ⟨His ware⟩-house point—and thence along the tide marks (*securing to myself the Rights* of the River & Shore as not injuring the Landing places for the Seins) to the foot of the Bluff or Cliff over which Colo. Williams threw a plumb line & measurd its perpendicular height to be 89 feet—thence in a line Eastwd. to where it will hit the Eastern boundary at the south side of the ridge level. The Colol: with Gilpins or plat, will easily explain these lines, & He guessd their contents to be about nine acres.

Now Sir for this Site, together with a contract or obligation upon me to dig & remove *all* the Earth (of which there is many thousands cubic Yards) *according to the plan & levels markd by Colo. Williams & Capt. Fenwick*,[2] I will take $25,000 Dollars. And for *the Site only* (securing to myself the rights of the River shore & not injuring the Landing places for the Seins, & not having any thing to do with digging or removing Earth) my Price is $15,000 Dollars. Or I will leave it to be adjusted to any 3 or five disinterested Gentlemen who may know the spot or be informd as to the value of such a situation—extra of any advantages it may possess as to its favourable position for defending the River upwards.—It has been generally & greatly overrated to what I ask.

I am with great regard
Sir Yr. Obt. Servant
Thos. Digges

[Addressed:] The Honble./Henry Dearborne/Secy. at War &ca.

NA: Record Group 107, Letters Received by the Secretary of War, Registered Series, 1801–1860 (Microfilm M221, Roll 6), D-240.

[1] Col. Jonathan Williams (d. 1815), chief engineer of the army's corps of engineers.
[2] Probably John R. Fenwick, an officer in the engineering corps.

To Henry Dearborn

On March 12 the secretary had acknowledged Digges's reply of the day before and written: "If you will agree to add 500 Acres of your land, including your buildings the price would be less objectionable, but for 8 or 9 Acres of land, of no intrinsic value, to be lain out so as not to interfere with your fishery, your landing, or shore $15000 is far beyond what I could have imagined any reasonable man would have thought of, as a price.

"I am authorized by the President to agree to a reference, and I am ready to meet you for the purpose of selecting such Characters as we may mutually agree on as referees, reserving the right to object to any Man without assigning reasons" (NA: Record Group 107, Miscellaneous Letters Sent by the Secretary of War, 1800–1809 [Microfilm M370, Roll 3], 196).

Rhodes's Thursday. afternoon 17 March 1808
SIR.
  I have but just arrivd here, after several days absence from Home, & receivd Your Letter of the 12th in answer to my proposition about conveying away the Site for Fortifications at Warburton. I am obligd to go home tomorrow but will wait upon You at Your office tomorrow;

Merely to express my willingness to fulfill my offer of leaving *the price to reference*; But Sir it cannot be expected of me to assent to other than Referees who are acquainted with the circumstances & value of the spot (for it is a farce to say the contemplated Fortifications will not injure the Landing places & the Fisherys) as also the injury consequent to inroads through a long neck of Land close to my door & Garden—the having also an entaild vicinity of a Garrison of Soldiers—the making my dwelling a cake-house to every visitant &ca. &ca. &ca.

It is not *the acres* which can be estimated:—suppose for instance a Fort was necessary on the South point of Mr. Masons Island[1] between his house & the River—would You attempt to value the *acres only* which might be necessary for the Fort? Surely not.—There are a dozen other circumstances of more import than *the acres*.

As You have been pleasd to be facetious in saying "If I would agree to add 500 acres of your Land including the Houses &ca. the price might be less exceptionable" I will now mention a price *in cash* which was offerd me by Mr. Bingham,[2] witnessd by a respectable member of the Senate, who visited me on the occasion, for that very 500 acres adjacent to the point & within the water boundarys of the River & two creeks & a straight line from one creek to the other—The Estate being as I said before a long point of Land between two Creeks.—You may probably have heard of this offer for it is well known as any purchase made in the district.—It was 20 Guins. *per acre* or ten thousand Guineas for the 500 Acres. You may Say a fool & his money is soon parted—but I was fool enough to refuse it. There are dozens of respectable Gentlemen mostly all known to You as well as myself to whom I would trust my property to valuation; But I never will, otherways than by force assent to leave it to persons unacquainted with its local situation & advantages—make out a list of names & I dare say we shall agree; and I'll bet you a *rump & dozen* it will go higher than my offer.

Yrs. with Sincere Regard
Thos. Digges

Excuse haste & writing almost in owl light.

[Addressed:] The Honble./Henry Dearborn/Secy. of War &ca. &ca.

NA: Record Group 107, Letters Received by the Secretary of War, Registered Series, 1801–1860 (Microfilm M221, Roll 6), D-249.

[1] Analostan Island, located in the Potomac off Georgetown and opposite the mouth of Rock Creek, had carried the name of its owner of many years, George Mason IV (1725–1792), a friend of Washington's and Jefferson's, the author of the Virginia Bill of Rights and the state's constitution, and father of Gen. John Mason (1766–1849), his fourth son, whom he had settled on the island.
[2] Bingham's identity remains uncertain.

To Henry Dearborn

Rhodes's   Mar: 21. 1808

SIR

If You should have a wish to see, or write to me Be pleasd to observe that on Thursdy. Evenings weekly the mail is made up & I recieve my Letters from The *Piscataway* post on every fryday forenoon. Your letter of the *[blank]*th was directed to *Portobacco* instead of Piscataway—to which I am just setting off.

You know out of the 12 or 13 names I noted for selecting *five*, that you scored every one but D. Carroll Brent, & that I accepted of the whole five you noted Vizt. Jno.[1] Thompson[2] Mason—Genl. Rt. Bowie—D. Car[3]rol Brent, Genl. Thomp[4]son Mason & Colo. Jno. Co[5]oke.[1] I hold them all to be proper & good men (altho 4 & 5 I never spoke to) But there will be much difficulty in getting them to meet at one point on any fixd day when the survey may be made which You mentiond. My reasons are these. The first resides part of the Year beyond Hagarstown 75 miles westward, & partly at Leonard Town St. Marys about 50 miles South:—The 2d lives at Nottingham on Patuxent River about 35 miles Eastwd. and Colo. Cooke lives about 50 miles below this on the Potomack—The other two may be easily got & even Colo. Cooke comes frequently up here.

I suggest to You whether (& for reason only *to insure a more certain meeting*) that the first name be withdrawn, & as a substitute You take either Robt. Brent, Genl. Jno. Mason, or Colo. Steuart[2]—the last of whom possess's *by marriage* the Landing a little below mine on the point of Piscataway Creek South, and who, as well as Genl: Thompson Mason can be got to the spot on any day by sending a boat a cross for them: neither of them or a single one on Your List are my intimates or to my knowlege were ever visitants at Warburton. I want the matter concluded one way or other. Every person whom I have heard speak on the subject says it is the only proper spot of defence for the upper Potomack. If they fix on it, I will submit to the inconvenience of slopeing the earth from the Battery towards the shore (which will pinch & much injure the stand for waggons & Carts &ca. comeing there for fish) And I will even further forgoe (what I have been legally as well as in a friendly manner advisd to do) inserting in my Deed of conveyance to the United States a restrospective Clause that if in any *future* instance such Fort, or Wharf &ca. (Colo. Williams saying a Wharf was essential) should be provd injurious to the Landing or Fisherys that I should obtain redress therefor through the intervention of a Jury legally summond to assess such Damage.[3]

       I am with great regard
       Sir Yr. Obt. Sert.
       Thos. Digges

[Addressed:] The Honble./H. Dearborn/Secy War &ca.

NA: Record Group 107, Letters Received by the Secretary of War, Registered Series, 1801–1860 (Microfilm M221, Roll 6), D-252.

[1] John Thomson Mason, the recently elected state senator and a nephew of George Mason IV, was a lawyer; Gen. Robert Bowie (1750–1818) had served as governor of Maryland, 1803–1806, and was at present a justice of the Prince George's County Levy Court; Daniel Carroll Brent (1770–1841), whose family owned a considerable tract between the Potomac and Aquia Creek, Va., had an interest in the stone quarries there, was one of the incorporators of the Washington Canal Company, and was U.S. marshall of the District of Columbia; General Thomson Mason (1759–1820) was a son of George Mason IV, and Col. John Travers Cooke (1755–1823) was a son-in-law.

²Brent, an older brother of Daniel's and Washington's continuing mayor, was in July to become paymaster of the U.S. Army. Gen. John Mason spent his summers on Analostan and his winters in Georgetown or Alexandria. Col. Steuart—Philip Steuart, or Stuart (1760–1830)—was a veteran of the Revolution and a future Federalist member of the House of Representatives from Port Tobacco in Charles County. On Mar. 28 Dearborn agreed to substitute Brent and arranged for a meeting of the referees at Warburton on Apr. 6 (NA: Record Group 107, Miscellaneous Letters Sent by the Secretary of War, 1800–1809 [Microfilm M370, Roll 3], 209).

³On Apr. 15, in an indenture between him and Jefferson, Digges conveyed to the president of the United States and his successors for $6,000 a part of Warburton Manor containing three acres and 127 perches of land, along with all waters, channels, woods, rights, members, and appurtenances appertaining. In his own behalf and in behalf of his heirs, Digges warranted the property against all future claims and stated as a proviso "that the said United States do not in any wise incroach or infringe upon the said Thomas A. Digges' fishing stations as now used, or upon the Banks or Soil without the limits of the boundaries aforesaid, but that in all respects as little injury shall be done thereto respectively as the nature of things will admit" (NA: Record Group 60, Attorney General's Papers: Letters Received—War Department, Box 1).

To Philip Barton Key

What had occasioned Key's involvement in Digges's affairs at this time must be inferred from circumstantial evidence. Surviving documents show that on June 7, 1797, Thomas Holmes and Samuel Hartley, both of Portland Place in the county of Middlesex, England, had come before a London notary to constitute as their attorney Phineas Bond (1749–1815), a loyalist during the Revolution, the British consul in Philadelphia in 1786, and now a lawyer there, and to give him wide authority to recover from Digges (still in London) sums due them by taking security, real or personal, for Digges's debts, by pursuing attachments, and by proceeding against garnishees. Digges owned property in Virginia, as well as in Maryland, and for some reason the suit against him had been instituted there. On September 25, 1805, the Virginia Superior Court of Chancery in Richmond, noting that the defendant was "out of this country" and had neither entered his appearance nor given security, had authorized the sale of 1,940 acres of Digges's land in the county of Loudoun, from whose proceeds Holmes and Hartley would each be paid what was respectively due them, with 5 percent interest computed from August 31, 1797: Holmes, £691 stg. ($3,071.11); Hartley, £247/15 stg. ($1,101.05). Any two or more of six named commissioners had been empowered to conduct the sale. There then having been no bidders, Digges had, as his letter to Key explains, bought back his own land and, it would appear, succeeded in depriving Holmes and Hartley of the money sought. Bond had apparently next turned to Maryland and elicited the help of lawyers in that state, among them Philip Barton Key (1757–1815) and his nephew, Francis Scott Key, a junior partner, both of whom had been long acquainted with the Digges family, Philip on at least one occasion litigating against some of its members. Philip especially, who had joined the British forces as a loyalist in 1777, become a captain in a Maryland loyalist regiment in 1778, been captured and released on parole, and then moved to England until after the peace, when he had reestablished himself in Maryland with no difficulty, had earned a reputation as a brilliant lawyer. In 1800 he had been appointed chief justice of the Fourth United States Circuit Court; in 1806 he had been elected to Congress as a Federalist.

Washington 28. May 1808.
DEAR SIR,

I have been so seldom at home that I but lately got your Letter of 11th Inst. or I should have sooner answerd it:—I suppose it is on the same business you last spoke to me upon in your City; But as I am at a loss to know *how* "a decree in favor of Holmes & Hartley against me in Virga." can now arrise as a claim you will oblige me very much by stating *whence* & from whom it comes &ca. &ca.

It is due, from my regard for you, to state somewhat of that matter, tho' I now hastily do it and without documents at hand.

In order to avoid a risk of being brought in as a partner in the London House of Lane, Son & Frazer, afterwards Lane, Son & *Boilston of Boston* (who was a very wealthy fugitive American in London and who after me became Indorser to their paper) that House failed.—It turned out ruinous to Boilston,[1] altho before his connection, the Commission receivd for my Indorsements was a help to me prior to my withdrawing.

I was threatned by the Agents of the Bankrupts, years after I had only indorsed their paper, to be brought in as a partner to the Trade:

And by advice of Mr. (now Lord Erskine) I took the advantage of a clause in an Insolvent act to free me therefrom by assignment of Property in Virginia, as well as in British America i.e. a Lot of 20,000 Acres in the Island of St. Johns Bay of fundy, which I had bought on the London Exchange many years before of Mr. Maitland the Army Agent, & was worth when I left England twelve or £1300–Stg: I nominated Mr. Holmes as a Trustee to this assignment—I believe a very worthy & good man and to whom I was indebted & was under some obligations—to whom also I have ever since wished to make payment. He by his adviser Mr. Hartley, chose the line of arrest & finally fell upon my Virginia property in preference to that in British America— Samuel Hartley was never a legally appointed Trustee, his bankrupt character being too well known.

At this period I had obtained the appointment, & was prepared to attend Mr. T. Pinkney from London thro Paris as Secretary to Mr. Pinkneys then successful Embassy to Madrid[2]—*where*, but for this rascal Hartley I might yet probably have been Agent or Minister.

I had a visiting & political intimacy (some years before & during my Agency business in London for American prisoners) with this S. Hartley while a Linen Draper in York Strt. Covent Garden, afterwards as Hartley & Francis also Linen Drapers, and as Hartley & Barber City Merchants trading to Africa India &ca. Barber residing abroad for the purpose of covering & as joint owners of Ships under false colours *& false oaths* during the later periods of the Revolutionary War.—My acquaintance with him was made thro his namesakes, very different men, no relatives of His & very amiable Gentlemen, David Hartley who made the Peace, & Colol. Hartley of Hampshire.[3] This Samuel Hartley is as sharp, trickey, & vile a rogue as came under my acquaintance. I have been witness to several of his scape gallows tricks, and I will narrate *one*, in which I am implicated too much myself, but I have the solace to say that I was (uninterestedly as to pecuniary profits) doing service to my Country and obtained the thanks of the best Man then in it for what I did.

It was usual, at this period of the War, and at times extremely irksome & troublesome to me (while acting a critical part in London) for several of the American Prisoners to bribe the Centinels, or breake prison & fly to me to get over to Ostend, Holland &ca. And I was armd with printed blank protections for them, & other Gentlemen passing homewards, written in four different languages & signed by the Ministers, which in case of capture would secure their persons & Baggage &c: I gave such pass's cheerfully & gratis to several Gentlemen wishin[g] to get home, as well as to our Captains &ca. (*among others to your friend Dr. Scott of Annapolis, The Revd. Heny: Addison, Dr. Smith, Capt. Belt of Queen Ann &ca.*)[4] and to five or six Boston Citizens & Captains who jointly with Captain Belt of Queen Ann purchased a Brig in London with a plan to take regular Convoy for New York but with intention to run into Delaware or Chesapeake.—My then intimacy with Hartley induced me to mention this, among the treasonable rogues He knew I had seen, of giving passports to escaping Prisoners which was nothing short of Treason.—He immediately struck upon making advantages or profits on it:—said he would Ship on board that brig 11 or 1200 Guis. worth of Articles most wanted in the American Army— Soldiers Cloathing, Blankets, Tent Linens Hosiery &ca. provided *I* would recommend them into safe hands in this Country—that without any advance from me as to the venture or outfit I should receive half profits on their Sales &ca. &ca. The Cargo was so consigned to Ridley & Pringle[5] at Baltme. or if put into the Delaware to Conyngham & Nesbit Philada.—They sailed & attended the British Convoy & trade to our Coasts, But the Boston Captains (who had also property on board) forced Capt. Belt into Boston & they all got safe & to an extraordinary high marked [market], some selling for 17. 18. & to 20– for one of first Cost & none under 1200 pr. Ct. The first news we had of the Brig was remittance from Ridley to Hartley of the first Cost amount in our Congress Bills on Grand the Paris Banker; and in some few months after He receivd the full amount of the greatest sales on Dry Goods I believe ever made in America. Yet so rascally did he behave, that I got not a stiver from his promise; and He even ultimately sued me on a loose money lending account of some 70 or £80. which I had at times borrowed!!—Nay he was so profligate as to make Insurance at Loyds to recover his outfit, and I believe attempted & did receive the Sum insured after it was proved *that* the *Brig had been* forced by its passengers into an American Port.—So much for a London Merchant.

I have the whole, & some &cas. detailed in print by way of an Anchovy for Saml. Hartley, & happy that Belt & other living witness's can attest it.

Mr. Wm. Cooke,[6] about 7. years ago, made an application to me about this Claim under Holmes's Trustee ship—I met, & thought I had satisfyd Him. Afterwards (& I guess thro Him,[)] I had to answer a solicitation from Mr. Dorsey[7] about the same—it then went back to Mr. Phineas Bond—I never heard an atom about it for six years, nor until Mr. Swan[8] wrote me there was a Court decree against my Loudoun Lands to be sold for its discharge; the whole run through, that Richmond court by Mr. Wickham[9] without my having *the least written or previous notification of such a suit until Mr. Swan Shewd me the decree*: and nothing I could say, or propose, could stay the actual puting up for Sale & public vendue of the Lands—There was no bidders & I bought them in at the Court House door of Leesburg.—My Sale of the 400 Acres to Jenings[10] had tried, & made my title doubtful, to say the least of it, and it is now at issue for trying the title (as You well know) in the Virga. District Court—and you also wrote the Deed (provisionally for 500 Acres of *Warburton*) to secure Jenings in his purchase, and which estate I have deeded to Dudley[11] also provisionally if when He is of age He chooses to take in preference to Jenings's 400 Acres should the title of the Virga. Land be found in Him. I certainly have somewhat of complaint to make against Mr. Wickham, for I cannot but look on it as ungentlemanly conduct in so Secretly running an important cause to me through the Richmond Court, for none of them even wrote or gave me the least item of it 'till I got it from Mr. Swan (who was Commissioned to Sell absolutely[)]. Whether this was the single act of Mr. Wickham, or of Messrs. Cooke, Dorsey, Bond, Wickham & Co. I know not. I am obliged by your mention of it to me & your last letter, And shall be more so for your further communications as to *how it now stands* so that it may be fairly met.[12]

     I am with regard Dr. Sir,
     Your obt. Servt.
     (signed) Thos. Digges

28 MAY 1808

You must excuse the length & hastiness of this scrawl. Mr. Brodie an English inmate in my house going to the City will drop it in the post at your City—the *Pisy.* [*Piscataway*] Post comes in every Fridy: Merning:

HSP: Cadwalader Collection, Phineas Bond section, Key Correspondence—*Digges* v. *Holmes & Hartley.* This document, not in Digges's hand, appears to be a copy made from the original, which Key sent John Francis Mercer on July 9, 1808.

[1] Lane, Son & Fraser was one of the leading mercantile firms in London trading with the eastern and southern United States. Phineas Bond had been their attorney. Thomas Boylston (1721?–1798), a Bostonian and first cousin of John Adams's mother, had become a loyalist during the Revolution and fled to England to invest his fortune in commerce. Committed to Newgate in 1793 in conjunction with the failure of his firm, he had never extricated himself from his difficulties and reportedly died in London of a broken heart.

[2] In Apr. 1795 Pinckney had been appointed envoy extraordinary and special commissioner to Madrid. Documents supporting Digges's claim to have been offered the appointment as Pinckney's secretary have not been found.

[3] James Hartley (1745–1799), David's half-brother, had distinguished himself by his military service in India.

[4] Scott's and Belt's attempts to return home are mentioned in letters Digges wrote Franklin during 1780. The date of Dr. Clement Smith's return is not indicated in the correspondence—he is simply listed among Forton's prisoners in 1777 (see Digges to Thornton, Dec. 1, 1777)—but Digges may have had in mind the Mr. Smith (John, Jr.) about whom he had written Franklin, Sept. 6, 1779. Addison (d. 1789), rector of St. John's in King George's Parish, Md., had, like Scott and Key, himself, been a loyalist. With his son he had taken ship for England in Sept. 1775, sailed back to New York in Oct. 1780, been denied a passport thence to Maryland, suffered the confiscation of his land the following year, and only in 1787, by an act of the state legislature, had restored to him land that remained undisposed of, enabling him finally to return home. There is no evidence, though, that Digges was ever supplied with "blank protections" or that anyone other than Franklin had issued them, and then at Digges's behest.

[5] The mercantile firm with which Matthew Ridley had been associated.

[6] Possibly the William Cooke (1746–1817) who had been one of Francis Scott Key's classmates at St. John's.

[7] Numerous members of that family were lawyers. This may be John, a correspondent of Bond's, or Walter, associated with Philip Barton Key in Federalist political activities and a future chief judge of the Court of Oyer and Terminer in Baltimore.

[8] Thomas Swann, a prominent lawyer, father of a future governor of Maryland, and one of those named as a commissioner empowered to participate in conducting the sale of Digges's property.

[9] John Wickham (1763–1839), probably Richmond's most prominent lawyer, a Federalist, and chief defense counsel during Burr's conspiracy trial in 1807.

¹⁰ Possibly Edmund Jenings (see Digges to Carmichael, Apr. 3, 1783, n. 1).
¹¹ William Dudley Digges, Thomas's nephew, who lived at Green Hill in Prince George's County, Md.
¹² The litigation would continue for some years: Francis Scott Key began proceedings in the Maryland courts later in 1808; Phineas Bond appointed Thomas Cadwalader of Philadelphia as his substitute to represent Holmes and Hartley in 1811; and Holmes and Hartley conferred new powers on their attorney in 1816. Documents to illuminate the sequel have not been found. (For some details of the legal actions in Maryland, see HSP: Cadwalader Collection, Phineas Bond section, Key Correspondence—*Digges* v. *Holmes & Hartley*, and also Bond's correspondence for 1808, 1809, and 1811, especially with the Keys, Wickham, Cooke, Thomas Buchanan, and, in 1811, Hartley himself.)

To Thomas Jefferson

Warburton Aug. 4. 1808

DEAR SIR

I got to the City very soon after Your departure from it, and was vexd & sorry not to have taken my ride thither on the preceeding day. After selecting a few Ewes from Bowies flock, I went to get the promisd Lamb You So kindly offerd from Your mixd flock, takeing Mr. Cocking (a well informd English *Farmer* living in Washington) with me the better to choose its form & feel its Fleece, for wool is the primary object with me, and I think I can improve the staple of Your City flock by a cross upon a few of my mixd Sort. Your absence however, and the want of penning them in the early part of that day made me defer it. I am going again in a day or two to the City and with the aid of Your Herdsman, & having Your permission so to do, I will take away one of the *no*-horned Ram Lambs—I do not care so much as You do for the many-*horned* sort, altho the old *Shetland* is a very fine but a wicked fellow.

The ardour of Sheep improvement is becoming more & more the commendable persuit of our Farming Gentry, I am urging them to it all I can though by indirect means. Those Gentlemen who have already obtain a good Stock to work upon, (which in my present purview has been from the mixture of the marinos and persian upon a tolerable good Mount Vernon flock) seem to be more bent upon getting a good price for thier tup Rams than in immitating which You have for Years blended into Your neighbourhood *by never cutting the Ram Lambs of the finer kinds but gratuitously offering them to Your Neighbouring friends for Breeders:*—hence I suppose Mr. Coles obtaind his fine flock —the sample of which that He shewd me is inferior to none I have seen of late, save those of Chancellor Livingstons[1] which You shewd me.

My avocations, and the continued vexations at the Fort (for I have them dayly, & too often nightly in the Robbery on my Garden & on my apple & Pear Trees) will I fear deprive me the gratification of seeing You at Monticello as I intended—May You long enjoy all the benefits & pleasures of that charming & healthy retreat.

I suppose my old friend & inmate Mr. Brodie has been, or soon will be there to visit you. My Compliments & best wishes to Him, & should You see Him, be so kind as mention there have been no Engh. Letters for Him altho I receivd a large packet by the Osage—also that I am in no kind of want of my horse & that He may use Him as He lists. I fear the late heavy rains (which had become much want[ed] for the Indian Corn) and the now Dog day Star heats & calm had retarded His ride towards Staunton Charlottesville &ca.

Fort Warburton is progressing with more than heretofore celerity—Its circular *stone* front towards The City & south Ends faceing to Virginia is about ¾ths finishd, & will of course be more interesting to Your view when You return to Us than when You left the City: And the Engineer Lieut. Bumford[2] seems indefaticably assiduous about it—He is an inmate with me—sober—very well directed & well informd. I have hardly ever seen so Young a Man so much up to his profession & he seems not to loose an hour for further improvements. I hope however This Fort, though necessarily wanted, will not be put to hostile use while We live. By my letters from England, together with a tolerable knowlege of things in that Country, I have every reason to believe that the John Bulls are not only uneasy but alarmd at the state of things, & that the thinking or sencible ones among them are now anxious to withdraw those unjustifiable Council orders, Edicts, &ca. &ca. under which our trade has been so injurd & thier own exports so diminishd. Yet the Anglo Foederal disturbers are more than ever at work (Electioneering perposes) to evince the policy of our joining "*our dear old friends*" at every risque. My creed is even yet to fight them both rather than join either. It looks as if the maddend King of Sweeden was galloping fast to his ruin;[3] & I am sorry, very sorry for the fate of Spain, because the present situation of that Kingdom may induce England to hit us a side blow by some act against the Florida's.[4]

Pray my Good Sir, if You can do it without much inconvenience, get Your Gardiner to save me a little Spanish-Broom Seed—if but a pint it will be a treasure—It is valuable to sow upon waste spots for the *winter food of Sheep*.

My Compliments to all the branches of Your Family, supposing they are nearly *all* as usual about You, And believe me with great Esteem

Your obligd & Obt. Sert.
Thos. Digges

P.S. At Your request last summer I had a survey made by Colo. Gilpin & two platts made by Him of the courses & bearings of the Shores, & Level heights of the ground &ca. at & adjacent to the Warburton Fort—Also men to stake out the Channel, its depths &ca. with a sketch drawing for the war office of the Banks & shape of the Channel. I have paid therefor, & shewd Genl. Dearborn the Charge which He did not disprove or think extravagant, but said He must have it certified as an order from You—I am sorry to trouble You about it, but as I am giving in my other accounts for Logs & poles found, Carting &ca. &ca., should be obligd to You for the necessary order to attach to the accounts so sending in with thier vouchers &ca.

T. D.

LC: Jefferson Papers, Series 1.

[1] Robert R. Livingston (1746–1813), a member of the committee chosen to draft the Declaration of Independence and later chancellor of New York, had served as Jefferson's first minister to France, 1801–1804. He had introduced the merino sheep in New York.

²George Bumford (d. 1848), a New Yorker who was pursuing a successful military career as an officer among both the engineers and those responsible for ordnance.

³Gustavus Adolphus IV (1778–1837), suffering from increasingly severe derangement, was proving incapable of coping with serious threats to his kingdom. He had joined Britain, Austria, and Russia against Napoleon, but when France and Russia had concluded a peace and Russia had then demanded that Sweden join the Napoleonic system, Gustavus, hostile to France, had chosen to stand by the English. Then, when Russia, along with Denmark, had attacked, occupying Finland, Sweden was imperiled. In 1809 Gustavus would be deposed.

⁴On Aug. 10 Jefferson, expressing his hope that Digges had taken his ram and promising to give Digges any broom seeds there might be, went on to concur with Digges's judgment of British attitudes: "I believe that the English ministers as well as people were coming over to the opinion that peace with us was their interest. But it is a nation more readily puffed up by small events than any one on earth. It is not improbable that the turn in Spanish affairs may mount them on their stilts again. It is a government with which no stable connection can be depended on. Their ministry is often changed, & with them their system. A new ministry so far from thinking themselves bound to observe what their predecessors had done, make a point of reversing it. It is a government of no faith, and the same may be said of France & Spain" (LC: Jefferson Papers, Series 1, [Reel 41]).

To Thomas Jefferson

Warburton Sepr. 20 1808

Dear Sir

I beg Your forgiveness for intruding on You the inclosd Letter to Mr. Brodie, which I suppose of some consequence to Mr. Brodie as comeing from His Family by the last British Packet. Should He not be at Monticello be pleasd to return it back to Me.

The Fort progress's towards its completion of its heavy wall work and begins to shew a handsome River front.—I have my dayly vexations about it as to depredations &ca., which will be removd when a regular soldiery is fixd in it—It is not the tradesmen workers who do the mischief, but a set of lounging Idlers, watermen & Labourers that pray upon my green corn, my stock, Hen roosts, all kinds of fruit even to garden vegetables:—The Engineer Lieut. Bumford (an assiduous, ardent & well informd Young Man) has also *his* troubles at not seeing enough of Masons & Bricklayers, for it is not more strange than true that such is the demand for House builders (*in these times of violent clamour about distress's difficulties & Embargo!*) that the latter description of tradesmen are not to be had hereabouts for 2$ per day, and in consequence the undertaker has had to resort to advertising for them. Buildings say they were never more rife, & there never was, at this season of the year, such empty warehouses & so little Flour, Indian Corn & wheat upon hand in this district of Columbia! We are all a little enlivend at a passing report, spread as coming by the late arrivals, that in consequence of the news by the St. Michaels packet to London in July, France having relaxd in Her restrictive Edicts & decrees, that England would shortly ease our commerce of thier mischevious proclamations Regulations &ca. &ca.[1] Altho it is probable in point of Justice, yet I fear it to be too good news to be true.

I have got home the Ram Lamb, & for which I am very much obligd to You—He is one of the no-hornd (which I preferrd) well shaped & not unlike His wicked Sire in form, shews a mixture with the Barbary broad taild & is tolerably well woold though a small sheep.

My Nephew John Fitzgerald with his relative Frs. Lightfoot Lee (a son of Rhd. Henry L., & who lately lost his wife my elder neice)[2] are out on a tour to Harpers Ferry, Winchester, and so down the fine vale of Land between the mountains and on to Staunton Richmond &ca. will of course try to see Monticello.

Mr. Lee is a young Lawyer of promising Talents good reading and amiable mind, and I think a far better politician & Patriot to His Country than any of His name. They have my solicitation to call on You & Mr. Madison. I hope to see You soon at Your return to the City and remain with great esteem & regard

Yr. Obt. Serv.
Thos. Digges

LC: Jefferson Papers, Series 1.

[1] In 1806 England through an order in council had attempted a partial blockade of European ports, interfering with American trade with Europe. Napoleon had retali-

ated with a decree declaring the British Isles under blockade. Further measures and countermeasures had followed through 1807, with the British soon gaining control of the seas.

[2] Francis Lightfoot Lee (1782–1850), a graduate of Harvard College, had married young John Fitzgerald's sister Elizabeth. In 1810, having become a widower, he married Elizabeth's younger sister, Jane.

To Thomas Jefferson

Rhodes's Wednesday morning [October 24, 1808]

DEAR SIR

I want very much to write to Dr. Wister of Philaa.[1] on the theme of placeing my two Nephews Attwood Fitzgerald & Geo. Carroll[2] at Philaa. as well for this & the next winters Lectures as also for the whole summer through; But I have no acquaintance with the Doctor but the short meeting we had on our return from Mr. Spriggs.[3]

They go by tomorrows Coach, and I should esteem it a great favour if You can conveniently do it, to give *Me* a line of introduction to the Doctor, so as that I could state to Him in writing the information I wish to obtain.[4] I will call about 11 or ½ past 11 oCk. & hope to find You so mended of Your Rhumatism as to induce a ride to the Race field.

Yrs. with Esteem & regard
T. Digges

MHS: Jefferson Papers.

[1] Dr. Caspar Wistar (1761–1818), successor to Benjamin Rush as professor of chemistry in the medical school of the College of Philadelphia in 1789, adjunct professor of anatomy, surgery, and midwifery at the University of Pennsylvania in 1792, and full professor of anatomy and midwifery there since July 1808, was earning his reputation for his work in anatomy.

[2] William Attwood Fitzgerald (1786–1819) was a son of Digges's sister Jane Fitzgerald; George Carroll was a son of Digges's sister Elizabeth.

[3] Probably Osborn Sprigg, who had an estate in Prince George's County.

[4] On Oct. 26 Jefferson addressed a note to Dr. Wistar in behalf of the two young men (LC: Jefferson Papers, Series 1, [Reel 42]).

To Thomas Jefferson

Warburton Feby. 20 1809

DEAR SIR

My Nephew Jno. Fitzgerald about to depart for His Military Station at Norfolk, & meaning to pay his farewell respects to You, gives me an oppertunity of handing You this.

I never left Washington with more regret, worse health and depressd Spirits (after a confinement of Sickness for three days in a dirty Tavern) than on Sunday last, or I would have made my departing congee to You. I got so dispirited Sir at the vile proceedings of a party in Congress, and at the long delay of the Union packet (which vessel will I hope soon put all things to right) that I could scarcely be comforted by the pleasurable Society of Your two Countrymen Judges Stewart & Holmes:[1] And who detail to me while chums in the same bed room the abominable speech of Mr. Gardineer on Saturday.[2]

Looking on the discomfiture to Britain in Her present persuits in Spain & Portugal as of most material moment,[3] at this juncture, to Our Country, I should, if any such News has arrivd, be very much gratified by perusing any of Your cast-by English or other news papers; for I am in a solitary nook here, & only recieve my Letters & Papers on every fryday.

My Nephew will recieve & forward them by a Servant returning on Wedy. or thursday.

I cordially wish You every happiness.

Thos. Digges

LC: Jefferson Papers, Series 1.

[1] Probably Judges Archibald Stuart (1757–1832) of Staunton, Va., and Hugh Holmes of Winchester, Va., friends of Jefferson's.

[2] On Feb. 18, during a debate in the House of Representatives concerning what became the Non-intercourse Act of Mar. 1, permitting commerce to be resumed with all countries except France and Britain, Barent Gardenier (d. 1822), a Federalist from Ulster County, N.Y., had not only expressed abhorrence of the destruction accomplished by Napoleon, but also defended Britain's right to have issued her orders in council that

since 1807 had hurt American shipping by forbidding trade with France unless the ships first put into English ports, where their goods were bound to be confiscated.

³A reference to shifting fortunes in the Peninsular War, whose outcome remained obscure.

To John Smith

Smith, chief clerk of the War Department, was serving as interim secretary pending the entrance upon his duties of Dearborn's successor, William Eustis (1753–1825), in April.

Fort Washington Mar. 15 1809

DEAR SIR.

I have before explain to my old freind Genl. Dearbourn & to Yourself the very disagreeable state in which my Sein-Landing place is left from a want of a removal of the heavy artillery, & more particularly the evil done & doing me by the drains to take the water from arround the Battery & fort being yet left without having *brick* or *Stone under drains* made up to prevent the deep gullies already made & still making by every rain that falls. We can, I hope, manage the heavy Guns as soon as the Soil gets a little more firm between them & about a forty five feet slope up hill to the battery.—Every days dripping down the two drains makes it more expensive to under drain; And the Gullys are now so deep as to preclude waggons & Carts crossing them by the only road to the fishery below: And they must if so left a fortnight or 3 weeks longer ruin my rents & income from the Fisherys.—I have ever avoided complaining though very considerable damages have been done me, & which the United States are bound to make good. I have too wrote twice or thrice to Mr. Bumford requesting him to state the evil to You & solicit its remedy—I expect eer this He has addressd You on the subject. As far as relates to His directions and Engineership, The work has been done well, & I am looking for his return with great anxiety.—There is no mortar work wanting for a small underdrain of brick, & the drain need not be more than one brick in breadth plaiced Lengthways, and one brick edgways laid thereon & coverd with the Soil—the Undertaking Mason yet lives here & has two or three workmen doing nothing until the weather gets mild enoug[h] for stone & brick work:—They cannot be employd better than upon these drains & the materials are at hand.

But the question is Who is to order them?

I have not heard of the Successor to the Secy. of Wars Office arrival in the City, But mean to wait upon Him on His arrival with a hope to explain more fully than I can write upon the Subject. I have a high opinion of His worth & hope to renew an acquaintance which had been pleasurably began while He was in Congress the last winter of His term,[1] generally meeting Him at my friends Saml. & Robt. Smiths.[2]

You will oblige me much my Good Sir by giving me a prompt Answer to this directing that answer to the Alexandria post office, from which I can obtain it in two or 3 days: But my usual mode of getting letters is by *Piscataway post* leaving the City only weekly, every *fryday morning early*.

I should be glad to know if You have had a letter from Mr. Bumford on the subject or whether the Secy. at War has arrivd, and to whom as well as yourself I profer every sentiment or regard &ca. &ca.

Thos. Digges

PS. If this letter should get to Your hands in time to put its answer into the Post office on *thursday night* it will if directed to me near Piscatawy. get to hand on *fryday forenoon*.

[Addressed:] The Honourable/The Secretary at War/City of/Washington

NA: Record Group 107, Letters Received by the Secretary of War, Registered Series, 1801–1860 (Microfilm M221, Roll 21), D-210.

---

[1] Digges is referring to the winter of 1804–1805. An ardent Jeffersonian from Massachusetts, Eustis had twice been elected to the U.S. House of Representatives. In 1800 he had defeated Josiah Quincy (1772–1864); in 1802, John Quincy Adams (1767–1848). In 1804 Quincy had beaten him.

² Samuel Smith, a Marylander and brigadier general in the state militia, had served in the House of Representatives and since 1803 in the Senate. He had long been a friend of Digges's (see Digges to Franklin, Sept. 6, 1779). His brother Robert (1757–1842) had been secretary of the navy since 1801.

To Thomas Jefferson

Warburton, Near Piscaty. Maryd. Sepr. 11th 1809

DEAR SIR

I have lamented extremely the not having it as yet in my power to pay You an intended visit at Monticello, as well as to have been with You nearly at the point of Your departure from the Presidoliad: And I trust You will not take my seeming neglect to any want of regard or my sincere wishes for Your health & preservation, (for there is none I regard more) but my mind & avocations having demanded more *of home* than I have ever before experiencd. I have nearly brought "an old House over my head" by attempting to repair a tottering, aged, and eighty years old family mansion & but to day only began the shingling. I have yet however hopes to get through with it, so as to spare a ride of eight or ten days, after our Elections, and thereby make another pleasurable visit to Monticello. Altho I have never *yet* made winds or weather an obstacle to journeying either on business or of pleasure, the late summer of remarkable coolness (altho too dry for Farming purposes in this vicinity) would have added to my incitements. The cause above stated, and that of looking a little after County Interests, for the Torey-Anglo Feds are assiduously at work, have wholly occupied my time—Thier dark policy as to present motives, are easier fathomd than what is thier actual or future intentions, for as yet they seem not to have got the text or cue upon which they are to blazen forth at our annual Elections the first Mondy. in Octor.

The old Currs, as well as the training Whelps, have got on the scent and yelp forth a strong cry against Genl. Smith[1]—They shamelessly propogate falsehoods, & even deny Him a military valor & intrepidity during our Revolutionary struggle:—But Toreys of 1776 are Toreys in 1809. They continue to abuse Him by Barbeque tub speakers & hand bills &ca. &ca.—Several news papers, & what we are distributing, already contain Answers to both the Charges against Him—That concerning the Bills of Exchange sold to The United States has been completely refuted by Mr. Purviances Statement, & by an extract of a letter from Washington to Annapolis. The charge against Him about the Contract with Barney (of St. Domingo memory) has also been refuted. The letter of Mr. Wilson fully disproves that Gen. Smith was privy to the partnership between Santhonax & Barney, And it is admitted that Smith stipulated that in case of a War with France the contract was to be void & at end: When it was made it was perfectly Lawful: But why should I intrude upon You what You already know. The motives of His Torey opponents is manifestly to keep Him from a seat in the Senate, & to get in one who as yet never did good to the party he espouses Mr. Harper![2] They think too by getting a Federal House of Maryland Representatives to finally undoe our Republican System; But I hope & fully believe thier manoevres & assiduity will be abortive, although our County is *yet* at risque from not getting a strong nomination—We want only honest, firm & upright Men. We have sustaind a loss by the move of The Covingtons out of it, and a particular one in the Death of Judge Ducket[3] who was a host of service about where he lived. I hear that Alexr. Scott of Geo. Town—Mr. Montgomery of Harford[4]—Mr. Trueman Tyler (our Register at Marlbro who holds an equally beneficial Employment[)] and Mr. Frank Digges[5] one of our late State Councellors, are competitors for the vacancy, & that some intrigues are going on to get it for Mr. Edmund Lee of Alexa.![6] I am well informd that Mr. Montgomery withdraws; in which case, in my humble opinion, Fr: Digges would be decidedly the fittest Man.— Those appointments should and doubtless will eminate from The President himself, who having been with You may perhaps have mentiond something of the appointment. I have not had it in my power to be with Him but one day since His Election, & missd him by half an hour when he departed last with Mr. Oaklys communications.

Expectation & surmise is now all agog as to how He will recieve the mighty Copenhagan Jackson (whom I formerly knew slightly in The foreign Department office under the Duke of Leeds[)][7] & his aid du Camp Mr. Hammond. Mr. Jackson arrivd a few days ago at Annapolis & is by this in the City. I know too well the faithless manoeuvres of His Court & present trickey employer to augre well of this his mission—England is not yet beaten enough in Her Continental intrigues (though she has contrived to ruin every one of Her allys) to make a fair & proper adjustment with Us. She never will forgive our prosperity & rivalship in Maratime Commerce.

I have varied from the purpose on which I sat down to write. It was, after appologizing for seeming neglects, to solicit Your aid in obtaining information how & through whom I can get the famous, or rather infamous Treaty of Tilsit. I never had an oppertunity to obtain it, & want to insert its substance in a paper meant to be read by the Toreys about St. James's palace & thier *amiable friends* hereabouts.

I am Yrs. with affectionate regard & Esteem
Thos. Digges

P.S. Lieut. Cherry[8] is at my Elbow & begs to offer You His respectful Compliments & best wishes for Your hea[l]th: Begs to return You his grateful acknowlegements & thanks for Your attentions & two different appointments in the Army & Volunteer Corps of The City Dragoons.

The Fort is very nearly completed & at present in nice order. Its compliment of men is but yet 25 privates & the Guns ready to the needful either against John Bull or any other Enemy.

Thos. Jefferson Esqr./Monticello

LC: Jefferson Papers, Series 1.

[1] The Federalists were charging that Gen. Samuel Smith, the senatorial incumbent, had been unscrupulous and unpatriotic in promoting his private financial and commercial interests. He had, they were alleging, bought bills of exchange by drawing on the house of Purviance & Degan when he had had no funds in their hands, and—possibly what rankled more—he had been profiting from a covert understanding with the disliked French even while the French were preying on the shipping of his countrymen. The evidence suggested that he had been a party to contracts Commodore Joshua Barney (1759–1818) had made with French officials in 1794 to deliver large quantities of flour to certain French ports. Barney, a native of Baltimore hostile to England, had been angered by the failure of the embargo on the shipping of foodstuffs to England, arranged for trade with the French that would bring him, Smith, and other merchants a solid return, and during 1796, while in France, accepted a commission in the French navy. To facilitate his commerce he had made use of close ties he had formed in Santo Domingo with Léger-Félicité Sonthonax (1763–1813), who had acquired influence on

the island as one of the French commissioners sent there in 1792 to establish order after the slave uprisings and who, it would seem, had been instrumental in providing passports that would protect Barney's ships against interference from the French navy. Although the situation in Santo Domingo had changed in 1797 with the rise of Pierre François Dominique Toussaint L'Ouverture (1743–1803), the contract with the French had extended unmodified well into 1807, so that when Barney had lately made claims against the French for payments due him, and when then Smith's name had appeared on a list of participating merchants, Smith's involvement had become public and placed him in the position of seeming to have enriched himself without incurring the large insurance expenses that his fellow citizens had had to bear in risking continuing French depredations of their shipping. The controversy as it reached the newspapers focused on how much Smith had shared in or known of Barney's claims against the French and how recently he had been a beneficiary of the trade. Statements and letters by various principals, including Smith, Barney, Robert Purviance, and Henry Wilson, who had loaded the cargoes in Cap Français, were now being printed and reprinted and cited by both Smith's defenders and his antagonists. (See, for example, *Hagerstown [Md.] Gazette*, Aug. 15 and 22, 1809.)

[2] Robert Goodloe Harper (1765–1825), a former South Carolinian and now a Baltimore lawyer, had been a member of his party's faction opposing John Adams in 1800 but since 1808 had been trying to unify the Maryland Federalists through the development of a tightly knit, statewide organization.

[3] Allen Bowie Duckett (d. 1809) had been a justice of the district circuit court since 1805.

[4] Thomas Montgomery, a lawyer and owner of a large plantation.

[5] Not a member of Thomas's family.

[6] Edmund Jennings Lee (1772–1843), who was Richard Henry Lee's son-in-law, "Light Horse Harry" Lee's brother, and Robert E. Lee's (1807–1870) uncle, was active in church and municipal affairs.

[7] Francis James Jackson (1770–1814) was replacing Erskine as Britain's minister to the United States. Erskine had failed to settle the difficulties arising from the *Chesapeake* incident (see Digges to Jefferson, Sept. 15, 1807, n. 3) in a way that the British government could ratify, and Jackson, whose nickname had derived from the dictatorial tone he had used in an effort to compel Denmark to unite her forces with Britain's against Napoleon in 1807, before the British had bombarded the capital, was expected to strengthen the British presence in Washington.

[8] Probably Robert Cherry (d. 1812), second lieutenant in the Second Infantry, stationed in the capital.

To Paul Hamilton

Warbn. Thursdy. 29th Nov./10

DEAR SIR

I have only a few minutes to catch the oppertunity of the Fort Boat (carrying up Cornet Beall to the War office) to forward this to

You with a solicitation (for which I hope for Your forgiveness) to free it to the Post master at N. York[1]—as I see an advertisement stating that letters must be put into that office for Engd. on or before the *1st Decr.* the packet to sail on that day; but I guess she will be *inducd* to stay for the first accounts of opening the Congress—the Presidents Message &ca. &ca.—No Ducks yet to be had hereabouts—I have requests out to get a few when *Shooteable* & I hope to send You some. I expect to be in the City on tuesdy.—being somewhat better of my Rhuematism.

         Yrs. with gt. regard
         Thos. Digges

NA: Record Group 45, Early Naval Records—Miscellaneous Letters Received by the Secretary of the Navy.

---

[1] Hamilton (1762–1816), a former governor of South Carolina, was secretary of the navy. Beall was probably Thomas Jones Beall (ca. 1792–1832), oldest son of the commander of Fort Washington, Capt. Lloyd Beall (d. 1817). Thomas had entered the U.S. Military Academy as a cadet in 1806 and could have held the rank of cornet before becoming a second lieutenant in 1811. Digges's accompanying letter has not been identified.

To Paul Hamilton

              Warburton 25 [23][1] July 1811

DEAR SIR

I am in afflication & several days confinement to my room with Rhuematic head & some &cas. or I would personally wait upon You. I mentiond lately to You & Mr. Goldsborough[2] my wish to get from on board the frigate of Commodore Rogers[3] a Seaman whose wife & small family (although His mother has left them some trifle of property) stands much in need of the husband & the Father.

James Gregory by name transferrd I believe from the Enterprize to Commode. Rogers's Ship & where I understand He now is & not knowing that his mother in Law is dead leaving them some trifle of property, and what is worse his wife almost gone in Consumption with three or four helpless Children the eldest & only adult of which a clever young woman has lost her sight. If a furlough for some months could be had for Him, or even His discharge on my procuring a substitute seaman I should be much obligd & it would prodigiously aid his afflicted family who live just on the edge of my Land adjoining Col. Lyles's at Broad Creek. Pray Sir assist me in it if You can, and further oblige me by information if the Frigate is yet at Annapolis or not—for to that quarter I am necessiated to go when able to take the saddle.

My head is extremely disorderd, & a confinement for several days & *no news* makes me low spirited. My Negro messenger who is going also to The Secy. of War[4] upon a Fort matter, will drop this at Your office. If You can give him a few news papers, You will add to the many kindness's conferrd on

Dr. Sr. Yours with sincere regard
Thos. Digges

Has the British frigate yet saild from Annas. [Annapolis]?[5]
Or is Mr. Barlow soon to take flight?

NA: Record Group 45, Early Naval Records—Miscellaneous Letters Received by the Secretary of the Navy.

[1] Hamilton's acknowledgment, referring pointedly to "your letter dated 25*th ins.*," is dated July 24; and Digges's letter of July 26 to John Rodgers refers to his letter to Hamilton as one written on July 23.
[2] Charles Washington Goldsborough (1779–1843), who had entered the Navy Department in 1798, was the department's chief clerk.
[3] Commodore John Rodgers (1773–1838) was the navy's senior officer; his frigate was the *President*.
[4] William Eustis.
[5] The reference is to the ship on which Joel Barlow (1754–1812), recently confirmed as minister to France, was to sail from Annapolis the following month, the *Constitution*, whose destination at the time of the letter Digges may have supposed was Britain.

To John Rodgers

In reply to Digges's letter of July [23] Paul Hamilton had written the following day: "Upon a substitute being furnished James Gregory may, if not in debt to the public be discharged, & this letter may be shewn to commre. Rodgers as his authority & direction to discharge Jas. Gregory accordingly.

"The Constitution is still at Anns. [Annapolis]" (NYHS: Commodore John Rodgers Papers, Reel 1).

Ft. Warburton Potomk. July 26. 1811

COMMODORE RODGERS
DEAR SIR

Upon making application to The Secy. of The Navy by letter on the 23d Int. and his [my] recieving His answer herein annexd, I have been under the necessity, from not exactly knowing *where* Your Frigate is at present stationd, to again trouble and solicit my good friend Secy. Hamilton to frank and forward this letter to You at N. York or at Norfolk whereever it is most likely for getting soonest to hand.

It is Sir the crys, distress's & wretchedness of His Family which made me an applicant for getting a Seaman, at this interesting crisis, dischargd from Your Ship.

James Gregory who went from the Enterprize I believe to Your Ship, is the person solicited for.—His family yet resides, where a few years back He lived on the edge of this my Estate, almost adjoining Colo. Lyles's at Broad Creek; and together with his earnings, and the provident help of a mother in Law, did tolerably well until his wife fell into a decline—Her mother died a short time back, and throws him for a time into additional distress from his eldest Daughter lately loosing Her eye Sight the only working support of two or three younger & helpless children. The mother of Gregorys wife (widow Jones) has left to Gregorys Children some trifling property which cannot be sold or divided until after Novr. Court; which, together with their wants, makes an imperious call upon James Gregory to get Home.

You will observe Sir from the terms of Mr. Hamiltons annexd Letter, the great difficulty I am put to so as properly to secure Gregorys discharge as to a substitute &ca., from not knowing where or to what quarter of the Union this letter may reach You, as well as the manner how I can get on board Ship a substitute for the Seaman in question; or indeed procure one sufficiently trust worthy to probe his way to You. I guess (from his having at times supplyd his wife with trifles of money, and once having a furlough to come & see Her either from the Enterprize or Your Frigate) That He is not in debt to the Country; But, if so, I will engage to punctually discharge that debt at the Navy Office, *where* I am very frequently & always see Mr. Secy. Hamilton: I will also pay any reasonable bounty money for His Substitute. For which purpose I have by this same mode of conveyance, I now write to my nephew Lieut. Jno. Fitzgerald in Fort Nelson (to whom I have before written relative to obtaining Gregorys discharge) to procure or aid me, in case Your Frigate comes into Norfolk, in getting a proper substitute for Gregory: For I am ardent as anyone to forward the Service of our infant Navy in which You are so distinguishd and honorable a Commander:—Go on my good Sir in doing services to Your Country, and recieve the benefits of it.

Should I be so lucky as obtain Gregorys discharge while the President Frigate is next at Norfolk, I should be obligd to You for a line by Him expressing where & to whom I can make the necessary payments for His defficiencies &ca. and it shall be gratefully done.

With great regard & Esteem and my very best wishes I remain
Yrs.
Thos. Digges

[Addressed:] Commodore Rodgers/United States Frigate President/ N. York City/Norfolk [*crossed out*]. [Franked:] Navy Depart./Paul Hamiltons

NYHS: Commodore John Rodgers Papers, Reel 1.

To Paul Hamilton

Warburton Jany. 4 1812

DEAR SIR

Understanding from Capt. Beall[1] That Mr. Charles Slade of Alexandria is an applicant to Your Department for a share of The Cordage Contract Four our Navy, I chearfully add my recommendation to those of others for Mr. Slades attainment thereof. I have known Him twelve or fourteen years as a partner in the respectable firm of Carne & Slade of Alexandria: And having jointly with His Son establishd the Rope making business on an extensive scale, and doing credit to Himself & the District in that persuit, I beg leave to recommend Him to Your usual attention & goodness with a hope that His materials may benefit our rising Navy.

> With great regard & esteem I remain
> Yours
> Thos. Digges

P.S. I am confind to my Chamber with a bad Scalded Leg & severe Cold, or I would have made one among You in the usual Christmass festivities & particularly at the Gala of the 1st Int.

NA: Record Group 45, Early Naval Records—Miscellaneous Letters Received by the Secretary of the Navy.

[1] Lloyd Beall, the fort commander.

To James Madison

Warburton 9th Feby. 1812

Mr. Digges's Compliments & best regards to Mr. Madison—He has been a miserable victim to confinement for the last fortnight or He would have waited on Mrs. & Mr. Madison: But *rubs*, at the age too of 68,[1] are the intermediate tributes that we are forced to Pay, in some shape or other, to our wretched nature, 'till we pay the last great one of all.

I cannot *complete* a white thorn Hedge at my lower garden for want of a few thorn sets of about 20 Ins. high: And on speaking to Your Gardiner (upon seeing some two or three dozen of such laid by in Earth near your old Ice House) He told me they were the overpluss of Your now flourishing Garden Hedge, & as He wanted but a very few of them for replacing where others had missd, He "was sure the President would spare some to me." If this is the case I should be obligd to You Sir to mention it to The Gardiner, and when my boat goes up next to Van ness's Wharf² I will make my Boatman call for them.

We have had here on yesterday a considerable rise in the Runs in & about Piscaty. from heavy rains just after the thaw:—My post Messenger had nearly been swept away Horse & all.—

If You have a cast by few *English Papers* I should be obligd by Some—I generally find some thing in them new and interesting to me. I am looking out for GOOD News from Windsor, & of the effect of The Prince getting into the Saddle unfetterd & with long reins.³

LC: Madison Papers.

¹ This would not be the last time Digges stated his age erroneously. He was, in fact, sixty-nine.
² Probably the wharf belonging to Gen. John Peter Van Ness (1770–1846), a former Democratic congressman from New York, who had become an officer of the militia of the District of Columbia in 1803 and made his home in the city.
³ George IV (1762–1830) had become prince regent with unrestricted powers in Feb. 1811, after his father had become permanently insane. What news there was, though, must have disappointed Digges because the prince was proclaiming that continuing maintenance of the empire's commercial and maritime rights must be a condition for any conciliatory discussions.

To John Carroll

Warburton 27 May 1812

DEAR & MOST RESPECTED SIR¹

By Chas. Robinson now residing at Hammonds ferry, going frequently to Your market, & long a Tenant here, I have the oppertunity of forwarding this letter to Your home, & thus offering my greetings, gratulations and best wishes: At same time to bore You with my afflictions my troubles, vexations and calls upon my personal exertions; Which very few at the age of 70 (Thanks to a Divine & omnipotant

Ruler) are more equa[l] to than myself. The day after I left You (*Wedy. the 20th Int. which will be long remembered in Prs. Geos. County*) I got such a complete soaking in my attempt to gain Ellicots Mills as obligd my return to Gadsbys & go drippingly & droopingly to bed; But it gave me an oppertunity of supping the next night (for there was no passage for Coach or horse traveller at Norwoods ferry on thursdy. the waters being very nearly as high as the rope) with the two Government messengers Biddle & Taylor[2] on their 24th day from Cherburgh, as also to Brakefast with them at Spurriers fryday morning. I am very sorry to have gatherd more as to the splendid appearances in France, her internal & vast improvements as to Roads, Canals, Bridges, Causeways, Her prime armys going out of and the Younger conscript miserables going into Spain, than I could learn as to the justice, performance of pledgd promises, good faith, or equitable decisions in their Courts of Marine Jurisprudence: Which rather outstrip those of Sir Wa. Scott and the Lords of appeal.—It is curious to see in some of these detaild decisions in the London papers, how the plain, old-fashiond & amiable Law of Nations are turnd & twisted from truth & justice to that of parsimony & subserviance to Courtly measures and the right of power—It is not more curious however than that this flower of The French Army moveing from Spain northward (which may not unlikely shake the Throne & capital of Russia) should give out "That they had conquerd Spain"!!

My purpose being to touch that quarter of Montgomery nearest to Baltio. and annarundel, & stop that night at my Sister Carrolls[3] for Electioneering purposes & find out what Billy was about, I took from Spurriers the detour towards the upper sources of Patuxent, the Snowdens upper new mill, so on to Brookville & thence to *Glenross* as Billy lately stiles it; And I arrivd there at 4 oCk. just an half hour after Billy had left it on a trip to & about Fredk.town, I hope on the very purpose I had contemplated to advise him about; Vizt. to publish his intentions to try for the succession of Mr. Keys seat in Congress,[4] to consult his leading friends in that quarter, & to state in His Circulars that He stood upon his former grounds & pretentions, and to Claim the aid of His Foederal friends &ca.

I found only my Sister & Nancy[5] at Home, & learnt from them there had been no publications on Williams side, but enough of them with reports &ca. on the other side—to my utter surprise & astonis[h]ment (what I cannot credit & only look upon as an Election report trick) That that Sloth & loggerhead Chas. Wharton had been at the first Rock-ville meeting or Hansons small call, and had there assented to go with that first flow of flood tide in favour of Hanson!—That Heny. Waring did nearly the like, & had given out "that but few of The Catholic Sect would vote for Wm. Carroll"!—That Chs. Jones even was slack & leaning to Hanson!![6]—That the heads of the Catholic Sect and even Bishop Carroll had advisd William not to contest the Election . . . & that some Deputation was soon to write to You (my belovd Bishop) to establish this last FACT!!!—But to pin up the whole, & from the same source too, I heard that The Revd. Mr. Plunket[7] had done William some mischief (I am convincd unintentionally) by accidentally dineing (I have forgot the name *where*) with some of Hansons adherents, Young Men of Rockville, & there expressing that He had always understood from the graver friends of Mr. Carroll as well as himself, that He had since his return from Ireland abandond all thoughts of again going into public life—This good Priest had hardly mounted his horse when one of that dineing party expressd himself thus "What has dropt from Mr. Plunket is as good as 200 Votes to Mr. Hanson.["] These items My Good Sir seemd to agitate & alarm my Sister & Nancy, more than upon reflection they had done me. I very accidentally & oppertunely met Mr. Plunket on Saty. 10 oCk. just as I came out of Mr. Fosters & where I had just taken a second Brakefast (for I had written Mr. Foster from Baltimo. I would call on Him that morning on a business of Jas. Pattens, *entre nous*, to obtain for him Mr. P. the appointment of British Consul for The District[8] & which I believe and have good hopes he will get) And I told the good man Plunket all I had heard.—He fully recollected the Conversation at a Captn. somebodys (for I forget the name) and he felt agitated & uneasy at any hurt it might do Wm. Carroll—that he had heard some days before what one of the Company had said respecting his expressions being worth 200 Votes to Hanson &ca. He perfectly satisfyd me as to His innocence, though at the same time I felt for its imprudence for every syllable is catchd at in Electioneering Contests.—I took the liberty to mention my recent parting with You & your approbation of Williams profer for going to Congress & the hope he would not withdraw. The Baltio., Fredk.town & Alexa. paper (as You will see by an inclosure a nefarious publication) are at work in favour of Hanson (who better knows than Billy Carroll possibly can do, the tricks & manoeuvres of Newspapers, how to gloss over falsities &ca.&ca.[)], And reports are certainly going about Montgomery of Your being averse to his standing a Candidate—That the basis of His support will be from The Democrats—this will cut a little; and assuredly every honest minded or sencible thinking Democrat would give Wm. Carroll a vote in preferance to such a Squatter in the County as Mr. Hanson, whatever their wishes might be in attainment of getting a Republican into Congress.

In my Saturdays ride & calling at several houses, I saw 14 or 15 Montgomery voters many of them very respectable, & I was not wanting in assiduity to evince that Billy was a declard Candidate for Congress—some of them had not heard He had offerd, and ALL were fully expressive of the issue being favourable & that he would far out poll his opponant—as there is to be a militia draft meeting at Gettings's on Saty. I hope to meet Billy Carroll there as I must be at Mr. Fosters & the War office on that forenoon. I left a letter on frydy. night for Billy at R. Creek stateing what I had done &ca. In the City I had only the oppertunity of converse with Mr. Rt. Brent on the subject—He had seen no publication of Billys. He advisd Billy to publish that He stood as a Federalist & entertaind no doubt of His success. If he now recedes or yeilds to Hanson (which that party is endeavouring to propagate He will do) He may throw his cap hereafter at a seat in Congress.

I come now, after troubling You too long, to the painful detail of The Storm, Whirlwind, Torrent, hail storm, hurricane, Tornado, or Whirlpool (for it has assumd all these qualities in its progress in the course of 30 or 40 miles & in a vein of but few miles in breadth acting differently close in the vicinity of one mischief to the other[)]. It seems to have commencd in Maryland & progressd from about Nangemoy & upwards to Pamunky, reaching this in a So.West course the same afternoon that I felt its watery effects only between Baltimo. & Ellicots where it was only a torrent of Rain with but little wind—*here* it was every thing but a hail storm, the wind in a few seconds shifting from So.E. to No.West & then going off with a water spout of Rain in a N.Et. direction—levelling trees of considerable firmness & magnitude as well as fruit trees & prostrating my favourite Locusts & those Majestic Lombardys in the Et. front of Warburton, (a punishment to me as the importer of this worthless 'tho stately tree) throwing down my largest wheat Stack Barn, and shaking the old brick dwelling to its very foundation. Very luckily I had but a few years back securd a new covering to the old displacd & tottering roof, or it would likely have gone in a body over & beyond the stables, the roof of which last in its middle elevation or *dome*-appartment was lifted intirely off & carryd in the air over its adjoining Cow-yard & part of a Clover lot against the Black smiths Shop about 150 yds. distance. At Dr. Marshalls point & Belvoir it was rather a whirlwind, & touchd but lightly on the Virginia side, hardly injuring but by wind & a torrent of rain the outskirts of Piscataway the Chapple & so on into Calverts mannor; where by inundation, washing up the lately planted Corn & loss of Fence rails it has injurd a number of poor Tenantry.

From this place in a direction to Mrs. Coombs's & on to Lyles[']s, Capt. Johns[']s Joe Edelins—Tolsons, into the Forrest about Duckets & Bowies—Mrs. Mullikans, Mrs. B. Youngs (whom it has but slightly injured) The Halls, neighbourhood of Marlbro, the White marsh Bellair &ca. The accounts of its ravages are dreadfull not a mill left in the whole course many Tobacco & dwelling houses & immense distruction from hail only to the Crops of Rye in particular & much of wheat & the lately planted Corn, distruction to trees &ca. Lyles & Mrs. Coombs cannot have sufferd less than six or seven thousand Dollrs. I shall get off for about one, Joe Edelin, & Kirby at High Park formerly Addisons near oxen hill at two or more thousands each—Wm. Bowie loss is said to exceed 4000 & F. Halls nearly as considerable. Bell-air is considerably injurd and I have only to hope, as is the case in all such first reports, that the disasters have not been so heavy[;] these of my Parish are fatally not exaggerations: But whatever is is right according to Divine lesson. I salute You with gratulations for Your continued good health & my every regard &ca.&ca.&ca.

           Thos. Digges

 We are well here, & I am going busily to work to save old nails, renew fresh timbers to broken down houses, making the prostrated Young trees take an erect possition setting Carpenters to work, with but scanty means for so doing:—My sister, Neice, & nephew George whom I am endeavouring to rig out for a western tour to obtain some accounts of his Fathers Lands are in their dayly arms of sleep, or they would profer their Respects—My bearer of *"these few lines"* is waiting.—

Right Reverend   }
 ArchBishop Carroll }

AB: Carroll Papers, 3C11.

---

[1] Carroll had been elevated to archbishop in 1808.
[2] They had carried dispatches from the American government to Joel Barlow, American minister to France. Taylor remains unidentified, but Lt. James Biddle (1783–1848), who had served as a midshipman on the *Constellation* and the *Philadelphia* and been nineteen months in prison after his ship had been grounded during the war with Tripoli, was soon to distinguish himself in the War of 1812.
[3] Elizabeth Digges Carroll's, Rock Creek. Her son Billy was considering a run for Congress.
[4] Philip Barton Key was completing his third term in the House of Representatives.
[5] Nancy was Billy's and George's sister, Anne (1777–1862).
[6] Of these political figures, the memorable one is Alexander Contee Hanson, the younger (1786–1819). A leading and vitriolic Federalist, he had founded the *Federal Republican*, a paper committed to attacking the policies and character of both Jefferson and Madison, had faced (and survived) court-martial proceedings in 1808 when, as a lieutenant in the Maryland militia, he had been charged with statements "mutinous and highly reproachful to the President," and in his continuing attacks on various authorities became the center of provocation of the bloody Baltimore riots in late July 1812. He succeeded Key in Congress and later became a senator.
[7] The Rev. Robert Plunkett (1752–1815), a former English Jesuit, had come to Maryland to serve as first president of Georgetown College (1791–1793), founded by Carroll, but he had left the post to serve the Maryland mission and in particular St. John's Church, Forest Glen, the Carroll family's chapel.
[8] Sir Augustus John Foster (1780–1848) was the British minister plenipotentiary.

James Patton had been vice-consul for some years and was a neighbor of Digges's (see Digges to John Borlase Warren, Jan. 14, 1813).

To Paul Hamilton

Warburton 28th May 1812

DEAR SIR.

I saught You but in vain in the City on Saturdy. morning last upon my return from Baltimore, wanting to speak to You on a matter of solicitation from Cap. Beall late of this Fort but now fixd at Fort McHenry: of which more hereafter, & I will try to see You soon.

The bearer Mr. Geo. Gant, son to a very respectable parentage of Chs. County near to Mr. Fenwicks[1] of Pamunky, is anxiously desirous of getting into our Navy as a Midship man. He is of unimpeachable Charactor, and I am perswaded is very capable of attaining the acquisitions necessary to do Credit to the service He wishes to enter into. I believe him sober & assiduous in any of his persuits, has lived with Credit in a store at Alexa. and acquird a good knowlege of accounts, figures, & writes a good hand. I have no hesitation in recommending Him to Your notice for the Service in which He seems bent upon entering into; not like too many of our Young Men to give it up soon but to continue & make his way in it. Any services You can render Him will be an addition to the many favours You have conferrd on

      Sir Yours with gt. regard & respect
      Thos. Digges

Piscataway

We have had a tremenduous storm here on Wedy. last and done me much mischief in blowing down & unroofing houses destruction of trees &ca. &ca. but I have fared some what better than my nearest neighbours whom some thousands of Dollrs. would not remunerate.

NA: Record Group 45, Early Naval Records—Miscellaneous Letters Received by the Secretary of the Navy.

[1] James Fenwick (d. 1823) had during the 1780s been a ship captain in the Potomac trade and later been associated with his brother Joseph, partner in the firm of Fenwick & Mason, Bordeaux.

To Paul Hamilton

Washington 23d June 1812

DEAR SIR

The application I before verbally made to You for admission or enrollment into The Navy was for Mr. Benjn. Beall the 2d Son of Capt. Loyd Beall late Commander at Fort Washington but now of Fort McHenry who seems fixd on keeping His Son into The Navy Service (His eldest being a Lieut. in The Regiment of Artillery)[1] And I can give You every assurance of the regular good Conduct of both those Youth—The latter regularly & well brought up by His parents a fine looking boy about 15 years old or 16.[2] His Fathers wish & desire is to keep Him a little longer under a teacher of Mathematics & in the eye of His Father: But at Your disposal & order as may best suit.

    With gt. regard
    Yrs.
    Thos. Digges

NA: Record Group 45, Early Naval Records—Miscellaneous Letters Received by the Secretary of War.

---

[1] See Digges to Hamilton, Nov. 29, 1810, n. 1.
[2] Benjamin Lloyd Beall (d. 1863) would be a cadet in the United States Military Academy, 1814–1818. Evidence of his serving in the navy has not been found.

To Paul Hamilton

Warburton Decr. 22d 1812

DEAR SIR

After writing You but a few days back merely to recommend Mr. Clarke to Your notice as a wisher to get into the Navy,[1] I am sorry to soon again trespass upon You; But my interesting Young friend Mr. James Pye (who is the second Son of a respectable & old Genteel Family in my neighbourhood) demands of me a grant of His request: Which is to get to You & report Himself at Your office, and to get attachd to some vessel for as early service as may be convenient. He was ardent to get into The Constellation Capt. Stewart[2] being known to many of The officers on board that ellegant frigate but He was too late. He is now in hopes that the Adams frigate will be the ship and having been much in the habit of voyageing about, & has a very good taste for naval drawings, as well as more up to being useful on ship board than Country youth are in general He would like to be assistant to the rigging & fitting out of that Frigate. He is to my knowlege a sober discreet & tolerably well educated young man & I doubt not but will do Credit to any employ he may enter into.

With great regard I remain Yours
tho yet too much indisposd to visit the City
Thos. Digges

I understand from Mr. Pye that He got His Commission dated in June last some considerable time after—& that He has been twice up to report himself but faild of seeing ——— like myself He knows but little of the mode for so doing.

NA: Record Group 45, Early Naval Records—Miscellaneous Letters Received by the Secretary of the Navy.

---

[1] This letter has not been found.
[2] The frigate *Constellation*, constructed under the authorization provided by Congress in 1794, was under the command of Capt. Charles Stewart. In Feb., encountering superior force, Stewart would have to put in at Norfolk and remain bottled up there for the duration of the war.

To John Borlase Warren

Promoted to the rank of admiral in 1810 and placed in command of a new, consolidated North American station in August 1812, Warren (1753–1822) had reached his headquarters in Halifax in September and sent a proposal to the United States suggesting a suspension of hostilities because of the repeal of the orders in council. If the United States accepted the proposal, he would halt operations; if not, he would open negotiations with disaffected sections of the nation, especially New England. Madison, through his secretary of state, James Monroe (1758–1831), had then made England's ending its impressment of American seamen a condition for any armistice, but because Warren had not been empowered to negotiate that question and his government was determined to continue the practice, discussions had stopped. Digges had, as the letter shows, known Warren socially some thirty-five years earlier and been associated with him at that time in buying land on St. John's Island (Prince Edward Island), which he located in the Bay of Fundy. Whether Digges had now initiated the correspondence with Warren solely on his own, or whether he had been encouraged to write by friends in Washington, is not known.

Fort Warburton Potomk: River
near Washington Decr. 28th 1812

DEAR SIR JOHN

Very soon after our news papers announcd Your arrival to the Halifax Station, and hail'd You as the Negociator, and as I *yet* hope the Harbinger of Peace between our reciprocal countries, I took the first occasion (altho' in bad health & in the advancd age of 72,[1] prompted too by the pleasurable feelings which Your negociating powers actuated) to address a letter to You my former good friend and pleasurable acquaintance. I shall never forget You; but perhaps a lapse of 35 or 36 years may have lost Your recollection of our intercourses & given You room to suppose me out of the land of the living: I therefore in my first letter (which I still hope You have recievd) dated about the 5th Novr.[2] for I rarely or ever keep copys, had to tease You somewhat in *detail* as to our primary meeting—afterwards in Lisbon—with passage to Falmouth—subsequent scenes in London, & with its then open hearted (Capn. T. Shirley) Ranger of the Green Park[3] & its pavillion banquets—Your L: Marlow scenes of Election to Parliament[4]—a few Bath & Portsmouth meetings &ca. &ca. &ca. I soon after the last enterd upon my disagreeable & 7 years vexatious occupation of Agent & Commissary for American Prisoners in England; in which my fund of health & usual ardency carryd me through, aided with the aleviating scenes among the gay *Venus's* of the Green Park, whom You parted with for the better embarkation on board the frigate Venus Capn. Williams if I remember right, where we last parted. I had however frequent & pleasurable accounts of You from Lord & Lady Howe,[5] Sir Geo: & Lady Warren,[6] admirals Sr. Jno. Lockt. Ross, Lord Keppell, Laforey,[7] &ca. at periods too when I had hardly time to write or to visit: often however requesting Mr. Stephens of The Admiralty (with whom I had much to do on the Cartel & Prisoners business, a valuable man) to inform me when You might be seen in London.

I wishd much to have seen You and *Your* Lady Warren soon after your marriage but was then only for a few days in London and obligd to a hasty return to Ostend & Antwerp.—Lady Cæcilia Johnson (an oracle of heraldry) had mentiond my distant relationship! for says She "Lady Diana Clavering & myself are Daughters of Lady Delawar, whose mother was a Digges of Chilham of which stock you are the lenial Heir & male Representative"—So indeed it is,[8] & so the world goes: My ancestor left that possession & His Castle of Chilham from the failure of Laws Mississippi bubble[9]—Settled in Maryland, and I now (an old gander batchelor) possess the Estate & reside in an old family farm House, nearly opposite to Mount Vernon, 15 Miles South of Washington City, & in full sight of it, of Alexandria & Georgetown; with humble viands for my *old* friend⟨s⟩ (whom I like better than *new* ones) and where no one would be more cordially welcome than Sir. Jno. Borlase Warren the *yet*, I hope, harbinger of Peace.

Mr. Baker[10] not being at the time in Washington to forward You my letter of the 5th Novr., and being pinchd for time to overtake a dispatch Cartel Vessel then at N. York, I freed the letter & inclosd it to The Postmaster there for forwardance by that or the first conveyance.—I have not heard of it since: I[t] was freely written after a too long introductory (like this) as to my opinion of men, of measures, and the probable approaching consequences of our unlucky disagreement with England, some recently receivd french news & measures &ca. I have not seen Mr. Baker for above two months from an accute malady which confines me to the House, & am thereby also denyd the usual free intercourses with Him & with our Executive Rulers, with all of whom I am intimate & have friendly intercourses; for I am among a large majority of my Country an adherent to those political principles which they adopt, however I may have felt for the Declaration of War.

I am much obligd to Mr. Baker for some English News Papers, together with a line from Him offering the forwardance of any letters to Engd.; And supposing He will do the like with this to You I shall make free to send it to Him—Sorry I am to find by his letter that He is likely soon to leave this Country. I will make every effort (& it is only an 18 miles ride to His hotel & *less by water*) to see Him before He departs. I hope nothing fresher than your proposition for suspension of Hostilities has caused His thought of departing—Be it as it may this shall go to Him; And whether I am doomd or not to see or hear from You hereafter, accept my cordial, most sincere & best wishes for Your personal safety & happiness.

It has been my fortunate lot Sir John to have personally known in England every Minister (save one) which has been sent from Your Country to this since its severation, & to have had an open intimacy with all—Hammond; Liston; Thornton; Merry; Erskine; Rose; Jackson but sligh[t]ly; Morrier, & Foster,[11] and it would be to me a happy climax to my Career (after a fifty years attention to political movements) to see You finish the blissful event of accomodating our differences.

It is but a *shadow* of no great national magnitude in the scale of our reciprocal Countries, which now seperates our Interests,—The right of Search for & taking our Seamen or Citizens, and those restrictive orders of Council denying us a fair open & neutral trad[e]. In my mind there may be an easy *adjustment by modification* for both; and I verily believe if there had been no *condition* tackd to the repeal of The orders of Council, that measure (very little if any way beneficial to England) would have been accomodated:—The *right* to seek for & take American Citizens is a more difficult pill to swallow, & surely requires some emolient. Be not discouragd by the rebuff of Your proposition for a sessation of Hostilities; put your back to the burthen once more; I have full confidence The Negociation will be renewd; And let us try to have

"a long pull, a strong pull, & a pull altogether"

vide Admiral Berkley[12]

I always lamented the *condition* which was implied in the British repeal of the orders of Council—better it had been done *un*conditionally and without reservation: I lament also two other evils emenating from Yourself—first for a seeming non assent for suspending (*pending the Armistice or Negociation*) the practice of taking from our Ships American Citizens.—2dly The implication in Your Proclamation that British Seamen are *seducd*, & have been *forced* into our naval service. It is more than probable many have been seducd or enveigled into the merchants service (where they obtain double or treble wages to that of our Navy) on board which they are inhibited when found to be British: and our *Laws* as well as our naval regulations, cannot *force* any person into public service.

I lament, & do sincerely lament, at such a *protraction* of Negociation: For delay may afford openings & probably will bring *profers* of *French fraternity* to Us; altho I firmly believe there is no prediliction in our Rulers in favour of France against Britain) [(] for I can pledge my honour that in a 13 or 14 years close intimacy & open intercourses with the last & the now President, that I never discoverd in them or their State Secys. any thing of such like tendency)—It would have shaken my attachments to them:—Yet my fears are now alive that something may, & likely will soon happen, through the pending French negociation in Europe to involve Us as an ally in the warfare with that Country—which may the Lord of His infinite mercy prevent.

The prompt, intrepid, and eagle-eyed avidity with which Napoleon catches at favourable incidents to forward His nefarious system of involving Nations in his means of destroying them, will naturally prompt Him to throw out (*at this onset of our Warfare with England*) every bait, lure, or favour to this Country for his sureer attainment of His primary wish . . . *the destruction of Britain*; & woe betide the remaining world if he does it. His home or channel seaports have already shewn prompt alacrity & considerable favours, in the reception & return outfits to many trading vessels lately got back to Baltimore & Philadelphia with cargoes of considerable value, and announcing every encouragement to others, together with assertions that Le *Grande Empereur* is to make good all his former rascally spoliations on our trade, in particular those seizures at St. Sebastians!! and many of our traders will be gull'd into a belief of it.[13] His invitation too to our Minister Barlow to meet Him forthwith at Wilna (& the Paris papers announce that Barlo left Paris in last month to go there) savours of no good to England.[14] Is it not more than probable then, should Napoleons career of mischief in the north extend further than Moscow & thereby menace Petersburgh (from which City it appears by the Engh. News papers they were early in Octor. embarking many ship loads of valuables & effects, and the Russian fleet ordered to England for safety) that He will either ruin or obtain an ignominious Peace from Alexander, excluding England again from an open Baltic Trade, and thereby be enabled to march his hords of cutthroats South, & again re-enter & ruin the Peninsula? Is it not likely too that He may *fraternally* offer Us Squadrons for protection of our sea board & Ports? more likely however to fall into the hands of some of Your Cruizers, than to do us any *ultimate* good. His machinations are diabolical as they are ruinous to civil & peacable Societies, and I cannot but fear His powers: I shall doubt the justice of the Almighty if he does not get a check in his career.

      I remain with great regard Your obligd
      and Obt. Servt. Thos. A. Digges

 P. S. Pray Sir John (when You can spare time from Your important concerns) be so good as inform me, what You have done with Your lott of 20,000 Acres Land on St. Johns Island Bay of Fundy; And did You fix setlers on it as we contemplated in 1777?—I bought the Lot No. not far distant *end ways* from Yours (but I have lost my map & platt of it[)]: And before I left London in 1798 I was offerd £1300– Stg. for it payable in English merchantile Debts (which I afterwards wishd I had taken as they turnd out good) But I had conveyd it by Power of Attorney to English *Trustees*: Who have neglected it almost intirely; and the Taxes, Royal Rents &ca. will of course injure and much reduce its worth—I hope You have profited more by Yours.
          T. D.

For Admiral Sir Jno. Borlace Warren
  Halifax

28 December 1812

SH: Warren Papers, Letters from Various Persons to Admiral Sir John Borlase Warren, 1792–1814, pp. 143–44.

[1] Once again Digges errs in calculating his age.
[2] This letter has not been found.
[3] Green Park, bordered by Piccadilly, was a milieu for the wealthy, the fashionable, and, apparently, the pleasure-loving.
[4] A resident of Little Marlow in his early years, Warren had been elected to the House of Commons from Great Marlow, where his family held property, for the ten-year period 1774–1784. Later he had represented Nottingham (1797–1806) and Buckingham (Mar.–Apr. 1807).
[5] Probably after 1778, when Richard Howe had resigned his American command. Lady Howe was Mary Hartopp of Welby.
[6] George Warren (1735–1801) had been elected to the Commons from Lancaster in 1758 and managed to hold his seat until 1780. He had then represented Beaumaris, 1780–1784, and Lancaster again, 1786–1796. Lady Warren was the wealthy Jane Revel, a fellow M.P.'s daughter with whom he had eloped during his first year in the House.
[7] Sir John Laforey (1729?–1796), appointed commissioner of the navy at Barbadoes and the Leeward Islands in Nov. 1779, had earlier taken part in the action off Ushant with Keppel and Ross.
[8] Digges's own notes on his ancestry, written during his visit to Chilham in 1794, are in MdHS (Ms. 246).
[9] John Law (1671–1729), a Scotsman who had as controller general of French finance persuaded the French regent, the duke of Orleans, to sell shares in the vast Louisiana territory in 1719, had along with associates brought speculation to a peak a year later; a reaction had then prompted the quick-witted to realize their gains and exchange their paper for coin, leaving the slower to discover the Royal Bank drained of coins and the state unwilling to honor its obligations. The so-called Mississippi Bubble had thus burst, and in the ensuing panic Digges's ancestor was among the sufferers.
[10] Anthony St. John Baker (d. 1854), legation secretary, who, after the American declaration of war and the breaking off of diplomatic relations between the U.S. and England, was left in Washington to manage British affairs and serve as agent for British prisoners. He was later consul general, 1816–1832.
[11] Unmentioned in earlier letters by Digges, Sir Edward Thornton (1766–1852) had been secretary to George Hammond in 1791, vice-consul in Maryland in 1793, secretary of the British legation in 1796, and acting chargé d'affaires, 1800–1804; Sir George Henry Rose (1771–1855) had been in Washington in 1807 on a special mission concerning the *Chesapeake* affair; John Philip Morier (1776–1853), following Jackson's departure for Europe in 1810, had been in charge of the British legation in Washington. Foster, after a year as minister to the U.S., had returned home when the U.S. had declared war, leaving Baker to carry on.
[12] As vice-admiral in command of the British squadron at the North Atlantic station in 1807, George Cranfield Berkeley (1753–1818) had been the officer responsible for ordering the search of the *Chesapeake* (see Digges to Jefferson, Sept. 15, 1807, n. 3).
[13] In his attempt to retaliate against Britain's blockade of French-held Europe, Napo-

leon had ordered the seizure of neutral carriers and their cargoes and sanctioned the repeated burning of American ships. Digges's reference to St. Sebastian is doubtless to Napoleon's retaliatory response to the Non-intercourse Act of March 1809. In May of that year an American schooner bearing cargo had entered the Spanish port in violation of none of Napoleon's decrees; yet Napoleon, apparently to prevent the proliferation of such commerce, had ordered the seizure and confiscation of the cargo, which he had then directed be sold in Bayonne, the money received to be placed in the "caisse de l'amortissement"—and he had announced that other American ships putting into port would be treated the same way. He had followed that action with seizures in Holland and Italy, as well as additional ones in Spain, where by May 1810 the total had numbered forty-four.

[14] Barlow had set out in Oct. to negotiate a settlement on trade and spoliation demands with the French foreign minister. But the course of military events and Napoleon's own movements had required deferring decisions, and by the time Napoleon had decided to leave Moscow for Paris, Barlow had died in Poland—two days before Digges's letter.

To John Borlase Warren

Ft. Warburton Maryland Jany. 14, 1813

DEAR SIR JOHN

I make free to refer You to my former letters, Vizt. (Novr. 5 which I have never yet heard if got in time for Your dispatch or Cartel vessel) and that of the 29th ulo. on that day put into the care of Mr. Baker just before He quitted his disagreeable avocation in Washington; And the present only serves my Good Sir to introduce to your notice & usual goodness my friend & neighbour James Patton Esqr. who has been for a number of years past (& the only one ever acting) as British vice Consul in this quarter, and in whose faith, rectitude and promptness, in whatever He may engage, I think you may with confidence rely— He having been in the close intimacy or agencys of every British Minister from Mr. Liston downwards. His house has ever been open to them all—He is by birth a Scotsman, & in His early teens engagd with his merchantile relatives in Alexandria—now united to a highly reputable Citizen Lady & residing on Her family property with a large & interesting progeny. There is no man more respected, nor was there any one in Alexandria more flourishing in trade & His agencys &ca.,

14 JANUARY 1813

(although He never took a dollar for His many years Consulage) But was suddenly *put all aback* by our unfortunate Embargo Law, which gave stoppage & ruin to some of His provision loaded vessels on their way to The British Forces in the West Indies &ca.[1]

I very cheerfully give these testimonials of Mr. Patton, whose intention is I believe to make some communications to You (whom I still hope to see here as a negociator & messenger of Peace) and I trust Mr. Patton may be benefited therein.

> I remain with great esteem & regard
> Yr. obligd & Obt. Ser.
> Thos. Digges

P. S. It may be necessary, or at least not amiss, to inform You That there has been (about the period of Mr. Purcivals unfortunate death[2]) an application made through Mr. Foster and others of The Prince Regents friends as well as the late Consuls Mr. Bond of Philadelphia and Colo. Hammilton of Norfolk,[3] to obtain for Mr. Patton, when a proper period arrivd for doing it, The appointment of British Consul to The District of Columbia, (which comprises the City, George town, and Alexandria) as from which by its late & encreasing Commerce, *particularly in Export of produce*, from a most abundant & extensive back Country has equalld the Port of Baltimore: And will, when the Trade opens fairly & properly be of great consequence to Britain & its dependencies, at least I believe & hope so. This application for Mr. Patton was of course, tho well backd at the time, suspended by the change of ministers on Mr. Percivals death.[4]

T. D.

[Addressed:] For/Admiral Sir John B. Warren/Kt. of the Bath &ca. &ca. &ca./Halifax

SH: Warren Papers, Letters from Various Persons to Admiral Sir John Borlase Warren, 1792–1814, p. 154.

[1] Commissioned in 1791 as vice-consul for "the Potowmack," Patton had subsequently built a house near Alexandria, which he had had to sell in 1809, when the embargo of the preceding year had made it impossible for him to repay debts he had contracted.

²Spencer Perceval (1762–1812), the prime minister, had been fatally shot on May 11, 1812, by a mentally deranged man with a grievance against the government.

³John Hamilton (d. 1817), a former American loyalist from Norfolk, had in 1791 been appointed consul for the Virginia district (which included Patton's), serving under Phineas Bond, consul general for the middle Atlantic and southern states.

⁴Digges must have given Patton this letter to forward in his own behalf, for among the Warren papers (SH) is a letter from Patton to Warren in Bermuda, Jan. 30, 1813, saying: "I now . . . inclose you a few lines introductory, from my Neighbour Thos. Digges Esquire, who appears to be an acquaintance of yours of some standing. . . . He is quite intimate, at the Presidoliad, and it has lately occurred to me, that it is not improbable but that his Letters to you in November last, were written with the knowledge & consent of the Executive—such is my conjecture. I sincerely wish to see my Friend Digges expectations of seeing you at Washington as a Negotiator reallized—".

To Jehu Chandler

Ft. Warburton *near Piscaty.* 19 Jany. 1813

Mr. Jehu Chandler
Dear Sir

I send You an advertisement for a Land Commission which pray be particular in inserting it in The Maryd. Republican[1] *once* every successive week for *five weeks*. My manager Mr. Frazer[2] going on business to Fort Madison[3] will drop this as he pass's Your Office & call as He comes out of town (probably early the following morning) for 20 or 30 printed Advertisements for letting a fishing Landing as inclosd within. Charge them to me & believe me among Yr. best well wishers & Obt. St.

Thos. Digges

I get your paper regularly & peruse it with grief & regret for the fallen & sunken political situation of Maryland & cordially dispise a majority of its representation.

[On verso]
Notice

The Subscribers intend to Petition The next April Court of Prc. Geos. County for a Commission to run, mark the lines, & place down sundrys of The boundary stones of Warburton Mannor & Frankland

(& also the adjoining tracts of Athys folly, Dalkieth, Addisons purchase &ca.)⁴ many of which boundaries have been wilfully or accidentally misplacd according to The acts of assenting in Such cases made & provided—And they invite any persons acquainted with the same to give testimony thereto.

     Thos. A. Digges ⎫ ⁵
     W. Dudley Digges ⎭

MdHS: Ms. 246.

¹ This Annapolis weekly, established in 1809, had become Chandler's with the issue of July 1, 1811.
² Henry Frazer.
³ At Annapolis.
⁴ These various tracts had been laid out in Lower Piscataway Hundred during the last half of the seventeenth century. "Athys" is usually spelled "Aitheys."
⁵ A copy of this notice, similarly worded, was, according to an endorsement in Digges's hand, "put up at Marlbro Court House Door—Broad Creek Church and Warburton Chappell by Natl. Soper—on the days as below—" (MdHS: Ms. 246).

To James Patton

Warburton 24 Apl. 1813

DEAR SIR

This will be dropt in the post office by the Captain of the dayly Fort Packet hither. I have been obligd twice to the City lately but necessiated to return same day: For I am envelopd in trouble with the Fishery, Corn planting (an essential which cannot be neglected) and just now entering on an engagement to find forthwith above 100 Locust & Cedar sleepers for the repairing platform of The Fort & which will closely occupy me for 8 or 10 days.

Have you heard anything from or about Colo. Barcklay,¹ or will he expect to remain in N. York or where—I guess He will not be allowd in N. York or any material seaport during the war.—Perhaps He may make Annapolis his residence—*the fleets* in the Bay to the contrary notwithstanding. Such armaments & such marauding excursions cannot *materially* (taken in a national view) do our Country the mischief which England & Her misguided Rulers seem to augre or expect; But must have the tendency to unite political discordants, and what hurts my feelings most, add fuel to the flame of enmity (for such there must be) against England: leaving thereby the sting against a *less favourd nation*, upon a consequent adjustment of present differances, instead of its remaining *first in favour*—The injury must & will lay heaviest against the manufacturing & carrying Interests of Britain.—This is as clear to me as any axiom in Euclid. For England, nor no other power, can injure or stop the progress of this Country if we are true to ourselves. If these excursions up our bays & Rivers are meant (as I believe they are) to divert or stop the hastening on Expeditions towards Canada, they will fail in the intended effect—EXERTION seems to be the order of the day for getting an adequate force to or over the Canada Line; and the militia, in my mind, will be found adequate to the Seaboard; for our present Enemy will, as in the case of the Revolutionary war, not venture far out of sight of their Fleets which alone afford the supply of their wants.

There has been a *second* intercepted Letter since that of the 2 Apr. obtaind by Government of more important contents as to *intention* and, to me, more afflicting *consequences*: as developeing names & treasnoble practices (under trickey covers) for supplying the Enemys wants &ca., which may go to the ruin (at least to the loss of *reputation*) of some hitherto respectable names in Merchantile persuits.—Phila., Boston & Baltimo. carrying on the drama.

The Frs: Freeling Packet saild mondy. evening from Annapolis for Bermuda some of the Chesapeak Squadron in sight above—I understand and believe from what I heard frydy. that the opening of Letters passing between Engd. & this Country by packets was an agred on regulation with England, & a usual matter with that Country for a few years back in their continental warfare—I rarely knew it practicd during my residence six years in London & while I was a coverd agent for American Prisoners—at the Close of that war I obtaind bags & sacks full of Letters *opend* during the naval warfare, as a *donation* from the succeeding minister to Ld. North (Rockingham) for my trouble & vigilence as messenger under them for the first overtures for Peace (*Independance the prelimary article*) to Amsterdam & Paris. The day of my return, in 8 days to & from Ld. Rockinghams, I did not sleep or hardly eat until I got a coachfull of those documents & Letters from the then foreign office of G. Jackson in Cleveland row.[2]

Gallatin has taken personal leave & it is with Mr. Bayard in Philadelphia they sail in a purchasd vessel (I believe from the Secy. of Navy his Brother its Captain) in 8 or ten days.[3] John Payne Todd[4] leaves the Presidoliad *today* to go as one of Gallatins Secys. to Petersburgh; and I wish I could have attended him as far as Patapsico or Elk[ton] but my avocations totally preclude it, & I am all but wearyd to death.

Lyes are flying dayly in the City as well as here where every thing going up are haild—Fryday Letters in the City from Norfolk asserted that 11 Sail of the Line &ca. had anchord in lynn haven bay—every body was of course at work & busily employd GUESSING their destination & object—Saty. mornings Letters proved it a fabrication—the Squadron on thursdy. was off Patapsico mouth, & inclining upwards tho in full sight of Baltio., but though threats were held out to the taken passengers on board a French town Packet going to Elkton there were not much fears *in* Baltio. though Familys were moving out. They will likely try thier Congreve rockets & probably with the same effect as at *"the walld Town, strongly fortified & with a full Garrison"* Lewis town[5] (see Warrens Letter) *cui bono?* Such work will unite all parties or they do not deserve the Country they live in.

—News of importance was hourly expected from Lake Ontao.— and troops were moving in every direction No.Westward. No likelyhood of *Armistice*, which would be for the present against us—sanguine expectations from the St. Petersburgh convention, both for amelioration of restrictions on the neutral carrying trade under the basis of the Law of Nations, as well as its being a leading path to Peace.—Gallatin gives himself to *Novr.* for his return home, but *Engld.* must, & will I fear, protract it all she can.

I have had no letter in reply to my three from Admiral Warren though I am pretty sure through an indirect & curious communication He has receivd my first congratulatory to Him at Bermudas on his arrival there as a Negociator—the 2d was under Bakers charge, & the third in consequence of seeing his Bermuda Proclamation[6]—from which my hopes as to Peace were intirely done away until the partys had enterd into a trial of strength and for the fate of which I have as yet entertaind no serious fears.

A Mr. Blackstone (one of the Blackstone Island family, of respectability & resident near the lower point of St. Marys, and who has an old relative neighbour a fisherman who found his road to the Deck of Admiral Warrens Ship) states the following as the *converse* of *St.* Marys, & what the Fisherman had from the Admiral—Can we get any Live stock or poultry from Your neighbourhood or can vessels water there? [The Admiral must have known this as the Fisherman saw on board his Ship a Smiths point pilot as if in pay of the Ship but not allowd to speak to Him.][7] His answer was We are in a poor district for cattle or stock, a few hogs & but scant of Poultry—no water but from Sandy springs & but brackish.—Do You know of any vessels in or about St. Marys outward bound?—None but bay traders and shallops in St. Marys River which are taking wood &ca. up the River and for Baltimo. to which place only *we* have any trade—As you live in Maryland you likely know a Mr. Digges & how far his house is up?—Very far up in sight of the City near Mount Vernon—has been up there some years back for Fish before the old General died.—Do you expect to go up soon? and if You go will You tell Him You saw me & I got his letter but cannot for the present pay the friendly visit which he may expect—is He a Congress man or assembly man?—I dont know, nor expects to go up but I can get some of the Craft Captains to take the Message to Him—Is there any frigate or Gun boats in the River?— The folks talk of some but they are far up by Crane Island—

A number of trifling &cas. The relater states the Admiral as a very fine Gentleman indeed & orderd him some beef & biscuit in his punt—States him as the finest dressd man in this world—His brod. [⟨brocaded⟩] goold lacd coat coverd with a fine broad ribband & cross's at his button holes with a monstrous big lacd hat. The talk at St. Marys was wondering how Digges could do so bad as write to Him but Digges was an Englishman &ca. &ca. Mr. Blackstone stoppd a tide at the wharf in a wood Loaded Schooner of his, and gave a detail of the boat Squadrons in & about St. Marys but had left the Potomk. going upwards a day or two before he started.

I wish the Admiral had written by The Fisherman.

I see Foster has got elected for one of the Devonshire Dukes Burroughs & I am promisd some parliamentary Debates by a messenger I am to send up on monday or tuesday to the war office & to Mr. Cutts *purveyors* office.⁸

The Regent I understand is in very bad health and getting into another scrape by a sort of underhand investigation into the Conduct of His wife and which causd the interesting Book from the pen of Percival stiled *"The Book."*—I should like much to get it from knowing *all* the Charactars (save one of two) left blank in *The Spirit* of *The Book* which I suppose you must have read, as eminating from the Princess of Wales herself.⁹

      Yrs. &ca. &c.
      T. D.¹⁰

NMM: LBK2, Admiral Warren's Correspondence with Lord Melville, American War, 1812–1814. Although no indication of the addressee appears on the face of this letter and no cover survives, Patton was clearly the recipient: a letter from him to Warren, April 28, 1813 (SH), concludes: "I have just received the inclosed from your old acquaintance. It may produce a smile." Perhaps Digges assumed that Patton, whom he had introduced to Warren in his letter of January 14, 1813, which he had given Patton to transmit, would pass it along. Warren in turn, writing to Robert Saunders Dundas (1771–1851), Viscount Melville and at that time first lord of the admiralty, on June 5, 1813, enclosed Digges's letter with this explanation: "I have sent by this conveyance a Letter from a Mr. Digges transmitted to me from Washington by the person to whom it was addressed: the former Gentleman I remember when in England in the former War with America, acting as Commissary General for prisoners: this person is a Friend of the present Cabinet in America & of course not well inclined to the Interests of Britain: Digges has written me several Letters offering his services, but as I had not any opinion of him none of these were answered & in the Letter enclosed your Lordship will [find] much useful matter as it shews the ideas of the Friends of Mr. Madison" (NMM: LBK2 . . .).

¹Colonel Thomas Barclay (1753–1830), a former loyalist and the British consul general for the eastern states during 1798–1812, had sailed for England with Foster at the outbreak of war but soon after, as prisoners on both sides had accumulated, had been appointed as British agent to distribute relief to those held in the U.S. In Jan. 1813 he had again taken ship, stopping in Bermuda on the way to confer with Admiral Warren, and on Apr. 1 had reached New York, whence he had hastened to Washington to present his credentials to Monroe and to confer with the American commissary general of prisoners, Gen. John Thomson Mason, for the purpose of drawing up preliminary agreements about the treatment and exchange of prisoners. He would then repair to

seclusion in Harlem, outside the military limits of New York, but, as Digges surmised, would not be permitted to remain anywhere close to military bases and have to move again.

² Digges's first allusion to this transaction is in a letter to Adams, Apr. 9, 1782.

³ Albert Gallatin (1761–1849), secretary of the treasury, and James Ashton Bayard (1767–1815), a leading Federalist, were to sail on May 9 to meet a British delegation at St. Petersburgh, where the Emperor Alexander was proposing to act as mediator between the two powers. The secretary of the navy, Paul Hamilton's successor, was William Jones (1760–1831), a merchant and former congressman who had had experience as a sea captain.

⁴ Madison's stepson (1792–1852).

⁵ The British had bombarded Lewistown on Delaware Bay earlier in Apr. Their solid shot had damaged houses; but their shells had fallen short, and their rockets had gone over the town—in fact, the Congreve rockets' terrifying screaming constituted their principal value: notoriously inaccurate, they accounted for only a single fatality in the entire war.

⁶ In Nov. 1812 Warren had been ordered by the ministry to establish a blockade of the Chesapeake and Delaware bays and had doubtless soon after that issued a proclamation of the blockade from his headquarters in Bermuda. But how Digges's third letter relates to it remains unclear, for his third letter to Warren appears to be the one dated Jan. 14, 1813, in which he devotes himself largely to introducing Patton.

⁷ The brackets are Digges's.

⁸ Richard Cutts (1771–1845), brother-in-law of Dolly Madison (1768–1849) and congressman from Massachusetts, 1801–1813, had just been appointed to the new office of superintendent general of military supplies.

⁹ The prince of Wales, the future George IV, had married Amelia Elizabeth Caroline of Brunswick-Wolfenbütel (1768–1821) in 1795. With the birth of their child, Princess Charlotte Augusta, in Jan. 1796, the prince, having conceived a dislike for his wife, had forsaken her and a few months later become formally separated, while at the same time asserting his right to restrict her social activities and her access to Charlotte. Then in 1802 Caroline had been given custody of a newborn child whom hostile tongues soon alleged to be her bastard. A commission appointed by the king (George III) to investigate her conduct had undertaken a secret inquiry and exonerated her, reproaching her mainly for a certain levity of manners, but had not published the evidence they had gathered. To help her clear her name publicly, Spencer Perceval, her appointed legal adviser, who had resigned as attorney general at Pitt's death and become a government critic, had in 1807 prepared the various letters, depositions, and other documents for publication and had had five thousand copies ready for distribution in Mar. 1808. The Grenville ministry had just fallen, though, and with the expectation of a friendly Tory administration's following, Perceval had judged publication gratuitous, if not impolitic, and ordered the edition burned. Yet, some copies had slipped into other hands, so that when the princess had continued to suffer from restrictions on her access to her daughter, when the continued protests had finally impelled the prince (become prince regent in 1811) to refer the matter to the cabinet on the ground that the Princess Charlotte's education was a matter of state concern, and when the cabinet had then authorized a new inquiry that had amounted to but another secret investigation of the old charges, she and her advisers had had at hand the volume whose publication they had concluded the time was now ripe for. Popularly known as *The Book*, it appeared in London in 1813

as *The Genuine Book, An Inquiry, or Delicate Investigation into the Conduct of Her Royal Highness the Princess of Wales*; *before Lords Erskine, Spencer, Grenville, and Ellenborough, The Four Special Commissioners of Inquiry Appointed by His Majesty in the Year 1806*.

[10] Although no additional correspondence between Digges and Warren or Warren's acquaintances has been found, Digges may have had further communications with Warren. On Aug. 23, 1813, Gen. Mason wrote Digges: ". . . we shall send a Flag very soon on Board admiral Warren, which you will have full permission to accompany—it will be requisite for You to be here early on *Wednesday* morning—to go of[f] to Annapolis to join Mr. Skinner our agent who will proceed on Thursday on board—the admirals Ship is of[f] Annapolis.

"I shall wish to have half an hour's conversation with you—" He then asked Richard Forrest, a clerk in the State Department, to convey the letter speedily to Digges. On both the envelope for this letter and the envelope for Forrest's covering note Digges made notations that suggest he did see Warren. On Forrest's he wrote: "For the going with propositions &ca. from Secy. of State to Admiral *Warren*." On Mason's: "Genl. Jno. Mason *Commy. of Prisoners* about my mission from Secy. of State to Admiral *Warren*" (MdHS: Ms. 246). Although such evidence is not conclusive, the word "mission" does imply a commitment likely to have been fulfilled.

To William Jones

Ft. near Warburton 16. Augt. 1813

Honble. The Secy. of The Navy
SIR

From my own knowledge of the tricks & manœuvres playd by some of the Alexandrians, (whose stations & appearance as merchants ought to induce more loyalty & patriotism to their Country) as well as what I hear from neighbouring farmer Residents on the shores of the Potomac near to Crane Island & in sight of Occoquan River, I am inducd to believe that supplys of Flour &ca. & ca. are now sending in small Bay & River Craft to The Enemys Fleets *from Ellicots Mills down the Occoquan River:* The mouth of which is very little below Crane Island & not more than 20 miles from hence—of course far above Maryland point. The Frigate while here, and the now Gun boats under Lieut. Reid[1] have done the needful hereabouts as to stopping, searc[h]ing or examining the passing vessels; But I see no kind of difficulty in the Craft of Alexandria passing regularly down by this, & proceeding to & from Occoquan River or Ellicots Mills with Cargoes of Flour &ca. &ca.

I trouble You with this merely to suggest if it would not be better that the two Gun boats *here*, take a station some where about Crane Island & Occoquan River, thereby to better look after these Craft as well from Alexa. as *Ellicots* where there are considerable Flour Mills. I often see & have had converse with the Commandrs. of these Gunboats upon the subject, & it appears obvious to them.

I am sorry Your hurry from hence led to such hasty Intercourses between Us. The Secy. at War[2] & his small staff were very agreeable inmates with me here—The troops remaining after Genl: Armstrongs departure were not so regular as might be expected, & did me much mischief, but it is all for the best. The Artillery Company of Capt. Peters;[3] The Virga. 10th Regiment under Col. Pickens,[4] and Captn. Bookers[5] volunteer Richmd. Company are strong exceptions to my Complaints—They were perfectly regular & orderly doing me no wanton mischiefs whatever.

I am with gt. regard & esteem
Yr. Obt. Ser.
Thos. Digges

P.S. Permit me to intrude upon You so far as to ask if any thing is likely to be done with the application for a Commission in the Marine Corps—For a worthy Young Man my neighbour, *Jas. Edelen Jnr.*, who about 3 months ago made application through Mr. Cutts for Mr. Madison & myself as Recommendators of Him—I have not seen or heard from him lately but understand He is volunteering His services with our Militia near Annapolis.

NA: Record Group 45, Early Naval Records—Miscellaneous Received by the Secretary of the Navy.

[1] No lieutenant with this name appears in the naval registers, but there is a George C. Read (or Reed) who does: a lieutenant since 1810, he rose to rear admiral before his death in 1862.

[2] Gen. John Armstrong (1758–1843), who had been instrumental in stirring up a mutiny among Continental officers during 1783, had become Dearborn's successor in Jan. after others had declined the office.

[3] George P. Peters (d. 1819), about to become major assistant inspector general and, by late Feb., captain of the Fourth Infantry.

[4] Andrew Pickens, of South Carolina, a lieutenant in the Tenth Infantry.

⁵Possibly Daniel Booker, a Virginian, listed in the historical register as a second lieutenant.

To John Armstrong

Warburton (near *Piscaty.*) Mar: 23d 1814

DEAR SIR.

In complyance with Your request to know my terms for selling to The U.S. the ridge westward of The Octagon battery including mostly all the slope or ravine *southward* down nearly to my meadow Fence, so as to include also the Octagon and about *20 yards Eastward* thereof (which Colo. Wadsworth¹ said was necessary for insuring a waggon road from thence to the lower stone North boundary of the Fort Lott) and to proceed thence to the other lower boundary neares[t] to Mount Vernon—thence under the Hill & nearly along the river course so as no way to interupt or injure the Fisherys until it passes south of the pitch of the high clift and touches or cross's the line of my meadow fence, & so on that line &ca. &ca.

These Sir are the outlines of what is expressd & wanted by Colo. Wadsworth.

On going round these lines, & taking a casual review thereof yesterday, I am of opinion they will contain about four times as many acres as the Fort lot within them (which is 3 acres 127 pers:) and of course will be highly estimated; But *I* am in no ways an extravagant *Exactor,*

It is essential, before doing any thing conclusive, That an accurate Surveyor comes *here:* Or at least such a person as Capt. Jas. Kearney² Your assist. Topographical Engineer, (who, I think, once sketchd this Hill promontary for You while in my house) And I would recommend His comeing forthwith hither bringing his impliments &ca.—I keep here a Survyors Compass Chain &ca., and I guess *He* can do the business in one day: And from His Sketch I can form a more satisfactory & accurate estimate.

I inclose Cap. Kearney an open letter of request to ride down here, & You will use it or not as You seem [see] fit; But at any rate to inform me *by fryday evenings post to Piscataway* whether He comes or not, as after tuesday night my business urges me to *our County Court* settings at Upper Marlbro.

With great respect & every regard
Yrs. &ca. &ca.
Thos. Digges

NA: Record Group 107, Letters Received by the Secretary of War, Registered Series, 1801–1860 (Microfilm M221, Roll 52), D-212.

[1] Col. Decius Wadsworth of the U.S. Engineers was commissary general of ordnance.
[2] Kearney (d. 1862), Irish-born, had achieved his rank in Apr. 1813 and rose to lieutenant colonel in 1838.

To John Armstrong

Washington: 9 April 1814

DEAR SIR

Captain Kearney will hand this to You together with His Survey & plat of The five Acres & 56 perches wanted by the Government in addition to what they hold in The Fort Lot of 3 acres 127 pers. sold in 1808 for $6000. It is nearly, as guessd it, double to what is contain'd in The Fort Line; and I ask somewhat more than its double price (Vizt. $13,000 Dolls.) for reasons that these additional lines will exclude & loose me (from the nature of The Ground) the two passages from the River shore over the ridge to an adjacent meadow and a fishing Landing, as well also as thier closely pinchng the high public road leading down to The Wharf and other Fishing Landings &ca. &ca.

If You like the bargain I will have a rough sketchd Deed made out from the original one on the file of your office to be submitted to The Attory. General[1] for Inspection & approbation, and the works may commence forthwith. I am obligd to travel homewards but will again be up on Monday if my Health & weather will permit.

I am with great esteem and Regard Yours
Thos. Digges

NA: Record Group 107, Letters Received by the Secretary of War, Registered Series, 1801–1860 (Microfilm M221, Roll 52), D-218.

¹ Richard Rush (1780–1859), son of Dr. Benjamin Rush and former comptroller of the treasury, had become Madison's attorney general in Feb. 1814.

To John Armstrong

McLoads Hotel [Washington] 14 Ap. 1814

Mr. Digges' Compliments & best regards to General Armstrong— He left with Capt. Kearney the 2d Int. a note for Genl: Armstrong together with a Sketchd Deed & the Survey &ca. of the lot of ground wanted at the Fort: And He solicits information thereupon, if convenient, by noon to day—He Mr. D. being more than usually wanted at home from leaving ⟨His⟩ house clear of any white assistant whatever and being in the hurry & bustle of the Fishery commencement (the glut being up)—And the obligation too which He is under to attend the rise of our Marboro. Court *where* our Republican party have an appointed meeting for Electioneering & political purposes.

Mr. D. thinks of going thence to Annapolis if He can accomplish it.

[Addressed:] For The Honble./The Secretary at War/&ca. &ca.

NA: Record Group 107, Letters Received by the Secretary of War, Registered Series, 1801–1860 (Microfilm M221, Roll 61), D-3.

To John Armstrong

Ft. Warburton Apr. 18 1814.

Dear Sir.

I have been in bed for several days from a throw from a horse when in the City, but I have hopes to be there on wednesdy. I have just been informd, 'though indirectly through Mr. Parker¹ (whom I submitted a Sketchd Deed for Your observation, & which I wish a return of as there is a slight mistake in one of its courses) That "my proposition from its unreasonable amount was inadmissable["]; And I am sorry for it although not from any impulse as to *self interest*: Some Gentlemen of high standing & judgement around the premises, and well knowing its evils in perpetuity, have rated it higher. I feel, as I ever have done, a proness to aid & assist The Executive Government in any measures for its defence and defeat of its now primary Enemy; And will concede to any reasonable proposition. Let me have Your, or Thier, sentiments upon the matter.

The original Lot of a supposd 3 acres, was valued by five Gentlemen chosen by the War office at $2000 per acre or $6000 with several conditions and obligations (*not one* of *which has been complied with*)—such as keeping up the Wharf for ten years, & now at the end of six years is unfit to land Cannon or any heavy article upon;—the making under drains from the Fort ditches, the want of which has much injurd my fishing shores by washing away the grass surface and covering with mud a clean gravel shore;—By trespass upon me without the lines of the Fort lot by digging ditches at its entry side, as well as building upon me the whole Bakehouse and ⅞ths of the Octagon stockade battery; and sundry rejected accounts not worth troubling You about. I therefore have only to remark that the price askd by me for the lot measurd off by Colo. Wadsworth & Capt. Kearney (which is intrinsically worth much more in point of acres & in position) of *about* 5¾ acres, is not, (all circumstances taken in view) for but a shade more than double the original lot of 3 acres which was sold for 6000$ an extravagant demand. But be it what it may it will never alter the regard & esteem with which I am

       Yours &ca. &ca.
       Thos. Digges

The Honble. The Secy at War

[Enclosure]

The Lines, as first proposd For addition to the Fort, nearly along the tide mark including the Bluff or Clift and lower down the meadow

3 MAY 1814   553

deep ravine back of the Octagon, would have taken in more than *six* acres—and of course been of higher value.

The Lot as now measurd & platted by Colo. Wadsworth and Capt. Kearney contains Acres 5 & 56 perches. The original lot sold to Government for *$6000*: or 2000$ per acre—contains Acs. *3 & 127* perches making the whole to The U.S. Acres 9—23 ps.

As 3 as.—127 ps. is to $6000
so is 5—   56   to $8461 $^{28}/_{100}$ $

N. B. The first Lot now belonging to The U.S. was valued by five Commissioners nominated by The War Officed Vizt. Genl: Bowie, Robert Brent, General Mason, Colo. Cooke & Martial D. C. Brent:[2] who fixd its value at 2000$ per acre or $6000—

As the addition of 5 As. & 56 pers. is of more value & intrinsic worth T. Digges thinks himself justified by askiing for it *the same price per acre* for which the first Lot was sold.

21 Apr. 1814

NA: Record Group 107, Letters Received by the Secretary of War, Registered Series, 1801–1860 (Microfilm M221, Roll 52), D-224. The document, dated April 21, 1814, was filed with Digges's letter of April 18 and apparently accompanied it.

[1] Possibly William Parker, a clerk in the auditor's office of the Treasury Department.
[2] See Digges to Dearborn, Mar. 21, 1808.

To John Armstrong

Warburton 3d May 1814

DEAR SIR

The Fort Boat (going up for supplys) affords me an oppertunity of getting this to You.

I should have been in the City but have yet a finish to put to my Fisherys but hope to see You in a few days.

I am necessiated, as an agent in the Business, to go soon by Coach to Norfolk—There to dispose of & place their proceeds in the Bank of some property in & about Norfolk mortgagd by Gilbert Robinson—Wheeler & Co. &ca. which must take me some days.

I shall naturally wish for a peep at & to inform myself about the invading Enemy at Lynhaven bay[1] &ca: and if You or any of Your Colleagues wish for any minute enquirys about them, or can point out any hint in which my review may be servicable I will cheerfully do it. I shall take the Alexa. packet to Potok. Creek & thence go in the Stage via Petersburg &ca.

>with great regard & esteem
>Yrs. &ca. &
>Thos. Digges

NA: Record Group 107, Letters Received by the Secretary of War, Registered Series, 1801–1860 (Microfilm M221, Roll 52), D-228.

[1] An arm of the Chesapeake, at its entrance in Virginia.

To John Armstrong

July 2d. 1814.

The Honble. The Secy. at War
DEAR SIR:

Our propos'd arrangement having faild for an additional limit to the Fort Warburton original lot of 3 acs. 126 pers., which I had supposd would be taken at the same price per acre & thereby have quieted my legal and just claims on the Government for trespass's on my soil & non fulfillment of agreements (as itemd below), induces me to request Your aid in getting Captn. Kearney the assistt. Tl. Engineer or Mr. King[1] the City Surveyor to go down and ascertain those encroachments &ca. &ca. on which I have every right to seek remuneration: And this will be more quietly and correctly done by either of those Gentlemen than my employing our County Surveyor. I think Capt. Kearney coud easily do it in one days visit.

I have before stated to Yourself and Predecessors in office, That a part of the front Ditch at the gate entry; The whole of the Bakehouse; and about ⅞ths of the Stockade Fort is upon my land out of the limits which the Government had valued & bought. The water battery also (which is a considerable inconvenience & obstruction to The Fishery), nor are any of the articles of agreement made with Genl. Dearborn comply'd with respecting under drains; slopeing the new road; keeping the *Wharf* in complete repair for ten years *though not now capaple to recieve cannon upon*; &ca. But these last are minor considerations & were formd for mutual convenience. An *essential* one to be done, after getting such a survey as is above requested, is getting a new Deed from me for the original Fort Lot, The Government Title to which being legally viciated *from a neglect in non recording*.—I had securd this title in my last Deed, as expressd in my letter covering that deed and yet in the Office; And I remain with a full belief that my Successor to the property will not be found hereafter so temperate in Sales of Soil or in good wishes to The Rulers of our Country as I have ever been & wish to be. I remain with great regard & esteem

Yours &ca. &ca.
Thos. Digges

I mean to be off to my harvest as soon as a bad sore throat will admit, and for the easier convenience will get Capt. Kearney to drop this with You He knowing the whole as to the Land lines &ca.

NA: Record Group 107, Letters Received by the Secretary of War, Registered Series, 1801–1860 (Microfilm M221, Roll 61), D-13.

[1] Robert King, Jr., whose father had worked in the surveying department and whose brother Nicholas had been the city official surveyor from 1803 to his death in 1812, had succeeded to Nicholas's position in 1813.

To John Armstrong

Warburton 22 July 1814

Dear Sir

By Lieut. Edwards[1] going in the morning to the War Office I have an oppertunity of sending this, and to state that Capn. Kearney who came hither yesterday afternoon and having soon finishd the work of marking out the encrochments upon my soil, & having a strong desire to take Nottingham & Barneys flotilla[2] in his detour back to City I mounted him on a hack for this purpose & he went off with his sur[v]ey notes &ca. this morning and is to soon furnish me with his result—all in good time. He first run the encroa[c]hment line from the Octagon Stockade (which is about ⅝ths or more in upon me at the door side) down to the north boundary stone of the original sold Lot making it a sharp angle below: And that line leaving the whole Bakehouse & a part of the Ditch at the fort Gate in upon me, I inducd Him to sketch another line thereby to leave a space sufficient for Cartage to turn at the Octagon Door,—this last to be taken or not, but it appears *essential*. The whole of these will not include more than three quarters of an acre or but very little more. As yet however it is but guess work, as He is hereafter to make his plat & measurement. He will likely be with You tomorrow or sundy. forenoon & of course give You the actual news from the Patuxent quarter, for the lies & falsities dayly put forth *here* (altho not more than 17 miles distant) are too vague for repetition.

The lye-order of the day is now from the St. Marys & Potok. River Quarter of which we hereabouts can get nothing certain but through Mr. Swann's[3] dayly report via the Post office in Washington; But I fear 'though I guess the invaders *there* to be only a division from the up-bay Squadron & not any recently arrivd force, is of itself bad enough. It has inducd some alarmists to move upwards effects & Negroes, and even in sight of me a little downwards some valuables, as I hear, have been movd into the interior Vizt. from Mr. Bonds, the Marshalls, &ca.[4]

They want WATER to a certainty, as well as Meats, and I suppose from the width of the River they can rather too uninterruptedly get up to Occoquan River & to Crane Island the last about 15 miles from hence & in full view of *Mount Vernon* for which I understand there is also some alarm where their barges could easily get in a nights tide. It is only their smaller vessels & capturd craft will likely come up that far for water, and I entertain no more fears than I did last July for this station.—There is I hear a want of Grape & Canister Cartrage in the Fort, but this is best known to the Department.

22 JULY 1814   557

The Commandt. Lieut. Edwards (who seems an active & dilligent Officer[)] will likely see You if he leaves this at the office. I shall not desert my Post.

I have (through Mr. Cutts for Mr. Madisons information) given some Bermuda information as to the there talkd of plans of the Enemy & their force in Ships & troops &ca.[5]—It comes from one who cannot be named but on whom I can rely—a professional man (with his family residing in sight of this) whose health obligd him to go to Bermuda 3 years ago, and from his practice, betterd by his move, & living much with the Naval & Military Gentlemen has favourable oppertunitys of knowing more than he would venture to write.—His intention is to get a passage out in some of their Men of War & get through a manoeuvre on shore & be speedily with his family—I am looking out for him but as yet no tidings.—If I get any You shall of course have it by express.

I have thought & thought much, about my late proposition for the requird additional acres to the Fort lot; And think it no ways unreasonable at *the rate per acre* for *which the first lot was Sold*: I am confident it will not be had so low from my Heirs, and it seems an essential.—I mean to charge the same price for the now small encroachments: *all of which*, together with sundry other just & old claims I have upon the Fort: I meant to throw into the bargain as deeded to The President on the 6th ultio. I mean by just claims as follow the non-fulfillment of any of the agreed upon as to under drains, the wharf kept in good repair for ten years—my Sodding account for all the Slopes within the Fort at which work I had a horse Cart & driver for 3 weeks to haul the sods from chosen spots on the farm, my negro Gardener & another prime hand for a longer space pegging the sods up, and got my charge 160 odd Dolls. insultingly markd *inadmissable*—also for the Surveys on Land & the various channel depths & bearings done by Colo. Gilpin of Alexa. by Mr. Jeffersons order—the account also markd inadmissable altho renderd by me under affidavit & the vouchers for what I had paid.—&ca. &ca. &ca.—but of this enough—

When I applyd for the 1600$ in part (the Ballance to remain) I was pushd for it by Obers & another failure in Geo. town—I cared not how long the remainder rested with Government. So I think I expressd in my letter to You leaving the Deed &ca. in Office.

I beg pardon for intruding so long upon Your time & numberless calls by Letter & with hopes that all will soon go smoother remain with great regard & esteem

Yr. Obt. Thos. Digges

[Addressed:] The Honble./The Secretary at War/*private*

NA: Record Group 107, Letters Received by the Secretary of War, Registered Series, 1801–1860 (Microfilm M221, Roll 61), D-21.

[1] James L. Edwards, a Virginian, was stationed at the fort as its commandant.
[2] Digges's syntax is curious. Commodore Barney was carrying out orders to keep his thirteen barges and a sloop in the Patuxent within reach of both Washington and Baltimore and had accordingly placed himself at Nottingham, a small village approximately forty miles from the capital.
[3] The Post Office had employed Thomas Swann, living in St. Mary's County, Md., to report British naval activity in the Chesapeake Bay area.
[4] The Bond family owned property near the mouth of the Piscataway; the Marshall family, whose seat was Marshall Hall, was established a little farther south on the Potomac, below and across from Mount Vernon.
[5] Bermuda was the center for Britain's naval operations along the Atlantic and Gulf coasts, whose direction had passed from Adm. Warren to Vice-Adm. Sir Alexander Cochrane (1758–1832) on Apr. 1.

To James Madison

The Madisons had had to flee Washington on August 24, shortly before the British had taken possession of it and set fire to the White House and other public buildings.

Warburton tuesday night Augt. 30 1814

MY DEAR GOOD SIR

In haste & almost fatigued to death I sit down to address a line to You while my nephew Dr. F[itzgerald][1] and a Gentleman, whom You know, are taking a mouthful of refreshment by one of whom You will I hope soon get this.

You can more easily immagine than I can describe my own troubles & vexations, and the deep anxieties I have felt for You & Mrs. M. since Wedy. last of the 24th Int. near the Capitol—since which I have heard not one *correct* account about You or the disasters of that fatal day. "Whatever is is right" a divine lesson & I hope will turn out for the best.

Mr. Loughborough[2] was the first account I got on Sundy. evening last about You, & his stay was but momentary as M. Manigaults[3] the bearer is likely now to be for He is determind to return forthwith. Mr. Loughborough will have dropt my Memorandum & detaild all proceedings up to that day respecting the unfortunate issue of the station here. I have been employd to day (altho the earth is rather too hot for walking upon within the walls) in taking a list of its ruind contents & which I will soon furnish.—Every thing within it is ruind save the two Columbiads of 52 lb. each—the rest are all useless as Cannon—The walls of The Fort & octagon stockades have not been touchd by a shot & seem as perfect as ever save in the ribband edge of the top brickwork thrown over by the explosion or burnt down by the grass dryd & yet hot fire of the sod.—Every voice I heard from the Fleet officers expressd great admiration of the well placd position for repelling water attack—exclaiming too that with 100 Artillerists or some of thier chosen crews they woud have destroyd in a very short space more than thier force of ships brought against it.

This force was as follows
The Seahorse 38 Gun frigate *Capt. Gordon*[4] Commodore
The Euryalus 36-------------- Cap. Napier
The Etna Bomb--------------- 2 mortars   } All Ship riggd
The Meteor do. --------------- do.   } but few Guns
The Devastation Do. -------- do. Cap. Alexander }
The Erebus a Rocket Ship
The Schooner Anna Maria of 4 Guns late a N. York Privateer

The Commandr. Lieut. Grey, & a Midshipman Mr. Dunkan (a relation to Dunkan Earl of Camperdown[5][)] who has spent part of the day with me. I am sorry to find through Him they are making severe exactions against The Citizens of Alexandria—She came down to near Swan point at 8 this morning & is station'd there to prove if anything is moving below, or arm'd men on the banks hereabouts for which He express'd some fears—I have hopes as well from the Commodores promise on Sunday as by a note of to day from Command'r Gray that my house & property will be secur'd; but I nevertheless fear they have an eye to The Negroes hereabouts as they pass down. This will not likely take place for two or three days—I have lost every thing between the Fort & River shore, & had the pleasure to hear & see dozens of Mortars. Rockets &ca. pass in direction very nearly over my house & some not far from my Well & within my front fields—but all this is nothing—a thunder bolt on Saty. before did me more mischief than all thier firein[g]. The fort has been neglected & shamefully abandond without any slur upon the officers. Dyson[6] I am sure did his duty & I have every reason to speak in high terms of Lieut. Edwards son to Mr. Edwards of the War Office.[7]

With sincere regard & Affection & with a hope to soon see You & Mrs. M. I remain Yrs.

Thos. Digges

LC: Madison Papers.

[1] William Attwood Fitzgerald, mentioned by Digges to Jefferson, Oct. 24, 1808, as a prospective medical student, had become a doctor.

[2] Nathan Loughborough (1772–1852), a Virginian resident in Washington for the past fourteen years and well known in financial and political circles, was serving as a lieutenant with numerous scouts at his command and functioning as a principal source of information for inhabitants of the outlying regions about the results of the British invasion of the city.

[3] Unidentified.

[4] Capt. James Alexander Gordon (1782–1869), senior officer in command of the squadron that forced its way up the Potomac to capture Alexandria. Whether Digges's list of ships is accurate is uncertain, for Adm. Cochrane in a letter to John Wilson Croker, Sept. 2, 1814, listed "Euryalus, Devastation, Ætna, Meteor, Manly, Erebus" (PRO: ADM 1/506, letter no. 267).

[5] Adm. Adam Duncan (1731–1804) had been created viscount of Camperdown in 1797 while winning a name for exploits as commander in chief in the North Sea.

[6] Capt. Samuel T. Dyson, the officer in charge of the garrison when the fort was evacuated on Aug. 27, had, instead of ordering the guns to be fired, ordered the fortifica-

tions to be blown up. He was tried before the General Court Martial and cashiered in Oct.

[7] James Lewis Edwards, after whom his son was named, was a clerk in the department.

To James Monroe

After the invasion of Washington, General Armstrong, widely blamed for the loss of the capital and other military failures, had resigned as secretary of war, and Monroe, at Madison's urging, had become acting secretary, while remaining at the head of the State Department.

Sundy. Eveng. 25 Sept. 1814

DEAR SIR

As I am about sending to The War Office a stated Account for what is due me for the surpluss trespass's upon my Soil as per The Account renderd by Captn. Kearney amounting to $751 : Dollrs. (extra for the space coverd by the lower or *Morris's* battery & for supplys to The Army horses &ca.), I here again fulfill Your request as to the progress of the works about The Fort Vizt.[:]

The Engineer Major, as usual, is ardently at it sundays not excepted[1]—Seems well pleasd at what He is about, but I am an utter stranger to Engineering Fortifications.

Andrew Bartle The W[h]arfinger & Bridge builder of Alexanda. (whom I mentiond to You as a fit and very industrious Artist) came hither with His apparatus & hand fryday last: has been actively busied & done considerably towards the repair of the Wharf:—has erected & will finish off on tuesday about one half of what is intended for a temporary plant Barrack for accomodation of all Labouring workmen Stone masons, Bricklayers Carpenters &ca. a quantity of materials ready here & the mansonry about to commence—This day though *Sunday* he has hired 26 or 28 additional men & fifty expected tomorrow. He has much too of large Timber to place down.

The Alexandria squad has diminishd since my last letter[(] although many are expected to join tomorrow) eight in number those who volunteerd for the weeks work ending last night.

The Fort Soldiers are working on as usual but shew signs of dislike at such labour & all is progressing well altho the last few days of rain is unpropitious for spadeing up earth. I think a week more will shew a very handsome begining—The Commissary Major Marsteller[2] aiding & pressing on the works.

       Yours with gt. regard & esteem
       Thos. Digges

I give You joy on the recently receivd news of the repeated advantages obtaind over The Invincible Anglo Canadian Army.[3] Ca ira—ca ira—

If You can without trouble pray give the bearer a few cast by news Papers.

NA: Record Group 107, Letters Received by the Secretary of War, Registered Series, 1801–1860 (Microfilm M221, Roll 61) D-44.

[1] Maj. L'Enfant had at Monroe's request, Sept. 8, begun to direct the reconstruction of the fortifications.
[2] Maj. Ferdinand Marsteller, descendant of a family that had moved from Lebanon, Pa., to Alexandria after the Revolution, was quartermaster general.
[3] At the battle of Plattsburg on Sept. 11 the American flotilla on Lake Champlain had forced the British ship *Confiance* to strike her colors, and the British land forces, informed of the naval defeat, had withdrawn, ending the last offensive planned for North America.

To James Monroe

       Warburton tuesdy. evening
       27 Sept./14

DEAR SIR

From an accident to my only negro Messenger, I could not send Him up, as I expected to do on yesterday morning, & in consequence my inclosd letter of *Sunday*[1] was delayd for want of conveyance; But I shall send my Messenger up with my account & claim early tomorrow.[2]

Major Marsteller now at his persuits among the various works going on in & about the Fort gives me an oppertunity to cover it with this to You and He can of course best explain the minutiæ of the transactions here.

I am pleasd to see the zeal & activity with which they are progressing. The platforms for battery below are going on, but not with so many digging hands as we were given to expect—The Engineer Major has had a feverish attack & headach for the last two days, but it diminishes not his ardor for he pushes out (though complaining & [in] fear of an ague) as usual. The Stone Masonry has been begun at the south point—Triangly fixing to get the dismantled Guns out of the old platform (which I fear will be a work of two full days at least) and the Soldiery, [(]though complaining of the task work) employd in taking down & clearing away the old south-round point of the Fort.— The Barrack for accomadation of all workers will be complete to night, & Mr. Bartle seems more than usually anxious in getting all forward—He seems to have as many hands as can well work for the present, & is well acquainted with the process of lifting up heavy articles by triangle or other purchases—some of the Guns are now in the way, & all but the two 52 pound Caronades are useless but for re-melting. Some additional men have just arrivd from Alexa. and they have plenty of material for actively working upon Vizt. Large & small Timber Trees, Stone, Brick Lime, scantling & plank &ca. &ca.

I remain as usual Yours
Thos. Digges

[Addressed:] The Honble./The Secretary at War/&ca.—/Washington/per favor/Major Marsteller

NA: Record Group 107, Letters Receivd by the Secretary of War, Registered Series, 1801–1860 (Microfilm M221, Roll 61), D-43.

[1] Digges to Monroe, Sept. 25, 1814. Monroe was now permanent secretary of war.
[2] Digges to Monroe, Sept. 28, 1814.

To James Monroe

[September 28, 1814]

The United States   Dr. To Thos. Digges
For Land in addition to Fort Warburton Lot

| 1814 Sepr. | To seventy six perches of Land for an addition to Fort Washington, an encroachment & trespass upon Warburton Manor, according to the orderd Survey made by Captn. J. Kearney & his plat & return made to The War Office: at the same rate per Acre which the original Lot of 3 acs. 127 pers. was purchasd at ---------------------------------- $ Errors Excepted   Warburton Sepr. 28h. 1814   Thos. Digges | 751–Dolls. |

NA: Record Group 107, Letters Received by the Secretary of War, Registered Series, 1801–1860 (Microfilm M221, Roll 61), D-43.

To James Monroe

Warburton frydy. morning
[September 30, 1814]

DEAR SIR

I very reluctantly intrude upon You in Your now moments of fatigue & disquiet.

My ignoramus black messenger returnd from the City wedy. night saying "an answer to my Letter was not necessary". I trouble You for an explanation.

All is progressing well about the Fort. The dismantled cannon was I believe got over its wall last evening save the two 52 pounders not necessary to move out of it.

Yrs. with great Esteem & regard
Thos. Digges

NA: Record Group 107, Letters Received by the Secretary of War, Registered Series, 1801–1860 (Microfilm M221, Roll 61), D-43.

To James Monroe

Ft. Warburton Feby. 27. 1815

DEAR SIR

I cannot (from dire necessity) longer refrain from asking of You my good Sir some advances towards my claim upon The Government: And to remind You (as I have frequently done to Your two last Predecessors in office) "that the Government Title in the originally sold Fort Lott of 3 acres 127 perchs., is *defective*, from a neglect in The War office of *not legally recording my Deed of it*, and with repeated assurances too that I have ever been ready to renew it." The cause of the first delay thereto, arose from the extraordinary mistake in its builder in fixing the Block-house battery full ⅝ths of it in upon my line; which line also went through the front gate ditch, and took in the whole of a well built Bakehouse.

Upon a second arrangement with Secretary Armstrong, it was agreed that a sharp angular addition should be measurd off from the begining No.west boundary so as to include the Octagon Block house (giving room for a waggon turn at its door) on my Land; and for which I was to be paid at the rate per acre as the Fort lot had been originally valued at by the Agents chosen by General Dearborne for its valuation.

The whole ground was explain to & viewd by General Armstrong while an inmate here in Augt. 1813; its terms afterwards agreed to; Captain Kearney Your Topographical Engineer, surveyd and markd the angular additional lines purchasd (amounting to 76 perches and its estimate $750—and a fraction); and His plott & Survey was deposited in the War Office; But the postponement of payment then, was from a contemplation of adding more acres to this scite of defence:—And early in the last spring, the contemplated addition was accurately designated; a Survey & platt thereof by Colonel Wadsworth & Capt. Kearney was renderd to the office; and our agreement concluded; But from the irruptions of the Enemy its finali was suspended.

There should, or ought to be (for I am aged, & You will not find my Successor so lenient and holding up so high as I do the worth & estimation of the Administration) forthwith perfected a *new Deed for the original Fort Lot of 3 acres 127 pers: together with the surveyd tresspass or surplussage of 76 perches*, distinct from the new contemplated large purchase (of which there is also a platt & survey in the Office) as now working on by the Engineer Majr. Le Enfant:—I say *seperate* or *distinct* deed, for reason that notwithstanding my first *for the Lot and its surplussage* would be ample as to legal Title, it would now require a second person joind with me (Vizt. my Nephew Dudley Digges to whom I have lately made a deed of Gift of this Estate after my demise)[1] to give a proper, perfect & legal Title to The United States *of what is to be added to the old Fort lot & its surplussage*. What I now solicit, I trust will not be viewd as any way unreasonable. I want at present a warrant for $750— so long my due on the Sale of Soil so tresspassd upon, And I can assure You Sir it will not cover the total of demands & calls upon me. Hereafter, and as soon as The Major Engineers plans & lines may be limited (which I trust & hope cannot be but triflingly more than the designated plott & Survey of Colo. Wadsworth and Capt. Kearney) You shall have a proper & satisfactory Deed for it submitted to The Attorney General—To Whom, to Yourself, to Mr. President, and all the worthys in our late glorious drama of happy and honourable Peace be all gratitude and Praise.

                                        Yrs. with grt. truth
                                        Thos. Digges

The Honble. James Monroe
    Secy. at War &ca.

NA: Record Group 107, Letters Received by the Secretary of War, Registered Series, 1801–1860 (Microfilm M221, Roll 61), D-118.

¹William Dudley Digges had Jan. 21, 1815, filed a statement with the War Department, care of George Graham, chief clerk, asserting his title (NA: Record Group 107, Letters Received by the Secretary of War, Registered Series, 1801–1860 [Microfilm M221, Roll 61], D-157): "The original plat of Fort Washington contains three acres and a quarter. The price or damages awarded by the Commissioners appointed by the Secretary of War, was Six thousand dollars, something less than two thousand dollars per acre. It was expressly understood among the Commissioners, that if the United States should at any future period wish to extend or add to this plat, they were to pay for such addition at the price per acre given for the original scite of the Fort. The [*hole*] ⟨title⟩ of the Warburton is vested in me, and without my concurrence no legal title can be given by Thomas A. Digges except for the period of his own life.
William Dudley Digges"
Dudley's interest was qualified by a life estate in Warburton that Digges had given his sister Jane Fitzgerald on Dec. 24, 1811 (MdHR: Prince George's County, Land Records, JRM 15, fol. 58–61; NA: William Dudley Digges to [⟨George Graham⟩], Sept. 3, 1815 [NA: Record Group 107, Letters Received by the Secretary of War, Registered Series, 1801–1860 (Microfilm M221, Roll 61), D-159]).

To George Graham

Ft. Warburton Landing 24 Ju[ne]/15

DEAR SIR

While waiting in the Clerks quarters for the approach of the steamboat to take on board Capt. Reid,¹ (going on furlough to Philaa. for better surgical aid or operation in a critical case) I take an oppertunity of recommending Him as a very worthy Man as well as a vigilent & good Officer to Your notice & civility—He urges on to Philaa. & hopes for a return to this station in 4 or 5 weeks. I shall trouble Your Office in a day or two with my Accounts for Smithswork, Cartage & Labour hire &ca. from 1st Jany. up to June 1st which I have been backward in heretofore sending in from knowing the push & run upon Your Office as well in Army disbanding measures & the press upon the treasury: But principally delayd by me on account of want of due signiatures from a too frequent remove of Clerks, overseers of the works &ca. &ca.—after Capt. Eveleths death & quitting this early in March, it was for a long time doubtful who was the Clerk —at times none—then a wish in Mr. Bartle to put in his Son (a small tho clever little boy)—then a seemingly very proper one Mr. W. Harper of Alexa. (brother to the late Surgeon of the Station Docr. Harper) with whom, probably from over exactness as to measurements of Cargos of falls Stone & supplys too lumpingly thrown in to the Government works) and which has often requird all the watchfulness, vigilence & strict integrity to The Engineer to counteract) producd dissentions & uneasiness between the contractor for the works & the new & yet Clerk Mr. W. Harper—You know all or more than I do of the matters yet at issue between the Commissary paymaster and the contractor whose accounts are so varient as to the causes of failure in trifling payments to Labourers & Workmen in want of their due—that it was impossible to listen to or deside which was in fault, The War office having constantly & I believe regularly paid every well authenticated demand upon it—money has stuck to the fingers somewhere, but *where* I know not and You will mind that my communications are to be *entre nous.*

There are mano[e]uvres now to displace & get in a more convenient or bending *Clerk* than Mr. W. Harper whose rectitude I have in some instances observd & to be a very faithful one to the station, and it is unknown & in justice to Him I mention this to You or those whom it may more immediately concern.

With great respect & best wishes
I remain Yr. Obt.
Thos. Digges

[Addressed:] For Mr. Wm. Grahame Esqr./Departmt. of War/Washington/per favor/Cap. Jas. Reid

NA: Record Group 107, Letters Received by the Secretary of War, Registered Series, 1801–1860 (Microfilm M221, Roll 61), C-177 [D-177].

---

[1] James Reid was the fort commander.

To George Graham

Ft. Warbn. Augt. 10th 1815

DEAR SIR

Among the number & increasing mischiefs to me and particularly to my Farm, the frequent calls upon me for *Fire wood for the Garrison* is not the least and there is a continuation ever since last fall, and at times too when (from the Ice & severity of the weather) it was impossible to give a due & regular supply: *six, eight* & nine Dollrs. would have been cheerfully given for it at *times* when from sleets & snow it could not be hauld. I have at times & by the year supplyd it for four $s and never chargd more than 5$ for its delivery at the Fort; But I have been obligd to give up the supply and must abandon it—although in exigencies which have frequently happend lately, I feed the station with it by cords or two at a time for 5$, and it now seems essential that some regular plan is persued to yeild the supply which will at least be six Cords per week; or *better* for a winter stock to be laid in now to be had likely as low as 4½$ instead of the unmerciful demands for it in freezing weather of 7 to 8$ per cord—it was once at ten last winter.

I had some conversation with Mr. W. Harper about it yesterday supposing he was yet the Clerk (& a very proper one he seems to have been) but he tells me he quits this to day as his functions cease. A. Bartles supply of wood suddenly ceasd about a month ago, as well as all other works under His contracts here. All is a dead inactive scene ever since, as far as regards the public opperations at the Station & from appearances the Government is dayly injurd thereby—more especially as to the *wharf*, which being only partially & not one fifth part *filled in* is on every full tide discharging its earth & ruining the adjoining depths of the water extra of the evils done me by the Loads upon loads of blocks of Aquia Stone, falls Stones, & logs &ca. dropt fully as far out as halftide & low-water marks. The loss of my Rents for the present & comeing next years fishery (for they are under Lease till June 1816) are trifles comparatively to the probable ruin in future of these valuable fisherys—an encreasing property of above 1000$s per year for the Fishery only. But to the *wood* business—I have orderd some printed handbills to be fixd up at the Ferrys in Alexa., & below this profering to recieve proposals for a Contract for fire wood supply to the Garrison, to be deliverd Corded upon the Warburton wharf or above tide water mark for at least six Cords per month the finders to be paid monthly, altho it had better come in a large quantity, & *I* could contrive to see the boat men so paid (for they are averse to taking & seek payment of treasury warrants). Vizt. suppose for every six Cord Deliverd 30$s—which I could add to my accounts when sent into office for payment. There can be no harm whatever in hearing what the woodsetters will contract for whether 5$ or under per Cord and I will inform You when ever any profer is made. It is impossible for me to give the Garrison supply of wood, & most assuredly their easiest mode of getting it is by boats. Besides my fallow ploughings and seeding time, I have engagd to supply 200 Cord of mixd, down, & all sorts of fuel fit for brick-kiln deliverd where there are already above a million of Brick made & stackd & I shall fall short of my supply. My Contract for this was with Bartle & Taylor on which not a cent has been paid tho I was to have had 1000$ for Earth &ca. in advance. By the general break up, & distress among the Brick makers &ca. &ca. they have all some days back returnd to their business in Alexa. & only two as protecting watchmen are there left. I should be glad to know how it will all end & if likely that any public works are likely to commence hereabouts again. Pray drop me a line in reply directing Your Letter via *Pisy. [Piscataway] P. Office.* I am not in good health & have much to do or I would go to the City—and without any second assistant in my house cannot at present leave it. It would be a great obligation if You could send me a few cast by *English* news papers.

Yours with gt. regard & best wishes
Thos. Digges

My weekly regular post day to Pisy. is *Saty.* If you drop me a line in the City P. Office *frydy. evening* I shall get it by 10 oCk. *Saty.*

[at the bottom of a blank page]
Out of my $2000 treasury warrant payment end of May last I profered Dudley the aid of some of it say half—I have got as yet &

that with difficulty only 250$ lately out of its proceeds though much wanting the residue. He seems to be careless of answering Letters, or as to his outgoings, and but an indifferent manager of his own affairs, for he ought to be down *here* looking after Bartle making rather too free in his adjoining to me woods. In particular I want of him the sketchd *outline* of our Deed to Government for at least so much as includes *Kearneys Survey*, (for I hear nothing of late as to The Engineers return). It ought to progress. This is all *entre nous* & tear this off Your Letter as soon as read.

[Addressed:] Piscataway Md./10 Augst./For George Grahame Esqr./War Office Dept./Washington City

NA: Record Group 107, Letters Received by the Secretary of War, Registered Series, 1801–1860 (Microfilm M221, Roll 61), D-153.

To John Carroll

Ft. Warburton Augt. 18th 1815

DEAR & MUCH RESPECTED SIR

Our Fort Surgeon Docr. o'Connor, and His good little wife, being on the very point of packing up their all for Baltimo. (being succeeded by another Philaa. bird Dr. Tremble[1]) suggests to me the writing to You by so favourable an oppertunity:—an Effort rather a duty which I have long wishd to perform, and indeed had often *schem'd* a better substitute by personally paying my respects; But Sir necessity, dire necessity for remaining at home & *at my post* during the last two years irruptions by a vandal Enemy, has prevented it. I am still *hopeing* for that gratification by having, in trust, some London Bill Exchange business to transact in Baltio., where I hear six & 7 pr. Ct. can be obtaind above their par of Exchange at the short dates I am empowerd to draw for. The Doctor has done very well in this his station of Surgeon, being strictly sober, attentively regular, and more clever in His profession &ca. than I at first supposd.—I am the more His friend from being the only one of the knott *against the measure* (of which my *nephew Doctor*[2] playd more than a second fiddle) in so shamefully & abominably abandoning & blowing up the old Fort! and of which measure I knew not a tittle 'till after they had Spiked up the whole of the cannon!!

A new Fort is progressing and but slowly advancing since Octo. last—approvd of by judges—and under direction of a finishd & I believe able Engineer LeEnfant—upon additional ground & heights of six to seven acres to the old 3¼ acre Lot; But every thing has been thrown back, & at present not a single workman or artist since the 7th July, where & a little time before some 150. to 200 & more hands had been in constant employ: All *owing* to the depredating, extortions, and unfair handlings of public money by The Deputy Commissary Paymaster, the contractor for the Buildings and Supplyers of materials—who had made secret partnerships to plunder the Public and even went to forgeries of names on Receipts given upon exaggerated supplys of materials for the works, Carts hire, Labour &ca., and there is likely to be a defecit to the Treasury of some 12 to $15,000—. Majr. LeEnfant is still a guest with me, & has ever shewn himself *here* as a faithful agent to his Employers and an inflexibly honest upright Man —*slow* & sure in his Surveys but with too strong appetites to extend the works beyond the prudent survey for our Country. I have kept him however within the ravine Sloped road down to my fishing Shores.

The Doctor can give You a full account—

I have had for years and yet have dayly heart-achs consequent to this too close Military station. It has alterd, more than You can concieve, the rural comforts, and to age & thoughtfulness, readings, &ca.&ca., those delights which quiet retirement alone can give. In the *commence* or 1st Instance, with a Family *here*, who rejected & slighted the well-meaning though plain & worthy neighbours, *for Town visitants*, an idle ride-about youth, military spriggs of spittle with little more in their heads than Tobacco smoke Grog drinkings & conversants only upon disputed politics, my house or Company was seldom *my own*, & I had to *groan* for a year or two: It was but a cake house for *the idle*, and the expences of it encreasd with my inability to serve as I wishd (*though I did it in full share & little thanks*) my *wanting* & properly conducted Relatives. My 2dly troubles during about two years progression, I was sorely afflicted with two or three idle lounging relatives, whose rides out were troublesome and whose only bent (save at mealtimes) was up & down to The Fort often to late night hours: The Elder, (from whom I have not only receivd bad treatment but personal insult) was in my perview long ago a free *drinker* & of late become a confirmed Sot. The Second (in whom however I never discoverd those propensities) but who had quitted only a second rate station for phisical advantages, turning his back on a 2000$ per year incomeing, absented from it suddenly (I believe by some loss's in gameing) and was for *a year & a half*! an Idler here & constant visitor twice or thrice a day up & down to the Fort—doing nothing whatever for himself!! his mother & sister most of the time acquiesant lookers on. The third, & who once I thought was the only industrious one, I had arranged every thing & promisd to free Him to a studency of Law (at that time his own choice) under *Mr. Morsell of Geo.town* (F. Key having wrote to me that his office was over full) and to board him for two years with *Mr. Fenwick* near the College, because he could there attain the knowlege of practical Surveying, and by the College Teachers get the Spanish & French Languages—It was finally *rejected*, and by a part of the Family too, on account of Morsell (now a judge) NOT BEING A GENTLEMAN!! He subsequently attempted Law reading in Alexa. & has become a Captain in the Militia! They are all three now with my Sister & neice in Bladensburgh trying by another *tug at the Yoke* to get the Doctor restord or reinstated in his former beneficial practice.—I have my fears there will be a want of *Industry* added to prudence.[3]

Your namesakes have conducted themselves better; but both have yet *to tug at the yoke*. The "hopes of the Family" as to name & consequence, although You Sir have heretofore expressd to me his having "sown his wild oats & got domesticated" *I fear has not yet reap'd those wild Oats*. Besides imprudencies & extravagancies, He is not enough *at home* to be happy:—The causes however I know not & I am afraid to enquire—I have a short time back (fearing it might get into *worse hands & sooner get to the hammer,[)]* perfected to Dudley[4] *& his heirs* a deed of Gift for above 800 Acres of this point of the warburton estate all within a certain line from Swan Creek to Piscaty. Creek.—I did it to this direct Heir and *"hopes of the Family,"* although his Fathers estate has been long & is yet owing me £1050–Sterg. with some 16 or 18 Years Interest (a very heavy sum & which I have frequently wanted) and it remains to be proven *what good* He will do therewith—I have my doubts—Et spes non fracta: It is impossible to put old heads on young shoulders. Of His negligence & inattention (*entre nous*) to his own affairs I have had a few unpleasant proofs lately—i.e. although warn'd repeatedly in good time, he did not attend or defend the survey of a 7 or 8 acres of *Vacancy* in the *first* instance taken from his estate near this by Mr. D. Brents[5] letting a Land Warrant expire; & secondly carryd into effectual loss on mondy. the 14 inst. by his own non attendance after my notification by special messenger the fryday before, & by a duplicate letter of same day trusted to Lieut. Brent[6]— he has also for months past let an unprincipled Timber getter, Bartle, ravage unmolested his woods adjoining me—even very recently by cutting 8 trees on the very Vacancy a full cause for Lawsuit & damage.

In a third case & most afflictingly at this period to me (for I have been days past without a second Dollar, much to purchase, & with an over-filld house) He withholds a 750$s. ballance due me Vizt. about the end of May I obtaind with great difficulty a *two thousand Dolls.* War-Office warrant in part of Acres sold in addition to the old Fort, and being confind to my room I empowerd Dudley to recieve & apply it for shares in the Patriotic bank—offering him a part thereof even unto an half!—with much difficulty I got about a month back 250$! but a *mite* as to my wants & it went the same day through my hands: The remainder 750 is yet *in nubibus*, & I just now hear from his home he is *out on a frolic*, altho I have a man waiting there to see him for the last three nights & not to quit without his answer—che sara sara.

It is high time on this overleaf sheet to proceed to what I at first only intended to write upon; Especially too as eer this, Your patience will be a little *worn* by its perusal. The Doctor & Dame o'Connor packing up (perhaps to be off today) suggested to me the sending You The Print from Sir Joshua Reynolds's fam'd picture of *Faith*, given me by an old acquaintance, Boydell, to-gether with HOPE & CHARITY its companions, distinguishd[l]y admir at that period as chef d'Ouvres of Reynolds pinxt., Bartilozi, & others Engravers to the London Picture Gallery of Alderman Boydell & Son who was then a pupil of Bartilozi & a finishd *drawer*.[7]—Pray accept it as a keep-sake from me: for those sort "of things" are only lookd on *here* and soon disregard'd as much as the pencil'd profiles of family miss's taken at half a crown a head and admird as much for their guilt frames as for their likeness's! —Our Country is naturally & will be for centuries (I hope) behind hand with The Louvre of Paris. I very well remember your too appropriate Wit while getting at the history of this print (then over my Side board) i.e. of its not being *framed* in time, & thereby savd from the fate *of loss at Sea* of the Alexa. Ship in 1798 on which I lost above £800- worth of valuable moveables never since heard of—"But however Sir (sayd You) I am very well pleasd to find You have retaind Your *Faith*":—I have done it, my good & valuable friend, fully I think as much so, 'tho not perhaps in every minutiae, as any of my relative exuberant deciples of Gortina: And I continue to affirm Crusi dum spiro fide. And why not? for few very few have experiencd or been more benignly favourd by Our Omnipotent Ruler!—I am now Sir in my 74 year of age, and for a continued half century of that time never had to lay by one hour, to my recollection, from bodily pain or sickness; I continue my temperate habits of riseing at daylight as I have done for many years; detesting night settings up; useing the aid of body Servants less than any other intimate; making my own bed or rather hard-mattrass; Shaving myself at any hour of the night or day without a glass; And but for a lame knee and periodical Piles attack for a few years back, can work, walk, or ride down any nephew I have!—Thanks, full thankfullness to The Almighty!

I am just apprizd of the Bearer being ready to take boat. I still hold an expectance of seeing You, hope You continue to enjoy good health and that You will believe me with great truth & regard

Yours &ca.&ca.
Thos. Digges.

[Addressed:] The Right Reverend/ArchBishop Carroll/Baltimore pr. fav. Doctor/O'Connor with a Print

AB: Carroll Papers, 3C12.

¹ According to the 1816 register of the government's officers and agents, the doctor's name was James Trimble. The puzzling use of the word "another" in the parenthetical phrase is the result of Digges's first thinking that Trimble came from Baltimore: he wrote "Baltio." originally, then inserted "Philaa." above that, an accurate revision.

² William Attwood Fitzgerald, who appears to have been living at Warburton. Digges had been instrumental in assisting him in his medical career (see Digges to Jefferson, Oct. 24, 1808).

³ Although Digges's relatives and Mr. Fenwick cannot be identified with certainty, the second of the idlers is most likely young William Fitzgerald. It is surely his career that was being discussed at Bladensburgh, where his mother, Jane Fitzgerald (Digges's sister), and sister, Jane, also wife of the younger Francis Lightfoot Lee), were living. Morsell's first name was James.

⁴ Digges's nephew, William Dudley Digges.

⁵ Daniel Carroll Brent, the archbishop's nephew—Robert's younger brother—was now a clerk in the State Department, destined to become chief clerk and afterward U.S. consul in France.

⁶ Which of the younger members of the Brent family this was it has not been possible to determine.

⁷ The pictures were reproductions of three of the panels Reynolds had designed for the west window of the New College chapel at Oxford in 1780. Engravings in stipple had been executed by Georg Sigmund Facius and Johann Gottlieb Facius, two brothers (b. ca. 1750) who had left the Continent for London in 1776 to work for John Boydell (1719–1804), who had walked from Shropshire to London in his twenty-first year to apprentice himself to an engraver and subsequently became an established publisher of prints. In 1785 Boydell had published a set of reproductions of the panels. Boydell had also been, as Digges indicates, a political figure. In 1782 he had been elected as alderman from Cheapside; in 1785 he had become sheriff; and in 1790 he served as lord mayor of London. Digges is correct in associating Francesco Bartolozzi (1727–1815), a native of Florence, with Boydell, for Bartolozzi had even earlier than the brothers Facius—in 1764—settled in London to work for Boydell, but his name is not recorded in conjunction with the prints Digges had been given.

To [⟨George Graham⟩]

Ft. Warbn. 24 Augt./15

DEAR SIR.

My Nephew Dudleys departure just now for the City gives me the oppertunity of acknowledging Your favour of 18 int. receivd per Saturdays post. Majr. Hite¹ has already advertisd for proposals as to a supply of fire wood for the Garrison, which is at the present intirely out of my power to furnish from other engagements.

I never chargd more for 2 or 3 years at the first than 4½$ deliverd *at the fortGate*, & only at 5$s latterly. At which price or lower I have every reason to believe he will get furnishd if he gets *at it* before the frosty weather sets in—in times of ice & sleet 7–8. or 9 $s would not obtain it—& by delivery of the wood *upon the wharf* or above tide water, it will be by far the cheapest way of getting it. In the mean time my Cart supplys (of which there have been 8 or 10 Cords since the commencement of Reeds command) will suffice them.

As I doubt more than half of what Bartle tells me, I cannot guess whether he was exact or not in saying the Government would pass over those public horses, after a fair valuation, unto Him. On Sunday Majr. Hite and myself, with good judges as *to age*, rated them seperately and when alone amount 320 $s—many of them far in their teens & but one under 10 Years—all have been mall treated & are low in flesh. Bartle not being yet down I know not whether a profer of them has been made to him at thier valuation—one of his managers tells me he will object at thier high price: And I have expressd to Majr. Hite what I now profer to the Office *to take them myself at that valuation* passing the valued amount to my Credit in Account and which, without anything like disguise, I really think the best mode for getting rid of them. It is however at the will of the concernd. I intend being up to the Office on tuesday upon the matter of passing conveyance by Deed &ca. too long neglected! *for as yet the Government possess no title even to the old Scite or the adenda according to Kearneys Survey.* The Deeds, Dudley tells me will be fully perfected before tuesdy. & ready for signing, at which time too I have by Colo. Lears[2] direction or shall make out a new & less complicated account than that put into His Office from 1st Jany. last. I am pushd for this & have only time to add I am wh. gt. regard

       Yrs. &ca.
       Thos. Digges

NA: Record Group 107, Letters Received by the Secretary of War, Registered Series, 1801–1860 (Microfilm M221, Roll 61), D-155.

[1] Maj. Robert G. Hite (d. 1823), a Virginian, recently major assistant adjutant general, now captain in the artillery corps.

²Tobias Lear (1762–1816), Washington's private secretary, 1785–1792, and his military secretary with the rank of colonel in 1798, had been president of the Potomac Canal Co. in 1795, a consular officer in Santo Domingo during Jefferson's first administration and in Algiers later during both Jefferson's and Madison's presidencies, and since June 1814 the War Department's accountant.

To George Graham

Fort Warburton Novr. 11 1815

DEAR SIR

I have been long confind to my home by sickness and now a lame foot, or I would have waited upon You and the Secy. at War,¹ with whom I am not personally acquainted altho I have met Him at the Presidoliad & much respect His Character.

Mr. Bartle (who has fulfilld his contract for the 150 Cord wood deliverd at the Fort & obtaind a receipt therefor from your Commander[)] will deliver this to You. I hope soon to regain my beat in your pleasurable circle; but have much, very much to look after here.

Lieut. Maurice² has been getting on well with the works since his commence about 3 weeks past; But we are again thrown back, by a mandate from headquarters as to *Ration* allowances, and our Labourers engagd at *ten $s* per day [month] for 26 working days with rations of meat, far under the City prices now going, are departing from us to seek better wages & a sufficientcy of food—The City prices for Labour is 1$ per day & not under 75 Cents

the rate of 10$s per month of 26 days is   38 Cts.
and the double ration is found here for — <u>32 Cts.</u>
                          making — 70 which is under the lowest rate workman in the City, Lads, &ca. for 75 Cts. but notwithstanding this, & the prosperity on which Lieut. Maurice was going on, there came an order yesterday to Him that no *double* ration woud be allowd (tho it is not more than sufficient for the sustenance of a Labourer[)]—They are in consequence murmering & several have gone off: and we fear that very few will be seen at work on the monday. It is an illadvisd order & must stop the progress of the works *here*.

Mr. Bartle is going well on towards the completion of the wharf and the south side of it is nearly finishd & filld in.—He has shewn me a paper remonstrance to which among others I put my attestations, and You have of course seen His memorial &ca. eer this. It certainly will be severely hard upon Him *at this time* to be thrown out of competition with any other Contractor for the *now* & hereafter supply of fall *Stone* & other materials: He having supplyd himself with the necessary vessels Sloops, Lighters &ca. for their conveyance down and at this time too when [⟨with⟩] the completion of the Wharf all heavy articles can be more easily and cheaply than in time of warfare be conveyd to the Fort. He had to combat the heavy evils of a War price for those materials & when Lime &ca. &ca. could not be got Hither by coasting commerce, which made an extravagant rise upon Lime, Timber, scantling, &ca. &ca.

He seems assurd if some further investigations was made before fixing on a new Contract, that he would not be injurd, and from His now possessing the carrying Craft or vessels, He could do the business as well and [at] a cheaper rate than any other contemplated or offering Contractor. He further assures me, That as to the charge against him relative to the *old materials*, & wanting to run The Government out of them, can now in most instances be amply cleard up. I never knew any thing or heard of any Interest or profits exacted from Him Bartle by The Agent, and am yet intirely unacquainted with the terms of His contract nor knew of any Copartnership dealings among Them.

       I am with great regard
       Dr. Sir Yrs. &ca. &ca.
       Thos. Digges

[Addressed:] For George Grahame Esqr./War Office/Washington/ per Mr. Bartle

NA: Record Group 107, Letters Received by the Secretary of War, Registered Series, 1801–1860 (Microfilm M221, Roll 61), D-180.

---

[1] A former senator and minister to France, William H. Crawford (1772–1834), a Georgian, had become head of the War Department in Aug.

²Lt. Theodore W. Maurice (d. 1832) was assistant engineer. L'Enfant, whose plan to remove some of the old fort had been questioned, had been offended by the War Department's criticisms and refused to submit reports of his progress; work had been suspended in July and L'Enfant dismissed in Sept., when Lt. Col. Walker K. Armistead (d. 1845) had been appointed to replace him as director of the reconstruction.

To James Madison

Ft. Warburton Nov. 27 1815

I hope my valued and highly esteemd Friends Mrs. and Mr. Madison will not attribute my long absence & a seeming withdrawing from Them, to any want of respect regard or affection, but place it to the true causes—i.e. that of the eventful incidents during the Autumn & fall of 1814, which occupied my whole mind and vocations, (adding thereto the weight of age: 76,¹ with Sickness, Rhuematics & achs for the last six months) and as yet denying me the free use of the saddle: For Sir I have not been outside of my own gates or ridden 20 miles since I parted with You on the Bladensburgh road on the memorable (and in my mind *happy* day for our Country as it broke *party Spirit & opend the eyes of many*) the *day of conflagration*. I have been but twice in the City, & then per Steam boat, since that period, and am more than commonly anxious for another voyage in Her since hearing of Your return.

I am convalessant & hope soon to spend some days in the City, having unsettled accounts since 1st Jany. last to settle in the War Office wanting due vouchers & verifycations from the disgraceful *break-up* of Marsteller, Bartle & Co. on the 7 July last.

In the circle of 10 to 20 miles round this we planters & Farmers have been afflicted with shortest Crops of Corn & small grain ever known—not even a quarter of Expected Crop has been obtaind— The poor class's have of consequence experience[d ⟨suffering⟩] & will severely suffer through the winter—there is not food or forage for ⅓d of thier cattle, & in this way I am a sufferer myself, & should have sufferd eer this most severely for farming incomes, but from the relief given me by shipments of my laid by housed Tobaccos per first Ship which started from the Rivr. for Amsterdam consignd to Willinks & Son[2] and which neated me on Sales there above 32£ 15/–Strg. per Hhd. for common Tobaccos upon which sales & remittance to Murdoch[3] I got 10 pr.Ct. on the Dutch Bill remitted therefor to London and 18 pr.Ct. premium on my bills on Murdoch—This was for common Crop not heavy & some of them seconds—Wheat (what little I had saleable) at 175–180 Cts. per bushell—Oats 75 Cts. and Corn selling at 5½ $ per barrel while the Crop was green. Labourrs wages now hardly under a dollar a day—Tradesmens twice or thrice higher.

But yet Sir "The Country is ruind" "Trade at a Stand" ["]Marine Commerce all but broken up" "all confidence lost in an imbecile & profligate-expending Government" "taxing the poorer people above thier means" &ca. &ca.—Such was the assertions of the tub-Orator federalists at the last Piscaty. election & doubtless many of the listening ignoramus's swallowed it as fact—Those Torey a[n]glefied Demagogus seemd to be getting more boldness & violent in their assertions at a time when thier party voters were getting less and when to every impartial observer The Country & its encreasing Commerce were obviously progressing for the better. Many must have felt the difference of the last winters price 3$ pr.Ct. for Tobacco while it was buying up in Octor. for 10$ per hundred.

I hope You Sir have been one of the many sufferers by this "ruin to our Country" in getting from 15 to 25$s per 100 for Your mountain Tobaccos and Your 180 Cts. for wheat in lieu of the late shamefully restricted Sales for that article—I hear Tobacco has been as high as 27$ per 100 at Richmond an unheard of "*ruinous*" price.

I long to read the articles of what I concieve a most happy & advantageous Peace[4]—The planners of which as well as the actors in the negociation deserve well of their Country—The subsequent measure of chastisement to the Barbary Rascals is a happy climax to our Marine Warfare[5] and must vex John Bull in the proportion of the high Credit & ex[a]lted situation our Country is put in by the whole of Continental Europe. Go on my good Sir in doing well for our rising & happy Country & recieve the benefits of it.

      I am wth gt. sincerity
      Yrs.
      Thos. Digges

Majr. Nourse⁶ & two others harbourd with me late last night as comeing from the Steam boat. From Confinement to my room I have not yet seen him but will ask Him to drop this at your *Hotel.*

My Compliments to Mr. Cutts & would be much obligd by his aid in forwarding me any Cast by French or Engh. Papers.

LC: Madison Papers.

¹Once again Digges miscalculates.
²Willem and Jan Willink, Amsterdam bankers with whom Americans dealt; they had joined with other firms in the Netherlands to raise the first Dutch loan to the U.S. in 1782.
³Murdoch, Yuille, Wardrop & Co., in Madeira, shippers of wine and other merchandise.
⁴The Treaty of Ghent had been ratified in Feb., but the claims of each side awaited the acceptance of an Anglo-American commercial treaty, now ready. Because Congress was in recess until Dec., the text remained secret.
⁵In response to hostile acts of the dey of Algiers, Congress, at Madison's behest, had declared war against Algiers in Feb., and Commodore Stephen Decatur (1779–1820) had led a strong squadron into the Mediterranean, where after the capture of an Algerine frigate and a large brig the dey had agreed to the immediate release of ten long-captive American seamen, with indemnification, and to a peace that would end the tribute system.
⁶Charles J. Nourse (d. 1851), major assistant adjutant general.

To George Graham

Ft. Warburton 22d Decr./15

Mr. Geo. Grahame
Dear Sir

Lieut. Maurice got down here this Evening—returns to Alexa. for a matter He has to adjust with Colo. Armistead, is to return hither tomorrow to pay off the workmen &ca, expecting to take packet the same evening for Norfolk on a visit to His family for some month or two, and of course suspends for this time the heavy public works here,—a proper measure, I think, from the probable severity of those two winter months.

He has been a welcome inmate with me since Colo. Armisteads appointment, and which gave the old Major¹ "the go by" and whose situation must be an uneasy one to him since Sepr. last although enjoying every comfort which my *Hotel* afforded from the period of his debut here soon after the conflagration; I call it a *Hotel*, for it was at times, & very often nothing better, & myself little less troubled than the bar keeper of a Tavern—All however pro bono Publico.

I have not been able to absent from home but one night since the memorable 24th of Augt.—Age, infirmity & bad health, is demanding of me a short & quiet retreat in the City for Phisical aid (*none here*) warm batheing, & the settlement of too many open accounts. I cannot however do it & leave my house *open* to a trustless set of Young Negroes and a most abominable set of theiving old ones. My tatterd old house has been long since uninhabitable to any of my *female* relatives; and I have no assistant but in an illiterate though well-meaning overseer. If I could but absent myself at times even for a week or two, & locking it up 'till my return, I could make it out: But how Sir can I do it with The old Major a seeming fixture therein? for although himself temperate, quiet, worthy and ever orderly, my doors opend to Him would become the Conductor to dinners, loungeing night visitants, &ca. &ca. &ca., and You as a family man can guess the result. I cannot bring myself to give Him a distant hint, but recently have entertaind hopes (from some lately passing Letters to & from yourself Mr. Monroe & him) that a lucky call of The Major to The Office of War Department might favour my so *escaping from Home*. I have always found him persevering, faithful to His employers, incorruptably honest, and in no instance staining his hands with public money—a mere mite serving for all his personal outgoings and habilliments. We never had the least variance or warmth but on (*what I knew to be the Wish of Government*) the theme of keeping within the limits of Kearneys Survey *north Eastward only*, and for the vast & expensive *extension* of The Wharf, which is a manifest injury done to my two Sein-hauling births adjoining it.

Pray excuse this my intrusion on You—I am personally unacquainted with The Secy. at War although well knowing & feeling His Public Worth: I have too often troubled my able & good friend Mr. Monroe; But if You can serve me by any way informing me as to the disposal of this good old Major (whom I would by no means injure) it would be some comfort or at least a guide to me: Keeping the matter as I promise to You entirely *entre nous*. I remain with great regard and best wishes—

Yours &ca. &ca.
Thos. Digges

[Addressed:] George Grahame Esq./War Office/Washington

NA: Record Group 107, Letters Received by the Secretary of War, Registered Series, 1801–1860 (Microfilm M221, Roll 69), D-24.

[1] L'Enfant.

To William H. Crawford

Ft. Warburton 26 Octo. 1816

The Honble. The Secy. at War
SIR.

Always unwilling & reluctant to trespass upon Your more important avocations, I have only at present to solicit a return of those papers as inclosd & requested in my last communication Vizt. The writ against Queen & Moore[1] and The Councils Opinion thereon that I could not without a loss of Costs of Suit sustain an action against them for my loss of the two or three last years Rents of my Fort Fishery because they had an indubitable fair plea of the premises not being fitly occupant for want of due accomodation & more so from the Government obstructions laying on its shores &ca.—I thought by sueing out the writ to get the fulfilment of the $600–penalty on my five years Lease ending in June last, or at least to get the last few years Rent. After getting the writ & placing it with the Shereff, I wrote to the Office of War that I had sued them; but afterwards from good legal Advice I discoverd that after a usual process in the Court they would foil and burthen me with the expences thereof from the causes of the obstructions as above stated. For which claim either they or myself have an indubitable claim upon the Government.

When I receivd Mr. Grahames official communication from the Office on the 7th Sepr.[2] (on which very day my inclosures went through his hands) as follows "In Your statement You say that You have sued Queen & Moore for fulfilment of Your agreement, & as that agreement included the year 1815 Mr. Craufurd has declind acting in the case until the suit is decided" I could then not act otherways than still to claim my right from the Government, and through the War Office Department try to prove the justness of that claim from the obstructions *laid by Government Agents* on the Shores while Mr. Monroe himself was in the habit of viewing those obstructions while acting as Secy. at War in the worst of times. I have this day by letter to Mr. Monroe solicited Him to wait on You & explain satisfactorily as he can do the whole matter of those obstructions as being a bar to any Fisherman or Sein hauler at that time useing those Sein births. And further Sir as I have been more than once pushd for vouchers from Commissarys (where there were no Commissaries) I have now the satisfaction to inform You that the actual *then* Commissary Major Marsteller, who from some defficiencies in the War Office better known to You than myself, has recently returnd to His residence & family in Alexandria, where I have (though but momentarily while he was very ill) seen him; And he can, I guess, more fully hereafter prove "whether it was Government Agents or others who placed the Fort building materials & particularly those obstructions" on the Shores to my ruin of a very valuable fishing berth. Mr. Monroe will probably also recollect somewhat about them & how often I have troubled him thereupon while his hands were over filld with other more important & highly interesting matters than materials for fort building.

As I shall be obligd to be in Alexa. on a law matter with the Mayor, & probably a day or two looking after the Commissary Major (who always acted fairly & properly in such transactions at the Fort as I had any knowlege of) to find out by whose orders those materials were deliverd on my shores, I will that you Sir to send me the requested Inclosures under a Cover to the *Post Masr. at Alexa.* our Piscataway Post not comeing in but weekly on the Saturdays.

With great regard & Esteem I remain
Sir Yr. Ob.
Thos. Digges

[Addressed:] For The Honble./The Secy. at War/Washington

NA: Record Group 107, Letters Received by the Secretary of War, Registered Series, 1801–1860 (Microfilm M221, Roll 69), D-94.

[1] Queen & Moore had leased two landings (see Digges to Monroe, Oct. 26, 1816).
[2] For the War Department's copies of this and related documents see NA: War Department, Secretary's Office, Letters Sent, Military Affairs, May 2, 1816–January 31, 1818 (Microfilm M6, Roll 9): Graham to Digges, Sept. 7, 1816; Crawford to Armistead, Sept. 10, 1816; Crawford to Digges, Sept. 10, 1816.

To James Monroe

Ft. Warburton Octo. 26 1816

DEAR SIR

I have every relyance on Your forgiveness and forbearance by thus intruding on You and soliciting Your aid in some explanations to The War Office respecting claims which are rejected there as wanting *Commissariate vouchers* when there was no Commissary at this Station! and requiring proofs from Me whether the serious and *to me* afflicting evils of placing vast heaps of *falls* and Aquia Stone, Bricks, Timber, and building materials, below the tide marks round my old Wharf, to manifest evil if not total Ruin of a very valuable Fishery: And which, by compact from all the former Secretarys at War, *were in no way to be injurd by the Fort works.*

Those two Landings adjoining each side the old Wharf, were (as I have heretofore stated to You) Let by Lease to Queen & Moore for *five* years expirable on the *15th June this year*, under a penalty from each of $600–. It became impossible for any Seine hauling gang, either to put out & Land a Seine, or get accomodation on the shore, after commencing & placeing thereon such vast heaps of wharf timber, Loads of Falls Stone, near an hundred huge acquia blocks, and thousands of Bricks mostly all of these at or without the low tide water; besides the Cargoes of scantling, boards, and several hundred Lime tierces, all of which Yourself must have seen while in our walks with Major L'Enfant, Marsteller the then Commissary & paymaster,

Bartle the Barrack builder & wharf Contractor &ca. The Wharf is yet not ⅓d of it filld in, and the unreasonable long expansion of its wings, extending to where the Shad & Herring nets dischargd their abundant drafts, and where *there is yet* remaining on the shores in & about the north wing about sixty or 70 of those huge acquia blocks of Stone which are under water every tide:—The *southern* birth has yet two or three lighter loads of Falls Stone laying outer of the low tide mark, and that part is filld up & dayly filling up by the slideings down of earth from the Clift precipice (in consequence of denuding it of its trees & shrubs and by throwing earth over my lines by Kearneys Survey) that there is now not more than three feet water where & before the digging commencd there was at least a 15 feet depth—to the manifest injury if not ruin of that seine birth.—The northern one yet remains to be proven whether it injures or not the Landing. Mr. Bartle however (without my assent, for I could not give it without being liable to the 600 $s penalty) made an attempt in Apr. last to clear it, he having 50 or 60 Negro wood Cutters at a short distance therefrom, and did actually by encircling a glut of Herring get on Shore 372,000 Fish—a miraculous & unprecedented haul! giving me my ample family supply though I never got any moneyd rent from Him or Queen & Moore for the last three years of their Lease.

To all these circumstances as to obstructions I have given to The War Office my own affidavit, and added thereto the Certificates of ten or eleven creditable neighbours, some of them heretofore renters of these Landings and all of them in a dayly or weekly habit of viewing those present mischiefs.

I had Sir a running Account against the Office from Jany. 1 1815 up to Augt. last of many hundred Dollrs. amount for Cord wood supplyd the Fort—timber & knees for a larg[e] Crab winlass—Cedar & Locust Logs—Negro hire—Carts hire—Smiths Shop supplys—&ca. &ca. and on giving it in it was scrutinizd with an ex[a]ctness that ill comported with the many thousands worth of waste & ruind articles on & about the Shores. This account was *partially* paid in Augt. last by a warrant for $190⁹⁰⁄₁₀₀ but sent back to me on account of my charging in it *one years* lost Rent (when I ought to have exacted *three* years) of 400 $s for lost Rent.—At first there was a demur to this charge as not passable in that office, which made me resort to affidavits and to prove by Certificates the justness of it:—which dozens of respectable persons can attest *that these Rents* were a loss to me from the obstructions the Government Agents placed & have left thereon. After that, by an Office letter, I was put to prove, whether they were Government Agents or not who put those obstructions in upon me!—How could I Sir but suppose that the old Engineer, or Majr. Marsteiler then & for long acting as a Commissary & Paymaster, or Bartle a contractor for buildings & the Wharf were other than Government Agents? [By the by Marsteller is returnd to his usual dwelling in Alexa. where I have seen him, though very low *in health*, & mean again to see him on this theme.]¹ I had often, with You my good & highly esteemd friend, trod over those wastes & heaps of those very obstructions while You aided with Your meritorious services as the acting Secy. at War to Your more important Office of State. As fairly might it be requird of me to prove that the present & worthy Engineer, His Deputy Lieut. Maurice, or their Clerk were or were not the Government Agents.

I write to The Secy. at War by this conveyance, and it will be doing me a great favour if You will state to Him what You recollect of those obstructions & their consequent evil as loosing me some years of Rent. I have long since & too repeatedly troubled You & the War Office with my complaints & uneasy omens I feel for the intire ruin of *this fishery*, of infinitely more importance as to clear annual profit than this my comfortable Farm and which I fear I shall soon be obligd to quit from dayly vexations, tresspass, & robbings upon it.

Accept my warmest salutations & wishes for Yr. health long life—&ca. &ca. while I remain

truly Yrs.
Thos. Digges

The old Major is still an inmate with me—quiet harmless, & unoffending as usual—I fear from symptoms of broken shoes, rent pantaloons, out at elboes &ca. &ca. that he is not well off—manifestly disturbd at his getting *the go by*—never facing towards the Fort though frequently dipping into the Eastern Ravines & hills of the plantation—picking up fossils & periwinkles—early to bed & rising—working hard with his instruments on paper 8 or ten hours every day as if to give full & complete surveys of his works &ca., but I neither ever see or know what his plans are (never Enquiring of any Engineer what he is about &ca.) and believing him always incorruptedly honest & with the cleanest hands as to *public money* &ca. &ca.[2]

[Addressed:] The Honble. James Monroe/Secy. of State/Washington/Private

[Note below in pencil]
N. B. Mr. Monroe went as requested to the Office, & made the necessary explanations to Mr. Grahame & Mr. Wagner[3] leaving this letter with them, & it came with Sundry others from The Wagners Office to me[—]see inclosed Wagners indorsement on this envelope. 28 octo./16

LC: Digges-L'Enfant-Morgan Papers, 3:531–32.

[1] Digges's brackets.
[2] A letter from Graham to Digges, Jan. 1816 (LC: Digges-L'Enfant-Morgan Papers, 3:534), shows that Digges had been active in helping L'Enfant make good his claims for compensation long withheld.
[3] Although a vehement Federalist and editor of the *Federal Republican*, Jacob Wagner was chief clerk of the State Department during both the Jefferson and Madison administrations.

To George Graham

Ft. Warburton 6th Novr. 1816

DEAR SIR

I very reluctantly solicit Your friendly aid to inform me in what shape or form I am to apply to The War Office (the late Secy. having removd from it to The Treasury)[1] for my claim to an heretofore non-passd account for the want of some *Commissariate* or other vouchers: The last Treasury warrant of \$190$^{90}/_{100}$ being only a small part payment thereof.

I got the requird papers from Your Office in consequence of my letter To The Secy. Mr. Crauford on the 26th ultio. On the same day I was necessiated to trouble the Secy. of State with a second request (I had his promise in July last of his calling in Your Office for the purpose) That he would step into & explain to Mr. Crauford, the justice & temparance of my Claim for the Fishing Rent of 400$—solely arising from The Government building obstructions placd in the Fishing births while He Colo. Monroe acted as Secy. at War who was often down with *Marsteller* the Commissary & paymaster!, and together with myself viewing those heaps of mischiefs (many even *yet* to be seen) and of which I have repeatedly complain'd.

The stoppage of my *means* arising from the sale of the Lot as per Kearneys Survey, together with those other retard'd payments on a runing account (altho paid through You in part) have placed me in the situation of *dire necessity*; and altho all my debts and wants are under 8 or 900 Dollars, I cannot *from the times* and other family circumstances, meet as heretofore some imperious demands which I am in anxiety to discharge.

Yours wth. gt. regard & Esteem
Thos. Digges

I am trying hard to get to the City for a few weeks, but my old Chum Major, the want of a housekeeper &ca. yet prevents me.

NA: Record Group 107, Letters Received by the Secretary of War, Registered Series, 1801–1860 (Microfilm M221, Roll 69), D-97.

[1] Upon Crawford's departure on Oct. 22, Graham had assumed the duties of head of the War Department.

To George Graham

Washington Hotel
March 5th. 1817

Mr. Digges hopes that Mr. Grahame has examin'd The Letter & sundry papers relative to Fort Warburton, & the causes for his having partially stopt the works by The Writ of Injunction on the 5 Decr. &ca.: And which Mr. D. solicited Mr. Grahame to communicate To The Engineer Colo. Armistead whom He expects has arrivd at the works.

Mr. D. is the more anxious & solicitous about the matter, from the near approach & setting in of The Fisherys: as without the aid of the building a new house & the usual *Shed accomodation* for the Sein haulers, no one will think of renting the two *Wharf Fisheries*.

Mr. D. only awaits for the Receipt of The Office Warrant on the Ballance due Him (as mentiond to Mr. Grahame yesterday) to depart from hence to Warburton.

NA: Record Group 107, Letters Received by the Secretary of War, Registered Series, 1801–1860 (Microfilm M221, Roll 73), D-24.

To George Graham

Ft. Warburton 16th Apr. 1817

DEAR SIR.

Adhering to my former purpose of informing You (and through You for communicating the same to The Engineers of the Fort) of every circumstance I take in consequence of obtaining the Writ of Injunction in Sepr. last to stay or stop the work at & near a particular or No.Wt. point of the Fort which has severely injurd my fishing births near the Same, I send with this (after shewing it to Lieut. Maurice Colo. Armistead being on a journey) the steps I was necessiated to take at the now Marlbro. Apr. Court. Vizt. the Court writ against the two Engineers, & my statement, partly on affidavit, for obtaining the same.

I thought it best to solicit, & have obtaind *leave* of the Court & Sheriff, to hold the actual writ in my possession; to be used hereafter if found necessary, & which from recent converse with Lieut. Maurice I have full confidence will not be further acted upon, in order thereby to spare the Engineers being intruded upon by any vulgar Sub Sh[er-i]ff. It was impossible for any one to forbear longer than I did & am yet doing at seeing destruction progressing to the Ruin of such valuable fishing Shores as those two adjoining the Wharf—in fact the southern & *shad birth* 'twixt the Wharf & Clift is already ruind & the *moneyd* rent thrown on my hands.

The *fishermen* are still living in a deckd Lighter, (the largest & I believe best on the River) but I hear from Bartle that Colo. Armistead has bought it to bring his quarrying Stones, & promisd the accomodation of a Shed as last year *now* clearing out of the Lime, when a half of the fishing month *Apr.* has passd!—*when over*, & proofs shewn as to its filling in, & the shores untenable for sein hauling, I shall have to get some 5 or seven Gentlemen to certify thier opinions of it, & they will of course be lookd on as being fully as well informd of Fishing matters as any Officer or Engineer can be—at least this is my opinion.

From the prompt openess of Lieut. Maurice as to moveings of Earth & the accomodations in lieu of what I had pulld down i.e. a Cellar &ca. I have no doubt all will be accomodated without further recourse to Law, which no man detests more than I do. Those now acting Engineers are not blameable for my loss's near the River Shores, & there are materials in the bottom of the Majors water battery capable for the building a Cellar &ca. which are dayly progressing to be envelopd by the slideing-down Earths into it.

[First enclosure]

At Marlbro. Court 10 Apr./17
T. A. Digges submitted to Jno. Law & Fs. Key
His following Statement

The inclosd Writ of Injunction and Subpoena obtaind by Thos. A. Digges in Sepr. 1816 will best shew the nature of his complaint against The Engineers their agents & workmen at Fort Washington: And although *Injury* was then apprehended and indeed *Seen* in the throwing large quantitys of Earth from within the Fort limits upon his soil near to the River fishing Shores, He *did not* from wishing in no way to obstruct the Public Works, as well as out of civility to The Engineers (who thereby might have been troubled to attend the last *Sepr. Court* or its adjournment to *Decr.*) use otherways the Injunction but by informing The Engineers That He possessd it, and leaving the Writ itself in The War Office for the due instructions to be given to The Engineers.

On the 1st Decr./16 all the public works at The Fort were *suspended* from that day until the 1st March—And upon the *5th Decr.* T. A. Digges servd The Writ of Injunction (Colo. Armistead being absent on a journey to No. Carolina) upon Lieut. Maurice the assistant Engineer, and upon Belitha Lawes the directing Master Mason; at the same time informing The War Office of Every step he had been necessiated to take prior to The Re-commencement of the Public Works in March.

The said Works were recommencd early in March under direction of Colo. Armistead (his assistant Enginr. being then absent on duty in Norfolk) and, notwithstanding the Injunction, sundry Carts were employd during the first week of March to draw from the Fort limits and throw Earth over so as to continue the Envelopement of the solid flat below.—On the 28 March, The Engineer Colo. Armistead not being there, I saw & calld sundry persons to view the Carts still so injuring me (Vizt. Mr. Belitha Lawes the contracting & head Mason for the Works, Heny. Frazer,[1] and two of The Goverment Overseers Feilder Jewell and Loyd Pumphrey &ca. to witness that my Injunction Writ had not been attended, & that I should be obligd to complain thereof to The Judges of The Court at the approaching Apr. term 7th April, and I went forthwith and informd the acting Secy. at War of the renewd tresspass and the measures I intended to persue.

In additional aggravation of this, and notwithstanding the Injunction includes the protection to be given to sundry Sheds, Workmens buildings &ca. &ca. (all of which are distant and without the lines & limits of The Fort) Yet the Soldiers (who said "*they were doing it* by orders of The Commandr. Colo. Jones[2] & Colonel Armistead["]) committed the Outrage of pulling down & took away one of those workmens Sheds as sp[e]cified in Deponents Bill of complaint.

T. Digges, in consequence of those repeated mischiefs and the great loss he is likely to sustain thereby, wishes for a motion to be made to The Court & obtain an order for stopping or restra[in]ing the same, either by Bill of Complaint on His own affidavit, or bringing into Court Witness's to prove the foregoing statements.

If any new Injunction, attachment, or other form is granted by the Court thereupon, He has particularly to request That *himself* possess the same, so as for him to use the said Court Order, or attachment, &ca. *discretionally* and with all possible delicacy & forbearance towards The Engineers: He having full confidence, when the acting Secy. at War has more leisure to see & consult the Engineers that they will rectify the mischiefs of which He complains.

Thos. A. Digges
Marlbro. Court 10 Apr. 1817.

[Second enclosure]

Copy of The Court order, or Writ for Attachment which writ T. A. Digges *had permission & yet holds in his possession*, to be servd hereafter, *if necessary*, & is witheld from The Sheriff, or His Deputies, thereby to save The Engineers &ca. from any uneasiness or trouble by any hasty Service thereof—It will be shewn to Colo. Armistead & Lieut. Maurice by T. A. D.—16 Aprl. 1817—
Prince Geos. County State of Maryland &ca.
To The Sheriff of Prince Georges County Greeting.

You are hereby commanded to attach the Bodies of Walker K. Armistead and Theophilus[3] W. Maurice if they shall be found in Your bailiwick and Them have before the said County Court of the County afforesaid, as a Court of Equity to be held at Upper Marlbrough Town in said County on the third monday in June next, to answer unto the State of Maryland touching a certain Complaint of Thomas A. Digges after being thereto legally Summond on 5 Decr. last. Hereof fail not at Your peril and have You then & there this writ. Witness The Honble. John Johnson Chief Judge of the first Judicial District the 7h Day of April 1817—

Issued the 15th day of April 1817

> John Read Magruder
> Clk.

[Addressed:] For George Grahame Esqr./Acting Secretary at War

NA: Record Group 107, Letters Received by the Secretary of War, Registered Series, 1801–1860 (Microfilm M221, Roll 73), D-45.

[1] Digges's manager.
[2] Col. Roger Jones, who later became the adjutant general.
[3] This must be Theodore. No other given name for Maurice appears in the registers.

To Charles Bagot

Sir Charles Bagot (1781–1843), former undersecretary of state for foreign affairs in the British cabinet, had arrived in Washington in March 1816 as Britain's first postwar minister to the United States.

> Washington Hotel 30th May/17.

Mr. Digges's Compliments to Mr. Bagot and returns with thanks the Londn. Papers sent Him last evening: From which he is gratified to find matters progressing for the better relief to the needy manufacturing and other poor of Britain.—He has also attaind by these Papers much illustration of the hitherto darkend measures & movements in Spanish America as to its revolutionary movements, about which we get *here* such incoherent & contradictory accounts. The Royal Commandrs. by imprudent Severitys & punishments (such as disgracd the first conquerors Pizarro & Co.) have seemingly contrivd to make The bigotted Priesthood Enemys to The Royal cause generally; and thereby hastening the probable loss of that fine Country to The Spanish monarchy,—an event so highly interesting to all maratime & commercial Countrys, in my mind very soon & likely to be effected. The yet undeveloped proposition from Madrid through Mr. Vaughan to the British Cabinet (as stated in those Papers) may soon throw fresh light upon it.[1]

Yrs. wth. gt. esteem & regard
Thos. A. Digges

[Addressed:] Mr. Baggot

YU: Walter F. Pforzheimer Collection.

[1] Spain, quarreling with Portugal over the revolutionary movements in Buenos Aires, was attempting to involve the British in the dispute, first as a mediator and then, failing mediation, as an ally of the monarchy against the rebellious colonists. Sir Charles Richard Vaughan (1774–1849), Britain's acting minister plenipotentiary in Madrid, had informed his government of Spain's wishes on Apr. 1.

To George Graham

Washington Hotel 11 July 1817

T. A. Digges makes free to thus submit some matters (*upon Fort Warburton Incidents*) To The Acting Secretary at War, for further illustration or determination thereon.

He submits his account for this years *moneyd Rent* $400– of the two Seine births adjoining the Wharf (the southern one of which being apparently ruind as a Shad Fishery) and which causd Him to yeild up those Fisherys to The Government by His communication to The War Office in April last: Or until a Jury of some *five* or more Gentlemen may be chosen by the Secretary out of about thirty names given in and who either own or are concernd in Fisheries between the City and Crane Island, the Government, by compact, being bound to make good any damages or ruin to those Fisherys *consequent to the* public works at The Fort.—The Account is accompanyd by Mr. Bartles statement per letter of His reasons for non payment of the agreed on *moneyd Rent* for the late & present years—and which Letter Mr. Digges begs a return of; He having already got the last years 400$s rent by a War Office warrant.

Colonl. Armistead has been apprizd of Major Kearneys promise to go down on Monday & await the Cols: convenience to attend *The ReSurvey* so highly essential and so long delayd, as some of the corners and other boundary marks are thrown down and the now deep-digging-Ditches are either over or closely upon the lines: And, until such *Resurvey* is made & assurances are given for replacing the Brick dwelling house &ca. which had been dug under & thereby destroyd by the former Engineer and workmen, He cannot withdraw the now in force District Court writ of Injunction granted Him in *Sepr. last* for stopping The public works *at* particular points thereof where the injury is visible to any observer; Nor can He make any deviations from Wadsworths & Kearneys Surveyd Lines (as expressd in the Deed of Conveyance) nor yeild any other alienation of Soil as lately spoken of & wishd for by Colo. Armistead towards the back ravine of the Garrison.

T. Digges also solicits information—Whether his now running Accounts against The Garrison for Fire-Wood Supplys, Smiths shops work, &ca. are necessiated to be Audited & examind (as was heretofore the Case) prior *to their being paid at The Garrison?*—In the summer & fall of last Year payments were made through The Engineers; But on sending in a letter to Colo. Armistead such Accounts, they were returnd to me with a verbal message by the Cl[er]k Mr. Murray that those Accounts must go to Lieut. Ansart,[1] lately appointed paymasr. and Quarter Master, and that the older ones up to 5 Decr./16 would be setled by Colo. A. whenever presented.—I have not since seen Lieut. Ansart, and on account of the Death of Lieut. Lee I missd of Colo. Armistead at The War Office yesterday.

I intend down this evening per Steamboat but will call at the office between one & two oCk. and if I can be favourd with this 400$s payment it would be an aid & a great convenience to me.

Yours with every regard & best wishes
Thos. A. Digges

11. JULY 1817

[Enclosure]
The United States Dr. To Thos. A. Digges

1817
June 10th To The *moneyd* Rent of my two Fishing Sein births at Warburton Landing (extra of Fish) and which I have lost for a few years back from the obstructions given thereto by The Public Works the last years however being paid to me by the War Office.............. $400–00

Thos. A. Digges
Washington 5 July 1817

[Addressed:] For the Acting Secretary at War/ &ca. &ca./ Washington

NA: Record Group 107, Letters Received by the Secretary of War, Registered Series, 1801–1860 (Microfilm M221, Roll 73), D-80.

[1] Felix Ansart, a first lieutenant in the artillery corps.

To George Graham

Ft. Warburton
Thursdy. afternoon 7th of Augt. 1817

DEAR SIR.

Pray be so good as give an order to Majr. Kearney for his visiting the Station here & makeing a Resurvey of the Fort Lot with the Engineers here. It is singular how long I have been trying to get them at it, & *faild*; but no ways owing to Majr. Kearney, for since You gave the first order He has ever been ready to come; and was down with me on *monday week* last. The Colo. Engineer was unfortunately absent on a visit to Mr. Masons fishing or venison hunting—Mr. Maurice not then returnd from Norfolk but got here this day week after Majr. K. had returnd home. I have not seen Colo. Armistead since; but on Lieutenant Morrice's appointing tuesday last, I sent up for Majr. Kearney & got but an odd Answer verbally from my drunken Negro "That He was at that time a little hurryd, & thought it best to get an Office order for his comeing on *the survey*" which is very essential to be done forthwith—the works now touching my lines, & in want of some trifling yeildings up of soil by me no ways of any value & what I am willing to do, (altho I have a serious account to settle with the Office, extra of my inju[n]ction to stay the works a⟨s⟩ a material point); But it seems Majr. Kearney cannot any where obtain a proper telescope Theodolite to work with, the City or even *the Office of War* not affording such an instrument though the Cost is not more than 50 or 55 Dollrs.!! I wish some of the boat money, nearly to the tune of 1000$, had been laid out for such an Instrument—(this however is *fun* tho not for "Unkle Sammy" but to remain entre nous). I expect a call to the City dayly to bring my Sister Carroll[1] down per steamboat from Mr. Brents, and await only for Major Kearneys business.

I am with gt. regard & esteem
Yrs. Thos. A. Digges

NA: Record Group 107, Letters Received by the Secretary of War, Registered Series, 1801–1860 (Microfilm M221, Roll 73), D-102.

[1] Elizabeth, wife of Daniel Carroll, III of Rock Creek, Md., was related to many of the Brents; the context does not establish which one of them she had been visiting.

To George Graham

Ft. Warburn. 19 Augt. 1817.

DEAR SIR

Let me again My Good Sir solicit You to urge The Topogra[p]hical Engineer Majr. Kearney to come hither to make the Re-survey of the Fort Lines: The diggings of which some very deep ones now walling up, & others building upon & adjoin[in]g the *out*side of the Fort limits (very manifest) making the survey highly essential. There are other reasons for having this resurvey made too long to deliniate in this letter, and which I must act up[on] in the now pending Suit of Injunction *to Stay the Works*! at our next district Court the first week of the comeing month, Be the same however unpleasant to The War Office or the Engineers as it must ultimately be. One of the best, or the Shad landing is already ruind by the works, & the other or North one is fastly progressing in a like manner to be.

It is hardly to be credited that the public offices, or the District, or the station *here*, can [not] produce a Theodolite Instrument with a Telescope fit for the sighting or survey of exact lines; and which, had I known it in time, (for I have been labouring to get this survey for two or three years) I could have obtaind from a Mathematical Instrument maker in Baltimore for 50 or 60$s!

Pray Sir inform me by a line whether I am to expect Major Kearney or not & which I solicited You upon some 8 or 10 days back:— one or other of the Engineers are ready to recieve his visit *here* for the purpose; although the Colo. has been very seldom here only a few short visits since Mr. Maurice returnd from Norfolk about *monday* last was 3 weeks.—Extra of the greivous loss of those fisherys (which the Government by compact as well as by my Deed are bound to make Good) I am a sufferer by loss of the fishing Rents (the last of which refusd payment by You) also by the loss of the brick house essential to the Renter of the Land & other accomodation for a Gang of Seine haulers which was destroyd by the former Engineers diggings under it—after some promises and expostulations I yet see no likelyhood for the rebuilding a similar one absolutely *necessary* to me.

With gt. regard Yrs. &ca. &ca.
Thos. A. Digges

NA: Record Group 107, Letters Received by the Secretary of War, Registered Series, 1801–1860 (Microfilm M221, Roll 73), D-102.

To George Graham

F. Warburton 25 Augt./17

DEAR SIR

After a variety of attempts to get the *Re*survey of the lines & distances of the Fort Lot as mentiond in my last letter to You (but not until it was *visibly requisite* from the diggings of The Works) The two Engineers on fryday last got to probeing out the lines &ca. by a Copy of them from Kearneys Survey, but still without his aid or assistance from the want, I believe, of a proper Theodolite.[1]—I send Majr. K. by this oppertunity a rough Memorandum sketch of what the Engineers did, with my reiterated request for his furnishing himself with one & as soon as convenient to come again upon that business (which need not occupy 3 or four hours to perfect) jointly with the Engineers. I hope for Your aid inducing him to come.—Messrs. The Engineers could make out nothing definitive thereon—save that by sighting the short river line from the 7th boundary stone $\frac{7}{FWB}$ to the begining an English Oak tree both of them very near the sharp lower point of Fort (and *which are the chosen spots by Genl: Dearborne & other officers for the basis beginings of the first Fort*), And they found that line as well as the long *given* line up from the tree towards the Clift were BOTH CORRECT; But in every other line, & particularly as to lingth in Chains & links *were* INCORRECT and extended further in upon me! So that in respect to *errors* either on one party or the other (extra of the diggings) it becomes actually *essencial* to get those lines rectifyd & that speedily.

Here stops this matter of the *Resurvey for the present*; after a two years assiduous endeavour on my part to get it made while I was looking at the progressing evils of that as well as the ruin of one Fishery; the non performance of erecting houses destroyd by the works & the promisd accomodation (for the fishing month only) necessary to Sein hauling Gang: And so it is likely to go on Sir for another two years! But "Uncle Sammy" is a Herculean pay*master* though not quite so patient under sufferings as John Bull:—Mine are such, as justice to myself & my necessities require to redress; And I shall in the course of the comeing week (when our Circuit Court is to sit) renew, or rather keep alive by affidavits and motion to its Judges, my pending Injunction writ against The Engineers for suspending the works near to the point of The Fort where I am agreivd by diggings & the washings down of Earth and the non noticing the promisd erection of a brick Cellar with an upper room of about 18 ft. cubic sqr. similar to the one which the public works have destroyd, & which I must myself rebuild & get paid for through the Office, or have one erected by the now public workmen.

I have again to apply to The Office for payment of my moneyd yearly Rent of $400 as per inclosd Account; And solicit You Sir either to pass that account for a Treasury warrant, or mark down on it The *Office rejection,* as it will stand a part of my affidavit before the next weeks District Court:[2] And pray add to the favour I ask, that of forwarding it to me by the *Piscaty. Post.*

         With great regard & respect I remain
         Yrs. &ca. &ca.
         Thos. Digges

Geo. Grahame Esqr.
Acting Secy. at War

[Addressed:] For George Grahame Esqr./Acting Secretary at War/ Washington

NA: Record Group 107, Letters Received by the Secretary of War, Registered Series, 1801–1860 (Microfilm M221, Roll 73), D-99.

 [1] On Aug. 26 Graham wrote Digges that Kearney had received instructions to procure a theodolite and to resurvey the land purchased by the U.S. from Digges (NA: War Department Secretary's Office, Letters Sent, Military Affairs, May 2, 1816–January 31, 1818 [Microfilm M6, Roll 9], 345).
 [2] Graham returned the account saying it "cannot be admitted by this department" (ibid.).

To George Graham

            Ft. Warburton 9th Octor. 1817

Dear Sir

 Mr. Thk. Lee,[1] who has spent a few days with me gives me an oppertunity of forwarding this.

 After refering to You my communications of the 24th ulto.[2] (& to which I have not been favourd with an answer) and my verbal statements to You on the 5th inst., no ways conclusive or satisfactory to me, as relating to my then expressd Claims, the requests for my ceeding more Soil; and especially as to the *Re*-survey by the Engineers & Major Kearney; I have only to say That it yet remains as it has done for more than a year past: And which more clearly evinces to me the adhereance to my line for acting as expressd in my letter to You of the 24th ulo. a substance copy of which was put into the hands of the Depy. Engineer here on the 22d Sepr.—a resort I shall very reluctantly enter into.

My claims for *mischiefs Done* are, unfortunately for me too obvious to any disinterested observer to need *the proofs* which You seemd to require on the 5th inst: The President Himself; His then Commissary, who certified to me the destruction of my brick house which he had used with my Shed Store; and a dozen of others of the *now* principal workmen yet here are proofs enough for me.—The former Engineer was not of such bending stuff as to "give me a Certificate of the mischiefs his diggings for the water batter[y] had done my property on the flat"; Nor would the present Engineer be likely to give His Certificate that by the throwings over of mounds of earth from the Fort Limits, have perfected, *as it obviously has done*, The ruin of the south comeing-in-Sein-birth *westward*. Just in like manner would go the northern fishing birth, were I to assent to more earth being thrown over on me at the *east* point of the works. Most assuredly *without a previously built wall*, this will be the case, whatever The Engineers may say to the contrary.

It is now Sir within six weeks of the usual & last years period for suspending until the 1st Mar. next all works of Masonry &ca. &ca. at this Station, and I have yet had no assurance from the War office (which is an essential to me) whether or not even my thrown down Brick Cellar & its top dwelling is to be Reestablishd together with effectual promises given for removal of other greivances and for The Fishermans accomodation in due time the next spring under one of the temporary Sheds as was heretofore the case but not yeilded in due time in the last Aprils fishery—Until this is done & my last years *moneyd* Rent paid I hope to be excusd from acting further as to yeilding up more Soil or granting further favours: for be it rememberd I claim nothing but my Rights.

      With gt. regard & esteem I remain
      Yrs. &ca. &ca.
      Thos. A. Digges

I have heard nothing from The Topographical Engineer (whom I left here on Saty. noon last the 4th int.) nor from any other about the event of The Resurvey of the Fort Lot. I understood when they last met, That their Surveying Instruments were so varient, some of them differing from 30 to 40 minutes per the needles, that they had determind to run from the two chosen & old boundarys of the first Fort & make their measurements by angular surveys, thereby to ascertain what is in those old boundaries.

Geo. Grahame Esq.
    The Acting Secy.

[Addressed:] George Grahame Esqr./Acting Secy. at War

NA: Record Group 107, Letters Received by the Secretary of War, Registered Series, 1801–1860 (Microfilm M221, Roll 73), D-113.

[1] Theodorick Lee (1766–1849), one of the less celebrated members of the celebrated Virginia family.
[2] This letter has not been found.

To George Graham

                              Washington Hotel Suny. 19th Octor. 1817
Jno. Grahame Esqr.[1]
Acting Secy. at War
DEAR SIR

I got up per steam boat last evening with Major Kearney who has been at the work of sighting lines, placing down two of the stone boundarys near the Bluff &ca. and done every thing so far which He could do in the absence of Colo. Armistead, whom I have not seen since our joint walk of this day week. Majr. Kearney with Lieut. Maurice has *sighted* the contemplated straight line from the Bluff boundary to the spot designated by me to be *the end* of that Ravine line, & which can*not be further extended* as it meets the point of a very sharp declivity which meets another deep ravine at the meadow road: And from that spot at a locust tree there is a necessity to make (in order to keep the edge of the grass level) a short course of about 21 yards to a trimmd & markd Cedar, from which I designated the line across the grass pasture (which leaves towards the Fort almost the intire *commanding height where the tents stand* which is said to be necessary for The Fortification) to another trimmd Cedar with a white brick on its body & which I shewd You with Colo. A—— [The Colo. seemd to want the line a very little lower towards the foot of this commanding hill slope eastward.][2]—From this Cedar Majr. K. & Lieut. Maurice sighted the course & line through the thicket of Cedars also on a sharp slope so as to take in the whole of the Graveyard & Bakehouse Lot, continuing the same line across the dip or drain where a wall is essential to preserve the *north* comeing-in fishing birth.—The space between this line & the River Shore is all that can be yeilded, because it is necessary for full as much space for the resting place or stopping spot of the waggons, Carts, & Horsemen comeing to the Landing for Fish: And This line too hits the spot where the promisd wall cross's the said drain and goes up to the road near the fort Gate & nearly through the middle of the *upper Stone Cutters Shed.*—Here the matter ended Saty. afternoon. And it is but about six weeks to come before the works as heretofore are to be suspended from begining of Decr. to the 1st March: and not a single step yet taken as to the fulfillment of what I think my rights, although dayly am I pressd with *verbal* solicitations (which I have earnestly requested to come in writing) about permitting earth to be thrown in upon me and for the yeilding this, that er 'tother, & for additional sales of Soil & where too it would be injurious to the property to give up without absolute written assurances not in any way to stop the now existing high roads and first building walls to save the remaining shores.

I am necessiated Sir to refer You to my letter of 24th Sepr., similar to what I have given in in writing to The Engineers, as well as to my conversation to You on Sundy. the 5th Int. of what I expected in the first instances to be done for myself Vizt. The payment of my moneyd Rent this year;—the begining to build, or giving a firm promise, to have my pulld down brick house rebuilt this fall; no more earth to be thrown over upon my Soil until the wall for salvation of the north fishery is built if but for a few feet up at first; together with some &cas. as to the slope for the So.Western Glacis towards the wharf is settled how far to Extend? For Majr. Kearney only ye[s]terday evening had shewn me a pole put down where he thought it was necessary to extend this slope or Glacis to; And which no less strange & afflicting to me was exactly in the middle of the former comeing-⟨in⟩ Sein birth where from three to six thousand Shad were taken out at a haul before the excrated extension of the wings of the wharf were put down!

I again Sir solicit Your answering IN WRITING as to these few propositions & in particular to that of payment for the *moneyd Rent*. Your silence will be taken as an index of refusal to me, and thereby no further visits of Mr. Kearney will be for the present necessary: and however it may afflict my feelings, I shall use my Writ of Injunction authority when ever I can see & prove injury done me by the works and which will necessarily lead to final & legal adjustments of the District Court.

       With great regard & respect
       Yr. Ob. Ser.
       Thos. A. Digges

[Addressed:] George Grahame Esqr./Acting Secretary at War/Washington

NA: Record Group 107, Letters Received by the Secretary of War, Registered Series, 1801–1860 (Microfilm M221, Roll 73), D-122.

[1] John Graham was chief clerk in the State Department, but was not the intended recipient. The letter's cover shows that Digges repeated his error in the address and then corrected it.
[2] Digges's brackets.

To George Graham

           Washn. Hotel 6 Nov. 1817

DEAR SIR

My inability to walk or go about as usual, and the recovering a Valisse (stolen from the Steam boat on my way home thursdy. last) has prevented my calling on You.

The period for suspending for the winter the public works at Ft. Washingn., and my having as yet no assurance whether the pulld down; the proposed wall to stop the slidings down of Earth into the River; and the pay for the last years lost fishing Rent; Are or are not to be done, induc'd my writing to Lieut. Maurice for information thereon, and the inclosure is his Answer.[1] I have not seen Colo. Armistead since You was down only en passant for a few minutes in the week of the Races (and while I was confind to the House here) Nor have I had any promise or assurances from Him. I therefore have to request a line from You informing me the Office determination on those points as above stated and what I have to expect; And by which I am to be guided.

Yours with gt. Regard &ca. &ca.
Thos. A. Digges

NA: Record Group 107, Letters Received by the Secretary of War, Registered Series, 1801–1860 (Microfilm M221, Roll 73), D-131.

[1] On Nov. 4 Maurice had written: "It is impossible for me to say positively that the celler is to be built but I believe that it is understood between Col. Armistead & the Secretary that one will be built & that the Wall in the ravine will also be built. My Papers & Rolls are at Col. Armistead, and are expected down to day" (ibid.)

To George Graham

Washington Hotel   20 Nov/17

DEAR SIR

I have just returnd from my business with Mr. Rush at Annapolis (whom I guess will embark to day),[1] and being unable to walk about as usual, I am obligd to send Mr. Power[2] with this to inform that I am yet without any reply, as requested in my sundry letters, to what I think *a necessary* before I act what is a very repugnant measure to my feelings, *That of* the enforcement of my writ of Injunction to stop the public works at two very material points of the Fortifications; *Where*, as I am informd the washings-down of the dug up earth is likely to much injure my property outside of the ⟨Fort⟩ Limits, and to remedy which there appears to be no steps yet taken.

I have not seen Colo. Armistead or receivd any answer to my requisition to Him, since Your walk with us in Sepr. round the works nor at the Resurvey of Majr. Kearney; nor has the material Stone boundaries been placd down by Majr. K. and The Engineers.

I have the renewd Injunction writ & Sheriffs order to his Deputy to serve it—But before doing it all I request (which will not take up a quarter of an hours time) is to be informd by a line whether I am to have the brick dwelling rebuilt which was lost to me by the public works;—If the stone wall over the north ravine or drain is to be made for the saveing from ruin the upper Fishing birth, the South one being already ruind;—also the *Shed* accomodation for Sein haulers next spring; And the payment of $400– for my lost moneyd Rent of last springs Fishery: For Sir without these are insurd to me I should not be doing justice to myself and be subject to the redicule of others.

Yours with great regard and esteem
Thos. A. Digges

NA: Record Group 107, Letters Received by the Secretary of War, Unregistered Series, 1789–1860 (Microfilm M222, Roll 19), D-1817.

[1] Richard Rush had just left his post as attorney general to sail for England as the American minister in London.
[2] Unidentified.

To John C. Calhoun

Washington City Hotel
25 Feby. 1818

Mr. Digges of Fort Warburton will be very much obligd to The Honble. The Secretary at War[1] for a reply to His Requisitions, heretofore given into The Office, Relating to the Fishing Shores adjoining The Fort, whenever His more important avocations will admit.

Mr. D. is necessarily urged thereto by the near approach of a few weeks only when the Fishery will commence: And there being as *yet* no appearance of rebuilding, as *promisd*, a lost dwelling house in consequence of The Public works, as well as the yeilding up one of the many temporary Sheds on his premises for the month of April only as a necessary cover for a Gang of Sein haulers. Mr. D. is obligd from indisposition to reside at The Washington City Hotel, where Mr. Lambert & Mr. Laub[2] are fellow Boarders; And they could conveniently bear any answer or Commands from the Secretary at War to Him.[3]

NA: Record Group 107, Letters Received by the Secretary of War, Unregistered Series, 1789–1860 (Microfilm M222, Roll 20), D-1818.

[1] Calhoun (1782–1850) had been appointed secretary of war in Oct. and assumed his duties in early Dec.
[2] William Lambert, best known for having marked the first meridian of the U.S., and Jacob Laub were both clerks in the War Department.
[3] Calhoun forwarded Digges's claims to Col. Armistead for a report on which a decision could be based (Calhoun to Armistead, Feb. 25, 1818, and to Digges, Feb. 27, 1818 [NA: War Department, Secretary's Office, Letters Sent, Military Affairs, February 2, 1818–February 19, 1820 (Microfilm M6, Roll 10), 20 and 23]).

To John C. Calhoun

City of Washn. Hotel Mar. 7th 1818

SIR

Having submitted my Statement of the former and now actual situation of my property surrounding the limits of Fort Warburton (*more especially as to The Fisherys*), and yesterday recieving The Engineers reply thereto under date the 1st inst.,[1] which is refuteable in many instances as I shall prove in the next April district Court, I have only to notify to You (as I had done the last year to The Acting Secretary at War) That I now yeild up to The Government of The United States and relinquish those two Fisherys on the *south* and *north* sides of The Warburton Wharf. I have not been able to realize The Rents from them for some years back,—Solely on account of obstructions on their Shores and by the Public Works as expressd in my memoir to You of the 3d ultio:[2] and I mean to proceed by a due course of Law to bring the subject into Court thereby to ascertain by a Jury the damages to which I am entitled.

> I remain with great esteem & regard
> Your Obt. St.
> Thos. A. Digges

The Honble. J: C: Calhoun
Secretary at War

NA: Letters Received by the Secretary of War, Registered Series, 1801–1860 (Microfilm M221, Roll 77), D-20.

[1] Armistead's unfavorable report was enclosed in a letter from Calhoun to Digges, Mar. 5, 1818, disallowing Digges's claim (NA: War Department, Secretary's Office, Letters Sent, Military Affairs, February 2, 1818–February 19, 1820 [Microfilm M6, Roll 10], 25).
[2] No letter of that date has been found.

To Christopher Van Deventer

City Washn. Hotel 15 March 1818

Thos. A. Digges of Ft. Warburton wishing always to apprize The Engineer & Fort Commander (*through the medium of The War Office*)[1] of any steps He is obligated to take for repelling any trespass's or mischiefs done Him *outside of The Fort limits*, Has now to state His intention of serving Legal Notice on The Engineers &ca. to stay or stop the works at particular points where injury may be done, and particularly to the throwing over dug Earth past or beyond the Fort Limits as per Majr. Kearneys Survey of The Fort Lot in Apr. 1814.

In this case He must serve on them The Writ of Attachment emenating out of His Bill of complaint & Injunction issued from the District Court commanding such stoppage: Upon the Service of which by the Sheriff or Depy. They will have to go into the said Court or incur a punishment for contempt.

This service will bring the Case in dispute between Mr. D. and

15 MARCH 1818   611

The War Office, before the Court & a Jury and determine the point as to damages & injuries of which He complains. The Court sits at Marlbro. the first monday in April—His Statements together with copys of The Injunction & Attachment writs were all put into the Office. The President himself knows of & has seen the mischiefs, and for evidenc[e] in the Case He shall resort To The Paymaster Brent, Mr. Geo. Grahame, The Fort Commanders during the time as Captn. Reid, Lieut. Edwards, Colo. Beall and many neighbours acquainted with The Shores.

For Majr. Vandeventer
    War Department

[Enclosure: newspaper clipping]

Warburton Fishing Landings

The subscriber hereby informs the usual customers to those landings, that he has been reluctantly obliged on the 7th instant, to throw upon the hands of the government, (as he had done to the acting Secretary at War in the last season) his two seine births on each side of the wharf—the south one being already ruined solely by the envelopement of dug earth, and the slidings down of mounds of earth, with its trees, shrubs, stumps, &c. from the acclivity, upon the tide beach below; thereby filling in the river for many yards beyond the former low-water mark, (insomuch that there is not now three feet depth of water where a very few years back there was above ten feet); and not in consequence, as has been lately stated, of any hang from a sunken vessel, or flat, in said birth; which flat had been taken up a few years ago, and her keel, timbers, anchor, &c. brought to the shore, as witnessed by dozens of fishermen. The sunken schooner, too, never in this birth, but directly westward of the fort clift, on the edge of Piscataway channel, was long ago lifted out, so as to float down the river, to Mr. Lyle's shore, who had a considerable sum to pay for getting her broke up and removed from his fishery. It is now believed there is no hang or obstruction whatever in the Warburton landings, save what arises from the immense accumulation of earth from the fort slope downward and to well known heaps of sunken stone, &c. now covered over by the same, beyond the former low-water mark; and over which it has been proved that a deep and heavy seine cannot be drawn without rolling up. There wants nothing but a review or examination to verify this.

Mr. Bartle means to fish the north shore from the wharf up to, and at the Swan landing, and will deliver fish as usual either on the shores or wharf, to which the old and public roads will be kept open. The clift or meadow-bars landing is let to Jenkins & Frazer, expressly to fish on the shore only, and no passage whatever allowed through the meadow to it. The Piscataway clift landing, lastly in operation of Mr. Burch, & the others above it, are from necessity obliged to be discontinued as public fisheries, from the yearly ruin done to ditches and inclosures, as well as destruction to grain fields, by turning cattle thereon: And all trespassers within the inclosures, (and especially the soldiers, the fort workmen, and brick yard laborers) will be duly noticed, and are hereby again requested to use only the public high road to their avocations, it being decidedly, too, the nearest way.

THOS. A. DIGGES.

march 11—

NA: Record Group 107, Letters Received by the Secretary of War, Registered Series, 1801–1860 (Microfilm M221, Roll 77), D-22.

[1] Maj. Van Deventer (ca. 1789–1838), who had been an assistant adjutant general and deputy quartermaster general, was now chief clerk of the War Department.

To John C. Calhoun

[May 19, 1818]

The United States   Dr. to Thos. A. Digges.

1818

Feby. 3d   To three years loss of *moneyd* Rents for The Fisheries adjoining the Fort Warburton Wharf, as per statement given into the War

[19 May 1818]

Office: And which *by Compact* The Government is bound to make good "if any stoppage or Injuries are done those Fishing Landings in consequence of The Fort Works" & which Compact is on file in the War Office............. 3 years at 300$— $900–00
 Errors Ex[cepte]d Ft. Warbn. 3d Feby. 1818

Thos. A. Digges

N.B. This account was returnd to T. A. Digges as not allowd on the 5th Mar. 1818. I nevertheless have now to claim it with The following addition

1818
May 20th The United States Dr. To Thos. A. Digges Dr.
 For this present seasons loss of the moneyd Rent of his above stated Fishery & by the afforesaid causes as can be demonstrably proven extra of the following Deposition $300–00
 Errors Ex[cepte]d Washington 19th May 1818 $1200–00

Thos. A. Digges

District of Columbia   S/s
 Washington County

  Personally appeard before me one of The Justices of The Peace for the County afforesaid Thos. A. Digges of Ft. Warburton and being duly sworn Deposeth & Saith That for several years back He has Rented or Let, first unto Messrs. Queen & Moore, and laterly unto Andrew Bartle: His two fishing Landings closely adjoining the north & south side of a former & present new Warburton *Wharf* and to a benefit unto Him the Deponent in the *moneyd* together with a quantity of Fish Rents to more than one thousand Dollars per annum:—That from the new Wharf, and its too-far extended *Wings* (*particularly that to the south*) and to which This Deponent always & uniformly objected and never in any way assented to, It has intirely en-

veloped the shore at the centre of a comeing-in Seine birth heretofore a very valuable Shad Fishery; And which, together with the dug Earth thrown from within the Fort lines & limits of the Survey, and the mounds of Earth and its slideings down to outside of the usual low water mark, and also by the unloadings of bricks, Stone &ca. &ca. within the said tide marks, The Said Shad birth has been destroyd by the afforesaid causes, so as not to leave a two foot depth of Water where the River was a few years back above ten feet deep, & which now prevents any sein from being hauld therein:—That Deponent verily believes & can bring many others to certify those to be *the causes* for the loss of that Fishery; and that there has not been for some few years back any hang of a sunken or drifted vessel &ca. in the said Shad birth between the wharf end & the pitch of the Clift: That the said shore continues to be filling in by the slideings down from the acclivity, and in a partial way by the cartings down of Earth from within the Fort limits over his line, and has been the cause of his obtaining a District Court Writ of Injunction to stay or stop the public Fort works wherever apparent injury is doing Him.
and further the Deponent saith not—   Thos. A. Digges

[Not in Digges's hand:]
Subscribed & Sworn to this 19 May 1818 }
before   R. S. Briscoe J. Peace   }

[Addressed:] For The Honble. The Secretary at War

NA: Record Group 107, Letters Received by the Secretary of War, Registered Series, 1801–1860 (Microfilm M221, Roll 77), D-53.

To Thomas Jefferson

Washington 30th May 1818
Tennisons Hotel

DEAR SIR.
  A variety of untoward incidents, to which we are all doomd, has for the last three summers rebutted my attempts to Visit You and our

good friends at Montpellier,[1] and I was peculiarly vexd in Octor. last that I could not by a proferrd seat in Mr. Bagots Barouche to Mr. Madisons & to have partaken of the pleasurable scenes they enjoyd there and of which they yet speak in rapturous delight:—The Minister having concievd a quite different character of The *President* to what He had found in the lively converse & abilities of The *Man*. I have enjoyd his Mr. B.'s descriptions of our friend very much, and although he repeats His regret for his non visit to Monticello, I have yet had no clue *as to why* it was not so contrivd as to His seeing You.

My mother *Atwoods* family migrating from the close vicinity of Lord Bagots seat in Staffordshire and my frequent Summers visits in it to Sir Fs. Burdetts, Lord Littletons[2] &ca. &ca. gave me an oppertunity of knowing more of that Shire & the central parts of England with the elder Inhabitants of it, has caused much laughter & fun between Us—He has uniformly been much liked *here*, and Mrs. B. (of the Wellington Irish Stock) is all affability & attention—very different from the Dame Merry, who it seems yearns & is very anxious to get back to Her former elevation.

Your neighbour Mr. Nelson[3] (who was all the last session a fellow liver in this hotel *where I keep a room*) got hither last night from a detour round by Winchester, and lost by a few hours only, the seeing The President & party gone on the survey of the lower Chesapeake, or I guess the Judge would have made one of the party Voyagers from Annapolis.—On my consulting him I have concluded to send You to the care of Mr. Faris[4] the Coach & mail contractor at Fredricksburgh, a peck or somewhat more of English-growth Spring Sown seed Wheat. I can get to Faris's without trouble or expence per the dayly going Steam boat, (the only vehicle I can at present travel in from a fistula complaint) and it will find safer conveyance either by Coach or Waggon by boxing it in preferance to a bag too apt to rub or get cut in the common conveyances. I got some of this spring-growth seed wheat rather too late for trial this year although I have put a quart of it on trial in a garden bed, & reserve the bulk for next Spring. I have seen at times a great portion of Spring sown wheat at the Mark-lane London Market sold at equivalent prices with thier other common wheats and have also observd its utility & commendations in Gloucestershire, Kent, Mr. Cokes of Holkum in Norfolk,[5] the Isle of Thanet

&ca. and have every belief it would answer well with us which I hear it does do in the State of N. York. I am determind to give it a fair trial from my remembrance in early life, (though I am now only 77[6]) that it was a very rare experiment in this quarter to sow wheat in the fall! May it not in some measure remove the Evil of the *Fly*? for although my home farm at Ft. Warburton (all but ruind by a lawless Soldiery & the Fort workmen) being on a high peninsula between two Side Creeks & the River in front towards Mt. Vernon and never afflicted with the fly, yet the neighbouring wheat fields are very often destroyd by it.—The Seed which I send is of a medium sizd excellent grain, rather dark in colour & weighs 63 lb. per struck bushl.

The Kind of wheat *now* generally used hereabouts (for we have lost that of the *early white* small graind of better weight) is of the Red or golden stemmd colour & is very apt to loose its seed in handling if not cut a little unripe.

I hope You continue to enjoy good health—accept my kindest & most grateful remembrances & good wishes & with compliments to all Your amiable Family I remain

      Yr. obt. &ca. &ca.
      Thos. A. Digges

  Since writing the above, I am pressd to do an act of service to a very deserving and respected Clerk in The Treasury office Mr. Columbus Fenwick the only Son & representative of Mr. Joseph Fenwick whom You may have known as the *French* partner of Genl. Jno. Mason, many years our Consul at Bordeaux and whose numerous family, highly respectable, are of the stock of our first Setlers in St. Marys Coy. Maryland.—It is Sir (if You know Mr. Geo. Washington Campbell[7] our lately appointed Minister to Russia) to give my friend Mr. Columbus Fenwick a Recommendatory to Mr. Campbell as a Secretary of Legation.

When Mr. Campbell, [(]with whom I am very intimate) left this, to return hither in a few weeks, leaving his family in Mrs. Wilsons, to proceed to His Embarkation at Boston in the Gurriere frigate, He had proferrd to the subject of this Solicit[at]ion the takeing Him into His family as a private Secretary, He Mr. Campbell *then* nor any one

30 MAY 1818

here supposing but that the Resident *Secretary of Legation* was Still to be continued at Petersburgh: But it seems He has resignd, and that Mr. Pinkney just now announcd to be arrivd at Annapolis[8] and there waiting to meet The President & party (who this morning left the City for embarking from thence to view the lower waters of the Chesapeak) Has left his Son, a very promising Young man though yet in his teens, as temporary *Secy. of Legation* at Petersburgh.

Mr. Columbus Fenwick, although more Independent than Clerks generally are, from the acquirements of His Father who maintains a most honorable & fair name as well as the attainment of an independant fortune, could not prudently yeild up His present Salary for the uncertainty of what Mr. Campbell could afford to give Him.

I have always noticd and regarded Mr. C. Fenwick on account of His acquirements and Gentlemanly intercourses within the first circles here and particularly with all the foreign ministers from a full knowlege of the French & Spanish languages; And nothing but such would induce my presumeing thus upon Your time.

Any item from You to Mr. Campbell might probably produce a mutual benefit to both, and gratify the Father, whom I have ever respected as an honorable minded and well directed Man & good Citizen of these States meaning very shortly to fix and remain therein—[9]

Thos. Jefferson Esqr.
    Montecello

LC: Jefferson Papers, Series 1.

[1] The Madisons.
[2] Sir Francis Burdett (1770–1844), who had entered Parliament from Boroughbridge, now represented Westminster; Sir Edward Littleton (ca. 1725–1812) had served Staffordshire as sheriff and later as a member of Parliament.
[3] Judge Hugh Nelson (1768–1836), a congressman, practiced law in Albemarle.
[4] Hazlewood Farish.
[5] Thomas William Coke (1752–1842), of Holkham Hall in Norfolk, was also known widely as "Mr. Coke of Norfolk," the "first Commoner of England," and "a downright Whig, trained to hate all Tories." In 1778, taking up agriculture, he had become the first in Norfolk to grow wheat instead of rye as the main crop.
[6] Digges seldom managed to report his age accurately.

⁷A former senator and secretary of the treasury, Campbell (1769–1848) had been appointed minister to Russia in Apr.

⁸William Pinkney (1764–1822) had left Russia in Feb. to resume private practice as a lawyer and had reached Annapolis on May 23.

⁹Acknowledging Digges's letter on June 15, Jefferson expressed sympathy for him in his various afflictions, mentioned his own feebleness, and explained that he had some time ago resolved "to renounce all solicitation of the government" in order to enjoy "the state of rest and tranquility which is the summum bonum at our age" (LC: Jefferson Papers, Series 1, Reel 50).

To James Madison

Tennisons Hotel Washington 17th July 1818

DEAR SIR

I have had the misfortune, from ill health and an accute disorder, to be confin'd here ever since the 30th April and am likely to be a longer resident in it from having my old family mansion nearly ruind by the severe hail storm of 21st May; and the more *feeling* ruin & depredations done & doing the Farm by an ungovernable vile Soldiery too close in my vicinity and the nightly plunder of the labouring herd on the Fort works; who not only ravage my outstock and domestic poultry, but hardly leave me any thing of the vegetable productions of the Farm,—And, after a fourth or fifth years trial, I am obligd to give up the growth of Indian Corn, Potatoes, Turnips &ca. so very essential to twenty odd field Negroes & a flock of 70 or 80 unprofitable ones.—But for the old Major¹ (a harmless honorable minded man & though a Great Oddity I believe as good an Engineer as any one we have) I should have eer this closed up its doors and used the place only as a *Tobacco plantation* until the Fort works are completely finishd; betaking myself to a secluded room in Tennisons Hotel—and I have done it noc timerē nec timidē.

I am much with our good friends Mrs. and Mr. Cutts, frequently hearing from Montpellier, talking about Ye, and myself anxiously desiring for another trip to Orange and Arlbemarle, but alas Sir it is inadmissable.

17 JULY 1818 619

I am about to send, per Steam boat conveyance as far as the Coach Inn at Fredricksburgh, two light boxes of about a peck in Each, of early spring seed Wheat the growth of Mr. Arthur Youngs place in Sussex Engd.[2]—It came to me in a teirce a welcome present, but arrivd too late in *May* (it is usually sown in Engd. the first open weather in March) for me to risque its whole sowing this spring; But I made immediate trial of about a pottle of it sown in drills in a border of my garden—distributing some of it hereabouts & writing to Mr. Jefferson I would forward some to him as above intimated for trial next spring. —It came up very well though in a bad period as to frosts & hail; grew vigorously of good stalk and by a sample sent me yesterday of one medium head is in a blossom & soft grain of 4½ to 5 ins. long tolerably well set. We are now in our first weeks cutting of red Straw bearded as it's here calld—of a good produce in my home front field, which on the 10th Apr. was so unpromising that I had condemnd the field to be put into Tobacco naturally of Good Soil & well plasterd Land, and it surprizes every one to see how it laterly & well came on.—This has been very much the case with all Wheat lands in a circle of 20 miles round this, and I hope You have experiencd a similar benefit in Your more extended fields of Wheat.

I hope the *peck boxes* may get safe to hand, and had a wish to have placd them in the foot of a gig-chaise and once more have got down to Monticello and Montpellier; but alas Sir the decrepities of age and various vexations from and at Fort Warburton puts it for the present out of the question. I am unluckily too at disputations or rather war with the War Office! where I am treated but scurvily on a claim for 300$s a year for a few years loss of my *moneyd* rent for the south birth fishery *filld in & ruind intirely in consequence of the Fort Works.* Engineers are not easily brought to acknowledge MISTAKES, (and there are more than *one*) nor can the Secy. at War or his chief Clerk, neither of whom have ever been at the station or know any thing of the works & mischiefs done me, be expected to be competant Judges. I fear I must have recourse to a possessd Legal Injunction Writ, once before used to effect, for stopping the works outside of the Fort Limits where Injurys were doing me—but mean first to try the effect of giving in 20 or

30 most unexceptionable names, & for the office to choose any seven or nine of them to view & decide whether I am injurd or not. My *recourse* as by original compact signd & witnessd by Genl. Dearborne, Genl. Bowie, Paymasr. Brent & Genl. Mason being that if any injury is done my Fisherys or soil outside the Fort limits The Government would remunerate me therefor.

But why have I troubled & trespassd thus on You. My wish was to state the benefits likely to arise from sowing or trying in part *Spring Wheat*. I am old enough to remember when no other but spring Wheat was sown in this vicinity and several were laughd at who first introducd fall sowings: And viewing, as I have personally done the benefits of *Spring* sown Wheat in several of the grain Countys of England, & seeing very large quantities of it *admixt* with the London Marklane weekly Sales, I cannot but think a trial of it at least may be advantageous in our districts—thinking too it might check in some way the ravages of the *Mexican fly*. I hope, from hearing less about it than heretofore, You have not been injurd by this pest. *I* have been lucky never to have had it at Warburton.

I can hardly bear the unusual hot weather accompanyd with distresing calms in the night—The Thermometer has often been at 93, and N. York, Newark &ca. it is stated to have been at 97 to 99!—It adds to my depressions at absence from a cooler home. I contrive however to bear my ills patiently, but uneasy thoughts will arrise on reflecting at What has been the scenes at Warburton before these aggravations & delapidations took place but spero meliora—.

My grateful & best respects to Mrs. Madison—I will not relinquish the hope of seeing You both again, nor cease from prayers for a long continuance of Your health & happiness.

Thos. A. Digges

[Addressed:] James Madison Esqr./Montpellier

LC: Madison Papers.

[1] L'Enfant was still living at Warburton.
[2] Arthur Young (1741–1820) had been apprenticed at the age of seventeen to learn

banking but soon became a political pamphleteer and after that a farmer. Traveling widely to survey agricultural conditions and practices, he had written several books on farming before the end of the century.

To John C. Calhoun

Strothers Hotel [Washington] 16 August 1818

Thos. Digges (through the aid of Colol. Bumford) to whom He has submitted the perusal & examination of The Paymaster Mr. Brents Certificate of His being one of the five Comissioners and *a Witness* to The Compact or Agreement made between the then Secretary at War Genl. Dearborn & Thos. Digges for the Sale of the first Fort Warburton Lot (and which Certificate he will this day shew to General Swift,[1] and also to Colo. Wadsworth who designated and attended the *R*esurvey of the Fort Lot in April 1814) Begs permission to submit to The Secy. at War as follows.

That he should have got The Paymasters *personal explanations* as to the above in preference to His *written* Certificate, but from Mr. Brents calamitous attack of Paralitic &ca. &ca.: And it behooves Mr. Digges to clear up the misconceptions expressd against Him in The Engineers report to The War Office of the 1st of March last as to "His belief there was no written Contracts" and "that he knows not of any injury done to the Fishing Shores &ca. &ca."; As from which Report (by the common rule of the War Office) I am kept out of some years *moneyd* Rents of my Fisherys (very well known to be occasiond by the public or Fort Works thereon, and the necessary Sheds-accomodation & covering to a Sein hauling Gang) although I had been paid the first year, 1814 under Colonel Monroes Secretaryship of the War Office— and who knows better than most other men my severe loss's under the Invasion, the shameful blowing up of the Fort & its consequent ruin to three or four Fishermens houses in its close vicinity, and the too manifest Ruin of one adjoining Fishery.

Those *evils* were most of them antecedant to Colo. Armisteads first view of the Station in the autumn of 1815, and although *taken unitedly*, caused the necessity for my obtaining & seeking remedy through a Writ of Injunction from our District Court: Which Writ is still alive and in full force against "The Engineers their workmen and hirelings, as well as against The Military Commander of the Station," who will have to attend their legal Summons's for a hearing in the next months term, or to incur a contempt of The Court.

But Sir, to avoid legal process through a County Jury (which I guess would be best for my pecuniary Interests[)], and to remove all doubts as to whether I am aggrievd or not, I propose that any five or seven out of the thirty odd unexceptionables as exhibited to Colo. Bumford, most of whom have possessions on one or other side of the River from Geo:town to below Mount Vernon (I care not by whom the seven are selected), Shall meet, take occular & other testimonys on the spot, and decide whether or not I have lost a valuable Shad Fishery and this done by the public Fort works.

In addition to Mr. Brents testimony, I have a belief but cannot trust my memory, That my patent Deed for the resurvey of the Fort Lot by Colo. Wadsworth & Majr. Kearney of Apr. 1814 (which I suppose is on record in the War Office) will express somewhat of *the terms* of my first agreement or Compact with the Commissioners & Genl: Dearborn, to whom I have written on the subject (by way of gratifying The Engineers doubts as to there being no agreement) and I am hourly expecting His The Generals answer having had a satisfactory one from Mr. Jefferson.

Upon every consideration, and evincement my claim is a very temperate one, I cannot but think the same as put in The War Office in February under affidavit as to loss of my rents (to which I can get a dozen attestations witnessing it as being under rather than over-*rated*) may be attended to and allowd me.

Thos. Digges

To The Honble. The Secretary at War.

[Addressed:] To The Honble./The Secretary at War

NA: Record Group 107, Letters Received by the Secretary of War, Registered Series, 1801–1860 (Microfilm M221, Roll 77), D-65.

[1] Brig. Gen. Joseph Gardner Swift (d. 1865), chief engineer of the army and superintendent of West Point.

To John C. Calhoun

Washington Sepr. 15th. 1818

Thos. A. Digges of Ft. Warburton begs permission of The Honle. The Secretary at War to represent to The War Department as follows.

That it having been disbelievd or denyd in The War Office "that Mr. Digges had enterd into no orriginal Compact or agreement with the then Secy. at War Genl. Dearborn & President Jefferson, or the Commissioners appointed under them respecting the purchase & terms of the original Fort Lot & especially so as to subsequent Surveys: And that there was no record deed thereof on file in the War Office": And which he believes he had himself deposited in said Office) He now takes the liberty to inclose, for the inspection of The Honble. Secretary, an Office copy from the Maryland State Records of the Deed & compact under which he conveyd to President Madison from the survey of Colol. Wadsworth & Majr. Kearney of Apr. 1814 the now Fort Lot & its limits; and which Deed He is under promise to restore to the Office of Our Court of Appeals.

Mr. Digges yesterday submitted the said & inclosd Deed to the view of The Attory. General, who inspected the clause as to secureing His Fisheries, and He expressd his opinion of its being a binding and conclusive compact.

Mr. Digges will call for a return of the Deed: And He respectfully [requests] The Secretary at War to review His claim as put into The Office in Feby. last supported by his subsequent affidavit, for His lost *moneyd* Rents in consequence of the public works and which is assuredly a very temparate one.

From the frequent movement of officers at the Fort Station and some &cas. Mr. Digges has been necessiated to renovate His Injunction Equity Bill & consequent Subpoenas from the District Court in force ever since its sittings in Sepr. term 1816, Which Injunction was granted & now Stands in force since the 9th inst.: directed to Colo. Walker K. Armistead Engineer, Lieut. Theodore W. Maurice Depy. Engineer, thier Agents workmen & hirelings, and also to Capn. Isaac Roach[1] & Leiut. Felix Ansart & to The Commander of The Garrison for the time being—to forbear trespassing or doing any further mischiefs outside of the Fort Lines or limits.

NA: Record Group 107, Letters Received by the Secretary of War, Registered Series, 1801–1860 (Microfilm M221, Roll 77), D-70.

[1] Roach (d. 1848), who had become a captain in the infantry in 1813, had been in the artillery corps since 1815.

To J. W. Harris

On December 18 Digges received in Washington the following letter from Harris:

Fells Point Baltim. 8th Decr. 1819

DEAR SIR,

After leaving a message for you with your Negro Carter Ned, who shewd me into the Fort while our water Kegs were filling slowly out of a once more *redundant spring (near your ruind fishery[)], it would have been the height of ingratitude in me to have passed your hospitable mansion (in which I have received so many benefits & comforts) without expressing my grateful thanks to you,—But* ingratitude *Sir, is not among the catalogue of my sins—But as our Packet was gliding very slowly by your* odly *constructed wharf, & nearly spent flood tide—limited to time by our Captain (who was without water, save the turbid and somewhat* brackish *water alongside,) and every object at and about the Fort as new to me as if I had never resided in the* old *one, I could not go to your house.—*

I am with a few relatives from Charleston, & a brother Officer here *met, bound to Lancaster.—We spent some days in Norfolk, and there [⟨met⟩] with some officers who knew you and expressed full knowledge of your Warburton*

8 DECEMBER 1819 625

Station & an officer of the Columbus 74 [⟨who⟩] came to St. Marys with us—.

We have taken the stage for tomorrow, and it will be the highest gratification to me my good Sir, to get a line from you directed to care of the Post Master Lancaster, stating your better health; for both Mrs. Frazer [wife of Digges's manager] & your Carter Ned told me you was confind to your bed room:— and, as I know your readiness to oblige others, pray add a little in answer to my perhaps too freely made questions, *for I have heard* the fortifications rediculed, *as well as* handsomely approvd of, *'though* generally *said to be commanded from two heights, and some* mistakes *(which all great works are in some measure liable to) as* one of which, *our Captain, a Baltimore trader, said he had often watered his Packet out of a fine & abundant well, in the old, or first Fort, and for four or five years past there had not been a gallon of drinking water within the lines of the new Fort—and that a point of the* new South West bastion *was likely to slide down! for want of a supporting wall along the tide mark!—I had but a momentary run up thro the sally port to see along the top wall the handsome parade—But is it not* commanded *from your pasture heights Eastward of the Garrison?*

—Who commanded the Station after those two expert *officers Captn. McGuire,*[1] *and Major Marsteller; and the* much lamented *Ritchie?*[2]*—The Fort seems pinched in its limits, and why are they not enlarged, especially* eastward? *for I have heard the Engineers well spoken of:—Is it true the officers in general keep hired double horse Carts?—Why was not this curious Wharf properly filled in to preserve its outside fine depths of tide water, for they told me it could be* walked *round at low tides:—Who was the architect or builder? for I have no where seen better work or materials:—I am going into Country practice, near my native burth place, and among my freinds after a too long absence from them.*

I depend on having a letter from you, & remain with heartfelt remembrance & thankfulness, for your many Kindness's

Yr. Oblidgd. & Obt. Servt.
J. W. Harris

[Addressed:] Thomas A. Diggs, Esq./Fort Warburton/near Pisscataway/Md.

The next day Digges drafted a reply, beginning his letter on the second page of Harris's. Whether such a letter was actually sent to Harris or simply remained as an intended letter cannot be determined.

Strothers hotel Washington 19th Decr. 1819

DEAR SIR

I got hither, from my tatterd & comfortless home on yesterday with a hope that in a warm room (which I keep in it for *going & comeing* purposes) to attain some amelioration in spasm complaints in my ankle joints & Rhuematics in my Shoulders & neck joint, afflictingly bad at times although *internally* in good health.—What is *Your remedy for* SPASMS?—You see I *begin* with questions although You *end* your pleasurable Letter to me of the 8th int. with some *tight* ones for *my* answering; because I know little of Fortifications, *less* of the interior, & of thier works & ["]*mistakes*", than I do of remedy for my Spasms—Of the evil, from the Forts in too close vicinity to me & mine I shall likely feel STRIKEING EVILS for two Years to come.

I regreted very much the loss of the old Fort well, which had abundant water of fine quality. It was dug close to an ancient spring head, and though only dug 30 feet below the grass, it was constantly about half filld by that spring, so that a number of passing vessels got Hhds. of water out of it; But it was *necessarily* destroyd by a main outside Wall of the new Works takeing a direction exactly over it. Since its loss about the year 1814 or *1815*, I believe there has been *no drinkable* water within the limits of Fort Warburton now calld Fort Washington!!

There has been attempts this last summer & probeing many feet deeper than the old well (which You likely remember) and perhaps from going as deep as the tide level the water was turbid & somewhat foetid:—An attempt is now making, & I am told likely to succeed, within the north bastion (nearly halfway up the hill from the old well) in a hard gravelly-clay soil: The southwesterly *bastion point*, is not on so firm a foundation & which You question me about *as likely to slide down*—I have heard susp[i]cions of such an Event as likely to happen, and a preventive wall is to [be] built between *that point* & the high water mark.—The Soil under it is not unlike that which surrounded the *bower* coverd fine Spring under which You have seen boating partys Regale; but that spring was *enveloped* and lost by a large body of earth sliding from the grass level of the high acclivity above it, and the water found its way out where Your kegs were supplyd.—These slideings-down have injurd, (together with a far too-*extended wings* of a

[30 July 1820]

Wharf) if not *ruind* the South Sein birth. But the Engineer has *reported* to the *Contrary*, though I believe he stands Single in that opinion.

The pasture hill brow was SEVEN or nine feet *higher* than the grass on the hard gravelly knowle about the old Block ⟨hou⟩se; but this knowle was levelld down sixteen feet to form the parade You mention & a very fine one it is, but this hill [is] generally said to command the works both above & below. I have agreed however for an addition of Land along that side so as to include that commanding height to come within the Garrison works, and *works* are to be erected upon it to remedy that evil.—Some of the officers had two horse Carts employd in the works, as well the Colonel Engineer in 1818 as now Engineer Captn. Mauri[c]e; His Clerk; the Doctor; Lieut. now Commanding, another Lieut., and Sergeants Sutler &ca., *and why not?* The old teems were ricketty or bad, & theirs producd more good work: For besides three or four constantly hauling water from the River up to the summit works there was an immensity of Bricks to cart near a mile to the well finishd & prime works—the wharf & its filling in excepted, and which has injurd my adjoining Fisheries very much. I shall be glad to hear of *Your* pleasurable settlement & wellfare among Your old friends & expe[c]ting a reply remain Yr. wellwishr. & obt. &ca.

Thos. A. Digges

MdHS.

[1] Possibly Samuel McGuire, who had become a captain of the Thirty-fifth Infantry in May 1813 and resigned in Sept. 1814.

[2] Possibly John Ritchie, a captain in the artillery corps, who was killed in the battle of Niagara Falls in July 1814.

To Pierre Charles L'Enfant

[July 30, 1820]

The following is the Exact copy of Capn. Maurice's Letter to Majr. LeEnfant as receivd this day Sundy. *30th July* by the messenger boy Charles.[1] T. A. Digges.

I am necessiated to keep the original to shew in office, haveing a belief that the Capn. M. had no such order *from the Department*, or the Secy. at War. Colo. Armistead, the head haveing been for some weeks out of it & now up at his Brothers in Fauquier County sick.

"Major Le Enfant Fort Washn. July 26. 1820
"Sir

"Haveing been calld on by the Engineer Department to report to it, by what authority the buildings now occupied by the Labourers were constructed on Mr. Digges Land—whether they were put up by Mr. Digge's consent and upon what conditions.—As I am not possessd of any information as requird by the Department, I must request of You (believing that You were here when those buildings were constructed) to do me the favour as to give me any information You may possess about them—Whether they were erected by the consent of Mr. Digges and upon what conditions.—You will also oblige me as to inform me if Mr. Digges consented to the erection of the wharf now used by the U. States. I am Sir

Yr. obt. Sert.
Theo. W. Maurice
Captn. Engineers"

T. A. D. is necessiated to keep for a few days the *original* of which the above is a copy. Either the *Secy. at War*, or *Capt. Maurice* is in error or misrepresentation for the words of the Secy. to me a few days ago (for Mr. Maurice has not seen me) are varient. But this in no ways concerns *You*. At present I have only to say you shall assuredly get a return of his actual letter to You.

I now Subjoin a Copy of Your answer to The Fort Engineer Capn. M——

Minute
"Capn. Maurice of the Engineers Warburton July 26. 1820
"Sir

Acknowledging the reception of Your letter of this date, in purport of a request, to be informd of—'by what authority & upon what conditions the Buildings now occup[i]ed by your Labourers, and the Wharf now used by the U. States were constructed on Mr. Diggs land'. In reply thereto Sir I can only observe on the case well known of the Engineers and War Department offices, that at the time to which I presume You refer of the begin[ning] of those constructions of the Barracks & Wharf, that these were affairs solely of the concern of the Quarter Master; the duties of whose office it then was, as had uniformly been on former military Establishments, to provide materials and suitable places for the deposit and workings—as also for the accomodation of Labourers & head workmen &ca. &ca.—therefore I had no power over terms and conditions, with Mr. Diggs—All what I had to do while acting as Chief Engineer at this place was limited to the Work of fortification and I did nothing more respecting such provisional construction of Barrack & Wharf as You mention than point out the situation & extent consistant to what in my judgement was convenient to have facilitated the service of the different works of my direction. I am Sir Yr. Obt. Sert.

P. ch. L——
late principal Engineer to the U. States["][2]

LC: Digges-L'Enfant-Morgan Papers, 3:557.

[1] L'Enfant was still at Warburton, and Digges, while assisting him with his various unsatisfied claims, was still pressing his own against the federal government.

[2] There are minor differences in spelling and paragraphing between this copy and one that appears to be either the original or a copy made by L'Enfant.

To John C. Calhoun

Mansion hotel [Washington] 14th Augt. 1820

The Honble. The Secy. at War

SIR

    Wishing to be correctly understood in our finishing converse a few hours ago as to refering my Case litigated between Us & arrising from my Claim only of lost *moneyd Rents* of a valuable Fishery (too well known to be ruind in consequence of The Fort & Public Works) I had no idea of referring that matter to The President Monroe: For it is a legally prov'd, just, and very temperate demand, which I have no doubt to obtain, notwithstanding The Engineers contra Report; And which I deny in almost every instance, But "the *opinion* of an Indiv[id]ual" cannot or ought not to controul the operation of Law and Equity.

My proferrd referance to The President arose from His better knowledge than that of any Engineer or officer I have since seen at that Station: While He as Mr. Monroe was acting in various important State avocations & many times a visitor to Warburton—a Witness to my various loss's and destructions of a Warehouse & the burnings and pulling down houses on the river Shore, the blowing up the first built Fort, the robberry of a valuable negro &ca. &ca.—for which I never dreamt of asking remuneration from my Country & to a far larger value in amount than my rejected Claim for lost MONEYD fishing Rents of 300$ per year.

It was for those reasons, and His personal *viewings* of the injurious Fort diggings and slideings thereof into The Seine births (denyd by The Engineer!) together with The authorities requiring me to yeild some additional Soil; the Resurvey of IRregular run lines in April 1814; And the securement of *Title* to some lotts nearly adjoining the Fort boundary Eastward, which I promisd Gratis, and as yet The U. States have no title in that I suggested a referance to The President. If the case requires any further measure in me, as I guess it must, I will give You information of such; For every act of mine has been uniformly left at The office generally by myself, and of course may be found; but sure I am *some* of such communications which have been referrd have not met the reading or have been thought unworthy of answer.

With every regard & esteem I remain
Sir Yr. Ob. Sert.
Thos. A. Digges

[Addressed:] For The Honble./The Secretary at War/Washington
    To be sent to Mr./C.'s House. Augt. 14th

NA: Record Group 107, Letters Received by the Secretary of War, Registered Series, 1801–1860 (Microfilm M221, Roll 77), D-12.

To ———

Digges, in Washington, was being kept informed of conditions at Warburton by L'Enfant, who on August 25 had given the young slave Charles a note to Digges:

          Warburton Augt. 25 *1820*
dear Sir
  The Boy charles *going up to morrow I have only to say I do not known of any thing worth mentioning only that the sickness continues amongst the people and childern—dr. Seems [Simmes] attend them.—they have began cutting tobaco all full ripe on the first planted tract.*
  I heard Mr. duddly was on his way home the day before yesterday so you will probably have ere now seen him.
           your obt. Sert.
           P: chs. *L'Enfant*

[Addressed:] *Mr. Thoms. A. diggs/City of Washington/by Boy charles*

On August 26 Digges jotted down on this note what must have been additional information provided by Charles. Whether he used this as the basis of a reply cannot be determined.

  Charles is to go back on his father's lame horse at 5 this evening. He says big Ned who is very lame was at the Tobacco Sticks *Gusty being* Sick—Dick was helping Buschs man to get timber—Vulcan wanting shoes was in the Black Smiths shop—Patience still ill—people cutting the Tobacco near Capt. Ansarts—Bett got out to work—Lawes not come up but expected on 2d of next month—which is a pay day *at the* Garrison. The Wells both very low and wants cleaning out—Brick yard well given out—the house water supplyd from the Rock Spring up in Triall [⟨Trail⟩]—The only *drinking* water in the Garrison is got from the river sprout spring. A shamefull & disgraceful *mistake* or negligence within it—

LC: Digges-L'Enfant-Morgan Papers, 3: 559.

To ———

On August 30 Charles had set forth from Warburton with another note from L'Enfant to Digges:

Warburton Augst. 30 1820
[(By Digges:) *he left* Warn. Tuesday 30th 10 oCk. *Warbn. & recd. by Chas. on in the City at 3 oCk.*—]
De[ar Sir]
the Boy charly was expecting to go by the Stone Yott this morning—and receiving your package from Capt. Ansart but this moment. I am unable to write any things of communication of matters you desire—labouring now and since of upward of 7 days past under an Intermittent Fever which particularly last Sunday and yesterday has been very severe—and rather of the hot *than of the aigue kind*—I am so feeble I can hardly old my pen—on the next opportunity I shall write you as you desire.
O— S—
P. chs. L'Enfant
[Addressed:] Mr. Thoms. A. Diggs/City washington/by Boy charly

Again Digges jotted down on L'Enfant's note additional information received from Charles.

Chas. says Dr. Simmes is very sick, not been to Warn. since *Saty. week*—That *Jack's* child is dead himself not well. Gusty & one of his children sick—but Gusty got about *today* & is at the Barn at work—Big Ned poorly—Patience still sick, as is Geo. Gray, and house girl Rachael—also his Father sick—Dominick complaining

& Vulcan without shoes. Patience still sick—all hands cutting Tobacco near the Wash. Landing. Tobacco as high as a man—The *wells* getting better as to water—Brick yard well *none*—

LC: Digges-L'Enfant-Morgan Papers, 3: 560.

To [⟨Paymaster General's Office⟩]

Digges was helping L'Enfant get from the government money owed him for his work as chief engineer during 1814–1815.

5th Sept. 1820

Chas. Philip Le Enfant [Pierre Charles L'Enfant] (who plannd the City) was for some years a rated Major in the U. S. Army: and when acting as *Engineer*, from the Invasion and blowing up of the *first Fort Warburton* had the additional allowance only of a Lieut. Colonels pay & two rations; until Colonel Armistead's succeeding him as Engineer in 1815 at Fort Washington—I think in June or July.

A little before Mr. R. Brent (the paymaster) was taken ill the Major applyd thro Mr. Digges for a statement of what was due him on the army books, which Mr. Robt. Brent then furnishd an item of for the Major to draw for, but he did not do it at the time.

I think it was Mr. John Brent then & now a Clerk in the pay office who gave Mr. Digges the *statements* & *mode* by which Majr. Le Enfant might draw for his pay—. That paper has been mislaid & He now requests to know what is due on his said Pay.

T. A. Digges[1]

LC: Digges-L'Enfant-Morgan Papers, 3: 561.

[1] A reply (in an unidentified hand) is written on the face of this letter: "No Payment appears ever to have been made to Majr. Le Enfant by the late Paymaster General but it is believed that some monies were paid him by the then Secretary of War, Mr. Grahame

[*name inserted by Digges*]; but for what grade or to what amount can not be ascertained from the books of this Office. Probably some information relative to the compensation in question may be drawn from the 3d auditors office, where it is belived all the papers for disbursements about that period are deposited.

Pay Mr. Genls. Office

To James Monroe

Strothers Hotel 4th March 1821

DEAR & RESPECTED SIR

It is with deep regrets I trespass on Your patience to state my hard Case, and this at a time too when Your multifarious exertions (highly appreciated by the whole of my circle of acquaintance) are admiring Your beneficent and patriotic measures: It is to solicit the boon of Your information to The Secretary at War, as to what was observance & state of my loss's by Fires, the explosion of the Fort Magazine and mischiefs done at the shores at periods of the Invasion; and for which I never had the least intention of claiming remuneration.

During the very worst of those Invasion times and while acting in various high and important Stations, You Sir, then my frequent visitor and viewer of those Scenes, knew more of them than any of the Heads or minor State Officers; or even some Scores of others who before and for years after partook of the open hospitality of Warburton house: This was the reason for my last winters Solicitation for obtaining a conferance [with] Yourself and Mr. Secy. Calhoun; who with all His ability, worth, & goodness, is even yet but slightly acquainted with the Fort Station.

Early in the last Spring I gave into The War Office a Statement under my own affidavit for six years lost *moneyd* Rents only for $300 – per year (getting my agreed for Family quota of Fish) and my affidavit was backd by above a dozen certificates from most respectable nieghbours and owners & Renters of adjacent Fisheries; proveing that The Sein births on each side of the ridiculous *triangle* Wharf (more especially the south shad birth) *"was ruind in consequence of the Fort & public works"* which indubitably can be proven, and I pledge You my honor that *it is* so, whatever The Engineers may say a Contra.

But the Secretary at War haveing doubts, and wanting additional evidence to the above stated, General Philip Steuart (the propriator of the adjoining next lower Landing amply acquainted with every fishery thereabouts) purposely went to Secy. Calhoun in May last, and on satisfying those doubts, He promisd The General as he has twice done to myself (upon my mentioning that The President well knew of such damages done me) that I should be paid my $1800– Claim early in the summer. I have not yet obtaind it although in great present want thereof.

I am disabled at present from severe Rheumatic pains, to personally attend to my business or from visiting You as heretofore, But have hopes that Genl. Steuart is again assisting me in it.—Both The Engineers seem averse to my obtaining a Topographical proper Resurvey on the three *eastern* lines of the Fort which are acknowledgd by Thier Surveyor Colo. Wadsworth to *be "irregular & erroneous"* by His and Major Kearneys Survey of Apr. 1814 & known to be so by both Engineers; And which has causd the building the point of the north bastion a very few Yards in & upon my premises: But which has been renderd secure from my yeilding gratis a trifle of Soil to make those *three* courses *one* straight line. ——— ——— There are some *mistakes*, AND THERE HAS BEEN SOME AT FORT WARBURTON; where *yet* a due Title to The U. States is still wanted to some very few Acres (such as the burial ground & the Bakehouse Lots &ca. &ca.) But my conditional *promise* is out & shall be faithfully fulfilld when the essential Resurvey is made and which can be done within the space of one day in fair weather.

I rely on Your goodness for forgiveness of this intrusion and am with sentiments of the highest esteem & friendship

Dr. Sir Your Obedt. Sert.
Thos. A. Digges

For The President of The United States (private)

NA: Record Group 107, Letters Received by the Secretary of War, Registered Series, 1801–1860 (Microfilm M221, Roll 88), D-56.

To [⟨William Dudley Digges⟩]

On March 29, 1821, at two o'clock, Digges received from Charles at his Washington hotel a note written earlier that day by L'Enfant:

Warburton March 29, 1821

DEAR SIR

Charles having to go by Mr. Simmes in his way to you to carry Mr. Simms message to Mr. duddly d. I deed not thought of sending him so Early in the morning as he can not of course return until to morrow: indeed the weather was so severe frost yesterday that I was quiet sick of Rumatism; and went to bed without tinking of his going of earlier to day. The Snow torm of the day befor and which turned out to great wind the most cold has done here the mere Injury to Every vegetable thing than could be Imagined. All our peas—and other things which began to appear above ground are lost and the peach tree and grape vines I fear destroyed.

Nothing else new—Captn. Ansart has for this two day past discharged above 24 men most of which are already gone up to the city to receive their pay. So much loss of the marrauding party wifes and childrens included.—It is Sayd The work at the fort will begin again on monday next.

Yr. obdt. ser.
P. ch. L'Enfant

[Addressed:] Mr. Thoms. A. Diggs / Washington City / by boy charles

At the foot of the letter Digges jotted down in a shaky hand what seems to be a message to be carried by Charles to William Dudley Digges.

Chas. will be his best detailer of news to You—Simmes was not at home—gone to Virga. to be back *fryday* somewhat about Cart Wheels—People all well except two women—Gusty about—Had stuff—Smiths burning of Coal Kiln—many Soldiers dischargd[—]works at fort to begin next monday—The old Majr. had been very sick—kept his bed one day—Dick helping Gusty—people going to make another Tobacco bed—Butterwick still harboard with his horse at Joes house—⟨Fielding⟩ will stay in with Lesby—Jack in the Garden is sowing Potatoes—Majr. not in the Garden for 2 or 3 days past—the family of G. Lee still in Dicks house—

LC: Digges-L'Enfant-Morgan Papers, 3: 586.

Index

"Account of the Late Disturbances in London, An," 237 n
Achilles, 196–97
Adam, William, 117, 118 n
Adams, 531
Adams, James, 92, 94 n, 95
Adams, John, xlviii–l, lii–liv, 132, 133 n, 133–35, 139, 144, 146, 156–57, 169 n, 183, 202, 391 n, 403; books and pamphlets for, 198–99, 205, 219–21, 221 n–23 n, 234, 236–37, 329, 345–46; opinion of British, 256–57, 311, 343, 345 n; reaction to Conway's motion for conciliation, 207 n; attitude toward Franklin, 133–34; view of Irish agitation, 185 n; criticism of Laurens's imprisonment, 310–11; view of parliamentary reform movements, 185 n; and peace negotiations, 352–68, 370 n, 371
  Letters to: 160, 170, 172, 181, 183, 189, 198, 205, 211, 215, 226, 234, 241, 245, 246, 252, 253, 256, 269, 277, 281, 286, 291, 294, 296, 299, 303, 304, 305, 307, 310, 316, 319, 320, 329, 331, 337, 339, 340, 341, 345, 348, 349, 350, 351, 352, 362, 364, 367, 371, 373, 375
Adams, John Quincy, 513 n
Adams, Peter Boylston, 172, 172 n, 177
Addington, William, 295
Addison, Rev. Henry, 502, 504 n

Administration Dissected, 219, 221 n
Admiral Edwards, 204 n, 240 n
Adventure, 163 n, 165, 207–8
Ætna, lxxvi, 559, 560 n
Affleck, Adm. Philip, 456, 457 n
Alert, 11 n
Alexander, Capt., 559
Alexander, Emperor, attempt at mediation during War of 1812, 546 n
Algiers, American declaration of war against, 581, 582 n
Allen, Andrew, 49, 50 n, 52, 206
Alliance, 10 n
Almon, John, 56, 83, 163
Amelia Elizabeth Caroline of Brunswick-Wolfenbütel, princess of Wales, 546–47 n
American commissioners and representatives, quarrels among, 2, 7 n, 11–14, 17 n, 26, 33, 68–69, 101, 123, 133 n, 145
Amerique, 28
André, Maj. John, li, 328, 329 n, 333 n, 338
Angelica, lvi, 400, 401 n, 412
Anglo-American commercial treaty (1815), 582 n
Anna Maria (Dutch merchant ship, 1779), 57, 62
Anna Maria (British armed schooner, 1814), 559
Ann Mary Ann, 414
Annual Register of World Events, 140

639

640 INDEX

Ansart, Lt. Felix, 597, 598 n, 624, 631–32, 636
Anti-Catholicism in England. *See* Gordon riots
Appleton, John, 278, 279 n
Appleton, Nathaniel, 172, 172 n, 177, 279 n
Arbuthnot, Adm. Marriot, 43, 45 n, 88, 117, 118 n, 284 n, 287
Archer & Byde, 39
Ardent, 210
Ariadne, 10 n
Arkwright, Sir Richard, 425, 427–28 n, 429, 439
Armistead, Lt. Col. Walker Keith, 580 n, 582, 591–94, 597–98, 604–5, 607–8, 610 n, 622, 624, 628
Armstrong, Gen. John, 548 n, 561, 565
Letters to: 549, 550, 551, 553, 554, 555
Arnold, Benedict, lii, 328, 329 n, 330–31, 333–34, 336
Arthur, Lt. John, 8, 11 n
Artois, 375
Artois, Charles Philippe, comte d', 42, 44 n
Ashurst, Sir William Henry, 392 n
Associations, the, 167, 169 n, 183
Astorga, Giovanni Oliviero, 122, 129 n; trios (*Six Sonatas . . . op. III*), 125 n, 166
Attwood, Ann (TD's mother), xxiii–xxiv, xxvi; property of, xxiv–xxv
Attwood, George (TD's great-grandfather), xxiii
Attwood, George (TD's grandfather), xxiii–xxiv, xxv; property of, xxiii–xxiv
Attwood, Elizabeth (TD's great-aunt), xliii
Attwood, Mary (TD's cousin), xliii
Attwood, Peter (TD's great-uncle), xxiii
Attwood, Rev. Peter, xxiv
Attwood, Thomas (TD's great-uncle), xxiii, xxv, xlii
Atwood, Ursula (TD's cousin), xliii

Attwood, William (TD's great-uncle), xxiii, xliii
Attwood family, 615
Aubarede, Guillaume-Claude, marquis d', 419–20, 422 n
Austin, Jonathan Loring, 190, 191 n, 192
Letter to: 15
Avery, John, 264
Ayre, Baron, 390

Bagot, Sir Charles, 615
Letter to: 595
Bagot, Mrs. Charles, 615
Bailey, Benjamin, 8, 10–11 n
Bailey, Samuel, 196–97
Baird, Sir James Gardiner, 73, 75 n
Baker, Anthony St. John, 533–34, 537 n, 538, 543
Bakewell, Robert, 448, 449 n
Baldiacam, 385
Balsamão, Luis Pinto de Sousa Coutinho, visconde de, 279 n
Baltimore, 414
Bancroft, Dr. Edward, xliv, xlvi, 11–14, 38–39, 41, 125 n, 362 n, 391 n
Banks, Sir Joseph, 165, 168, 169 n, 179, 187–88, 204, 205 n
Barber, Mr. (of Hartley & Barber), 137–38, 141–42, 147–48, 150, 165–66, 501
Barclay, Thomas (American consul), 393, 395 n
Barclay, Col. Thomas (British consul), 541, 545–46 n
Barlow, Joel, 519, 519 n, 536, 538 n
Barnes, Maj. George, 458–60
Barnet, Capt. James, 216, 226, 230–31, 243–44, 248
Barney, Commo. Joshua, lxxv, 515, 516–17 n, 556, 558 n
Barré, Col. Isaac, 376, 377 n
Barrington, Rear Adm. Samuel, 27, 30 n, 375
Barron, James, 324
Barry, Edward, 143, 167, 169 n, 177–78

Bartle, Andrew, 561, 563, 574, 578–80, 587–88, 592, 596–97, 612–13
Bartle & Taylor, 570
Bartlett, Capt. Nicholas, 138, 141 n
Bartolozzi, Francesco, 574–75, 576 n
Bathurst, Henry, 2d earl of, 113, 114 n
Baubetrang, Lt. Col., 11 n
Bayard, James Ashton, 543, 546 n
Bayley, John. *See* Bailey, Benjamin
Baylor, Mr., 4
Beall, Benjamin Lloyd, 530, 530 n
Beall, Capt. Lloyd, 518 n, 521, 522 n, 529–30, 611
Beall, Cornet Thomas Jones, 517, 518 n
Beauchamp, Francis Seymour Conway, Viscount, 358–59, 361, 361 n, 390
Bedford, John Russell, 4th duke of, 45 n
Bedford party, 43–44, 45 n, 54
Beekman, James, 1, 2 n
Behemus, 195–97, 198 n
Belfast News-Letter, lx
Bell, John, 48, 50 n, 136, 137 n, 149
Belson, Mons., 83–84
Belt, Capt. Walter, 150–51, 152–53 n, 153, 158, 164–66, 356–57, 502–3, 504 n
Benton, Mark, 477, 479 n
Berckel, Engelbert van, 291
Berkeley, Vice Adm. George Cranfield, 534, 537 n
Berkely (*or* Barclay), Capt., 293 n, 334
Bermuda Proclamation, 543, 546 n
Bernard, Gov. Francis, 34, 36 n, 314–15, 316 n
Bertrand, Pierre J. (*also* V. J.) (TD's pseudonym), 22, 30, 80
Biddle, Lt. James, 524, 528 n
Bingham, Mr., 496
Bingham, William, 393, 395 n
Blackburne, Mr., 461, 463 n
Blackstone, Mr., 544
Blount, Sir Walter, xxxiii
Blount, Gov. William, conspiracy of to seize Spain's possessions, lxix, 457, 460
Board of Associated Loyalists (N.Y.), 52 n

Board of Sick and Hurt Seamen, 48–49, 49–50 n, 57, 92, 100–101, 131, 137 n, 141 n, 159, 166–67, 213, 249, 264, 265, 277, 279–80, 307, 325–26
Bob, 151
Bond family (Potomac residents), 556, 558 n
Bond, Phineas, 499, 503, 504 n, 539, 540 n
Bondfield, John, lv
Bonhomme Richard, 17 n, 90 n, 102 n
Booker, Lt. (*or* Capt.) Daniel, 548, 549 n
Boucher, Jonathan, 220; *The American Times*, 223 n
Boulderson, Capt. John, 130, 131 n, 131, 166–67
Boulton, Matthew, 441–45, 446 n, 446–49, 464
Bourbon Compact, 326
Bowens, François, 114, 115 n, 166, 169, 189, 199–200, 209–10, 213, 215, 223, 230, 238, 243, 248, 284–85, 306–7, 322, 324–25, 343, 351
Bowie, Dr. John, 477, 479 n
Bowie, Gen. Robert, 497, 498 n, 505, 553, 620
Bowie, William, 527
Bowman, John, 255–56, 284, 303
Boydell, John, 574–75, 576 n
Boylston, Thomas, 500, 504 n
Boyne, 270
Brackenridge, Mr., 5
Brailsford, William, li, 337 n, 350, 394, 396 n
Brant, Capt. Joseph, 46, 462–63 n
Brehon, Dr. James, xliv, xlvi, 11 n, 48, 49 n, 55, 57, 63, 122, 138–39, 244
Brent, Anne, 472 n
Brent, Catherine. *See* Digges, Catherine Brent
Brent, Daniel Carroll, 497, 498 n, 553, 574, 576 n
Brent, John, 633
Brent, Lt., 574, 576 n
Brent, Robert, lxix, lxxiv, 470, 472 n,

498, 499 n, 553, 611, 620–22, 633
Brereton, William, 20, 21 n
Brett, Alexander (TD's pseudonym), 218, 225
Brickwood, John, 380, 382
Bridgen, Edward, xliv, 36, 37 n, 95–96, 102, 118–19, 123, 161, 204
Brighton affair, 150, 356–57, 393, 502–3
Briscoe, Richard S., 614
Brodie, Francis, 478, 479 n, 490, 504, 506, 508
Bromfield, Henry, 257, 259 n, 260, 281, 283–84, 286, 291, 329
Brooke, Maj. Robert, 409, 410 n
Brookes, Benjamin, lxvii
Brown, George (pseudonym). *See* Austin, Jonathan Loring
Brown, Mr., xlv
Brown, Thomas, lxi
Brown, Collinson & Triton, 166, 169 n
Bryant, Lt. James, 8, 10 n
Buford, Col. Abraham, 237 n
Bull, Frederick, xliv, 270, 271 n
Bumford, Lt. (*later* Capt.) George, 506, 508 n, 508, 512, 621
Burch, Mr., 612
Burdett, Sir Francis, 615, 617 n
Burdy, Thomas, 79, 80 n, 82
Burgoyne, Lt. Gen. John, 12, 27, 30–31 n, 37–38, 47 n, 50 n, 159; *A State of the Expedition from Canada,* 160 n, 221, 223 n, 329
Burke, Edmund, 155–56, 158 n, 159, 230 n, 237, 270, 376, 390; *The Letters of Valens,* 141 n; *Speech of,* 219, 221 n; *Thoughts on the Causes of the Present Discontents,* 238 n
Burke, Richard, *The Letters of Valens,* 141 n
Burke, William, *The Letters of Valens,* 141 n
Burn, William, 174–75, 178, 210–11, 213, 230, 240–41, 249, 387
Burn, Messrs. Edward, & Sons, 174–75, 178, 384, 386–87
Burr, Aaron, conspiracy of, 491 n

Butler, John, bishop of Cork, 469, 472 n
Butler, Col. John, 132, 133 n
Butterwick, Mr., 637
Byrne, William, 466
Byrne Book Sellers, 437
Byron, Adm. John, 23–24, 25 n, 27–28, 51, 52 n, 54, 72–73, 90 n, 96, 98, 116

Cadwalader, Thomas, 505 n
Calef, Capt. John, 104 n, 107, 122
Calhoun, John C., 609 n, 634–35
 Letters to: 608, 609, 612, 621, 623, 629
Calvert, Edward Henry, 477–78, 479 n
Camden, Charles Pratt, 1st earl of, 163, 164 n, 371, 373 n
Camden, S.C., British victory at, 297–99, 304, 332 n, 336
Campbell, Col. Archibald, 23–24, 25 n, 27, 34
Campbell, George Washington, 616–17, 618 n
Campbell, James, 267–69
Campeche, Bay of, 242, 243 n, 244
Candid and Impartial Narrative of the Transactions of the Fleet under Command of Lord Howe. See Meath, bishop of
Carbery, Capt. Henry, 396 n
Carleton, Gen. Guy, 374, 375 n, 376
Carlisle, Frederick Howard, 5th earl of, xliv, 24, 25 n, 390
Carlisle commission, xliv–xlvi, 25 n
Carlos III, 65 n
Carmarthen, Francis Godolphin Osborne, marquis of, 368, 370 n
Carmichael, William, xlv–xlvi, lv, 6, 7 n, 18, 117, 118 n, 121, 124, 139, 146–47, 169 n, 183, 276
 Letter to: 383
Carne & Slade, 522
Carpenter, Capt. Benjamin, 161, 163 n, 164–65, 175–76, 274; TD's certificate for, 207–9, 326–27
Carr, Mrs., 87

INDEX 643

Carr, Samuel, 478, 479 n
Carroll, Anne, 524–25, 528 n
Carroll, Charles, 477, 479 n
Carroll, Daniel (of Ballycrenode), 471
Carroll, Daniel, III (TD's brother-in-law), xxvii, lxxi, 465 n
Carroll, George Attwood (TD's nephew), 468, 472 n, 528
Carroll, James, 471
Carroll, John (of Liscariff), 471
Carroll, Archbishop John, lxx–lxxi, lxxiii, lxxv; opinion of TD, xxvii–xxviii, 467–68
  Letters to: 467, 523, 571
Carroll, William (TD's nephew), lxxi, 464, 465 n, 470, 524–25, 528 n
Cartel, ships and problems of, xlviii, 49, 50 n, 57, 69, 81, 86, 89, 92–93, 95, 99, 101, 105, 108, 114, 118–19, 124, 130–31, 133 n, 134, 137–38, 142–43, 147–49, 151–52, 155–56, 159, 166–67, 169 n, 177, 183, 185 n, 192–93, 194 n, 204, 210, 211 n, 213, 217, 224, 233 n, 239, 262, 269, 274–75, 281, 303, 378
Cartwright, Charles, 425, 427 n, 429
Cartwright, Rev. Edmund, 425, 427 n, 429
Cartwright, Maj. John, 425, 427 n, 429
Carysfort, John Joshua Proby, 1st earl of, *Letter from the Right Honourable Lord Carysfort*, 219, 222 n
Catharine, 411–12
Catholicism: and British politics, 469–70; and Maryland politics, 525
Cavendish, Lord John, 390, 392 n
Cazneau, Capt. Isaac, 183–84, 185 n, 187, 199, 204, 216
Champion, Richard, 37, 39, 40 n, 275, 283, 285, 304, 322
Chance, 415
Chandler, Jehu
  Letter to: 540
Chandos, James Brydges, 3d duke of, 43, 45 n
Channing, John, 248, 251 n
Chapman, Charles (of 80 Corn Hill), 449, 452 n

Chapman, Charles (of Leaden Hall St.), 383
Chapman, Henry H., 477, 479 n
Charles (Warburton Negro carter), 627, 631–32, 636–37
Charleston: 1778 riots, 23, 25 n, 34; defense of, 70, 71 n, 74–76, 93–94, 200–201, 203, 205, 210, 218; British hope for, 161; British capture of and reaction to, 204 n, 227–29, 233–34, 237 n, 258, 260, 273; rebel uprisings in vicinity of, 283, 284 n, 287, 290, 299
Charlotte Augusta, Princess, 546 n
Charters of the British Colonies in America, The, 140, 141 n
Chaumont, Jacques Donatien le Ray de, 12, 17 n, 216, 224, 226, 230, 243–44
Chaumont, Thérèse Joguer, Mme de, 16, 17 n
Cherry, Lt. Robert, 516, 517 n
Chesapeake incident, 488, 489 n, 517 n
Cheston, Mr., 270
Chilham Castle, xxiii–xxiv, 533; TD's claim on, lxv–lxvii, 457 n
Chisholme, John D., 457–62, 463 n
Christie, Gabriel, 477, 479 n
Church, John Baker, 401 n
Church, William Singleton (W. S. C. and S. W. C.) (TD's pseudonym), l, 57, 87, 93, 100, 137, 154, 160–61, 171, 176, 182, 191, 204, 211–13, 224, 236, 242, 245, 251, 253–54, 256, 259, 261, 263, 266, 271, 278, 281, 288, 291, 293–97, 299, 301, 303–5, 307–9, 313, 320, 327, 331, 340, 342, 350–51
Civil Usage, 5
Clark, *Latin Exercises*, 329
Clark, Christopher, 138, 141 n
Clark, Lt. Col. George Rogers, 78 n
Clark, Peter, 397
Clark, R., lxv
Clark, William, 480 n
Clarke, Mr. (British vice-consul, Lisbon), 387
Clavering, Lady Diana, 533

644 INDEX

Clinton, Sir Henry, xliv–xlv, 25 n, 27, 58, 61 n, 76, 98, 161, 182, 184, 187, 198, 200, 202–3, 204 n, 205, 210, 213, 218, 224, 234 n, 242, 246–47, 250, 252, 255, 259–61, 277, 284 n, 286–87, 289–90, 348 n, 349
Cochlan, Jerea., 143
Cochrane, Sir Alexander, lxxv, 558 n
Cocking, Mr., 505
Cockings, George, 223 n
Coffin, Capt., 138
Coinage, lxv, 95–96, 204 n, 441–56, 464–65, 466 n
Coke, Thomas William, 615, 617 n
Coles, Mr., 506
Colley, Capt., 148
Collier, Sir George, 92, 94–95 n, 116, 120, 124, 153 n
Collins, Charles, 371 n
Collins, Capt. Lewis, 461, 463 n
Colt, Peter, 401 n
Columbus, 625
Commission for Sick and Hurt Seamen. *See* Board for Sick and Hurt Seamen
Committee of Secret Correspondence, 4 n
Confederacy, 118 n, 258, 261
Confiance, 562 n
Congreve rockets, 543, 546 n
Connor, Timothy, 10 n
Conqueror, 227
Considerations upon the French and American War, 140, 141 n
Constellation, 531
Constitution, 519 n, 520
Constitutionalist, *Letters to the Electors & People of England*, 220, 222 n
Content, 329
Conway, Gen. Henry Seymour, 201–4, 206, 228, 232, 355, 361 n, 367, 371, 373 n, 390; motion for conciliation, 207 n
Conway, Gen. Thomas, 111 n
Conyngham, David H., 180 n
Conyngham, Capt. Gustavus, l, 8, 11 n, 60, 61–62 n, 78, 80 n, 81, 85–86, 91–92, 94–95 n, 97–101, 104 n, 105, 107–8, 123, 126, 131, 138, 193, 204, 235, 244, 248–49, 251 n, 279, 325, 329–30, 351–52
Conyngham, Redmond, 180 n
Conyngham & Nesbitt, 178, 180 n, 394, 424, 432, 438, 502
Cook, Capt. James, 154–55 n, 168
Cooke, Col. John Travers, 497, 498 n, 553
Cooke, William, 503, 504 n
Coombs, Mrs., 527
Cooper, Mr., 342
Corbet, Lt. Gov. Moyse, 348
Cornplanter (Capt. John Abeel), 461, 463 n
Cornwall, 227
Cornwall, Charles Wolfran, 313, 313 n, 315
Cornwallis, Lt. Gen. Charles, 2d Earl, 24, 25 n, 49, 50 n, 56, 59, 68, 116, 161, 275, 287, 290, 297–99, 308–9, 311–15, 348 n, 362 n
Cotton manufactures, 408–10. *See also* Pearce, William
Coulthard, Capt., 247 n
Countess of Scarborough, 191
Courrier de l'Europe, xliv, 163
Courts, Dr. Richard H., 482–83
Coventry, George William Coventry, 6th earl of, 163, 164 n, 359, 362 n
Covington, Leonard, 474, 475 n
Cowdry, William, 96 n
Craig, Maj. Isaac, 461, 463 n
Craig, James, 13, 15 n
Craik, George Washington, 482, 482 n
Craik, Dr. James, 482 n
Crawford, William H., 579 n, 589–90
 Letter to: 584
Critical Review, xxxvii
Croker, John Wilson, lxi, lxxv
Crop failure (Maryland, 1815), 580–81
Croy, Emmanuel, duc de, 174 n, 177, 179, 188
Cruger, Henry, 270, 272 n
Culloden, 23–24
Cumberland, 153 n
Cumberland, Richard, 236, 237 n

INDEX 645

Cunnim, Capt. Michael, 414
Currie, Capt. Alexander, 84, 102 n
Curson, Samuel, lviii–lix, 405, 407 n
Cutting, James, lxvi
Cutts, Richard, 545, 546 n, 548, 582, 618
Cutts, Mrs. Richard, 618

Daily Advertiser (London), xxxi
Dalling, Sir John, 167, 169 n, 177–78, 244, 245 n
Dalrymple, Col. William, 282, 284 n, 287, 290
Dana, Francis, 132, 133 n, 133, 242
Darby, Vice Adm. George, 262, 263 n
Darnall, Henry (TD's great-uncle), xxiv
David, 148
Davis, Mr., 394
Day, Thomas, xliv
Deakins, Col. William, 411, 415, 417 n
Dean, 275
Deane, Silas, xli, xlvi, 4 n, 7 n, 11–14, 29, 38, 117, 123, 181 n, 384, 391 n; "Address . . . to the Free and Virtuous Citizens of America," 14 n, 30 n, 33
Dearborn, Gen. Henry, lxxiii, 485 n, 492, 507, 512, 555, 565, 620–23
  Letters to: 485, 492, 495, 497
De Calb, Baron. *See* Kalb, Johann
Decatur, Stephen, 582 n
Defence of Admiral Keppel, The, 140, 141 n
De Grey, Thomas, 81, 85 n, 86
Dekay, Charles, 8, 10 n
de la Hay, Charles. *See* Dekay, Charles
De Lamotte, L'air, 153 n
De Lancey, James, 34, 36 n, 49, 50 n
Delawar, Lady, 533
Denmark, neutrality of, 201, 202 n. *See also* League of Armed Neutrality
Dennis, Robert, 477, 479 n
Devastation, lxxvi, 559, 560 n
Dick (Warburton Negro), 631, 637
Dick, Capt. Alexander, 8, 10 n, 18, 21
Dickinson, Gov. John, 424, 427 n, 432, 438

Digby, Adm. Robert, 170, 171 n, 262
Digges, Ann (Nancy) (TD's sister), xxv, xxx, lxx–lxxi, 472, 473 n
Digges, Anna Maria (TD's niece), xxxi
Digges, Anne (TD's aunt), xxiv–xxv
Digges, Catherine Brent (Mrs. George) (TD's sister-in-law), xxxi, 467
Digges, Charles (TD's grandfather), xxiv–xxv
Digges, Charles Attwood (TD's brother), xxv–xxvi, xxviii–xxix, lxix
Digges, Sir Dudley (TD's ancestor), xxiii
Digges, Gov. Edward (TD's great-great-grandfather), xxiii
Digges, Elizabeth (Mrs. Daniel Carroll III) (TD's sister), xxvi, xxx, lxx–lxxii, 465 n, 491, 524, 528, 599
Digges, Frances (TD's sister), xxv
Digges, Frank, 515
Digges, George (TD's brother), xxv–xxvi, xxviii–xxxi, xliv, xlvi, lvii, lxv, lxxii, lxxiv, 4, 6, 6 n, 54, 378, 394, 424, 432, 448, 449 n
Digges, Henry (TD's brother), xxv
Digges, Jane (Mrs. John Fitzgerald) (TD's sister), xxvi, xxx, lxx–lxxii, lxxiv, 567 n
Digges, John (TD's great-uncle), xxiv
Digges, Joseph (TD's brother), xxv–xxvii, xxx, xlviii, 53, 55 n
Digges, Mary (TD's aunt), xxiv
Digges, Mary (TD's sister), xxv
Digges, Susane (Susanne, Susanah) (TD's sister), xxv, lxx
Digges, Teresia (Teresa, Tracy) (TD's sister), xxv, xxx, lxx
Digges, Thomas (mathematician) (TD's ancestor), xxiii
Digges, Thomas Attwood: ancestry and birth, xxiii; inheritance, xxv, xxviii–xxxi, 394; education, xxvi; journey to Portugal, xxviii, 1–2; knowledge of Portugal and Spain, xliii, xlix, 68–69, 174–75, 236, 249, 384–87, 473; relationship with Elizabeth Tyler, xxxviii; arrival in En-

gland, xxxviii; publication and reception of *Adventures of Alonso*, xxxi–xxxiii, xxxvii; autobiographical and political elements in *Alonso*, xxviii, xxxiii–xxxviii; purchase of land on Prince Edward Island, xxxix–xl, 501, 532, 536
Revolutionary period in England: as agent to assist American prisoners, xlvi–xlviii, lxviii, 5, 7–9, 18, 21, 48, 49 n, 55, 86, 89, 100–101, 104 n, 105, 138, 149, 151, 166, 173, 174 n, 233 n, 244, 251 n, 256, 279 n, 307, 329, 344, 345 n, 352, 377, 381, 501–2; signer of oath of allegiance, xlvii, 40–41; as shipper of military supplies and "useful articles" to America, xxxix–xlii, xlvii, 35–36, 57, 83, 91, 165–66, 176, 185, 187, 324, 352 n, 357; and reprinting of American news, 184, 188, 202 n, 249, 272, 317 n, 342; connections with arrested Americans (see Hutchins, Thomas; Laurens, Henry; and Trumbull, John); financial and accounting difficulties, xlviii–l, lv, lxix, 48, 89, 105, 119, 122–23, 138, 329, 344, 347, 356–58, 361 n, 407 n, 411; recovery of seized papers, 359–61, 362 n, 372, 384, 542–43; and St. Eustatius papers, lvii–lx, 402–7, 407–8 n; efforts to assist peace negotiations, liii–liv, 132, 135, 139, 352–76; reputation, xxvii–xxviii, xliii–xliv, lii, liv–lv, lxi–lxiv, lxvii–lxviii, 104 n, 356–58, 361 n, 407 n; claimant to property in Worcester, xlii–xliii; use of pseudonyms (*see* Bertrand, Pierre J.; Brett, Alexander; Church, William Singleton; Drouillard, Jacques Vincent; Dundas, T.; Du Vall, Pierre J.; Ferguson, William; Fitzpatrick, William; Forbes, Donald; Forbes, William; Hamilton, Allen; Hamilton, Arthur; Hammilton, Alexander; M., W.; McKinLock, Alexander; McPherson, A.; P——, W.; Ross, Timothy D.; Ross, William S.; Russell, William; Sinclair, Robert; Thompson, John; W., J.; W., S. C.; Williamson, Alexander; Williamson, T.; Wister, D.)
Post-revolutionary period abroad: promotes emigration of skilled workmen, indentured servants, and tenant farmers, liv–lvi, lx, lxv, 389, 392–93, 399–400, 408, 412–13, 423–24, 437–42; interested in manufactures and machinery, liv–lv, lx, lxv, 389–90, 422–49, 464 (*see also* Pearce, William); interested in coinage, lxv, 441–56; visits Ireland, lv, lxi–lxiv, 398–441; possible author of "A Representation of the State of Politics, Commerce and Manufactures, in Ireland, in 1785," lvii; associates with United Irishmen, lxi–lxiv, 418; arrested, lii, lvi–lvii, lxi–lxiii, 407 n; claimant to Chilham Castle, lxv–lxvii, 457 n; offered appointment as Pinckney's secretary, 501, 504 n; suit by Samuel Hartley and Thomas Holmes, lxix, lxxiv, 499–505; helps investigate Blount conspiracy, 457–62
Later years at Warburton Manor: homecoming, lxix; negotiates sales of sites for Fort Washington, lxxiii–lxxiv, 484–90, 492–98, 499 n, 549–58, 564–66, 567 n, 577; reports on construction, and reconstruction, of fort, lxx, lxxiii, 485–90, 506, 561–63, 572–73, 578–79, 580 n; seeks reimbursement for property damage and loss of income from construction and use of fort, lxx, lxxiii, 512–13, 561, 569, 572–73, 584–90, 597–614, 616, 619–30, 634–35; secures injunction to stop work on Fort, 590–95, 599–600, 608, 610–11, 619–20, 622–24; laments British impressment and orders in council during War of 1812, 534–35; opinion, of Napoleon, 535–36; opinion of British marauders, 541–42; reports on

INDEX 647

British naval movements in 1814, 554, 556; interested in cattle and sheep breeding, 448, 505–6, 509; interested in grains, 473–74, 615–16, 618–20; anti-Federalism of, lxx, 474, 476–78, 483, 506–7, 508 n, 511, 524–26, 581; commitment to Catholicism, lxxi (*see also* letters to Archbishop John Carroll); death, lxxvii
Digges, Col. William (TD's great-grandfather), xxiv
Digges, William (TD's father), xxiii–xxvi, xxviii–xxx, lv, lxxi, 394
Digges, William Dudley (TD's nephew), xxxi, lxxiv, lxxvi, 470, 472 n, 503, 505 n, 541, 566, 567 n, 573–74, 576 n, 631
 Letter to: 636
Disorders and uprisings in England (1783), 389. *See also* Gordon riots
Dispassionate Thoughts on the American War. *See* Tucker, Josiah
Dispatch, 415
Dodge, John, 76; "A Narrative of the capture and treatment of John Dodge," 77–78 n
Dohrman, Arnold Henry, 249, 251 n
Dominica, capture of by French, 27, 31 n
Doorn, Capt. Claas (*or* Klaas), 139, 146, 191
Dorrington (seaman), 197
Dorsey, John, 504 n
Dorsey, Lloyd, 479 n
Dorsey, Mr., 270
Dorsey, Walter, 504 n
Dover, 6 n
Downer, Dr. Eliphalet, 8, 11 n
Dragon, 415
Drayton, William Henry, 116, 117–18 n
Drouillard, Jacques Vincent (*also* Vincent Jacques, V. J., *and* P.) (TD's pseudonym), 37, 47, 54, 67, 69, 71, 74, 84, 88, 106, 110, 114, 132, 152, 178, 193
du Barry, Jean-Baptiste-Adolphe, Vicomte, 19–20, 21 n

Dublin Chronicle, lix
Dublin Gazette, lvi, lxi
Dublin Journal, lvii, lix, lx
Ducket, Thomas, 477, 479 n
Duckett, Judge Allen Bowie, 515, 517 n
Duffy, Edward, 373 n
Dumas, Charles Guillaume Frédéric, 317 n
Duncan, Adm. Adam, viscount of Camperdown, 560 n
Duncan (midshipman), 559
Dundas, Henry, 461, 463 n
Dundas, T. (TD's pseudonym), 163, 164 n, 171
Dunkin, Capt. Edmund, 151, 153 n, 187, 262, 271
Dunning, John, 219, 222 n
Dunstan, Mr., 397
Dury, Mr., 122
Du Vall, Pierre J. (TD's pseudonym), 22, 35
Dyson, Capt. Samuel T., 560, 560–61 n

Earl of Hertford, 2 n
Echlin, Sir Henry, 83, 85 n
Edelen, James, Jr., 548
Edelin, Joseph, 527
Eden, William, Lord Auckland, xl, xliv, 14 n, 24, 25 n, 51, 362 n, 390
Edmonds, Richard, 463
Edwards, Lt. James L., 555, 557, 558 n, 611
Edwards, James Lewis (father of Lt. James L.), 560, 561 n
Edwards, Adm. Richard, 292, 294
Effingham, Thomas Howard, 3d earl of, 163, 164 n
Ellis, Mr., 82, 87
Ellis, Welbore, 63
Ellison, R., 81 n, 82, 87
Ely, Daniel, 197
Emigrations. *See* Digges, Thomas Attwood: Post-revolutionary period abroad
Endeavour, 428
Enquiry into, and Remarks upon, the Con-

648   INDEX

duct of Lieut.-Gen. Burgoyne, 220, 222 n
Enterprise, 518
Erebus, lxxvi, 559, 560 n
Erskine, David Montagu, lxix, 492, 492 n, 517 n, 534
Erskine, Thomas, 1st Baron, 501
Erskine, Sir William, 59, 61 n, 73
Estaing, Charles-Henri, comte d', 22–24, 25 n, 27–28, 51, 73, 96, 98, 106, 108, 116, 120, 124, 127, 130, 133 n, 134, 145
Euryalus, lxxvi, 559, 560 n
Eustis, William, 512, 513 n, 519 n
Eveleth, Capt., 568
Examination [of Adm. Keppel], 140, 141 n
Examination of Joseph Galloway, Esq. . . . before the House of Commons, 220, 223 n
Experiment, 116, 130

Fabroni, Mr., 106, 108, 125 n
Facius, Georg Sigmund and Johann Gottlieb, 576 n
Fair American, 332 n
Fairfax, Mr., 137
Fairy, 292, 293 n
Fancy, 96 n
Farmer, Capt. George, 96, 96–97 n
Farish, Hazlewood, 615, 617 n
Faulkner (English Jesuit), 419
Fawcett (or Faucitt), Gen. William, 134, 135 n, 151, 361, 362
Federal Republican, 528 n
Fenwick, Columbus, 616–17
Fenwick, James, 529, 530 n
Fenwick, Rev. John Ceslas, 469, 472 n
Fenwick, Capt. John R., 494, 495 n
Fenwick, Joseph, 530 n, 616
Fenwick, Mr., 573
Fenwick & Mason, 530 n, 616
Ferguson, Capt., 325–26
Ferguson, James, 433 n
Ferguson, Maj. Patrick, 161, 163 n, 348 n

Ferguson, William (TD's pseudonym), 132
Field, Nicholas, 373 n
Fielding (Warburton Negro), 637
Fielding, Sir John, 81, 84 n, 86
Fisher, Jabez (or Jebas) Maud, 49, 50 n, 51–52, 59
Fitzgerald, Elizabeth (TD's niece), 510 n
Fitzgerald, Jane (Mrs. John) (TD's sister). See Digges, Jane
Fitzgerald, Jane (TD's niece), 510 n
Fitzgerald, John (TD's brother-in-law), xxvii, xxx, lvi–lvii, lxvii, 390, 392 n, 394, 399, 401 n, 411, 413, 415, 424, 428, 432, 465, 484
Fitzgerald, Lt. John (TD's nephew), 482, 484–85, 487–88, 509, 510 n, 511, 521
Fitzgerald, Richard, 471
Fitzgerald, William Attwood (TD's nephew), 510, 510 n, 558, 560 n, 572–73, 576 n
Fitzpatrick, Col. Richard, 390, 392 n
Fitzpatrick, William (TD's pseudonym), 308–9, 315, 321, 391 n
Fitzwilliam, Lord William Wentworth, 390, 392 n
Fizeau, Grand & Co., 128, 139–40, 146, 191
Fletcher, Capt. John, 264, 326
Florida-Blanca, José de Moñino y Redondo, conde de, 384
Fontana, Mr., 107–8
Foot, Samuel, 197
Foote, Caleb, 279 n
Forbes, B. (proposed pseudonym for Franklin), 122, 137
Forbes, Donald (TD's pseudonym), 121
Forbes, William (TD's pseudonym), 125
Forgoson (seaman), 197
Forrest, Richard, 547 n
Forrest, Uriah, 474, 475 n
Forsyth, David, 398
Fort Mifflin, 85 n
Fort Omoa, 172, 173 n, 174
Forton Prison, xliii, xliv, 7–11, 50 n, 70 n, 86, 93, 99, 139, 141 n, 142, 173,

INDEX   649

192–93, 249, 256, 275, 307, 325, 328 n
Fort St. Juan, capitulation of, 241–42, 244
Fort Stanwix, reported capture of, 134, 135 n
Fort Warburton. *See* Fort Washington
Fort Washington: negotiations for U.S. purchase of sites, lxxiii–lxxiv, 484–90, 492–98, 499 n, 549–58, 564–67, 623; construction of, lxx, lxxiii, 485–90, 506–9, 512–13; damage to in War of 1812, lxx, lxxvi, 559–61, 571–72; reconstruction problems, lxx, lxxiii, lxxvi–lxxvii, 561–63, 572–73, 578–79, 580 n, 584–95, 597–614, 616, 619–30
Foster, Sir Augustus John, 487, 525–26, 528 n, 534, 544
Fothergill, Dr. John, 262, 263 n, 306, 327
Four Courts Marshalsea, lvi–lvii, 479 n
Fox, Charles James, 117, 118 n, 230 n, 270, 390, 392 n, 395
Frances, Louis (Franklin's pseudonym), 22
Francis Freeling, 542
Franco-American alliance: British attempts to break, 24 n, 29–30, 33, 148–49, 163; efficacy of, 130, 157. *See also* Revolution, American: Anti-French feeling in America
Frankland: TD's inheritance of, xxv, xxviii–xxx; rents due on, lxv; threat of confiscation of, lxvii–lxviii
Franklin, Benjamin, xli, xlvi–lv, lxviii, 2, 11–14, 16, 29, 79, 128, 133–35, 156–57, 208, 329, 337 n, 353–57, 361 n, 363, 365–66, 409, 410 n; books ordered for, 114, 125 n, 127–29, 140, 141 n, 146, 166, 176; Congressional dissatisfaction with, 133; TD's defense of, 133; opinion of British, 179 n, 335; opinion of TD, 356–57; Royal Society's proposed medal for help to Capt. Cook, 154, 155 n, 168, 169 n, 174 n, 179, 187–88, 205; Trumbull's portrait of, 344
Letters to: 18, 21, 26, 31, 36, 41, 42, 45, 46, 48, 50, 52, 55, 62, 65, 66, 67, 70, 72, 75, 78, 81, 85, 90, 91, 95, 97, 98, 103, 104, 106, 107, 112, 115, 118, 121, 126, 131, 137, 141, 142, 147, 150, 153, 158, 164, 171, 173, 174, 175, 180, 185, 191, 194, 195, 198, 202, 209, 212, 214, 223, 230, 238, 243, 247, 254, 260, 261, 263, 267, 272, 279, 284, 289, 293, 295, 298, 301, 305, 309, 314, 318, 322, 323, 324, 333, 335, 343, 354
Franklin, Gov. William (BF's son), 51, 52 n, 58, 60
Franklin, William Temple (BF's grandson), 52, 137, 166, 192; maps and books ordered by, 114, 125 n, 127–29, 138–40, 146, 191–92
Letters to: 127, 146, 240
Frazer, Henry, 540, 541 n, 593
Frazer, Mrs. Henry, 625
Frazer's Magazine, li
French & Hopson (or Hobson), 67–68, 215, 226
Frères Aubert Tollot & Co., 175, 178
Friend at Plymouth, 91, 101, 123, 166, 193. *See also* Heath, Rev. Robert
Fuller, Son & Co., 65, 67, 247
Fullarton, William, 317, 318 n

Gallatin, Albert, 543, 546 n
Galloway, Joseph, xliv, 34, 35–36 n, 47, 52 n, 59, 63, 68, 109, 206, 220, 223 n, 369; *Account of the Rise and Progress of the American War*, 221, 223 n; *Cool Thoughts on the Consequences . . . of American Independence*, 220, 222 n; *Historical and Political Reflections on the Rise and Progress of the American Rebellion*, 220, 222 n; *Letters to a Nobleman*, 220, 222 n; *Letter to . . . Lord Viscount H——e*, 220, 223 n
Gant, George, 529
Gant, Levi, 474
Gardenier, Barent, 511, 511–12 n

650   INDEX

Gardiner, Luke, xxiv
Gastón, Commo. Don Manuel, 164 n, 167
Gates, Gen. Horatio, 127, 127 n, 287, 290, 297–99, 333 n
Gazetteer and New Daily Advertiser (London), xxxi
Geary, Adm. Francis, 210, 211 n, 236, 262
General Advertiser (London), 206, 212 n, 329
General Glover, 98–99, 116
General Pickering, 277, 279 n
Gentleman's Accomptant, The, 128, 146
Genuine Book, An Inquiry . . . into the Conduct of . . . the Princess of Wales, The, 546–47 n
George III, 12, 47 n, 218, 314; speeches of, 112–13, 225, 311, 313 n, 316–19. *See also* "White Eyes"
George IV, 523, 546–47 n
Gérard, Conrad Alexandre, 117, 118 n, 132
Germain, Lord George, lviii, 44, 45 n, 47 n, 59, 68, 86, 259, 264, 269, 295–96, 300–301, 330, 369, 403, 407 n
Ghent, treaty of, 581, 582 n
Gibraltar, 64–65 n, 72, 116, 132, 144, 146 n, 151, 162, 170, 171 n, 237 n, 317, 319, 326, 347, 352
Gibson, Jacob, 477, 479 n
Gildemeester, Jan, 249, 251 n
Gilman, Nicholas, 171, 172 n, 177
Gilpin, Col. George, 484, 485 n, 493–94, 507, 557
Glassford, John, & Co., xxvi
Glover, Col., 380
Goddard, J., 254–55, 256 n, 260–62, 265–66, 275, 303, 305–6, 327
Golden Eagle, 277, 279 n
Golden Rule, 414
Goldsborough, Charles Washington, 518, 519 n
Goldsborough, Robert Henry, 477, 479 n
Gordon, Lord George, 219, 221 n, 225

Gordon, Capt. James Alexander, lxxvi, 559, 560 n
Gordon, William, 58, 60–61 n; *A History of the Rise, Progress, and Establishment of the Independence of the U.S.A.*, 60–61 n
Gordon riots, 217–18, 221 n, 224–25
Gouverneur, Isaac, lviii–lix, 407 n
Gower, Granville Leveson-, 2d earl, 45 n, 113, 114 n
Grafton, Henry Fitzroy, 3d duke of, 43, 45 n
Graham, George, lxxvii, 585, 589, 611
  Letters to: 567, 569, 576, 578, 582, 589, 590, 591, 596, 598, 599, 600, 602, 604, 606, 607
Graham, John, 604, 606 n
Graham, William, 61 n
Grand, Ferdinand, xlix, 31, 35 n, 66–68, 70, 80–81, 86–87, 92, 99–101, 105, 108, 118–19, 122, 125 n, 137–38, 198, 200, 216, 276, 303, 307, 327, 502
Grand, George, 141 n, 192
Granger, Gideon, 482, 482 n
Grant, Capt., 80 n, 86
Grant, Maj. Gen. James, 27, 30 n
Grantham, 97, 100
Grantham, Thomas Robinson, 2d baron, xli–xlii
Grattan, Henry, lxiv
Graves, Rear Adm. Thomas, 182, 183 n, 184, 187, 189–90, 192, 233, 235, 239, 247, 260, 286–87, 289, 294; mutiny aboard ships of, 189–90, 192
Gray, George, 632
Green, Capt. John
  Letter to: 377
Green, V., 345 n
Gregory, James, 518–21
Grenada, French capture of, 73, 90–91, 92 n
Grenville, William Wyndham, Baron, lxv, 418, 458, 459 n, 461
Grey, Maj. Gen. Charles, 24, 25 n, 49, 50 n, 56, 59, 68

INDEX 651

Grey, Harrison, 337 n
Grey, John, 337
Grey, Lt., 559–60
Grimshaw, Nicholas, 440, 441 n
Grosett, Diana (Mrs. Robert Walpole), 393, 395 n
Guichen, Adm. Luc Urbain de Bouëxic, comte de, 189, 192, 194 n, 233, 245, 287–88, 290, 330
Gustavus Adolphus IV, 507, 508 n
Gusty (Warburton Negro), 631–32, 637

Hake, Mr., xxxiii
Haldimand, Gen. Frederick, 125, 126 n
Hall, F., 527
Hall, William, 423–24, 427 n, 432, 434–35, 439–40
Hamilton, Alexander (TD's pseudonym). *See* Hammilton, Alexander
Hamilton, Alexander, *Report of the Secretary of the Treasury ... on ... Manufactures*, 437, 441 n
    Letter to: 436
Hamilton, Allen (TD's pseudonym), 52
Hamilton, Arthur (TD's pseudonym), 46
Hamilton, Dr., 479–80
Hamilton, Lt. Gov. Henry, 76, 77–78 n
Hamilton, Col. John, 539, 540 n
Hamilton, Paul, 518 n, 519–20
    Letters to: 517, 518, 521, 529, 530
Hamilton, W. (TD's pseudonym), 319
Hammilton (*or* Hamilton), Alexander (TD's pseudonym), 102, 104, 317
Hammond, George, 461, 463 n, 534, 537 n
Hammond, Mr. (friend of David Hartley's), 148, 156
Hammond, Mr. (Francis James Jackson's aide de camp), 515
Hamond, Sir Andrew, 49, 50 n
Hancock, 151, 153 n
Hancock, John Gregory, 442–43
Hanger, Capt. George, 163 n
Hanson, Alexander Contee, 525–26, 528 n

Haraden, Capt. Jonathan, 279 n
Hardy, Sir Charles, 77 n, 210, 211 n
Harland, Sir Robert, 376, 377 n
Harper, Robert Goodloe, 515, 517 n
Harper, W., 568–69
Harrier, 106 n
Harrington, Joseph, 413–14
Harris, J. W., lxxvii
    Letter to: 624
Harris, Capt. John, 8, 10 n, 69, 70 n
Harris, Nathaniel, 195–96
Harrison, Gov. Benjamin, 401 n
Harrison, Benjamin, & Son, 400
Harson, Daniel, xl
Hart, Gov. John, xxiv
Hartley, David, 7, 12, 38, 69 n, 74, 90 n, 96, 101, 119, 137–38, 141–42, 144, 148, 160, 169 n, 188, 204, 242, 252, 357, 363, 501; advocate of negotiation and accommodation, xlvii–xlviii, liii, 29, 42–43, 44 n, 47 n, 55 n, 56, 64, 163, 206–7 n, 228, 230 n, 232, 239, 352–53, 355; role in expediting prisoner exchange, xlvi, 15 n, 44 n, 49 n, 56–57, 92–93, 99, 115 n, 124, 144, 152, 159, 164, 224; *Letters on the American War*, 20–21, 29, 135, 136 n, 219, 222 n; *Two Letters from D. Hartley...*, 219, 222 n
    Letters to: 19, 71, 129, 133, 134, 135, 136, 148, 155, 364
Hartley, Col. James, 501, 504 n
Hartley, Samuel, liii, lviii, lxix, lxxiv, 84, 102 n, 137, 141–42, 150 n, 156, 166, 212–13, 223–24, 238, 248, 252–53, 284, 356, 380, 499–503, 505 n
Hartley, Mrs. Samuel, 240–41, 248
Hartley, Winchcombe Henry, 150 n
Hartley & Barber, 137, 141–42, 165–66, 501
Hartley & Francis, 501
Harvey, David, & Co., 268
Harvey, Mr. (owner of the *Washington*), 401 n
Haslar Royal Hospital, 69, 70 n
Hawk, 104 n
Hawke, 84, 96

Hawkins, George F., xxviii
Hawkins, John, 107, 111 n
Hayes, Thomas, 425, 428 n, 429
Hayley, George, 270, 271 n
Heath, Rev. Robert, 90 n, 106 n, 111 n, 115 n, 121 n, 173, 174 n, 251 n, 361 n. *See also* Friend at Plymouth
Heath, Maj. Gen. William, 141 n
Henley, David, 140, 141 n
Henry, 84, 102 n
Hessian troops, 135 n, 161, 206
Hill, Capt. Benjamin, 10 n
Hill, Clement (TD's uncle), xxiv
Hill, Capt. Peter, 130–31, 131 n, 166–67
Hillsborough, Wills Hill, earl of, 113, 114–15 n, 300–301, 321–23, 348, 359, 369
Hite, Maj. Robert G., 576–77, 577 n
Hocken, Joseph, 195–96
Hodgson, William, xliv, lv, 15 n, 156, 158 n, 160, 164, 168, 176, 281 n; and distribution of relief to prisoners, 4 n, 115 n, 173, 174 n; role in expediting prisoner exchange, 114, 115 n, 119, 144, 149, 152, 159, 169 n, 192, 194 n, 224, 239, 279–80, 307, 325; opinion of TD, xxvii, liv, 356–57
Hodgson, William, & Co., 214–15, 226, 256
Holland: reported plan of mediation, 88; neutrality of, 201, 202 n, 236 (*see also* League of Armed Neutrality); relations with U.S., 291–92, 296, 348 n; relations with Great Britain, 27, 102–3 n, 202 n, 296, 340–42, 343 n, 352, 371, 374, 376; Britain's declaration of war against, 346, 347–48 n, 349–50
Holmes, Judge Hugh, 511
Holmes, Thomas, lxix, lxxiv, 499–501, 505 n
Holstein, Agosto Antonio de Souza, 279 n
Honorable Board of Associated Loyalists, 121 n
Hood, Rear Adm. Sir Samuel, 315, 317, 318 n

Hopes, Messrs., 335, 338
Hopkins, Capt. John Burroughs, 61 n, 73, 74–75 n
Horneca, Grand & Co., 56–58, 62, 89, 90 n
Hornet (Continental sloop), 8, 11 n
Hornet (diplomatic courier ship), 475, 475 n
Hotham, Sir Beaumont, 392 n
Hotham, Commo. William, 27, 30 n
Howe, Mary Hartopp, Lady (wife of Viscount Richard), 533, 537 n
Howe, Adm. Richard, 4th Viscount, 25 n, 33, 35 n, 43, 47 n, 50 n, 59, 115 n, 140, 141 n
Howe, Maj. Gen. Robert, 331, 333 n, 334 n
Howe, Sir William, 35 n, 43, 47, 47 n, 50 n, 59, 329
Hughes, Rear Adm. Edward, 28, 31 n
Humberton, Thomas Mackenzie, 318 n
Hunt, John, 24 n, 29, 31, 357, 361
Huntington, Gov. Samuel
  Letter to: 411
Hussey, Thomas, 111 n, 236, 326
Hutchins, Capt. Thomas, xlvii, 79–80, 80 n, 81–82, 86–87, 92, 105–6, 112, 137, 178
Hutchinson, Gov. Thomas, 34, 36 n, 115 n

Ibetts, Capt. Nanne, 329
Indentured servants, sending to U.S., lv–lvi, 392–93, 399–400, 411–17
Independence, British attitudes toward, 23, 29, 32–34, 58, 63, 88, 109, 163, 183–84, 186, 190, 206, 228, 259, 272–73, 280–81, 288, 330, 368, 371
Inglis, Charles, *Letters of Papinian*, 220, 221 n
Invasion of British Isles, fear of, 27, 64, 70, 80 n, 94, 190–91
Invincible, 192
Ireland: conditions in, 43, 45 n, 54, 109–10, 112–13, 121, 162–63,

INDEX 653

167–68, 201, 203, 273; emigration from, lx, 399–400, 423–24, 437; sending of convicts as indentured servants, 411–17
Irving, Lt. Gov., 348
Irving, Washington, *Life of Washington*, xxvi
Izard, Ralph, xlii, xlvi, 12, 18, 92, 101, 103 n, 118, 120, 123–24, 133–34, 145, 150
  Letter to: 2
Jack (Warburton Negro), 632
Jackson, Francis James ("Copenhagen"), 515–16, 517 n, 534
Jackson, George, lviii, 265, 267 n, 276, 327, 359, 362 n
Jackson, John, 133 n, 143–44, 167
Jackson, Jonathan, 6 n
Jackson, Tracy, & Tracy, 5
Jägers, 161, 163
James, 165, 207
Jameson, William, 423–24, 427 n, 428, 432, 434–35, 439–40
Jane, 267
Jarvis, Capt., xxxiii
Jason (British armed frigate, American prize), 60, 61 n
Jason (Capt. Manley's), 153 n
Jason (British man-o-war), 206
Jay, John, liii, 7 n, 117, 118 n, 121, 124, 132, 133 n, 139, 146, 222 n, 353, 365, 383
Jebb, Dr. John, 395, 396 n
Jefferies, Capt., 438
Jefferson, Martha, 475 n, 479 n, 480
Jefferson, Thomas, liii, lxxiii, 78 n, 181 n, 365, 432, 438, 447, 449, 452, 472 n, 495, 557, 622–23; comment on significance of July 4, 475 n; 6th annual message to Congress, 480; indenture between TJ and TD for sale of Fort Washington site, 499 n; judgment of English attitudes (1808), 508 n
  Letters to: 408, 422, 441, 464, 466, 472, 473, 476, 479, 481, 482, 483, 487, 489, 491, 505, 508, 510, 511, 514, 614

Jenings, Edmund, xliv, 384, 387, 391 n, 503, 505 n
Jenkins & Frazer, 612
Jennings, Daniel, 383
Jennings, Richard Downing, lix
Jenny, 8
Jewell, Feilder [Fielder?], 593
Johnson, Capt. (of *Mount Vernon*), 464
Johnson, Lady Cæcilia, 533
Johnson, Capt. Henry, 7
Johnson, Judge John, 479 n, 595
Johnson, Joshua, xlvii, lxvii, 5, 6 n, 19, 53, 67, 119, 121 n, 122, 135, 136 n, 248, 391 n, 394, 424, 436, 441, 447–49, 465
  Letter to: 456
Johnson, Thomas, xlv–xlvi, lvii
Johnson, Capt. William, 461, 463 n
Johnston, Christopher, xlvi
Johnston, William, 106
Johnstone, Gov. George, xliv–xlvi, 23, 24–25 n, 34, 43, 51, 282, 283 n, 420, 422 n
Jones, Charles, 525
Jones, Maj. Gen. Daniel, 73, 75 n
Jones, Capt. John Paul, 17 n, 88, 93, 102–3 n, 149 n, 151, 153 n, 190–91, 194 n, 251 n
Jones, Mr. (defrauder of Franklin), 256 n, 262, 263 n, 265–66, 303, 305–6, 327
Jones, Col. Roger, 593, 595 n
Jones, William (secretary of navy), 546 n
  Letter to: 547
Jones, Sir William (fellow of Royal Society), 154, 155 n, 168, 174 n, 235, 272, 276 n, 306, 312, 325, 351
Jordan, John, 443, 447
Joy, Capt. Benjamin, 323–24

Kalb, Johann (baron de Kalb), 488, 489 n, 490
Kearney, Capt. James, 549–50, 550 n, 551–56, 561, 564–66, 571, 577, 590, 597–602, 604, 622–23, 635
Kellock, Katharine, xxvi

Kelsey, John, 432–33 n
Kemble, Col. Stephen, 244, 245 n
Kent, Dr. Joseph, 474, 475 n
Kentish Chronicle, lxvi
Keppel, Adm. Augustus, Viscount, 25 n, 28, 140, 141 n, 371, 373 n, 376, 533
Keppel, Capt. George, 291–93, 300, 302
Ketland, Thomas, 442
Key, Francis Scott, lxxiv, 215 n, 500, 573
Key, Philip Barton, lxix, lxxiv, 524, 528 n
    Letter to: 499
King, Robert, Jr., 554, 555 n
King, Rufus, lxix
    Letters to: 457, 459
King George, 2 n
Kirby, Mr., 527
Kirkman, John, 270, 271 n
Knox, Col. Henry, 129 n, 331, 333 n, 333
Knox, Lt., 69
Knox, William (British undersecretary of state), lviii, 12, 15 n, 81–82, 85 n, 86, 403, 408 n
Knox, William (American, brother of Col. Henry Knox), 128, 129 n, 138
Knyphausen, Lt. Gen. Wilhelm, baron von, 252, 253 n, 259, 284 n

Labor, cost of in 1815, 578
Lady Elizabeth, 139, 191
Lafayette, Marie Joseph Paul Yves Roch Gilbert du Motier, marquis de, 111–12 n, 384
Laforey, Sir John, 533, 537 n
Lambert, William, 609, 609 n
La Motte Picquet (Picquet de la Motte), Toussaint-Guillaume, Comte, 51, 52 n, 189
Lane, Son & Boylston. *See* Lane, Son & Frazer
Lane, Son & Frazer, lxix, 500
Langara, Adm. Don Juan de, 146 n

Laub, Jacob, 609, 609 n
Laurance (American prisoner), 325
Latrobe, Benjamin Henry, 466, 466 n
Laurens, Henry, 384, 391 n, 394; capture and imprisonment of, l–liv, 291–92, 293 n, 293–305, 307–18, 320–23, 326–40, 345 n; and peace proposals, 353–54, 358, 365, 367 n, 367, 369, 370 n, 371, 372 n, 374, 376–77; papers of, 406
    Letter to, mentioned, 353–54
Laurens, Henry, Jr., li, 299–300, 301 n, 301–3, 316, 318 n, 320–23, 336, 338, 362
Laurens, Col. John, 30 n, 34, 332 n
Law, John, 533, 537 n
Lawes, Belitha, 593
Lawrence, John, 143
League of Armed Neutrality, 202 n, 250, 251 n, 258, 261, 273, 348 n, 352
Leake, Robert, 143
Lear, Col. Tobias, 577, 578 n
Lee, Arthur, xli–xlii, xliii–xliv, xlvi–xlvii, 3, 4 n, 6 n, 7, 16, 17 n, 18, 29, 33, 65 n, 69 n, 78 n, 117, 120, 123–24, 125 n, 134–35, 145, 181 n
    Letters to: 11, 37
Lee, Gen. Charles, 9, 11 n, 30 n, 311, 314, 316 n; "General Lee's Vindication," 30 n, 33–34
Lee, Edmund Jennings, 515, 517 n
Lee, Francis Lighfoot, 509, 510 n
Lee, G., family of (Warburton Negroes?), 637
Lee, Henry ("Light Horse Harry"), 124, 126 n
Lee, James, 8
Lee, Lt., 597
Lee, Thomas Sim, lvii
Lee, Richard Henry, 17 n
Lee, Theodorick, 602
Lee, William, xliii–xliv, xlvi–xlvii, 6–7 n, 13, 17 n, 18, 69 n, 78 n, 92, 125–26 n, 145, 181 n, 291
Lee-Van Berckel treaty, 291–92, 296, 348 n
Leeke, Frank, xxix

INDEX 655

Legear, Lt. Edward, 11 n
L'Enfant, Maj. Pierre Charles: and selection of site of Fort Washington, 484–85, 489 n; and reconstruction of fort, lxxvi–lxxvii, 561, 562 n, 563, 566, 572, 586; dismissal of, 580 n, 582–83; last years, 588–90, 618, 627–36; claims on government, 629 n, 633, 633–34 n
 Letter to: 627
Leonard, Daniel, lviii–lix
Leonard, Mr., 397
Leopard, 489 n
Le Patriote, 377
Lesby (Warburton Negro), 637
Leslie, Maj. Gen. Alexander, 347, 348 n
Letters of Valens, The. See Burke, Edmund
Levant, 5, 10 n
Lewis, John, 197
Lewis, Meriwether, 480 n
Lexington, 8, 11 n
Lilly, William, xliii
Lily, William, *Grammar*, 329
Lincoln, Maj. Gen. Benjamin, 59, 61 n, 71 n, 75, 124, 127, 130 n, 133 n, 145, 203
Linton, John, 410
Lion, 377
Liston, Robert, 457, 461, 534, 538
Little, Joseph, 198 n
Littleton, Sir Edward, 615, 617 n
Liverpool Blues, 28, 32
Livingston, Robert R., 506, 507 n
Lloyd, John, 37, 39, 40 n, 214, 215 n, 226
Lloyd's coffee house, 54, 59, 72, 227, 231, 252, 271, 274, 282, 288, 290–91
Lloyd's Evening Post (London), xxxi
Logan, Dr. George, 189, 191 n, 191, 200, 213, 480
London Chronicle, xxxi, 21 n, 25 n
London Courant, lii, 163, 199, 205, 219–20, 251 n, 256 n, 267 n, 293 n, 341–42
London Evening-Post, li, 199, 205, 219–20
London Gazette, 70, 73, 130, 132, 170, 205, 223, 283, 294

London Magazine, xxxi
London Packet, 199, 205, 219–20
London Review, xxxi
Long, Samuel, 197
Long & Richard, 2 n
Long Island, popular revolt on, 120, 121 n, 124–25
Loudoun County (Va.): TD's property in, xxiv–xxv, lxv
Loughborough, Baron. See Wedderburn, Alexander
Loughborough, Nathan, 559, 560 n
Lovell, James, 311, 314, 316 n
Lowe, Col. Henry (TD's great-grandfather), xxiv
Lowe, Susannah Maria (TD's grandmother), xxiv
Loyalists, American, in England, 47, 50 n, 257–58, 379. *See also* Galloway, Joseph
Luard, Peter Robert, 90–91, 91 n, 92, 98, 119, 122, 137, 144, 147, 160
Lunt, Lt. Joseph, 69, 70 n
Lupton, George. *See* Van Zandt, Isaac
Lyles, Col. William, Jr., 474, 475 n, 477, 479 n, 527, 611
Lyttelton, William Henry, xxxv–xxxvii

M., W. (TD's pseudonym), 334
Macatter, Edward, 369, 370–71 n, 372, 376
Macaulay, Catherine, 16, 58; *The History of England . . .*, 16, 17 n
McBride, Capt. John, 375, 376 n
McCabe, Thomas, 423–29, 432 n, 435, 436 n, 438–39
McCausland, Conolly, 267–69, 326
McCausland, Marcus, 267–69
McCormick (white- & blacksmith), 434
McCulloch, James H., 477, 479 n
MacDermot, Frank, lxiv
McElderry, Thomas, 477, 479 n
McGuire, Capt. Samuel, 625, 627 n
McHenry, Dr. James, 477, 479 n
McIver, J., 492 n
Mackenzie, John (Lord MacLeod), 31 n.

See also McLeod's Highlanders
McKinLock, Alexander (TD's pseudonym), 174
McLeod's Highlanders, 28, 32. *See also* Mackenzie, John
McPherson, A. (TD's pseudonym), 77
Madison, Dolly, 522, 559, 580, 620
Madison, James, lxx, 472 n, 490, 492, 509, 515, 532, 545 n, 548, 611, 615, 623
  Letters to: 522, 558, 580, 618
Magellan (Magalhaens), Jean-Hyacinthe de, 144, 145 n, 176
Magruder, John Read, 595
Mahratta Confederacy, 246 n
Maitland, Mr., 501
Manigault, Gabriel, 90 n, 108
Manigault, Mr., 559
Manley, Capt. John, l, 151, 153 n, 166, 169 n, 173, 177, 193, 194 n, 204, 244, 249, 277, 279 n, 279, 325, 329–30, 351–52
Manly, lxxvi
Manning, William Coventry, 292, 298 n, 298–303, 320–22, 332
Mansfield, William Murray, Baron, 85 n, 110, 218, 224
Manufactures, development of, lx. *See also* Digges, Thomas Attwood: Revolutionary period abroad
Marie-Antoinette, 376
Marriott, Sir James, 376, 377 n
Marshall family, 556, 558 n
Marsteller, Maj. Edward, 562, 562 n, 563, 585–86, 588, 590, 625
Marsteller, Bartle & Co., 580
Martin, Mr., 283
Maryland politics, 476, 524–26, 528 n, 540, 581. *See also* Digges, Thomas Attwood: Later years at Warburton Manor: anti-Federalism of
Mason, George, IV, 496, 497 n, 498 n
Mason, J. F., xxviii
Mason, Gen. John, 497 n, 498, 499 n, 547 n, 616, 620
Mason, John Thomson, 477, 479 n, 497, 498 n

Mason, Gen. Thomson, 497, 498, 498 n, 553
Mathew, Gen. Edward, 282, 284 n
Maurice, Lt. (*later* Capt.) Theodore W., 578, 580 n, 582, 591–94, 600, 604, 607, 624, 627–28
Maxwell, John (American loyalist in England), 49
Maxwell, Dr. John (Maryland state senator), 477, 479 n
Maxwell, Brig. Gen. William, 333 n, 333
May, John, xxxvii
Meath, Thomas Lewis O'Beirne, bishop of, *Candid and Impartial Narrative of the Transactions of the Fleet under Command of Lord Howe*, 140, 141 n; *Considerations on the Late Disturbances*, 238 n
Meddowcroft, J., lxvi
Mediterranean trade, 28
Melville, Robert Saunders Dundas, Viscount, lxxv, 545 n
Mendez, Padre Heres, 420
Mends, Benjamin, 378, 379 n
Mends, C. S., 379 n
Mercer, John Francis, 476, 478–79 n
Mercury, 291, 333 n
Meredith, Sir William, 59, 61 n
Merrell, Thomas, 197
Merry, Anthony, 469–70, 472 n, 534
Merry, Mrs. Anthony, 615
Meteor, lxxvi, 559, 560 n
Mexico, discontent with Spanish rule in, 418–22
Miflin, 92
Milford, 48, 49–50 n, 69
Miller, Sir J., 20
Milligan, Mr., 100
Mill Prison, 7, 50 n, 80 n, 81, 86, 93, 94 n, 95, 99–100, 142, 151, 153 n, 173, 193, 249, 256, 325, 328 n, 329–30, 369, 371 n, 377
Miró, Estevan, 422 n
Mitchell, Capt. Henry, 133 n, 143, 151, 159, 163 n, 165, 167–68, 176, 208–9, 217, 225, 262, 265, 271, 275–76, 327

INDEX 657

Mitchell, John, 460–61, 462 n
Molleson, Robert, 5, 6–7 n
Molleson, William, 5, 6–7 n
Monroe, James, lxx, lxxv, 532, 583–84, 589–90, 621, 630
  Letters to: 561, 562, 564, 565, 586, 634
Montgomery, 8
Montgomery, Thomas, 515, 517 n
Monthly Review, xxxiii
Montresor, Col. John, 49, 50 n
Moore, Alexander, 8, 10 n
Moore, Mr., 458
Morann, Lt. William, 11 n
Mordaunt, William, 473
Morier, John Philip, 534, 537 n
Morlaix, port of, for prisoner exchange, 49, 50 n, 56–57, 95 n, 105, 108
Morland, George, lxxii
Morning Chronicle and London Advertiser, xxxi, lix
Morning Post and Daily Advertiser (London), xxxi, xlvii, 212 n, 329
Morris, Capt. Richard Valentine, 468, 472 n
Morris, Robert (American financier), xlv, 179–80 n, 377, 391 n
Morris, Robert (British subject in Blount conspiracy), 460, 462 n
Morris, Theodore, 49
Morris, Thomas, 396 n
Morsell, James, 573, 576 n
Mosquito, 8, 10 n
Moulton, Joseph, 198 n
Mountmorres, Hervey Redmond Morres, 2d Viscount. *Considerations on the Intended Modification of Poynings' Law*, 219, 222 n
Mount Vernon, 464
Moylan, Francis, bishop of Cork, 469, 472 n
Muir, John, 391 n
Mulcaster, Mr., 348
Murdoch, Yuille, Wardrop & Co, 581, 582 n
Murray, Lt. Gen. James, 27, 30 n
Murray, Mr., 597

Nancy, 411, 414, 416
Napier, Capt., 559
Napoleon: and treaty of Tilsit, 487 n, 516; internal improvements under, 524; and War of 1812, 535–36, 537–38 n; and Russia, 536. *See also* Peninsular War
Napper, Capt., 415
National Intelligencer, lxxvii
Neave, Richard, 79, 82, 87
Neave, Richard, & Co., 80 n
Ned (Warburton Negro), 624–25, 631–32
Neilson, Sam, lxi
Nelson, Judge Hugh, 615, 617 n
Nepean, Evan, 403, 408 n
Nesbitt, 377
Nesbitt, John Maxwell, 180 n
Nesbitt, J. M., & Co, 180 n
Netherlands. *See* Holland
Neufville, Jean de, li, 248, 251 n, 275, 291, 309 n, 316, 352
Neufville, Jean de, & Son, 316, 332, 346, 351
Neufville, Leendert de, li–lii, 308, 309 n, 310, 336, 338, 340 n, 341, 345 n, 347
Nevin, Capt. Duncan, 414–15
Newnham, Nathaniel, 270, 271–72 n
New Prison, 79, 81
New Protector, 192
"New Whigs," 45 n
Nicholson, Capt. James, 11 n, 247
Nicholson, Capt. John, 7, 8, 11 n
Nightingale, 280
Nolcken, Baron Gustav Adam, 354
Non-importation (U.S. during Revolution), 34–35
Non-intercourse Act (1809), 511–12 n, 537–38 n
Norris, Lt., 292, 300, 302
North, Frederick, Lord, xxxix, xlvii, liii–liv, 12, 29, 38, 44, 45 n, 47 n, 54, 121, 131–33, 144, 167, 389–90; early indirect peace discussions with Franklin, 46–48; later peace preliminaries, 353, 358–59

Northampton, 10 n
Norton, Sir Fletcher, 313, 313 n, 315
Notre Dame, 10 n
Nourse, Maj. Charles J., 582, 582 n
Nugent, Lord Robert, 359, 362 n

Oakly, Mr., 515
O'Beirne, Thomas Lewis. *See* Meath, bishop of
Obers, failure of, 557
O'Brien, Mrs., 471
O'Connor, Dr. and Mrs., 571–72, 574
O'Grady, James, lxi
Old Mill Prison. *See* Mill Prison
Oliver, Andrew, 115 n
Oliver Cromwell, 8
O'Mara, Capt., 468
O'Mara, Richard, 468, 470
O'Neill, John, 1st Viscount, 432 n
Ore, Col. James, 460, 462 n
Orvilliers, Adm. Louis Guillouet, comte d', 65 n
Osage, 491, 506
Out-of-Door Parliament, The, 221, 223 n
Owen, Robert, 456

P——, W. (TD's pseudonym), 64
Palliser, Vice Adm. Hugh, 25–26 n, 262, 263 n, 282
Panchaud, Isaac, 53–55, 57, 63
Papinian, Letters of. See Inglis, Charles
Paradise, John, 154, 155 n, 168, 174 n, 179, 235, 272, 276 n, 306
Parker, Adm. Sir Hyde, 189, 191 n
Parker, Capt. Timothy, 401 n, 411–13
Parker, William, 551, 553 n
Parliamentary reform movements, 158 n, 162, 167, 169 n, 183, 185 n, 186
Parliamentary Register, 140, 141 n
Partridge, John, 477, 479 n
Patience (Warburton Negro), 631–33
Patterson, Brig. Gen. James, 334
Patterson, John, 49, 59 n
Patton, James, lxxv, 525, 529 n, 538–39 n
    Letter to: 541
Pearce, William, 423–34, 440, 441 n, 442
Pearson, John, 5
Peirson, Maj. Francis, 348, 349 n
Peisley, James, 79, 80 n, 81–82, 86
Pembroke Prison, 86
Pendennis Castle, 80 n, 81, 97, 100
Penelope, 187
Peninsular War, 491, 492 n, 511, 512 n
Penn, Mary Masters (Mrs. Richard), 393
Penn, Richard, 37, 40 n, 53, 55, 300, 301 n, 302, 358–59, 384, 393
Pensacola, 151, 153 n, 182
People's Barrier against Undue Influence, The, 219, 221 n
Perceval, Spencer, 539, 540 n, 546 n
Perkins, William, 383
Peters, Capt. George P., 548, 548 n
Peters, Richard, 46 n
Peters, William, 45–46, 46 n, 48, 53, 55, 57, 65–68, 70, 72, 75, 78, 81, 138, 247, 251 n
Petrie, Samuel, 276, 276–77 n
Pettice, Capt., 197
Petty, William. *See* Shelburne, 2d earl of
Phillips, Maj. Gen. William, 116–17, 118 n
Philpot, Thomas, 414
Pickens, Col. Andrew, 548, 548 n
Pickett, Lt. William, 95, 96 n
Pickles, Capt. William, 291, 293 n, 332
Pierce, Dr. J. Harvey, 194
Pike, Zebulon Montgomery, 480 n
Pilgrim, 325–26
Pinckney, Thomas, lxv, lxix, 446 n, 464–65, 501, 504 n
    Letters to: 446, 449, 452
Pinkney, William, 617, 618 n
Pitt, Thomas, 395, 396 n
Pitt, William, the Younger, 387, 391 n
Platt, Ebenezer Smith, and habeas corpus, 312, 313 n
Plattsburg, battle of (1814), 562 n

Plunkett, Dr., 198
Plunkett, Rev. Robert, 525, 528 n
Poetical Epistle to His Excellency George Washington, A, 219, 222 n
Political Magazine, li
Pollock, William, 403, 408 n
Polly, 133 n, 143, 151, 159, 163 n, 208
Polly, Capt. Heden de, 84, 96
Pombal, Sebastião José de Carvalho e Melo, marquês de, xxxiv–xxxv
Poona, 246, 246 n
Porten, Sir Stanier, xl
Portland, William Henry Cavendish-Bentinck, 3d duke of, 390, 392 n, 460
Portugal: neutrality of, 201, 236, 285; reported embargo by, 278, 281–82; proposed commercial treaty with U.S., 385–86; Napoleon's invasion of, 491, 492 n
Potomac Canal, lvii
Potts, Capt. J., 2 n
Potts, Richard, 477, 479 n
Powel, Lt., 148
Powel & Hopton, 379
Pownall, Gov. Thomas, 183, 185 n, 186, 202; *Administration of the Colonies*, 185 n, 186, 188; *A Memorial . . . to the Sovereigns of Europe*, 183, 185 n, 186, 188–89 n, 219, 296
Poynings' Act, 162, 164 n, 167
President, 519 n, 521
Preston, 270
Prevost, Maj. Gen. Augustine, 58–59, 61 n, 70, 71 n, 73–76, 127, 130
Price, Dr. Richard, 58, 61 n, 235, 395; *An Essay on the Population of England*, 220, 222 n, 297
Prior Documents, 219, 221 n
Prisoners, American, xlvii–xlviii, lxviii, 5, 7–11, 13, 142–43, 325, 352, 374 (*see also* Forton Prison, Mill Prison); exchange of, during Revolution, 38, 48–49, 50 n, 56, 78 n, 99, 101, 102–3 n, 115, 126–27, 130–33, 143–44, 153 n, 194 n, 211 n, 249, 264–65, 267–69 (see also Cartel, ships and problems); exchange of, during War of 1812, lxxv, 547 n
Proceedings of a Court-Martial . . . for the Trial of Colonel David Henley, 140, 141 n
Protestant petitioners. *See* Gordon riots
Providence, 92
Public Advertiser (London), lix
Pulaski, Count Casimir, 74, 75 n
Pumphrey, Lloyd, 593
Purnell, Zadock, 477, 479 n
Purviance, Robert, 515, 517 n
Purviance & Degan, 516 n
Pye, Charles, 463–64
Pye, James, 531
Pym, Capt. John, 2 n

Quebec, 96
Queen & Moore, 584–85, 586 n, 613
Queen of France, 377
Quids, 476, 478–79 n
Quincy, Josiah, 513 n

Rachael (Warburton Negro), 652
Radford, Lt. William, 11 n
Rainbow, 210
Randolph, Thomas Mann, Jr., 480 n, 483; *Letter of . . . to His Constituents*, 474–75, 475 n
Raspe, Rudolf Erich, 75, 77 n, 84, 85 n, 101, 103 n
Rattan (Roatán), island of, 242, 243 n, 244
Read (*or* Reed), Lt. George C., 547, 548 n
Reid, Capt. James, 567, 568 n, 577, 611
Reid, Lt. *See* Read, Lt. George C.
Remembrancer, 56, 114, 140, 183, 221 n
Renny, Mr., 212
Renommé, 148
Reprisal, 8, 10 n
Revenge, 11 n, 60, 62 n
Revolution, American: American disunity during, 22–23, 26–27, 32–34, 58, 63; Anti-French feeling in Amer-

ica during, 23, 25 n, 132, 133 n; British attitudes toward prosecution of war, 6, 20–23, 26–27, 32–34, 43–44, 54, 56, 63, 67–68, 88, 115–16, 120–21, 129–30, 132, 134–35, 145, 161–62, 167, 170, 190, 193, 201–4, 228–29, 231–35, 257–59, 270, 272–74, 280–82, 285–90, 297–99, 301–2, 316–20, 336, 339, 352, 367–68, 373–74; loyalist plan for revolt in Jerseys, 51–52, 58, 60; British reaction to loss of East and West India fleets, 252–55; British peace proposals, 29–30, 33, 54–56, 58, 352–68, 371–72, 375 n, 376 (*see also* Independence, British attitudes toward); Digges memorandum, 365, 370 n; peace negotiations, 132–35, 150, 201–2; British attitude toward post-war commercial relations, 387–89, 395

Reynolds, Sir Joshua, lxxii–lxxiii; "Faith," lxxiii, 574, 576 n; "Hope" and "Charity," 574, 576 n

Rhode Island, American possession of, 127

Rice, Count, 19–20, 21 n

Richmond, Charles Lennox, 3d duke of, 63, 65 n, 390, 418

Ricketts, Mr. and Mrs., 393

Ridgeley, Gen. Charles, 477, 479 n

Ridley, Anne (Mrs. Matthew), 395

Ridley, Essex, 395

Ridley, Matthew, xlii–xliv, xlvi, liii, lv, 3, 16, 19, 119, 120 n, 122, 277, 284, 391 n, 502
    Letters to: 4, 392

Ridley & Pringle, 356, 502

Ridout, Horatio, 479 n

Ridout, Mr., 270

Riedesel, Friedrich Adolph, baron von, 116–17, 118 n

Ringgold, Samuel, 477–78, 479 n

Riots. *See* Gordon riots

Rising States, 70 n, 141 n

Ritchie, Capt. John, 625, 627 n

Roach, Capt. Isaac, 624, 624 n

Roberts, Mrs., 53, 57, 66

Robertson, Maj. Gen. James, 59, 61 n

Robertson, Robert, 111 n

Robertson, William, *History of America*, 420, 422 n

Robinson, Charles, 523

Robinson, Gilbert, 553

Robinson, John (clerk, British treasury department), xxxix–xli

Robinson, John Read (passenger on *Polly*), 143

Robinson, Capt. Joseph, 325, 328 n

Rochambeau, Jean Baptiste Donatien de Vimeur, comte de, 234 n, 288

Rockingham, Charles Watson-Wadsworth, 2d marquis of, 24 n, 43, 45 n, 155–56, 158 n, 159, 365, 368, 403

Rodgers, Commo. John, 518, 519 n
    Letter to: 519

Rodney, Adm. Lord George Brydges, lvii–lviii, 99, 102 n, 109, 146 n, 151, 162, 164 n, 167, 170, 212, 226–27, 231, 234–35, 239, 245, 270, 273, 285, 328–29, 405–6, 408 n. *See also* St. Eustatius papers

Roeloffs, Christiaan, 57, 62

Rogers, Mr., 19–20

Rolf, Enock, 197

Romayne, Dr. Nicholas, 460, 462 n

Rose, Duncan, 324

Rose, Sir George Henry, 534, 537 n

Ross, Rear Adm. John Lockhart, 88, 90 n, 144, 146 n, 533

Ross, Timothy D. (TD's pseudonym), 341 n

Ross, William S. (W. R.) (TD's pseudonym), 6, 117, 193, 202, 307, 344, 347, 376

Rowley, Sir Joshua, 27, 30 n

Rowley, Owsley, 379, 381–82

Royal Society's medal, proposed for Franklin and other protectors of Capt. James Cook, 153–54, 154–55 n, 168, 169 n, 173–74, 179, 187–88, 205 n, 235

Rozier, Henry, xxv

INDEX   661

Ruggles, Capt. 138
Rumford, Count. See Thompson, Benjamin
Rush, Richard, 550, 551 n, 607, 608 n
Russell, 203
Russell, John (Irish linen draper), 433 n
Russell, John (brother of Irish nationalist, Thomas Russell), lxiv
Russell, Capt. John (nephew of Irish nationalist, Thomas Russell), lxi, lxiii
Russell, Thomas (Boston banker), 426, 428 n, 432, 437
Russell, Thomas (Irish linen expert), 433 n
Russell, Thomas, (Irish nationalist), lxi–lxiv, 418
Russell, William (TD's pseudonym), 206
Russia: neutrality of, 201, 202 n, 236 (see also League of Armed Neutrality); navy of, 258, 273; and Napoleon, 536; attempted mediation during War of 1812, 546 n
Ryan, Luke, 369, 370–71 n, 372, 376

Sackville, George. See Germain, Lord George
St. Asaph, bishop of. See Shipley, Jonathan
St. Eustatius papers, lvii, lx, 402–7, 407–8 n
St. George, Capt., 327
St. James Chronicle, 92
St. John's Island (S.C.), 74–75
St. Lucia: capture by British, 30 n; Adm. Byron's leaving, 72, 72 n, 73
St. Luke's Hospital (London), 381, 397
St. Petersburgh convention, 543
St. Vincent (Cape Verde Isls.), British naval defeat at, 259–60 n, 261, 273–74
St. Vincent (W. Indies), capture of by French, 72 n, 73
Sally, 84, 96
San, Fernando Raymond (J. Adams's pseudonym), 160

Sandwich, John Montagu, 4th earl of, 33, 35 n, 57, 63, 65 n, 70 n
Saratoga, Burgoyne's surrender at, 30–31 n
Sarley, Jacob, 364
Sarsfield, Guy-Claude, comte de, 16, 17 n
Sartine, Antoine Raymond Jean Gualbert Gabriel de, comte d'Alby, 137, 140 n, 239, 240 n
Savage, Arthur, lviii–lix, 403, 405, 408 n
Savannah, British victory at, 130 n, 132, 134
Savile, Sir George, xliv, 163, 164 n, 228, 230 n, 404
Sawbridge, John, xliv, 156, 158 n, 270, 272 n
Schorn, Hendrik, 351
Schuyler, Angelica, 401 n
Schuyler, Gen. Philip John, 331, 333 n, 333
Schweighauser, Jean-Daniel, 56, 77, 78 n
Scott, Alexander, 515
Scott, James, 477, 479 n
Scott, John. See Trott, John
Scott, Capt. Robert, 277, 279 n, 279
Scott, Dr. Upton, 214, 215 n, 225–26, 230, 255, 502, 504 n
Seaguer (or Seger), George, 8, 10 n
Seahorse, lxxvi, 559
Searle, James, 312, 313 n, 316, 320, 331, 351
Senegal, 28, 31 n
Serapis, 90 n, 102 n
Seton, William, 424, 427 n, 432, 438
Sewall, Elizabeth (TD's great-grandmother), xxiv
Sewall, Henry (TD's great-great-grandfather), xxiv
Seward, Capt., 428
Shaaf, Arthur, 477, 479 n
Shannon, Mr., 415
Sheffield, Capt. Aron, 150, 153 n
Shelburne, William Petty, 2d earl of, xliv, xlvi, liv, lviii–lix, 15, 28–29,

33–34, 35 n, 43, 45 n, 63, 117, 365, 367–69, 371, 401–3, 407 n, 419, 422 n
   Letter to: 376
   Memorandum for: 365, 370 n
Shipley, Georgiana, 42–43, 44 n, 58, 210, 213, 239, 284, 322, 325
Shipley, Jonathan, bishop of St. Asaph, xliv, 42–43, 44 n, 58, 163, 164 n, 211 n, 213, 306, 345 n
Shipley, Mrs. Jonathan (Anna Maria Mordaunt), 44 n
Shirley, Capt. T., 532
Shriver, David, 477, 479 n
Shuldham, Adm. Molyneux, 27, 30 n
Shute, Robert, 332, 332 n
Simmes, Dr., 631–32, 636–37
Sims, Dr., 55
Sinclair, Robert (TD's pseudonym), 127
Sinclaire, Mr., 433 n
Sketch of the Operations before Charlestown, 221, 223 n
Skinner, Baron, 390
Skinner, Mr. (U.S. State Dept. agent), 547 n
Slade, Charles, 521–22
Smith, Dr. Clement, 8, 11 n, 55 n, 502, 504 n
Smith, John (American prisoner), 371 n
Smith, John (boatswain on *Mosquito*), 8, 10 n
Smith, John (chief clerk, U.S. War Dept.)
   Letter to: 512
Smith, John (passenger on *Polly*), 143
Smith, John, Jr. (Baltimore merchant), 83, 85 n, 91, 150, 504 n
Smith, Joseph, 461, 463 n
Smith, Robert, 513, 514 n
Smith, Lt. Col. (*later* Gen.) Samuel, 83, 85 n, 513, 514 n; charges of profiteering against, 514–15, 516–17 n
Smith, W. *See* Smith, John, Jr.
Snelling, Capt. John, 175, 180, 185
Society for Establishing Useful Manufactures, 427 n
Somerset, 23

Somerset, Catharine (TD's ancestor), xxiii
Sonthonax, Léger-Félicité, 515, 516–17 n
Sousa, John de, xxxv–xxxvii
Southey, Robert, xxxvii–xxxviii
Spain, 27–28; relations with Great Britain, 54, 55 n, 63, 64–65 n, 236, 237 n, 326; assistance to U.S., 70–71, 151, 153 n, 156–57; attitude toward American independence, 383–84; colonial discontent with rule of, 418, 595–96
Spencer, Lord Charles, 109, 111 n
Sprague, William, 194
Sprigg, Osborn, 474, 475 n, 510
Sprigg, Samuel, 475 n
Spuyt, Jan, 351
Stack, Rev. Richard, 434 n
Stafford, Capt., 415–16
Stafford, Miss, 79, 82, 87
Stedman, Capt., 460, 462 n
Stedman, Capt. John Gabriel, *Narrative, of a Five Years' Expedition, against the Revolted Negroes of Surinam*, 460, 462 n
Stephens, Philip, 57, 60 n, 144, 155, 159, 262, 533
Stephenson, John, 84, 85 n, 96
Sterry, Cyprian, 82–83, 87, 91, 99, 138, 150
Steuart, Charles
   Letters to: 396, 398
Steuart (*or* Stuart), Col. (*later* Gen.) Philip, 498, 499 n, 635
Stewart, Capt. Charles, 531, 531 n
Stewart, David (TD's cousin), lxiv, 62 n
Stewart, Dr. George (TD's uncle), xxiv, xxvii, 60, 62 n
Stewart, Dr. William, 267–69
Stewart & Campbell, 3 n
Stewart & Plunket, 415
Stickney, Capt., 401 n
Stirling, William Alexander, earl of, 311, 314, 315–16 n
Stockdale, H. W., 416
Stockdale, John, 340, 341 n, 360, 364

Stock-jobbing and speculation, 13, 37–39
Stoddert, Benjamin, lxxiii
Stormont, David Murray, 7th Viscount, 113, 115 n, 300-301, 321–23, 390
Story, Enoch, 49, 50 n
Stratton's madhouse, 380–81, 397
Street, Francis, xlii
    Letter to: 1
Strettel, Mr., 380
Strothers Hotel, lxxvii
Stuart, Judge Archibald, 511
Stuart, Lt. Col. Charles, 24, 25 n
Stuart, Gilbert, li, 336, 337 n, 338
Suffolk, Henry Howard, 12th earl of, xxxix–xl, 33–34, 35 n, 113, 115 n
Sullivan, Gen. John, 25 n, 311, 314, 315–16 n
Sullivan, Lt. John (mutineer), 396
Sumter, Gen. Thomas, 349, 349 n
Sutton, D. J., 459–62
Swallow, 70 n
Swallow (Capt. Joy), 324
Swann, Thomas, 503, 504 n, 556, 558
Sweden, neutrality of, 201, 202 n. *See also* League of Armed Neutrality
Swift, Brig. Gen. Joseph Gardner, 621, 623 n

Taney, Roger Brooke, 477, 479 n
Tarleton, Lt. Col. Banastre, 235, 237 n, 311, 314, 349, 349 n
Taylor, Jesse, 435, 436 n
Taylor, John, 168, 170 n
Taylor, Mr., 524
Temple, 264–65, 280
Temple, George Nugent-Temple Grenville, 2d Earl, 390, 392 n
Temple, John, 101–2, 103 n, 118–20, 124, 126, 187, 193, 247, 254–55, 319–20, 333 n
Temple, Robert, 254, 254 n, 255, 262–65, 271, 274, 279 n, 280, 284, 303
Tennison's Hotel, 618
Ternay, Commo. Charles Louis d'Arsac, chevalier de, 182–83 n, 233, 234 n, 234–35, 239–40, 246–47, 254–55, 259, 261, 271, 274, 289, 330
Tessier, Louis, 122, 125 n, 200, 216
Tew, Capt. James, 69, 70 n
Texel, the, 101, 102–3 n, 121, 125 n
Thaxter, John, Jr., liii, 355
Thomas, William, 477, 479 n
Thompson, Benjamin (Count Rumford), lviii
Thompson, John (TD's pseudonym), 240
Thornton, Sir Edward, 534, 537 n
Thornton, John, xliii, 12, 38
    Letter to: 7
Thurlow, Chancellor Edward, 113–14, 115 n
Tilsit, treaty of, 487 n, 516
Todd, John Payne, 543, 546 n
Tone, Theobald Wolfe, lxiii–lxiv
    Letter to: 418
Tory subversion in America, 51–52, 58, 60
Toussaint L'Ouverture, Pierre François Dominique, 517 n
Townshend, Lord Thomas, 43, 45 n, 390
Tracey, Capt., 138
Tracy, John, 6 n, 262, 263 n, 264
Tracy, Nathaniel, 6 n, 262, 263 n, 264
Trade restrictions: British embargo during American Revolution, 27; American non-importation (Revolutionary period), 34–35; Pitt's proposals of 1783, 387–88, 391 n; British and French blockades during Napoleonic wars, 509, 509–10 n; Non-intercourse Act (1809), 511–12 n, 537–38 n; U.S. embargo on exports to England, 516 n
Traill, Robert, xlix, lv, 396–99
    Letter to: 379
Traill, Robert, Jr., 379–83, 396–99
Trant, Thomas, lv
    Letter to: 399
Treaties (1688–1771), 234, 236 n
Trimble, Dr. James, 571, 576 n

Trott, John, 6 n
Troy, James Thomas, archbishop of Dublin, 467
Trumbull, 247
Trumbull, John, l–li, lxviii, 336, 337 n, 338, 343–44, 345 n, 350, 361 n, 384, 406
Trumbull, Gov. Jonathan, li, 337 n
Tryon, Mrs., 59
Tryon, Gov. William, 117, 118 n, 282, 284 n, 331, 334
Tryon, Lt. William, 8, 10 n
Tucker, Josiah, *Dispassionate Thoughts on the American War*, 220, 222 n
Tumulte de Londres, 237
Tyler, Elizabeth, xxxviii
Tyler, Maj. John Steel, lii, 336, 337 n, 338, 350
Tyler, Trueman, 515
Tymmonds, Mr., 382

Ulster Magazine, lxi
United Irishmen, lxi–lxiv, 418
U.S. Mint, 446 n, 447, 453
Ushant, battle of, 25–26 n, 164 n

Vandalia scheme, 12, 115 n
Vandam, Mr., 460
Van Deventer, Maj. Christopher, 612 n
 Letter to: 610
Van Horne, Archibald, 474, 475 n
Van Ness, Gen. John Peter, 523, 523 n
Vansittart (spy). *See* Van Zandt, Isaac
Van Zandt, Isaac, xliii, 14–15 n
Van Zandt, Jacobus, 14 n
Vardill, John, xliv, 14–15 n
Vaughan, Benjamin, xliv, 4 n, 90 n, 91, 101, 108, 145 n, 165–66, 168–69, 255
Vaughan, Mrs. Benjamin, 166, 168
Vaughan, Sir Charles Richard, 596, 596 n
Vaughan, Gen. John, lvii–lviii, 93, 182, 406. *See also* St. Eustatius papers
Vauguyon, Paul-François de Quéland de Stuer de Caussade, duc de la, 103 n
Velse Prison, 84, 96
Vengeance, 84, 102 n
Venus, 533
Vergennes, Charles Gravier, comte de, liii–liv, 355, 359, 363
Vestal, 291–94, 332 n
Veuve Babut (Vieve Babet) & Co., 335, 337
Viebert, Lt. Col., 11 n
Virginia, 282, 285–90
Volunteer's Journal (Dublin), lvii, lix
W., J. (TD's pseudonym), 24, 372, 375
W., S. C. (TD's pseudonym), 340
Wadsworth, Col. Decius, 549, 550 n, 552–53, 566, 597, 621–23, 635
Wadsworth, Jeremiah, 401 n
Wagner, Jacob, 589 n
Walker, W. & Alexander, 442
Wallace, Charles, 391 n
Wallace, Sir James, 116, 130, 130–31 n, 162, 168
Wallace, Johnson & Muir, 387, 413
Walpole, Sir Robert, 393, 395–96 n
Walpole, Mrs. Robert. *See* Grosett, Diana
Walpole, Thomas, 12, 100, 102 n, 396 n
Walsingham, Commo. Robert N., 162, 164 n, 167, 170, 184, 187, 233
Warburton Manor: acquisition by Digges family, xxiv; TD's inheritance of, xxv, xxviii–xxx; George Washington's visits to, xxvi, 484; TD's claim against, lxv, lxxiv; threat of confiscation of, lxvii–lxviii; sale to William Dudley Digges, lxxiv. *See also* Fort Washington
Ware, Mr., 5
Waring, Henry, 525
Warner, Jonathan, 171, 172, 177
War of 1812: American attitude toward British orders in council and impressment of seamen, 532, 534–36; British proposal for truce, 532, 534; British marauding, 541–42; naval threat to Baltimore area, 543; Poto-

mac trade with enemy, 547–48; British naval approach to capital, 554, 556; destruction of Fort Washington, 559–61, 571–72; taking of capital, lxxv–lxxvi, 559, 561
Warren, Jane Revel, Lady (wife of Sir George), 533, 537 n
Warren, Sir George, 537, 537 n
Warren, Adm. John Borlase, xxxviii–xl, lxxv, 537 n, 543–45, 547, 558 n; blockade of Chesapeake and Delaware bays, 546 n
  Letters to: 531, 538
Warren, Lady (wife of Adm. John), 533
Warren, Winslow, li–lii, 293 n, 332–33 n, 337 n, 349–50
Washington, lvi, 399
Washington, George, lvii, lxix–lxx, 30 n, 58–59, 76, 134, 247, 259, 261, 286–87, 289–90, 331, 362 n, 423–44, 439, 465, 484, 490; friendship with Digges family, xxvi–xxvii, xlv–xlvi; opinion of TD, lxvii–lxviii; Trumbull's portrait of, 343–44; insurrection of Lancaster (Pa.) regiment against, 394, 396 n
  Letters to: 428, 434, 463
Waterman of London, lv
Watson, Prof. Richard, bishop of Llandaff, *A Sermon Preached before the University of Cambridge*, 219, 222 n
Watt, 247 n
Watt, James, 443, 446 n, 447, 464
Waugh, Lt., 348
Wedderburn, Alexander, Baron Loughborough, 114, 115 n, 390, 392 n
Weeden, Brig. Gen. George, 324, 324 n
Wemys, Dr., 407 n
Wentworth, Paul, xliv, 361, 362 n, 362
West, Benjamin, li, 337 n
West, Col., 73
West India Merchant, The, 140, 141 n
Westminster Magazine, 236
Westwood, Obadiah, 442, 446 n, 448–49, 452 n
Weymouth, Thomas Thynne, 3d Viscount, xxxv, xli, 43, 45 n, 113, 114 n
Wharton, Charles, 525
Wharton, Joseph, Jr., xlvi, 12, 19, 37 n, 37–39, 81–82
Wharton, Samuel, xlvii, 12, 15 n, 36, 37 n, 79–80, 80 n, 86–87, 105–6, 110–11, 114, 166
Wheeler & Co., 553
White, Capt., 138
White, Lt. Thomas, 8, 10 n, 69, 70 n
"White Eyes," 300, 302, 313–14
Whitely, William, 477, 479 n
Whitley, Col. William, 460, 462 n
Wickes, Capt. Lambert, 8, 10 n, 377
Wickham, John, 503, 504 n
Wilkes, John, 58, 61 n, 151
Wilkinson, Gen. James, 490, 490–91 n, 492
Williams, Capt., 533
Williams, Rev. David, 101, 122, 128, 146; *Lectures on the Universal Principles and Duties of Religion and Morality*, 103 n
Williams, Grace Harris, 181 n
Williams, John, 13, 15 n
Williams, Col. Jonathan (U.S. army engineer), 493–94, 495 n
Williams, Jonathan, Jr. (Franklin's grandnephew), lvi, 13, 15 n, 180, 181 n, 407 n
Williams, Thomas, 477, 479 n
Williamson, Alexander (TD's pseudonym), 247
Williamson, T. (TD's pseudonym), 246
Williamson, William, 387
Willing, Anne, 395 n
Willing, Thomas, 179 n
Willing & Morris, 178, 179–80 n, 377
Willink, Willem and Jan, 582 n
Willinks & Son, 581
Wilmington, 438
Wilson, Henry, 515, 517 n
Winthrop, Capt. Robert, 411–13, 416, 417 n
Winthrop, William, 417 n
Wistar, Dr. Caspar, 510
Wister, D. (TD's pseudonym), 3 n

Woods, J., 20
Woolsey, George, 423, 428
Wren, Rev. Thomas, 10 n, 173, 174 n, 251 n, 256, 276, 299, 361 n
Wright, Sir James, 47, 47–48 n
Wright, Joseph, 235, 240 n
Wright, P., xl
Wright, Patience Lovell, 240 n, 248, 251 n
Writtle, William Petre, baron of (TD's ancestor), xxiii
Wyld, Henry, 409–10, 410 n

Yawkins, Capt. William, 196–97
York petition, 156, 158 n
Yorke, Sir Joseph, 150, 150 n, 236, 274, 277, 335, 346
Yorkshire Association, 158 n, 222 n
Yorktown, 362 n, 365
Young (seaman), 197, 332
Young, Arthur, 619, 620–21 n
Young, Rev. Dr. Matthew, 433 n
Young, Mary Carroll (Mrs. Notley Young), 469, 472 n
Young, Maj. Moses, 292, 293 n, 334 n, 481, 482 n

Zephyr, 192

OHIO UNIVERSITY LIBRARY

Please return this book as soon as you have finished with it. In order to avoid a fine it must be returned by the latest date stamped below.

QTR. LOAN
JUN 2 8 1983

SEP 2 8 1983

QUARTER LOAN
MAR 3 0 1992

JUN 0 7 1992

CF